THE COMPLETE BLUEPRINT TO BUILDING A HIGH-SCORING (MAN-TO-MAN) OFFENSIVE SYSTEM BOOK 2 OF 2 BOOKS

JOHN KIMBLE

ISBN: 9798330290093

Printed in the United States of America

This book is dedicated to our grand-daughter, Lila Elizabeth who was born as this book

was being written. This beautiful little girl has given her parents as well as us so much

happiness, joy and love in such a short amount of time. This is to tell her how much her

grandparents and parents love and appreciate her

ACKNOWLEDGMENTS

This book is dedicated to all of those who have influenced my basketball coaching life and to all the committed basketball coaches that have spent countless hours at coaching clinics, reading books, and "X and Oing" it with their colleagues. I have been a player, a fan, a teacher of the game, a student of the game, a coach and a lover of the game. As a student and a coach of the game, there have been several influences that have impacted my coaching beliefs. These influences range from summer basketball camps, coaching clinics, coaching textbooks and written publications, video tapes, observing other coaches' practices, and the countless informal coaching clinics with many other coaches trying to learn just one more drill, defense, or play. Personal influences in my coaching life have been from many of the most top-notch coaches of the game: The Doug Collins Basketball Camp (Doug Collins and Bob Sullivan), The University of Illinois Basketball Camp (Dick Nagy and Lou Henson), The Indiana Basketball Camp (Bob Knight), The Dick Baumgartner Shooting Camp (Dick Baumgartner), The Iowa Basketball Camp (Lute Olson and Scott Thompson), The Washington State University Cougar Cage Camp (George Raveling, Tom Pugliese, Mark Edwards and Jim Livengood), The Snow Valley Basketball School (Herb Livesey), The Notre Dame University Basketball Camp (Digger Phelps and Danny Nee), The Illinois State University Basketball Camp (Tom Richardson), The Millikin University Basketball Camp (Joe Ramsey), Eastern Illinois University (Don Eddy), The Purdue University Basketball Camp (Lee Rose), The Oregon State University Basketball Camp (Ralph Miller and Lanny Van Eman), The Troy University Basketball Camp (Don Maestri), the Maryville (TN) College Basketball Camp (Randy Lambert) and the Kansas State University Basketball Camp (Jim Wooldridge, Mike Miller, and Chad Altadonna). Just a few of the most memorable and outstanding speakers I have heard at some of the many coaching clinics I have attended have been, Coach Doug Collins, Coach Hubie Brown, Coach Bob Knight, Coach Dick Nagy, Coach Don Meyers, Coach Lute Olson and Coach Rick Majerus. The most outstanding authors of coaching books have been Coach Del Harris, Coach Dean Smith, Coach Bob Knight, and Coach Fran Webster. Coach Lute Olson, Coach Hubie Brown. Coach Don Meyer and Coach Jerry Krause, Coach Del Harris, and Coach Dick Baumgartner have been authors of some of the most outstanding video tapes I have observed and learned a great deal. Coaching colleagues with whom I have worked are: Benny Gabbard, Doug Collins, Steve Gould, Bob Sullivan, Norm Frazier,Dave Toler, Brian James, Tom Wierzba, Steve Laur, Ron Roher, Will Rey, Mike Davis, Dennis Kagel, Don Eiker, Bob Trimble and Ed Butkovich. I was fortunate to always be involved with tremendous coaching staffs with outstanding coaches, who were even more outstanding as people and friends to me than as coaches. These good friends were outstanding people such as Benny Gabbard, Mitch Buckelew, Scott Huerkamp, Phil Barbara, Chris Martello, Don Tanney, Les Wilson, Al Cornish, Ron Lowery, John Lenz, Doug Zehr, and Ken Maye. To all of these people, I say "Thank you for your loyalty, commitment, hard work and effort!"

I would like to say "thanks" to the many players I have coached, to the extra-ordinary non-player students that were big parts of the basketball programs—the managers, the student statisticians, the film-takers, the student athletic trainers, and student helpers. I hope that I conveyed to each and every one of them the fact that they were important parts of the program and that they all deserved credit for the successes of their basketball programs that they were a part of.

I want to also say "thank you" to the special adults that I have met and become friends with in the different communities where I have coached. These are people that participated in the development and the successes of the basketball programs where I coached. These people were contributors, supporters of the program, faithful fans, and loyal friends. Some were parents of players, while some were parents of students and some were just fans of the game. These people are Bob and Ro Flannagan, Ed and Roseanne Moore, Ron and Mary Roher, Dick and Sharon Payne, Don and Bev Hiter, Dave Gregory, Norm Frazier, John and Pam Russell, Ken and Judy Sunderland, Fred Prager, Mark Henry, Carlan and Dee Dee Martin, George Stakely, Charles Owens, Dutch VanBuskirk, Kelly Stanford and so many other good people.

This book is dedicated to all of those who have influenced my personal life. I was brought up by inspirational parents who always taught me to go the extra step, to never be satisfied until the job was done right. I hope I have succeeded in accomplishing that goal with the writing of this book. My wife, Pat, was my biggest source of encouragement to write this book. She was my constant positive reinforcement and support. My daughter Emily and son Adam also were sources of personal encouragement that helped me continue this endeavor. My two brothers, Joe and Jim, who also offered support as I slowly progressed through the ordeal of organizing and writing. And also to my parents, who were always positive role models and constant sources of encouragement and support. Mr. Jerry Krause (friend, coach at Gonzaga University, author and an invaluable source of information) also was of great help and encouragement; as was Mr. Murray Pool (former high school coach and current publisher of Basketball Sense, friend, and source of information). Benny Gabbard was the one person who got me started in my junior college coaching career and showed great faith and confidence in me in my first years of coaching junior college basketball.

This book is dedicated to all of those "students of the game" who have the same love and passion for the game as I have always had.

FOREWORD

Coach John Kimble has once again written a basketball coaching book which stimulates thinking on how to utilize all types of fundamentally strong offensive techniques and methods within the framework and structure numerous offensive plays/entries from many different offensive alignments/sets that, if not producing a good shot will smoothly flow into the final phase of the offensive attack—various continuity offenses. Coach Kimble wrote this detailed and thorough book not to create an occasional winning season for one team but to create a fundamentally sound offensive system that will produce successful winning teams for all squads within the program. Those teams could include 6th, 7th, and 8th grade teams all the way through the entire high school levels both for all of the girls' as well as all the boys' teams, including possibly post high school teams.

Coach Kimble has integrated his overall plan of action with seamless transitions from each of the three progression and skill levels, which closely fit the characteristics and skill levels of those teams, whether the teams are elementary, middle school/junior high or high school to post high school teams.

This plan is designed to include identical offensive concepts, techniques, and methods at the appropriate skill levels, philosophies that can progress from the elementary phases into the highest levels within the entire program.

When players mature and improve their skills and understanding (in addition to the coaching staff also growing), so should the sophistication of the new team's playing and competition levels. Therefore, the fundamental skill levels should improve as well as the methods, techniques, and plans of action for all players as well as the coaching staff.

Coach Kimble has created a blue print for each level of development to have a seamless transition from one level (or squad/team) to the next level. Therefore, a program with the same offensive system will be able to maintain a high degree of consistency and therefore success.

In addition, Coach Kimble has included various man-to-man plays/entries (to be used by the specific level of talent) that are begun out of various man-to-man offensive sets/alignments. Each of those plays will have smooth and immediate conversions from this initial phase of the offense (the alignment and then the play) to the final offensive spot-ups that will allow a smooth flowing transition into the final phase of the attack—various offensive continuities that will also fit the specific team's offensive skill levels and the team's actual strengths and weaknesses being taken into account.

This is a system that players can continually progress and grow in. Successful coaches adapt their strategy to take advantage of their talent. This book demonstrates how to make adjustments, depending on that talent, while maintaining a solid system that players will know inside-out. The game has changed greatly over the past years and the *Designing a Blueprint to Building a Successful Man-to-Man Offensive System* book has ideas which keep pace with those changes. The book can be used for both men's and women's, boys' and girls' teams from elementary to post high school programs.

Bob Ociepka (Retired)

NBA Assistant Coach (25 years)

Los Angeles Clippers	Portland Trailblazers	Chicago Bulls	Minnesota Timberwolves
Milwaukee Bucks	Detroit Pistons	Cleveland Cavs	Detroit Pistons
Orlando Magic	Philadelphia 76ers	Los Angeles Clippers	Indiana Pacers

Head High School Coach at Gordon Tech High School

Chicago, Illinois And York High School

Elmhurst, Illinois

TABLE OF CONTENTS

While on the surface, this offensive system may appear to be complicated with the many details and nuances, once the coaching staff learns it; they will be able to effectively teach the system to their players.

Again, while the appearance leads to speculation the system is complex; this system has very simple primary objectives. The two objectives are that all of the various actions and schemes are to simply position (and continually reposition) individual players into situations where each player can have a maximum number of opportunities to succeed offensively. This can be accomplished first with careful evaluations of each individual player.

Each player must clearly have his individual skills assessed so that the more outstanding skills of each player can be utilized by placing that player in a situation where he/she can have the greatest opportunity to succeed. Players who have inferior skills must be individually worked with to improve those deficiencies with specific drills in practice, while also manipulating those players in games so that they will not be forced to execute those lesser skills during games. Specific situations must be created for individual players to be able to utilize their strengths while avoiding for the most part the offensive actions that have lesser chances for success. While eluding those types of situations in games, every individual player's lesser offensive skills and talents must be worked on in practices to build up those offensive weaknesses into strengths. The greater the number of offensive strengths a player has, the more weapons that offensive team has in its arsenal that can be used to attack opposing defenses. This can be even more effective when an opposing team's defensive weaknesses are discovered, a player's corresponding offensive strengths can be used to even exasperate the discovered defensive weaknesses. This obviously gives the offensive team a much greater probability of success.

An obvious and simplistic example would be for an offensive system not to create many opportunities and instances for a short offensive player that does not have the necessary offensive post-up skills. But a successful and well-thought out offensive system that has a presumed 'perimeter type player' possessing notable offensive post-up skills in addition to facing an inferior post-up defender should be placed in those types of offensive scenarios (without greatly disrupting the overall offensive plan of action.) This plan would benefit both the individual player as well as the overall offensive team's chances of success.

When an offensive system can have several individual players placed in offensive situations where success is more likely for the team. In addition, a team's overall offensive skills must also be observed and evaluated so that as a team, those skills should included in the design and blueprint of the offensive attack. Conversely, a team's overall general deficient skills must be avoided more often than they are used.

Another simplistic example would be a team that lacks team depth, overall ball-handling skills and perimeter shooting skills to implement a spread offense with many '3 point' shot scenarios.

As a team addresses and works to improve individual players' skills, so should that same team work on improving that same team's overall offensive deficiencies. The more overall offensive strengths a team possess, the more weapons that offensive team has in its arsenal that can be used to attack opposing team defenses. As an offense probes and discovers an opponent's general weaknesses, offensive system should have methods to take advantage of those team defensive weaknesses. This obviously gives the offensive team a much greater likelihood of success.

A simple and short way to address these primary objectives to players could be to state, "constantly attempt to put players in situations/scenarios/positions where they have the best chances for success and avoid those instances where players have a much lesser chance for overall offensive success."

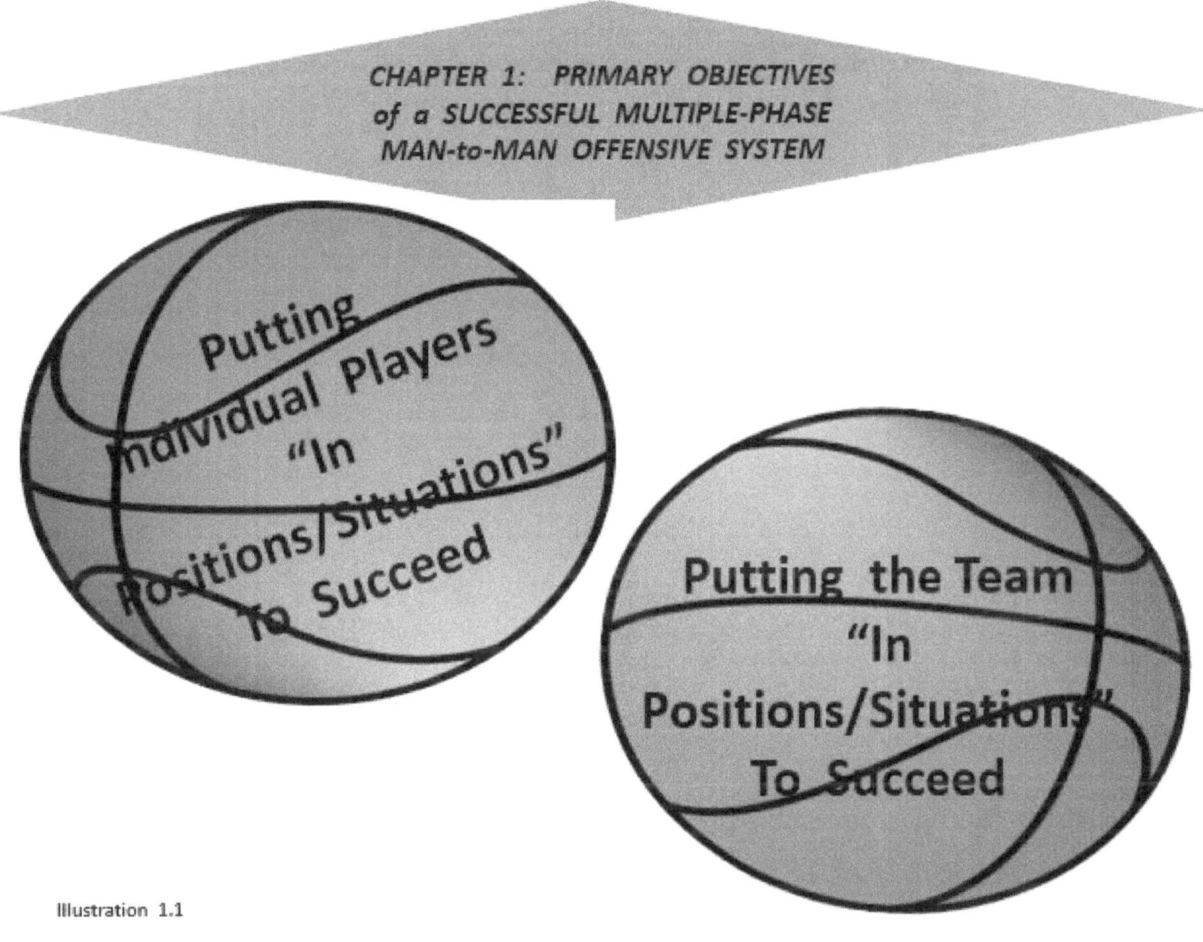

Illustration 1.1

The BLUEPRINT Pieces of a Successful Multiple-Phase Man-to-Man Offensive System

(Chapters 1 – 8)

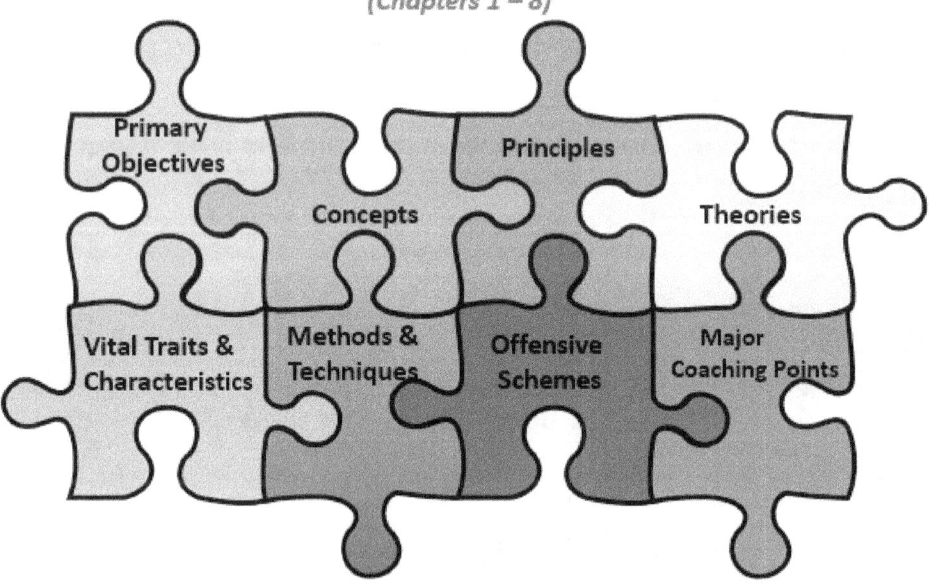

The Important Phases in a Successful Multiple-Phase Man-to-Man Offensive System

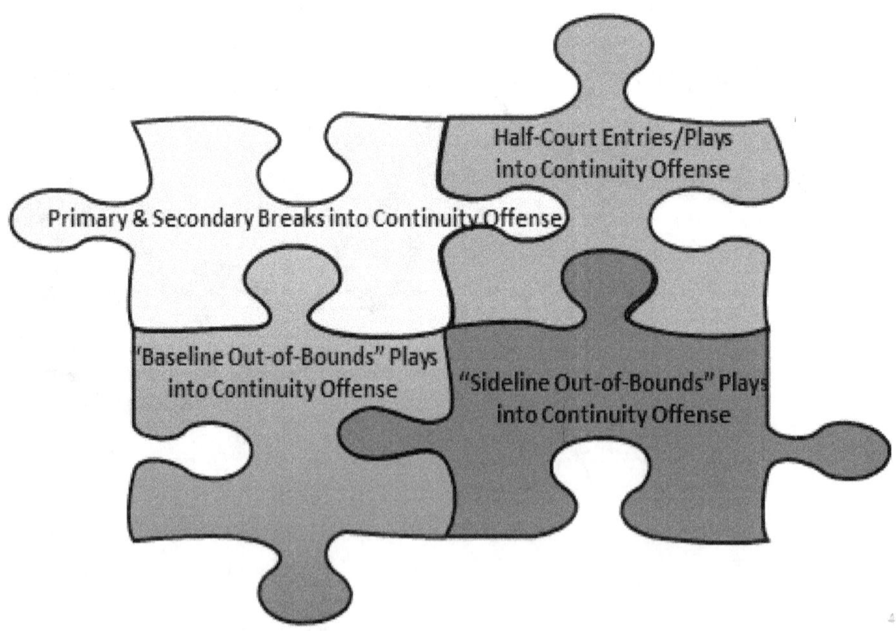

CHAPTER 2
BASIC CONCEPTS APPLIED IN A SUCCESSFUL MULTIPLE-PHASE MAN-TO-MAN OFFENSIVE SYSTEM

⊛ *CONCEPT 1:*

PRIMARY OBJECTIVES OF MULTIPLE-PHASE OFFENSIVE SYSTEMS
(FOR ALL FULL-COURT AND HALF-COURT OFFENSIVE SITUATIONS)

The Primary Objectives of a good offensive system are to "always place all individual offensive players in positions/locations and situations to succeed." This means that the initial objective of every play/entry is to immediately "place the right people in the right place" so that those players can utilize and highlight their specific strengths, minimize their individual Weaknesses and therefore have better opportunities to score quickly and directly off of the play. The offensive action is to allow that team to be the team that initiates the 'action' while also forcing the defense to always be the reactionary team and to adjust to the strategies and movement of both the ball and the offensive players. This is combined with another objective of always having any of the five possible basic phases or levels within the offensive system. Another major (but not immediate) objective of each play is that if the entry does not produce a shot, all five offensive players end up in what we call the "spot-ups" of the specific continuity offense that is utilized.

⊕ *CONCEPT 2:*

THE FIVE PHASES OF A MULTIPLE PHASE OFFENSIVE SYSTEM

The five basic ways that an offense can begin attacking the opposition's defense have been thoroughly discussed. During every game, each of these five methods, will be the initial attacking wave or phase of the offensive system. When shots are not taken from this particular phase but possession of the basketball is retained, there is always a smooth & seamless transition into the continuity phase of the offensive attack. Primary Fastbreaks that flow into Secondary Fastbreaks can have an extra phase of attack that flows into the designated continuity offense or the motion-type offense. Never do we want to run a Fastbreak or a half-court play and when no shots are taken, then back out of that phase to again restart or "set up" the offense. The Multiple-Phase Offensive System never gives the opposition's defense any breathing room and always maintains constant pressure on the opposition's defense.

The five main phases mean that an offense can begin attacking the opposition's defense by utilizing:

A. A Primary Fastbreak that should flow into a Secondary Break attack that could then possibly have various "Options" and "Counter-Options" that would then flow into the designated continuity offense or motion-type offense.

B. A Press Offense that could flow into (the same) Secondary Break attack. If there are no immediate scores or shots, the same "Secondary Break Options" could be executed that could then also flow into the designated continuity offense.

C. Half-court plays (also called entries or quick-hitters) that could also sometimes flow into some of the same "Secondary Break Options" that would then seamlessly transition into the desired continuity offense. Other half-court plays that immediately and fluidly flow into the continuity offense.

D. Baseline Out-of-Bounds (B.L.O.B.) plays could be the first wave or phase of attack that would then flow into the same designated continuity or motion-type offense.

E. Sideline Out-of-Bounds (S.L.O.B.) plays that could also be the initial phase of the attack. If no shots are produced could then also flow into the same continuity or motion-type offense.

⊕ *CONCEPT 3A:*

UTILIZE EVERY POSSIBLE FULL-COURT
DEFENSIVE SITUATION-TO-OFFENSIVE SITUATION

We want to utilize various first phases of our offensive attack, but always finish with the same last phase or wave of attack—a designated Continuity or Motion-type offense (that fits that specific season's offensive personnel's skill levels.) We want to implement an offensive scheme that can begin from several different beginning points before ending up seamlessly and smoothly flowing into a (half-court) continuity offense that maintains a continuous attack on the opposition's defense. The first group of starting points could/should begin from the defensive end of the court and can be incorporated from the team's defense into different offensive avenues of attack such as from all "Defense-to-Offense" conversions that begin with Primary Fastbreaks that transition into Secondary Fastbreaks and then flow into the desired continuity offense. Specifically, this could start out of Full Court Press Offenses into Primary Fastbreaks, on into Secondary Fastbreaks and then flow into the designated continuity offense.

⊕ *CONCEPT 3B:*

ALWAYS HAVE SMOOTH TRANSITIONS FROM ANY OFFENSIVE PHASE
INTO THE NEXT PHASE OF THE OVERALL OFFENSE

Coaches should continually be looking for new ways to place all of their offensive players "in positions to succeed." This means that every offensive play/entry out of every offensive set/alignment should have multiple objectives. The initial objective of every play/entry is to immediately "place the right people in the right place" so that those players can utilize their specific strengths, minimize their individual weaknesses and therefore have better opportunities to score quickly and directly off of the play. Another major (but not immediate) objective of each play is that if the entry does not produce a shot, all five offensive players end up in what is called "spot-ups." These "spot-ups" are the five specific locations/positions on the floor that allow the designated continuity (or motion) offense to immediately flow from the finished entry into the designated continuity offense—giving the opposition's defense absolutely no time to adjust or recover from their attempt of defending the offense's entry.

⊕ *CONCEPT 3C:*

ALWAYS HAVE SMOOTH TRANSITIONS FROM ANY OFFENSIVE PHASE INTO THE NEXT PHASE OF THE OVERALL OFFENSE

This philosophy of flowing smoothly and immediately from half-court entries/plays (that do not produce shots) should and is incorporated from the other offensive avenues of attack—Press Offenses flowing into Primary Fastbreaks that flow into Secondary Fastbreaks and eventually into the designated continuity offense. In addition, there should be a seamless conversion from "Defense-to-Offense" Primary Fastbreaks that flow into Secondary Fastbreaks and then into the desired continuity offense. In addition, all Baseline and Sideline Out-of-Bounds plays should also possess the ability of smoothly and instantly flowing into the continuity offense that is to be executed.

⊕ *CONCEPT 4:*

ALWAYS MAXIMIZE THE NUMBER OF "FASTBREAK OPPORTUNITIES WHICH ARE AVAILABLE"–

Full Court pressure defenses are practical weapons on the defensive side of the ball that can help control tempo of the game and can affect the physical, emotional and mental conditioning of the opposition. But there is no rule that says that a team cannot magnify that same weapon by "full court pressing on offense." That means that a team that is equipped to be able to pressure an opponent on defense should be able to apply that same degree of pressure with an organized fastbreak system that can not only attack after the opposition after turnovers and missed shots, but after made shots. This quick in-bounding after "their scores," can also be an effective deterrent against the opposition's defensive attempt to try to full-court pressure your team's offense.

ALWAYS HAVE A SMOOTH CONVERSION FROM
EVERY PRIMARY AND SECONDARY FASTBREAK OPPORTUNITY
INTO THE NEXT WAVE OR PHASE OF THE ATTACK--

Utilize full court press offensive attacks and a primary and secondary fast break system that is compatible with and that fully complements the overall man-to-man offense package. The continuity offenses that are selected should have the capabilities to be able to easily transition from the Primary Break immediately into the Secondary Break and on into the desired continuity offense. This gives the offense a perpetual attack on the opposition's defense and to maintain a constant attack on the opposition's defense, therefore preventing the opposition from ever recovering or reorganizing in its defensive transition phase. A key to winning is to control the tempo of the game. A team can control tempo when they have a smoother, quicker and more effective defense-to offensive transition than the opposition's offense-to defense transition.

Secondary Fastbreak Options are designed to be "accelerated full-court plays" that are similar to half-court plays/entries in several ways. Just like half-court plays/entries, the first objective of all Secondary Break Options is to place offensive personnel in situations where they can succeed. This can be done by utilizing offensive players' strengths and minimizing those player's weaknesses as well in different types of options out of the Break.

In addition, the Secondary Break Options will attack defensive weaknesses of individual defenders as well as the opposition's overall team defensive weaknesses.

A primary objective of the offensive attack is that if and when the Secondary Break Options have not created the shot desired, the Break has at least moved players and repositioned players into new locations where they can succeed. Those locations are the designated spot-ups of the Second Phase or Wave of Attack— the team's designated Continuity Offense. If the Primary Break does not produce the desired shot, the Primary Break flows effortlessly into the Secondary Break Option. If the selected Secondary Break Option does not create the shot wanted, the offense can then smoothly and fluidly flow into the next form (or phase) of attack—the designated Continuity Offense.

As is our philosophy in our half-court man (and zone) offensive philosophies, we would very much like to be multiple in the various methods of attacking defenses in the fastbreak part of our offensive attack. After determining our team's physical as well as mental strengths and weaknesses, we would like to have multiple weapons in our overall offensive scheme. We would like to have a balanced inside and perimeter attack as well as have plays or options that can highlight various individual players' offensive strengths. This can make the offensive attack less predictable and therefore more difficult to defend. This means that we could have specific Secondary Break Options to fit our offensive personnel's strengths and needs for both sides of the floor. Ideally, the Secondary Break could have separate and different options that start from each side of the floor to attack the defense possibly in entirely two different manners.

As stated previously, any one or two from this list of options could be actually used at the end of the Secondary Fastbreaks. Again, it must carefully be determined which should be used at the conclusion of Secondary Breaks from the left side of the floor and which one from the right side of the floor. These fundamentally sound and successful options include:

A. The "Bump & Flare-Cut" Option,
B. The "Back-Screen" & Quick Ball-Screen/Roll,"
C. The "Brush-Screen," the "Give-n-Go Cut,"
D. The "Iso Duck-In Cut,"
E. The "Veer Cut," the "Early Ball-Screen/Roll,"
F. The "Chase & Early Screen/Rim-Run,"
G. The "Chase & Early Screen/Down-Screen," the "Late Ball-Screen/Roll," and
H. The "Duck-In Cut & Late Ball-Screen/Rim-Run" and the "Flex & Weave."

⊕ *CONCEPT 6:*

**UTILIZE VARIOUS "1ST PHASES" BUT ALWAYS USE
THE SAME LAST PHASE—
THE MAN CONTINUITY OFFENSE (OR MOTION-TYPE) OFFENSE PHASE---**

One offensive philosophy is to implement an offensive scheme that can begin from various locations before ending up seamlessly and smoothly flowing into a continuity offense that maintains a continuous attack on the opposition's defense. The offense could begin from the full court location from the various types of conversion from defense to offense such as after turnovers, defensive rebounds after opponents' missed field goals and free throws, or after opponents' made field goals or free throws, or various Full-Court Press

Offenses. Other ways to implement the same offensive scheme could begin after offensive baseline and sideline out-of-bounds situations while the most frequent situation is after offensive half-court plays/entries that do not produce shots. With no shot taken or loss of possession of the ball, all five offensive players should be relocated into important locations or positions on the floor that are defined as the continuity offense's "spot-ups."

◕ *CONCEPT 7A:*

**CHOOSING MOTION OFFENSES OR CONTINUITY OFFENSES
AS THE FINAL PHASE OF THE OFFENSIVE ATTACK--**

Some coaches believe in choosing various forms of motion offenses (when the play/entry does not create a shot) that will then give freedom to their offensive players and also create a high level of unpredictability to opposing defenses. Coaches disagreeing with this type of philosophy will state that unpredictable movement is good, but movement with no purpose or fundamental value is not good. It is difficult for the proper player to have proper movement at the proper time. This "motion" philosophy may also give individual offensive players so much freedom that their indecisiveness in choosing their movement may actually stifle the movement desired. Many offensive players (and teams) may need more structure in their offensive play and more help in their offensive decision-making.

Another group of coaches believe in maintaining a high level of controlling what their individual players can and cannot do, based on the coaching staff's evaluations of individual and team" offensive abilities. This can be achieved by utilizing half-court continuity offenses that provide structure to offensive players. Opponents of using the continuity offense philosophy complain that it makes the offensive players too predictable in their movements and the predictability makes it easier for opponents to defend. Additionally, some coaches believe that it makes offensive players "robots on specific tracks."

Other coaches adhere to the philosophy of choosing various forms of motion offenses that will then give freedom to their offensive players and also create a high level of unpredictability to opposing defenses. Opponents of using the continuity offense philosophy sometimes complain that it makes the offensive players too predictable in their movements and the predictability makes it easier for opponents to defend. Additionally, some coaches believe that it turns offensive players into "robots on specific tracks."

⚫ *CONCEPT 7B:*

CHOOSING MOTION OFFENSES OR CONTINUITY OFFENSES AS THE FINAL PHASE OF THE OFFENSIVE ATTACK— (WITH REASONS TO CHOOSE CONTINUITY OFFENSES):

Often times, coaches disagreeing with this last type of philosophy will state that unpredictable movement is good, but movement with no purpose or fundamental value is not good. It is sometimes difficult for the proper player to have proper movement at the proper time. This "motion" philosophy may also give individual offensive players so much freedom that their indecisiveness in choosing their movement may actually stifle the movement desired. Many offensive players (and teams) may need more assistance and organization in their offensive decision-making. And by using continuity offenses that are fundamentally sound in concept, these continuity offenses can then also serve as a "base offense" and a type of security to the offensive players (when other phases of the offensive attack have broken down or are not as successful as usual.) This gives that offensive team somewhat of a "security blanket" that they can always rely on when entries break down with no productive shot taken.

⚫ *CONCEPT 8:*

CREATING A MIXTURE OF BOTH CONTINUITY AND MOTION TYPES OF HALF-COURT OFFENSES (FOR THE SECOND PHASE OF ATTACK)

Coaches could institute somewhat of a blend of both philosophies and try to get the best of both worlds. And that is a continuity offense that can smoothly transition from one phase to the final phase, which is a continuity offense that has some freedom as well as a structure in the form of rules. Every time a player has the basketball and makes a pass to one of his other four teammates, there is a rule that provides structure and helps guide the movement of all five players. It is not a rigid offense because the player with the ball realistically has at least three (of his four) teammates that he can almost always pass the ball. Each pass from any of the five "spot-up" locations then has at least three potential pass receivers. Therefore, there is the freedom of making the pass to different players and thus a high degree of unpredictability of what movement takes place after the unpredictable pass is made.

REQUIREMENTS OF ALL CONTINUITY OFFENSES: SMOOTH AND IMMEDIATE CONVERSION FROM PLAYS/ENTRIES TO CONTINUITY OFFENSE

Every continuity offense that is selected should have the capabilities to be able to flow seamlessly, smoothly and instantly from the initial phase/wave of attack into the final phase-the designated continuity offense. This gives the offense a perpetual attack on the opposition's defense and to maintain a constant attack on the opposition's defense, therefore preventing the defense from ever recovering or reorganizing in its defense.

⊕ *CONCEPT 9B:*

REQUIREMENTS OF ALL CONTINUITY OFFENSES: THE SELECTED CONTINUITY OFFENSE MUST FIT THAT TEAM'S SPECIFIC SKILL-LEVELS:

There are numerous continuity offenses that exist that a coaching staff can select. A coaching staff should carefully evaluate that season's team skill-levels in regards to the team's general ability, the overall talent level of its opponents for that year before then deciding on the appropriate continuity offense. The continuity offense must also fit the chosen style of play and the overall staff's coaching philosophy. In addition to selecting the appropriate team defense for the season as well as the specific style of play the staff wants the team to play, this could very well be the biggest and most important decisions a coaching staff will make for that specific season. Choosing the correct plays/entries from the right offensive set or alignment is another vital decision that must be made. But, offensively, the most crucial decision might be in picking the most efficient and productive continuity offense.

**REQUIREMENTS OF ALL CONTINUITY OFFENSES:
CONTINUITY OFFENSES MUST EXECUTE
FUNDAMENTALLY SOUND PASSES MADE FROM EACH
SPOT-UP LOCATION TO THE OTHER FOUR SPOT-UP LOCATIONS
WITHIN THE CONTINUITY OFFENSE:**

Based on which continuity offense is utilized, there are many different types of movements that both the one 'on-the-ball player' and the four 'off-the-ball offensive players' could make before or after the various types of offensive pass is made. These fundamentally sound types of action all have specific purposes and objectives that will attack defenders both individually as well as an entire defensive group. The actions will literally reposition players into locations and situations that will give offensive players as well as the overall offensive team advantages to more easily attack and defeat the opposition's defense.

Once again, the opposition will have trouble recognizing and then actually defending the high volume of the types of offensive movements and actions that can exist within the structure of the continuity offense. These many types of movements and cuts, when controlled by the many types of passes that can be made will give the offense a degree of structure, but still provides freedom of fluid and unpredictable movement by all offensive players.

⚆ *CONCEPT 10:*

**"THE IMPORTANCE
OF A CONTINUITY OFFENSE'S SPOT-UP LOCATIONS"—
PROVIDES AN INSTANT AND FLUID TRANSITION FROM THE 1ST PHASE TO THE LAST
PHASE OF THE OFFENSIVE ATTACK—**

After a selected play/entry from a set/alignment is executed and the offensive team maintains control of the ball with no shot taken; the next phase of the offensive attack begins by smoothly and seamlessly flowing into a variety of continuity offenses or types of motion offenses. This next phase or wave of the attack from different types of offenses must begin with players beginning in specific locations on the court after the play/entry has been concluded (with no shot or loss of possession of the ball.) These important locations or positions are defined as the continuity offense's "spot-ups." The concern that a defensive opponent is able to predict the offensive action should be somewhat minimal, especially if there are multiple plays/entries that are used with some options and counter-options within the continuity offense. When plays or entries are run but the desired shot is not taken, but possession of the ball remains with the offensive team and then flows into the designated continuity offense, defenses will not be able to recognize the actual continuity offense because of the spot-ups of all five offensive players. And from those spot-ups, there will again be an immediate and fluid conversion into the continuity offense that actually is the second and final wave or phase of the overall offensive attack.

Spot-Ups of a continuity offense become a conduit between a team's plays/entries & the team's Second phase of attack—be it a continuity offense or a motion-type offense. It also becomes a means to be able to smoothly continue after Secondary Breaks, Baseline Out-of-Bounds, and Sideline Out-of-Bounds Plays that do not produce shots. 'Spot-Ups' are a way to camouflage a continuity offense because many times the offense will score or lose possession of the ball during the entry before the actual continuity is utilized. Therefore opposing teams will not even see the continuity offense many times and therefore, not necessarily be accustomed to defending it.

⊕ *CONCEPT 11A:*

**"SPOT-UPS OF CONTINUITY OFFENSES" WILL CREATE AN
EVENLY BALANCED AND THEREFORE AN UNPREDICTABLE AND CONTINUOUS SCORING
ATTACK"—**

Chuck Daly, once Head Coach of the Detroit Pistons, has stated, "Offense is spacing and spacing is offense."

Good man-to-man offenses maintain good floor balance and good spacing between offensive players. (Appropriately 15 feet to 18 feet between most players.) Proper spacing will (vertically as well as horizontally) stretch the overall strength of the defense and helps make ball-reversals much easier and safer as well as skip passes. Spacing also discourages double-team traps both on the perimeter as well as "double-downs" when the ball is passed inside to an interior player.

This multi-phase offensive attack produces a potent and fluid type of offense that fits many types of philosophies and styles of offensive play. Using plays from various sets that then smoothly flow into this continuity offense can give the team various styles of offensive attack such as an up-tempo or a slower ball-control type of attack which can both be executed, making the attack a different kind of "balanced attack." Passing rules in this continuity offense allow an offensive team to have both an "inside oriented" as well as an outside or "3-pt. oriented" or a mixture of both—making it an even different type of balanced (and more difficult to defend) method of attack. In addition, various types of plays can provide a balanced scoring attack as well.

The concern that a defensive opponent is able to predict the offensive action should be somewhat minimal, especially if there are multiple plays/entries that are used with some options and counter-options within the continuity offense. When plays or entries are successfully executed with no shots taken and the play transitions into the continuity, the smooth beginning of the continuity is camouflaged by the play's action so that the continuity is not even recognized or distinguished as that continuity offense. Still, the spot-ups will smoothly flow into the designated continuity offense that becomes the second wave phase of the offensive attack.

As stated, every man-to-man offensive continuity can be a very effective and productive way to attack opposing man-to-man defenses. The selected continuity eventually gives every player equal opportunities both on the perimeter and on the interior to perform and utilize their offensive talents and skills. The continuity places individual offensive players in all of the various spot-up locations that can give every player a distinct and immediate "position advantage" that can be taken advantage of immediately. The continuity provides specific spot-ups so that each play can smoothly and seamlessly flow into that continuity to therefore become the final phase or wave of attack. It should be emphasized that each team must select the appropriate plays and just as importantly (or maybe even more so) the proper continuity or motion offense that is the right fit for their team.

"SPOT-UPS OF CONTINUITY OFFENSES" WILL CREATE BALANCED LOCATIONS AND SPACING FOR EVERY INDIVIDUAL OFFENSIVE PLAYER—

A Continuity Offense's Spot-Ups provide excellent positions for maximum offensive success by allowing for ideal spacing both on the perimeter as well as the interior, by spreading the opposition's defense both vertically and horizontally. The Spot-Ups of the designated continuity offense give offensive players good cutting, screening and passing angles to utilize in the offensive action. The continuity's spot-ups provide opportunities for inside and outside shots. The spot-ups of the continuity offense also provide spacing for aggressive (but under control) dribble-attacks to the basket. In addition, these Spot-Ups can offer the offensive team fundamentally sound opportunities for successful offensive rebounding and also for efficient defensive transition.

⊕ *CONCEPT 11C:*

CONTINUITY OFFENSES MUST PROVIDE THE OFFENSIVE TEAM WITH AN "EVENLY BALANCED INTERIOR AND PERIMETER SCORING ATTACK"—

Outstanding man offenses should have somewhat of a balanced attack by having an "inside-out" perimeter shooting attack as well as an "outside-in" type of attack. Starting an attack in one particular location to force opposing defenses to react, adjust and commit to stopping that form of attack before the offense itself countering to the other type of scoring attack is invaluable in keeping defenses off balance and off guard. Make the opposition "pick their poison" on which they attempt to defend—the inside or the perimeter.

⚉ *CONCEPT 11D:*

"SPOT-UPS OF CONTINUITY OFFENSES"
WILL CREATE BALANCED FLOOR LOCATIONS FOR PLAYERS AND THEREFORE HELP CREATE MORE OF A
BALANCED AND UNPREDICTABLE AND CONTINUOUS SCORING ATTACK—

A Continuity Offense's Spot-Ups provide excellent positions for maximum offensive success by allowing for ideal spacing both on the perimeter as well as the interior, by spreading the opposition's defense both vertically and horizontally. The Spot-Ups of the designated continuity offense give offensive players good cutting, screening and passing angles to utilize in the offensive action. The continuity's spot-ups provide opportunities for inside and outside shots. The spot-ups of the continuity offense also provide spacing for aggressive (but under control) dribble-attacks to the basket. In addition, these Spot-Ups can offer the offensive team fundamentally sound opportunities for successful offensive rebounding and also for efficient defensive transition.

Each entry that does not produce a shot from the half-court alignment the play was executed from will at least place all five offensive personnel in either a (Balanced or Unbalanced) "4-Out/1-In" set of continuity spot-ups or from a (Balanced or Unbalanced) "3-Out/2-In" continuity spot-ups. These same spot-ups should be filled at the conclusion of any Secondary Fastbreaks, Baseline Out-of-Bounds (B.L.O.B.) or Sideline Out-of-Bounds (S.L.O.B.) plays. Again, players having repositioned into these designated spot-ups allows the offense to smoothly, seamlessly, and immediately flow into various continuity offenses or different forms of motion offenses. This makes the designated continuity offense even more crucial to the overall success of the offense.

⚉ *CONCEPT 12:*

CONTINUITY OFFENSES ARE ABLE TO AND WILL PROVIDE
AN OFFENSIVE TEAM WITH OFFENSIVE STABILITY THAT WILL THEN DELIVER POTENTIAL OFFENSIVE SUCCESS-

Coaching staffs should use continuity offenses that are fundamentally sound in concept that can also serve as a "base offense" and a type of security to the offensive players (when other phases of the offensive attack have broken down or are not as successful as usual.)

This gives players somewhat of a "safety blanket" where confidence can again be instilled so that an offensive team can "weather the storm" and again become successful and productive.

✪ *CONCEPT 13:*

COACHES MUST ALSO SELECT THE MOST EFFECTIVE ENTRIES/PLAYS FOR EACH SPECIFIC TEAM-

Coaches must select the most effective entries/plays as well as the most effective continuity/motion offenses for each specific team. This is the philosophy behind each and every man-to-man continuity offense and its package of entries/plays that is firmly believed in. There are numerous continuity offenses that can possess families of plays/entries from various offensive alignments/sets that can have its plays quickly, easily and fluidly flow into the designated continuity offense's "spot-up" positions. It must also be emphasized that a team can have an excess of entries/plays as well as too many different continuity man offenses. Therefore, a coaching staff must study which continuity offense best suits their team's personnel and then pick the most productive and efficient plays that fit their players as well as the chosen continuity offense. In addition, the coaching staff should evaluate their personnel both physically and mentally to make sure the correct offenses and the correct plays and the appropriate number are chosen.

✪ *CONCEPT 14:*

COACHES SHOULD UTILIZE DIFFERENT ENTRIES/PLAYS THAT ARE EXECUTED FROM DIFFERENT SETS/ALIGNMENTS—

Possessing and executing multiple entries/plays from a variety of various alignments/sets can greatly improve the overall offensive package. Coaching staffs should be able to integrate different entries/plays out of various sets/alignments to be more varied to become less predictable to the opposition while still maintaining a degree of simplicity for their own team. An offensive package limited to just one primary scorer when other players could also become higher level scorers if given the proper scoring chances in specific plays gives the offensive team a greater level of balance and unpredictability as well as making the offensive package more of an "equal opportunity scoring attack."

⊕ *CONCEPT 15:*

COACHES SHOULD UTILIZE THE SAME OR VERY SIMILAR ENTRIES/PLAYS THAT ARE EXECUTED FROM DIFFERENT SETS/ALIGNMENTS—

Using multiple plays and also multiple sets can greatly improve the overall offensive package. Coaching staffs should be able to integrate similar or possibly identical entries/plays out of various sets/alignments to appear to be more complex to their defensive opponents while keeping it simplified to the offensive team. This can make the offense appear to be more unpredictable to the defense and easier for the offense to comprehend, understand and become more productive.

⊕ *CONCEPT 16:*

COACHES SHOULD SELECT AND UTILIZE ENTRIES/PLAYS THAT WILL HIGHLIGHT INDIVIDUAL OFFENSIVE PLAYERS' STRENGTHS AS WELL AS MINIMIZE THOSE SAME PLAYERS' WEAKNESSES—

Capitalize on the strengths of the offensive alignment/set by distorting the shape of the original man defense to stretch it both vertically as well as horizontally, as well as to initially place individual defenders in potentially unsuccessful positions. Capitalize on various offensive player's individual strengths via various entries/plays or different alignments/sets while attacking weaknesses of both individual defenders as well as the overall team defense in the form of quick-hitting plays. These plays can also serve as a conduit to smoothly flow into the designated continuity offense. The entries can move the opposing man-to-man defenders as well as disguising how the offensive team is proceeding to attack the defense. This adds another layer of unpredictability to the overall offensive attack. The opponent's defense must first place all attention and effort into attempting to stop the entry/play and without any time for reorganization or regrouping to then attempt to defend the continuity man-to-man offense.

⊕ *CONCEPT 17:*

COACHES SHOULD SELECT AND UTILIZE ENTRIES/PLAYS AND CONTINUITY OFFENSES THAT WILL SUCCESSFULLY ATTACK OPPOSING TEAMS' OVERALL DEFENSIVE WEAKNESSES—

Every opposing man-to-man defense has inherent team weaknesses. Coaching staff should learn the opponents' particular styles of the defenses that are being used so that the offense may attack and take advantage of the general weaknesses of each defense. Every man-to-man defense has specific strengths and weaknesses of the overall opposition's man defense. Coaches should study and know the particular styles of the man-to-man defense being used against their team to avoid the strengths and probe the inherent weaknesses of that style of defense. An opponent's seemingly defensive strength might be able to be converted into a weakness with the proper offensive scheming. While also searching for that defensive weakness, the opposition's defensive transition skills might be the key weakness. Once discovered, those weaknesses can be attacked and capitalized on by the offense.

⊕ *CONCEPT 18:*

EVERY OFFENSIVE PLAY AND CONTINUITY OFFENSE MUST HAVE CLEARLY DEFINED RULES FOR EACH PLAYERS' DEFENSIVE TRANSITION RESPONSIBILITIES-

Make sure that defensive transition responsibilities (preventing opponents from getting into THEIR own fastbreak offense) are clear-cut and carried out by everyone after every single offensive possession. Not only should it be clearly defined as to whom "gets back," but what "getting back" really means—as far as "how far back and where (on the court.) We want that assigned defender to quickly sprint to the center jump circle, giving depth as well as balance to be able to cover both sides of the floor.

EVERY OFFENSIVE PLAY AND CONTINUITY OFFENSE MUST HAVE CLEARLY DEFINED RULES FOR EACH PLAYERS' OFFENSIVE TRANSITION RESPONSIBILITIES—

Just as important are the offensive rebounding responsibilities are also clear-cut and carried out by everyone. The three best qualified and most skilled offensive rebounders are called "fullbacks," to clearly describe their one and only assignment is to hit the offensive boards with a "full" commitment toward that assignment. It is important that all offensive rebounders understand that "long field goal misses" mean "long rebounds." "Fullbacks" must learn to read the angles of missed shots and the techniques of beating the opposition's defensive box-outs. The attitude should be instilled to those three offensive rebounders that they look as every offensive shot is "THEIR" offensive rebound ('Stick-back' opportunity.)

The fourth most qualified offensive rebounder is titled the "halfback" as he specifically splits his responsibilities as "half" offensive rebounder and "half" defensive transition.

The fifth offensive player is descriptively called the "tailback." Regardless of where he is located when the offensive shot is taken, the "tailback" must devote his full attention and energy to properly getting his "tail" back on defense.

⊛ *CONCEPT 20:*

COACHES SHOULD IMPLEMENT OFFENSIVE BOTH BASELINE AND SIDELINE OUT-OF-BOUNDS PLAYS-

Another initial phase of the offensive attack, while still finishing with the same designated Continuity or Motion-type offense (that matches offensive personnel's skill levels) could and should be from all Baseline Out-of-Bounds and Sideline Out-of-Bounds plays that are utilized. This would be only as long as these plays also possess the same ability of easily and instantaneously being able to immediately flow into the designated continuity offense.

⊕ *CONCEPT 21:*

**EVERY OFFENSIVE PLAYER
SHOULD VALUE AND UTILIZE THE DRIBBLE PROPERLY—**

Man-to-man offensive players should know the value of the dribble and utilize the dribble properly. They should utilize the dribble in an efficient manner to either advance the ball down-court, to attack the basket to score, to "drive & dump" to a teammate for an inside pass, for "penetrate & pitch" action to a perimeter teammate, to improve passing angles to make passes to teammates, to reverse the ball from one side of the floor to the other side or to escape defensive double-team traps.

⊕ *CONCEPT 22:*

**ALL OFFENSIVE PLAYS AND CONTINUITY OFFENSES
MUST BE ABLE TO FLATTEN DEFENSES
AS WELL AS TO UTILIZE BALL-REVERSALS—**

Flatten the defense by getting the basketball down to the baseline and then reverse the ball quickly to the opposite side of the floor. This is another way of stretching the defense first in a vertical manner and then in a horizontal manner. This movement of the ball from one side of the floor to the opposite side causes ballside defenders and helpside defenders to be in constant movement as well as to change defensive assignments, stances and locations. Ball reversals by means of reverse passes, skip passes or dribbles will force the opponents to defend both sides of the floor, thereby forcing all five defenders to move and forcing all defenders to become both ball defenders as well as off-ball defenders. This can exploit major weaknesses of all individual defenders. Ball-reversals are so revered by some coaching staffs that they keep a detailed statistic on how many ball reversals take place in their offensive schemes.

⊕ *CONCEPT 23:*

**ALL SUCCESSFUL OFFENSES MUST UTILIZE VARIOUS METHODS TO ELIMINATE
OPPONENTS' HELPSIDE DEFENSES**

A major objective of various types of continuity offenses (as well as offensive plays/entries/quick-hitters) can also be to eliminate or weaken helpside defenders to attack the opposition's post defenders as well as to isolate post defenders with either flash-post action and/or to occupy helpside defensive opponents with 2 or 3-man games on the offense's weakside.

⚫ *CONCEPT 24:*

ALL SUCCESSFUL OFFENSES MUST UTILIZE VARIOUS "SKIP PASSES" IN VARIOUS LOCATIONS—

Perimeter players should not hesitate on making "skip-passes" across the court. "Skip-passes" are an instant method of reversing the ball from one side of the court to the other side. Reversing the ball is an integral concept for successful offenses to be able to attack both inside and also on the perimeter. "Skip-passes" will also discourage "man defenses" from providing good helpside defense in the lane from the weakside of the offense, off of the "skip pass." After "skip passes" are made, post players should seal off the post defenders that deny them the ball on the original ballside and be prepared to receive the pass from the original weakside. "Skip-passes" can provide offenses with open "catch & shoot 3's" or opportunities to "shot fake & create." When man-to-man defenders react to the "skip pass," a second "skip pass" back to the original ballside can be very effective. A phrase "One good skip pass deserves another" should be taught and utilized in every type of offense that is utilized.

⚫ *CONCEPT 25:*

INSTRUMENTAL TO OFFENSIVE INDIVIDUAL AND OVERALL OFFENSIVE TEAM SUCCESSES ARE THE USE OF PASS FAKES AND SHOT FAKES--

Coaches should always stress to every offensive player to always use good passing and shot fakes against the opposition's defenders.

Basic passing fakes can sometimes move multiple defenders in their eagerness to play good defense, causing defensive problems for the opposing defenses.

Shot fakes can create many more opportunities to drive to the basket and to draw fouls on the opposition. To be successful, shot fakes do not have to cause the defender to leave the ground, but to just slightly move that defender or straighten the defender's legs. Defenders cannot play defense with their legs straight. Defenders will not be able to jump or make any quick lateral defensive moves. Shot fakes made earlier in the game will give shooters more space to take those jump shots later in the course of the game.

⚉ *CONCEPT 26:*

SUCCESSFUL MAN OFFENSIVE PLAYS AND CONTINUITY OFFENSES MUST HAVE PRESSURE RELEASE OPTIONS TO COMBAT OPPOSITION'S DENIAL PRESSURE--

Teams should have simple and easily understood methods to combat aggressive defensive overplays and denials (both on the perimeter and in the post) for their entries as well as their Second Phase/Wave of Attack—whether it is a continuity or motion type offense. "Backdoor Cuts," "Give-n-Go Cuts," "Blind Pig" Actions, "Iverson Cuts," "Barkley Cuts" (defined as "Iverson Cuts" by the offensive team's Post Players,) "Dribble Hand-Offs," "Fake Dribble Hand-Offs," "Counter Options" and other actions are ways to eliminate opponents' denial pressure on the perimeter. High-Low Flash post overloads and off-ball screens on the weakside are viable options to counter opponents' Helpside Defenses that are necessary in the opposition's aggressive and interior man-to-man defensive action.

⚉ *CONCEPT 27:*

COACHES AND PLAYERS MUST BELIEVE THAT OFFENSIVE PATIENCE IS INVALUABLE TO OFFENSES--

Offensive players should be patient and move the ball as well as themselves. They should force the defense to move, to react, and to work for extended periods of time to wear down opponents and provide more opportunities for defensive mistakes. Offensive players should always remember that "THEY" cannot score if "WE" have the ball. A team's patience on offense will ultimately affect both the opposition's defense as well as their own offense (by fatigue as well as offensive impatience.)

**SUCCESSFUL OFFENSIVE SYSTEMS MUST
INCORPORATE AND UTILIZE A WIDE VARIETY OF OFFENSIVE CUTS--**

Attack opposing man defenses with various types of offensive cuts both on the ballside and the weakside. Use a mixture of the different kinds of cuts by off-the-ball offensive players such as: "V-Cuts," "Pipe or Zipper Cuts," "Shuffle Cuts," "Duck-In Cuts," "Iverson Cuts," "Barkley" Cuts, "Michigan" Cuts, "Shuffle Cuts," "Scissors" Cuts, "Flex Cuts," "Veer Cuts," "Bump Cuts," "Curl Cuts," "Give-n-Go Cuts," "Backdoor Cuts," "Blind-Pig" Cuts, "Flare Cuts," "UCLA Rub-Off Cuts," "Bruin" Bump Cuts," "Flash Post Cuts," "Slash Cuts," "Blur Cuts," (Post) "Spin-Screen Cuts," and "Basket Cuts" (Ball-Screen Rolls and Rim-Runs).

🏀 *CONCEPT 29:*

**SUCCESSFUL OFFENSIVE SYSTEMS MUST
INCORPORATE AND UTILIZE A WIDE VARIETY OF "OFF-THE-BALL" SCREENS--**

Integrate the many different types of "off-the-ball screens" in the offense so that your team can to either completely eliminate or at least move the "helpside" defense, or to have personnel cutting towards the ball either on the perimeter or the interior. These "off-the-ball screens" could be in the form of "Big-on-Small," "Small-on-Big," "Small-on-Small" or "Big-on-Big" types of "off-the-ball screens." Another form of an "off-the-ball screen" is called a "Ram Screen" that makes the up-coming Ball-Screen even tougher to predict when it will develop and therefore more difficult to defend. Screens set by a different sized player on a different sized teammate helps discourage defensive switching or can quickly put defensive players in drastic mismatches that can and should be capitalized on.

🏀 *CONCEPT 30A:*

**SUCCESSFUL OFFENSIVE SYSTEMS MUST
INCORPORATE AND UTILIZE A VARIETY OF "ON-THE-BALL-SCREENS"—**

An offensive scheme should/could include "on-the-ball" screens with three different starting points and the six or more different "follow-up methods/techniques" that can effectively be executed. The locations of the initial ball-screen can also be on different locations of the court. Therefore having different starting points and locations, different types of ending action and different players setting as well receiving the actual ball-screen, in addition to the different combinations of players involved, can result in numerous offensive ball-screening scenarios that would be very difficult for defensive teams to adequately defend.

✪ *CONCEPT 30B:*

SUCCESSFUL OFFENSIVE SYSTEMS MUST INCORPORATE AND UTILIZE A VARIETY OF "ON-THE-BALL-SCREENS"—

There are five different fundamentally sound methods to initiate the ball-screen action. These ways are:

A. The traditional stationary ball-screen usually set near the top of the key or halfway from the top of the key and the high elbow areas,

B. The "Long Ball-Screen" where the designated ball-screener breaks into the designated screening location,

C. The "Flat Screen" action usually set somewhere near the middle "alley" just inside the 10-second timeline with the ball-screener setting the stationary ball-screen with his butt pointing directly towards the basket or

D. The "Double Wide" Ball-Screen (utilizing two offensive players side by side that set a wider ball-screen,)

E. The Ghost Ball-Screens that can start at various locations on the floor and can be set by all types of personnel,

F. The "Inside Ball-Screens" that are set at the high post elbow area for middle penetration drives.

✪ *CONCEPT 31:*

SUCCESSFUL OFFENSIVE SYSTEMS MUST INCORPORATE AND UTILIZE A VARIETY OF WAYS TO CONCLUDE THEIR "ON-THE-BALL-SCREENS"--

Various types of actions that could be utilized after executing 'Following (the-pass) Ball-screens'; could be any of the following such as:

A. The "Ball-Screen/Roll,"

B. "Ball-Screen/Rim-Run,"

C. "Ball-Screen/Slip" (Picking and Popping),

D. "Ball-Screen/Flare-Cut,"

E. "Ball-Screen/Re-Screen" or

F. Various forms of "Screen-the-Screener" action on either the interior or the perimeter player.

⊕ *CONCEPT 32:*

SUCCESSFUL OFFENSIVE SYSTEMS MUST INCORPORATE AND UTILIZE A VARIETY OF "COMBO SCREENS"--

A now popular offensive concept that is being applied is the series of action where the initial screener sets two (or more) different types of screens in a very short, smooth and fluid series of offensive action. Another newer type of action (called the "Chin Screen" action) is a reverse pass that initiates a back-screen for the ball reversal passer that is immediately followed by a ball-screen(with various types of action that could then follow that ball-screen.) Other forms of Combo Screens could be started with an off-ball screen and then finished with a second off-ball screen. Many types of Combo Screens can start with a ball-screen that is then followed with a second off-ball screen on a second teammate. These are fluid forms of action that give the screener's defender no time to read the type of screen and prepare to defend it.

⊕ *CONCEPT 33:*

SUCCESSFUL OFFENSIVE SYSTEMS MUST INCORPORATE AND UTILIZE VARIOUS FORMS OF BOTH THE WEAVE/DRIBBLE HAND-OFF AND FAKE DRIBBLE HAND-OFF ACTIONS--

There are many forms of offensive Weave/Dribble Hand-Off actions that can be integrated into a successful offense. The ball can easily be handed off before then dribbled towards the middle of the floor as a form of ball reversal. In addition, centering the basketball in the middle of the floor eliminates the defense's definition of a "ballside" and a "helpside." That means there will be a large decrease in defensive support. Utilize "weave/dribble hand-off action" can also highlight offensive players' dribbling and driving skills and talents. It can also invert post players into becoming perimeter players, which means opposing post defenders are forced to defend in possibly unfamiliar areas where they could very easily have weaknesses. The weave/dribble hand-offs can also provide opportunities in creating "big on small" or "small on big" mismatches that can be capitalized on by discovering individual defenders' weaknesses as well as utilizing individual offensive players' offensive strengths. To counter "Dribble Hand-Off" action, an offensive team can also have an option that incorporates "Fake Dribble Hand-Offs."

⊕ _CONCEPT 34A:_

SUCCESSFUL OFFENSIVE SYSTEMS MUST INCORPORATE AND UTILIZE VARIOUS FORMS OF "FLIP-PASSES" (ALSO CALLED "PASS HAND-OFFS")

There are several ways that an offensive "Flip Pass" action can be integrated to attack opposing defenses within the framework of several different offensive plays/entries. This action, that could also be called "Pass Hand-offs" (or PHOs) can have the same results as many Dribble Hand-Offs (DHOs) previously discussed. The ball can move in the direction both towards and away from the center of the floor. When the ball is dribbled towards the wing with the initial Passer following his "Wing Pass, " there will be indecision and a delay by the defense to read if the ball and the play continue in the same direction, if the ball remains at the FT Line extended or if the direction of the play is changed to move back towards the middle of the floor. This hesitation by the defense can often give the offense enough time to take advantage of that delay and be able to successfully attack the defense and the many disadvantages this type of action can provide for the offense. This action could be used as a counter to any of the countless times in a game when there is a "Wing Pass" that was made from the top of the key. After the use of a couple of "Flip Passes" are made, every "Wing Pass" is made afterwards, there could be a slight moment of doubt by the defense. When this action is used with a mixture of (traditional) 'big' and a 'small' players, defensive switching strategies would cause all types of defensive switches. These defensive switches could cause various types of defensive problems that the offense could take advantage of.

⊕ *CONCEPT 34B:*

**SUCCESSFUL OFFENSIVE SYSTEMS MUST INCORPORATE
AND UTILIZE VARIOUS FORMS
OF "FAKE FLIP-PASSES" (ALSO CALLED "FAKE PASS HAND-OFFS")**

While integrating "Flip Pass" actions within the offensive structure of the system, a form of deception and misleading of the defense in partnership with this type of action comes the use of the "Fake Flip Pass." There are several ways that after using the "Flip Pass" action, an offensive team can switch up its attack with faking the actual "Flip Pass" and following up with a different form of attack. When defensive opponents attempt to adjust their defensive "REACTION" to the initial offensive "ACTION" of the "Flip Pass," they will remain a step behind and forcing the defense to remain in that same 'reactionary mode of thinking and acting.' As in any "Flip-Pass" action, the same possibilities of misdirection, the covering up the actual objectives, the increase of confusion and hesitancy by the opposition, and the possible creation of 'position player mismatches' will also be created for the offense to make the most of.

⊕ *CONCEPT 35:*

**SUCCESSFUL OFFENSIVE SYSTEMS MUST INCORPORATE AND UTILIZE VARIOUS WAYS
TO IMPLEMENT AND UTILIZE THE
CREATION OF "POSITION MISMATCHES"--**

All continuity offenses can implement an offensive plan of attack that can be defined as creating "position mismatches." This means that the offense can force opposing defenders into having to defend offensive players they were not initially assigned to guard. This can be done by integrating "Big-on-Small" or "Small-on-Big" off-ball and/or on-ball screens within the rules of the continuity or very easily in the design of specific quick-hitting plays/entries. This could also be a form of forcing defenders to be inverted, while offensive players remain in their normal and customary locations.

SUCCESSFUL OFFENSIVE SYSTEMS MUST INCORPORATE AND UTILIZE VARIOUS WAYS TO INVERT OFFENSIVE PERSONNEL TO CREATE "POSITION MISMATCHES"--

Coaches should constantly look to invert offensive personnel to create "position advantages," such as a perimeter player ending up in the post area to have a possible "position advantage." These advantages could be one or more or a combination of height, strength, quickness and/or inside scoring skills advantages (through experience and training.) These types of action can be created by carefully designed plays as well as the continuity offense that is decided upon. Perimeter Players could be inverted with certain perimeter players repositioning themselves inside and Post Players could also be inverted to also take advantages of their offensive skills and the possible weaknesses of their opponents.

⊕ *CONCEPT 37:*

SUCCESSFUL OFFENSIVE SYSTEMS MUST INCORPORATE AND UTILIZE VARIOUS WAYS TO INVERT PERIMETER-TYPE OFFENSIVE PLAYERS--

One simple, but sound method of attack that can be a part of this offensive system is to "invert" perimeter players. This means that so-called "perimeter players" can be placed into post-up locations. After perimeter players have been taught and trained how to successfully post up their perimeter defenders inside, there are plays designed that will take advantage of those possible "position mismatches." The coaching staff takes the challenge of preparing "perimeter players" to be more prepared as offensive post players than opponents' perimeter players to be good post defenders and vice versa with the traditional "post players." Specific offensive plays, rules or special options within the continuity can then provide various players with "position advantages" by taking advantage of newly-found offensive strengths and newly discovered individual defensive weaknesses both on the interior as well as on the perimeter.

⊕ *CONCEPT 38:*

SUCCESSFUL OFFENSIVE SYSTEMS MUST INCORPORATE AND UTILIZE VARIOUS WAYS TO INVERT OFFENSIVE POST PLAYERS–

A Continuity offense (as well as many plays) not only can invert perimeter players "down on the blocks," but can also move and reposition certain offensive post players away from the basket; so that they can attack their defender on the perimeter as well. This attack could be because of that player's dominating quickness, ball-handling and/or perimeter shooting skills (or because of a specific defender's overall perimeter defensive weakness.) Inverting offensive post players could also be to pull defensive "bigs" away from the basket to take away defensive strengths, such as defensive rebounding and shot-blocking skills. This can give that designated player (be it a traditional so-called perimeter player or a post player out on the perimeter) an opportunity to use his driving, passing and/or perimeter shooting skills, as well as his offensive creative skills. These methods could be incorporated within the general rules of the continuity, in the counter-options or in specific plays executed for that primary reason.

⊕ *CONCEPT 39A:*

SUCCESSFUL OFFENSIVE SYSTEMS MUST INCORPORATE AND UTILIZE VARIOUS WAYS TO ISOLATE OFFENSIVE POST PLAYERS—

One way to attack opposing team's defenders is to place both the traditional as well as the so-called inverted perimeter players in the post with little or no interior support for those specific defenders. When opposing post players play behind the offensive post players, those "Inside Passes" should be able to easily be made to that particular post player. The properly selected continuity offense should have a plan of attack to neutralize double-teams from perimeter defenders with perimeter movement so that post players can then "kick the ball back out" for open perimeter shots. If post defenders try to full-front or three quarter front post players to deny them the ball, we want our offenses to be able to take away weakside defensive help so that lob passes can be made to the fronted post player. The positioning, repositioning and moving of offensive players can be accomplished within the framework of the selected continuity offense. This can give a coaching staff the ability to be able to not only place a designated player into the mid-post area, but to isolate that particular player so that he can attack a lone defender from a high percentage shot location.

⊕ *CONCEPT 39B:*

SUCCESSFUL OFFENSIVE SYSTEMS MUST INCORPORATE AND UTILIZE VARIOUS WAYS TO ISOLATE OFFENSIVE POST PLAYERS--

Still another method used to attack opposing defenders is to position both the traditional as well as inverted perimeter players in the post with little or no interior support for those defenders. If defensive post players play behind, we should be able to easily make the inside pass to that designated post player. We want to have a plan of attack to neutralize double-teams from perimeter defenders with perimeter movement so that post players can then "kick the ball back out" for open perimeter shots. If post defenders try to full-front or three quarter front post players to deny them the ball, we want our offenses to be able to take away weakside defensive help so that lob passes can be made to the fronted post player. The positioning, repositioning and moving of offensive players can be accomplished within the framework of the selected offensive plays/entries. This can give a coaching staff the ability to be able to not only place a designated player into the mid-post area, but to isolate that particular player so that he can attack a lone defender from a high percentage shot location.

⊕ *CONCEPT 40:*

SUCCESSFUL OFFENSIVE SYSTEMS MUST INCORPORATE AND UTILIZE VARIOUS WAYS TO ISOLATE OFFENSIVE PERIMETER PLAYERS--

If an offensive team can isolate players "in the post," that type of attack should be able to also isolate certain offensive players on the perimeter. Those players can attack their defenders on the perimeter as well, with those defenders able to receive much help from defensive teammates. This attack could be executed because of an offensive player's advantage in quickness, ball-handling and/or perimeter shooting skills (or because of a specific defender's overall perimeter defensive weakness.) This would provide that designated offensive player (be it a traditional so-called perimeter player or a post player out on the perimeter) an advantage and a chance to use his driving abilities, his passing and/or perimeter shooting skills, as well as his offensive creative skills. Various forms of off-ball screening on the weakside or overloading the ballside with offensive players can help eliminate helpside defenders to force the opposition into "one-on-one" defensive assignments on the interior. These methods could just as well be integrated somewhere within the structure of the continuity.

⊕ *CONCEPT 41:*

SUCCESSFUL OFFENSIVE SYSTEMS MUST INCORPORATE AND UTILIZE VARIOUS WAYS TO UTILIZE "FALSE (BALL OR PLAYER) MOTION"—

If an offensive team is mentally able to handle it, some offensive sets can be camouflaged by actually beginning in one alignment, then using a form of "false (ball) movement;" before "shifting" the location of both the ball and offensive personnel into the actual desired start point of the offensive attack. With some offensive sets, begin certain offensive plays/entries with "false (ball) movement" and/or "false (player) movement." The "false (player) movement" concept is somewhat comparable to a football team "shifting" from one offensive formation and actually ending up in a different offensive formation before the action actually begins. This somewhat simple action can cause a delay in the defense's read of the offense's objectives. The "(False) Motion" concept is when offensive personnel move from their original locations (on a designated time) after the ball and player movement—disguising what the offense's final alignment and intended action (to confuse and weaken the defense.)

⊕ *CONCEPT 42:*

SUCCESSFUL OFFENSIVE SYSTEMS MUST INCORPORATE AND UTILIZE THE "SHIFTING CONCEPT"—

The "shifting" concept is simply when offensive personnel move or shift (on cue) from their original locations to different locations before the play/entry/quick-hitter actually begins—changing the offensive set to a different offensive set. (Before the defense can adjust.)

SUCCESSFUL OFFENSIVE SYSTEMS MUST INCORPORATE AND UTILIZE VARIOUS WAYS TO IMPLEMENT THE "COMBO OFFENSE" CONCEPT—

The "Combo Offense" Concept is executing one continuity offense and when at a designated "trigger point," the offense simply converts to a compatible; but entirely different continuity offense with no delays or interruptions. This causes the opposition's defense to try to read and then react to a different set of offensive actions.

⊕ *CONCEPT 44:*

SUCCESSFUL OFFENSIVE SYSTEMS MUST INCORPORATE AND UTILIZE THE "DO-SOMETHING-DIFFERENTLY-THAN-WHAT-OTHER-TEAMS-DO" CONCEPT—

This may be construed as an unusual concept, but it is felt that it can be a very valuable concept to implement. It is believed that a portion of the offensive scheme that is used should be somewhat unique and different from the majority of teams (as long as it is still fundamentally sound and not a huge portion of the overall offensive scheme.) Regardless of how minor the action is, doing something different offensively than most teams means that the opposition has not seen the action from other teams and therefore not had the experience in defending that specific type of action or style. This then makes it more difficult for the opposing defenses to defend.

⊕ *CONCEPT 45:*

SUCCESSFUL OFFENSIVE SYSTEMS MUST INCORPORATE AND UTILIZE VARIOUS WAYS TO IMPLEMENT DECEPTION & DISGUISES—

Keeping the opposition off balance by not showing the defense the offense's actual plan of attack can be accomplished by executing plays/entries/quick-hitters from different alignments/sets and running counters to the plays that are most frequently used.

Showing different looks offers the offense even more deception and having "counter plays" can make the offensive action more deceiving, causing the defense doubt (and slower) in their (defensive) reaction times to the overall (offense's) actions.

✪ *CONCEPT 46:*

SUCCESSFUL OFFENSIVE SYSTEMS MUST INCORPORATE AND UTILIZE A WIDE VARIETY OF SCORERS
(AS WELL AS THE LOCATIONS OF THOSE SCORERS)—

Preventing the opposition's defense from knowing the offense's actual plan of attack can be accomplished by executing a play/entry that either attacks various particular defensive weakness or highlights/utilizes any number of different offensive player's dominant skills. Those skills of the various players could produce shots from various locations on the floor where those players are more efficient and skilled. If the desired shot is not taken, there still could then exist a smooth transitioning into the continuity offense that then either attacks the defense possibly with a different offensive scorer from a different location within the framework of the continuity offense.

✪ *CONCEPT 47:*

SUCCESSFUL OFFENSIVE SYSTEMS MUST INCORPORATE AND UTILIZE VARIOUS WAYS TO IMPLEMENT A WIDE VARIETY OF STYLES
(AS WELL AS THE LOCATIONS OF THOSE SCORERS)—

An offensive team that has the flexibility and the type of players that can thrive in various styles of play as well as the ability to use different game speeds in both the half court and the full-court phases of the game will have a tremendous opportunity for more offensive success. Different offensive styles of play that can be executed by an offensive team not only allow the team to highlight both individual and team offensive players as well as take advantage of defensive weaknesses. Having multiple styles and tempos of play that all can be successfully executed gives the offense another opportunity to succeed as well as also increasing the amount of unpredictability the defense must deal with.

COACHES AND PLAYERS SHOULD
BELIEVE IN, VALUE AND UTILIZE FUNDAMENTAL DRILLS"—

Every athletic team has practice to prepare for their games. What takes place is practice can and will make the difference in whether that team will succeed in the game or fail. It is very likely that a large portion of each of these daily practices will be the fundamental drills. Drills, the way those drills are taught and how they are incorporated in the daily practices will determine whether a coach is a good coach or not and whether the team has a chance to succeed in actual competition or not.

Drills, the way the drills are taught and how they are incorporated in the daily practices will determine whether a coach is a good coach or not and whether the team has a chance to succeed in actual competition or not. "Game-realistic" scenarios must be implemented to simulate "game-like" conditions in the form of drills. Drills must be created to practice the many necessary fundamental skills and techniques. The old cliché, "practice makes perfect" should not apply. A better philosophy that should be used in practices is this: "Perfect practice makes perfect!" That must come through "game-realistic" drills and conditions under a very watchful and scrutinizing coaching staff. Success must come in small consistent increments so that players' confidence in themselves, in their teammates, and in the "system" will slowly and gradually develop.

⊕ *CONCEPT 49:*

COACHES SHOULD BELIEVE IN, VALUE AND ALWAYS UTILIZE
THE CORRECT TEACHING/COACHING METHODS"—

Good coaches are outstanding teachers and motivators. In order for a basketball program to be successful, that coaching staff must demand that every player be fundamentally sound in how to perform all techniques in each of the many phases of the game. That staff then must be able to motivate every player in performing those fundamentals at their highest level of intensity. The staff's attention to detail must be crucial, as well as the positive and constructive criticism that must come with the teaching and the drill work. One successful method of teaching basketball skills is the "whole-part-whole" method with a great emphasis on the how and the why on every technique, every skill, on offense, defense, transition, or whatever technique is being taught to every player as well as the overall team. Players must have confidence in the coaching staff that the methods and the techniques that they are being taught are crucial to the improvement of each player as well as to the overall success of the basketball team.

⊕ *CONCEPT 50:*

COACHES SHOULD BELIEVE IN, AND ALWAYS VALUE THE IMPORTANCE OF DAILY PRACTICE PLANS:--

Good teachers have efficient lesson plans. Good coaching staff must have daily practice plans that are time efficient and productive so that all fundamental offensive and defensive skills, physical conditioning, as well as overall team offenses, defenses, special situations, the understanding of rules. These practice plans must be followed closely but coaches must still be flexible enough to modify the time frames that are pre-planned in the practices. An overall Master Practice Plan must also be designed, recorded, and evaluated for the staff to stay "on track."

⊕ *CONCEPT 51:*

COACHES SHOULD BELIEVE IN, VALUE AND ALWAYS UTLIZE STATISTICS IN PLAYER EVALUATIONS—

An old cliché "if it is worth doing, it is worth measuring" should be used to measure athletic performances both in athletic practices as well as in games. To maintain a good offensive system, that system must be constantly observed and evaluated not only by the number of wins and losses and by passing the "eye test," but also by an objective comparison to previous games, previous season and by opponents' performances. Stats and data analysis are becoming increasingly more important in many sports and basketball must follow that trend. While many of the traditional statistics are still of great value, there are other statistics that can also help a staff get a more accurate read on not only the performance of the system, but also of the current team as well as current individual players' performances. Using many of the traditional data, several ratios and frequencies can be implemented to give the coaching staff more assessment data and a clearer and objective evaluation tool in performances.

COACHES AND PLAYERS SHOULD BELIEVE IN AND VALUE BOTH INDIVIDUAL PLAYERS' OFFENSIVE AND DEFENSIVE GAME PERFORMANCE GRADES ALONG WITH THE OVERALL TEAM'S OFFENSIVE AND DEFENSIVE GRADES BY UTILIZING THE PERFORMANCE GRADING SYSTEM"—

To instill a team-first atmosphere (and not individual glory in the most common statistics such as "most points scored or most rebounds") and to motivate players as well as the overall team; both an Offensive and a Defensive Performance Grading System can and should be implemented. When a coaching staff builds its grading system, it can place a greater emphasis on what they value the most to fit their system and philosophy. Players should not only understand what the coaching staff values the most during games as well as in practices. Individual offensive and defensive grades on every player (regardless of the position and the amount of playing time) can be accumulated as well as overall team grades for both their own team as well as the opposition's grades. These team grades can be compared from game to game as well as from season to season; giving the coaching staff concrete evidence in the evaluation of players, teams and the overall performance of the system. When players see what types of offensive and defensive statistics are of the highest value to the coaching staff by their grades and how those highest grade leaders are recognized in the form of rewards; players will adjust their focus to the same values the coaching staff places on those specific aspects of the game. When those individual statistics are then integrated into the overall team's offensive and defensive grades, the team's attitudes will improve and success will then come to the team.

These are the concepts that serve as the foundation and the building blocks that can establish an effective and productive man-to-man offensive system that can withstand the weather of time. As players and their respective ability levels of both strengths and weaknesses change from one season to the next, in addition to opponents changing; a fundamentally sound offensive system can adjust accordingly without major disruptions or changes to the overall program. This consistency gives both the players and the coaching staff faith and confidence in the system.

CHAPTER 3
FUNDAMENTAL THEORIES
APPLIED IN A SUCCESSFUL MULTIPLE-PHASE MAN-TO-MAN OFFENSIVE SYSTEM

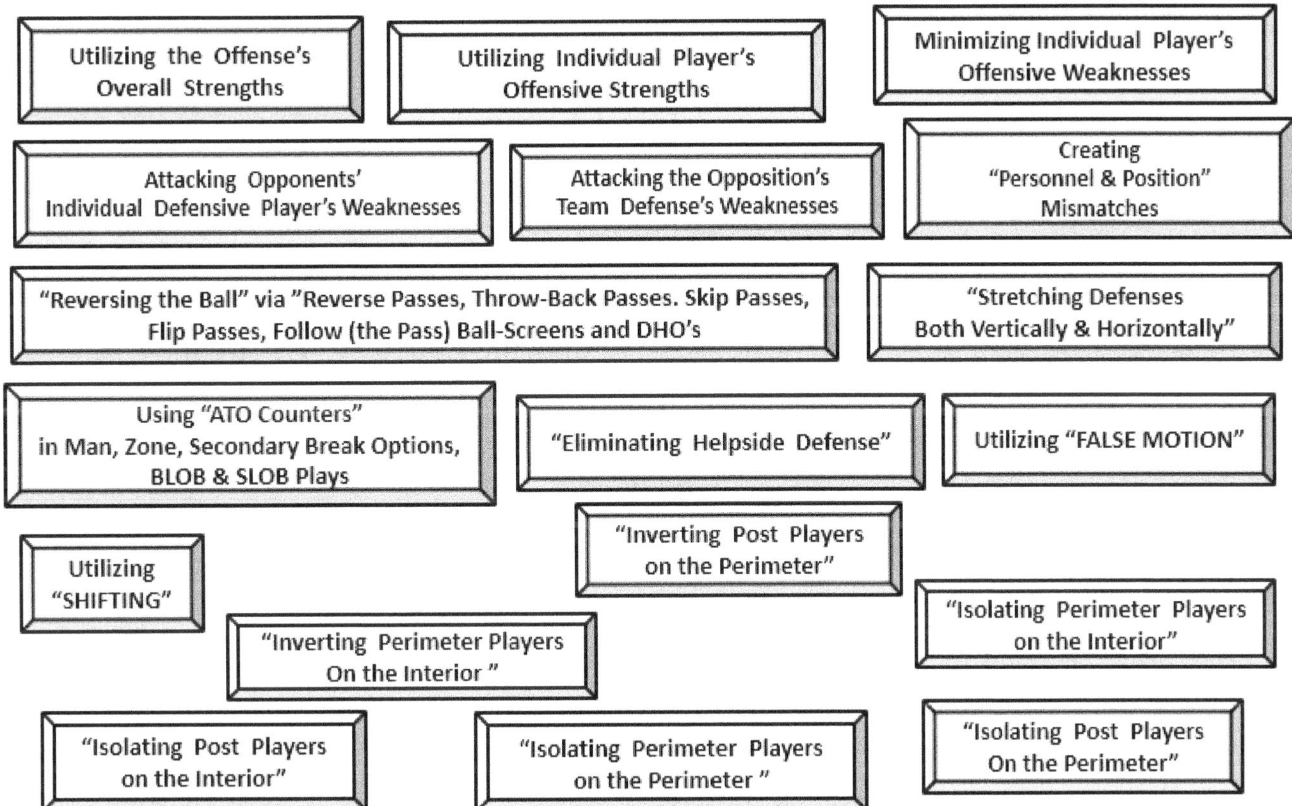

Utilizing the Offense's Overall Strengths
Utilizing Individual Player's Offensive Strengths
Minimizing Individual Player's Offensive Weaknesses
Attacking Opponents' Individual Defensive Player's Weaknesses
Attacking the Opposition's Team Defense's Weaknesses
Creating "Personnel & Position" Mismatches
"Reversing the Ball" via "Reverse Passes, Throw-Back Passes. Skip Passes, Flip Passes, Follow (the Pass) Ball-Screens and DHO's
"Stretching Defenses Both Vertically & Horizontally"
Using "ATO Counters" in Man, Zone, Secondary Break Options, BLOB & SLOB Plays
"Eliminating Helpside Defense"
Utilizing "FALSE MOTION"
"Inverting Post Players on the Perimeter"
Utilizing "SHIFTING"
"Isolating Perimeter Players on the Interior"
"Inverting Perimeter Players On the Interior "
"Isolating Post Players on the Interior"
"Isolating Perimeter Players on the Perimeter "
"Isolating Post Players On the Perimeter"

After the list comes the actual examples of the theories that is the text used in conjunction with the PowerPoint diagrams.

⚆ *THEORY 1:*

UTILIZING THE OFFENSE'S OVERALL STRENGTHS–

When the coaching staff determines the biggest strengths the team possesses should create plays/entries and a continuity offense(s) to then incorporate those strengths as much as possible.

⚆ *THEORY 2:*

UTILIZING INDIVIDUAL PLAYER'S OFFENSIVE STRENGTHS—

After the coaching staff analyzes and evaluates every player's top strengths, players' strengths should also be incorporated within the framework of plays/entries as well as the continuity offense that is to be executed. Individual offensive strengths used will give the overall offense even more weapons to utilize.

⚆ *THEORY 3:*

MINIMIZING INDIVIDUAL PLAYER'S OFFENSIVE WEAKNESSES—

Conversely, every player's weaknesses and offensive deficiencies should be avoided as much as possible within the offensive attack. Those deficiencies should not be ignored in practice sessions but worked on constantly to turn those weaknesses into strengths that can then be utilized more. Those newly developed and improved upon weaknesses can now become offensive strengths that produce even more benefits to the offense.

⚆ *THEORY 4:*

ATTACKING OPPONENTS' INDIVIDUAL DEFENSIVE PLAYER'S WEAKNESSES

After discovering the weaknesses of individual defenders, those should be attacked within the basic overall structure of the offensive attack, giving the offense another type of advantage over the defense.

⊕ *THEORY 5:*

ATTACKING THE OPPOSITION'S TEAM DEFENSE'S WEAKNESSES—

Just like the individual flaws in the structure and objectives of the opposition's defense, the offense should take advantage of that discovery and attack within the framework of the overall offense.

⊕ *THEORY 6:*

CREATING "PERSONNEL & POSITION" MISMATCHES—

Within the structure of the plays and the continuity offense(s), the offense looks to discover how offensive players can place themselves in offensive various types of advantages. See Play # 1.

⊕ *THEORY 7:*

**"REVERSING THE BALL" VIA" REVERSE PASSES, THROW-BACK PASSES.
SKIP PASSES, FLIP PASSES, FOLLOW (THE PASS) BALL-SCREENS AND DHO'S—**

The quicker and more often an offensive team can change the "defensive ballside" into the "defensive weakside" and vice versa; the more opportunities of success the offense will have available. See Play # 2.

⊕ *THEORY 8:*

"STRETCHING DEFENSES BOTH VERTICALLY & HORIZONTALLY"—

The more an offense can stretch an opposing defense, the thinner and weaker the defense becomes. This new weaknesses creates even more opportunities for offensive success. See Plays # 3 & 8.

🏀 *THEORY 9:*

USING "ATO COUNTERS" IN MAN, ZONE, SECONDARY BREAK OPTIONS, BLOB & SLOB PLAYS—

Using After Time-Out Counter Plays within the overall offensive system gives offensive teams moments to communicate and organize a play/entry that appears to the defense to be known and recognized, when in fact, has similarities with a drastic difference somewhere in the Counter Plays' action. This gives the offense still another offensive advantage. See Play # 5.

🏀 *THEORY 10:*

"ELIMINATING HELPSIDE DEFENSE"—

When an offense wants to attack a defense on the interior, opposing defenses will want to "load up" their interior defense with extra defenders. Offensive players on the "Ballside" are obviously bigger threats to the defense since they are closer to the ball, so defenses cannot adjust and move those "Ballside defenders" closer to the offensive post players. But offensive players that are on the opposite side of the ball are further away from the ball and are not as viable scoring threats because of their increased distance from the actual basketball. See Plays # 1, 2, 3, 4, 6, 7, & 8.

🏀 *THEORY 11:*

UTILIZING "FALSE MOTION"—

"When an offense needs to move and adjust specific player's positions and locations from its initial offensive set/alignment, to different locations that are necessary for the continuation of the play; this action (called "False Motion") is vital. See Play # 7.

🏀 *THEORY 12:*

UTILIZING "SHIFTING"—

This procedure has players shift from one location in an offensive set into a new location. This "shifting" from one set into another set before there is actual offensive action begins helps give the offense still additional offensive advantages by making offensive actions less predictable.

⊕ *THEORY 13:*

"INVERTING POST PLAYERS ON THE PERIMETER"—

When a defined offensive post-player is discovered with so-called "above average offensive talents" that can lead to advantages for that offensive player and the team via offensive players/entries, those situations should be used often. See Play # 8.

⊕ *THEORY 14:*

"INVERTING PERIMETER PLAYERS ON THE INTERIOR"—

Conversely, when a defined offensive perimeter-type player can use his discovered "above average offensive skills" in different locations such as in the Mid or Low post areas, other plays/entries should be built and utilized within the offensive package. In addition, moving so-called "perimeter-type defenders" that are forced to defend someone in the "post areas" should have distinct disadvantages such as lack of experience, training, height, weight, strength, etc. These all could be weaknesses that the offense should and could take advantage of. See Play #2, # 8 & 9

⊕ *THEORY 15:*

"ISOLATING PERIMETER PLAYERS ON THE INTERIOR"—

In addition to placing opposing defenders that are more of a "perimeter-type defenders" that have greater deficiencies and weaknesses in these abnormal situation, when these so-called weaker defenders would need extra help in the form of "double-down traps" or extra interior support. See Play # 8.

THEORY 16:

"ISOLATING POST PLAYERS ON THE INTERIOR"—

When offensive 'post-type players" are placed in these close-to-the-basket and high percentage scoring areas with no extra support defense, the advantages clearly would go to the offensive team. See Plays # 1, 3, 4, 5, 6, 7 and 9.

THEORY 17:

"ISOLATING PERIMETER PLAYERS ON THE PERIMETER"—

To simplify things, "isolating any defender on their so-called "perimeter-type" player in the wide open spaces of the perimeter places the defense in disadvantages for the defense which creates tremendous advantages for the offensive players. See Plays 6 & 8.

THEORY 18:

"ISOLATING POST PLAYERS ON THE PERIMETER"—

Isolating any type of opposing defender in interior areas that are close to the basket and are in high percentage scoring areas is a very difficult task for any type of defender in one-on-one settings. See Play 10.

CHAPTER 4:

PRINCIPLES
of a SUCCESSFUL
MULTIPLE-PHASE
MAN-to-MAN
OFFENSIVE
SYSTEM

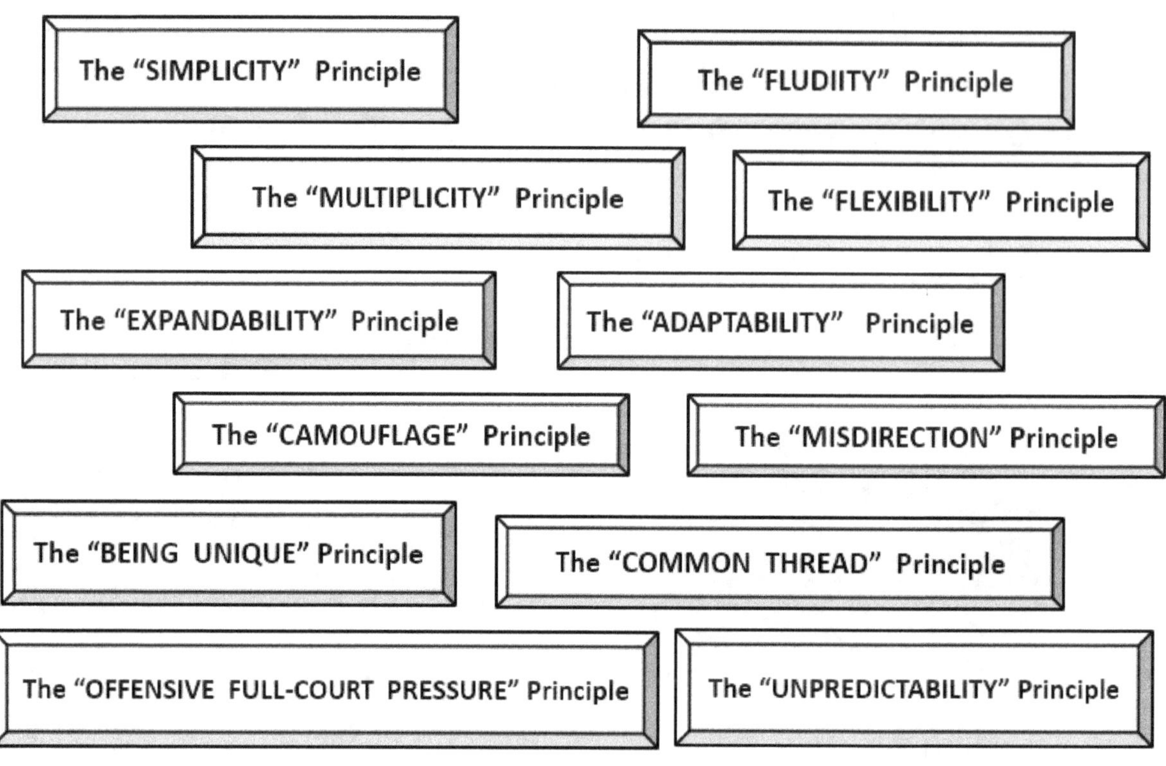

PRINCIPLE 1—

THE "SIMPLICITY" REQUIREMENT:

A successful man offensive package must require simplicity (for its own offensive players) possibly as its main component. Players must know what their assignments and responsibilities are in each phase of the overall offensive attack. Coaching staff must evaluate their team's mental abilities as much or more than their squad's physical skills and talents to determine its mental capacity and how much that team can utilize other important offensive characteristics and traits. The level of *"Simplicity"* is different in each specific team. This belongs in the same group of requirements that a successful team's man offense should possess, such as the "Simplicity," the "Fluidity," the "Multiplicity," the "Flexibility," the "Expandability," the "Adaptability" and the "Unpredictability" principles. From these comes the ability for man offenses to be so unpredictable to opposing man defenses that a team's man offensive scheme can be very productive, efficient and successful.

⊕ *PRINCIPLE 2—*

THE "FLUIDITY" REQUIREMENT:

Regardless of the number of offensive sets utilized and the number of offensive plays/entries/quick-hitters that are implemented; each play must have the ability to instantly, seamlessly and fluidly flow into the chosen continuity offense. This gives the offensive package separate (on paper) phases of offensive attack that blend so smoothly that it appears on the court to be one long continuous offensive assault on the opposition's man-to-man defense. This is the very important "Fluidity" requirement that each phase of the offense needs to be successful.

⊕ *PRINCIPLE 3—*

THE "MULTIPLICITY" REQUIREMENT:

Once the "Simplicity" and the "Fluidity" principles have been integrated into the multiple-phase offensive system, many other very important principles can be implemented, with the "Multiplicity" trait quite possibly being the next most important. This is because the "Multiplicity" principle is the bridge to many other more valuable principles. Being able to have multiple plays out of multiple sets/alignments and multiple continuities is invaluable to an offensive system. This allows the offense to be more varied and less predictable to opposing defenses, while still maintaining a degree of simplicity for your own team, but it must be stressed to NOT have too many plays or alignments. Being multiple offensively allows an offensive team to possess more "weapons" and more ways to attack and defeat opposing defenses. Some teams could also have more than one continuity offense; but again, too much could mentally hamper and diminish an offensive team's effectiveness. Each team will have its own set of limitations on how multiple it can be offensively. Having the correctly chosen continuity offense that every play in the offensive arsenal can smoothly transition into not only gives the offensive team still another vehicle to attack the defense, but a form of a security blanket. If the play breaks down, the team can go back to its continuity offense that a team has been accustomed to and can maintain its attack. Each play that does not create the desired shot can seamlessly flow into the (fundamentally sound) continuity offense that has its own methods and ways to successfully attack the defense. This would be a tremendous advantage to the offense and a huge disadvantage to the opposition's defense.

⊕ *PRINCIPLE 4—*

THE "FLEXIBILITY" REQUIREMENT:

An offensive package that is "Multiple" also allows the offense to be "Flexible," "Expandable," and "Adaptable." If an offensive team has the ability to change its method of attack because of its own specific strengths and weaknesses along with the opposition's defensive strengths and weaknesses, it will be a much more successful offense and add more ways to attack the opposition's defense. This "Flexibility" characteristic increases a team's offensive strengths exponentially.

⊕ *PRINCIPLE 5—*

THE "EXPANDABILITY" REQUIREMENT:

An overall offensive scheme that possesses the strength of also being expandable always gives the offensive team the potential to add other forms of attack as the season progresses to become a more explosive offensive team. This could be by adding extra plays either out of the same offensive set or out of an entirely different offensive alignment. The number of options and/or counter-options to the designated continuity offense could be expanded to give the continuity offense more fire-power.

⊕ *PRINCIPLE 6—*

THE "ADAPTABILITY" REQUIREMENT:

If an offensive team has the ability to change or vary its plan of attack because of middle-of-the-game "time and score" situations, because of its own personnel changes or the opposition's defensive actions and adjustments; then it increases a team's chance for a more successful season. This important requirement is called "*Adaptability*" Principle.

❀ *PRINCIPLE 7*—

THE "CAMOUFLAGE" REQUIREMENT:

Offensive teams in every sport are constantly attempting to fool its competitive defensive opponents to force those defenses into being more vulnerable and susceptible to the offense's actual plan of attack. Offensive teams try to also conceal their actual objectives until the very last moment in order to gain as much of an advantage as well possible over the opposition's defense. When offensive teams hide its own objectives, its strengths and its team weaknesses while at the same time looking to attack the opponents' weaknesses by camouflaging their methods of attack, it will always keep the opposition off-balance, confused and hesitant. This gives the offense advantages over the defense and allows the offense to be even more unpredictable. Deceiving the opposition can occur in the beginning parts of plays/entries by incorporating *"shifting" and "false motion" actions.* This allows the offense to utilize and take advantage of one of the more important principles in every offensive scheme and attack—and that is called the *"Unpredictability"* Principle.

❀ *PRINCIPLE 8*—

THE "MISDIRECTION" REQUIREMENT:

In addition to concealing until the last possible moment of what an offensive team is attempting to do and how it is attempting to attack an opposing defense at the beginning of the offensive action, an offensive team can also attempt to confuse and fool a defense by utilizing additional "false motion" further into the offensive movement and also by utilizing planned *"misdirection actions"* by using different techniques and methods. This can often help neutralize defensive strengths and actually turn those strengths into defensive weaknesses. This offensive principle also helps effectively utilize possibly the most important offensive principles that is needed in every offensive scheme and plan of attack—once again, the *"Unpredictability"* Principle.

⚉ *PRINCIPLE 9—*

THE "BEING UNIQUE" REQUIREMENT:

As stated previously, offensive basketball teams are constantly attempting to gain advantages over their defensive opponents. One principle that can be applied to for an offensive coach to thoroughly evaluate his/her own team's overall offensive skills and talents as well as the opposition. If a coach has very similar forms and methods of the offensive attack that his/her team's opponent utilizes. That means that defensive opponents that are accustomed to defending very similar offensive actions will become more proficient in defending those similar attacks and methods. Therefore, if a coach decides to use different methods of offensive attacks that defenses are not accustomed to seeing, not knowing how to properly defend those unique offensive actions, the defensive opponents will have a much more difficult time in understanding, preparing for and correctly defending those different types of offensive actions. A coaching staff should not make drastic changes to be different for the sake of being different, but if those changes will accent his/her team's skills, minimize his/her team's weaknesses and also force the opposition into preparing for and playing against those changes; the offense will be more successful. These changes in the offensive scheme can often help neutralize defensive strengths and highlight defensive weaknesses. This will help the offense with the *"Unpredictability"* Principle.

⚉ *PRINCIPLE 10—*

THE "FULL-COURT OFFENSIVE PRESSURE PLACED ON THE OPPOSITION'S DEFENSES" REQUIREMENT:

Full Court pressure defenses are practical weapons on the defensive side of the ball that can help the opposition control the tempo of the game and can affect the physical, emotional and mental conditioning of offenses. But there is no rule that says that a team cannot magnify that same weapon by applying offensive pressure and stress on the opponent's defensive team at the full court level. Our belief is to apply "full court offensive pressure on the opposition's defense." This means that a coach's offensive team could apply a large degree of pressure on the opposition's defense by utilizing every possible fastbreak opportunity that is created. These could take place immediately not only after the opposition's turnovers and missed shots, but also after opponent's 'made' shots. This quick in-bounding after "their scores," can also be an effective deterrent against the opposition's defensive attempt to try to full-court pressure your team's offense.

⊕ *<u>PRINCIPLE 11—</u>*

"COMMON THREADS IN ALL THE VARIOUS FORMS OFFENSIVE ATTACK" REQUIREMENT:

The full utilization and integration of all forms/methods of offensive attacks; be it half-court offensive attacks, offensive out-of-bounds attacks, full-court offensive attacks off of Full-Court Press Offensive attacks, as well as all transitions attacks must all have the same common threads that integrate the same offensive concepts and philosophies. These various forms of attacks begin at different points of time in all offensive/defensive positions that also begin in different locations of the court. While there are different origins and different times of initiation, the common threads will help make all of these attacks a more effective and successful attacks against the opposition's defenses.

⊕ *<u>PRINCIPLE 12—</u>*

THE "UNPREDICTABILITY" REQUIREMENT:

A Multiple-Phase Offensive System that is "Multiple," and/or "Flexible," and/or "Expandable" and/or "Adaptable" as well as able to "Camouflage" its objectives and often make it appear the offensive action is going in one particular direction before suddenly switching directions provides even more potential advantages and benefits to the offensive team. Conversely, those also create disadvantages and problems for the opposing defenses. These principles helps create the single most advantage for any and every offensive scheme and attack—the *"Unpredictability"* Principle. If an offensive team can make changes in how it attacks opposition's defenses from game to game and even from quarter to quarter of the same game, it makes it extremely difficult for any defense to attempt to solve the offensive plan that can constantly change. A defensive team that does not know what to expect from the offense has a much more difficult time to defend any offensive attack.

CHAPTER 5

VITAL TRAITS AND CHARACTERISTICS USED IN A SUCCESSFUL MULTIPLE-PHASE OFFENSIVE SYSTEM

⊕ *TRAIT 1:*

THE "SIMPLICITY" TRAIT/CHARACTERISTIC—

A successful man offensive package must require simplicity (for its own offensive players) possibly as its main component. Players must know what their assignments and responsibilities are in each phase of the overall offensive attack. Coaching staff must evaluate their team's mental abilities as much or more than their squad's physical skills and talents to determine its mental capacity and how much that team can utilize other important offensive TRAITS and CHARACTERISTICS. This trait belongs to the same group of concepts of a successful team's man offense should possess, such as: "Simplicity," "Fluidity," "Multiplicity," "Flexibility," "Expandability," "Adaptability" and "Unpredictability." From these characteristics comes the ability for man offenses to be so unpredictable to opposing man defenses that a team's man offensive scheme can be very productive, efficient, and successful.

⊕ *TRAIT 2:*

THE "FLUIDITY" TRAIT/CHARACTERISTIC--

Regardless of the number of offensive alignments/sets utilized and the number of offensive plays/entries/quick-hitters that are implemented; each play must have the ability to instantly, seamlessly and fluidly flow into the designated continuity offense. On paper, this gives the offensive package separate phases or layers of offensive attack that blend and transition so seamlessly and smoothly that it appears on the court to be one long continuous offensive assault on the opposition's man-to-man defense. This is the very important *"Fluidity"* characteristic.

⊕ *TRAIT 3A:*

THE "MULTIPLICITY" TRAIT/CHARACTERISTIC–

Once the "Simplicity," the "Fluidity," along with the "Deception & Misdirection" TRAITS and CHARACTERISTICS have been integrated into the man offensive package, many other very important characteristics/TRAITS and CHARACTERISTICS can be implemented, with the "Multiplicity" trait quite possibly being the next most important. This is because the "Multiplicity" characteristics are the bridge to many other more valuable TRAITS and CHARACTERISTICS. Being multiple in the number of plays, sets/alignments and possibly other continuities is an invaluable trait of an offensive system. This allows the offense to be more varied and less predictable to opposing defenses, while still maintaining a degree of simplicity for your own team. A philosophy is that an offensive team can have multiple plays/entries and can run out of multiple sets/alignments, but it must be stressed to NOT have too many plays or alignments.

⊕ *TRAIT 3B:*

THE "MULTIPLICITY" TRAIT/CHARACTERISTIC--

Being multiple offensively allows an offensive team to possess more "weapons" and more ways to attack and defeat opposing defenses. Some teams could also have more than one continuity offense; but we believe that no more than two continuities. Each team will have its own set of limitations on how multiple it can be offensively. Having the correctly chosen continuity offense that every play in the offensive arsenal can smoothly transition into not only gives the offensive team still another vehicle to attack the defense, but a form of a security blanket. If the play breaks down, the team can go back to its continuity offense that the team has been accustomed to and can maintain its attack. Each play that does not create the desired shot can seamlessly flow into the (fundamentally sound) continuity offense that has its own methods and ways to successfully attack the defense. This would be a tremendous advantage to the offense and a huge disadvantage to the opposition's defense. Therefore, the *"Multiplicity"* trait is an invaluable weapon to all offensive packages/schemes.

⊕ *TRAIT 4:*

THE "FLEXIBILITY" TRAIT"--

An offensive package that is "Multiple" also allows the offense to be "Flexible," "Expandable," and "Adaptable." If an offensive team has the ability to change its method of attack because of different opponents having varying strengths and weaknesses, the offensive package will be much more successful and add more ways to attack the opposition's defense, it increases its offensive strengths exponentially. This is the offensive package's important characteristic called the *"Flexibility"* trait.

⊕ *TRAIT 5:*

THE "EXPANDABILITY" TRAIT/CHARACTERISTIC--

An overall offensive scheme that possesses the strength of also being expandable always gives the offensive team the potential to add other types or forms of attack as the season progresses to become a more explosive offensive team. This characteristic is what we call the *"Expandability"* trait.

🌐 *TRAIT 6:*

THE "ADAPTABILITY" TRAIT/CHARACTERISTIC--

If an offensive team has the ability to change or vary its plan of attack because of game "time and situation" factors in the middle of a game or season because of personnel changes during a game or the season, then it increases a team's chance for a more successful season. Unexpected changes in personnel clearly could call in changes in styles, tempo of games, offensive plays, and/or continuity offenses. This is the important *"Adaptability"* characteristic that is a necessary trait for all successful offensive systems.

🌐 *TRAIT 7:*

THE "UNPREDICTABILITY" TRAIT/CHARACTERISTIC--

An offensive package that is "Multiple," and/or "Flexible," and/or "Expandable" and/or "Adaptable" and possesses "Deception & Misdirection" characteristics will very much possess the all-important weapon of being unpredictable to all opposing defenses. If an offensive team can make changes in how it attacks opposition's defenses from game to game and even from quarter to quarter of the same game, it makes it extremely difficult for any opposition to attempt to solve the offensive plan that can constantly change and adjust to the defense. This is the all-important *"Unpredictability"* offensive characteristic.

🌐 *TRAIT 8:*

THE "CAMOUFLAGING AND DECEIVING OF THE OPPOSITION" TRAIT/CHARACTERISTIC--

Offensive systems that can effectively deceive opposing defenses will increase defensive mistakes, confusion, breakdowns, and hesitancy. These defensive results will provide great amounts of offensive productivity, efficiency, and success in the offense's actions, plays, and continuity offenses. Many of the offensive sets/alignments discussed in this book are symmetrically balanced; each play could initially attack either side of the floor. This makes each play ambidextrous and therefore even more unpredictable for the opposition until the very last instant. Another method for offenses is to implement offensive counters, counter-options and/or ATOs. These organized and pre-planned, pre-taught, pre-coached actions by the offensive team will maintain the offensive advantage of preserving the unpredictability factor. This sustains the "offensive actions that attack defensive reactions" factor. "Shifting" and "False Motion" can also be integrated to add to the camouflaging, the hiding of the plays' objectives court just before the beginning actions of the entry/play/quick-hitter starts. It takes place after the ball has crossed the timeline but before there are passes by the Point Guard or before screens are set for that same Point Guard. We define the "False Motion" within offensive systems as the actual movement of both the ball and players that can also help deceive opponents in the ways an offensive team is attempting to attack the opposition's defense.

⊛ *TRAIT 9:*

THE "DISGUISE/HIDING/COVERING" TRAIT--

This important trait can be used so that every entry/play could be camouflaged in the same offensive set or in other alignments. This makes many offensive actions more unpredictable and therefore, tougher to defend; almost every entry could be executed with or without "Iverson Cuts." There can be very simple and basic offensive actions that can be implemented off and on that can change the entire cosmetic appearance of various offensive sets/alignments in addition to many plays/entries. Some entries could substitute Iverson Cuts with "L-Cuts" where both 03 and 02 break up and out from their initial Deep Corner locations to the FT Line extended, but remain on the same side of the floor. When and if "Iverson Cuts" are appropriate for a play, the designated "high cutter" (03 for example) and the "low cutter" (02) can be easily switched to give each play a different cosmetic look. Mixing in each play with "L-Cuts, with a crossing of the two players through the lane, or executing "Iverson Cuts" and switching whether 03 or 02 is the high Iverson Cutter and the opposite player being the low (Iverson) Cutter gives each individual play/entry many more different 'looks' that will momentarily cause the defense to hesitate at the initial action of the play/entry and therefore allow the offense to deceive defenses even more so. Opposing defenses may have to compete and defend these different ways the offense may attack defenses. Executing basically the same play, but out of various offensive sets, is another easy and simple method for the offense to utilize in the overall offensive system.

⊕ ***TRAIT 10:***

THE "VARIETY" TRAIT/CHARACTERISTIC--

The more opportunities an offensive team can have in implementing various players that also have different levels of athleticism and different offensive strengths, the more legitimate offensive weapons an offensive team can have. The more multiple the offense can be within its wide variety of offensive entries and also in the final phase of the offensive attack—be it a Motion Offense or a Continuity Offense, the more methods a team can successfully attack a defense. A successful offensive system can include a range of offensive phases, levels or waves of attack that all have the unique ability to be able to flow smoothly from one part to the next part of the offensive attack. A coaching staff cannot just become more multiple for the sake of being more multiple. A team's offensive system must be compatible with the coaching staff's philosophies as well as fitting the team's offensive personnel's overall basketball strengths and skills as well as its basketball intelligence. Too much of anything good can be bad. An offensive team cannot be bogged down mentally with too many offensive sets, too many offensive plays, too many continuity offenses, too many counter-options, etc. Another factor that can be implemented within an offensive system is a coaching staff that properly selects the proper style of play to maximize that particular team's success. Within reason, there can be a range of styles of play that meet an offensive team's overall strengths that can be chosen, changed, and modified from one season to the next. Adjusting and modifying the different varieties of tempo and style of play can play a vital role in the success of an offensive team. Implementing a wide range of methods to attack defenses with primarily inside oriented or perimeter oriented attacks can (and should be) altered to fit each team's needs for that specific season. The methods to attack the presumed opponents' defensive weaknesses with the current team's offensive strengths will have to be diversified from season to season and possibly from shorter time periods. The *"Variety"* trait is also a very important component of successful offensive packages/schemes.

THE "MISDIRECTION" TRAIT/CHARACTERISTIC—

The offensive teams in every sport are constantly attempting to fool its competitive defensive opponents to make them vulnerable and susceptible to the offense's actual plan of attack. With deception, the offensive team is trying to disguise its own strengths while hiding its team weaknesses while at the same time looking to attack the opponents' weaknesses. This trait is tied directly to the offensive scheme of "Unpredictability," again making the offense a more efficient form of attack. Deception can occur in the beginning parts of plays/entries by incorporating the invaluable *"Misdirection"* trait. This trait in the offensive scheme can often help neutralize defensive strengths and actually turn those strengths into defensive weaknesses. The *"Misdirection"* trait helps institute one of the other more important TRAITS and CHARACTERISTICS in every offensive (as well as defensive) schemes and attacks—the *"Unpredictability"* Trait.

⊕ *TRAIT 12:*

THE USE OF UNIQUE ACTIONS/SCHEMES DIFFERENT THAN MOST OPPONENTS' ACTIONS.

A successful offensive system does not have to be the same as most other offensive systems. In fact, the more unique an offensive system is in relationship to its opponents; the greater chance it can become a dominant and successful system. That is only when that specific offensive system actually fits not only the coaching staff's philosophies and beliefs but that it corresponds to the actual talent levels, strengths and weaknesses of the offensive personnel on that season's team. An offensive system that is unique for the sake of being unique will not make an offensive system successful or productive. But when philosophies and personnel strengths match and can fit in with that different type of offensive style, its tempo and its ways to attack the opposition's defenses; it can be a very successful system. Because of the uniqueness of the offense, opposing defenses will not have been able to acquire a knowledge of the system, will not have the experience to understand strengths, weaknesses, and objectives. To opposing defenses, this different offensive system will be more difficult to understand, harder to prepare opposing players to defend it and much more difficult to be able to predict the actions of the offense. These reasons simply start adding to more and more offensive advantages and widen the gap between an offense's "actions" that are attempted to be defended by an opposing team's "reactions."

There are many techniques that could and should be implemented in some manner within the framework of both the package of offensive plays as well as within the offensive continuity or motion offense's scheme. The more of these techniques used and applied by the offense's entries as well as the continuities used; the more weapons that offensive team can possess. More weapons help an offensive team probe opponent's defenses for both individual as well as overall team defensive weaknesses. These techniques could be categorized as either various types of cuts, various types of off-ball screens and diverse types of ball-screens that have ending types of actions following those different types of ball-screens. An offensive team wants to maximize those fundamentally sound techniques without overloading a team with too many techniques incorporated within the offense. The package of various entries/plays should be able to implement more of a variety of these techniques than the desired continuity or motion offense.

⚟ *TECHNIQUE 1:*

**ALL OFFENSIVE PLAYERS SHOULD REALIZE THE
OFFENSIVE EFFECTIVENESS AS
WELL AS TO BE ABLE TO EXECUTE THE "INSIDE PASS"—**

Offensive players should make bounce-passes "away" from the defenders of their interior pass receiver unless the post player is fronted. If the offensive post player is fronted, the passer should then lob the ball "away" from the fronting defender towards the corner of the backboard. We want all "inside passes" to be "bounce passes" except for "lob passes" when playing against fronting interior defenders.

⚟ *TECHNIQUE 2:*

**ALL OFFENSIVE PLAYERS SHOULD REALIZE
OFFENSIVE EFFECTIVENESS AS WELL AS TO BE ABLE TO
EXECUTE THE PROPER "INSIDE PASS" TECHNIQUES—**

Offensive players should make bounce-passes to their post-up teammate's hand that is "AWAY" from that interior defender unless the post player is fronted. If the post defender is ¾ fronting on the offensive post player's "high" side, the ball should be passed to the outstretched "low" hand of the post player. If the defender is ¾ fronting on the "low" side, the ball should be passed to the post player's "high" hand of that teammate. If the defender is winning the "battle of the feet" and is effectively denying the inside pass, a quick pass to another perimeter teammate should have a much better passing angle to make that successful inside pass. If the offensive post player is fronted defensively, the passer should then lob the ball "away" from the fronting defender towards the corner of the backboard. Another method would be to make a quick, accurate and safe "skip pass" and have the interior player then "seal off" his fronting defender. If the post defender is playing completely behind, the perimeter passer should make a hard bounce pass and slightly shade the pass either low or high to set the post player up for maximum shot effectiveness.

ALL OFFENSIVE PLAYERS SHOULD REALIZE OFFENSIVE EFFECTIVENESS AS WELL AS TO BE ABLE TO EXECUTE "SKIP PASSES"—

Perimeter players should not hesitate on making "skip-passes" across the court. "Skip-passes" are an instant method of reversing the ball from one side of the court to the other side. Reversing the ball is an integral concept for successful offenses to be able to attack both inside and also on the perimeter. "Skip-passes" will also discourage "man defenses" from providing good helpside defense in the lane from the weakside of the offense, off of the "skip pass." After "skip passes" are made, post players should seal off the post defenders that deny them the ball on the original ballside and be prepared to receive the pass from the original weakside. "Skip-passes" can provide offenses with open "catch & shoot 3's" or opportunities to "shot fake & create." When MAN defenders react to the "skip pass," a second "skip pass" back to the original 'ballside' can be very effective. A phrase "One good skip pass deserves another" should be taught and utilized in every type of offense that is utilized.

⊕ *TECHNIQUE # 4A:*

ALL OFFENSIVE PLAYERS SHOULD REALIZE OFFENSIVE EFFECTIVENESS AS WELL AS TO BE ABLE TO UTILIZE THE "THROW-BACK REVERSE PASS"--

Perimeter players should be able to execute the all-important 'Throw-back (Reverse) Pass' that could/should be used off of the dribble. This pass being made off of the dribble makes an even quicker misdirection actions that can surprise both the on-ball defender but also all of the off-ball defenders. With it being off of the dribble and reversing the ball, it prevents all defenders from being able to react as quickly to the pass. This immediate and most likely surprising pass makes it more difficult for the initial 'helpside defenders' to adjust and become the new 'ballside defenders,' as well as making it tougher from those initial 'ballside defenders' to adjust to become the new 'helpside defenders.' The likely surprise and the quickness of being able to execute the pass to a new offensive threat can create several types of defensive weaknesses, both on the interior as well as in the interior.

ALL OFFENSIVE PLAYERS SHOULD REALIZE
OFFENSIVE EFFECTIVENESS AS WELL AS TO BE ABLE TO
EXECUTE THE "HAMMER PASS"--

Perimeter players should also be able to execute a somewhat newer type of pass that is gaining popularity in the NBA and major college basketball. This pass comes after a ball-handler drives the baseline and when a 'helpside defender' rotates over to stop the ball, a weakside offensive player drifts down towards the Weakside Deep Corner behind the '3 Pt.' Line to receive the so-called "Hammer Pass." This driving action stretches the defense both vertically as well as horizontally. Even when the opposing defenders execute the fundamentally sound defensive rotations, there very likely will be an offensive player available for an open '3.' Again, with the "Hammer Pass" being executed off of the dribble and reversing the ball in a very unique manner, it keeps the opposition from being able to react as quickly to the pass. Just as the "Throw-back Pass" can attack defenses in somewhat of a unique way, the "Hammer Pass" will also cause the opposition's defense problems in the conversion from initial 'helpside defenders' becoming new 'ballside defenders' and vice versa.

⊛ *TECHNIQUE # 5A:*

ALL OFFENSIVE PLAYERS SHOULD REALIZE
OFFENSIVE EFFECTIVENESS AS WELL AS TO BE ABLE TO EXECUTE THE PROPER
DRIBBLING TECHNIQUES—

Another objective of this continuity offense is to have the capability for players at times to have the freedom within the structure of the offense to be able to attack individual defenders off of the dribble. This is done partially by giving offensive players the proper spacing to be able to create within the structure of the offense. Even though both dribbling techniques are primarily zone offense dribbling both the ball defender as well as helping defenders to create both high percentage inside shots as well as open "3s" as well as other pass receivers being able to drive to the basket. Any dribbler can either attack the initial on-ball defender and when that defender needs help, that dribble/driver can "penetrate & pitch" to a receiver on the perimeter for open shots or another driving opportunity or he can "drive & dump" to a post player close to the basket. Even if the shot is missed by the driver or the pass-receiving teammate, the "stick-back" opportunities are greatly enhanced because of less successful defensive box-outs by the defense's forced scrambling rotations.

⊕ *TECHNIQUE # 5B:*

ALL OFFENSIVE PLAYERS SHOULD REALIZE
OFFENSIVE EFFECTIVENESS AS WELL AS TO BE ABLE TO
EXECUTE THE VARIOUS FORMS OF "PERIMETER PULL" DRIBBLES"--

Offensive players must at times, have the freedom within the structure of the offense to be able to attack individual defenders off of the dribble. This is done partially by giving offensive players the proper spacing to be able to create within the structure of the offense. Offenses must constantly move both the basketball and offensive personnel quickly and efficiently. The more frequent and the quicker the movement of both the ball and personnel, the greater the chance for defensive breakdowns. Even though this dribbling technique is thought of primarily as a zone offensive dribbling technique, these 'perimeter pull' dribbles will attack both the ball defender as well as attacking all off-the-ball defenders. These various types of 'perimeter pull' dribbles will create both high percentage inside shots as well as open "3s" for off-the-ball offensive teammates. as well as other pass receivers being able to drive to the basket.

⊕ *TECHNIQUE # 5C:*

ALL OFFENSIVE PLAYERS SHOULD REALIZE
OFFENSIVE EFFECTIVENESS AS WELL AS TO BE ABLE
TO EXECUTE ALL OF THE VARIOUS FORMS OF "PERIMETER PULL" DRIBBLES"--

When an offensive player dribbles vertically down from the 'Wing' area down towards the 'Deep Corner' area, this particular 'Perimeter Pull' Dribbles could be specifically called 'Down-Dribbles.' 'Up-Dribbles' are vertical dribbles in the opposite direction, from the initial 'Deep Corner' up towards the 'Wing' area. Both of these types of dribbles can also serve as a method of improving the passing angle so as to deliver the ball to a Post player near the 'Ballside Block.' Both of these types of dribbles can stretch the defense vertically and therefore weaken the defense's interior. These dribbles also of these particular types of dribbles definitely force opponents' helpside defenders to move as the ball is moved either down towards the baseline or up towards the timeline. When helpside defenders have to provide interior support defense. When a ball-handler makes a 'perimeter pull' dribble across the top of the defense (called a 'Drag Dribble), the action not only reverses the ball to the opposite side of the floor, which causes opposing defenders to adjust to the movement of the ball, to switch their individual positioning, stances, and defensive responsibilities from 'helpside to ballside' or 'ballside to helpside' responsibilities. With all five defenders having to make those major types of changes and adjustments (with the offense possibly only moving one player that has the ball), the opportunities for the offense to capitalize on possibly several breakdowns is great. This simple 'Drag Dribble' also stretches the defense horizontally, and therefore again weakens the defensive interior.

⊕ *TECHNIQUE # 5D:*

ALL OFFENSIVE PLAYERS SHOULD REALIZE
OFFENSIVE EFFECTIVENESS AS WELL AS TO BE ABLE TO
EXECUTE THE VARIOUS FORMS OF "PENETRATION" DRIBBLES"--

Any dribbler can either attack the initial on-ball defender and when he slightly penetrates into one of the gaps between the ball and the next closest defender on either side of the ball. That action can force a defensive teammate to not only help but to then end up in a location and/or stance disadvantage when and if the ball is then passed to his specific man. That can then cause a defensive breakdown where a second defensive opponent must attempt to help the new ball-defender that is in trouble. This chain reaction can continue until the offense can attack the weakened and scrambling and out-of-position defense with an inside shot or an open perimeter shot. A situation can also take place where the on-ball defender does not have a perimeter teammate that can help out. That dribbler can then dribble and make an even deeper penetration and when that defender needs help, that dribble/driver can "penetrate and pitch" to a receiver on the perimeter for open shots or another driving opportunity or he can "drive and dump" to a post player close to the basket. Even if the shot is missed by the driver or the pass-receiving teammate, the "stick-back" opportunities are greatly enhanced because of less successful defensive box-outs by the defense's forced scrambling rotations.

ALL POST PLAYERS SHOULD REALIZE OFFENSIVE EFFECTIVENESS AS WELL AS TO BE ABLE TO EXECUTE THE VARIOUS LOW AND HIGH POST FLASH-CUTS—

All offensive players operating in the low post areas should understand the importance and how to execute flash post cuts to both the low post and the high post with or without the aid of off-ball screens. If screens are set for the flashing post player, that player should first set his defender up with more than one-step V-Cuts and then scraping shoulder to shoulder with the screener. In addition, the actual screener should be prepared to counter defensive switches by sealing off the new defender and also becoming a flash-post player.

⊕ *TECHNIQUE # 7:*

ALL POST PLAYERS SHOULD REALIZE OFFENSIVE EFFECTIVENESS AS WELL AS TO BE ABLE TO EXECUTE THE "DUCK-IN CUT"—

Post players should use the "Duck-In" Cut and be ready to then use either a "power" move or a "face-up" move. This is particularly effective when the ball is passed inside from the top of the key. Regardless of how the opposition's post defender tries to defend the "Duck-In" Cut, the offense has an effective method of defeating the defensive action. The "Spin-Screen and Post Up" move should also be implemented when the defense is fronting the "Duck-In" move (with help from a screen from a second interior player.)

⊕ *TECHNIQUE # 8A:*

ALL POST PLAYERS SHOULD REALIZE OFFENSIVE EFFECTIVENESS AS WELL AS TO BE ABLE TO EXECUTE THE LOW-POST, THE HIGH POST FLASH-CUTTING AND THE "DUCK-IN" CUTTING TECHNIQUES--

All offensive players operating in the low post areas (including "inverted" perimeter players) should understand the importance and how to execute flash post cuts to both the low post and the high post with or without the aid of off-ball screens. If screens are set for the flashing post player, that player should first set his defender up with multi-step V-Cuts and then scraping shoulder to shoulder with the screener. in addition, the actual screener should be prepared to counter defensive switches by sealing off the new defender and also becoming a flash-post player.

When the defense tries to play on the side of the offensive post player, those post players should be able to use the "Show & Go Opposite" Power Move and the "Olajuwon Whirl Move"

When the defense presents ¾ or full denial in the post, the offense should execute the "Seal & Lob Pass" action between passer and post player.

When the defense plays directly behind, the "Duck-In" Cut the "Sikma Move" should be executed o square up to the basket (before then executing the (perimeter) "Blast" or "Cross-Over" Move to attack the defender.

If there are defensive "Double-Down" traps executed, the offensive post player must be aware of offensive perimeter players that are making "Drift Cuts" to get open and be able to make the "Kick-Out" Pass to the open perimeter teammate.

⊛ *TECHNIQUE # 8B:*

**ALL PERIMETER PLAYERS SHOULD REALIZE
OFFENSIVE EFFECTIVENESS AS WELL AS TO BE ABLE
TO EXECUTE THE 'DRIFT CUTS' AFTER INSIDE PASSES ARE MADE--**

If the ball is passed inside to a post player, all each perimeter player should rotate ½ of an offensive spot-up location either towards the Ballside Baseline or away from that same Baseline that will neutralize the various types of double-teams and rotations that defensive teams could utilize to combat the offensive team's "inside game." Each perimeter player should immediately "get his feet and hands ready" and already "cheat" to begin getting his shoulders and toes squared up to the basket. He should prepare to catch the 'Kick-out Pass' and be able to shoot quickly off of that pass as well as to drive to the basket or to immediately make the 'extra pass' to a perimeter teammate or to make a second inside pass back to the same post player.

ALL OFFENSIVE PLAYERS SHOULD REALIZE
OFFENSIVE EFFECTIVENESS AS WELL AS TO BE
ABLE TO EXECUTE THE VARIOUS PERIMETER CUTS–

Teams that use a variety of different types of offensive cuts by all types of offensive players from different locations on the floor during the many phases of the offense makes the offense much less predictable and ultimately much more difficult to defend by both individual defenders as well as the overall opponents' team defense. These types of cuts force individual defenders to defend their men more often as well as to occupy themselves to help reduce the effectiveness of the opposition's ballside and helpside defense on support defense. These offensive cuts that could be utilized within the offense's frameworks are:

A. "V" Cuts,
B. "Pipe" or "Zipper" Cuts,
C. "Shuffle" Cuts,
D. "Flex" Cuts,
E. "Scissors" Cuts,
F. "Veer" Cuts,
G. "Flex Bump" Cuts,
H. "Curl" Cuts,
I. "Backdoor" Cuts,
J. "Give-n-Go" Cuts,
K. "Flare-Cuts,
L. "UCLA Rub-Off" Cuts,
M. "Bruin" Bump Cuts,
N. "Ghost-Screen" Cuts,
O. "Brush" Cuts,
P. "Iverson" Cuts and
Q. "Barkley" Cuts.

In addition, the traditional "Post Players" types of cuts that "inverted perimeter" players should be able to execute are:

A. "Duck-In" Cuts,

B. "Lob" Cuts, (High or Low)

C. "Flash-Post" Cuts,

D. "Slash" Cuts,

E. "Spin-Screen" Cuts,

F. "Basket Cuts ("Slip" Cuts, "Rolls," or "Rim-Runs.")

G. "Backdoor" Cuts,

H. "Blind-Pig" Cuts,

I. Give-n-Go" Cuts,

J. "V"-Cuts,

K. "L"-Cuts,

L. "Lift" Cuts,

M. "Drift" Cuts,

N. "Pipe" Cuts,

O. "Shuffle" Cuts,

P. "Iverson" Cuts,

Q. "Barkley" Cuts,

R. "Flare" Cuts,

S. "Lob" Cuts,

T. "Flex" Cuts,

U. "Bump Flex" Cuts,

V. "Veer" Cuts,

W. "Scissors" Cuts,

X. "Flash Post" Cuts,

Y. "Slash" Cuts,

Z. "UCLA" Cuts,

AA. "Bruin" Bump Cuts,

BB. "Michigan" Cuts,

CC. "Blur" Cuts,

DD. "Duck-In" Cuts,

EE. "Flash-Post" Cuts,

FF. "Spin-Screen" Cuts, and

GG. "Basket" Cuts (Ball-Screen Rolls or Rim-Runs)

⊕ *TECHNIQUE # 10:*

ALL OFFENSIVE PLAYERS SHOULD REALIZE OFFENSIVE EFFECTIVENESS AS WELL AS TO BE ABLE TO EXECUTE THE VARIOUS TYPES OF PIVOTS

Offensive players must understand the value of basketball and how devastating turnovers can be to the offensive production of both individual players as well as the overall offensive team. Pivots are needed with offensive players on the perimeter as they prepare to shoot off of the dribble, as well as off of the pass and cutting from either side of the court. The perimeter player's foot closest to the basket is called the 'Inside Foot' and that 'Inside Foot' should be the designated 'Pivot Foot' (for both players cutting and catching the pass before shooting off of the pass. Dribblers should also pivot off of their 'Inside Foot' as they are about to shoot off of the dribble. Post players that receive 'Inside Passes' and prepare to execute their offensive post moves must heavily depend on the proper pivot in different directions, with either foot being the designated pivot foot. Offensive rebounders need to be able the same type of pivots as all other offense players. When the opposition shoots the ball, those defensive players are about to become offensive players in transition. Therefore defensive players must first know how to execute front and reverse pivots with either foot being the pivot foot so as to defensively 'box-out' the opponent to defensively rebound the ball. They then must proficiently execute both types of pivots with either foot being that pivot foot to successfully outlet the ball to being their team's transition offense. Offensive players must also be able to successfully execute all types of pivots versus opponent's defensive double-team traps.

⊕ *TECHNIQUE # 11:*

ALL OFF-THE-BALL OFFENSIVE PLAYERS SHOULD REALIZE OFFENSIVE EFFECTIVENESS AS WELL AS TO BE ABLE TO EXECUTE THE PROPER TECHNIQUES OF CATCHING THE PASS (AND QUICKLY ATTACKING WITH A SHOT OR WITH DRIBBLE PENETRATION) ---

When catching the basketball, perimeter players should always be ready to become immediate offensive threats as shooters, passers, or driving threats. Off-ball receivers should always be prepared to receive the pass, immediately attack the basket with a dribble or be ready to shoot quickly and accurately off of the pass. They should always "have their feet and hands ready." They should always keep their shoulders at least partially squared up to the basket as well as facing the passer. Receiving the pass could come off of solo cuts, cutting off of the various types of screens available or floating on the weakside perimeter.

🏀 <u>TECHNIQUE # 12:</u>

ALL OFFENSIVE PLAYERS SHOULD REALIZE
OFFENSIVE EFFECTIVENESS AS WELL AS TO BE ABLE TO
EXECUTE ALL FORMS OF PASS FAKE AND SHOT FAKE TECHNIQUES–

All offensive players should realize the importance of good pass against defenders. A coaching point of emphasis can be taught with the phrases:

A. "Fake a pass to make a pass."
B. "Fake high and pass low or fake low and pass high."

Passing fakes should be as realistic as possible and that means the fakes should be executed at game speed. Basic realistic passing fakes helps relieve defensive pressure as well as reduce interceptions and deflections.

All offensive players should also realize the importance of good shot fakes against defenders. A coaching point of emphasis can be to look at the rim while making a shot fake and making the fake look as close to an actual shot is vital. The ball should be brought up through the nose and face with the eyes on the rim. The ball should then be yanked back down on the side in a protective location while the drive to the basket begins. Shot fakes can create many more opportunities to drive to the basket and to draw fouls. To be successful, shot fakes do not have to cause the defender to leave the ground, but to just slightly move him or straighten his legs. Defenders cannot play defense with their legs straight. Basic realistic passing fakes help relieve defensive pressure as well as reduce interceptions and deflections.

⊛ *TECHNIQUE # 13A:*

ALL OFFENSIVE PLAYERS SHOULD UNDERSTAND AND BE ABLE TO PERFORM THE TECHNIQUES OF HOW TO 'OBTAIN & MAINTAIN' "BODY POSITION ADVANTAGES" IN THE POST—

Coaches should teach every one of their post players (as well as their so-called "perimeter" players) the techniques of how to obtain and then maintain "body position advantages" over their post defenders. "Arm bars" and "target hands" should be used to obtain the inside pass from teammates. "Sealing" off an interior defender after pin-screening for a teammate, after skip passes or ball-reversals or defensive overplays. Versus interior defensive overplay such as ¾ or full fronting can be defeated by movement of the basketball along with the interior player then obtaining and then maintaining the position advantage over the aggressive defense.

Along with various methods of eliminating the opposition's helpside defense, offenses can get the ball inside to effectively attack the opponent's interior defense.

⊛ *TECHNIQUE # 13B:*

ALL OFFENSIVE PLAYERS SHOULD REALIZE OFFENSIVE EFFECTIVENESS AS WELL AS TO BE ABLE TO EXECUTE THE BASIC POST PLAYERS' MOVES AFTER RECEIVING THE INSIDE PASS–

If the post player catches the ball in the post area without any physical contact by the post defender; he should "bunny-hop and land on both feet simultaneously" as the ball is being caught. This enables either foot to be used as a pivot foot for the offensive post player.

Four effective offensive post moves that every offensive player should work on are:

A. the "Show-and-Go-Opposite" move,
B. the "Square-up & Up-and-Under" move,
C. the "Whirl" move and
D. The "Spin Screen" Action.

Each of these moves could/should have different types of shots that can be taken at the end of any of these offensive post moves.

🌐 TECHNIQUE # 14:

ALL OFFENSIVE PLAYERS SHOULD BE ABLE TO
INTEGRATE VARIOUS METHODS TO
ELIMINATE OPPONENTS' HELPSIDE DEFENSES

Vertically stretching as well as horizontally stretching defenses can take away many of the opposition's strengths and defensive reactions. Overloading the post with both high post and low post players with flash posts can also take away defensive help.

In addition, using 2 or 3-man weakside actions will help occupy or eliminate opponent's helpside defenses that are necessary to defend almost all offensive interior games.

This weakens the overall defense, giving the offense more opportunities to score from the interior. Reading helpside defenders properly can also give offenses possibilities to score from the perimeter as well. This action can give offenses a two-pronged attack that is very difficult to stop both forms of action.

🌐 TECHNIQUE # 15A:

ALL OFFENSIVE PLAYERS SHOULD REALIZE
OFFENSIVE EFFECTIVENESS AS WELL AS THE TECHNIQUES OF
SETTING AND RECEIVING 'ON-THE-BALL-SCREENS'—

Offensive plays and possibly continuity offenses should/could include "on-the-ball" screens with several of the different starting points and many of the different "follow-up ball-screening actions" that can effectively be executed. The actual offensive ball-screeners should be well-versed in performing the various individual offensive techniques that are needed to be successful in the different ball-screens, particularly the action just after the actual ball-screen has been set. The actual 'on-the-ball screeners' always should have a wide base and make sure they keep the legal distance from the defender as well as not reach out to hold or illegally hinder the defender.

There are many types of ball-screens that can be introduced, in addition to where those screens should be set. Also, there are many forms of action that follow these different ball-screens and the strengths and weaknesses of these. Many of these ball-screens should also be introduced before a coaching staff determines which types and locations should be integrated into their current season's offensive scheme. The starting points of the initial ball-screen can vary from different locations of the court.

Receiving as well setting the actual ball-screens from different starting points and different types of ending action as well as the different combinations of players involved can result in numerous offensive ball-screening scenarios that would be very difficult for defensive teams to adequately defend.

Dribblers that receive ball-screens must be able to set up and then attack the ball-defender with the proper angles before then "dribble-scraping" off of the screening teammate. After taking advantage of the ball-screen, dribblers should also be able to anticipate and attack the next wave of defense whether it is the initial ball-defender that is trailing him, or a switching defender that could be in the form of a defensive mismatch (in speed or height), or a double-team or a rotating defender and be effective as a driver, shooter and passer.

These different methods or types of ball-screens that could be utilized within each offensive team's frameworks are defined as:

A. "Big-on-Small" Ball-Screens,
B. "Small-on-Big" Ball-Screens,
C. "Long" Ball-Screens,
D. "Flat" Ball-Screens,
E. "Double" Ball-Screens,
F. "Twisted Double" Ball-Screens,
G. "Inside" Ball-Screens,
H. "Pistol Ball-Screens,
I. "Follow (the Pass) Ball-Screens,"
J. "Ram" Ball-Screens,
K. "Consecutive" Ball-Screens, and
L. "Stagger" Ball-Screens.

These most common and likely starting locations where "On-the-Ball-screens" can successfully be set are:

A. At the top of the key (for "Long Ball-Screens and any type of Double Wide Ball-Screens,
B. Near the elbow area on both sides of the floor (for "Inside Ball-Screens and "Pistols Ball-Screens,
C. Near the Wing areas for "Follow (the Pass" Ball-Screens and
D. Sometimes further out between the time-line and the top of the key for a (Ball) Flat-Screen."

The many and various types of actions that could be utilized that can follow any of the 'on-the-ball screens could be any of the following such as:

A. The "Ball-Screen/Roll,"
B. "Ball-Screen/Rim-Run,"
C. "Ball-Screen/Slip" (Pick and Pop),
D. "Ball-Screen/Flare-Cut,"
E. "Ball-Screen/Re-Screen" or
F. "Various forms of 'Screen-the-Screener' action on either the interior and the perimeter."

⊕ *Technique # 16A:*

**All Offensive Players Should Be Able To
Execute All Of The Techniques Of
Setting And Also Receiving 'Off-The-Ball Screens'—**

With ball-screens being a huge part of the offensive system, even more so should the large variety off-ball screens be an integral part of the offense. Every offensive player should thoroughly be able to execute the proper those off-ball screening techniques. They also should have a wide base and make sure they maintain the legal distance from the defender and not hold or illegally hinder the defender. The skills of the different options that can follow the off-ball screening action should also be emphasized and acquired. Cutters that receive screens must be able to set up and then attack the defender with the proper angles before then "scraping" off of the shoulder of the screening teammate with their "feet and hands ready." Cutters should be prepared to receive the ball and instantly become a threat to shoot off of the pass, to drive or to make the next pass to a teammate.

Integrate these many different types of "off-the-ball screens" within the framework of the designated continuity offense so that your team can either completely eliminate or at least move the "helpside" defense, or to have offensive personnel cutting towards the ball either on the perimeter or the interior. These "off-the-ball screens" could be in the form of "Big-on-Small," "Small-on-Big," "Small-on-Small" or "Big-on-Big" types of "off-the-ball screens." Screens set by a different sized player on a different sized teammate helps discourage defensive switching or can quickly put defensive players in drastic mismatches that can and should be capitalized on.

These off-ball screens could also be combined with other types of off-ball screens discussed to become a two-part form of screening action. Some of these screens can be called:

A. "Down-Screens" (with or without 'Seals' or Flash Post action,)
B. "Stagger-Screens," (Twisted or Not)
C. "Shuffle-Screens,"
D. "Chin Back-Screens,"
E. "Flare-Screens,"
F. "UCLA-Screens," (with or without UCLA Bumps Actions)
G. "UCLA-Screens," (With or Without 'Bump' Cuts,)
H. "Pin-Screens," (With or Without Seal-Offs)
I. "Interior "Spin-Screens,"
J. "Brush-Screens,"
K. "Elevator-Screens" or "Twisted Elevator" Screens,
L. "Interior Lane Exchange Cross-Screens,"
M. "Down-Screens,"
N. "Screen-the-Screener Screens,"
O. "Ram-Screens,"
P. Various "Combo-Screens,"
Q. "Dribble Hand-Offs,"
R. "Dribble Hand-Offs & Off-Ball Screens," and
S. "Dribble Hand-Offs & Rolls or Rim-Runs."
T. "Ghost Down-Screens,"
U. "Pin-Screens" (with or without Post Seal-offs,)
V. "Stagger-Screens" (Twisted or Not),
W. "Ghost Flare-Screens",

X. "Iverson,"

Y. "Barkley" Screens,

Z. "UCLA-Screens," (with or without Bump Cut Options)

AA.   "Brush-Screens," and

BB.(Interior) Spin-Screens"

A now popular offensive series of action is where the initial screener sets two (or more) different types of screens in a very short, smooth and fluid series of offensive action. Another newer type of action is a reverse pass that initiates a back-screen for the ball reversal passer that is immediately followed by a ball-screen (with various types of action that could then follow that ball-screen.)

Other forms of Combo Screens could be started with an off-ball screen and then finished with a second off-ball screen. Many types of 'Combo Screens' can start with a ball-screen that is then followed with a second off-ball screen on a second teammate. These are fluid forms of action that give the screener's defender no time to read the type of screen and prepare to defend it.

⊕ *TECHNIQUE # 17A:*

ALL OFFENSIVE PLAYERS SHOULD REALIZE OFFENSIVE EFFECTIVENESS AS WELL AS TO BE ABLE TO UTILIZE THE VARIOUS FORMS OF THE 'DRIBBLE HAND-OFF' AND THE POSSIBLE ACTIONS TO FOLLOW—

There are different manners that an offensive ball-handler can exchange the ball with one of his teammates. One method of giving up the ball to a teammate is by the dribbler simply handing the ball to a teammate. From there, the initial ball-handler now is the new off-the-ball teammate and the initial off-the-ball teammate becomes the new ball-handler who has the same three basic offensive possible roles: to become a dribbler/driver, a passer and/or a shooter. These three DHO options will be difficult for opposing defenses to defend, particularly when there are multiple options and each of the actions are similar but yet different, not easy to detect and therefore difficult to defend. The initial ball-handler making the hand-off becomes an offensive player without the ball and becomes a different threat to the defense. The offensive player that receives the DHO is now the offensive player with the ball and becomes a more dangerous type of player once having possession of the ball. All of the various types of drives to the basket, the passes to teammates and the wide range of shots falls into the hands of the new ball-handler.

🌐 *TECHNIQUE # 17B:*

ALL OFFENSIVE PLAYERS SHOULD REALIZE
OFFENSIVE EFFECTIVENESS AS WELL AS TO BE ABLE TO
UTILIZE THE VARIOUS FORMS OF THE
'FAKE DRIBBLE HAND-OFF' AND THE POSSIBLE ACTIONS TO FOLLOW—

A counter to the previously discussed offensive action is for two offensive players to fake the actual Dribble Hand-Off. This simple method of the two players exchanging their actions can very easily mislead and confuse the opposing defense. The initial ball-handler and teammate still must make the same close connection, but because there is no actual exchange of the ball; the dribbler must retain his dribble. Therefore, after deceiving the defenders; the initial ball-handler remains the ball-handler with the same three potential offensive threats that can be used against the defender. In addition, after faking the actual hand-off, the initial off-ball teammate retains the same off-ball offensive possible actions—making the various cuts, the possible setting of the various possible screens and the possibility of receiving screens from any of his offensive teammates.

There is still another effective method of executing another swift, short and safe offensive exchanges of the ball between the initial ball-handler and another one of his teammates. One method is the simple return of the ball from the initial Pass Receiver 'flipping' the ball back to the initial Passer, who has followed his pass to cut near the receiver and the ball. From there, the initial ball-handler again becomes the ball-handler with the same three basic offensive options: a dribbler/driver, a passer and/or a shooter.

These three options are again unpredictable to the opposing defense. The initial ball-handler is now the teammate that does not have the ball and has the same options as all other off-the-ball offensive players—making any of the possible cuts, setting screens or receiving screens. All the various types of cuts and different methods of screens are all possible.

The initial off-the-ball teammate has gained possession of the ball by receiving the 'Flip Pass' and now has the same options of all ball-handlers. All the various types of dribbles and dribbling attacks are open for the new dribbler/driver.

🌐 <u>*TECHNIQUE # 17C:*</u>

**ALL OFFENSIVE PLAYERS SHOULD REALIZE
OFFENSIVE EFFECTIVENESS AS WELL AS TO BE ABLE TO
UTILIZE THE VARIOUS FORMS OF THE 'FAKE FLIP PASS'
(OR 'FAKE PASS HAND-OFF') AND THE POSSIBLE ACTIONS TO FOLLOW—**

There is still another effective method of executing another swift, short and safe offensive exchanges of the ball between the initial ball-handler and another one of his teammates. To counter the "Flip Pass" action, the pass receiver can simply fake the expected 'Flip Pass' back to the initial passer and maintain the same stance so as to become the same 'Triple Threat' offensive player, with the initial 'Passer' now being the off-ball teammate that has the same off-ball actions.

🌐 <u>*TECHNIQUE # 18:*</u>

**ALL OFFENSIVE PLAYERS SHOULD REALIZE
OFFENSIVE EFFECTIVENESS AS WELL AS TO BE ABLE TO
EXECUTE THE TECHNIQUES OF ANY OF THE SECONDARY BREAK
SCREENING AND CUTTING OPTIONS**

Any one or two from this list of options could be actually used at the end of the Secondary Fastbreaks. Again, it must carefully be determined which should be used at the conclusion of Secondary Breaks from the left side of the floor and which one from the right side of the floor:

A. "The Techniques of the Bump & Flare-Cut" Option,
B. "The Techniques Back-Screen" & Quick Ball-Screen/Roll,"
C. "The Techniques Brush-Screen,"
D. "The Techniques Give-n-Go Cut,"
E. "The Techniques Iso Duck-In Cut,"
F. "The Techniques Veer Cut,"
G. "The Techniques Early Ball-Screen/Roll,"
H. "The Techniques Chase & Early Screen/Rim-Run,"
I. "The Techniques Chase & Early Screen/Down-Screen,"
J. "The Techniques Late Ball-Screen/Roll,"

K. "The Techniques Duck-In Cut & Late Ball-Screen/Rim-Run."

CLOSING

These are the proper fundamental offensive techniques and the correct techniques that serve as the fundamentally sound building blocks that can help establish an effective and productive man-to-man offensive system that will withstand the test of time. As players and their respective ability levels of both strengths and weaknesses change from one season to the next, in addition to opponents' skills and talents changing; a fundamentally sound offensive system can adjust accordingly without major disruptions or changes to the overall program. This consistency gives both the players and the coaching staff faith and confidence in each other and in the overall system.

CHAPTER 7

USING VARIOUS OFFENSIVE SCHEMES AND FORMS OF OFFENSIVE ATTACKS IN A SUCCESSFUL MULTIPLE-PHASE MAN-TO-MAN OFFENSIVE SYSTEM

There are many different philosophies on how to attack opposing defenses. This multiple-phase offensive system uses more than one phase/layer/wave of attack, with each phase/wave having a seamless and immediate conversion into the next phase/wave. While this system can be confusing to defenses and difficult to defend, this system can be properly taught and coached so that it can be easily understood and ultimately executed by players of many different levels of (physical talent, mental understanding, and playing experience.)

In addition, there are several types of offensive schemes and different ways within this system that offenses can attack their defensive counter-parts. Many of these can be integrated within the same offensive system that can attack defenses in various ways. The larger the number of schemes that can be successfully utilized and integrated within the same system, the greater the opportunity an offensive team can find the most efficient and productive schemes that can place both individual and the overall team in the best and most frequent "positions to succeed."

Each play has been carefully studied and evaluated to determine which level of talent and experience (for both players and coaching staffs) must be possessed for that specific team to be able to successfully execute the play. If players do not know how or are physically unable to execute the skills within plays, the play will not be able to be productive. Likewise, if coaching staffs do not or cannot effectively teach the skills, that play will not be productive. While it is obvious that the physical skills and talents must be possessed by the players, but the mental understanding of the game by all players and coaching staffs is mandatory for both. If either group fails, the offensive play will also fail.

The most sophisticated plays/entries would fall into one of the three levels all based on the team's physical talents and skills, the mental capacities and the overall team's game experience. In addition, the coaching staff must have a high degree of basketball knowledge as well as very high teaching and coaching skills to educate his/her entire basketball team. The proper breakdown drills must be thoroughly utilized to hone the fundamental skills and techniques needed for individual players and the overall team to execute plays that can be efficient, productive and successful. We define this family of plays as the "Level 3 category" of plays. This "Level 3" family of plays will have a much more complex offensive scheme that would require a very high amount of physical talent as well as requiring a greater amount of the players (to execute) and the coaches (to teach and coach) mental capacities and experience needed for the offense to be efficient, productive and successful. We feel plays in our defined "Level 3" category could possibly be successful for NBA teams, definitely for college teams and also for many high schools and older AAU teams.

The next classification or level of plays would be possibly slightly lower as far as sophistication, complexity and the actual 'length' of the play (and the number of passes, cuts, and screens used) in the play's overall scheme. While all "Level 2" plays in each of the chapters in this book remain to be fundamentally sound, these plays may lack the actual number of techniques/methods that are implemented within that play in comparison to the more advanced "Level 3" plays/entries. Therefore any team that successfully executes the highest "Level 3" plays/entries could/should easily be able to execute any of these so-called lower "Level 2" plays/entries, if so desired. Almost all high school teams should be able to execute successfully all aspects of the "Level 2" plays.

The final grouping of plays would be called "Level 1" plays and are not as difficult for offensive players to master the execution of them, both physically as well as mentally. Even though the techniques are still fundamentally, they may not be as complex to learn and understand in addition to being easier to physically execute.

"Level 1" plays would be lower in the scheme's complexities and the number of techniques used in the execution of this category of plays. Obviously, since these "Level 1" plays are still sound, but lack some of the methods used in the two previous more sophisticated and complex levels; these more elementary plays should be able to be utilized by any teams that use either of the two higher level plays. We feel that Middle School/Junior High teams as well as younger AAU teams or organizations should be able to utilize any of the "Level 1" plays successfully, with a possibility that some of those teams that are slightly more advanced (than other teams) could possibly use some plays located in the immediate next immediate level.

Ideas, concepts, and techniques from actual plays from teams of all three levels have been used to modify or to create different combinations of the various techniques and schemes used that will help prove these entries can be successfully used. This allows the author to create numerous plays that use the various schemes to build a library of fundamentally sound plays that will be unique and will be appropriate for the wide range of teams with the various ages and skill levels.

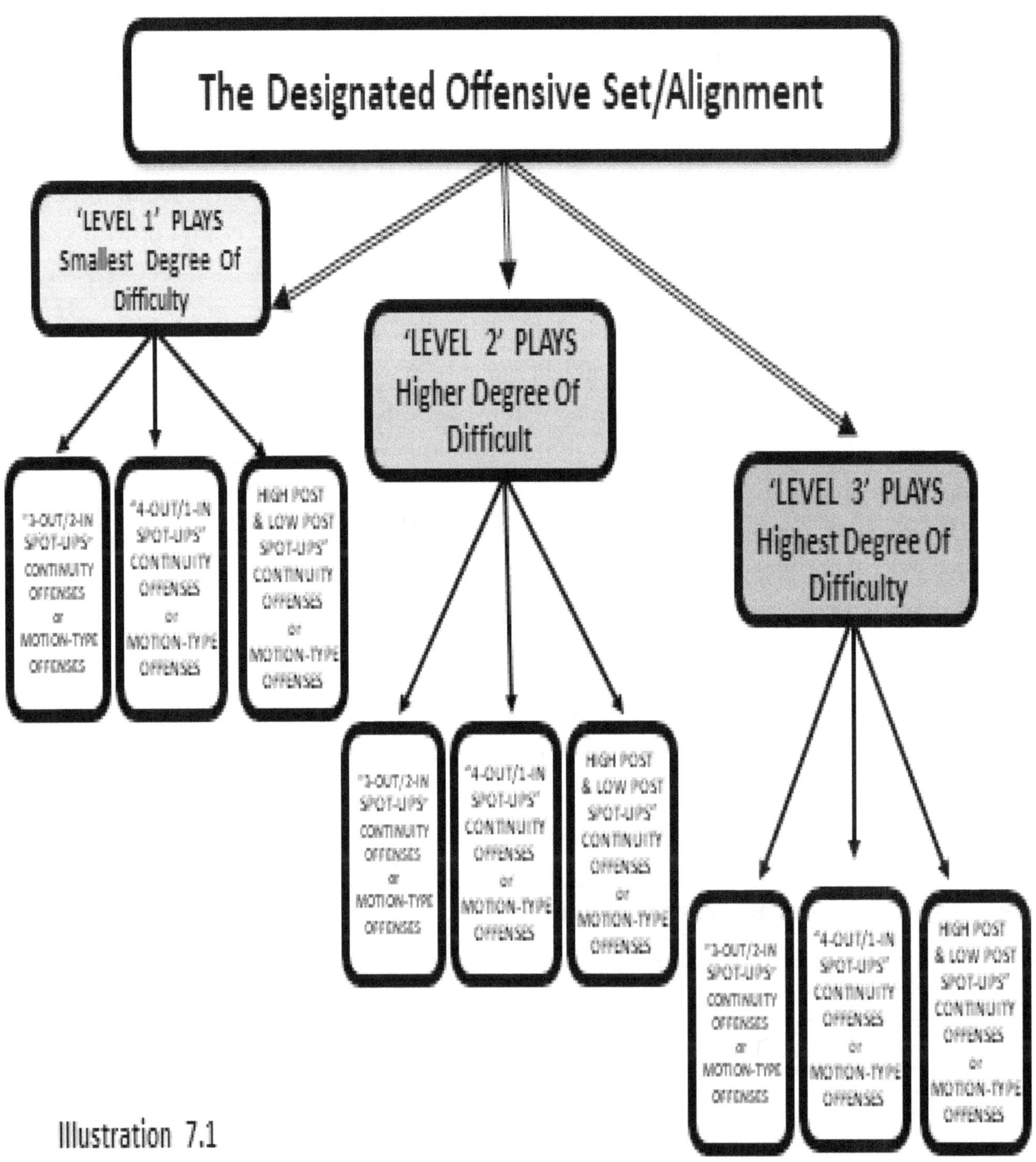

Illustration 7.1

In addition to the multiple-phase concept of this system, there are several types of offensive schemes and different ways that offenses can attack their defensive counter-parts. Many of these can be integrated within the same offensive system that can attack defenses in various ways. The larger the number of schemes that can be successfully utilized and integrated within the same system, the greater the opportunity an offensive team can find the most efficient and productive schemes that can place both individual and the overall team in the best and most frequent "positions to succeed."

Some of these offensive schemes that could be easily integrated include:

A. "Ball-Screen" Actions from Various Locations,

B. Different 'Off-the-Ball Screening" Action from Various Locations,

C. "Pistols" Action,

D. "Penetrate and Pitch" Actions,

E. "Drive and Dump" Actions,

F. "Dribble Hand-Off" Action Followed by "On-the-Ball" or "Off-the-Ball" Actions,

G. "Fake Dribble Hand-Off" Actions,

H. "Flip Pass Hand-Off" Action Followed by "On-the-Ball" or "Off-the-Ball" Action,

I. "Fake Flip-Pass Hand-Off" Actions,

J. "Chin-Screen and Cut" Actions,

K. "Flex-Screen and Various Cuts" Actions,

L. "Shuffle-Screen and Various Cuts" Actions,

M. "UCLA-Screen and Various Cuts" Actions,

N. "(Off-the-Ball) Screen the (Ball-)Screener" Actions,

O. "Consecutive Combination Screen" Actions,

P. "Mismatch On-the-Ball Screen" Actions,

Q. "Mismatch Off-the-Ball Screen" Actions,

R. "Blind Pig" and Other Types of "Basket Cuts" Actions,

S. "Hammer" (Drive/Pass/Flare-Cut) Baseline" Actions,

T. "Ghost Ball-Screens with various types of action following the screen and

U. "Ghost Off-Ball-Screens with the various types of action following the screen.

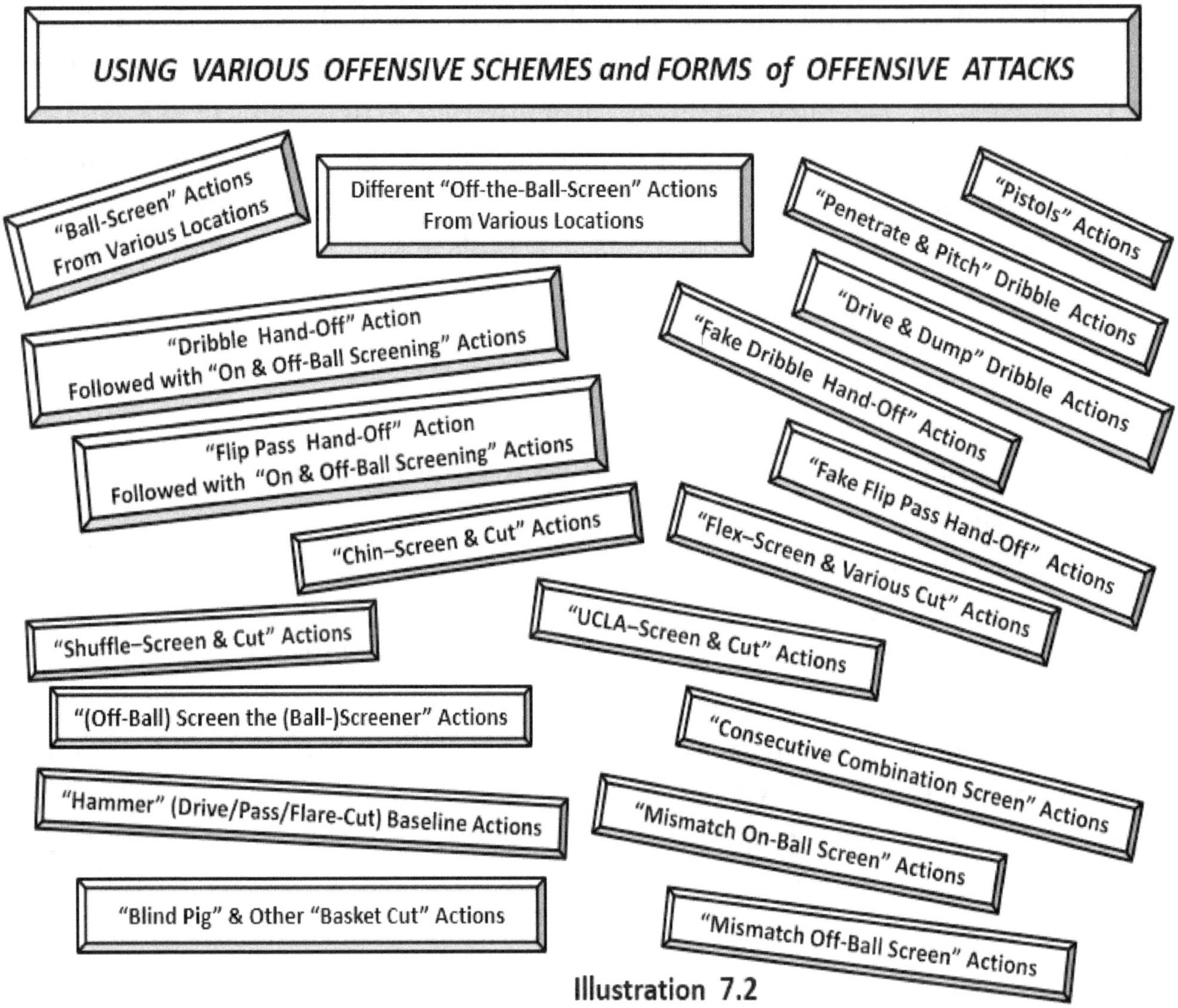

Illustration 7.2

CHAPTER 7:
USING VARIOUS PASSES in OFFENSIVE ATTACKS

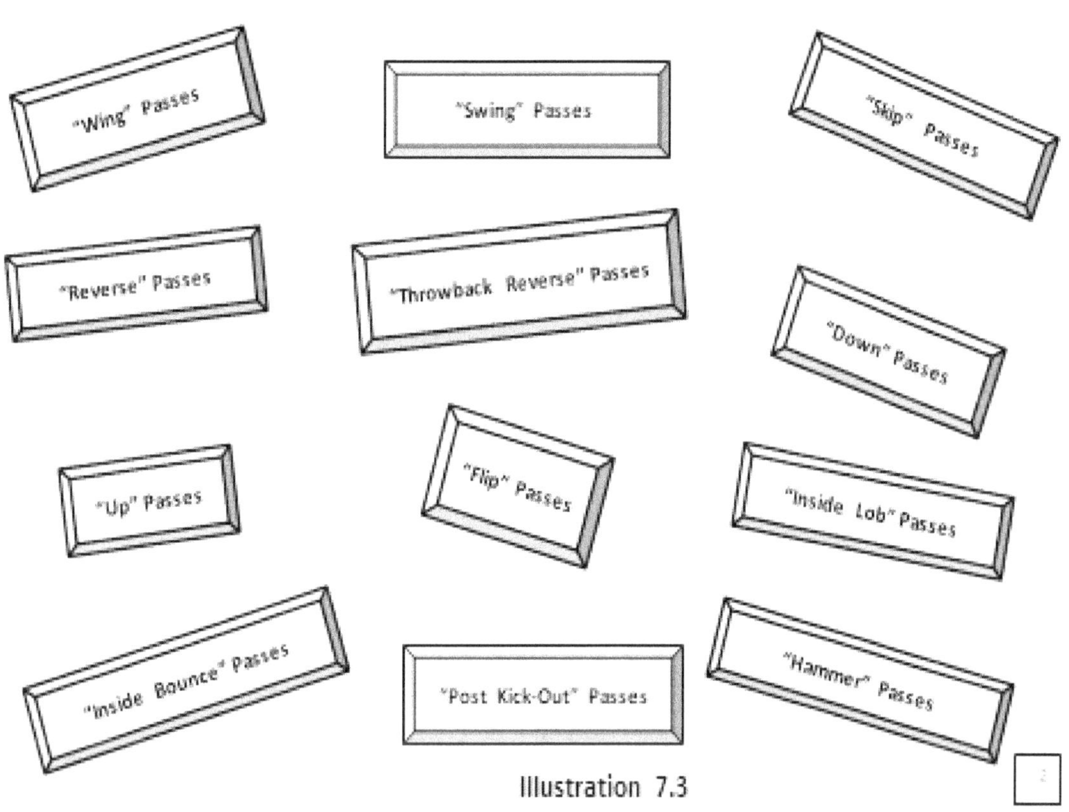

Illustration 7.3

CHAPTER 8
MAJOR COACHING POINTS OF EMPHASIS IN A
SUCCESSFUL MULTIPLE-PHASE MAN-TO-MAN OFFENSIVE SYSTEM

COACHING POINT 1:

OFFENSES MUST VERTICALLY & HORIZONTALLY STRETCH
THE OFFENSIVE FLOOR IN EVERY PHASE
OF THE OVERALL OFFENSIVE ATTACK

By stretching the offensive floor both horizontally as well as vertically, offenses force opposing defenses to guard and defend a wider and longer area of the floor. This stretching, pulling and thinning the defense can only weaken the defense; giving offense great advantages in the different phases of the offensive system. The stretching concept should be applied in the Full-Court part of the offense. Primary Fastbreaks, Full-Court Press Offenses, half-court plays/entries, Sideline and Baseline Out-of-Bounds plays in addition to the final level that each of these phases will eventually flow into—the designated continuity offense will all benefit with the stretching and weakening of the overall opposition's defense.

🌐 *COACHING POINT 2:*

COACHES MUST USE A
SYMMETRICALLY BALANCED OFFENSIVE ALIGNMENT

If the particular set/alignment is perfectly symmetrical, each entry can then possess the capabilities of being able to attack either side of the floor. Therefore, with each play being "ambidextrous," each play can be a duel threat as being able to initially attack both sides of the floor. In addition, each play could be inside-oriented or perimeter-oriented. A team can also create plays for every player that will capitalize on that player's strengths. So after plays and the desired side are called out, players will have time to comprehend their responsibilities and assignments for that play and then begin to execute those assignments in an efficient and productive manner.

🌐 *COACHING POINT 3:*

COACHES MUST HAVE A BALANCED AND UNPREDICTABLE ATTACK

This multi-phase offensive attack produces a potent and fluid type of offense that fits many types of philosophies and styles of offensive play. Using different plays from different sets can give the team various styles of offensive attack such as an up-tempo or a slower ball-control type of attack. Both styles could be utilized and executed, making the attack a different kind of "balanced attack."

Plays from this set can be "inside oriented" as well as outside or "3-pt. oriented" or a mixture of both—making it an even different type of balanced (and more difficult to defend) method of attack. Still, if the play/entry does not create a shot, the offense will always be able to smoothly and easily transition to the designated continuity offense.

COACHES MUST UTILIZE OFFENSIVE PLAYERS' STRENGTHS AND MINIMIZE THOSE SAME OFFENSIVE PLAYERS' WEAKNESSES

Different plays/entries designed especially for specific players can also utilize various offensive strengths that different offensive players can possess in addition to minimizing that player's offensive players' weaknesses. In addition, the correctly selected play can also attack both the opposition's individual as well as team defensive weaknesses, before then capitalizing and attacking those discovered defensive weaknesses. Various parts of the selected play/entry can also have their own general strengths and characteristics that make the play unique in its own way. The play can be utilized to not only accentuate individual offensive players' special skills and talents, but to also to attack both individual defenders' specific deficiencies as well as take advantage of the opposition's overall defensive weaknesses.

⚉ *COACHING POINT 5:*

OFFENSES MUST DISCOVER AND THEN ATTACK INDIVIDUAL OPPONENT'S DEFENSIVE WEAKNESSES

In addition to overall defensive weaknesses, coaching staffs should constantly be probing and searching for defensive weaknesses of individual opponents that they can attack. Those weaknesses could be in the form of a defender that cannot match up to his offensive responsibility because of a lack of height, strength, quickness, or knowledge/training in defending his man in a certain area of the offense. That opponent might be hurting your team by being an important offensive scorer, rebounder, ball-handler or play-maker. Attacking that player and getting him in foul trouble or even fouled out of the game could very well decrease or completely diminish his overall contributions to his team. Specific plays called to attack that opponent or using specific options of the continuity could allow the offense to attack that newly discovered defensive weakness and reduce that opponent's overall contributions.

❦ <u>*COACHING POINT 6:*</u>

OFFENSES MUST CREATE VARIOUS "POSITION MISMATCHES"

Another objective of different types of offensive action can be to create "position mismatches." This purpose is to force opposing defenders into having to defend offensive players they were not initially assigned to guard, mainly because those opponents are not matched with the defensive skills, strengths and experience to successfully be able to defend that specific offensive players. This objective can often be accomplished by the offensive team executing "Big-on-Small" or "Small-on-Big" off-ball or on-ball screens.

These offensive actions could also be a method of inverting opposing defenders while (from their normal and custom 'perimeter areas' or their 'interior areas;' while keeping offensive players in their normal and customary locations.

❦ <u>*COACHING POINT 7:*</u>

OFFENSES MUST INVERT OFFENSIVE PERIMETER PLAYERS

A fundamentally sound method of attack often used in this offensive attack is to "invert" perimeter players. This means that entries/plays can be created that include placing so-called "perimeter players" into post-up locations. After perimeter players have been taught and trained how to successfully post up their perimeter defenders inside, there are plays designed that will take advantage of those possible "position mismatches." The coaching staff takes the challenge of preparing "perimeter players" to be more prepared as offensive post players than opponents' perimeter players to be good post defenders and vice versa with the traditional "post players." Specific offensive plays can then provide various players with "position advantages" by taking advantage of newly-found offensive strengths and newly discovered individual defensive weaknesses both on the interior as well as on the perimeter. These created plays should utilize these concepts by giving every offensive player the opportunities to be positioned at both perimeter & post-up spot-up locations, so that those players can utilize their offensive skills in various manners.

⚇ COACHING POINT 8:

OFFENSES MUST INVERT OFFENSIVE POST PLAYERS IN VARIOUS MANNERS

Not only do we want to invert perimeter players "down on the blocks," we also want to be able to move and reposition certain offensive post players <u>away</u> from the basket; so that they can attack their defender on the perimeter as well. This attack could be because of that player's dominating quickness, ball-handling and/or perimeter shooting skills (or because of a specific defender's overall perimeter defensive weakness.) Inverting offensive post players could also be to pull defensive "bigs" away from the basket to take away defensive strengths, such as defensive rebounding and shot-blocking skills. This can give that designated player (be it a traditional so-called perimeter player or a post player out on the perimeter) an opportunity to use his driving, passing and/or perimeter shooting skills, as well as his offensive creative skills. These methods could be implemented in many different man-to-man plays/entries/quick-hitters.

⚇ COACHING POINT 9:

**OFFENSES MUST ATTACK THE OPPONENT'S
OVERALL TEAM DEFENSIVE WEAKNESSES**

Coaching staffs should study and know the particular styles of the man-to-man defense being used against their team, so that those inherent weaknesses of that specific style of defense can be discovered, attacked and then capitalized on by the offense in the proper fundamentally sound methods and techniques. Those techniques should already be built into various plays that can be used. In addition, those weaknesses can be taken advantage of within the framework of the designated continuity offense via options and counter-options.

⚇ COACHING POINT 10:

**OFFENSES MUST ELIMINATE HELPSIDE DEFENDERS
IN THEIR OFFENSIVE ACTIONS AND MOVEMENT**

A fundamentally sound objective of various types of offensive action is to eliminate or weaken helpside defenders that can help provide extra defensive support for interior post defenders. By minimizing or eliminating helpside defenders initially on the weakside of the defense away from the basketball, the offensive action can more effectively attempt to attack the opposition's ballside post defenders and to isolate those opposing post defenders. Offensive actions can be accomplished with either flash-post action (both high-post and low-post action) and/or with '2 or 3-man' games on the offense's weakside. Other offensive actions could be by executing Diagonal down-screens and stagger-screens could be utilized on the weakside to occupy helpside defenders and prevent those defenders to being involved with helping their interior ballside defenders.

⊕ *COACHING POINT 11:*

OFFENSES MUST ISOLATE OFFENSIVE PERIMETER PLAYERS
IN THE MANY VARIOUS MANNERS

If an offensive team can isolate players "in the post," we also want to reverse that type of attack by being able to also isolate certain offensive perimeter players out on the perimeter. Those players can attack their defenders on the perimeter as well, with those defenders not able to receive much help from defensive teammates. This attack could be executed because of an offensive perimeter player's advantage in quickness, ball-handling and/or perimeter shooting skills (or because of a specific defender's overall perimeter defensive weakness.) This can give that designated offensive player an opportunity to use his overall advantages in driving, passing and/or perimeter shooting skills, as well as his offensive creative skills. These methods could just as well be integrated within the framework of the correctly chosen offensive play or somewhere within the structure of the continuity that is used.

⊕ *COACHING POINT 12:*

OFFENSES MUST ISOLATE OFFENSIVE POST PLAYERS
IN DIFFERENT MANNERS

Still another method way we want to attack opposing defenders is to position both the traditional as well as inverted perimeter players in the post with little or no interior support for those particular defenders. If defensive post players play behind, we should be able to easily make the inside pass to that designated post player. We want to have a plan of attack to neutralize double-teams from perimeter defenders with perimeter movement so that post players can then "kick the ball back out" for open perimeter shots.

If post defenders try to full-front or three quarter front post players to deny them the ball, we want our offenses to be able to take away weakside defensive help so that lob passes can be made to the fronted post player. The positioning, repositioning and moving of offensive players can be accomplished within the framework of the selected offensive plays/entries.

This can give a coaching staff the ability to be able to not only place a designated player into the mid-post area, but to isolate that particular player so that he can attack a lone defender from a high percentage shot location.

COACHING POINT 13:

COACHES SHOULD IMPLEMENT "SHIFTING" WITHIN THE OFFENSIVE SYSTEM

Hiding from opponents the actual plan of attack until the last possible moment can be achieved in basketball by using a form of what football offenses also try to do. One of these simple methods of deception is what we call "shifting." Our definition of "shifting" is simply that offensive players can move or shift to a new location when the ball is in play just before it reaches the timeline, but obviously, before the first pass is made and the entry/play actually begins. This last second movement of one or more offensive players actually changes the cosmetic appearance of the offense by "shifting" from one offensive set /alignment to a new and possibly much different one that is the actual set/alignment that is desired. This keeps defenses from being able to predict and therefore know how to defend the offensive action. There is less time for the opposing defenses to react to the offensive alignment and before the offense executes the desired play/entry—thereby giving the offense another huge advantage.

COACHING POINT 14:

**COACHES MUST IMPLEMENT "FALSE MOTION"
WITHIN THE OFFENSIVE SYSTEM**

The second technique or method of deception is what we call "false motion." We define "false motion" as the offense actually making cuts, setting screens and passing the ball before then truly attacking in the desired manner. This could possibly take place when the ball is reversed, the true offensive action that is designed to attack the defense in the true manner then begins. Again, this is done to prevent defenses from being able to predict specific offensive action. The "false motion" is fundamentally sound and still makes the defense move, work & defend, but its goal is to deceive and camouflage the offense's true objectives. This is the other manner that disguises the true intentions and action of the offense and therefore giving the offense still another advantage for successful execution.

🌐 *COACHING POINT 15:*

OFFENSES MUST IMPLEMENT ONLY PLAYS/ENTRIES THAT FIT THE TEAM'S SKILL LEVELS

Coaching staffs should study which plays/entries (as well as the continuity or motion offense) that best suit their team's personnel and subsequently select the most productive and efficient plays and continuity offense that fit their players. There are numerous plays/entries from this offensive set or alignment that can possess families or groups of plays in which every entry can quickly, easily and fluidly flow into the designated continuity offense's "spot-up" positions. Each play can be executed to highlight an individual offensive player's skills, to attack an individual defender's weakness(es) or a discovered overall team defensive weakness. Each entry can be categorized by players' initial actions to begin the play. These various fundamentally sound categories include:

"Iverson" Cuts, "Barkley" Cuts, "Backdoor" Cuts, "Give-n-Go" Cuts, "Flex & Veer" Cuts, "Flex" Bump Cuts, "UCLA Rub-Off Action," "Bruin" Bump Cuts, "Wing Passes," "Post Pop-Out Passes," different types of "On the Ball-Screens," "Wing Pass & Follow (Ball-)Screens, various "Off-Ball-Screens," "Dribble Weave Hand-Offs," "Fake DHO" Action, "Low-Post & "High-Post" Flash Cuts" and "Inverting & Isolating" Perimeter and Post Players.

PLAYERS MUST USE THE PROPER TECHNIQUES WHILE EXECUTING ALL PLAYS/ENTRIES

There are many techniques that could and should be implemented in some manner within the framework of both the package of offensive plays as well as within the offensive continuity or motion offense's scheme. The more of these techniques that are used and applied by the offense's entries and by the continuities used; the more weapons that offensive team can possess. More weapons help an offensive team probe opponent's defenses for both individual as well as overall team defensive weaknesses. These techniques could be categorized as either various types of cuts, different kinds of off-ball screens and a wide range of ball-screens that have ending types of actions following those ball-screens. An offensive team wants to maximize those fundamentally sound techniques without overloading a team with too many techniques incorporated within the offense. The package of various entries/plays should be able to implement more of a variety of these methods than the desired continuity or motion offense.

⊕ *COACHING POINT 17:*

OFFENSIVE PLAYS/ENTRIES AND CONTINUITY OFFENSES MUST HAVE THE PROPER FLOOR BALANCE AND PROPER SPACING

Good man offenses maintain good floor balance and good spacing between offensive players (About 15 feet to 18 feet between most perimeter players). Proper spacing will horizontally and also vertically stretch the overall strength of the defense and helps make ball-reversals and skip passes much easier and safer to use. Proper spacing isolates defenders both on the perimeter and the interior. Proper floor spacing reduces the amount of pressure on the ball because there is less defensive help that can support ball-defenders and actually reduce the pressure that 'one-pass-away defenders' can apply to their offensive responsibility. Proper floor spacing aids in preventing defensive "help & recovers" on offensive dribble penetrations as well as also discourages double-team traps both on the perimeter as well as "double-downs" when the ball is passed inside to an interior player.

OFFENSIVE PLAYERS MUST ALWAYS USE THE DRIBBLE TO ATTACK DEFENSES

Another objective of various types of offensive action is to not only attack individual defenders but to also attack overall opponents' team defenses by forcing defenders to have to give help to their defensive teammates. This can be done giving offensive players the proper spacing and freedom and then have offensive players utilize their dribble to attack individual defenders to force off-the-ball defenders to have to help, creating openings for their own opponent they were guarding.

One of these two types of attacks could be called the "Drive & Dump." The dribbler drives into the lane and if there is interior vertical defensive rotation that arrives on time to stop the drive, an 'inside pass' can be made to the open man in the lane.

The second type of dribble-attack could be called the "Penetrate & Pitch." The dribbler drives into the lane and if there is outside defensive help, the dribble/driver "pitches" the ball out on the perimeter to the open teammate for an open "3." These dribble attacks that isolate defenders can be executed still within the structure of the offense.

⊕ *COACHING POINT 19:*

OFFENSIVE PLAYERS MUST ALWAYS USE
REALISTIC BALL FAKES AND SHOT FAKES

Coaches should constantly stress to offensive players that they always should use good ball-fakes as well as realistic shot-fakes against the opposition's man-to-man (or zone) defenses. A coaching point phrase could be "fake a pass to make a pass." In addition, it must be emphasized that shot fakes are extremely important before a shooter drives to the basket as well as after he has killed his dribble (particularly in the lane.) One part of a shot fake that is easily forgotten is for the offensive player with the ball to actually look at the rim during his shot fake and to bring the ball up through his nose for a more realistic-looking shot fake.

OFFENSES MUST ALWAYS USE VARIOUS CUTS IN THEIR PLAYS/ENTRIES

Teams that use a variety of different types of offensive cuts by all types of offensive players from different locations on the floor during the many phases of the offense makes the offense much less predictable and ultimately much more difficult to defend by both individual defenders as well as the overall opponents' team defense. These types of cuts force individual defenders to defend their men more often as well as to occupy themselves to help reduce the effectiveness of the opposition's ballside and helpside defense on support defense. These offensive cuts that should be utilized within the offense's frameworks are defined as:

A) "V" Cuts,
B) "Pipe" or "Zipper" Cuts,
C) "Shuffle" Cuts,
D) "Flex" Cuts,
E) "Flex Bump" Cuts,
F) "Flex Veer" Cuts,
G) "UCLA Rub-Off Cuts,
H) "UCLA Bump" Cuts,
I) "Curl" Cuts,
J) "Backdoor" Cuts,
K) "Give-n-Go" Cuts,
L) "Flare-Cuts,
M) "Iverson" Cuts,
N) "Barkley" Cuts,
O) "Duck-In" Cuts,
P) "Lob" Cuts,
Q) (High or Low) "Flash-Post" Cuts,
R) "Slash" Cuts,
S) "Spin-Screen" Cuts, and
T) "Basket Cuts (including cuts such as "Slip" Cuts, "Rolls," "Rim-Runs," "Ghost Ball-Screen Cuts," "Ghost Flare-Screen Cuts," "Ghost Diagonal Down-Screen Cuts," or "Ghost Pin-Down Screen Cuts.")

⊕ *COACHING POINT 21:*

OFFENSIVE PLAYERS MUST ALWAYS USE THE PROPER ANGLES TO IMPROVE PASSING TO THEIR TEAMMATES

Utilizing the proper angles in basketball is a very underrated concept in basketball. The proper angles in executing several different techniques and methods is a lost art. One example would be when a perimeter player with the ball is on a higher plane than his teammate that is posting up a defender on the "Block" is being front or ¾ fronted with that same defender shading the offensive player on the high side. If the ball can switch to become on the plane lower than the post defender, the offensive post player will be able to have a "position advantage" over his opponent. It is the post player's responsibility to maintain that new-found advantage with the proper pivoting, footwork and using his body to 'seal' off and keep that defender on the so-called high side of him (when the ball is lower than the defender.) Adjusting to the proper angle may simply require a quick pass to a perimeter teammate that is in better location to be able to have that improved "passing angle." Another method may simply require a short perimeter 'pull dribble' that not only improves the angle, but also stretches opposing defenses that will weaken the opposition's interior support defense.

⊕ *COACHING POINT 22:*

OFFENSIVE DRIBBLERS, CUTTERS AND SCREENERS SHOULD USE THE PROPER ANGLES TO IMPROVE ALL TYPES OF SCREENING ACTIONS

Both 'on-the-ball' and 'off-the-ball' offensive screens are implemented between (at least one screener) and the designated cutter that is to use the screen to free himself from his individual defender. Good defenders are conscious and aware of many upcoming screens that will be used to slow down or impair their defending their offensive opponent. It is imperative that the screener always set the legal screen with the legal distance between he and the defender with a wide base and to expect contact. The invaluable technique that seems to not be stressed enough is that the screener must also set the screen to offer the largest and widest "wall" or obstacle to prevent or slow down the defender's progress. The most forgotten technique is for that screener to have his butt directly pointing to the spot on the floor where his teammate needs to pass through on his cut or on his dribble.

The receivers of all 'off-the-ball' offensive screens must remember initially to set up their defender for the coming (various types of) off-ball screen being set for him. He then must make sure that he makes as close of contact as possible with the proper side of the screener before then turning to make the slight "angle" to square up to both the passer with the ball and also with the basket. In addition, we have the off-ball cutters prepare for the actual catch with hands in position and for the proper footwork (to stop the cutter's momentum to be able to quickly take the shot under control) and be ready for a possible immediate 'catch and shoot' or 'catch and create' offensive action. We use three phrases to emphasize and constantly remind offensive players to always execute those techniques:

A) "Scraping off of the (screener's) outside shoulder,"
B) "Getting your feet and hands ready (for the pass)" as well as
C) "Cheating your inside shoulder to square up to the ball and the basket."

Dribblers that are to receive 'on-the-ball' offensive screens must remember should also initially set up their ball-defender for the coming ball-screen. That dribbler must also make as close of contact as possible with the proper side of the ball-screener before then "turning the corner" to attack the basket. While the dribbler already in in possession of the ball, we still have the driver/dribbler prepare for the receiving of the ball with the hands in already in position in the 'shooting pocket.' In addition, we have the dribbler get his timing down to also prepare his 'Inside pivot heel' to square up to the basket as he makes the last dribble (the lowest and the hardest dribble that flows directly and quickly into the shooting pocket) just before his 'lift off.' We also stress getting the 'inside shoulder already starting its turn towards the basket even as the last dribble is being made. The same three phrases can be made to constantly remind offensive players to always execute those techniques "Dribble-scraping off of the (screener's) shoulder" and "getting your feet and hands ready" as well as "cheating your inside shoulder to square up (to the basket earlier)."

ALL OFFENSIVE PLAYERS MUST ALWAYS USE THE PROPER ANGLES TO IMPROVE 'DRIVES TO THE BASKET'

Football coaches constantly coach and emphasize their running backs to sometimes run "east and west," but mostly to run "north and south" or "downhill." While the phrase is coming into the basketball world, it still can be emphasized more so. We try to show players that on drives to the basket out from the perimeter, that the angle they begin with can reduce their driving distance and therefore driving time. We try to show players the imaginary 45 degree angles from each sideline diagonally towards the basket as being the perfect lay-up path. We then try to emphasize that unless a driver is vertically and horizontally trying to (passively) 'Perimeter Pull Dribble'" the ball to stretch interior defenders or is ultimately trying to drive the baseline; the best bet is to drive within the imaginary "cone" for more direct (and shorter/quicker) penetrations to the basket. Therefore, those driving angles should also be emphasized.

⊕ *COACHING POINT 24:*

ALL OFFENSIVE PLAYERS MUST UTILIZE A WIDE VARIETY OF "ON-BALLSCREENS"

Offensive schemes should/could include "on-the-ball" screens with as many as five different starting points and a maximum of six or so different "follow-up methods or techniques" that can effectively be executed. The starting points of the initial ball-screen can vary from different locations of the court. Therefore having different players receiving the ball-screen in addition to setting the actual ball-screens from different starting points and different types of ending action as well as the different combinations of players involved can result in a multitude of offensive ball-screening scenarios. These various scenarios could be applied to specific players that fit their offensive strengths and allow certain players to avoid some scenarios where there can be individual weaknesses. In addition to playing to individual players' strengths, to avoiding individual players' weaknesses, the various scenarios can be used to attack individual defenders' weakness. The various scenarios will also can a higher degree of unpredictability for opposing teams, making it even more difficult for defensive teams to adequately defend.

⚜ ***COACHING POINT 25:***

**OFFENSES MUST UTILIZE THE VARIOUS LOCATIONS
FOR ALL "ON-BALL SCREENS"**

These basic starting locations where the ball-screen can effectively be set are at the top of the key, an area between the top of the key and the elbow area on both sides of the floor, (for the ball-screener to set "Inside Ball-Screens" at the high post elbow area or for the ball-screener to attack the defender and the overall defense down the middle of the lane,) and near both wide deep corner areas.

Another area could be further out between the time-line and the top of the key for a "Big" to set a "Flat (Ball)-Screen" for the dribbler to shed his defender higher up, further from the basket and attack the middle interior of the floor.

⚜ ***COACHING POINT 26:***

**COACHES SHOULD UTILIZE OFFENSES THAT UTILIZE THE VARIOUS WAYS TO
INITIATE "ON-BALL SCREENS"**

These various types of (fundamentally sound) on the ball-screens that should/could be utilized within each offensive team's frameworks are defined as:

A) "Big-on-Small" Ball-Screens,
B) "Small-on-Big" Ball-Screens,
C) "Inside" Ball-Screens,
D) "Follow" (the Pass & Ball-) Screens,
E) "Long" Ball-Screens,
F) "Ram" Ball-Screens,
G) "Ghost" Ball-Screens,
H) "Flat" Ball-Screens,
I) "Double" Ball-Screens,
J) "Twisted Double" Ball-Screens,
K) "Consecutive" Ball-Screens,
L) "Stagger" Ball-Screens and
M) "Spain" Ball-Screen Action.

N) A fundamentally sound way to initiate the ball-screen action could be the traditional stationary ball-screen usually set near the top of the key or halfway from the top of the key and the high elbow areas.

O) Another method (the "Flat Screen") is action when the somewhat traditional stationary ball-screener sets his screen somewhere near the middle "alley" just inside the 10-second time-line with his back directly towards the basket—allowing the dribbler to dribble-scrape off of either of the screener's shoulder and directly in a straight line towards the rim.

P) Different or more modern methods of setting ball-screens could be the "Long Ball-Screen" where the designated ball-screener breaks from an initial low post position up to the designated screening location.

Q) Another method could be the "Ram-Screen" where one offensive player sets a a form of a "Down-Screen" for that specific cutter to use to break towards the ball (initially as a possible pass receiver), before then continuing towards the ball (and ball-handler) to then set an on-ball screen.

R) A third method (called the "Follow (ball-) Screen which is when a passer completes a pass to a teammate and immediately "follows" his pass to set an immediate ball-screen on the new ball-handler/dribbler.

⊕ *Coaching Point 27:*

Coaches Should Utilize Offensive Action That Always Use The Various Ways To Finish The Various Types Of "On-Ball Screens

Various finishes to the different types of 'ball-screens' that could/should also be integrated (dependent upon each team's strengths, weaknesses, style and staff's philosophies) could be any of the following such as the:

A) "Screen-Roll,"

B) "Rim-Run,"

C) "Lob-Cut" after Screen-the-(Ball-)Screener action,

D) "Flare-Cut (also called "Pick & Pop"),

E) Various "Off-the-Ball" Screening Actions after the initial Ball-Screen

F) "Back-screen the Ball-Screen on his roll" ("Spain" action.)

⊕ *COACHING POINT 28:*

COACHES SHOULD UTILIZE OFFENSES THAT UTILIZE A VARIETY OF THE DIFFERENT OFF-THE-BALL-SCREENS

Integrate these many different types of "off-the-ball screens" within the framework of the offense so that your team can either completely eliminate or at least move the "helpside" defense, or to have offensive personnel cutting towards the ball either on the perimeter or the interior. These could be in the form of "Big-on-Small," "Small-on-Big," "Small-on-Small" or "Big-on-Big" types of "off-the-ball screens." Screens set by a different sized player on a different sized teammate helps discourage defensive switching or can quickly put defensive players in drastic mismatches that can and should be capitalized on. These off-ball screens could also be combined with other types of off-ball screens discussed to become a two-part form of screening action.

⊕ *COACHING POINT 29:*

COACHES SHOULD UTILIZE OFFENSES THAT UTILIZE A VARIETY OF THE DIFFERENT OFF-THE-BALL-SCREENS

These various types of (fundamentally sound) off-the-ball-screens that should/could be utilized within each offensive team's frameworks are defined as:

Some of these "Off-the-Ball-Screens can be called:

A) "Diagonal Down-Screens" (with or without Flash Post action,)
B) "Pin-Screens" (with or without Post Seal-offs,)
C) "Stagger-Screens" (Twisted or Not),
D) "Elevator-Screens" (Twisted or Not),
E) "Shuffle-Screens,"
F) "Back-Screens,"
G) "Flare-Screens,"
H) "Flex-Screens" (with or without Bump Cuts or Veer Cuts,)
I) "Iverson Screens,"
j) "Barkley Screens,"
K) "Chin Back-Screens,

L) "UCLA-Screens," (with or without Bump Cuts),

M) "Brush-Screens,"

N) "Ram-Screens,"

O) (Interior) "Lane Exchange Cross-Screens,"

P) (Interior) Spin-Screens"

Q) "Various Ghost Off-the-Ball Screens,"

R) "Various (Off-Ball) "Screen & Re-Screen" Combo Actions.

Each of the following screens could be set with different types of offensive personnel both setting the screen and receiving the screen. These screens could involve either "Big-on-Small" screens, "Small-on-Big" screens, "Big-on-Big, screens" or "Small-on-Small Off-the-Ball-Screens." These four various combinations can cause opposing defenses problems if defensive switches are involved.

✪ COACHING POINT 30:

COACHES SHOULD EXECUTE OFFENSES THAT UTILIZE
A VARIETY OF "COMBO-SCREENS"

A popular offensive series of action now is where the initial screener sets two (or more) different types of screens in a very short, smooth and fluid series of offensive actions. The initial screener then screens a second teammate which gives the passer multiple pass receiving targets and therefore provides the offense with more scoring threats.

Some of these "Combo-Screens" could be:

A) Shuffle Back-Screen into a Ball-Screen,

B) Shuffle Back-Screen into a Stagger-Screen,

C) UCLA Back-Screen into an Inside Ball-Screen & Roll,

D) UCLA Back-Screen into an Inside Ball-Screen & Flare-Cut,

E) Ball-Screen into a Down-Screen,

F) Other Combos that can be created.

COACHES SHOULD VALUE THE IMPORTANCE OF A
CONTINUITY OFFENSE'S "SPOT-UPS"

After a selected play/entry from a designated offensive set/alignment is executed and the offensive team maintains control of the ball with no shot taken; the next phase of the offensive attack begins by smoothly and seamlessly flowing into a designated continuity offense or a particular type of motion offense. This next phase or wave of the attack from a wide type of offense must begin with players beginning in specific locations on the court after the play/entry has been concluded (with no shot or loss of possession.)

We define these important locations or positions as the continuity offense's "spot-ups." Each play in the team's arsenal must have the very same "spot-ups," so that the next phase of the offense will begin with all five players having filled those same "spot-up" locations.

The concern that a defensive opponent would be able to predict the offensive action should be somewhat minimal, especially if there are multiple plays/entries to be used and that there are options and counter-options within the framework of the continuity offense. When plays or entries are successfully executed, but with no shots taken and the play then transitions into the continuity offense; the smooth beginning of the actual continuity is actually camouflaged by the plays' action. Therefore, the continuity offense is not even recognized or distinguished as that continuity offense. Still, players in the correct spot-up locations will smoothly and easily flow into the designated continuity offense which then instantly becomes the second wave of the overall offensive attack.

Each entry/play/quick-hitter that does not produce a shot from the alignment/set will at least place all five offensive personnel specifically in either (Even-Front or Odd-Front) "4-Out/1-In" or (Balanced or Unbalanced) "3-Out/2-In" spot-ups. Particular groups of these spot-ups should also be filled at the conclusion of any Secondary Fastbreak actions, from every Baseline Out-of-Bounds (B.L.O.B.) or from each of the Sideline Out-of-Bounds (S.L.O.B.) plays. Again, this allows the offense to smoothly, seamlessly and immediately flow from an offensive play into various continuity offenses or different forms of motion offenses. This makes the designated continuity or motion offense even more crucial to the overall success of the offense.

Each entry/play/quick-hitter that does not produce a shot from the alignment/set will at least place all five offensive personnel specifically in either (Even-Front or Odd-Front) "4-Out/1-In" or (Balanced or Unbalanced) "3-Out/2-In" spot-ups. Particular groups of these spot-ups should also be filled at the conclusion of any Secondary Fastbreak actions, from every Baseline Out-of-Bounds (B.L.O.B.) or from each of the Sideline Out-of-Bounds (S.L.O.B.) plays. Again, this allows the offense to smoothly, seamlessly and immediately flow from an offensive play into various continuity offenses or different forms of motion offenses. This makes the designated continuity or motion offense even more crucial to the overall success of the offense. "Spot-Ups" of a continuity offense become a conduit between a team's plays/entries and the team's 2nd phase of attack—be it a continuity offense or a motion-type offense. It also becomes a means to be able to smoothly continue not only after half-court plays that did not produce a shot; but just as importantly after all Secondary Break actions, all Baseline Out-of-Bounds Plays and every Sideline Out-of-Bounds Play in the team's arsenal in which the action did not generate a shot. "Spot-Ups" are a way to also camouflage a continuity offense because many times the offense will score or lose possession of the ball during the entry before the actual continuity can begin and be utilized. Out of all of an offensive team's possessions, opposing teams often will not even face the continuity offense and therefore not necessarily be accustomed to defending it. These are the major points of focus that coaches should stress to all players to establish an effective and productive man-to-man offensive system that can withstand the weather of time. As players and their respective ability levels of both strengths and weaknesses change from one season to the next, in addition to opponents changing; a fundamentally sound offensive system can adjust accordingly without major disruptions or changes to the overall program. This consistency gives both the players and the coaching staff faith and confidence in the system.

CHAPTER 9

ON-BALL SCREENS USED IN A SUCCESSFUL MULTIPLE-PHASE MAN-TO-MAN OFFENSIVE SYSTEM

These thirty offensive actions all involved the use of the fundamentally sound and extremely successful action of the traditional "ball-screen" modified in various manners from the many different plays/entries (out of the many different offensive sets/alignments.)

Notice that the overall action of each quick-hitter/play/entry, regardless of what specific level the play is, repositions each offensive to move into one of the proper spot-ups of the designated continuity or motion-type offense. Therefore, if the various ball-screening actions of the play does not immediately create the desired shot, the action will at least allow for a smooth, immediate and fluid transition into that last phase of the offensive attack—the continuity or motion-type offense. This gives the opposition no opportunity to recover or regroup after just preventing a shot from initial entry.

The "Ball-Screen" action has long been a staple to offenses of levels of competition. From elementary teams to the NBA, the many ways that the various types of ball-screens are set, the different types of players that use the screen, various players that set the screens; the action can produce shots. In addition, defenses will have increasingly difficulties with the unpredictability factor, because of the many combinations of players that could be involved in the action. In addition, with the many different locations that the ball-screens could be executed increase that large amount of unpredictability. In addition, there are countless types of action that can be executed following the actual ball-screen.

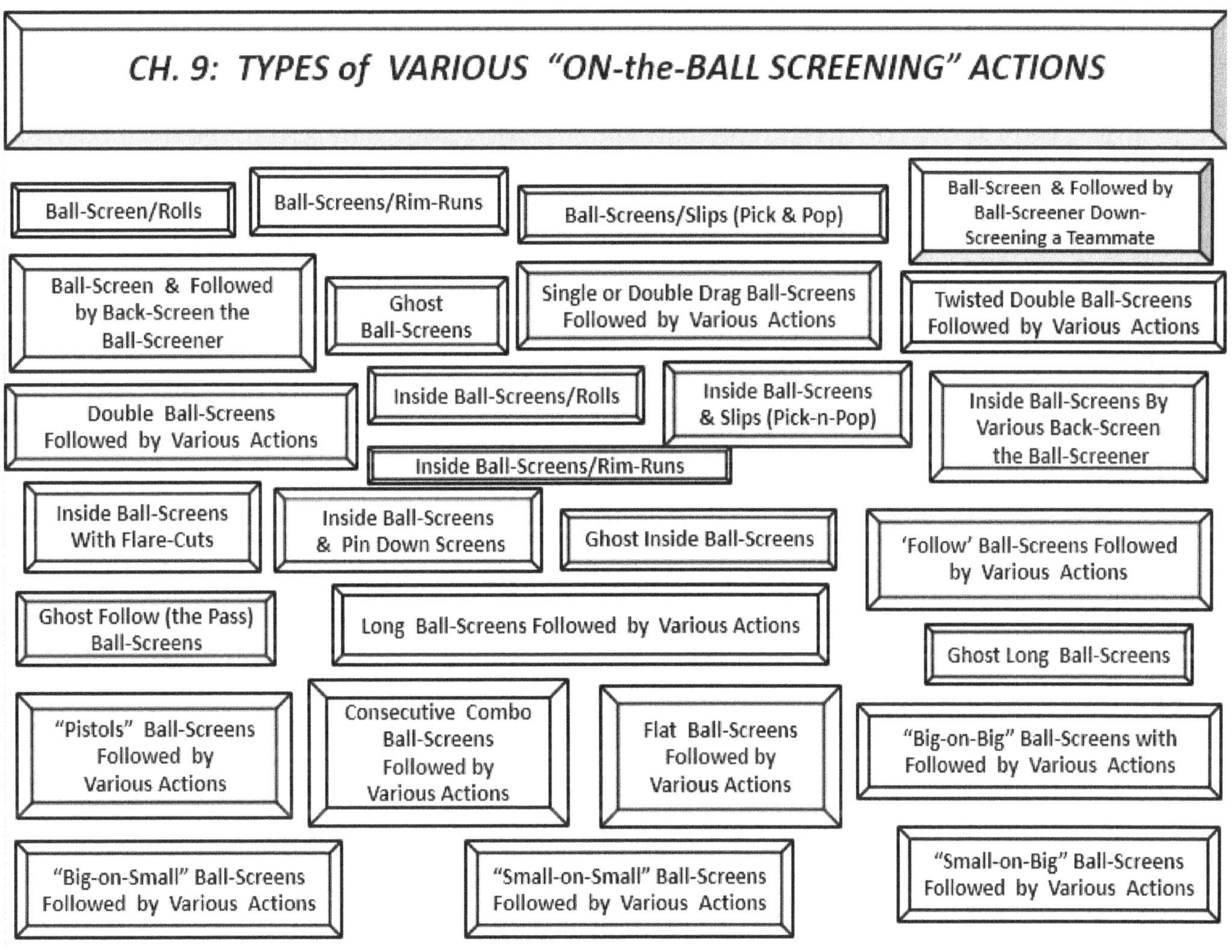

Diagram 9.1

Diagram 9.1 illustrates the very basic, but still extremely successful "Ball-Screen/Roll." This action can and should be included within the free-flowing but organized structure of several quick-hitting plays/entries from every level of play. This action could begin out of almost every offensive alignment, but this example is taken from an Offensive Baseline Out-of-Bounds (BLOB) situation, called "Jam."

The play begins with 05 back-pedaling out to the 'High Post Elbow' location and receiving 01's inbounds "Lob Pass." 03 immediately lifts to the FT Line extended to receive a Dribble Hand-Off from 05 and for 01 to have space to break towards the new "Ballside Deep Corner." As 03 receives the ball, 04 diagonally breaks up to set a "Big-on-Small Ball-Screen" to perimeter drag dribble across towards the opposite side's perimeter "Slot." As 03 "dribble-scrapes" off of 04's top (left) shoulder, 04 makes a reverse pivot off of his lower right foot to open up to the ball and rolls down the lane and looks for a possible "Inside Pass" from 03 (or possibly from 02 or 05). With 05 remaining near the new "Weakside Slot," the presumed biggest defender, X5, is taken away from the play and cannot help out his isolated defensive teammate, (either X4 or possibly X3). With 01 and 02 spotted up in the perimeter "Deep Corners" on both sides of the floor, 03 and 05 on the two perimeter "Slots," the initial "Ball-Screener," 04 will enjoy a dominating "position advantage" by completing isolating his defender in the vulnerable highest scoring area on the court.

Regardless of how the "Ball-Screen/Roll" action is played by the defense, whether it be: a) "straight up," "hedge" or "hard hedge," "switch," "trap" or "drop;" the offense should be able to capitalize on what the defense gives up and be able to create either "position advantages" or "player advantages" to get the desired shot by the desired player(s) directly from the entry.

Still, if the desired shot is not taken, all five players are in the "4-Out/1-In" Spot-Ups for the designated 2nd Phase of the attack to seamlessly begin. The defense cannot recover from defensive switches or being out of position attempting to defend the initial action of the play.

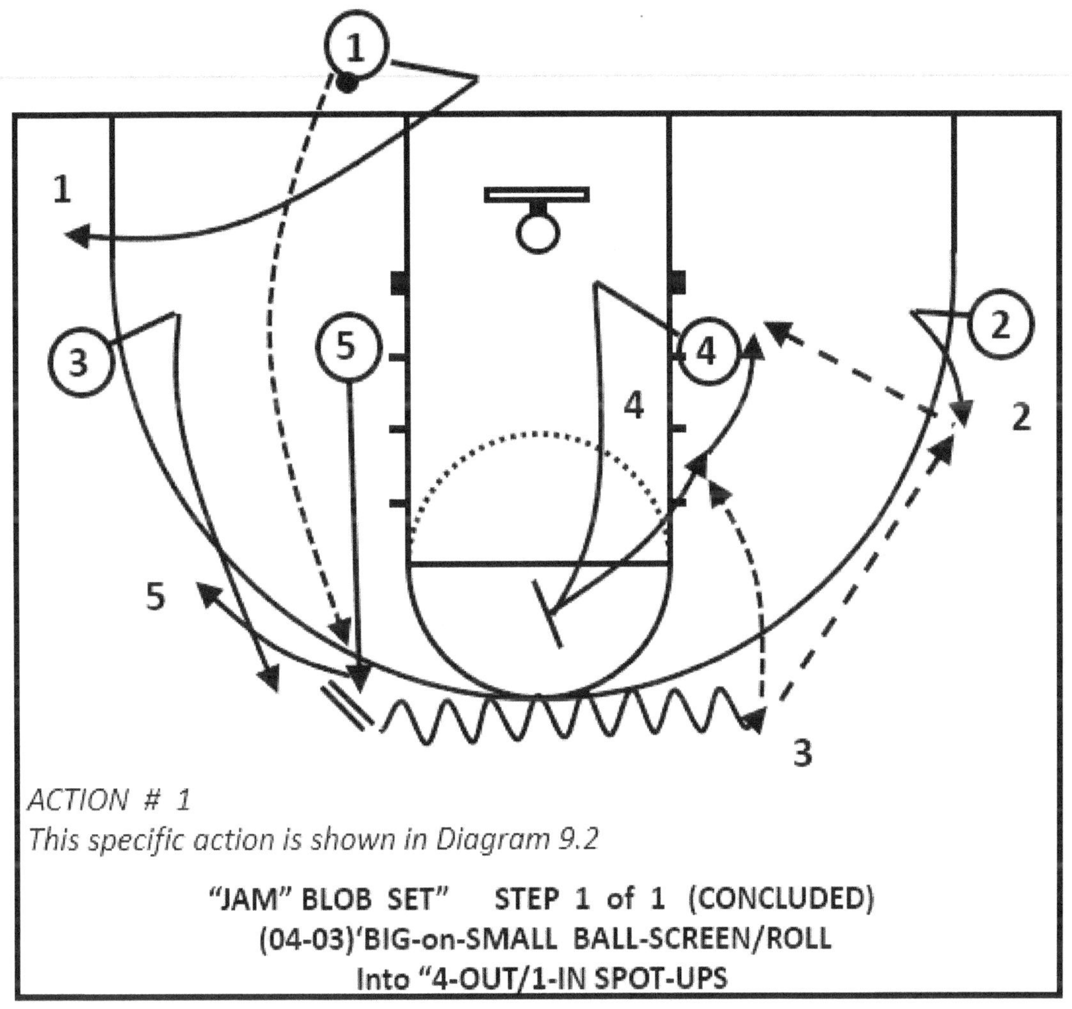

Diagram 9.2

🏀 PLAY # 2: "BIG-ON-SMALL BALL-SCREEN/RIM-RUN" ACTION

Out of the "Twins" Set, Diagram 9.3 illustrates another "Big-on-Small Ball-Screen," but this time with the action by the screener (04) setting the same screen near the top of the key. As the designated ball-handler (01) "dribble-scrapes" off of 04's top left shoulder and breaks contact with the screener, this time 04 makes a front pivot off of the same lower right foot to make a "Rim-Run" towards the basket and looks for 01's "Lob Pass."

As 01 starts dribbling towards 04, 05 makes a diagonal "Slash Cut" diagonally across the basket to the newly designated "Ballside Mid-Post Notch (above-the-Block.) 02 and 03's initial locations vertically stretch the defense and as 01 approaches the right "Slot," 02 breaks out to his "Deep Corner" to also then horizontally stretch the defense; further weakening the defensive interior for both 05 and his "Slash Cut" and then for 04 on his

"Rim-Run." 03 breaks up to the newly declared "Weakside Slot" with 01 filling the new "Ballside Slot." Interior shots first by 05 and then by 04, followed by perimeter shot options by 01, 02 and also by 03 can all be viable shot for this Play # 2.

Once again, all five players have attacked their individual defenders and weakened the overall team defense; with players in the correct spot-up positions for a seamless and fluid beginning to the designated continuity or Motion-type offense.

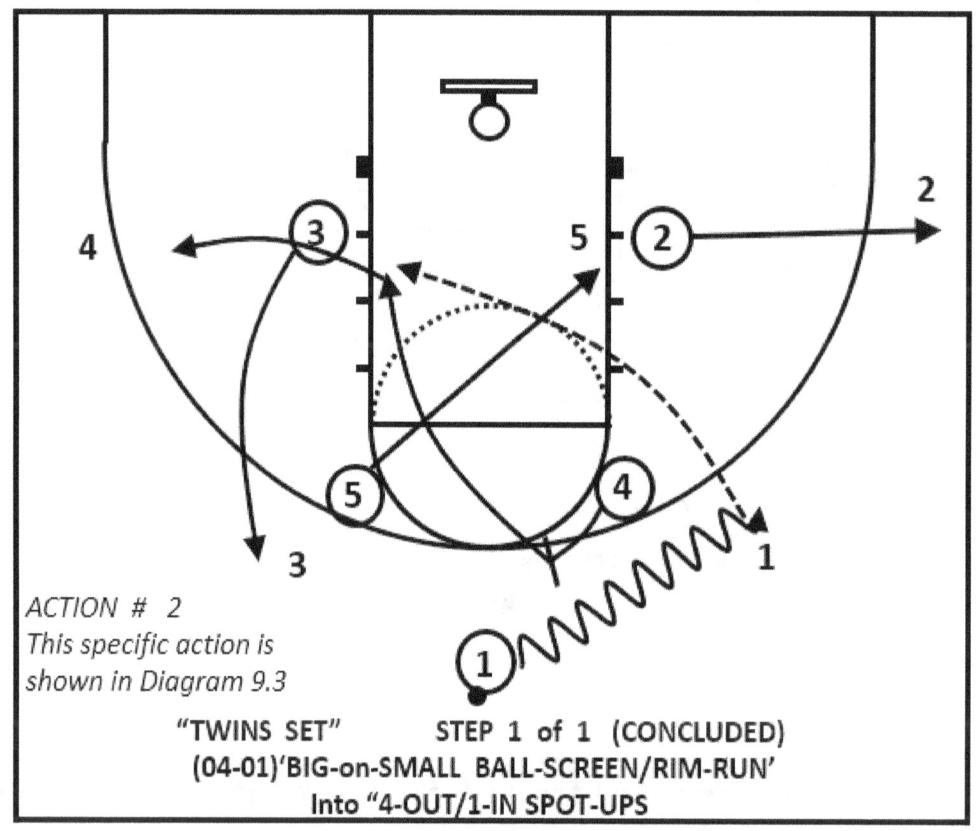

Diagram 9.3

PLAY # 3: "BIG-ON-SMALL BALL-SCREEN SLIP" ACTION

Diagram 4 illustrates another version of the "Ball-Screen," out of "2-Down Flat" Set. With 01 at the top of the key, 04 makes a strong and aggressive "Duck-In" Cut from his initial location. 01 looks to capitalize on making the pass to 04 on his cut as he dribbles towards 05, located at the high "Elbow" area on the left side of the floor. At the same time, 03 "drift cuts" towards his "Deep Corner," vertically and horizontally stretching the defense. 01 "dribble-scrapes" off of 05's top right shoulder. When defenses attempt to defend the ball-screen by "dropping (X5), "hard hedging" or "switching:' 05 can then "slip his screen and flare as far as to the opposite "Slot." This action is commonly also called "Pick and Pop" and was made popular with Bill Laimbeer and the Detroit Pistons years ago. It has been copied by many teams from all three Levels of play since then. If 05 has perimeter scoring skills, particularly "catch and shoot" skills from behind the arc; this action will be very successful. Keep in mind that even if 05 turns down his shot, 04 has still gained a "Position advantage" by isolating his lone defender in the highest scoring area on the floor—the lane just in front of the basket.

If no shots are taken, (particularly by 05 or 04) all players are once again in the "4-Out/1-In" Spot-Ups for the final phase of the offense, able to smoothly and immediately begin; giving the defense no time to regroup or recover.

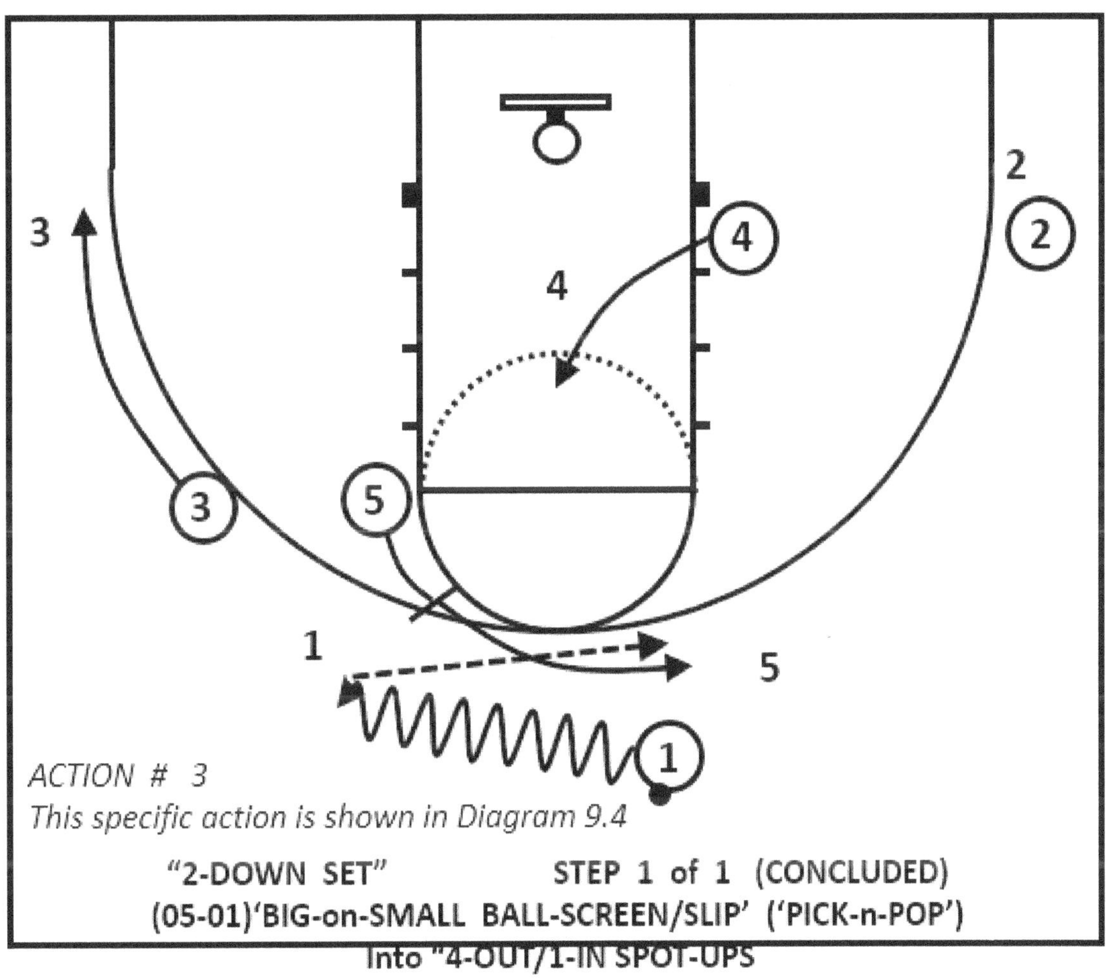

Diagram 9.4

⊕ Play # 4: "Big-on-Small Ball-Screen Pin-Down" Action

Diagram 9.5 illustrates an entry out of the "Horns" Set when it is felt that 05 is not an overwhelming perimeter scoring threat. To capitalize on 04's interior scoring skills, 05's lack of scoring skills and 02's perimeter scoring skills, this play utilizes players' strengths while avoiding other player's weaknesses. Another "Big-on-Small" (05-01) Ball-Screen initiates the action of this play.

01 again "dribble-scrapes" off of 05's top right shoulder and 04 immediately diagonally "Slash Cuts" across the lane to post up his defender in another isolation situation. With 03 and 02 both starting in their respective "Deep Corners," the defense is already stretched into a weakened condition. As 01 breaks contact with 05's top shoulder, 05 makes another front pivot off of his left lower foot to then go set a "Big-on-Small" (this helps discourage defensive switching) Screen for 02 to use to rub his defender off and break to the newly declared "Weakside Slot" for a "catch and shoot" shot behind the arc. 05's action not only frees up 02 for the open shot, but also pulls the most likely biggest defender (X5) away from the basket; to help further X4's situation. "4-Out/1-In" Spot-Ups are again easily and quickly filled; not only for another fluid transition into the next phase of the offensive attack, but also helping to contribute for better offensive rebounding opportunities as well as defensive transitioning success.

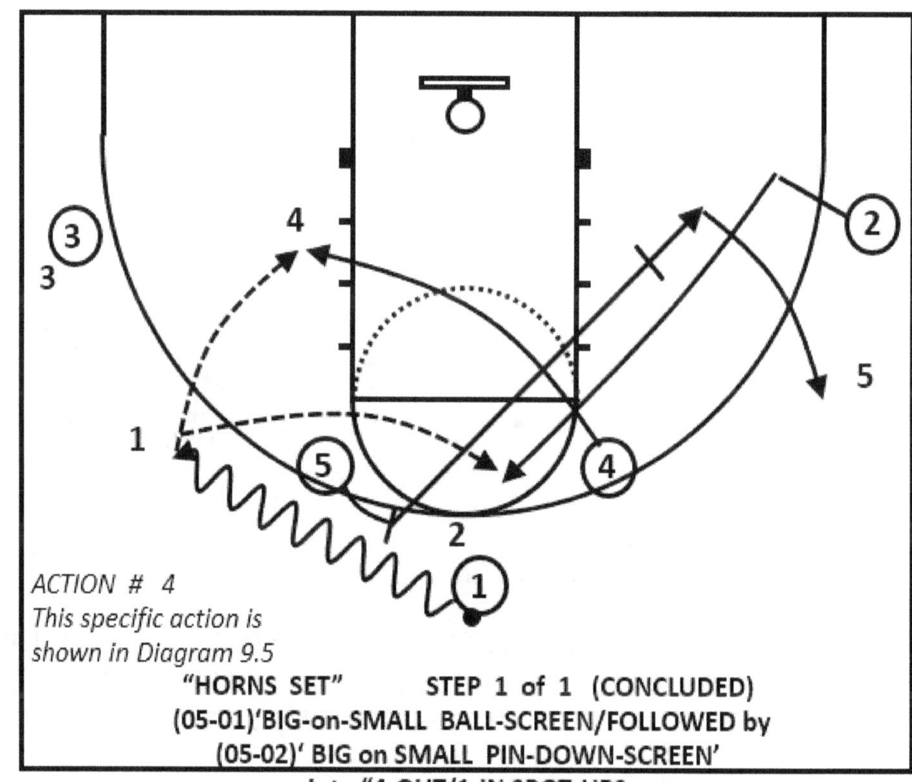

"HORNS SET"   STEP 1 of 1 (CONCLUDED)
(05-01)'BIG-on-SMALL BALL-SCREEN/FOLLOWED by
(05-02)' BIG on SMALL PIN-DOWN-SCREEN'
Into "4-OUT/1-IN SPOT-UPS

Diagram 9.5

⊕ Play # 5: "(Small-on Big Back-)Screen the (Ball-)Screener"

ACTION

Out of the "Hi-Lo Stax" Set, this quick-hitter starts with another "Big-on-Small Ball-Screen" with 01 closely dribbling off of 05's top shoulder while 03 "flare-cuts" to his "Deep Corner." At the same time, 04 flashes across the lane to isolate his post defender on the opposite side of the lane.

Another method of attacking opponent's "ball-screening" defenses is using different forms of "screening the (ball-)screener" action. Play # 5 has 02 diagonally make a long break to set a (02-05) "Small-on-Big Diagonal Back-Screen' for 05 to peel off 02's outside left shoulder and make a "Lob Cut" to the basket. With 02 screening for a "Big" (05), if defenses would switch this very difficult screen to defend; it would place a perimeter player (X2) on an offensive "Big" (05) near the basket. This gives the offense not only a "player advantage" but a "position advantage." 01 would still have an inside scoring option in looking to hit 04 on his isolation action. 01 and 03 both should have primary perimeter scoring opportunities.

If the play has not created the desired shots, it still has accomplished repositioning all five offensive players in the proper "4-Out/1-In" Spot-Up locations for an immediate transition into the last phase of the offensive attack.

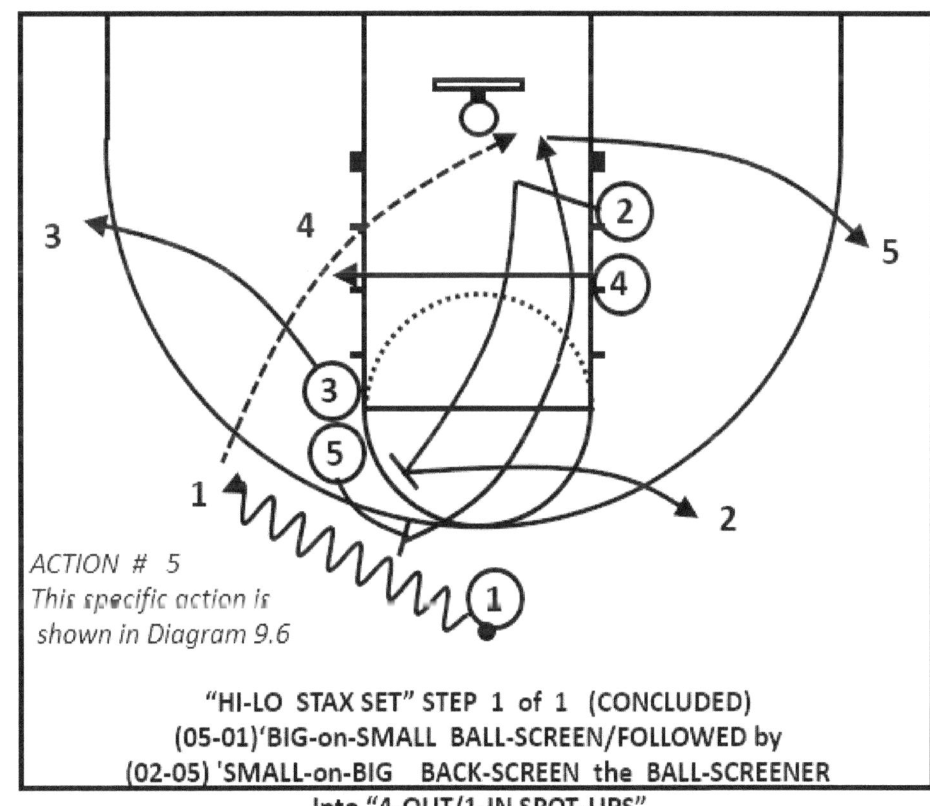

"HI-LO STAX SET" STEP 1 of 1 (CONCLUDED)
(05-01)'BIG-on-SMALL BALL-SCREEN/FOLLOWED by
(02-05) 'SMALL-on-BIG BACK-SCREEN the BALL-SCREENER
Into "4-OUT/1-IN SPOT-UPS"

Diagram 9.6

⚉ Play # 6: "Big-on-Small Ghost Ball-Screen/Slash Cut" Action

Play # 6 out of the "1-Down" Set is an illustration of another type of (counter-)attack to disrupt opposing defenses attempting to defend ball-screens. With 02 bringing the ball across the line himself or by receiving an early (01-02) "Reverse Pass," 02 starts towards 04. At the same time 04 breaks up as if to set a "Big-on-Small Ball-Screen" at the Slot. With X4 anticipating the screen, 04 breaks off of his screening path and makes a "Rim-Run" to the basket. To occupy his defender, 05 either flashes from across the left side of the lane to "Iso Post-Up" his defender or he begins on the same side of the floor as 04. This option of starting on either side of the lane gives the offense more looks and more deception and less predictability for the opposition. To occupy any possible weakside help defense, 03 steps up to set a (03-01) "Big-on-Small Flare-Screen." This gives 02 two possible '3 Pt. Scoring' Pass Receivers besides a back-up interior receiver in 05. If 05 is not immediately hit by 01, he should break out to the vacant "Deep Corner." This stretches and pulls the presumed biggest defender (X5) further away from the basket, leaving X4 in a more isolated and weakened defensive position/location.

If no shots are taken, all players are in the "4-Out/1-In" Offensive Spot-Ups—the initial starting locations for various other continuity offenses.

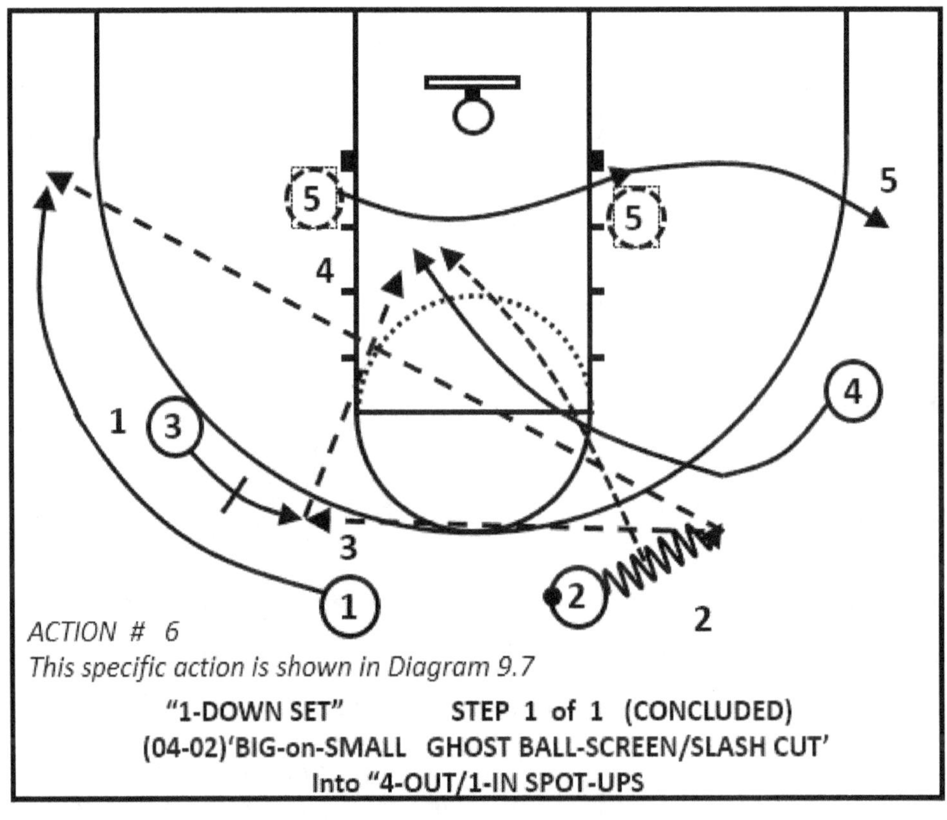

Diagram 9.7

Out of the "3-UP" Set Play # 7, 01 uses the Double "Big-on-Small Ball-Screen" set by both 05 and 04. After scraping and breaking contact with 04's top left shoulder, 01 dribbles towards the inside of the offense's right "Slot." If he can turn the corner and make a full dribble penetration, he should look to score, or to make a "Drive & Dump" pass to 04 or a "Penetrate and Pitch" pass to 02, flattened and spread out in the "Deep Corner. If 01 is "walled" off and cannot fully penetrate, he should make his dribble more of a "dribble pull" and stay out towards the "Slot."

With 04 making a "Rim-Run" and 05 making a "Slip" (again, sometimes called "Pick & Pop), the offense has stretched the defense both vertically and horizontally—further weakening the overall defense. If 05 is a strong perimeter scoring threat and/or X5 is a weak perimeter defender; 01 could reverse the ball to 05. 05 could look to score off of the "catch and shoot" or make interior or perimeter passes to his four teammates. This gives the offense not only immediate scoring threats but also places all players into the same "4-Out/1-In" Spot-Ups (for an immediate and fluid transition into the designated Continuity offense.)

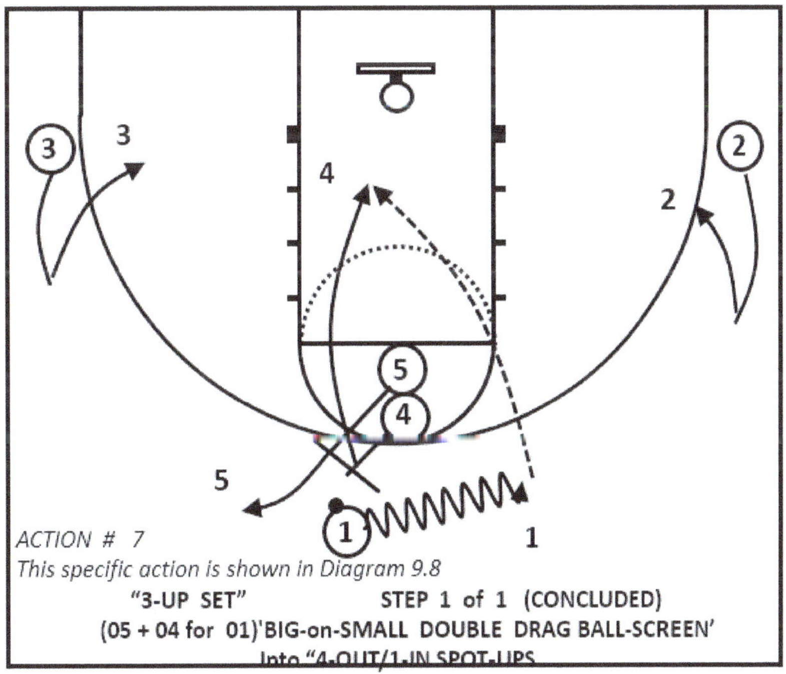

Diagram 9.8

 # PLAY # 8: "BIG-ON-SMALL TWISTED DOUBLE BALL-SCREEN (WITH SLIP AND RIM-RUN)" ACTION.

Diagram 9.9 illustrates a play out of the unique set, called the "Nail" Set. With 03 and 02 at the Free Throw line extended on their respective sides of the floor, 05 begins on the "Nail" with 04 stacked vertically just above 05.

This action could easily be executed out of the same "3-Up" Set (Diagram 9.8) and it simply has 05 step vertically above the stack to set the ball-screen with 04. This action is simply called the "Twisted (Big-on-Small) Ball-Screen. "Rolls" down the lane by 05 and "Slips" by 04 could be executed or 05 and 04 could reverse the rolls and slips; making the play even more unpredictable as well as giving 05 and/or 04 opportunities to accent their offensive advantages over their individual opponent.

This diagram illustrates Play # 8 with 01 "dribble-scraping off of 05's top left shoulder before 05 slips to the "Slot." This action then has 04 making a "Rim-Run" to the basket just as 01 breaks contact with 05 on his perimeter (or penetrating into the lane) dribble towards the right side of the floor. Both 03 and 02 drift down to their "Deep Corners" to vertically stretch the floor as their initial locations have already horizontally pulled their defenders further out of the middle. The "4-Out/1-In" Spot-Ups are once again filled so that the advantage of the fluid and immediate transition into the final phase of the attack remains.

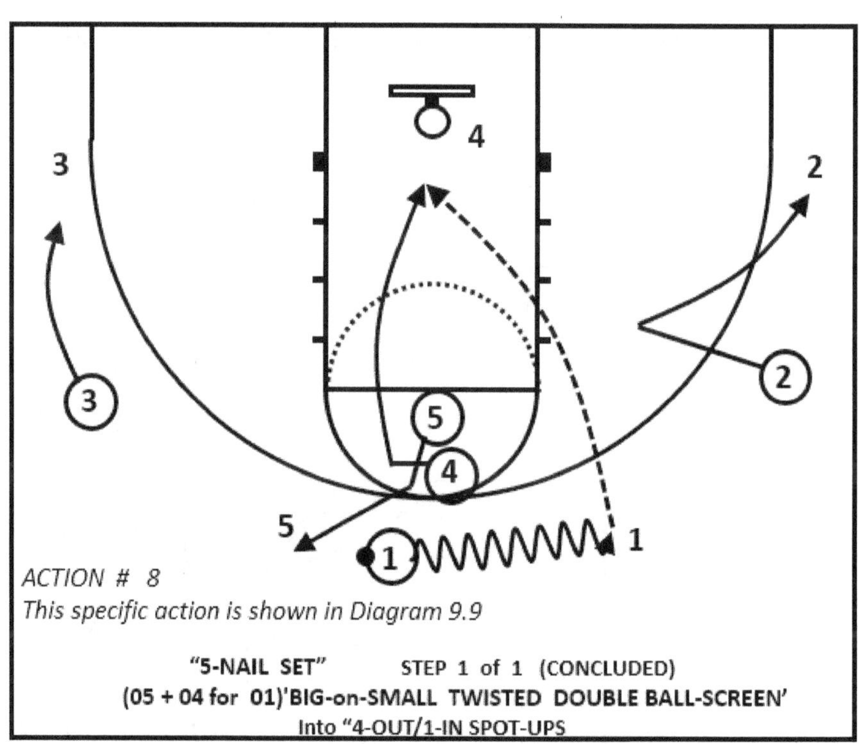

Diagram 9.9

⊕ PLAY # 9: "BIG-ON-SMALL DOUBLE BALL-SCREEN (WITH SLIP AND RIM-RUN)" ACTION.

Diagram 9.10 illustrates a play out of the "5-SQUEEZE" Set where 01 starts towards the right "Slot" area with 03 and 02 both making "Iverson Cuts" to the opposite "Wing" Spot-Up locations. As 01 then begins his change of direction with a cross-over dribble, both 05 and 04 break up to the top of the key to set their ball-screen action.

When 01 "dribble-scrapes" towards the offense's left "Slot" location off of 05's outside right shoulder 05 makes a front pivot off of his left foot to continue slipping to the newly designated weakside "Slot" position. At the same time, 04 makes a reverse pivot off of his inside right pivot to make an aggressive (and isolated) "Rim-Run" to the basket, looking for a "Lob Pass" from 01 or an "Inside Pass" from 02 on an "Isolated Post-Up."

If nothing is available on the left side of the floor, 01 could reverse the ball to 05, particularly if 05 has strong offensive perimeter skills from behind the arc. If the ball is reversed to 05 and/or 03 (with a 01-03 "Skip Pass" or a 05-03 "Down Pass,") 04 should "chase the ball to post up on the new "Ballside Mid-Post." With 02 and 03 both spotting up in the "Deep Corners," the interior support defense is again stretched vertically and horizontally to further isolate X4. In addition, the "4-Out/1-In" Spot-Ups are again filled for the same seamless and fluid conversion into the last phase of the attack.

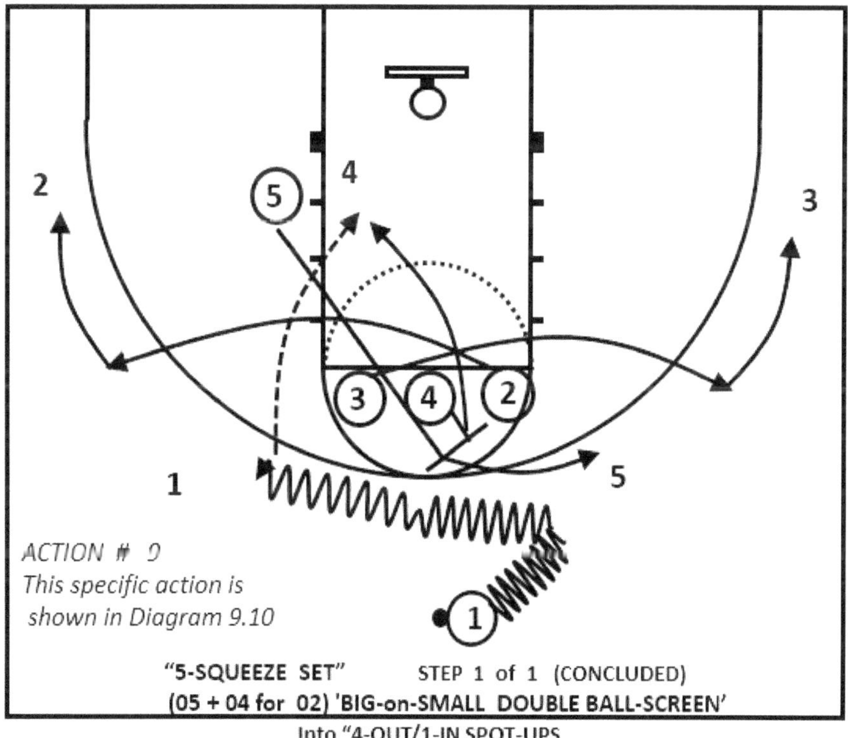

Diagram 9.10

⊕ PLAY # 10: "BIG-ON-

SMALL INSIDE BALL-SCREEN/ROLL" ACTION.

Diagram 9.11 illustrates a play out of the "2-SQUEEZE" Set. 02 breaks diagonally out from his initial "Mid-Post" location to the "Wing" spot on his initial side of the floor. As 01 makes the "Wing Pass" to 02, 05 quickly slashes to the new "Ballside Mid-Post," looking for a quick "Iso Post-Up." 03 breaks out to the FT Line extended and 01 flare-cuts to the new "Weakside Slot to both stretch the weakside defense.

If 05 does not receive an immediate pass from 01, 04 cuts towards 02 and the ball to set a "Big-on-Small Inside Ball-Screen" for 02 to use to either make a strong "penetrating dribble" into the lane or a "perimeter pull dribble" to move the ball to the other side of the floor and to stretch the defense even further. 05 steps out to the "Deep Corner" to pull his "defensive Big" away from the basket. After 01 "dribble-scrapes" off of 04's top right shoulder, 04 reverse pivots off of his lower left shoulder and rolls through the lane in his isolation cut towards the basket. 04 looks to receive the ball from either 02, 01 or 03. If 02 throws the ball back to 05, 04 should again "chase the ball and flash to the new "Ballside Mid-Post" location. If no shots are taken, regardless of the perimeter location of the ball; the "4-Out/1-In" Spot-Ups are filled for a smooth conversion into the next phase of the offensive attack.

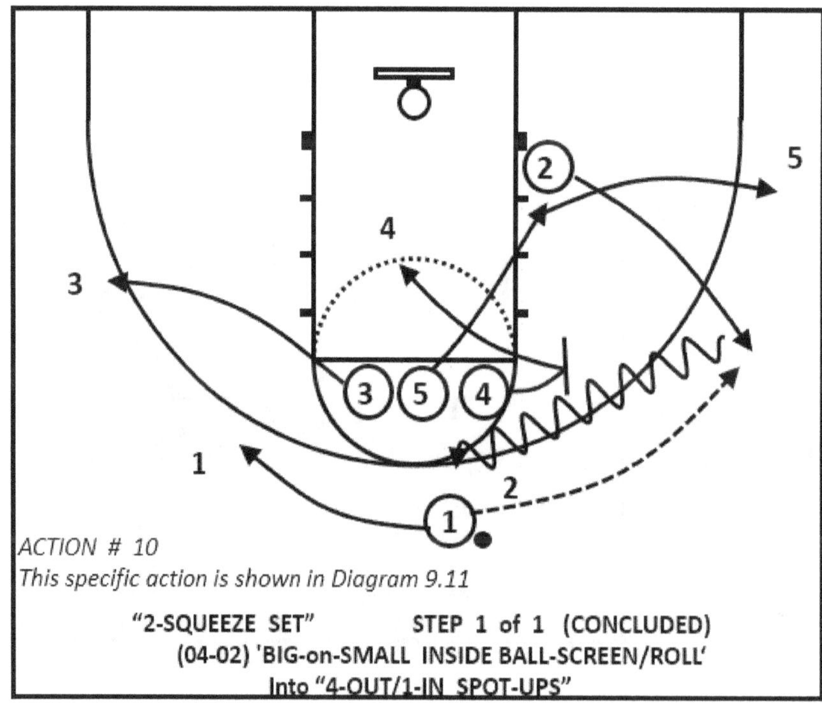

Diagram 9.11

⊕ PLAY # 11: "BIG-ON-SMALL INSIDE BALL-SCREEN/RIM-RUN" ACTION

Diagram 9.12 shows a play that has already been initiated out of the "3-ACROSS" Set with 04 starting on the left side of the lane. With 02 having the ball at the top of the key making a "Wing Pass" to 03, 01 has set a (01-02) "Flare-Screen" 02 to use to stretch his defender towards the new "Weakside Deep Corner." After screening for 02, 01 slips his screen and remains near the "Weakside Slot."

At the same time, 05 breaks from his initial "Nail" spot towards 03 and the ball to set a "ball-screen" for 03 to attack his defender out near the top of the key area. After 03 "dribble-scrapes" off of 05's top right shoulder, 05 then makes a front pivot off of his left foot to "Rim-Run" to the basket. 03 looks to either make a "Lob Pass" to 05. If 05 does not receive 03's "Lob Pass," 05 empties out of the lane to the vacant "Deep Corner." If 03 retains his dribble, he looks to make, a "penetrating dribble" into the lane (where he could "penetrate and pitch" to either 01 or 03 or make a "penetrating drive and dump" to 04.

If the desired shot is not found from the many options available, the "4-Out/1-In" Spot-Ups are once again to allow the offense to continue its relentless attack on the opposition's defense.

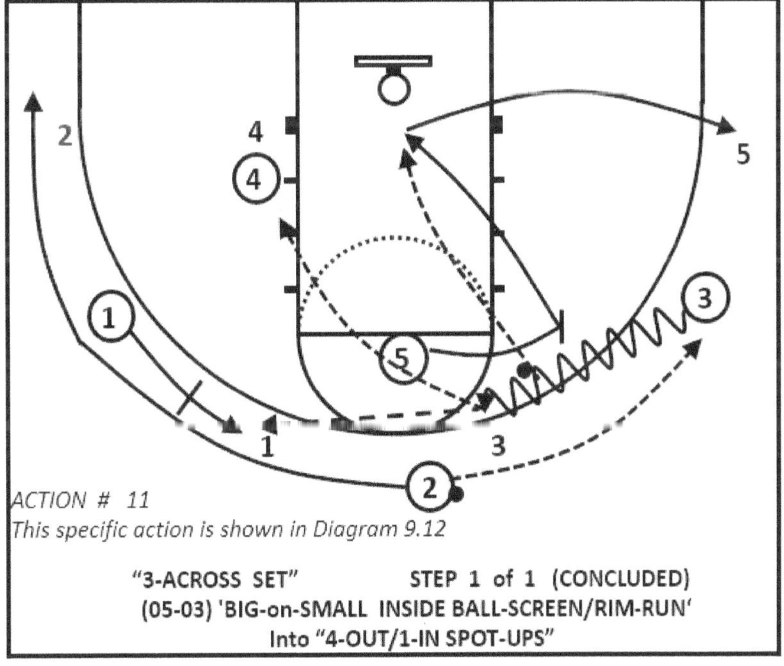

Diagram 9.12

⊕ Play # 12: "Big-on-Small Inside Ball-Screen/Slip" Action

Diagram 9.13 shows a play that has already been started with 02 having the ball on the FT Line extended, 03 at the "Weakside Slot," and 01 also on the weakside at the FT Line extended. 04 has isolated his defender on the "Ballside Block," and 05 stepping out from the "Ballside High Post" area. As always, when using ball-screens, 02 sets his defender up with jab steps and fakes before then "dribble-scraping" off of 05's to right shoulder. In this instance, two teammates other than 05 are going to attack the interior defense. 04 will make a strong Iso Duck-In Cut while 03 crosses his defender up from the appearance of a (03-01) Pin-Down Screen by "ghosting" the perceived action and diving to the basket. To make way for less congestion, 05 makes a front pivot off of his right foot and steps to the perimeter area that 02 has just vacated. This helps 04 on his isolation action and also for 03 on his surprise inside cutting action.

It is also even more effective when 05 has good offensive perimeter skills, such as "catch and shoot" (off of the pass) skills and/or perimeter passing skills. 05 could receive 02's "Reverse Throwback Pass," turn down a shot and then look to hit 04 isolated on the "Ballside Block."

A unique feature in this particular play is that a new set of offensive spot-ups are used—the "3-Out/2-In" Spot-Ups. This gives the offense a whole new set of continuity offenses that could be used as well as different Motion-types of offenses (with their own different set of rules).

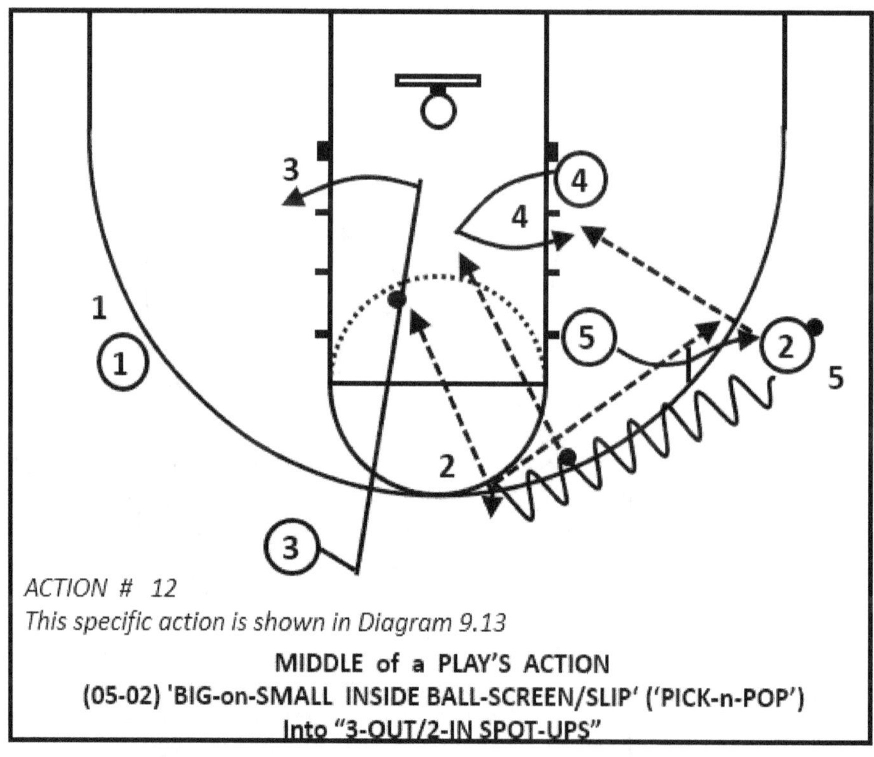

Diagram 9.13

⊕ Play # 13: "Big-On-Small Inside Ball-Screen Followed By

"Small-on-Big (Back-) Screen The (Ball-) Screener" Action

Diagram 9.14 shows a middle of a play where 01 has possession of the basketball on the offense's right side of the floor. 02 has isolated and inverted his perimeter-type defender with 05 at the Ballside High Post, 04 inverted out on the now designated "Weakside Slot" and 03 spotted up on the "Weakside Wing."

After 01 turns down the interior pass to 02, 05 again steps out on the perimeter to set his "Big-on-Small Inside Ball-Screen" for 01 to utilize his dribble with either "perimeter penetration" or "perimeter pull-dribbling" action. After "dribble-scraping" off of 05's top right shoulder and breaking contact with 05, 02 steps up to set a "Small-on-Big (Back-)Screen the (Ball-)Screen" for 05 to use. 05 front pivots off of his lower left foot and "scrapes" off of 02's left shoulder to then make a "Rim-Run" cut to the basket. After setting the screen, 02 slips his screen to reposition himself in the "Deep Corner" on the same side of the floor.

To provide the offense with scoring threats on the weakside of the floor as well as to occupy weakside defenders to further isolate 05 on his "Rim-Run," 04 cuts over to set a "Big-on-Small Pin Down-Screen" for 03 to break up to the "Slot" After screening, 04 drifts further into the "Deep Corner" area to further stretch the opposition's defense. When no desired shots are taken, the offense has still attacked various individual defenders and repositioned every offensive player so that the designated continuity offense associated with the "4-Out/1-In" Spot-ups can fluidly begin.

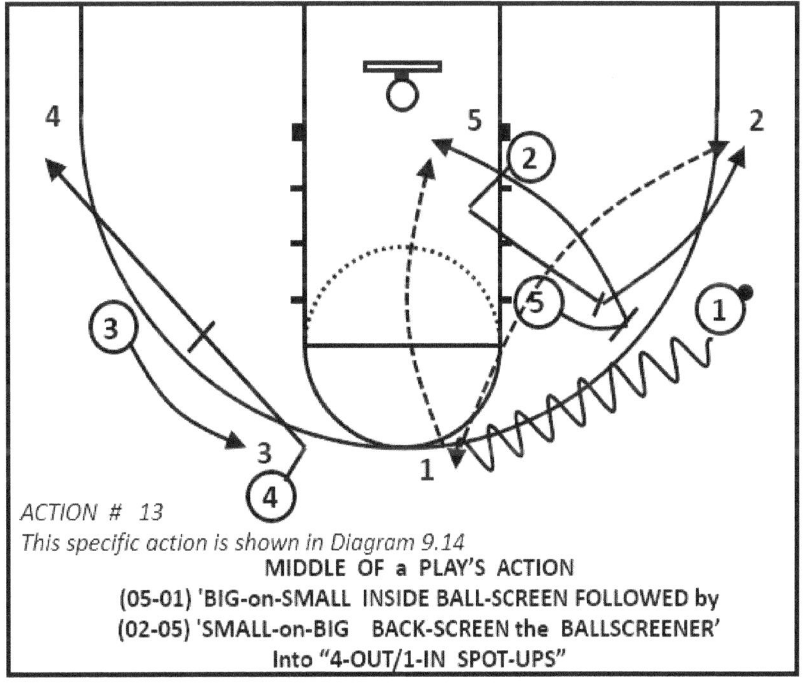

ACTION # 13
This specific action is shown in Diagram 9.14
MIDDLE OF a PLAY'S ACTION
(05-01) 'BIG-on-SMALL INSIDE BALL-SCREEN FOLLOWED by
(02-05) 'SMALL-on-BIG BACK-SCREEN the BALLSCREENER'
Into "4-OUT/1-IN SPOT-UPS"

Diagram 9.14

Diagram 9.15 illustrates the middle of a play that again places the ball in the hands of 01 at the FT Line extended on the right side of the floor. 05 is the player that has the advantage of posting up his isolated defender, X5, on the "Ballside Block" with 04 at the "Ballside High Post." 03 has ended up on the "Weakside Slot" and 02 at the "Weakside Wing."

When 01 turns down the interior pass to 05, 04 again steps out to set his "Big-on-Small Inside Ball-Screen" for 01 to use to make various passes to teammates or to look to use his "penetration dribble" into the lane or to use his "perimeter pull dribble" to vertically stretch the defense.

The weakside action of this particular play has 02 step up to set a "Small-on-Big Flare Screen" for 03. This gives 01 not one, but two perimeter scoring threats on the weakside while having a potential "Reverse Throwback" Pass opportunity to 04. This pass can be especially effective using misdirection and taking advantage of 04's possible perimeter scoring talents. In addition, it can be a way for the offense to attack X4's lack of perimeter defensive skills. 04 could also be the perimeter player that has an improved passing angle to deliver the ball to 05, isolated in the post.

If shots are not taken from the many options, all players are again repositioned into the "4-Out/1-In" Spot-Ups for the offense to continue its constant attack on the defense.

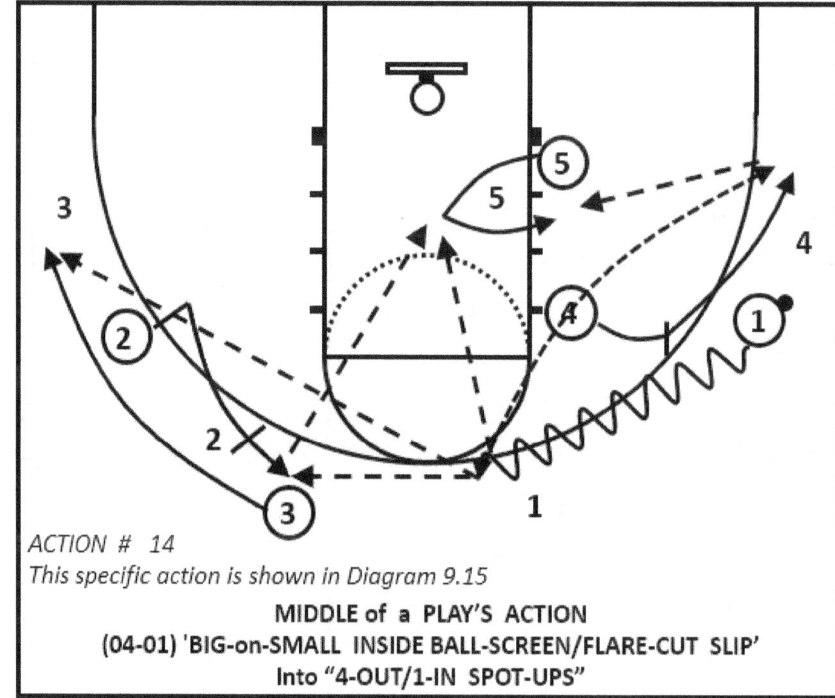

ACTION # 14
This specific action is shown in Diagram 9.15
MIDDLE of a PLAY'S ACTION
(04-01) 'BIG-on-SMALL INSIDE BALL-SCREEN/FLARE-CUT SLIP'
Into "4-OUT/1-IN SPOT-UPS"

Diagram 9.15

☠ PLAY # 15: "BIG-ON-SMALL INSIDE BALL-SCREEN/

FOLLOWED BY "PIN-DOWN SCREEN" ACTION

From the middle of the play, this diagram shows 03 having the basketball at the FT Line Extended, with 05 at the "Ballside High Post," 02 stretched out into the "Deep Corner, 01 at the "Weakside Slot" and 04 at the "Weakside FT Line extended.

When 03 "dribble-scrapes" off of 05's top right shoulder, 05's option in this play is to immediately break down to set a "Big-on-Small (05-02) Pin Down-Screen for 02 to fill the newly vacated wing area. After setting the screen for 02, 05 and slip his screen and "Rim-Run" (looking for interior passes from either 03 or from 02.

Weakside action has 04 start up to set a "Flare-Screen" for 01, but instead "ghosts the screen and continues to the "Weakside Block." 01 continues with his own "Flare-Cut" to the weakside.

02 has penetrating and perimeter scoring options off of his dribble, passing options to 02, to 05 to 04 or to 01. If these scoring options do not create the desired shot, the five offensive players have attacked and moved their own individual defenders as well as repositioned themselves into another set of offensive spot-ups. This is where a continuity or motion-type offense can begin out of these somewhat different "3-Out/2-In" Spot-Ups.

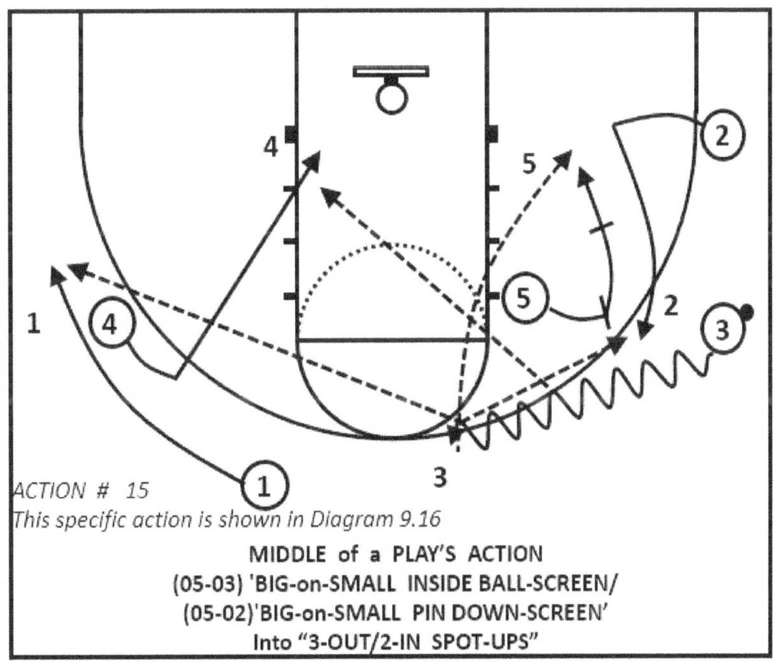

Diagram 9.16

⊕ PLAY # 16: "BIG-ON-SMALL GHOST INSIDE BALL-SCREEN" ACTION

From the middle of the play, this diagram shows 03 having the basketball at the FT Line Extended, with 05 at the "Ballside High Post," 02 stretched out into the "Deep Corner, 01 at the "Weakside Slot" and 04 at the "Weakside FT Line extended.

This play is unique in that there is a different form of deception in this play because 04 does not actually step out to set the "Inside Ball-Screen." Instead 04 sets a "Ghost Inside Ball-Screen" and quickly slashes to the basket, while looking for the quicker, earlier surprise pass from 01. If 01 still makes his "perimeter penetration dribble" or "perimeter pull dribble" (as he always has done in the previous plays) he looks again to make the pass to 04, a possible "Reverse Throwback Pass" to 03, who has lifted up to fill 01's initial "Wing" spot. 01 could look to hit 05 making a "Backdoor Cut" to the basket or to 02 on his "Flare-Cut" to the FT Line extended.

If shots are not created with all of the action described, the offensive players have forced their defenders to react and to move; while repositioning themselves into the proper "3-Out/2-In" Spot-Ups for a different type of Continuity or Motion Offenses than "4-Out/1-In" Spot-Ups utilize.

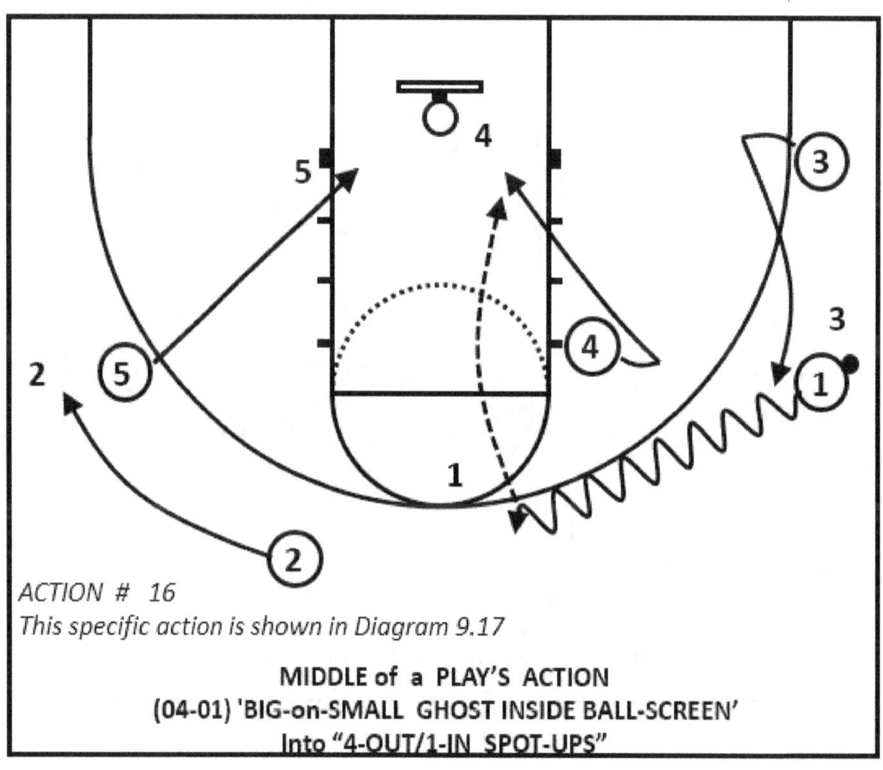

Diagram 9.17

⊕ Play # 17: "FOLLOW-(the-Pass) BALL-SCREEN/RIM-RUN" ACTION

Diagram 9.18 illustrates the entire Play # 17 that begins from the "2-TWIST" Set.

This entry starts with 01 bringing the ball across the time-line and making the 01-02 "Reverse Pass." 01 immediately follows his pass by cutting across to set a "Ball-Screen" for 02 to use and he "dribble-scrapes" off of 01's top right shoulder to proceed with his "perimeter pull dribble." As 01 breaks contact with 02, 01 makes a front pivot off of his left foot to then "scrape" off of 05's "Big-on-Small Back-Screen the Ball-Screener" to then make an inverted "Rim-Run to the basket. 05 breaks then slips his screen and slides out to the new "Weakside Slot." At the same time, 03 makes a "Flare-Cut" to the new Ballside Deep Corner" while 04 makes an aggressive "Iso Duck-In Cut" on his side of the lane.

01 looks to highlight his inverted leaping and post-up scoring skills and/or to attack X1's individual interior defensive skills. If 01 does not receive 02's "Lob Pass," he then empties out to the new "Weakside Deep Corner." This places the final offensive player into the correct "4-Out/1-In" Spot-Up locations, allowing the offense to maintain a constant pressure on the defense.

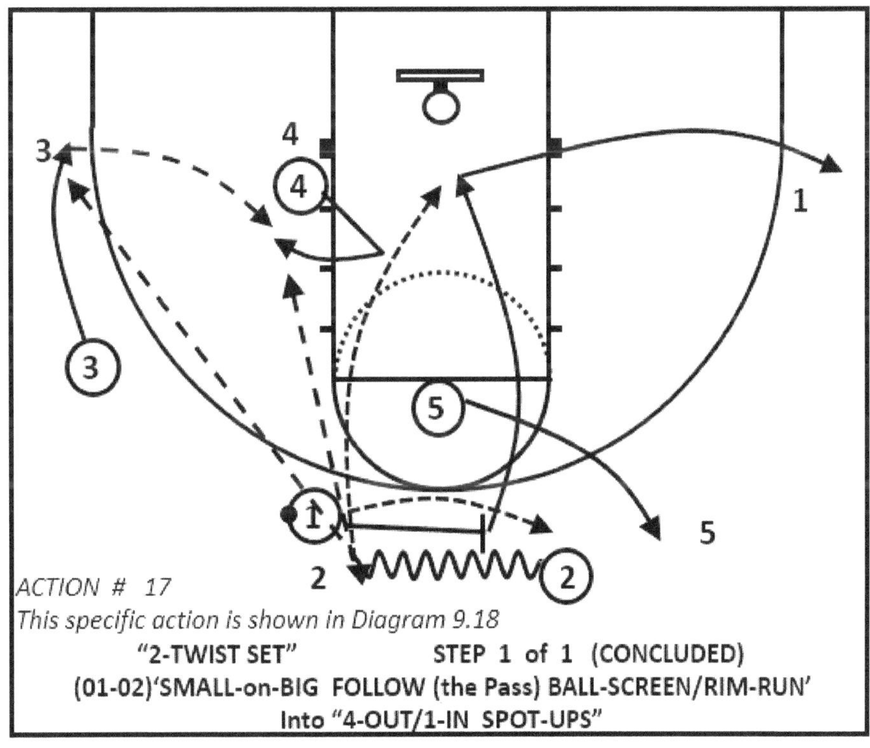

Diagram 9.18

PLAY # 18: "SMALL-ON-BIG FOLLOW-(THE-PASS) BALL-SCREEN/ROLL"

ACTION

From the "2-UP" Set, this play/entry shows the same type of ball-screen from a similar location, but with a different set of actions that follow the screen. 02 is the designated player to make the (02-01) "Reverse Pass" to 01 and then follows his pass to set a "Ball-Screen" for 01 to use. 01 then "dribble-scrapes" off of 02's top left shoulder. At the same time, 05 steps up and out to get out of the way of 02's following action. When 01 dribbles tightly off of 02's top shoulder to deflect his defender, 02 makes a "Reverse Pivot" off of his lower right foot. From there, he can open up to the ball and to 01 as he rolls down the lane to invert and isolate his perimeter-type defender, X1.

With 05 inverting the presumed biggest opposing defender away from the basket and occupying his weakside defender with a "Drift Cut" down towards the new "Weakside Deep Corner;" these actions not only stretch the defense vertically as well as horizontally, but also occupy them (so that 02 can further isolate his perimeter-type defender sliding down the lane.

If 02's skills and position advantage" does not help create the ideal shot, the "4-Out/1-In" Spot-Ups so that the offense can remain in fluid movement and attack mode.

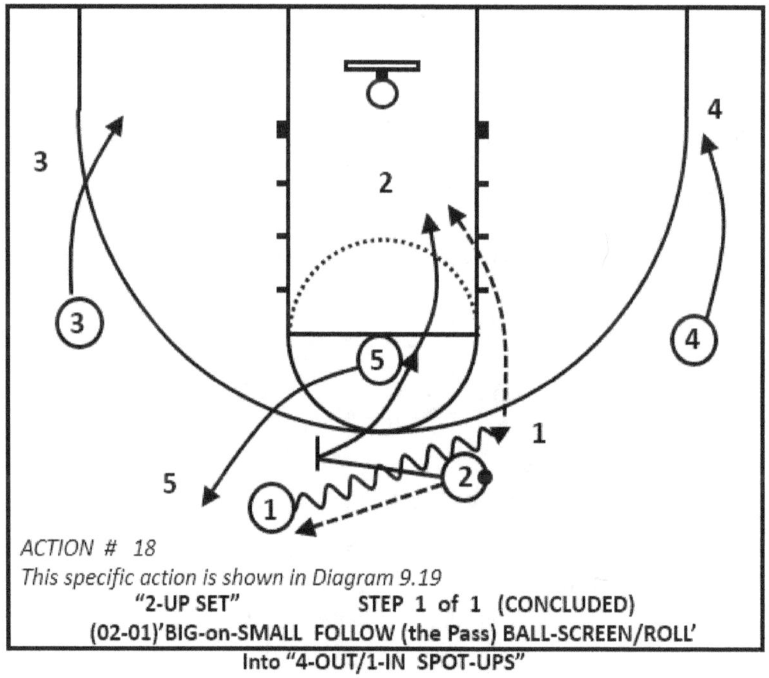

Diagram 9.19

ACTION

Diagram 19.20 shows another play/entry out of the same symmetrically balanced "2-UP" Set with making the initial "Wing Pass" to 04. Instead of going to set a "Follow-the-Pass Ball-Screen, 02 uses conception and fakes the action by simply making the Ghost action and immediately cuts to the basket. This action is actually a simple "Give-n-Go" Cut with a fake "Follow the Pass Ball-Screen" towards 04. 01 rotates over with 05 inverting to the new "Weakside Slot" area and 03 "Drift Cutting, positioning all five players into the proper "4-Out/1-In" Spot-Ups.

This play could easily be executed with a 02-01 "Reverse Pass," that is followed by a quick (1-03 Wing Pass." The next action would be for 01 to disguise his "Follow-the Pass Ball-Screen" presumed action with his own "Ghost" action.

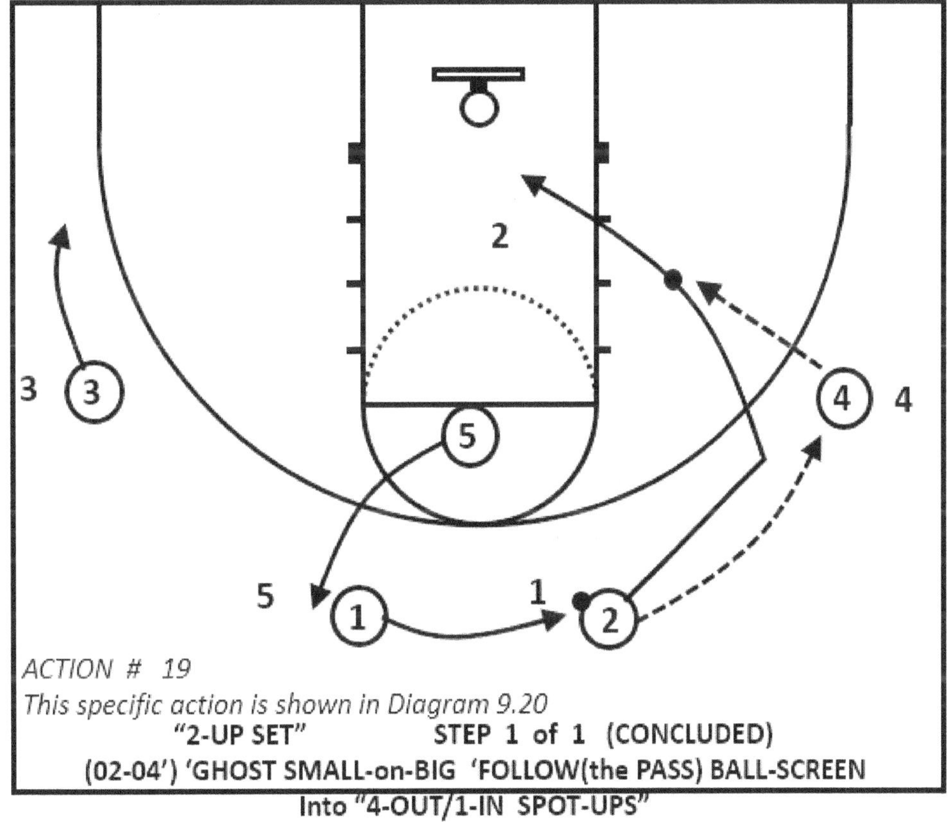

Diagram 9.20

Diagram 9.21 shows another form of ball-screening action that is different and can be more effective than the traditional ball-screen action for several reasons. This action could obviously be used in the half-court play setting as all other examples have been in this chapter. But to expand, we chose to show it as a Secondary Fastbreak setting.

After using other Secondary Break options that have 04 "chase the ball across the lane" while looking for the perimeter pass first from 02, then 01, then 05 at the top of the key and finally from 03 on the opposite Wing (from 01); this Secondary Break option uses deception by first having 05 and 03 change locations at the very end of the Primary Break.

During this Secondary Break, when 03 ends up at the top of the key at the very end of the Primary Break, he is the player that receives the "Reverse Pass" from 01. 02 immediately runs the baseline from one "Deep Corner" to the opposite "Deep Corner," looking for a possible (03-02) "Lob Pass."

Instead of 03 looking to make the "Inside Pass" to 04 cutting through the lane and/or to continue the swing of the ball to 05, 04 changes his route and breaks diagonally up towards 03 and the ball. Initially, this action appears to be and could actually be an aggressive "Duck-In Cut into the lane. If 03 cannot make that pass to 04 during his different cut, 04 continues into the direction of 03 to then set his "Big-on-Small Long Ball-Screen.

03 then fakes a drive or a pass towards 05 and "re-reverses" the ball via dribble. 03 should then "dribble-scrape" off of 04's top outside left shoulder as he advances the ball towards the initial "Ballside Slot." As contact is broken, 04 "reverse pivots" off of his top left shoulder to open up to the ball, to 03 and to 01 as he makes a "Drift Cut" down the sideline. This gives 03 space to

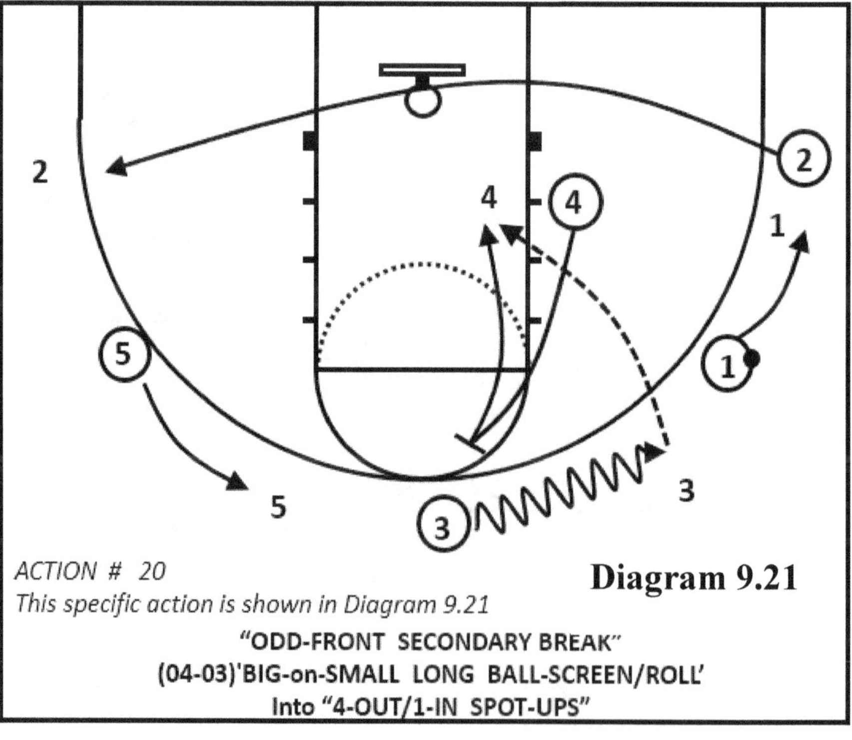

Diagram 9.21

dribble towards the "FT Line Extended" for a better passing angle and can also create a new and improved passing angle for 01 to make the interior pass to 04 as he rolls down the lane. If the passes are not there, players have attacked and moved their individual defenders as well as repositioned themselves not in random locations, but in the same "4-Out/1-In" Spot-Ups that will allow the offense to seamlessly flow into the Continuity Offense that is wanted.

⊕ PLAY # 21: "BIG-ON-SMALL LONG BALL-SCREEN/RIM-RUN" ACTION

Diagram 9.22 illustrates another half-court play from beginning to end out of the "1-DOWN" Set with 02 making the "Reverse Pass" to 01 and immediately making a "Given-Go" Cut to the basket. If 02 does not receive the ball from on the 01-02 pass, 02 empties out to the sideline as he then drifts down to the new "Weakside Deep Corner." 04 breaks up to the now vacant "Slot."

As this action takes place on the new "Weakside," 05 breaks up from the new "Ballside Block" to set a "Big-on-Small Long Ball-Screen" for 01 to use. As 01 "dribble-scrapes" off of 05's outside right shoulder, 05 makes a front pivot off of his inside left foot to then "Rim-Run" to the basket.

04 now spots up at the "Slot" behind the arc, stretching the defense vertically. 03 "Drift Cuts" towards the new "Ballside Deep Corner," becoming a strong '3 Pt.' Shooting threat. In addition, 03 becomes a potential and likely threat to be the actual player to make the "Inside Pass" to 05 on his "Iso Post-Up (after finishing his "Rim-Run" to the basket. 01 has the ball outside of the arc and 02 ends up in the "Weakside Deep Corner." This action places four players outside of the arc with 05 completely isolating his lone defender.

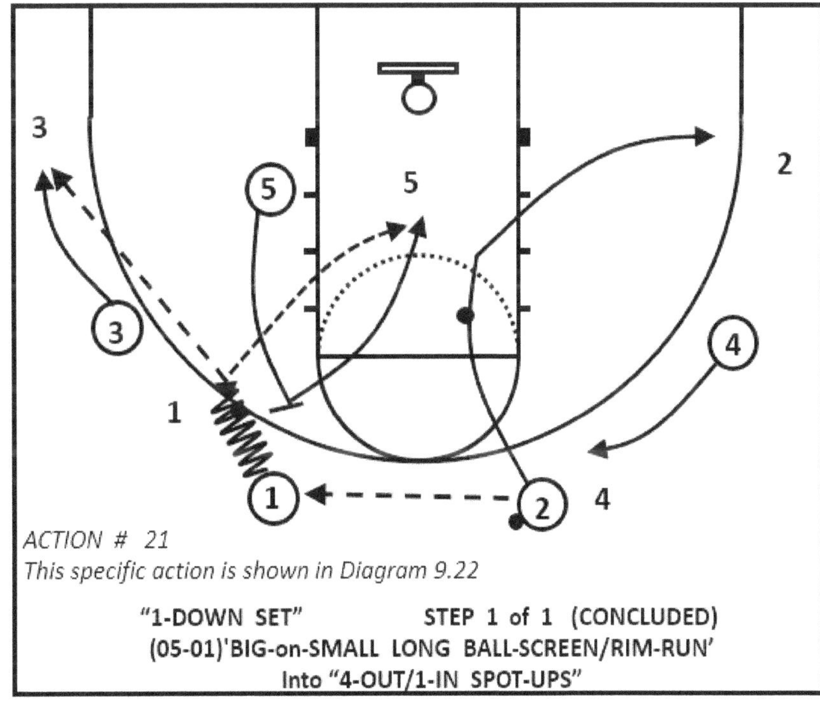

ACTION # 21
This specific action is shown in Diagram 9.22

"1-DOWN SET"   STEP 1 of 1 (CONCLUDED)
(05-01)'BIG-on-SMALL LONG BALL-SCREEN/RIM-RUN'
Into "4-OUT/1-IN SPOT-UPS"

Diagram 9.22

If shots are not created, the offense once again has attacked various individual defenders and have repositioned each offensive player so that the designated Continuity Offense that can smoothly and instantly begin once the "4-Out/1-In" Spot-Ups have been filled.

⚉ PLAY # 22: "BIG-ON-SMALL GHOST LONG BALL-SCREEN/RIM-RUN"

ACTION

Diagram 9.23 illustrates an entry out of the "4-DOWN" Set that could be executed after the action illustrated in Play # 21 has been executed two or three times in a game. With 01 centering up the ball at the top of the key, he could elect to drive towards either 05 and his side of the floor or towards 04 and the "Slot" on his side of the floor.

In this example, 01 dribbles towards 04's side of the floor. This keys that 05 immediately makes a "Vertical Elbow" Cut outside of the arc. 04 immediately breaks up as if to begin his "Big-on-Small Long Ball-Screen" (as done in various plays executed before.) But in this specific play, there is deception with 04 breaking off his route towards 01 as 04 actually sets a "Ghost Ball-Screen" and "Rim-Runs" to the basket much sooner than usual, catching X4 off guard. This is especially effective against teams that like to either "hard hedge," "trap" or "switch" all ball-screens.

04 and 05's actions isolate X4 and with 03 and 02 spotted up in their respective "Deep Corners;" the floor and the opposing defense has been stretched both vertically and horizontally-further weakening the overall defense.

In addition, the "4-Out/1-In" Spot-Ups are instantly filled; so that the designated 2nd Phase of the offense can also instantly begin its constant attack on the defense.

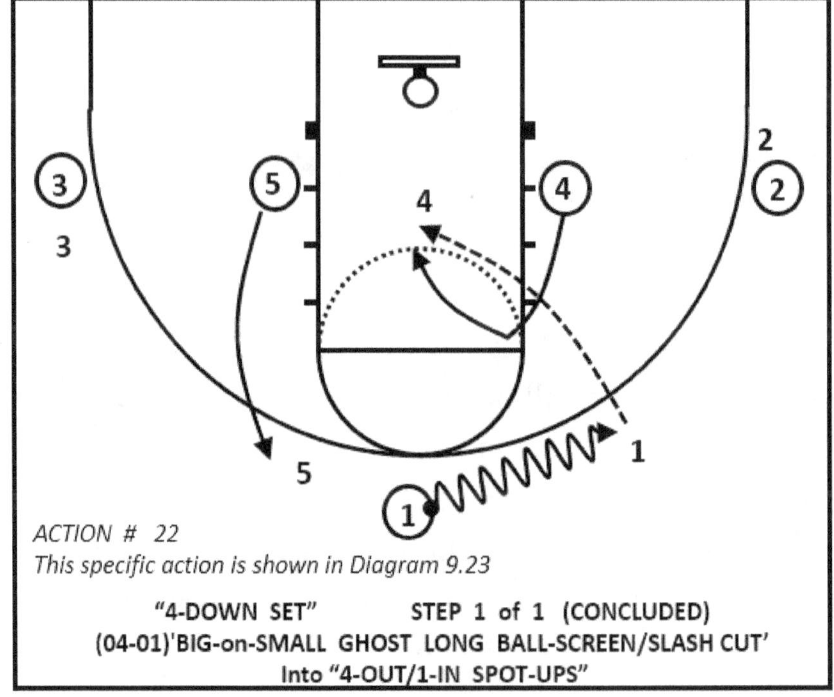

Diagram 9.23

Diagram 9.24 illustrates a half-court entry/play that begins from the "Nail" Offensive Set/Alignment—a symmetrically balanced alignment where each play could be executed towards either side of the floor. In this example, 01 starts the action by dribbling towards 02. With 02 faking a "Backdoor Cut" to relieve the denial pressure, he then reverses direction to receive the ball on the (01-02) Dribble Hand-Off. As the ball exchanges hands, 04 slashes to the initial "Ballside Block," while 05 steps up and over to immediately set his "Ball-Screen" for 02 to get his defender X2, lost in the offensive maze between 01, 05 and his man.

As 02 "dribble-scrapes" off of 05's top right shoulder, 05 then "reverse pivots" off of his left foot to open up to the ball and to 02 as he rolls through the lane; searching for the pass from 02 (or from 03 (who has drifted down into his "Deep Corner." As the ball is dribbled across the (imaginary) center line by 02, 04 should empty out to the new "Weakside Deep Corner" and 01 should step back up to fill the new "Weakside Slot" location. This action not only isolates 05 and his vulnerable defender, X5 but also repositions all offensive players into the "4-Out/1-In" Spot-Ups. Again, the offense has the position advantage of all five players to immediately flow into the designated 2nd Phase of the offense.

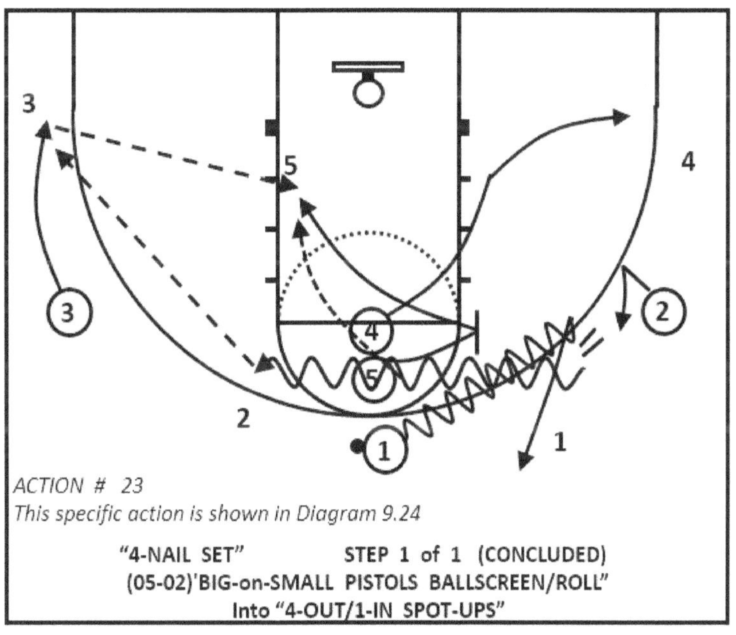

Diagram 9.24

PIN DOWN-SCREEN" ACTION

Diagram 9.25 illustrates another Primary Fastbreak situation that has smoothly flowed into a specific "Even Front Secondary Fastbreak" Option. With 01 possessing the ball at the Ballside Slot, the "First Trailer," (04) on the new "Ballside Block," 02 spotted up in the "Ballside Deep Corner, 05 settling in as the "Second Trailer" at the new "Weakside Slot," and 03 stretched out on the "Weakside Deep Corner;" both 01 and 02 look for the best possible passing angle to deliver the ball to 04 on the "Block."

The ball could be both "Down-Passed from 01 to 02 and then also "Up-Passed" from 02 to 01. When 01 receives the "Up-Pass," 05 should step over to set a "Big-on-Small Ball-Screen" for 01 to be able to freely move the ball on the perimeter to the opposite side of the floor. When the ball crosses the (imaginary) center line, 04 works aggressively hard to "chase the ball across the lane while actively looking to receive 01's "Inside Pass."

To occupy the presumed biggest defender, X5, and to eliminate the only other helpside defender (X2), as well as to free up one the presumed better perimeter shooters (02); 02 should scrape off of 05's outside right shoulder to break up to the new "Weakside Slot" for an open '3.'

05's screen for 01 should free 01 up to make an easier "Inside Pass" to either the isolated 04 on the interior or the wide open 02 on the perimeter. The "4-Out/1-In" Spot-Ups are once again filled so that immediately after the Primary Fastbreak flows into the Secondary Break Options and from there, the designated continuity offense can then smoothly begin.

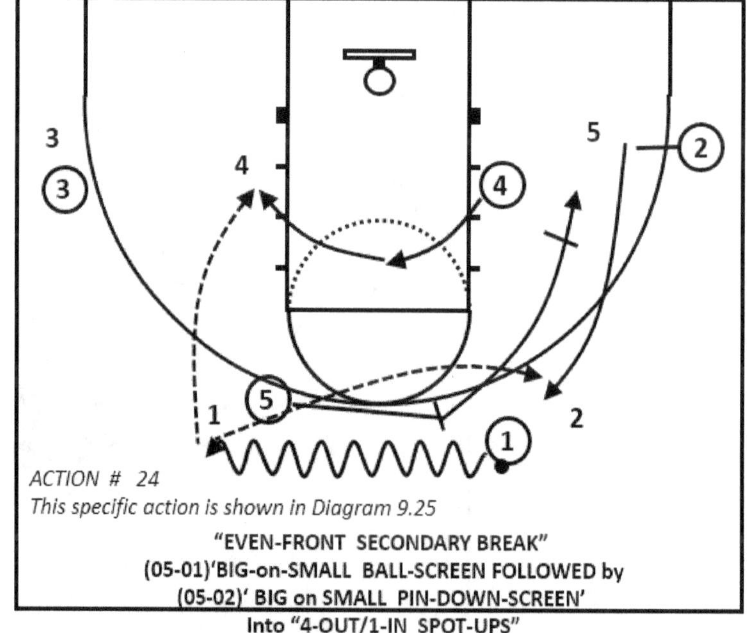

"EVEN-FRONT SECONDARY BREAK"
(05-01)'BIG-on-SMALL BALL-SCREEN FOLLOWED by
(05-02)' BIG on SMALL PIN-DOWN-SCREEN'
Into "4-OUT/1-IN SPOT-UPS"

Diagram 9.25

⊕ PLAY # 25: "BIG-ON-SMALL FLAT BALL-SCREEN/SLIP" ACTION

Diagram 9.26 illustrates another half-court entry out of the "3-DOWN" Set with 01 attacking his defender by "dribble-scraping" off of either shoulder of 04 and looking for a hard penetrating dribble towards the lane and the basket. 05 should read his defender and when X5 steps up to help X1, 01 should look to make the "Lob Pass" to 05. During his penetrating dribble from the top of the key, he looks for "penetrate and pitch" pass receivers on both sides of the lane. As 01 gets into his lane, 03 and 02 can both slightly lift from their initial "Deep Corner" locations. This makes it more difficult for X3 and X2 to help out X1 on the dribble penetrating drive as well as to protect shots outside of the arc. After screening for 01, 04 drifts slightly to the side of the floor opposite of the side 01 has chosen. The "4-Out/1-In" Spot-Ups are somewhat filled for the designated continuity offense to smoothly and instantly begin its own fundamentally sound fluid (but structured) offensive attack.

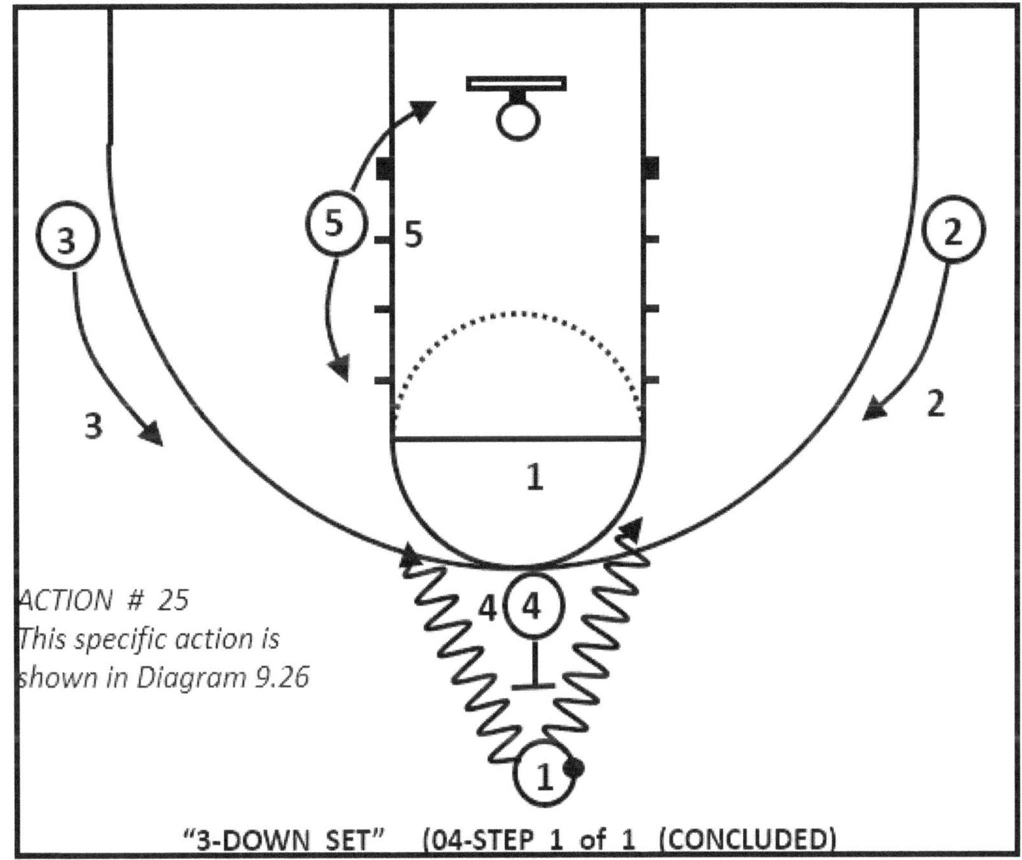

Diagram 9.26

Diagram 9.27 illustrate a quick-hitting entry out of the "5-UP" Set—another symmetrically balanced offensive set. This means the play could be "mirrored" and run to either side of the floor.

Even though 05 and 03 could be the players on the initial side to attack, it has been designated that the right side would be the beginning action side. 04 is the player that steps out just outside of the arc to receive 01's initial pass. As 04 catches the ball, 02 should immediately make a hard "Backdoor Cut" to the basket and look for the quick bounce pass from 04. If 02 does not receive the quick and deceptive pass, he should then pop back out to his beginning spot-up location.

As soon as the pass is made, 03 should break up quickly to set a "Big-on-Small Flare-Screen" for 01 to use to "Flare-Cut" to the area outside of the arc between the FT Line Extended and the "Deep Corner" on the new "Weakside" of the floor. 03 then slips his "Flare-Screen" to break to the new "Weakside Slot," stretching the overall defense and giving 04 two legitimate '3 Pt.' scoring threats.

At the same time of the action of 01, 03 and 02; 05 cuts across the FT Line to set a "Big-on-Big High Ball-Screen" for 04 to use to attack the perimeter defensive skills of his defender. 04 dribbles across the floor by "dribble-scraping" off of 05's top right shoulder and looks to penetrate-dribble or to make passes to any of his four teammates. As 04 breaks contact with 05's top shoulder, 05 should reverse pivot off of his left foot to open up to the ball and to 04 and roll through the lane looking for an "Inside Pass" from whomever has possession of the ball.

This action can isolate both X4 and X5 and look for defensive weaknesses as well as utilize offensive strengths possessed by either 04 or 05.

If shots are not taken, the "4-Out/1-In" Spot-Ups are again filled for an immediate and smooth conversion from the half-court play/entry instantly into the designated continuity offense.

Not shown or discussed, but a Counter Play to Play 26 could be 05 making the same "Ball-Screen" for 04 and then make a "Rim-Run" to the basket. Executing "Rim-Runs" when the defense attempts to defend "Rolls" can give the offensive team several "position advantages."

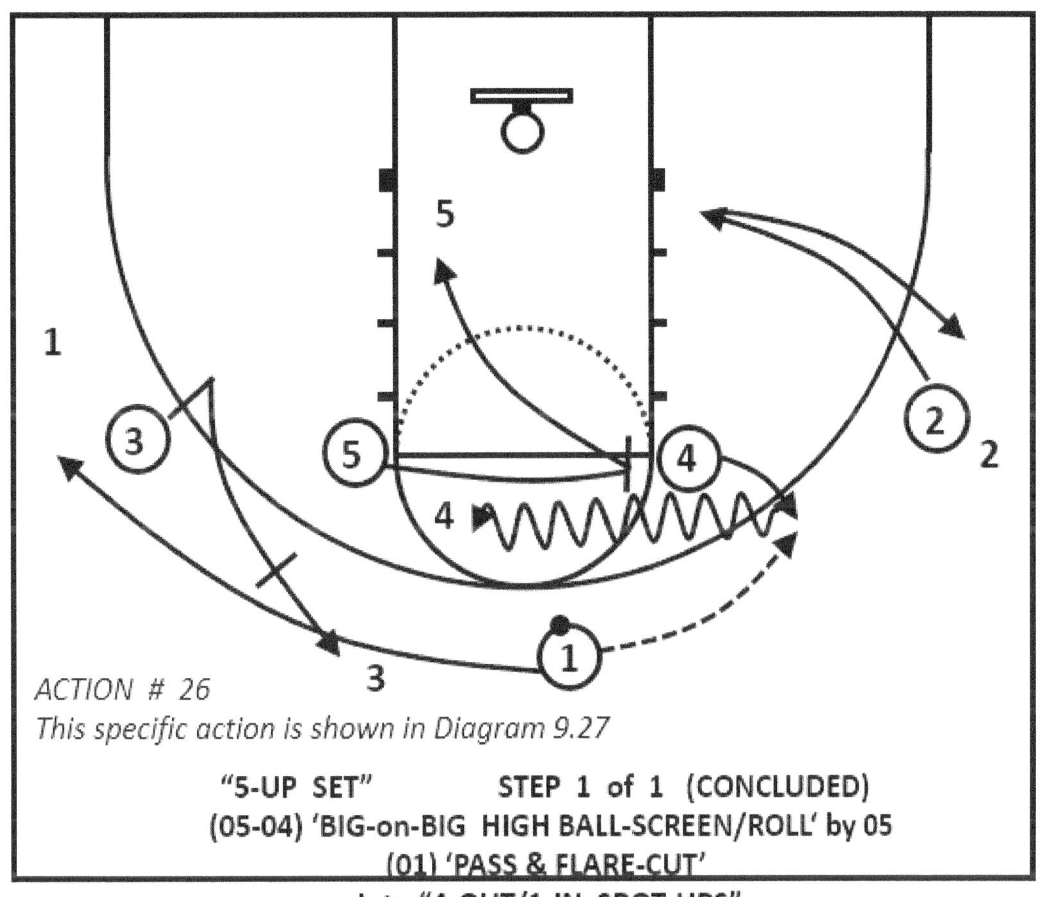

ACTION # 26
This specific action is shown in Diagram 9.27

"5-UP SET"   STEP 1 of 1 (CONCLUDED)
(05-04) 'BIG-on-BIG HIGH BALL-SCREEN/ROLL' by 05
(01) 'PASS & FLARE-CUT'
Into "4-OUT/1-IN SPOT-UPS"

Diagram 9.27

Diagram 9.28 illustrates an entry out of the "HORNS" Set—another symmetrically balanced offensive set/alignment. This again means that any entry shown could be "mirrored" to the other side of the floor.

It appears that 01 has decided to attack the side of the floor so that 04 steps up to set his "Big-on-Small Ball-Screen" At the same time, 05 makes his "Diagonal Slash Cut" across the lane to the new "Ballside Block" to isolate his defender, X5. At the same time, 02 drifts and moves his defender for X2 to lose sight of him. On the new Weakside of the floor, 03 "Lift" Cuts up, while staying outside of the arc to become an immediate "catch and shoot off of the pass" threat.

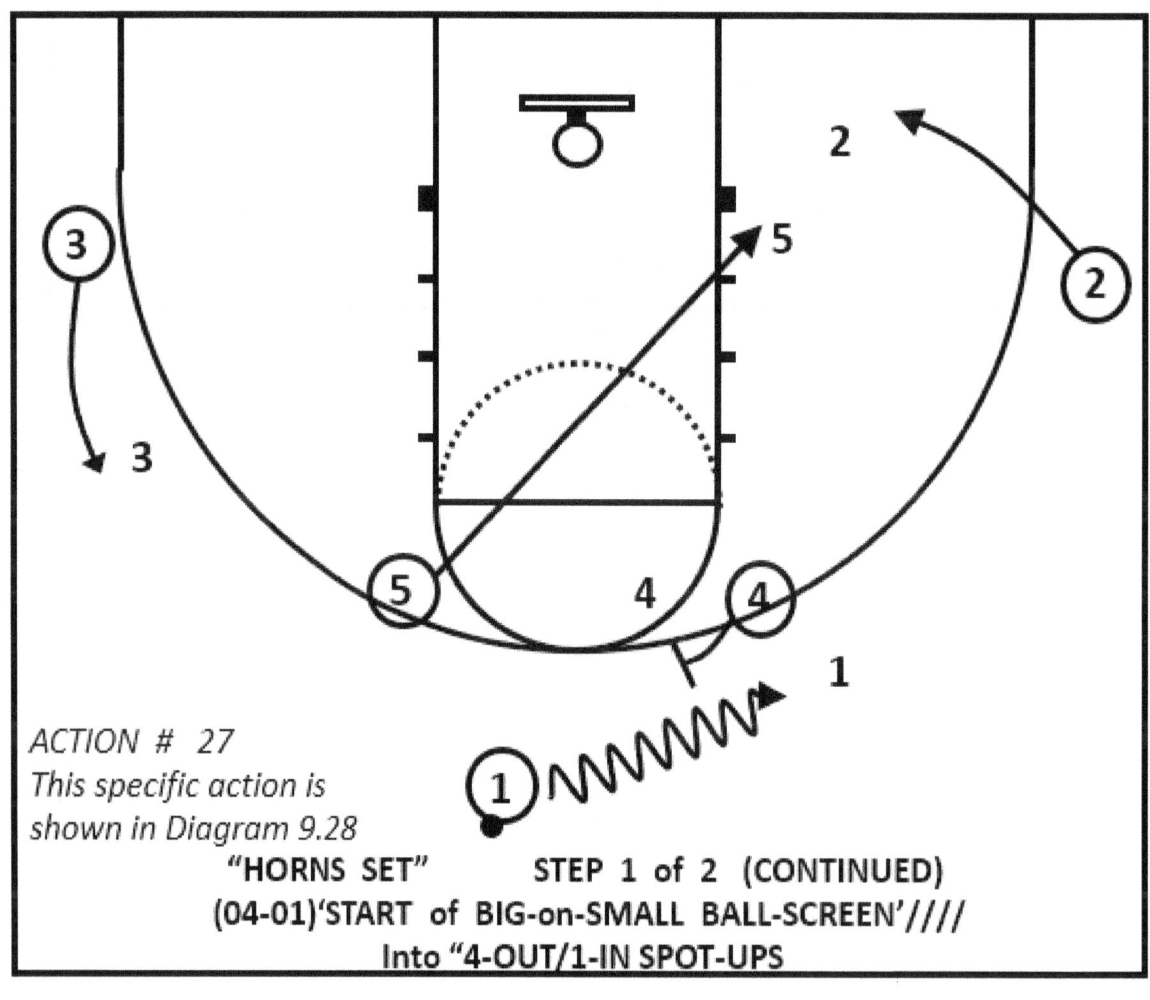

Diagram 9.28

⊕ PLAY # 27 (PART 2): "REJECTION OF BIG-ON-SMALL BALL-SCREEN"

ACTION

As 01 approaches 04 at the beginning of the action in Play # 27 players are in the locations shown in Diagram 9.29. With planned deception, 01 suddenly rejects the expected (04-01) Ball-Screen and reverses the direction he started and was expected to go to make a hard aggressive "perimeter penetration dribble" towards the open-spaced opposite side of the floor.

At that time, 03 puts his defender in a bind by making a "Drift Cut" towards the "Deep Corner, while remaining outside of the arc. 03 puts his defender in a defensive bind, in that X3 does not know whether to help out on his isolated teammate, X1 or to stay with his man to prevent the "penetrate and pitch" action between 01 and his own man. 02 remains along the baseline to set up his next offensive move—to then break up off of the "Big-on-Small Stagger Screen" set by 05 and 04.

This action not only occupies all three defenders on the offense's new weakside of the floor but also gives 01 on his penetrating drive to the basket a "Drive and Dump" passing option to 05, a "Reverse Throwback" option to 02 near the "Ballside Slot," and a "Penetrate and Skip Pass" option to 04 near the "Weakside Wing."

On the ballside of the floor, 01 has "Pull-up Jumper" or "Power Lay-up" scoring options as well as a closer and safer pass option to 03.

It seems unlikely that any one of the five offensive players would not get off an open shot from this (two diagrammed series of actions), but the "4-Out/1-In" Spot-Ups are again filled for the next wave of offensive attacks to continue smoothly.

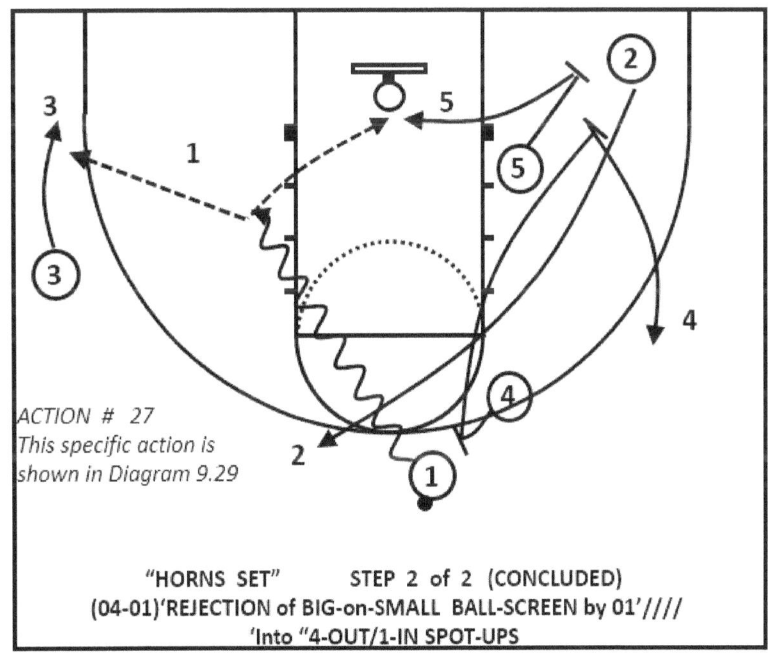

"HORNS SET"   STEP 2 of 2 (CONCLUDED)
(04-01)'REJECTION of BIG-on-SMALL BALL-SCREEN by 01'////
'Into "4-OUT/1-IN SPOT-UPS

Diagram 9.29

Diagram 9.30 shows this offensive action that begins out of the "5-TIGHT" Offensive Set/Alignment. This is another perfectly symmetrically balanced offensive alignment that will allow every play to be able to be executed on either side of the floor. This makes the plays even more unpredictable and therefore more difficult to defend.

This action has 02 be the designated perimeter player (either 02 or 03) to be the player that breaks up to the top of the key to set the "Small-on-Small Ball-Screen" for 01 to "dribble-scrape: off of his top left shoulder. 03 cuts through the lane to "invert and isolate" his perimeter-type defender, X3, on the opposite side's new "Ballside Block."

As 01 breaks contact with 02, 02 continues cutting across to the opposite side's now vacant "Weakside Wing" spot-up area. 05 curls over the top of 04 to cut to the "Ballside High Post Elbow" area; while 04 then pops to spot up at the top of the key. 01 finishes his dribble near the "FT Line Extended," looking to make "Inside Passes" first to 03, then to 05, a possible (01-04) "Reverse Pass" or a possible (01-02) "Skip Pass."

Players are now in a different set of offensive Spot-Ups, called the "High-Post/Low-Post" Spot-Ups" These spot-up locations will then allow other different continuity offenses to immediately begin and continue the pressure on the opposition.

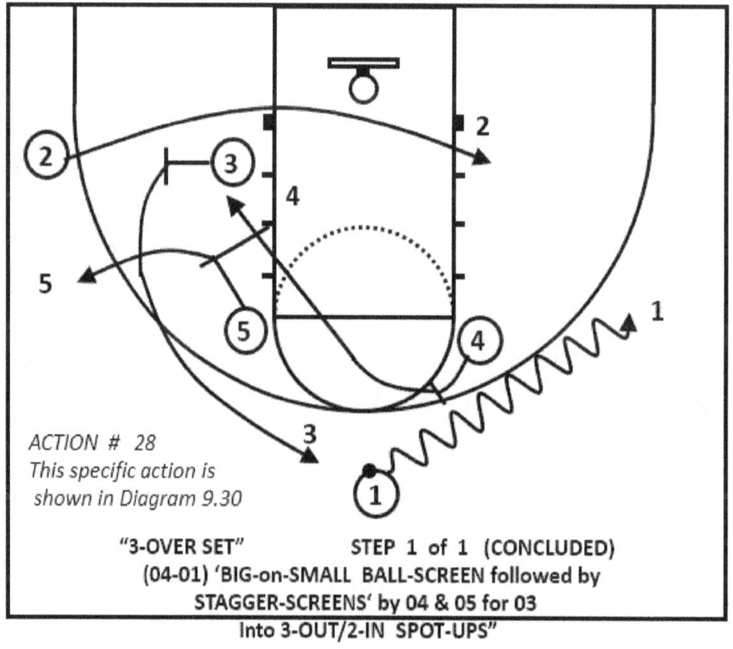

Diagram 9.30

Diagram 9.31 shows an example of an entry out of the "3-OVER" Set where 01 immediately takes advantage of attacking his defender on the more open side of the court with a (04-01) "Big-on-Small Ball-Screen."

In this particular alignment, as soon as 01 starts towards 04, 02 cuts off of the "Big-on-Small Flex Back-Screen" Set by 03 on the new weakside of the floor. After 01 "dribble-scrapes" off of 04's top left shoulder to drive to the FT Line extended, he looks to make the Interior Pass to the now inverted and isolated perimeter player, 02. After 01 breaks contact with 04, 04 makes a front pivot off of his lower right foot to then diagonally break down (with 05) to set a "Big-on-Small (Diagonal Stagger-)Screen the (Flex-)Screener. 03 "scrape-cuts' off of 05's outside left shoulder and prepares for a quick "catch and shoot" pass from 01 by "getting his feet and hands ready" before and during his cut to the top of the key. After screening, 05 slips out to the new "Weakside Wing" area and 04 remains on the new "Weakside Block." This places all five offensive players in the "3-Out/2-In" Spot-Ups for the various continuity offenses that are "family" to these spot-ups. The designated continuity or motion offense will be able to seamlessly begin as soon as 01 delivers the ball to a teammate. This quick conversion puts even more pressure on the opposition's defense.

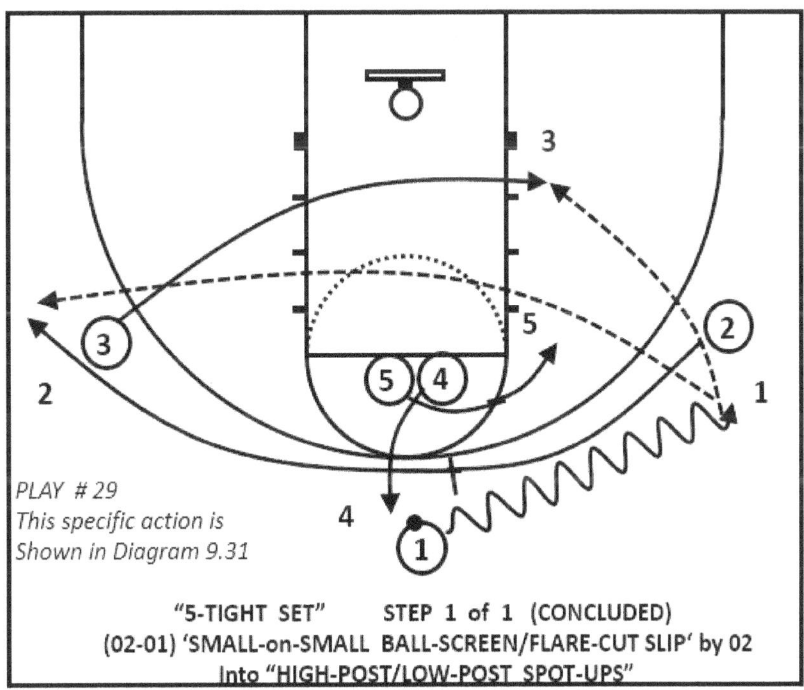

Diagram 9.31

⊕ PLAY # 30: "SMALL-ON-BIG BALL-SCREEN/SLIP" ACTION

Diagram 9.32 shows action in the middle of a play where all five offensive players have moved to various different locations and the plan was to then get the ball into 05's hands out at the top of the key.

With perimeter-type players, 02 and 03, at both "Wing" locations, either player could become the designated screener. In this illustration, 02 steps up to become the actual "Small-on-Big" Ball-Screener for 05 to attack his defender. After screening for 05, 02 makes a front pivot off of his inside right foot to instantly spot-up at the top of the key "with his feet and hands ready" for a quick "Reverse Throwback" Pass from 05. This action has also been traditionally called the "Pick and Pop" and when the 'picker' is a legitimate perimeter-type player with perimeter scoring skills and the defense switches the screen (with a presumed slower and less experienced perimeter defender, X5); there can be an immediate "position and player advantage" for 02.

This type of isolation on the perimeter is created with 03 setting a "Big-on-Small Pin Down-Screen on the one side of the floor with 04 making an "Iso Duck-In Cut" on the opposite side. With 05 having the ball at the "Wing" Spot-Up location, he has pulled the presumed biggest defender away from the basket, allowing 04 to also be able to isolate his own defender in a very vulnerable area-the "Ballside Block." Many scoring advantages can be created in the middle of this play, with the final advantage being that all players are in the "3-Out/2-In" Spot-Ups. As always, these and the other two types of spot-up discussed give the offensive team immediate advantages by being able to flow into the last phase of the offensive attack.

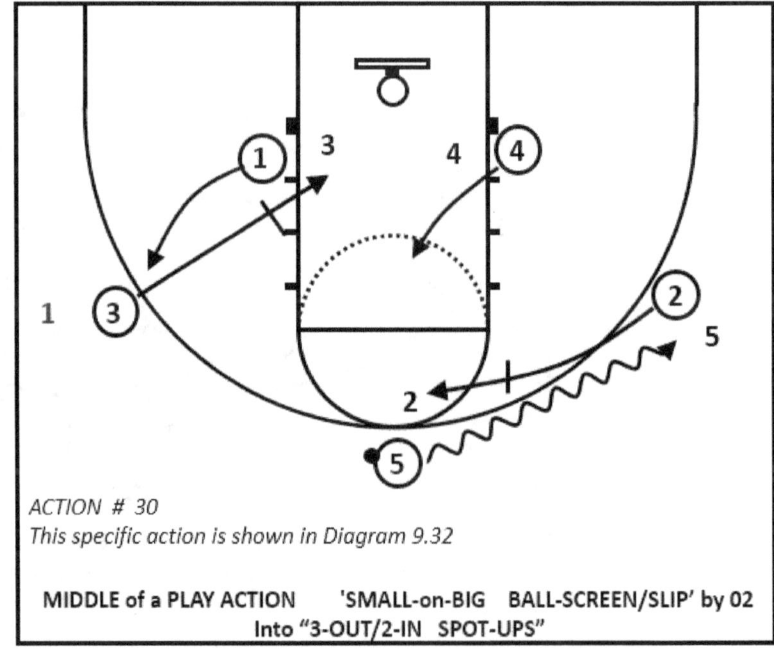

ACTION # 30
This specific action is shown in Diagram 9.32

MIDDLE of a PLAY ACTION   'SMALL-on-BIG   BALL-SCREEN/SLIP' by 02
Into "3-OUT/2-IN   SPOT-UPS"

Diagram 9.32

CLOSING

These thirty Ball-Screening types of action are all fundamentally sound and can be executed by various combinations of players in various locations on the floor and with countless finishing forms of action (after the actual screen has been set.)

These actions are shown out of various offensive sets/alignments and they all end in one of the three groups of offensive spot-ups. There are different continuity offenses or motion-type offenses that exist than can easily and fluidly begin from those offensive spot-ups.

Coaches should be able to pick and choose the right combinations from this chapter that fit the staff's philosophies, personalities and most of all the team's talent and skill levels to help improve the team's offensive production and efficiency.

CHAPTER 10:
PLAYS/ENTRIES EXECUTED FROM THE "1-DOWN SET/ALIGNMENT

There are many different philosophies on how to attack opposing defenses. This multiple-phase offensive system uses more than one phase/layer/wave of attack, with each phase/wave having a seamless and immediate conversion into the next phase/wave. While this system can be confusing to defenses and difficult to defend, this system can be properly taught and coached so that it can be easily understood and ultimately executed by players of many different levels of (physical talent, mental understand and playing experience.)

In addition, there are several types of offensive schemes and different ways within this system that offenses can attack their defensive counter-parts. Many of these can be integrated within the same offensive system that can attack defenses in various ways. The larger the number of schemes that can be successfully utilized and integrated within the same system, the greater the opportunity an offensive team can find the most efficient and productive schemes that can place both individual and the overall team in the best and most frequent "positions to succeed."

The plays/entries carefully diagrammed down to the small and seemingly unimportant 'V-Cuts' made by countless players before making their more important following cut are also described in detail.

Each play has been carefully studied and evaluated to determine which level of talent and experience must be possessed for that specific team to be able to successfully execute the play. This includes all players' physical skills as well as their mental understanding of the game. Coaches must also have the experience and the associated level of understanding of the game as well as their coaching/teaching of the nuances of each play.

The most sophisticated plays/entries would fall into the first of the three levels all based on the team's physical talents and skills, the mental capacities and the overall team's game experience. In addition, the coaching staff must have a high degree of basketball knowledge as well as very high teaching and coaching skills to educate his/her entire basketball team. The proper breakdown drills must be thoroughly utilized to hone the fundamental skills and techniques needed for individual players and the overall team to execute plays that can be efficient, productive, and successful. We define this family of plays as the "Level 3 category" of plays. This "Level 3" family of plays will have a much more complex offensive scheme that would require a very high amount of physical talent as well as requiring a greater amount of the players (to execute) and the coaches (to teach and coach) mental capacities and experience needed for the offense to be efficient, productive and successful. We feel plays in our defined "Level 3" category could possibly be successful for NBA teams, definitely for college teams and also for many high schools and older AAU teams.

The next classification or level of plays would be possibly slightly lower as far as sophistication, complexity and the actual 'length' of the play (and the number of passes, cuts, and screens used) in the play's overall scheme. While all "Level 2" plays in each of the chapters in this book remain to be fundamentally sound, these plays may lack the actual number of techniques/methods that are implemented within that play in comparison to the "Level 1" plays/entries. Therefore any team that successfully executes the highest "Level 1" plays/entries could/should easily be able to execute any of these so-called lower "Level 2" plays/entries, if so desired. Almost all high school teams should be able to execute successfully all aspects of the "Level 2" plays.

The final grouping of plays would be called "Level 1" plays are not as difficult for offensive players to master the execution of them, both physically as well as mentally. Even though the techniques are still fundamentally, they may not be as complex to learn and understand in addition to being easier to physically execute.

"Level 1" plays would be lower in the scheme's complexities and the number of techniques used in the execution of this category of plays. Obviously, since these "Level 1" plays are still sound, but lack some of the methods used in the two previous more sophisticated and complex levels; these more elementary plays should be able to be utilized by any teams that use either of the two higher level plays. We feel that Middle School/Junior High teams as well as younger AAU teams or organizations, should be able to utilize any of the "Level 1" plays successfully, with a possibility that some of those teams that are slightly more advanced (than other teams) could possibly use some plays located in the immediate next immediate level.

Ideas, concepts, and techniques from actual plays from teams of all three levels have been used to modify or to create different combinations of the various techniques and schemes used that will help prove these entries can be successfully used. This allows the author to create numerous plays that use the various schemes to build a library of fundamentally sound plays that will be unique and will be appropriate for a wide range of teams with various ages and skill levels.

With this book having plays in these three presumed categories or levels, the book will reach out and benefit a much larger group of serious basketball coaches from elementary school age to the highest skilled levels that exist.

In addition, an experienced and resourceful coach may be able to mold some plays that include all of the offensive techniques that he/she desires could reshape a specific play that begins in one specific offensive set/alignment and reshape it so that it could begin in a different offensive/set that is more favorable to that coach and his/her coaching staff's liking.

Conversely, that innovative and creative coach may completely like the specific offensive set/alignment and favor the very same offensive actions included in a certain play, but can modify that play so that the ending spot-ups of all five players are conducive to being able to begin the final phase of the offensive attack by using a more favorable offensive continuity offense.

PLAYS/ENTRIES THAT END in the "3-OUT/2-IN" OFFENSIVE SPOT-UPS

After the entry/play/quick-hitter has been executed but no shots have been taken, all five players will end up in a different group of offensive spot-ups. These "3-Out/2-In Spot-Ups" will have players moved about the court with any of the five ending up in the "Ballside Block," the "Ballside Wing," the "Weakside Block," the "Weakside Wing," and the "Point" (at the top of the key). These five positions can provide the offense with safe and easy types of ball-reversals, large gaps for dribble penetration, opportunities to deliver the ball inside to whomever (perimeter-type or post-type players) is posting up their defender on the "Ballside Block," and a player that can be a perimeter-scoring threat and a legitimate offensive rebounding threat from outside of the arc on his "offensive crashing of the boards." The "3-Out/2-In Spot-Ups also provide ample opportunities for constant and effective defensive transition responsibilities.

Diagram 10.1 illustrates the "1-DOWN SET." 05 is the designated player that has the ability to post up on the 'Mid-Post' on either side of the lane. 01 and 02 are the guards that bring the ball down the floor to initiate the offense and the designated play/entry. The two remaining players (03 and 04) are "spotted up on the "Wing" locations, on both sides of the lane outside of the arc at the FT Line extended. With 05 being able to post up on either side of the lane and therefore start on either side of the lane, the offense will have two diverse cosmetic looks and therefore gives the offense a higher level of unpredictability. In this diagram, 05 posts up on the offense's right side of the lane, below 04's initial right "Wing" spot-up location.

There is a significant number of philosophies on how to attack the various types of opposing defenses. This multiple-phase offensive system uses more than one phase/layer/wave of attack, with each phase/wave having a seamless and immediate conversion into the next phase/wave. While this system can be confusing to defenses and difficult to defend, this system can be properly taught and coached so that it can be easily understood and ultimately executed by players of many diverse levels of (physical talent, mental understand, and playing experience.)

In addition, there are several types of offensive schemes and different ways within this system that offenses can successfully attack their defensive counter-parts. Many of these can be integrated within the same offensive system that can attack defenses in various ways. The larger the number of schemes that can be successfully integrated within the same system, the greater the opportunity an offensive team can find the most efficient and productive schemes that can place both individual and the overall team in the best and most frequent "positions to succeed."

The plays/entries carefully diagrammed down to the small and seemingly unimportant 'V-Cuts' made by countless players before having those same players then make their more important cuts are also described in detail.

Each play has been carefully studied and evaluated to determine which level of talent and experience must be possessed for that specific team to be able to successfully execute the play. The most sophisticated plays/entries would fall into the latter of the three levels all based on the team's physical talents and skills, the mental capacities and the overall team's game experience. In addition, the coaching staff must have a high degree of basketball knowledge as well as very high teaching and coaching skills to educate his/her entire basketball team. The proper breakdown drills must be thoroughly utilized to hone the fundamental skills and techniques needed for individual players and the overall team to execute plays that can be efficient, productive, and successful. In addition to the sophistication of the plays as far as the various offensive techniques used, it is almost certain there is a larger number of the various offensive techniques that are weaved into the offensive entry or play. Therefore, there will be additional steps of parts of the higher sophisticated "Level 3" plays.

We define this family of plays as the "Level 3 category" of plays. As just stated, this "Level 3" family of plays will have a much more complex offensive scheme that would require high amounts of physical talent as well as requiring a greater amount of the players (to execute) and the coaches (to teach and coach) mental capacities and experience needed for the offense to be efficient, productive and successful. We feel plays in our defined "Level 3" category could possibly be successful for NBA teams, definitely for college teams and also for many high schools and more experienced AAU teams.

The next lower classification or level of plays would be somewhat lower as far as sophistication, complexity and the actual 'length' of the play (including the number of passes, cuts, screens and other techniques used) in the one particular play's overall series of actions. While all "Level 2" plays in each of the chapters in this book remain to be fundamentally sound, these plays may lack the actual number of techniques/methods that are implemented within that play in comparison to the "Level 3" plays/entries. Therefore, any team that successfully executes the highest "Level 3" plays/entries should easily be able execute any of these so-called lower "Level 1 and 2" plays/entries, if so desired. It appears most high school teams should be able to execute successfully all aspects of all of the "Level 1 and 2" plays.

The final grouping of plays would be called "Level 1" plays and are not as difficult for offensive players to master their execution of the plays, both physically as well as mentally. Even though the techniques are still fundamentally sound, they may not be as complex to learn and understand in addition to being easier to physically execute. These plays will not take as long of a time to execute the full play because of the lesser number of actual offensive actions implemented within the play.

"Level 1" plays would be lower in the scheme's complexities and the number of techniques used in the execution of this category of plays. This means that these plays will be executed in shorter periods of time before the end of the play and therefore the beginning of the designated continuity offense. More than likely, the fewer number of diagrams will relate to the number of offensive techniques and actions; therefore the lower level of complexity in that particular play/entry.

Obviously, since these "Level 1" plays are still sound, but lack some of the methods used in the two previous more sophisticated and complex levels; these more elementary plays should be able to be utilized by any teams that use either of the two higher level plays. We feel that Middle School/Junior High teams as well as younger AAU teams or organizations should be able to utilize any of the "Level 1" plays successfully, with a possibility that some of those teams that are slightly more advanced (than other teams) could possibly use some plays located in the immediate next immediate level.

Various concepts, techniques and methods taken from other plays/entries from teams ranging in all three levels could be utilized to produce other plays with the various combinations of those concepts to create different plays. This provides the imaginative and resourceful coach endless boundaries to be different and creative in developing newer plays for his system.

Any team that has the capabilities of executing "Level 3" plays (sometimes called quick-hitters or entries) would then be able to execute the somewhat less complicated and complex plays categorized in both the "Level 2 and Level 1" groups.

Also, any offensive team that can execute "Level 2" plays should then be able to incorporate and implement (the somewhat lower) "Level 1" plays/entries.

The "Level 3" plays that are discussed in this chapter should most likely be slightly too complex for teams that use the Level 1 and 2 plays. Some teams may be able to handle some particular plays that are just a step up from their normal family of plays, such as a team that predominately implements "Level 1" plays may have the capabilities of adding a very small number of "Level 2" plays. Or a team that has a majority of "Level 2" plays may only on rarely have instances to successfully incorporate a "Level 3" play.

With this book having plays, in these three presumed categories or levels, the book will reach out and benefit a much larger group of serious basketball coaches from elementary school age to the highest skilled levels that exists.

In addition, an experienced and resourceful coach may be able to mold some plays that include all of the offensive techniques that he/she desires could reshape a specific play that begins in one specific offensive set/alignment and reshape it so that it could begin in a different offensive/set that is more favorable to that coach and his/her coaching staff's liking.

Conversely, that innovative and creative coach may completely like the specific offensive set/alignment and favor the very same offensive actions included in a certain play, but can modify that play so that the ending spot-ups of all five players are conducive to being able to begin the final phase of the offensive attack by using a more favorable offensive continuity offense.

Diagram 10.1 illustrates the beginning of Play # 1 with 02 bringing the ball across the timeline and looking to make the "Inside Pass" to 05 on his "Iso Duck-In Cut" into the Dotted Circle. At the same time, 01 steps over to set a "Small-on-Big Pin Down-Screen" for 03 to break up to 01's initial "Slot" location. If 02 does not make the pass to 05, 05 continues across the lane and 02 then looks to make the perimeter pass to 03. When 02 makes the (02-03) "Reverse Pass," 04 then steps up and over to set a "Big-on-Small Flare-Screen" for 02 to attack his defender and "Flare-Cut" to the "Weakside Wing" area. 02 scrapes off of 04's outside left shoulder and immediately "gets his feet and hands ready" for a "Catch-and-Shoot Skip Pass" from 03. See Diagram 10.1

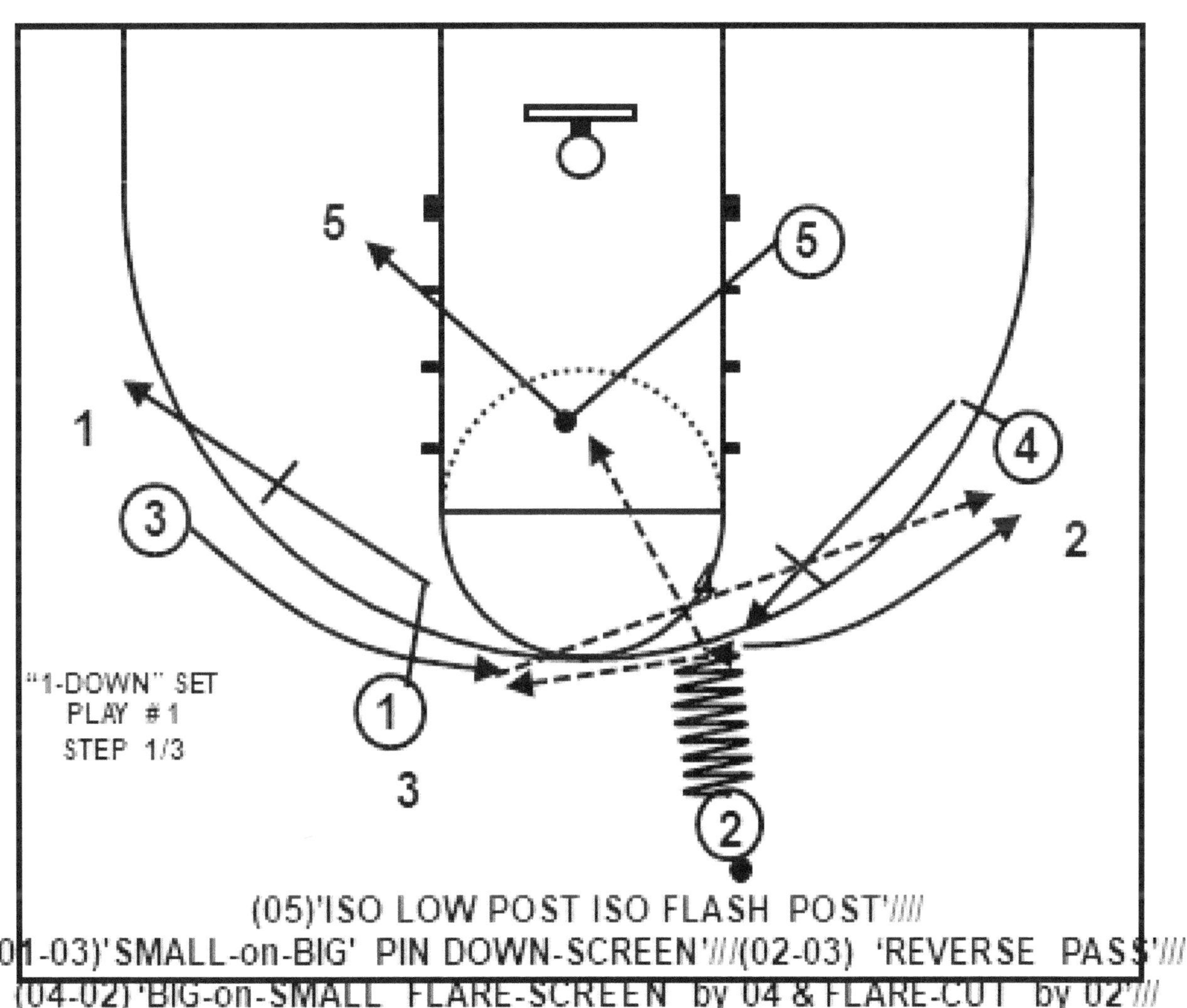

Play # 1   Diagram 10.1

Diagram 10.2 illustrates the continuation of Play # 1 with 03 not making the passes to any of his teammates, but instead starting his "perimeter pull-dribble" to drag the ball across the top of the key. 04 breaks towards and behind 03 as if to receive a hand-off from 03. Instead, this particular play (with 03 likely being the better ball-handler), 04 fakes the hand-off, so that 03 reverses the ball to the opposite side of the floor via dribble. As 03 crosses the imaginary center line, 05 makes his second "Iso Duck-In Cut" into the same Dotted Circle area (but starting from the opposite side of the lane.) If 03 cannot make the pass to 05 or if he cannot improve the passing angle (to make the pass to 05, now on the "Block,") 03 can look to make the "Wing Pass to 02, (who should have an excellent passing angle to deliver the ball to 05.) See Diagram 10.2

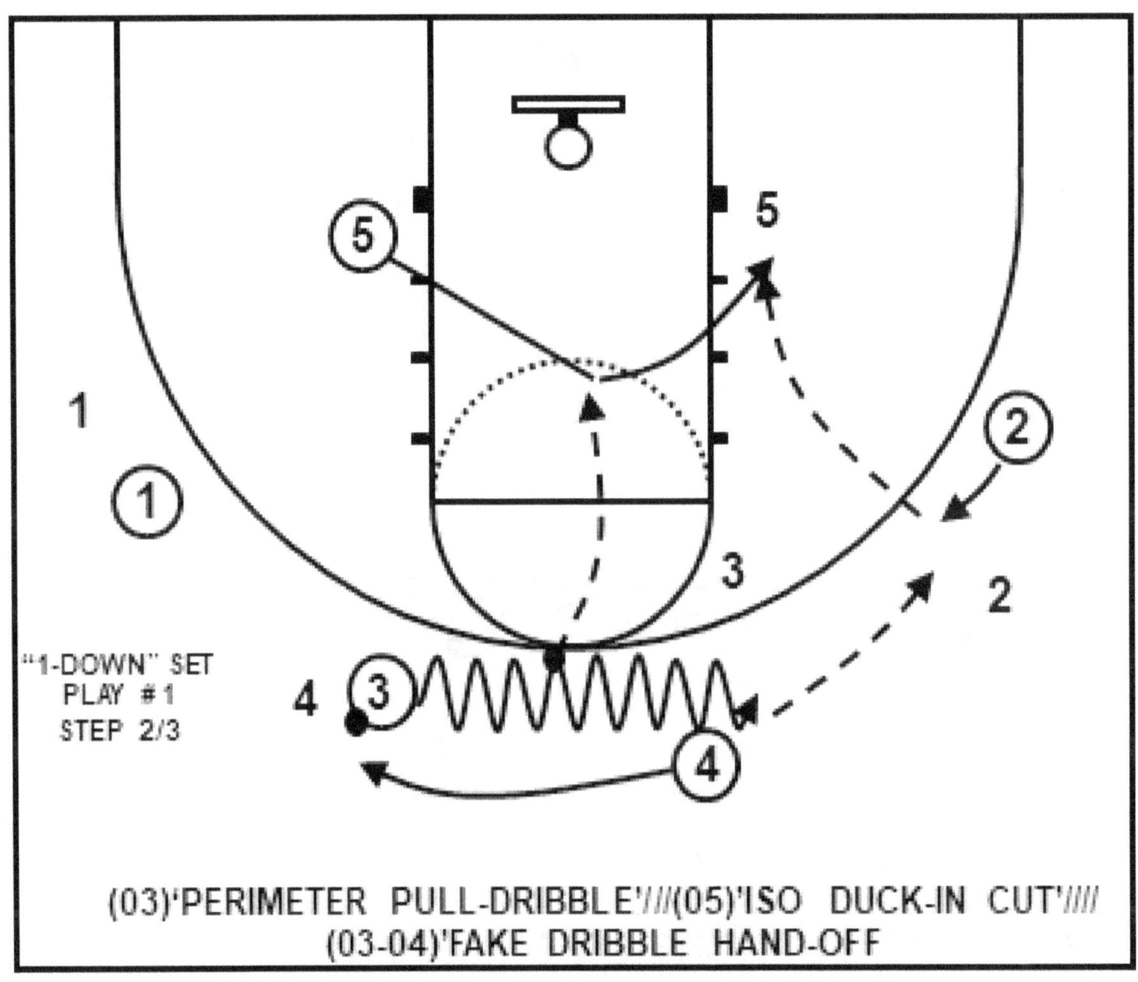

Diagram 10.2

Diagram 10.3 shows the last component of the play with 03 or 02 not being able to make the "Inside Pass" to 05. 03 reverses the ball to 04 with 05 immediately stepping up and out to set a "Big-on-Small Back-Screen" for 02 to rub his defender off of 05 as he cuts through the lane to the opposite side of the lane. 05 then continues his cutting action with stepping further out to set a (05-03) "Big-on-Small Flare-Screen" for 03 to use to make a "Flare-Cut" to the now vacant new "Weakside Wing" area.

With 04 having the ball out on the perimeter and 05 moving out on the perimeter, both defensive "Bigs" are vertically stretched out away from the interior. This gives 02 an "inverted and isolated" post-up advantage on his perimeter-type defender. If 04 cannot make that "Inside Pass" to 02 on his cut through the lane, he can swing the ball over to 01, who presumably should be an outstanding passer and should possess an improved passing angle (to deliver the ball to the isolated and inverted 02). After making the pass to 01, 04 should receive the (05-04) "Diagonal Back-Screen" for 04 to make a "Lob-Cut" to the basket. If 04 does not receive the "Lob Pass" from 01, 04e stays at to the "Weakside Block" (for two major reasons.)

One reason is to prevent X4 from attempting to "double-down" on the ball to 02 in the post. X4 must honor 04's cut to the basket and know that 01 should have the ability to make that pass to 04. The second reason is that with 04's cut, all five players are now in the proper "3-Out/2-In" Spot-Ups so that the next pass made will smoothly and instantly begin the designated continuity offense. See Diagram 10.3

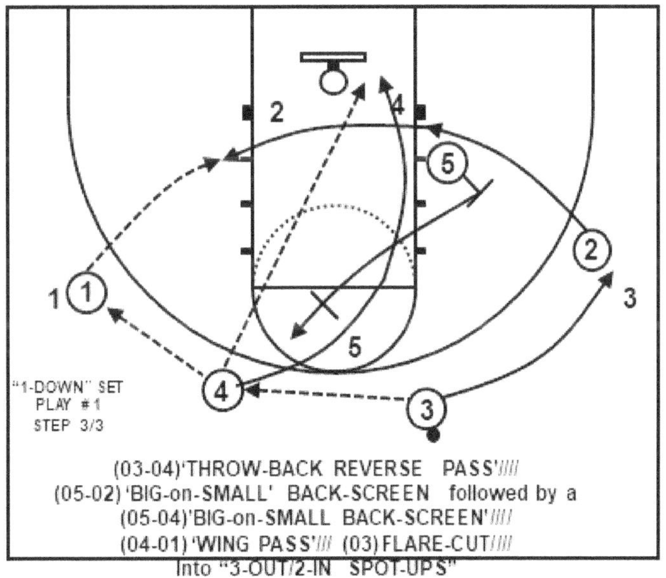

Diagram 10.3

This play has added value in that there can be subtle, simple, easy, and minor changes to the play to have multiple counter plays that all can be married to this particular play.

Diagram 10.4 demonstrates the beginning of Play # 2. As 01 brings the ball across the timeline, 03 steps up as if to set a "Big-on-Small Ball-Screen." Instead, 03 "ghosts" the action and breaks off his screening route to make a hard and aggressive cut towards the basket. After killing his dribble, 01 looks to make the pass to 03 before then making a "Reverse Pass" to 02. If 03 does not receive the pass, 03 then pops out to the FT Line extended on the same side of the floor. After passing the ball to 02, 02 looks to make an "Inside Pass" to 05 on his "Iso Duck-In Cut." 01 follows his pass to set a "Small-on-Big Follow-the Pass Ball-Screen." See Diagram 10.4

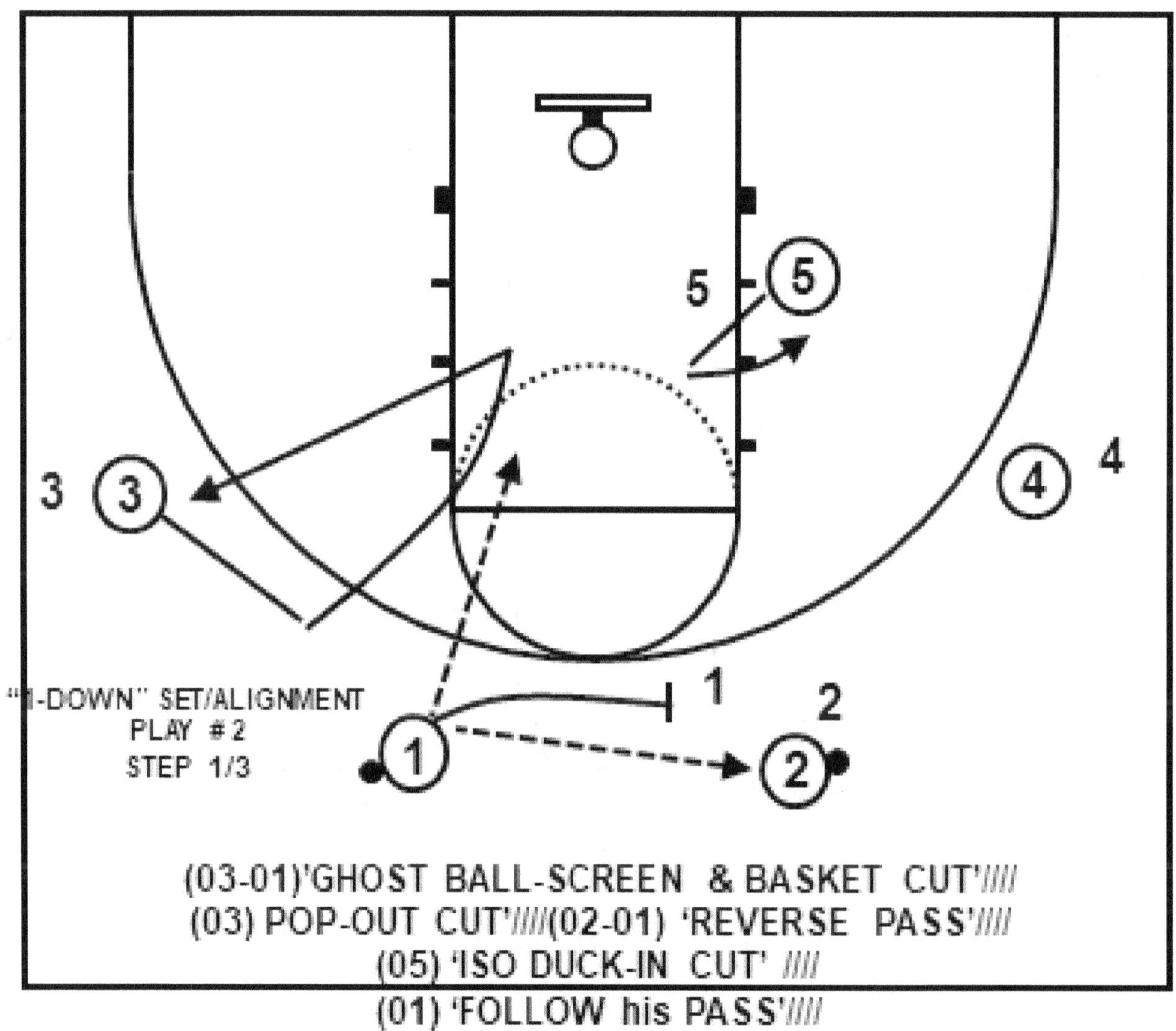

Play # 2   Diagram 10.4

After making the (01-02) "Reverse Pass, 01 follows his pass to set his (01-02)"Small-on-Big Ball-Screen." After 02 crosses the imaginary center line, 04 uses 05 as a "Big-on-Small Back-Screen." 02 then "dribble-scrapes" off of 01's outside top right shoulder towards the opposite side's "Slot."

After (01-02) "Ball-Screen," is set, 05 then steps up to set a "Big-on-Small (Back-)Screen the (Ball-)Screener" for 01 to make his "Flare-Cut" to the new "Weakside Wing." On 02's dribble, 02 looks to make the "Inside Pass" to 04, a "Throwback Reverse Pass" to 05 or a "Skip Pass" to 01, who is now spotted up on the new "Weakside Wing." See Diagram 10.5

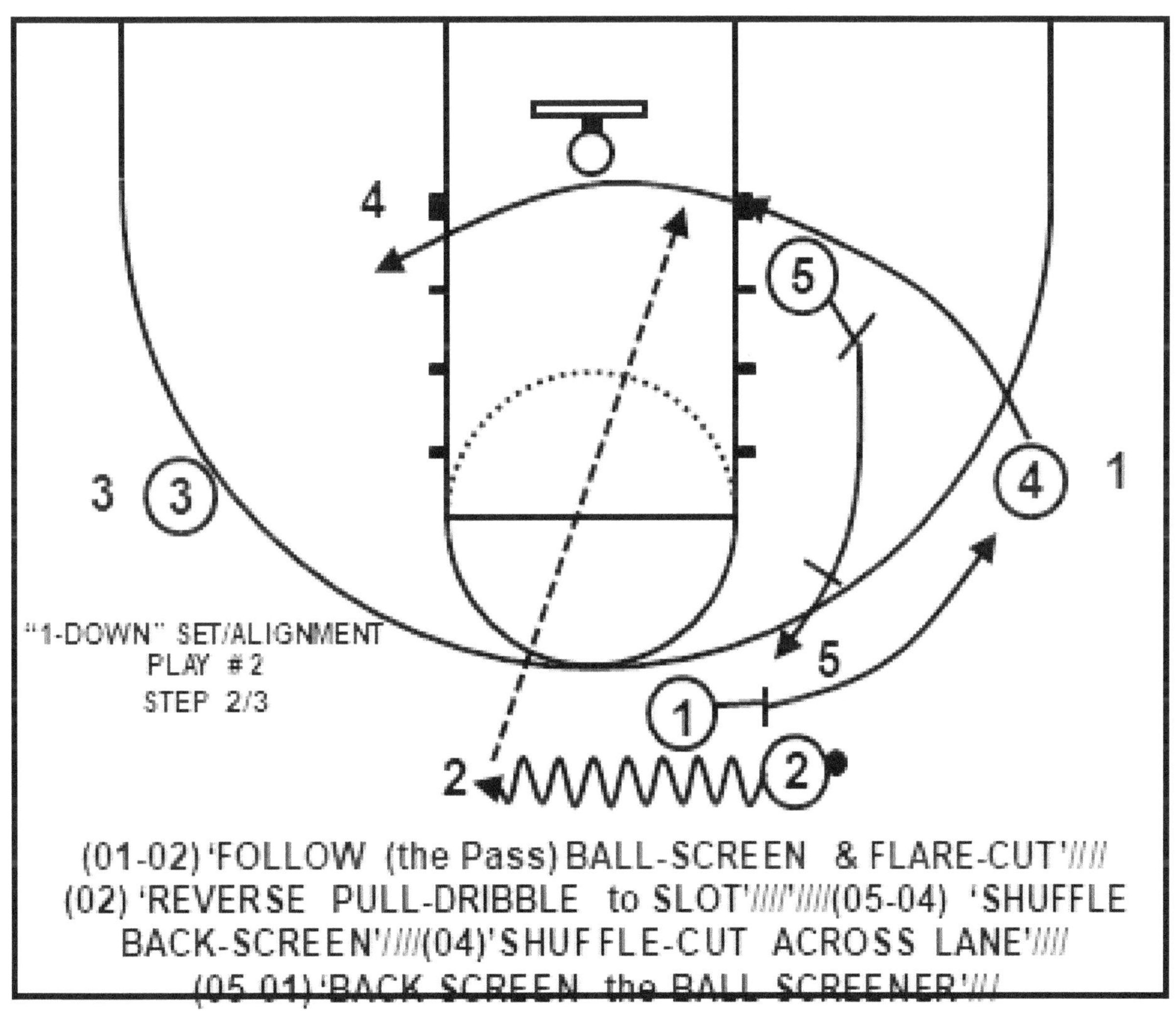

Diagram 10.5

Diagram 10.6 illustrates the end of the entry with 02 turning down all passes until he makes the "Wing Pass" to 03. With an improved passing angle, 03 looks to make the "Inside Pass" to 04. With the pass to 03, both 02 and 05 break diagonally over to set a "Twisted Stagger-Screen" for 01 to use. Setting stagger-screens on the weakside of the court helps to eliminate helpside defense as well as the twisted action helps confuse defenders and helps prevent defensive switches. This gives 04 an outstanding isolation post-up opportunity, particularly with 05 and his defender, X5, (presumably the biggest opposing defender) further from 04 and the basket. This action also makes 01 the primary receiver on the perimeter with 04 remaining as the primary interior receiver. If shots are not taken, this action attacks and moves individual defenders as well as placing all five offensive players in the proper "3-Out/2-In" Spot-Ups for the designated continuity offense to seamlessly begin. See Diagram 10.6

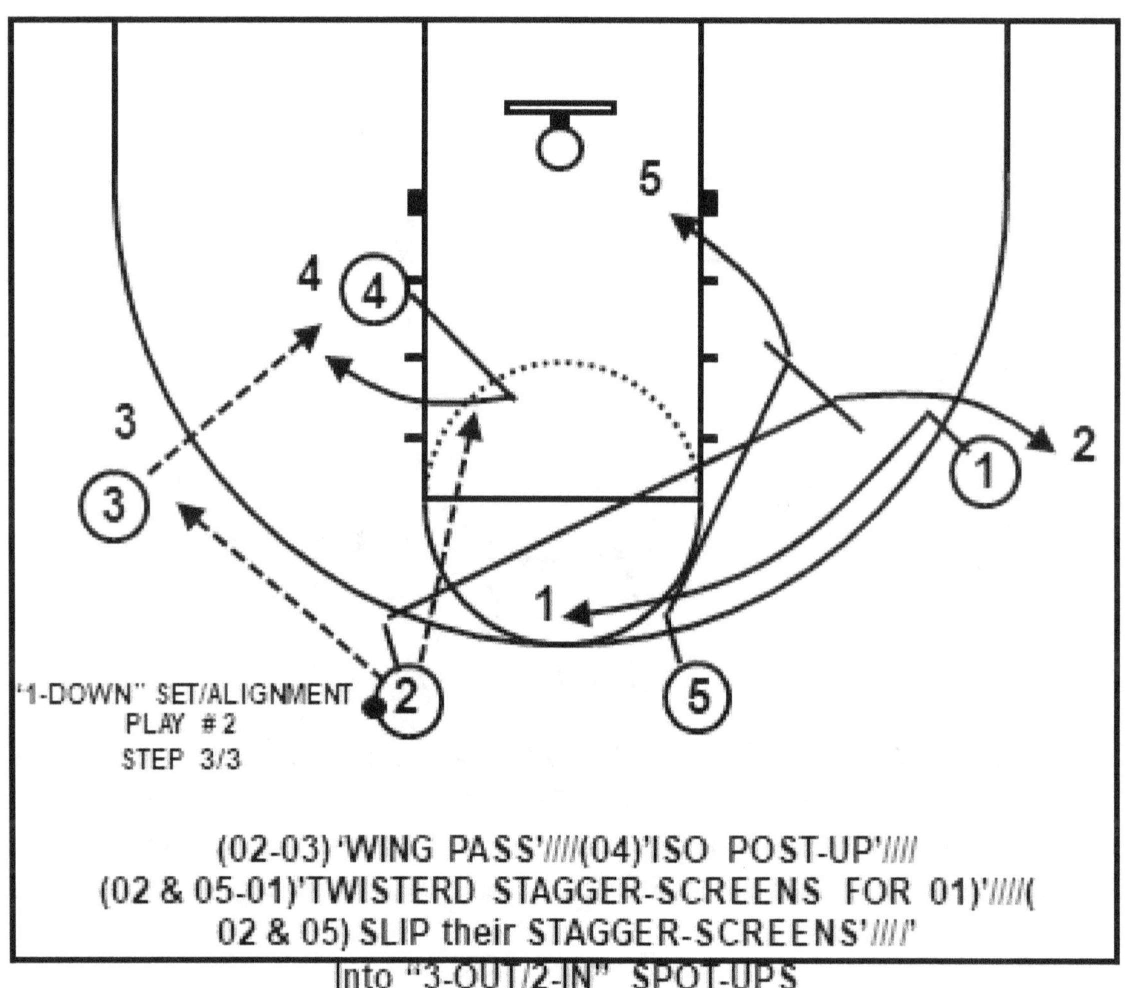

Diagram 10.6

Diagram 10.7 also shows the beginning of Play 3 out of the "1-DOWN" Set. With either 01 or 02 bringing the ball across the timeline and 05 on the left side of the lane, the ball should end up with 01 dribbling directly at 03. This causes 04 to set a "Big-on-Small Flare-Screen" for 02 to "Flare-Cut" to the new "Weakside Wing" and spot-up for a potential "Skip Pass" from 01 or from 03. As this action occupies the weakside of the defense, 05 is able to attack his lone interior defender with an "Iso Duck-In Cut" into the middle of the lane. See Diagram 10.7

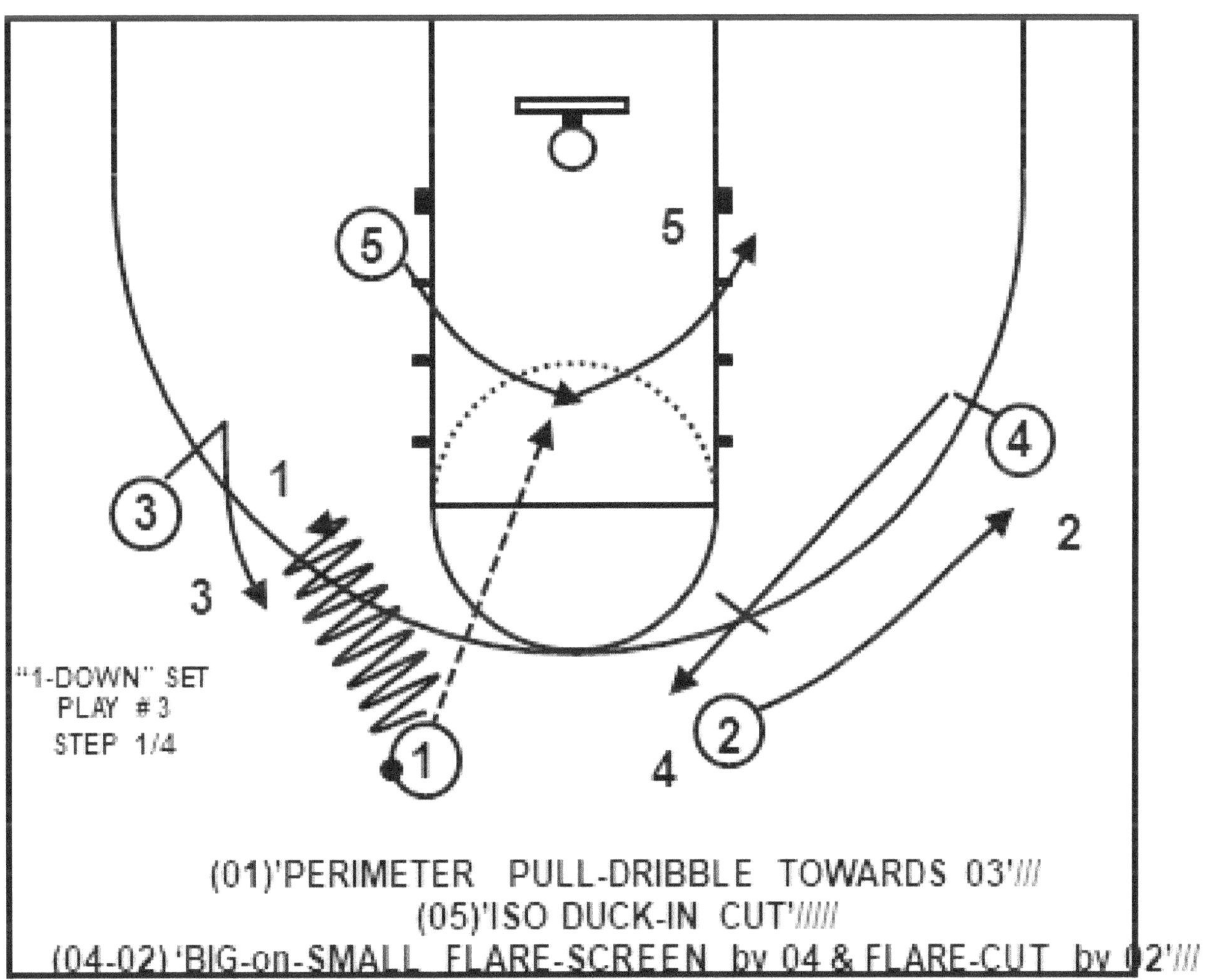

Play #3   Diagram 10.7

Diagram 10.8 illustrates 01 making the "Small-on-Big Dribble Hand-Off with 03 and slipping to the "Weakside Wing." After setting the "Flare-Screen" for 02, 04 slips the screen and inverts his 'post-type defender' at the "Weakside Slot," becoming the primary perimeter receiver for 03. After making the (03-04) "Reverse Pass," 02 cuts down towards 05 to set a "Small-on-Big" Pin Down-Screen" to invert and isolate the perimeter-type defender X2 as well as to invert 05's post-type defender, X5 out at the FT Line extended. 03 and 01 stay spotted up on the weakside of the floor to further help 02 in his new "position advantage" over X2. See Diagram 10.8

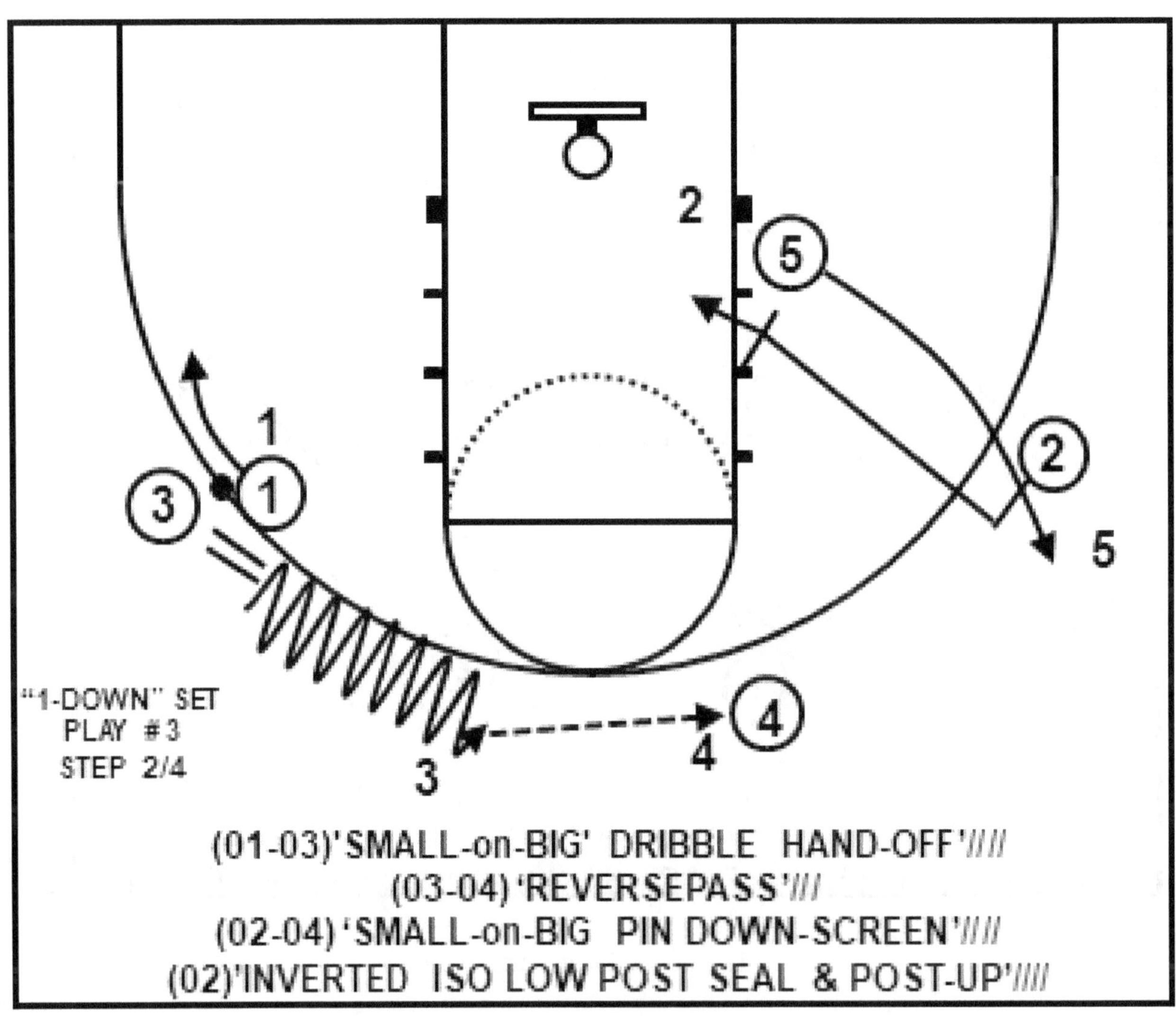

Diagram 10.8

Diagram 10.9 shows 04 then making the "Wing Pass" to 05, who has inverted his defensive "Big" out on the perimeter. 02 then breaks up to set a "Small-on-Big Long UCLA Back-Screen" for 04 to vertically break down to the new "Ballside Block." This mismatch off-ball screen will discourage defensive switches, because X2 would be 04's newly isolated defender down on the "Block." With 04 being the cutter off of the "UCLA Screen," his defender's (X4) defensive reaction should be unique and therefore possibly not being able to be performed efficiently as the so-called 'perimeter-type defenders.' This gives the offense another possible advantage that can be utilized. See Diagram 10.9

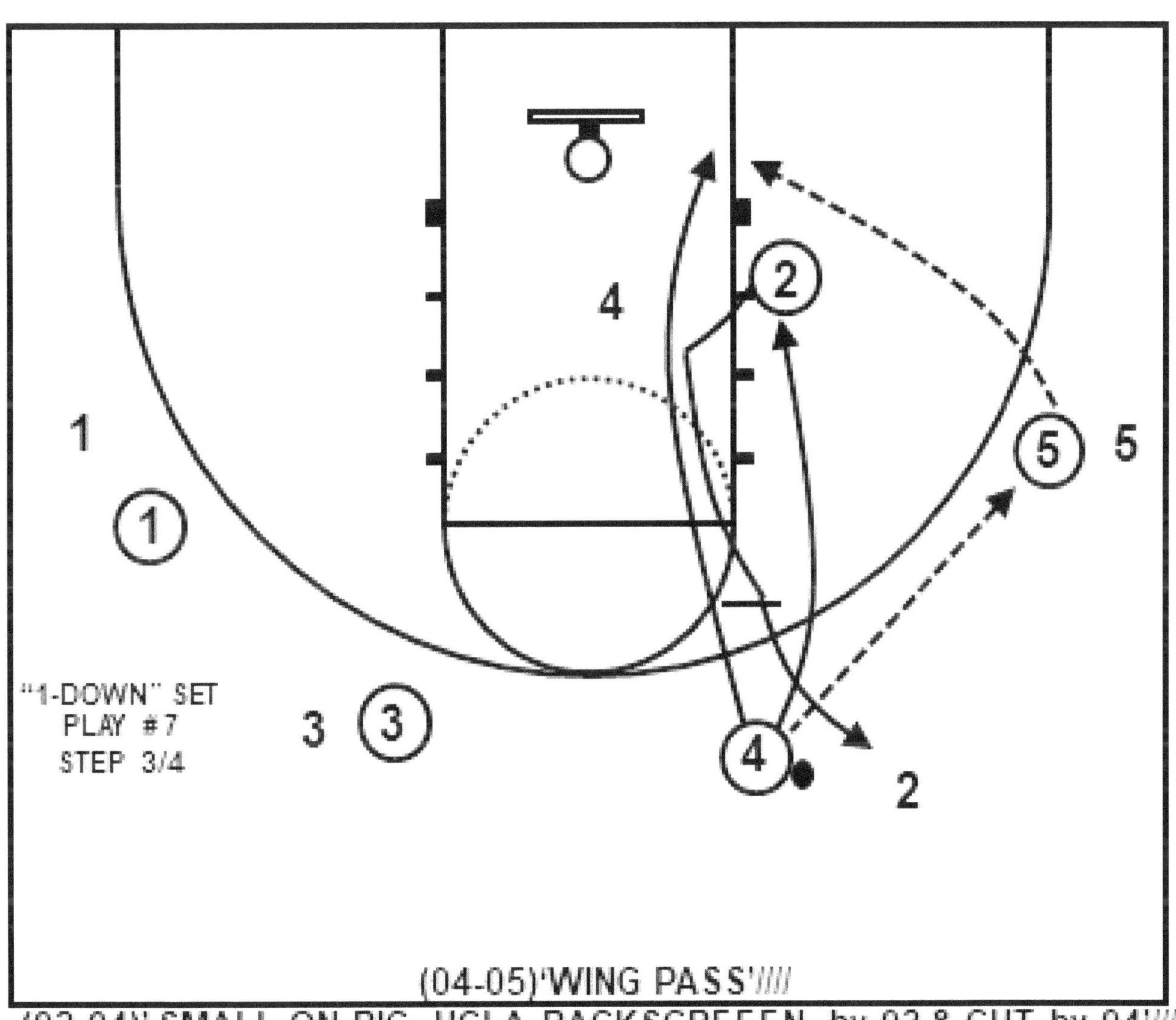

Diagram 10.9.

Diagram 10.10 shows the conclusion of Play # 3. If 05 does not make the "Inside Pass" to 04, he would pass the ball back to 02, stepping out on the "Slot."

03 would then break to set a "Big-on-Small Ball-Screen" for 02 to drag the ball across the horizontal perimeter outside of the arc. After 02 dribble-scrapes off of 03's top right shoulder, 04 attacks his isolated defender with a "Duck-In Cut" into the Dotted Circle area. At the same time, 03 should then make a front pivot off of his inside left foot to make his "Rim-Run" to the basket; looking for the "Lob Pass" from 02.

If X4 denies 04 the ball, 02 could make a "Lob Pass" over X4, or a "Throwback Reverse Pass" to 05, (stretched out on the "Wing,") or a "Wing Pass" to 01 on the opposite side of the floor. If 02 cannot deliver the ball to 04, either or both 05 and 01 should have improved passing angles to make the "Inside Pass" to 04. If no shots are taken, the "3-Out/2-In Spot-Ups are also filled so that the designated continuity offense could immediately begin. See Diagram 10.10

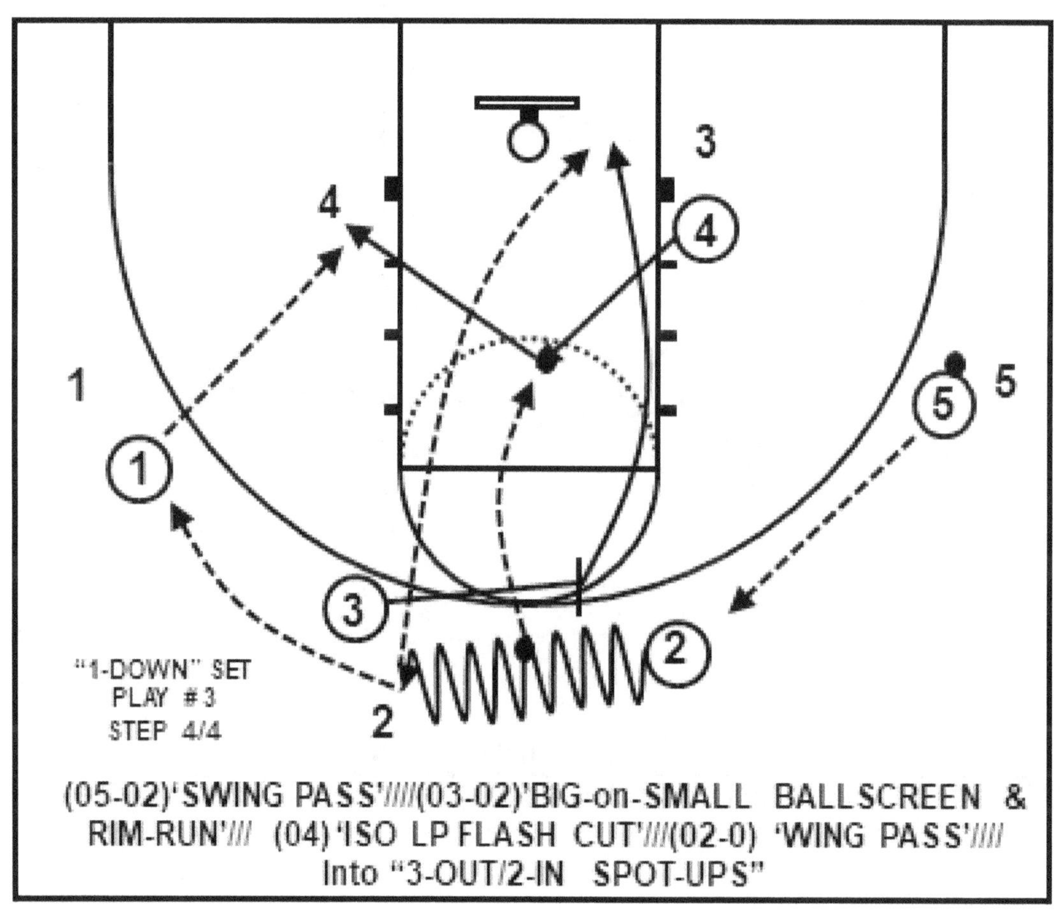

Diagram 10.10

This play/entry started outed out of the "1-DOWN" Set and that the conclusion of the play that does not produce the desired shot will flow into any of the several continuity offenses that can begin from the "3-Out/2-In" Spot-Ups. These entries could fall into either the Level 2 or Level 3 types of plays. Other entries from the same set or from the large selection of other alignments/sets can also be used.

PLAYS/ENTRIES THAT END in the "4-OUT/1-IN" OFFENSIVE SPOT-UPS

The difference in the following plays/entries are that all five players will end up in a different group of offensive spot-ups. These "4-Out/1-In Spot-Ups" will have players moved about the court with any of the five ending up in the "Ballside Deep Corner," the "Ballside Slot," the "Weakside Slot," the "Ballside Post," and the "Weakside Deep Corner." These five positions can provide the offense with safe and easy types of ball-reversals, large gaps for dribble penetration, opportunities to deliver the ball inside to whomever (perimeter-type or post-type players) is posting up their defender on the "Ballside Block," and a player that can be a perimeter-scoring threat and a legitimate offensive rebounding threat from outside of the arc on his "offensive crashing of the boards." The "4-Out/1-In Spot-Ups also provide ample opportunities for constant and effective defensive transition responsibilities.

Diagram 10.11 shows the beginning of a section of the chapter with plays only ending up the "4-Out/1-In" Spot-Ups. These plays can be started out of various sets/alignments as well as fall into the various levels of play. Play #8 shows another play beginning out of the same "1-DOWN" Set. As 01 brings the ball across the timeline, 05 makes another "Iso Duck-In Cut" that puts his defender into another precarious location in the high percentage scoring area for 05. Maintaining his dribble, if 01 does not make passes to either 05 or 03, he then dribbles towards 02. 02 sets his defender up before cutting back towards 01 for a "Small-on-Big Dribble Hand-Off." After the hand-off, 01 slips to the new "Weakside Slot," while 02 fills the new "Ballside Slot." See Diagram 10.11

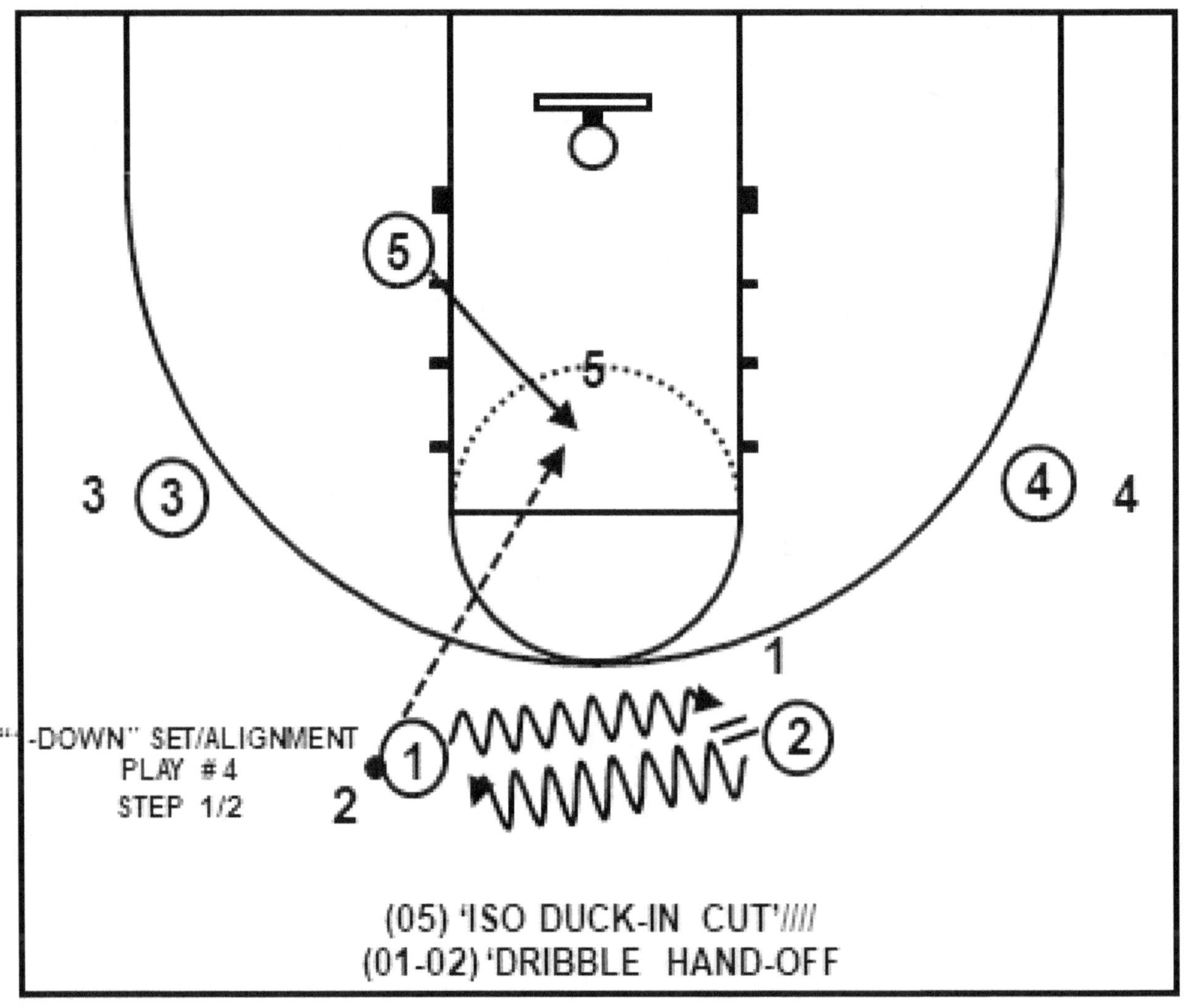

Play # 4   Diagram 10.11

Diagram 10.12 illustrates the continuation of Play # 4 with 01 making a "Wing Pass" over to 03. With that pass, 01 cuts away from the ball towards the weak side of the rim. On the way, 01 will set a "Big-on-Small Brush-Screen" for 02 to use (before 02 then receives the "Big-on-Small Nail Shuffle Back-Screen from 05.) 01 then uses 05's same screen and scrapes off of 05's ballside right shoulder. 02 ends up on the new "Ballside Block" and 01 empties out to the new "Weakside Deep Corner." After setting screens for both 02 and 01, 05 pops out to the new "Ballside Slot," while 04 stretches the defense by stepping out to the "Weakside Slot."

03 looks to make a "Lob Pass" to 01 and to hit 02 anywhere on his cut from the perimeter to the new "Ballside Block." 03 has the freedom to make a "Down-Dribble" to the "Deep Corner" for driving opportunities, perimeter jump shots and better passing angles to make the "Inside Pass" to 02. 03 also has possible perimeter passes to either inverted post-type players, 05 and 04 (in the "Slots.")

If shots are not taken, the (different group of) "4-Out/1-In" Spot-Up locations are filled for a different type of continuity offense to again be able to seamlessly begin. See Diagram 10.12

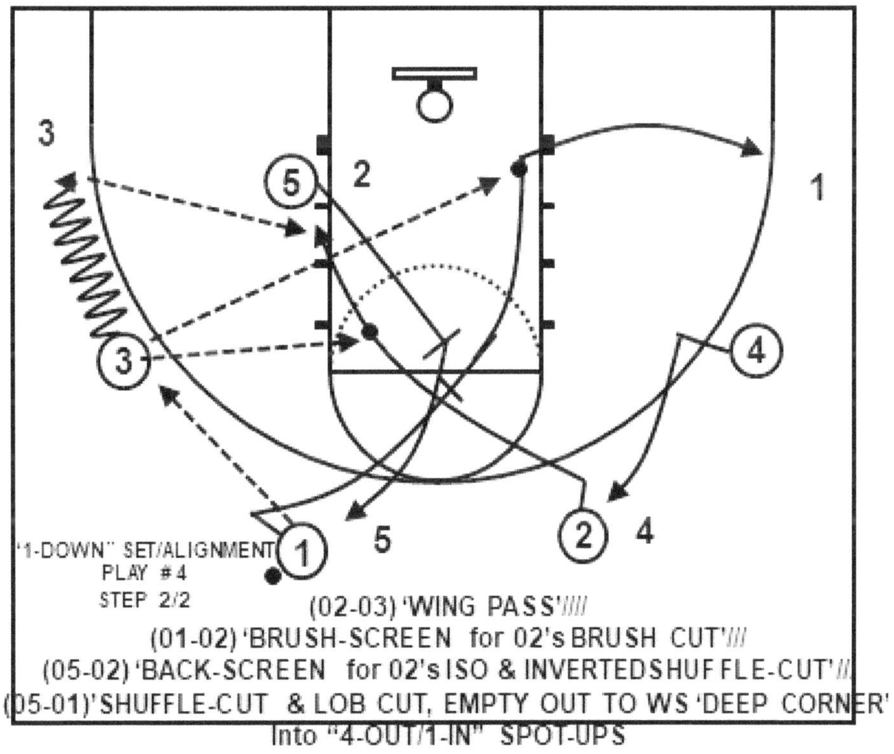

Diagram 10.12

Diagram 10.13 shows the beginning of Play #5 with 02 bringing the ball up the court and 05 starting on the same side of the lane as 02. 02 continues the dribble and 01 then approaches 02 for a "Small-on-Big Ball-Screen & Slip" near the top of the key and the imaginary center line.

This "Drag Ball-Screen" between 01 and 02 results in both 01 and 02 exchanging their two initial "Slot" locations. At the same time, 04 breaks down to set a "Small-on-Big Pin Down-Screen" for 05 to invert and isolate his "Defensive Big" out on the perimeter's "Wing" area. After setting the (04-05) Pin-Screen, 04 slips the screen and makes a deceptive but aggressive "Iso Duck-In Cut" into the lane (and eventually across the lane,) looking for 01's "Duck-In Interior Pass." See Diagram 10.13

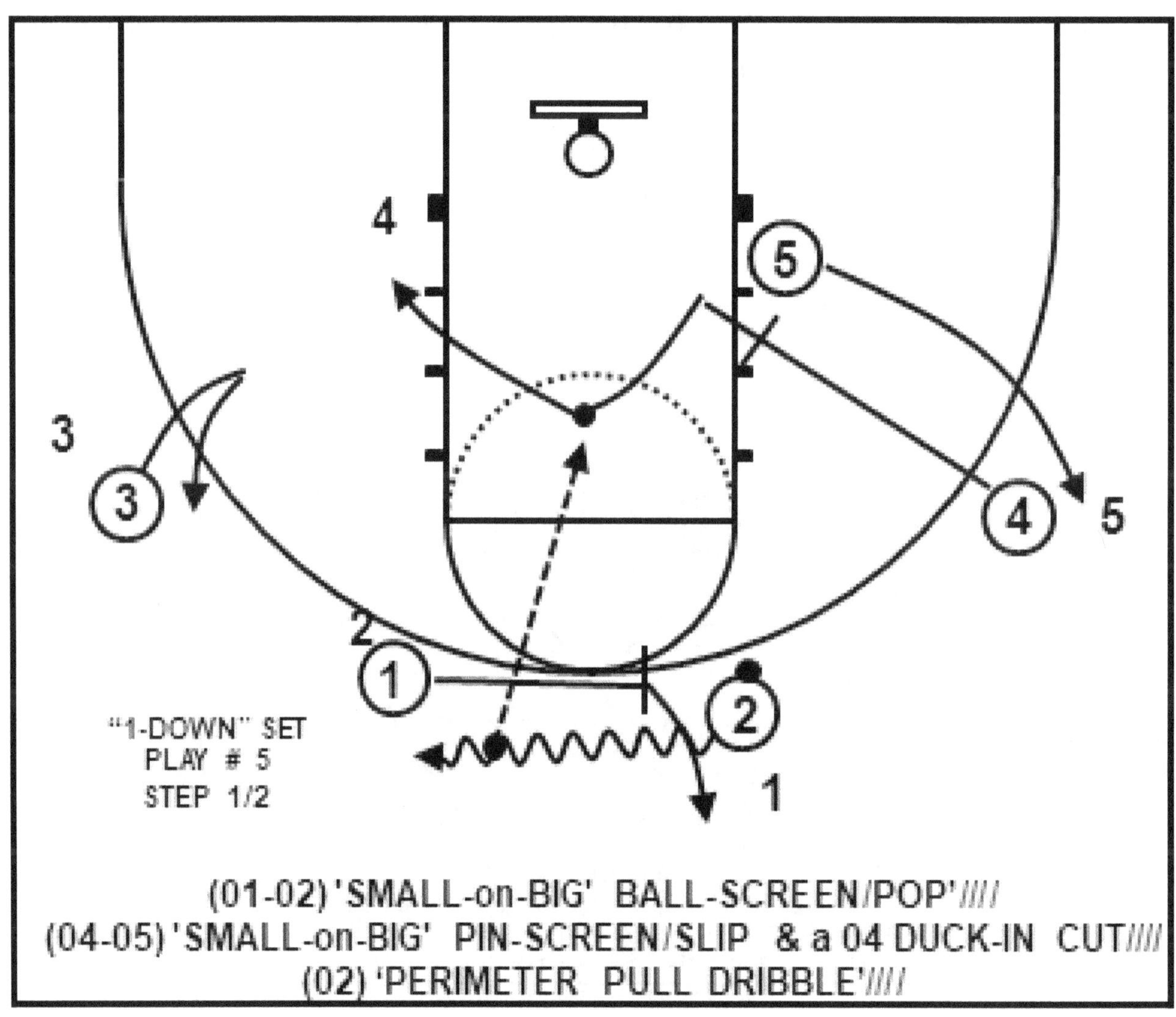

Play # 5   Diagram 10.13

Diagram 10.14 demonstrates the conclusion of the entry (and the beginning of the last phase of the offensive attack.) As 02 approaches 03, 05 steps up to set a "Big-on-Small Flare-Screen" for 01 to use to "Flare-Cut" to the opposite side's "Wing" area. If 02 does not make the possible "Skip Pass" to 01 or a "Throwback Reverse Pass" to 05; he must look to continue his dribble for a (02-03) "Small-on-Big DHO" near the FT Line extended.

After the DHO, 03 then takes the ball and makes his "Perimeter Pull Dribble" towards the top of the key looking for three perimeter pass receivers, primarily 01, 02, and 05. As the ball is dribbled towards the imaginary center line, 04 again attacks his lone defender with an "Iso Duck-In Cut" and looks to receive the ball first from 03, from 05 or from 01.

If shots are not taken, this action attacks various defenders and also repositions all five offensive players into the appropriate "4-Out/1-In" Spot-Ups for a specific continuity offense to seamlessly begin. See Diagram 10.14

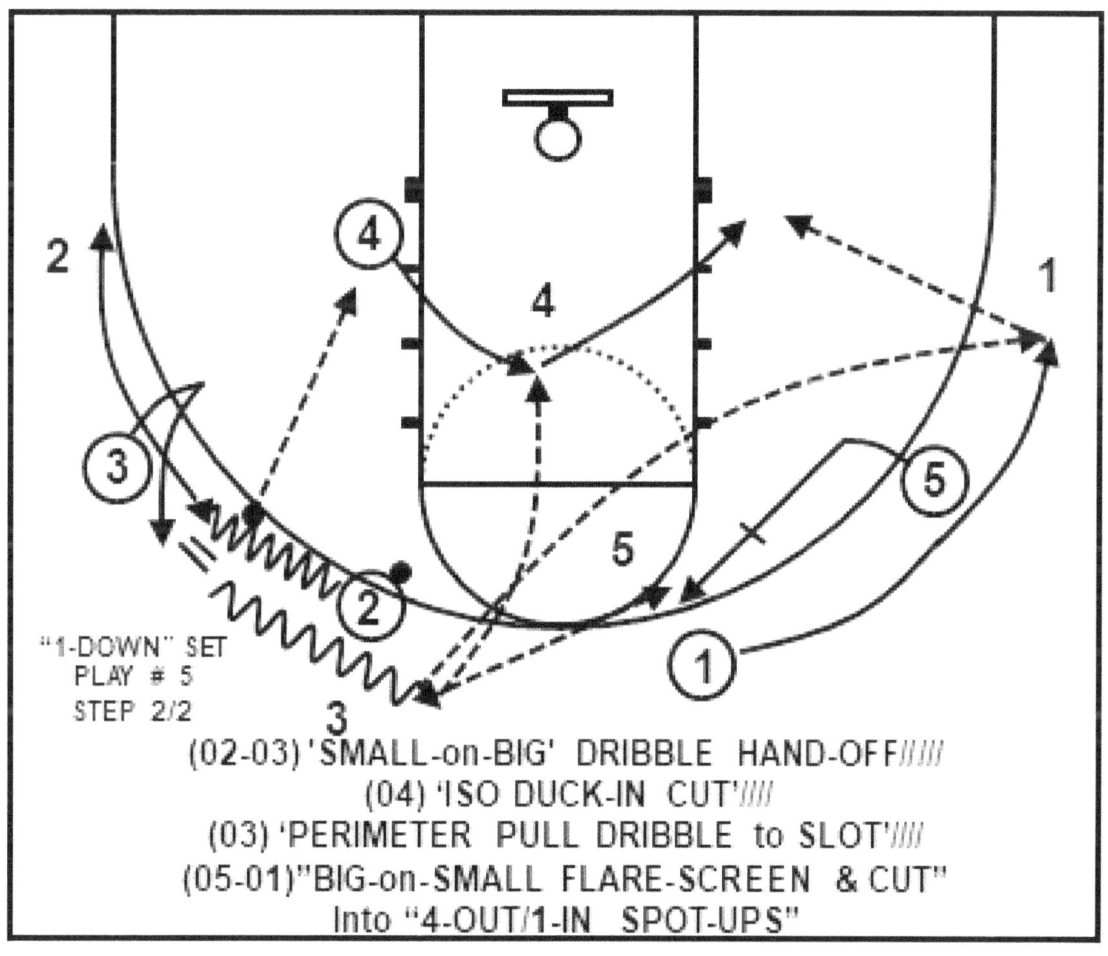

Diagram 10.14

Diagram 10.15 illustrates the initial action of Play # 6. After 01 crosses the timeline and approaches the "Slot" location, 05 makes a strong "Iso Duck-In Cut" into the middle of the lane, looking for the basketball. If 01 turns down the pass to 05, 01 makes the 01-02 "Reverse Pass" and quickly follows his pass with a "Small-on-Big Follow-(the Pass) Ball-Screen" for 02 to use to drag the ball across the top of the key. After 02 "dribble-scrapes" off of 01's outside right shoulder and breaks contact with his teammate, 01 continues to the new "Weakside Wing" after receiving 04's "Big-on-Small (Flare-)Screen the (Ball-)Screener. 04 slips his screen and inverts his post-type defender by slipping to the "Weakside Slot."

As 02 dribbles across the imaginary center line, 05 finds the right time to attack his isolated defender with his aggressive "Duck-In Cut" into the Dotted Circle area. See Diagram 10.15

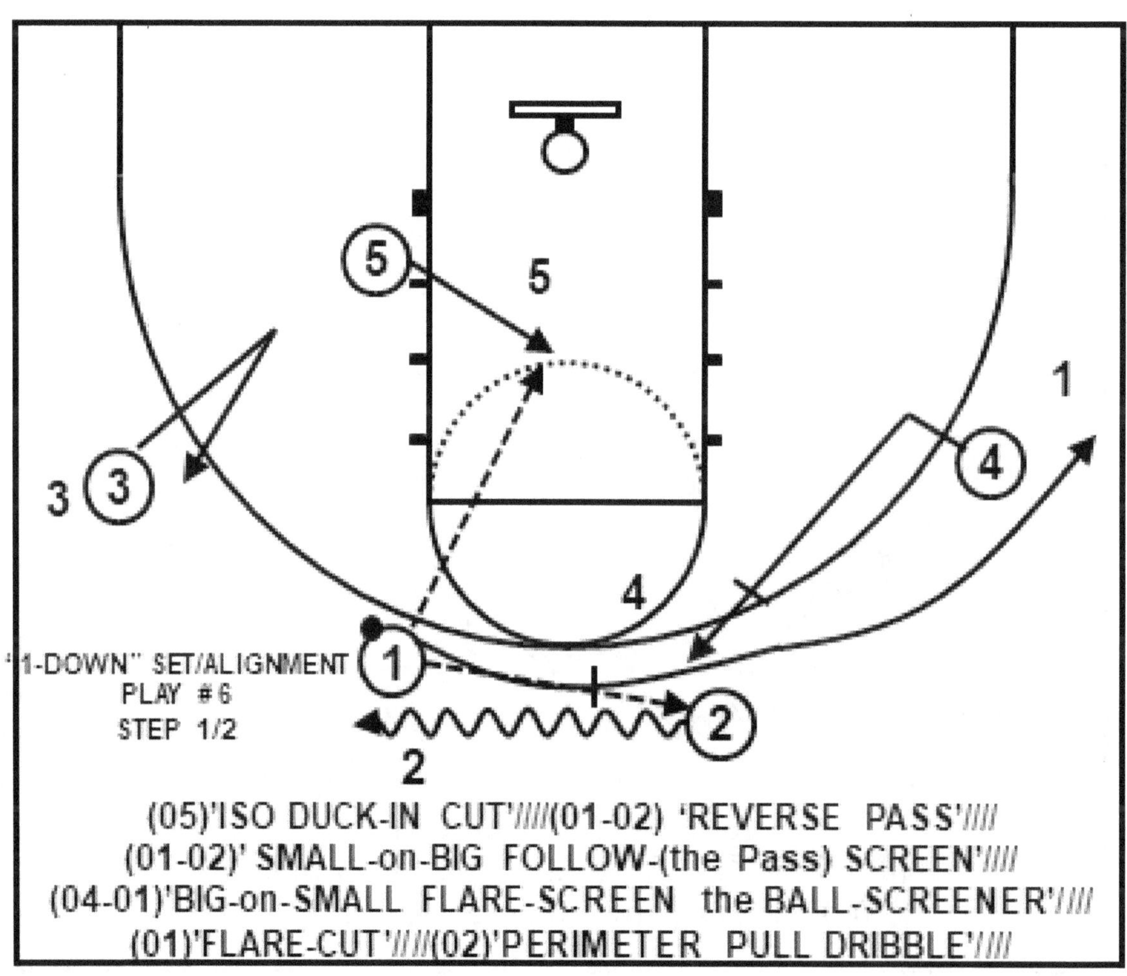

Play # 6   Diagram 10.15

Diagram 10.10 continues and ends the play with 02 looking for his two primary receivers: one on the interior, to 05 in the lane; or two 01 for a "Throwback Reverse Skip Pass" to 01 after his "Flare-Cut" to the wing area.

05 looks to "chase the ball" and flash to whatever side of the lane the ball is passed. In this case, 03 receives the ball and looks to improve the passing angle to make the pass to 05. All players are in the necessary "4-Out/1-In" Spot-Ups for the designated continuity offense to immediately begin. See Diagram 10.10

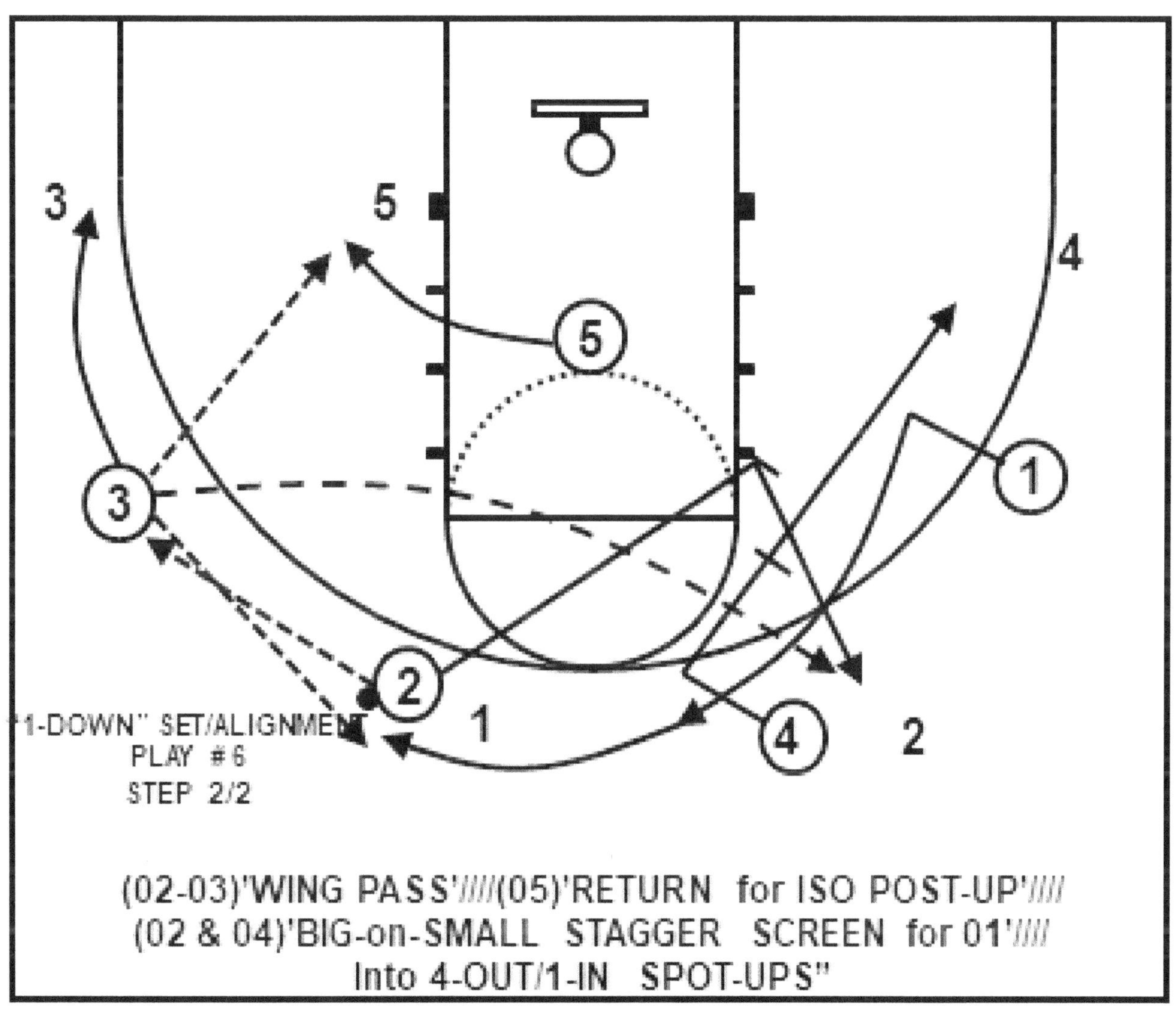

Diagram 10.16

Diagram 10.17 shows Play # 7 with 01 being the primary ball-handler and 03 stepping up to set a "Big-on-Small Ball-Screen" near the "Slot" location. 01 "dribble-scrapes" off of 03's outside right shoulder and when contact is broken, 05 makes an "Iso Duck-In Cut" into the lane to look for 01's pass. If 05 does not receive the pass, he empties out to the opposite side of the floor. After screening for 01, 03 slips the screen and remains at the "Slot." See Diagram 10.17

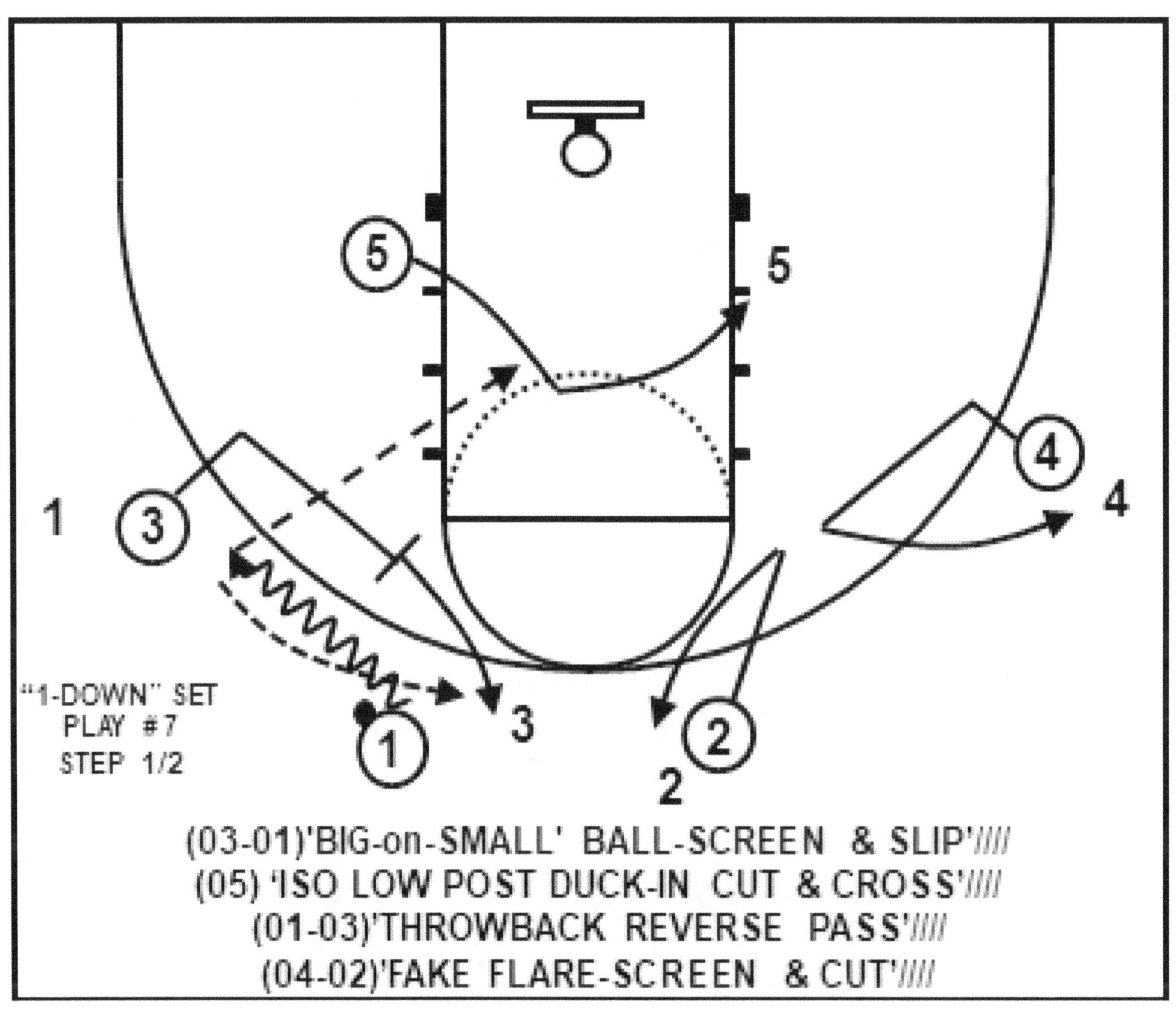

Play # 7   Diagram 10.17

Diagram 10.18 shows 01 unable to make the pass to 05 and not having a good shot of his own. He then makes the (01-03) "Up Pass" for 03 to then reverse the ball to 02 on the other side of the floor. 03 immediately then turns to set a "Big-on-Small Pin Down-Screen" for 01 to return to his initial "Slot" location. This action gives 02 two viable and potential perimeter targets on the weakside of the floor as well as to occupy both possible helpside defenders that X4 would need.

Upon 02 receiving the ball from 03 out on top, it appears that 04 is going to repeat a ball-screen near the "Slot" on the opposite side of the floor. Instead, 04 breaks off of his screening route to make his action a "Big-on-Small Ghost Ball-Screen" followed by a cut through the lane. With 05 inverting his own post-type defender, 05 breaks out to the "Deep Corner" (to occupy his defender) and allow 04 to not only surprise his defender but to isolate him on his cut through the lane. This action gives the play perimeter options as well as interior options for both offensive "Bigs." The action also moves players into the fundamentally sound "4-Out/1In" Spot-Ups for the final phase of the offense to begin. See Diagram 10.18

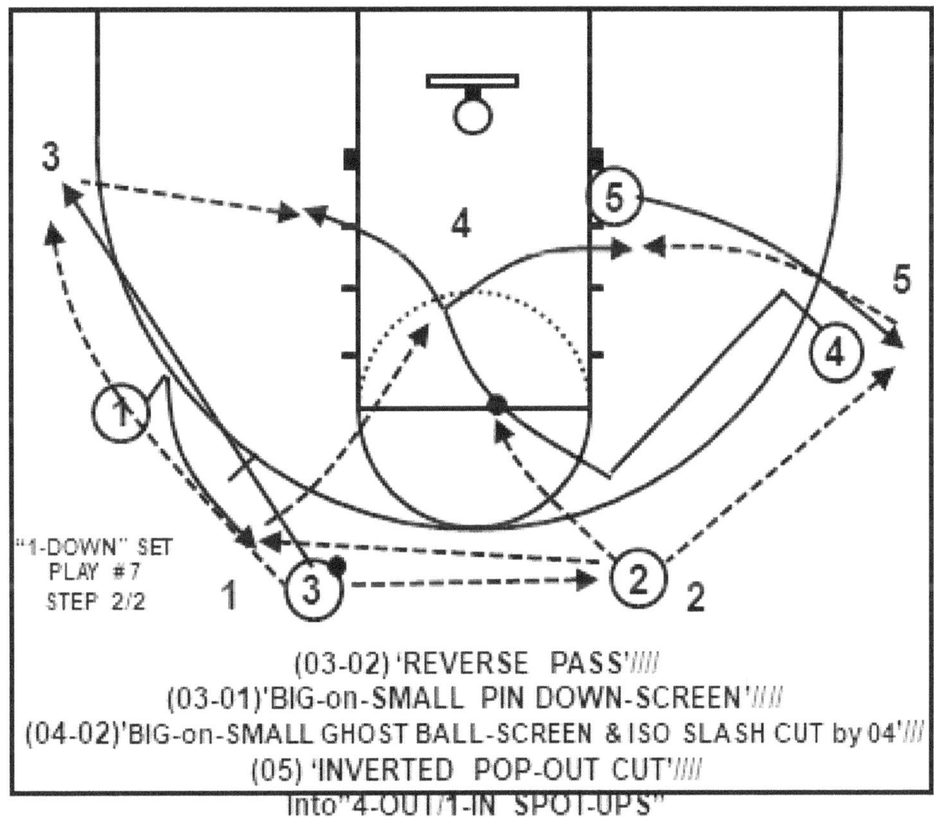

Diagram 10.18

Diagram 10.19 begins Play # 8 with identical action of all five players as Play # 7. 03 steps up to again set the (03-01) "Big-on-Small Ball-Screen," followed by 03 again slipping to the "Slot" position vacated by 01. After breaking contact with 03, 01 looks to attack 05's isolated defender again on the new "Ballside Block." 02 and 04 occupy their newly defined "weakside defenders for better isolation situations between 01 and 05. See Diagram 10.19

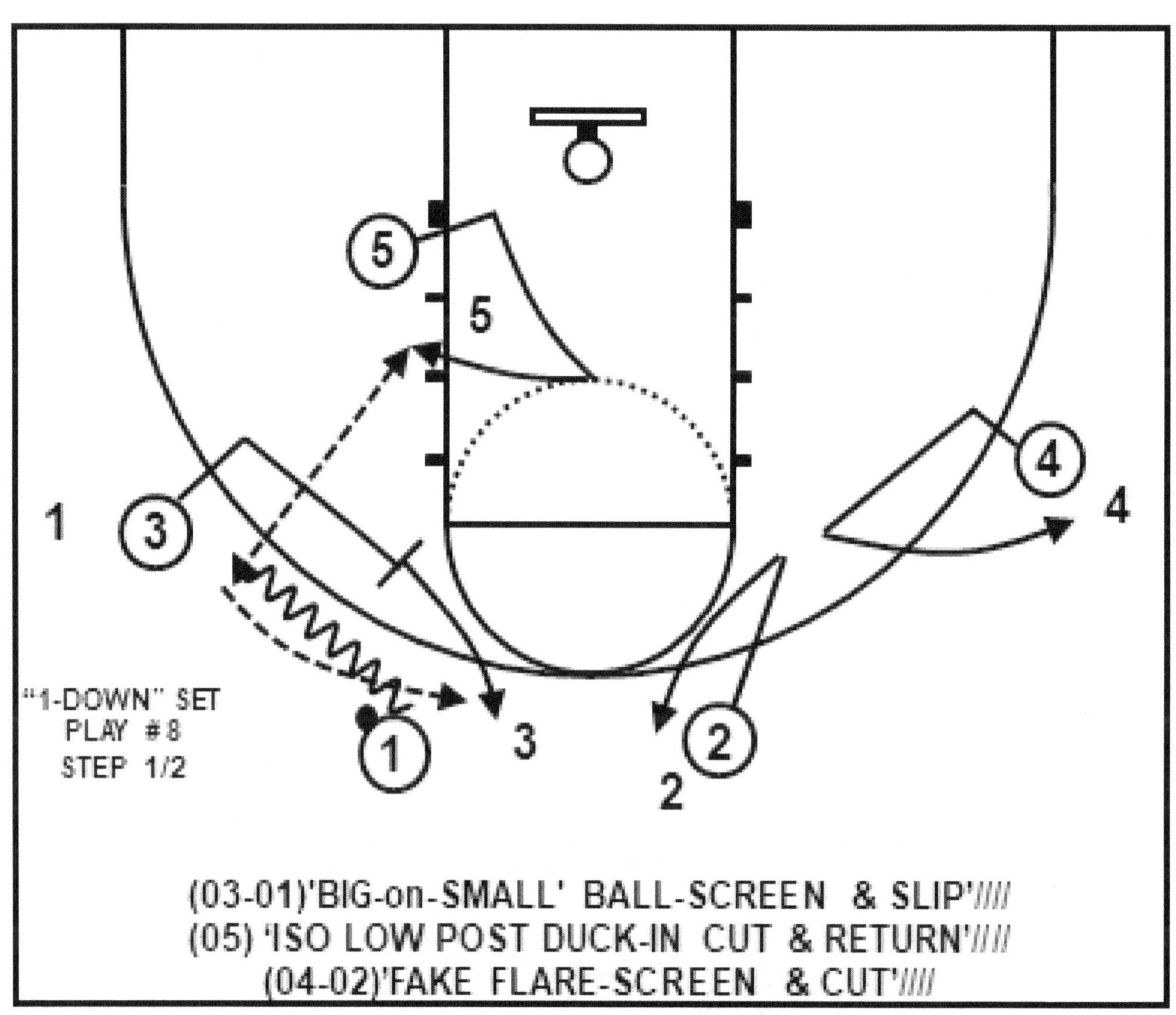

Play #8   Diagram 10.19

Diagram 10.20 shows the continuation and conclusion of Play # 8 with 01 again having the opportunity to make a "Throwback Up-Pass" out to 03. This action is still identical to the previous play. With the opposition possibly getting familiar with the action, 04 and 02 change things up with an actual "Big-on-Small Flare-Screen" by 04 and "Flare-Cut by 02. 02 can also make his cut wider and deeper. This action is not by accident, in that after 03 makes his (03-04) "Reverse Pass," he will surprise his (newly inverted and isolated) defender, X3 with an immediate "Give-n-Go" Cut diagonally through the lane to the newly declared "Ballside Block." During that pass, 01 also makes his own "Drift" Cut wider and deeper towards his own "Deep Corner" to further stretch the defense. In addition, as the ball leaves 03's hands, 05 makes a vertical "Elbow Up" Cut to the new "Weakside Slot." This action by all off-the-ball offensive cutters will fully occupy all off-ball defenders, further isolating X3, in the lane.

If shots are not taken, the "4-Out/1-In" Spot-Ups are once again filled (as they are in Play # 7 and all previous quick-hitters/entries/plays; allowing a smooth conversion into the last phase of the offense. See Diagram 10.20

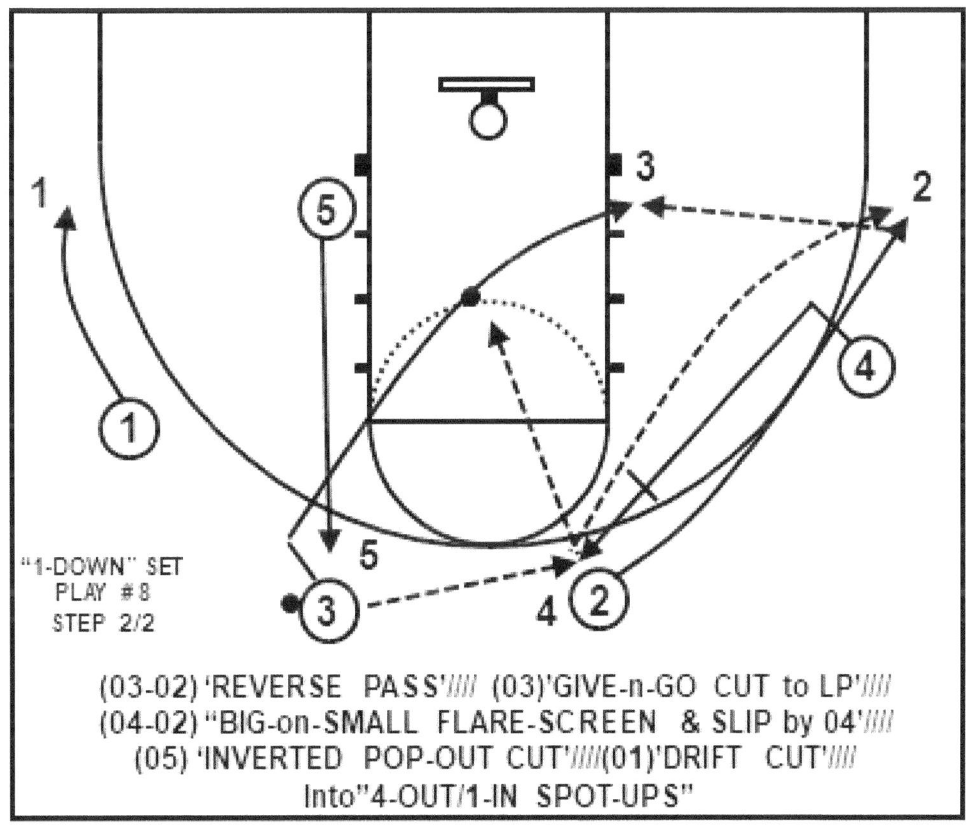

Diagram 10.20

Diagram 10.21 shows Play # 9 beginning with 01 making the (01-02) "Reverse Pass" to 02 with 03 then stepping up to set a "Big-on-Small Flare-Screen" for 01 to use on his "Flare-Cut" to the new "Weakside Wing." Once the ball is in 02's hands, 05 makes what appears to be his standard "Iso Duck-In Cut" into the Dotted Circle area.

05 could begin this cut first "by getting into his defender and either making a "front pivot off of his outside left foot and swim with his right arm over or through the defender." Once 05 has X5 caught on his inside right hip, 05 uses his right forearm as his "arm bar" to seal off the defender as he side-step shuffles further into the lane. The methods of a good defensive box-out are basically the same techniques used once 05 has gained his offensive "seal-off" position advantage.

The second technique is for 05 to step in between X5's feet with his outside left foot before "reverse pivoting" and swinging his right foot around to gain that initial "seal-off" position. Once again, the same defensive box-out techniques of using the same footwork, hips and legs and arms are all used to maintain that "position advantage" so that the ball can be received in that vulnerable area.

02 dribbles towards 04 to gain a possible better passing angle to make that pass to 05, working hard on the "Block" to receive the ball. See Diagram 10.21.

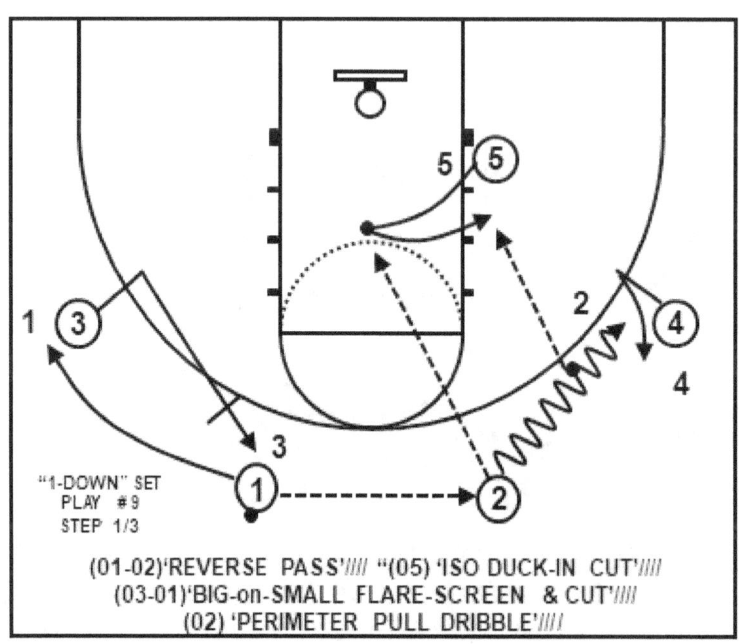

Play # 9   Diagram 10.21

Diagram 10.22 illustrates 02 unable to make the pass to 05 and continuing towards 04. 04 then breaks back up towards 04 to receive the (02-04) "Small-on-Big Dribble Hand-Off. 04 further inverts his post-type defensive "Big" by dribbling out towards the newly vacated "Slot," while 02 then slips the DHO with a "Flare-Cut" towards the "Deep Corner."

As 04 dribbles out on the perimeter, 03 prepares to receive the "Reverse Pass" from 04, before then making a hard "Give-n-Go" Cut to the basket, looking for the pass from 04. If 04 does not hit 03, 03 empties out to just behind 05 on the "Block" and 04 continues his "Inverted Perimeter Pull-Dribble" to the opposite side's "Slot."

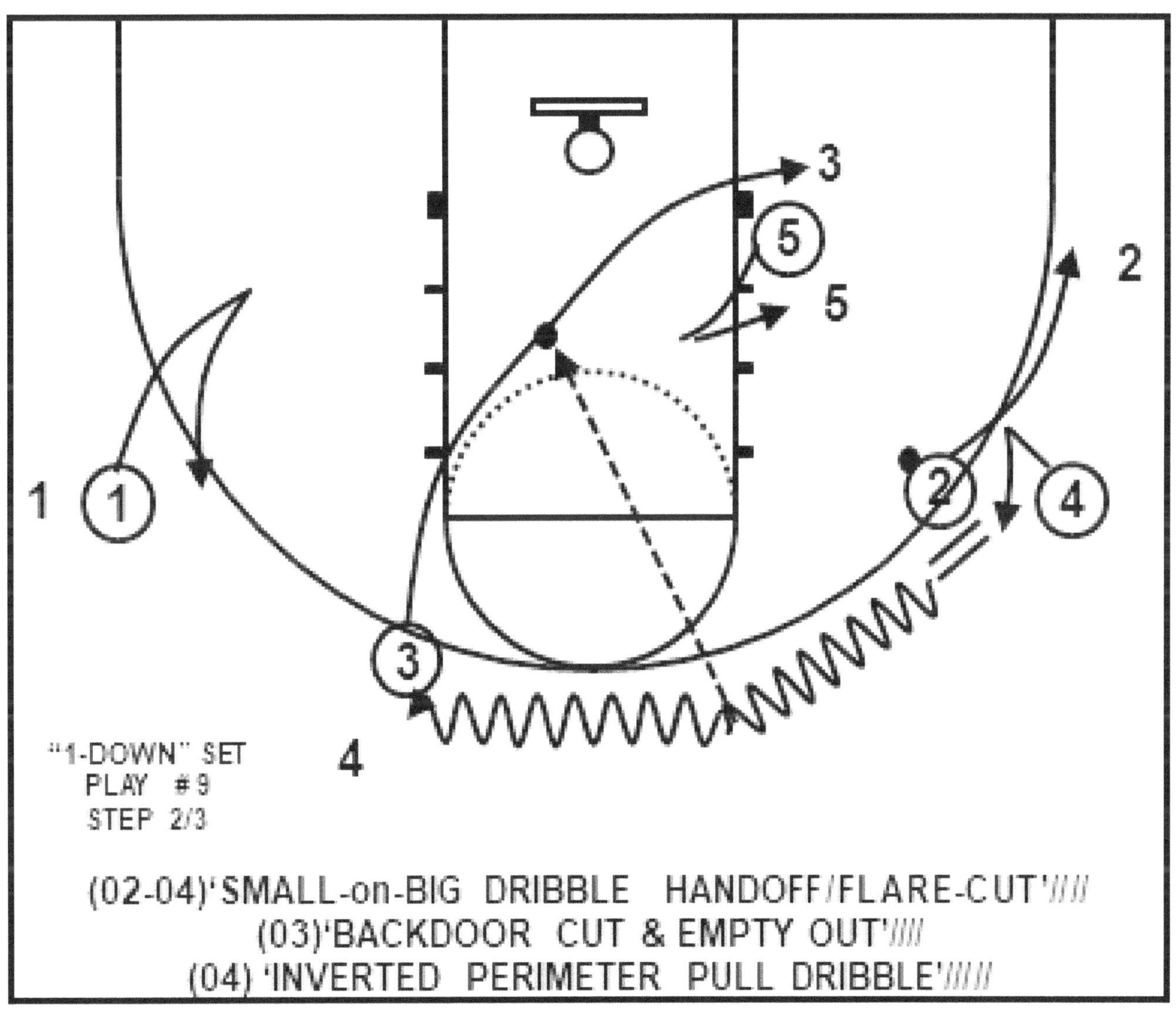

Diagram 10.22

Diagram 10.23 shows the continuation and the end of the play with 04 then making a "Big-on-Small DHO" with 01—presumably the best ball-handler and passer. With 04 handing the ball off, he has kept presumably the opposition's second biggest defender away from the basket.

As 01 receives the DHO and starts towards the middle of the floor, 05 breaks diagonally up from the opposite "Block" to set a "Long Big-on-Small Ball-Screen" for 01 to rub/bump his defender off.

After 01 "dribble-scrapes" off of 05's top left shoulder and breaks contact with him, 05 makes a "front-pivot" off of his inside right foot and continues to make a "Lob-Cut" to the basket. If 01 does not make the "Lob Pass" to 05, 05 empties out to the "Weakside Deep Corner."

As 01 "perimeter pull dribbles" and drags his defender across the top of the key, 02 makes a "Drift Cut" towards his "Deep Corner" while 03 begins from his "Deep Block" location to make his "inverted and isolated Duck-In Cut." If 01 cannot make interior passes to either 05 or to 03, he has two potential perimeter pass receivers in 02 or 01. In addition, 01 has the option to make an aggressive "penetration dribble" (off of 05's ball-screen).

With all of the options, the offense will still reposition all players in the "4-Out/1-In" Spot-Ups, allowing the next phase of the offensive attack to continue. See Diagram 10.23

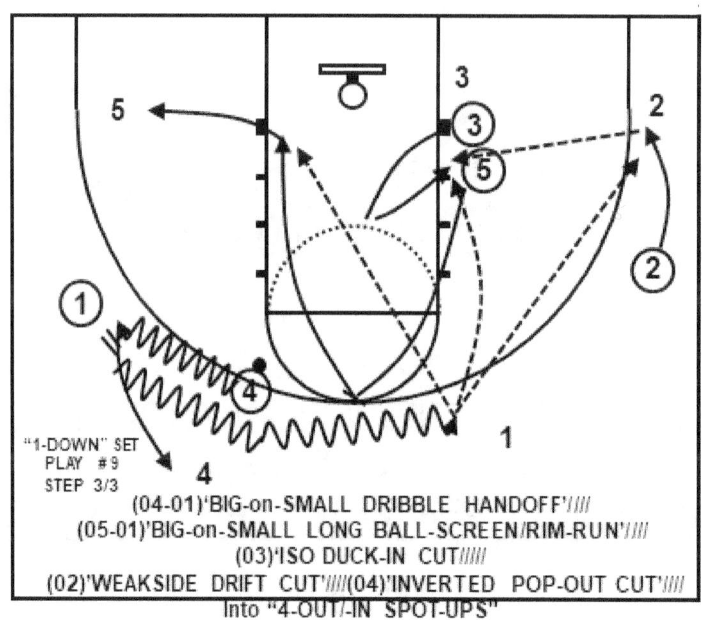

Diagram 10.23

Play # 10 in Diagram 10.24 shows 02 dribbling towards the "Slot," with 05 making his usual "Iso Duck-In Cut" and looking for the pass from 02. If 05 does not receive the pass, 02 then reverses the ball over to 01. After the pass is made, 04 steps up to set his "Big-on-Small Flare-Screen" for 02 to use to make his "Flare-Cut." 02 should scrape off of 04's outside left shoulder and cut towards the "Wing" area. This action horizontally stretches the defense as well as occupy two off-ball defenders to keep them away from the ball. See Diagram 10.24

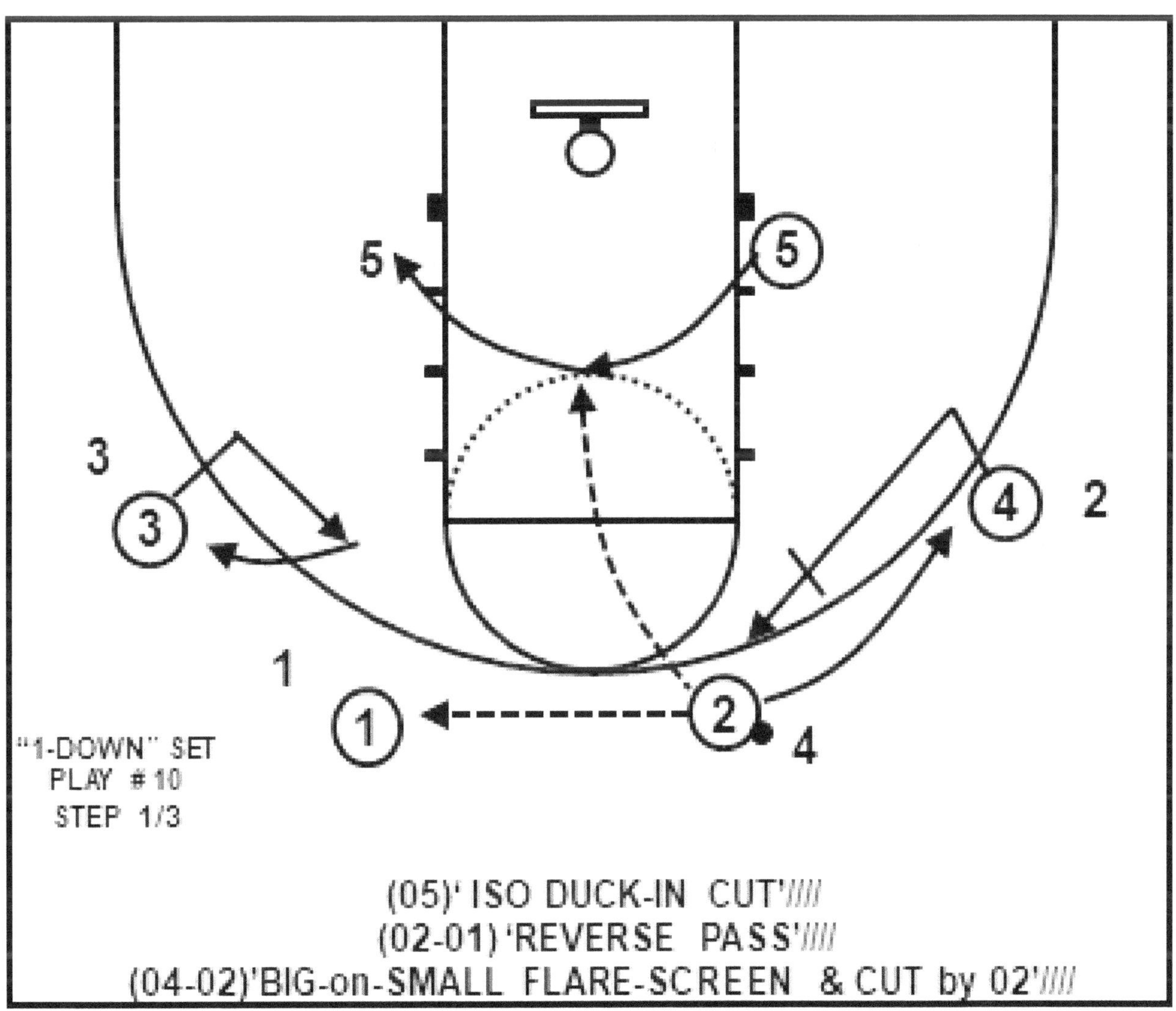

Play # 10   Diagram 10.24

Diagram 10.25 shows the next phase of the play, with 01 looking to make an "Inside Pass" to 05 or a "Wing Pass" to 03. At the same time, 04 slips his initial screen before stepping across the top of the key to set a (04-01) "Big-on-Small Ball-Screen" for 01 to use. 01 "dribble-scrapes" off of 04's top left shoulder and looks for "dribble penetration," or a "perimeter pull dribble" to then make an "Inside Pass" to 05, now on the new "Ballside Block" or a perimeter pass to 02. After ball-screening for 01, 04 remains at the "Slot" on that side of the floor. See Diagram 10.25

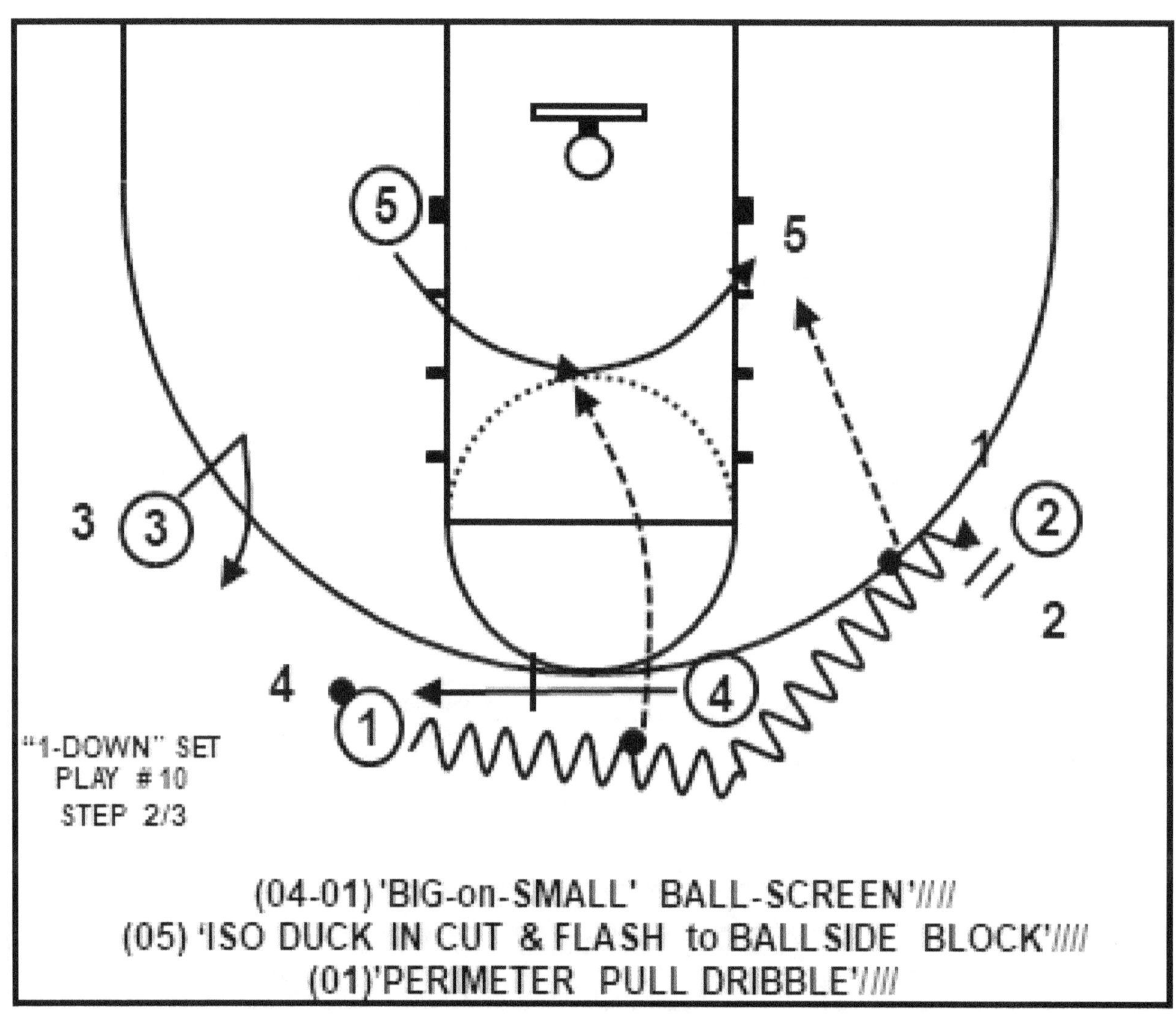

Diagram 10.25

Diagram 10.26 shows the final components of this play. When 01 elects not to make the pass to 05, he dribbles towards 02 to make the "Small-on-Big DHO"

Immediately after giving up possession of the ball to 02, 01 receives 05's "Big-on-Small Back-Screen" for 01 to attack his perimeter-type defender with a "Lob Cut" to the basket. If 02 does not make the "Lob Pass" to 01, or a "Throwback Reverse Pass" to 05 who has inverted his defender out to the "Wing," area, 02 continues dribbling out towards the top of the key towards 04.

While the defense could easily expect 04 to set a "Ball-Screen" for 02 or for a "Pin Down-Screen" for 03; 04 can cross up the defense and its expectations with a (04-02) 'Big-on-Small Ghost Ball-Screen" by 04 and instead make a diagonal "Slash Cut" to the rim. At the same time, 03 lifts out to the now vacant "Slot." If 02 does not make the pass to 04, 04 empties out to the "Deep Corner" on his side of the court. This places both 05 and 04 out on the two respective "Deep Corners," vertically and horizontally stretching and thinning out the defensive interior. This action leaves X1 completely alone in the interior in a highly vulnerable area where he most likely has defensive weaknesses and a lack of defensive experience. This gives the offense the advantage and opportunity to attack X1 and his weaknesses and/or to utilize 01's outstanding post-up and possible "Inside scoring" skills.

Still, if no shots are taken, the offense has moved players into the "4-Out/1-In" Spot-Ups for the final phase of the offense to maintain its constant and fluid attack on the scrambling defense. See Diagram 10.26

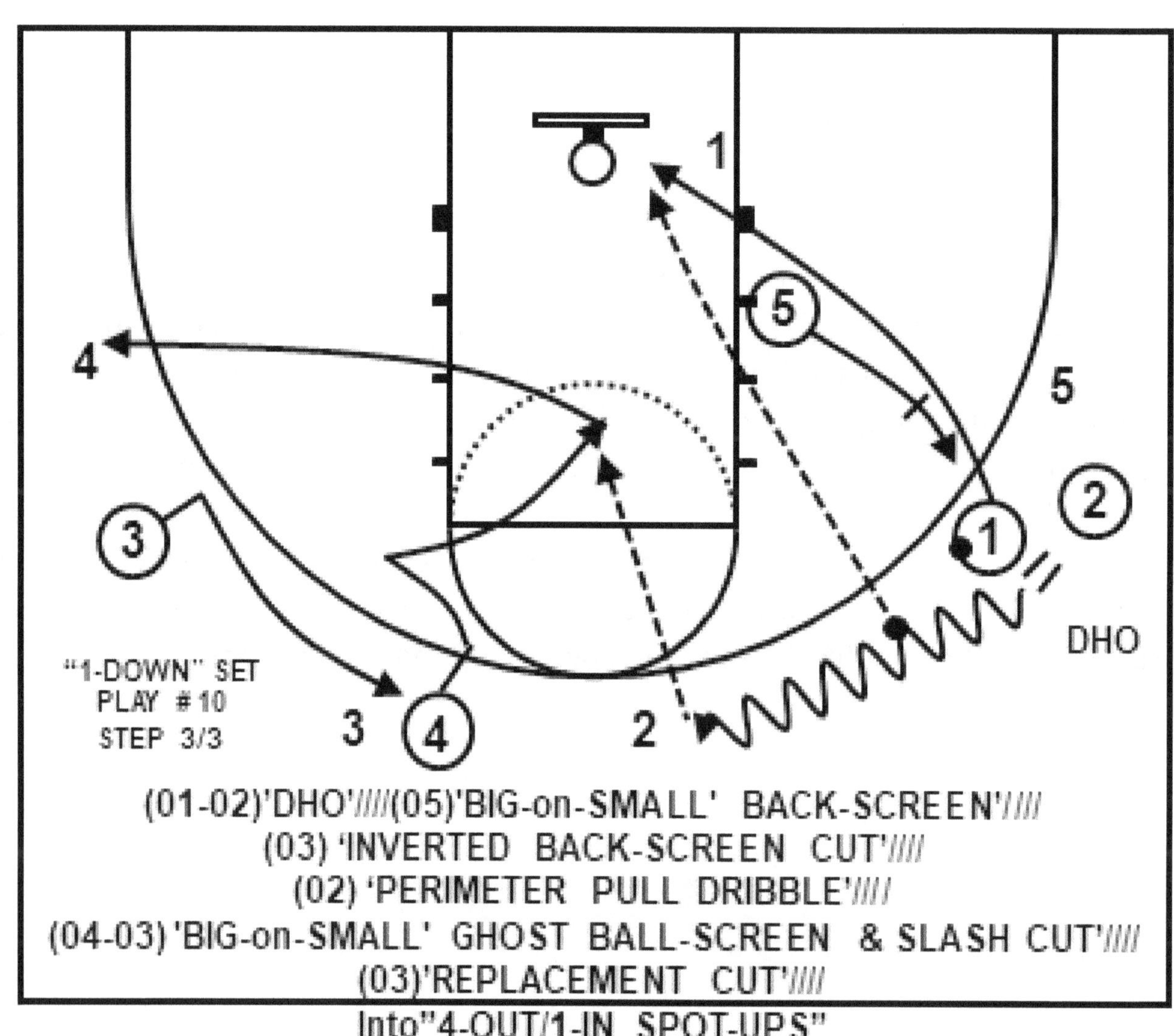

Diagram 10.26

Play # 11 in Diagram 10.27 has 02 bring the ball down the floor before reversing the ball to 01 (and the side of the floor where 05 starts.) Upon 01 receiving the ball, 05 again steps into the lane to execute his "Iso Duck-In Cut." 02 immediately scrapes off of 04's outside left shoulder to execute his "Flare-Cut" to the new "Weakside Wing." If 01 elects not to make the "Inside Pass" to 05, the "Skip Pass" to 02 on his "Flare-Cut" or to 04 on his "Slip Cut;" 01 makes the "Wing Pass" to 03. After making the "Wing Pass" to 03, 01 immediately cuts towards 03 to receive 03's "Flip Pass" or "Pass Hand-Off." See Diagram 10.27

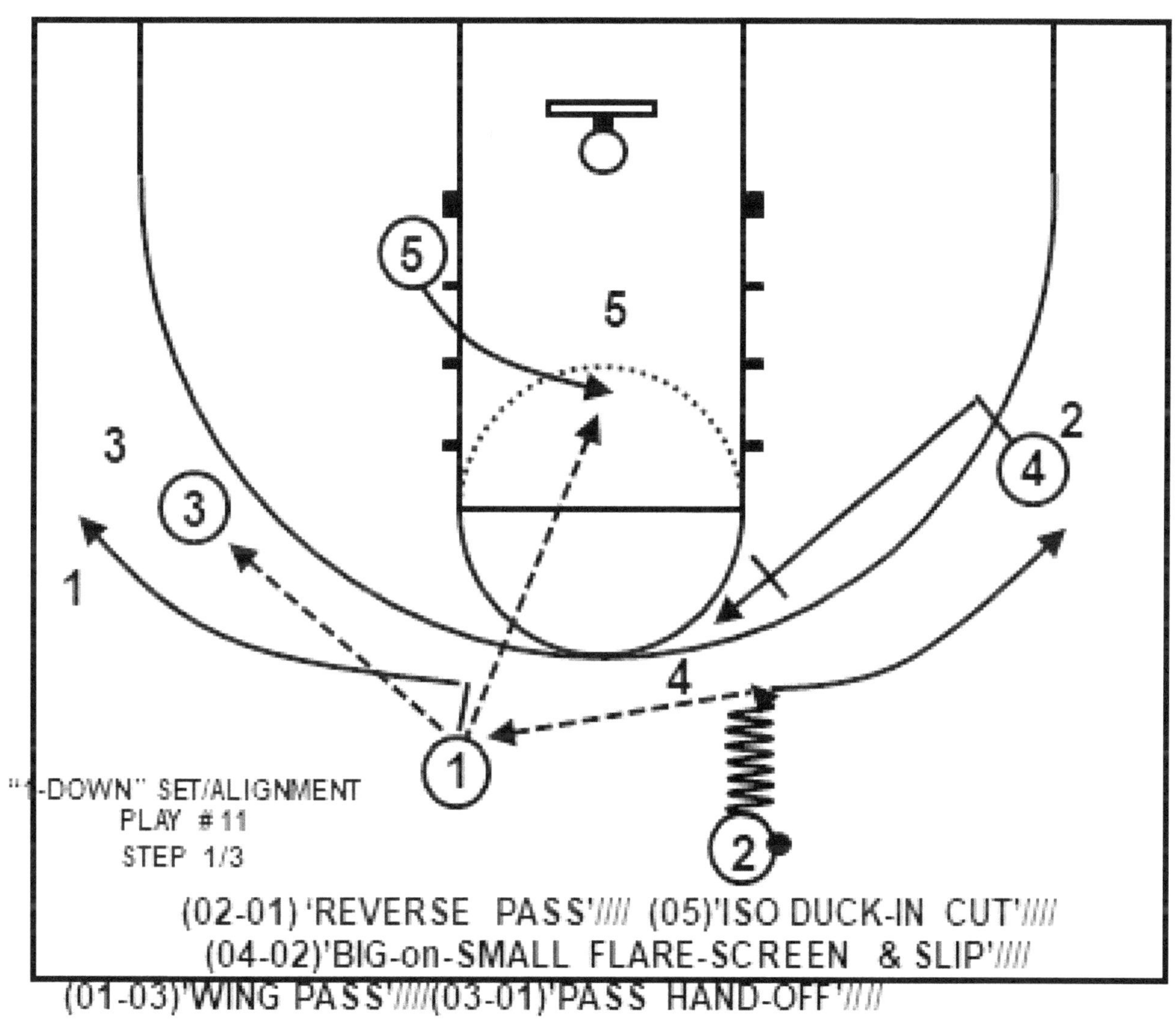

Play # 11   Diagram 10.27

Diagram 10.28 shows 01's cut towards 03 and at the same time, 05 steps up and out to set a (05-04) "Big-on-Small Shuffle Back-Screen" for 04 to use to make his "Inverted and Isolated Slash Shuffle Back-Screen Cut." With 04 pulling out his defensive "Big" out on the perimeter, when 05 screens X4; this defender will not have the experience or the skills to successfully defend this type of offensive perimeter screening action. 05 then slips his screen to keep the opponents "Big" defender away from the basket. See Diagram 10.28

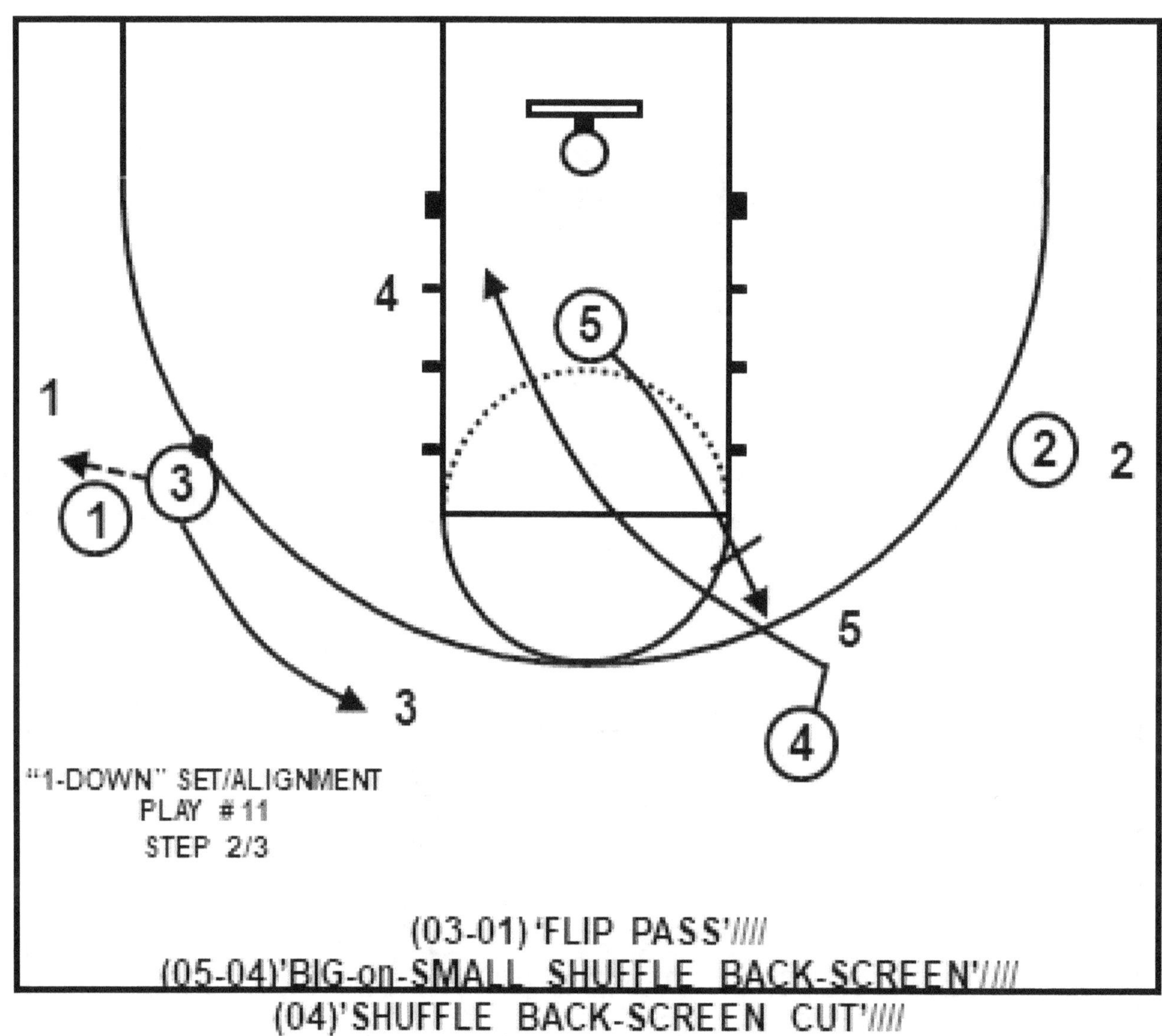

Diagram 10.28

If 01 cannot make the quick "Inside Pass" to 04 on his cut, 01 should make his "Perimeter Pull Dribble" down towards the baseline to look for a better passing angle to deliver the ball to 04, now posting up. 01 could have driving or shooting options. In addition, Play # 11 has moved offensive players into the "4-Out/1-In" Spot-Ups for the next and final phase of the offensive attack. See Diagram 10.29

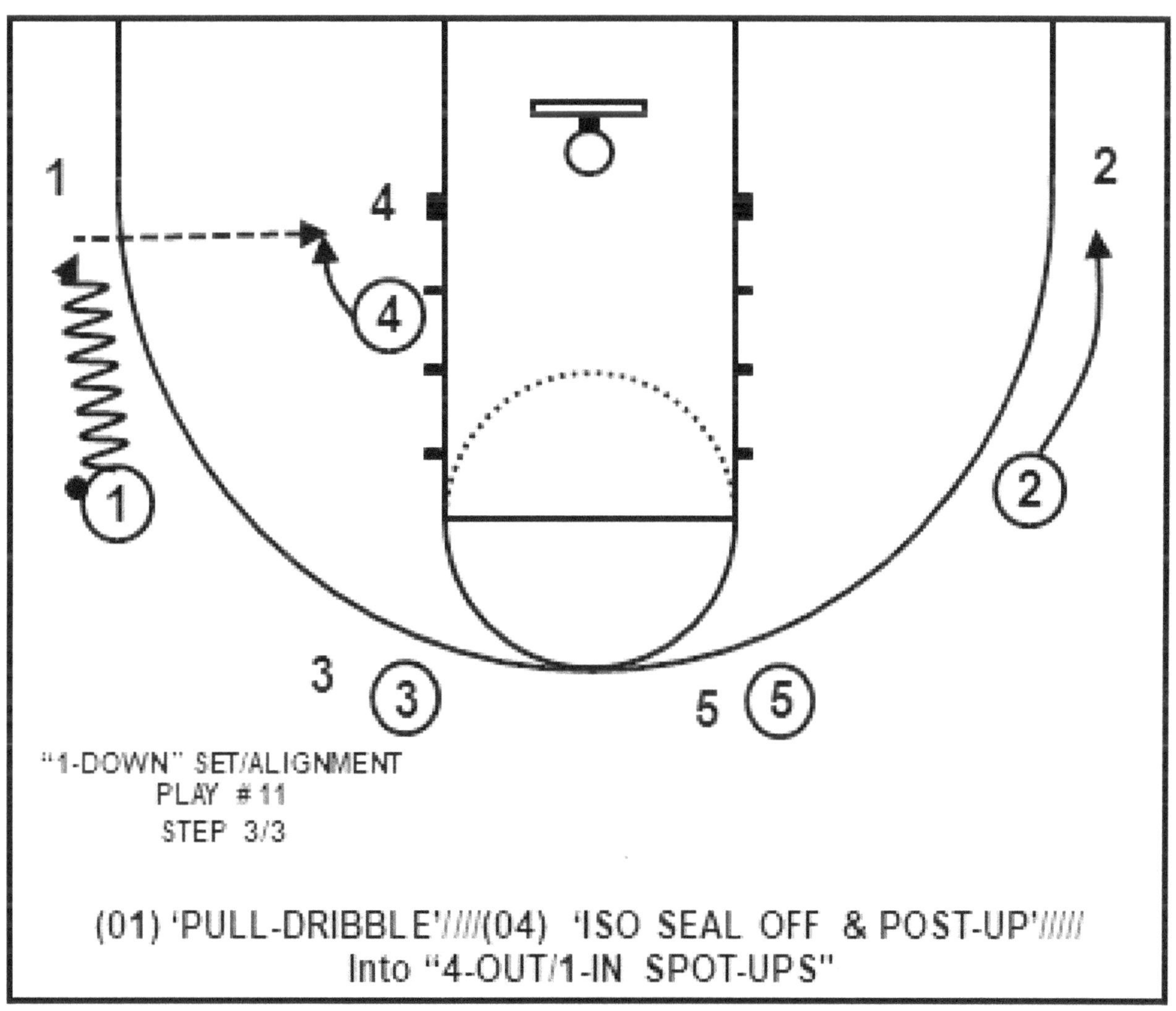

Diagram 10.29

Diagram 10.30 shows the beginning of Play # 12 with 02 first looking and then turning down the "Duck-In Pass" to 05 before then making the (02-03) "Slot Pass" after the two-man action between 01 and 03 (a "Big-on-Small Flare-Screen/Slip" by 03 and a "Flare-Cut" by 01.) 05 "chases the ball" across the lane to make another "Iso Post-Up" on the opposite side of the lane.

After making the pass to 03, 02 also receives a "Big-on-Small Flare-Screen" from 04. 02 rubs his defender off of 04's outside left shoulder and makes his "Flare-Cut" to the new "Weakside Wing" area, all the while "getting his feet and hands ready" for a quick "Catch-and-Shoot Skip Pass" from 03. After screening for 02, 04 slips his screen and steps to the new "Weakside Slot," also ready to receive the ball. See Diagram 10.30

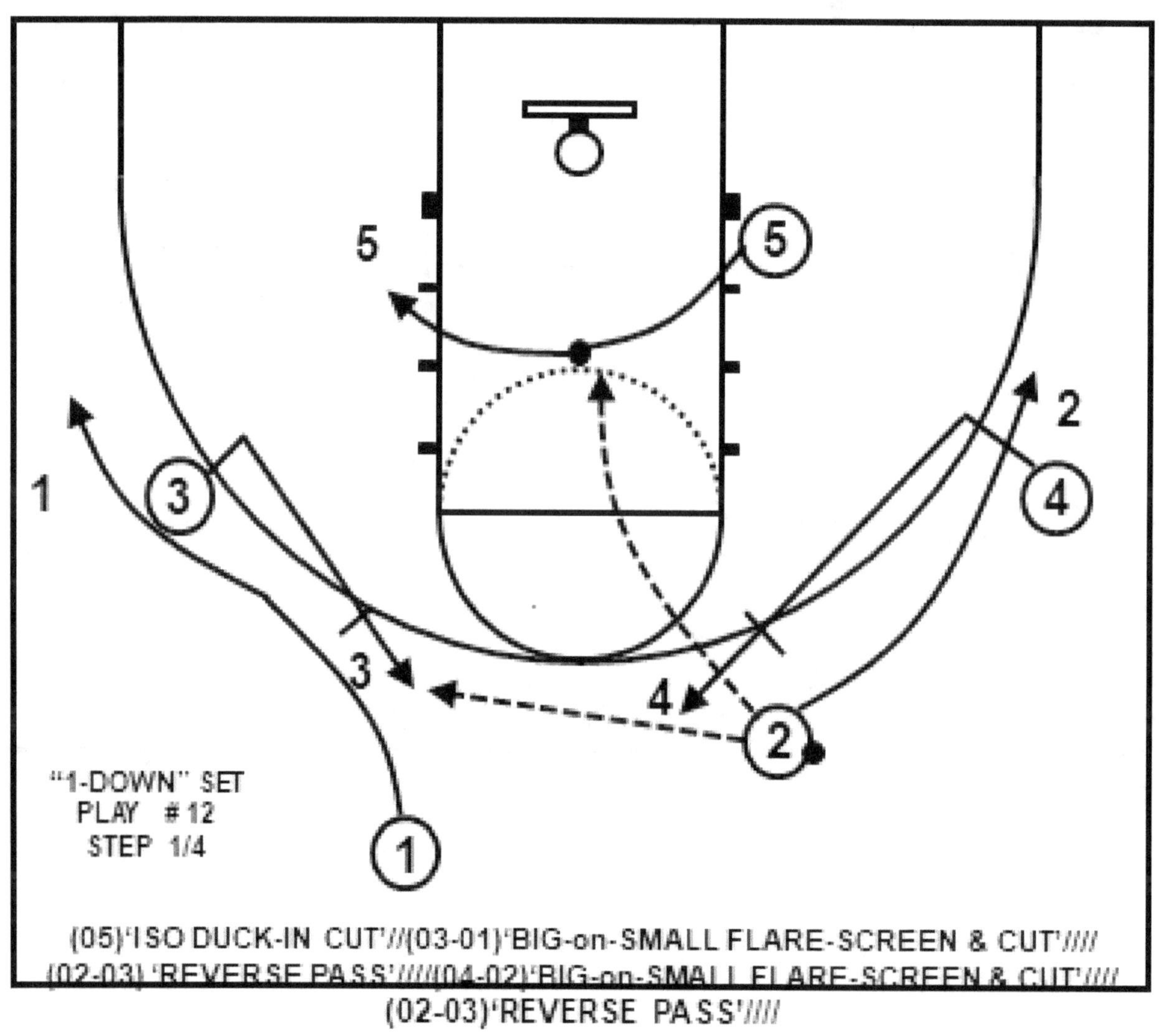

Diagram 10.30

Diagram 10.31 shows 03 turning down passes to both 05 and 01 and simply reversing the ball to 04 (after his "Flare-Screen Slip.") Again, 05 follows the perimeter passes and cuts across the lane to post up on the opposite side of the floor as the ball moves across the floor. 04 then dribbles directly at 02, with 02 setting his defender up for the "Big-on-Small DHO" near the "Wing" area. See Diagram 10.31.

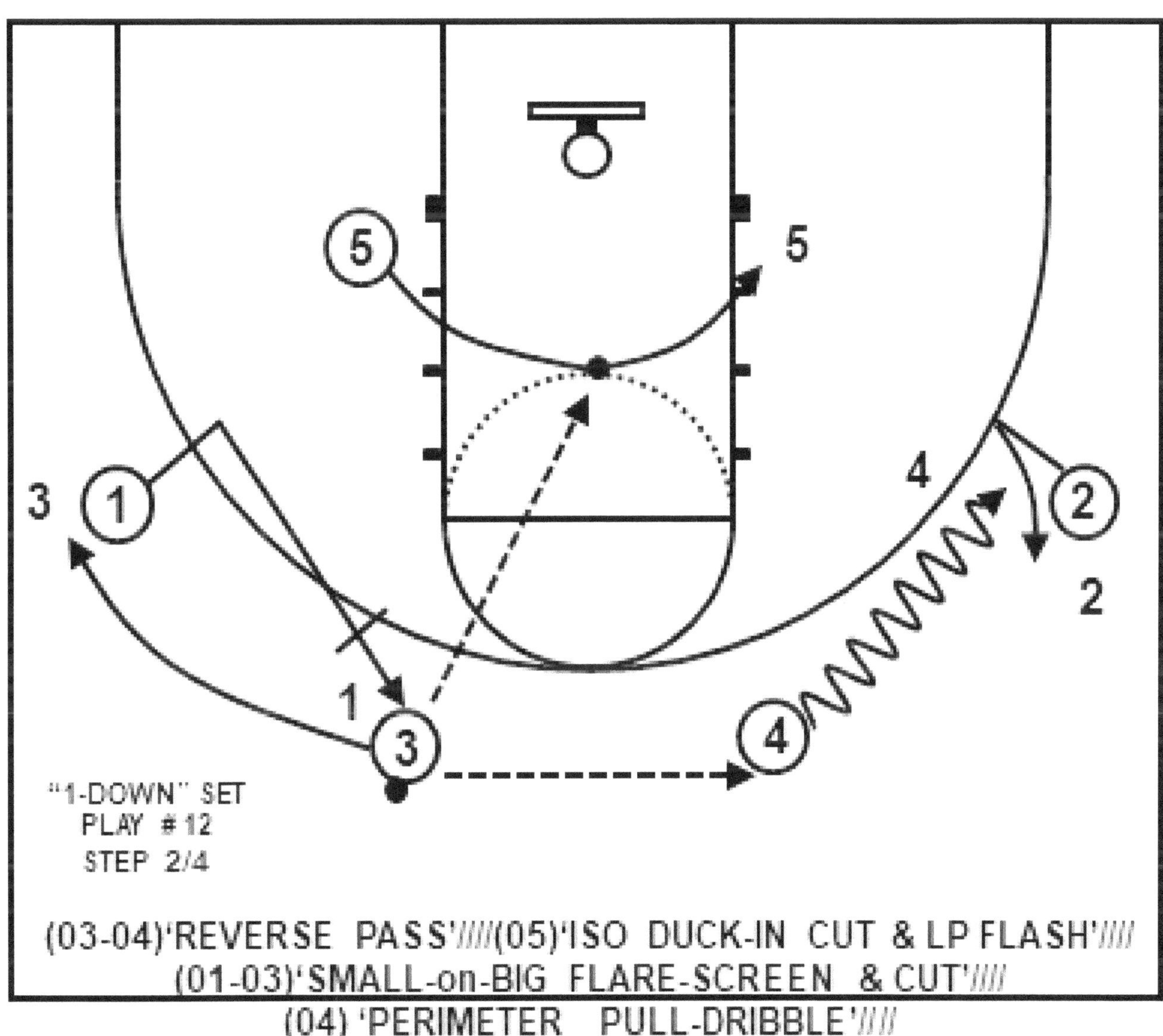

Play # 12   Diagram 10.31

Diagram 10.32 continues the action with 02 receiving the DHO and 04 continuing his cut towards the "Deep Corner." As 02 dribbles out past the "Slot" and towards the top of the key towards his teammates, 03 and 01; 03 steps up as to set another "Flare-Screen" for 01. Instead, 03 breaks off of his screening route to make a hard "Slip" to the basket, looking for the surprise pass from 02. As the "Ghost Flare-Screen is executed by 03, 01 continues his "Flare-Cut" to the "Weakside Wing" (but without the screen.) If 02 does not hit 03 on his "Slash Cut" to the basket or his "Skip Pass" to 01; he maintains his dribble all the way to the "Slot" on the opposite side of the floor. See Diagram 10.32

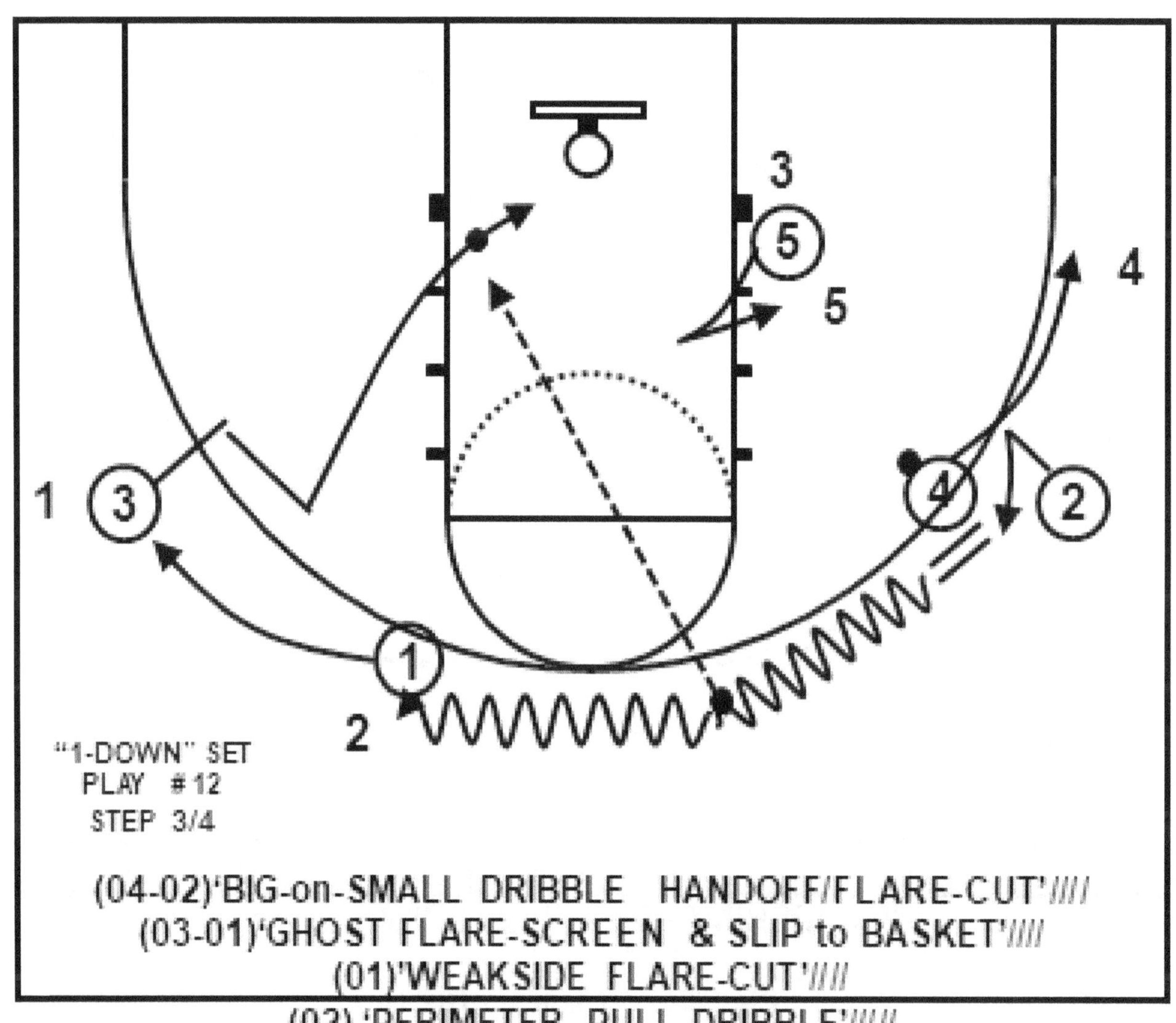

Diagram 10.32

Diagram 10.33 shows the continuation and conclusion of Play # 12 with 02 killing his dribble and waiting for 03 to cross the lane and set a "Small-on-Big Lane Exchange Cross-Screen" for 05 to use (to flash across the lane to post up.) After screening 05's defender, 05 breaks up vertically to the new "Weakside Slot" location. This action further attacks X5 or the switching X3 to give 05 even better opportunities to score.

If shots are not taken, the "4-Out/1-In" Spot-Ups are properly filled so that the designated continuity offense or the designated Motion(-type) offense can smoothly and instantly begin. See Diagram 10.33.

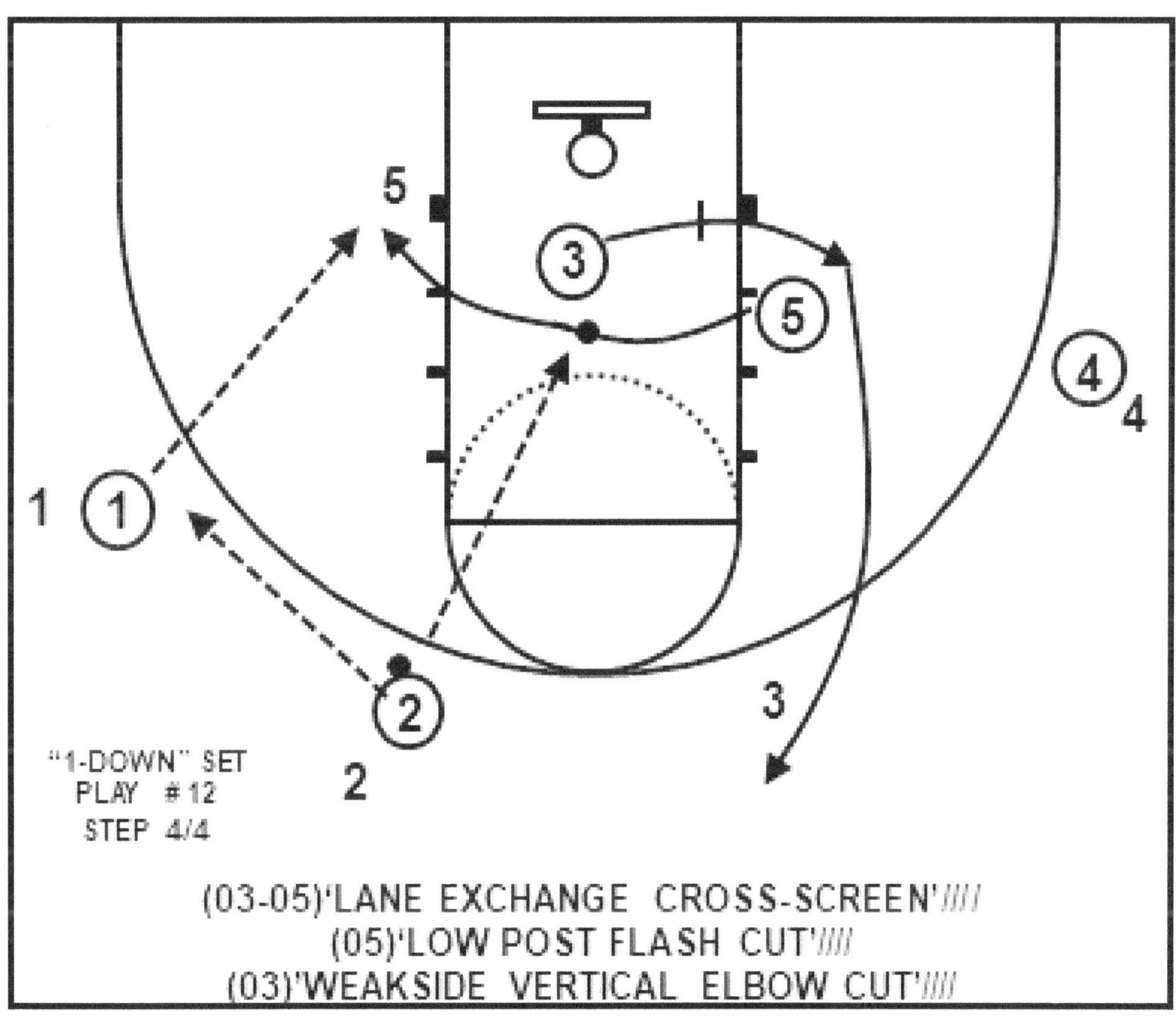

Play # 12   Diagram 10.33

Play # 13 in Diagram 10.34 demonstrates 01 turning down the "Inside Pass" on 05's "Iso Duck-In Cut" and instead, reversing the ball to 02. 04 immediately steps up to set a "Big-on-Small Ball-Screen at the "Slot," while 05 continues across the lane to the new "Ballside Block" area. See Diagram 10.34

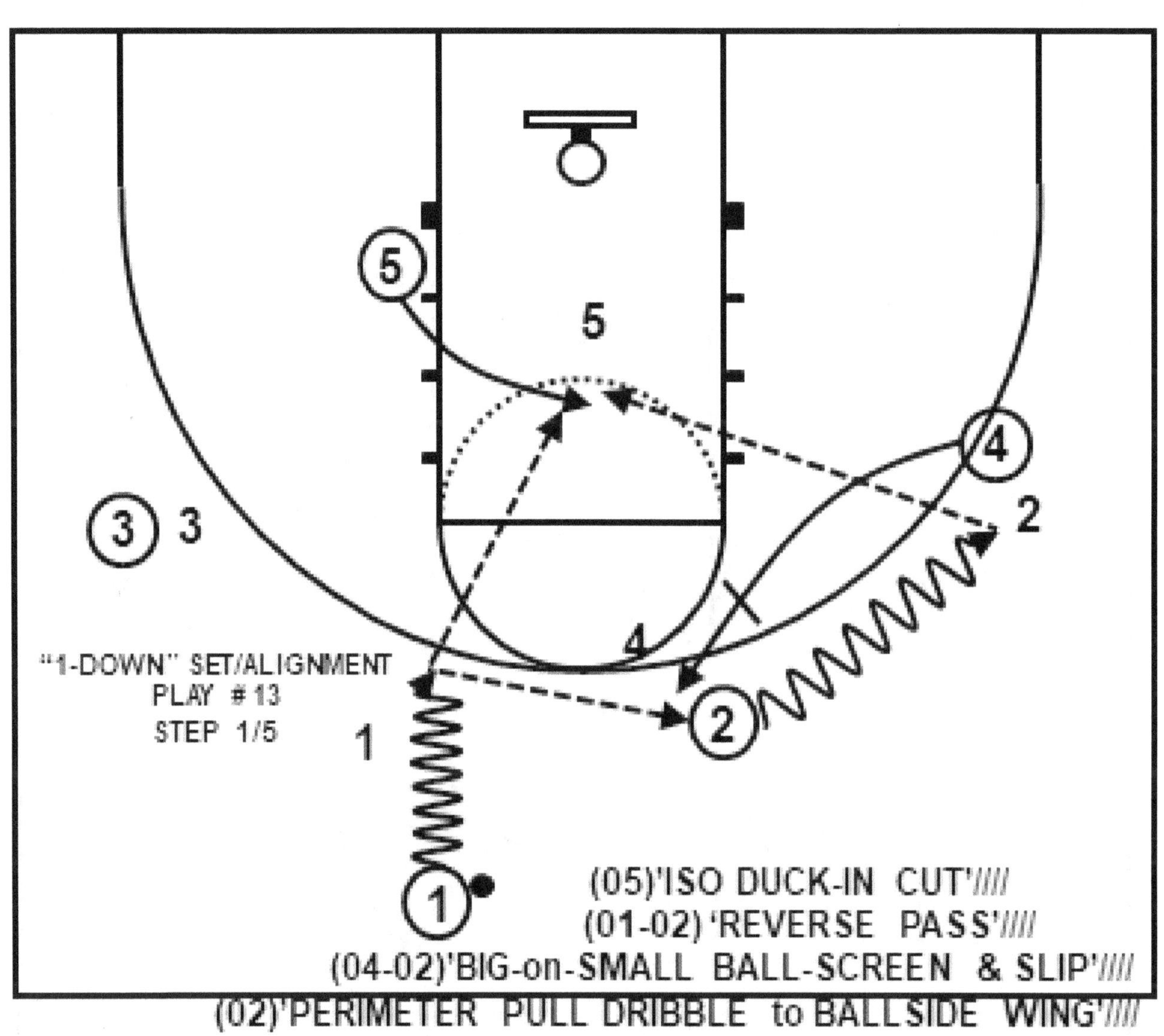

Play # 13   Diagram 10.34

If 02 continues his dribble (to improve his passing angle to 05) and does not hit 05 on his "Iso Post-Up," he should make a "Throwback Up-Pass" to 04. 04 immediately reverses the ball to 01 and quickly follows his pass with a "Big-on-Small Follow(-the Pass) Screen. 01 uses the screen by dribbling back towards the right side of the floor, while 04 continues across the floor to then set a "Big-on-Small Pin Down-Screen" for 03 to use. On 01's "Perimeter Pull Dribble," he looks to make another "Duck-In Cut Pass" to 05. With 04 screening for 03, the defensive weakside is fully occupied so that X5 is once again "on an island, trying to defend his man completely by himself. See Diagram 10.35

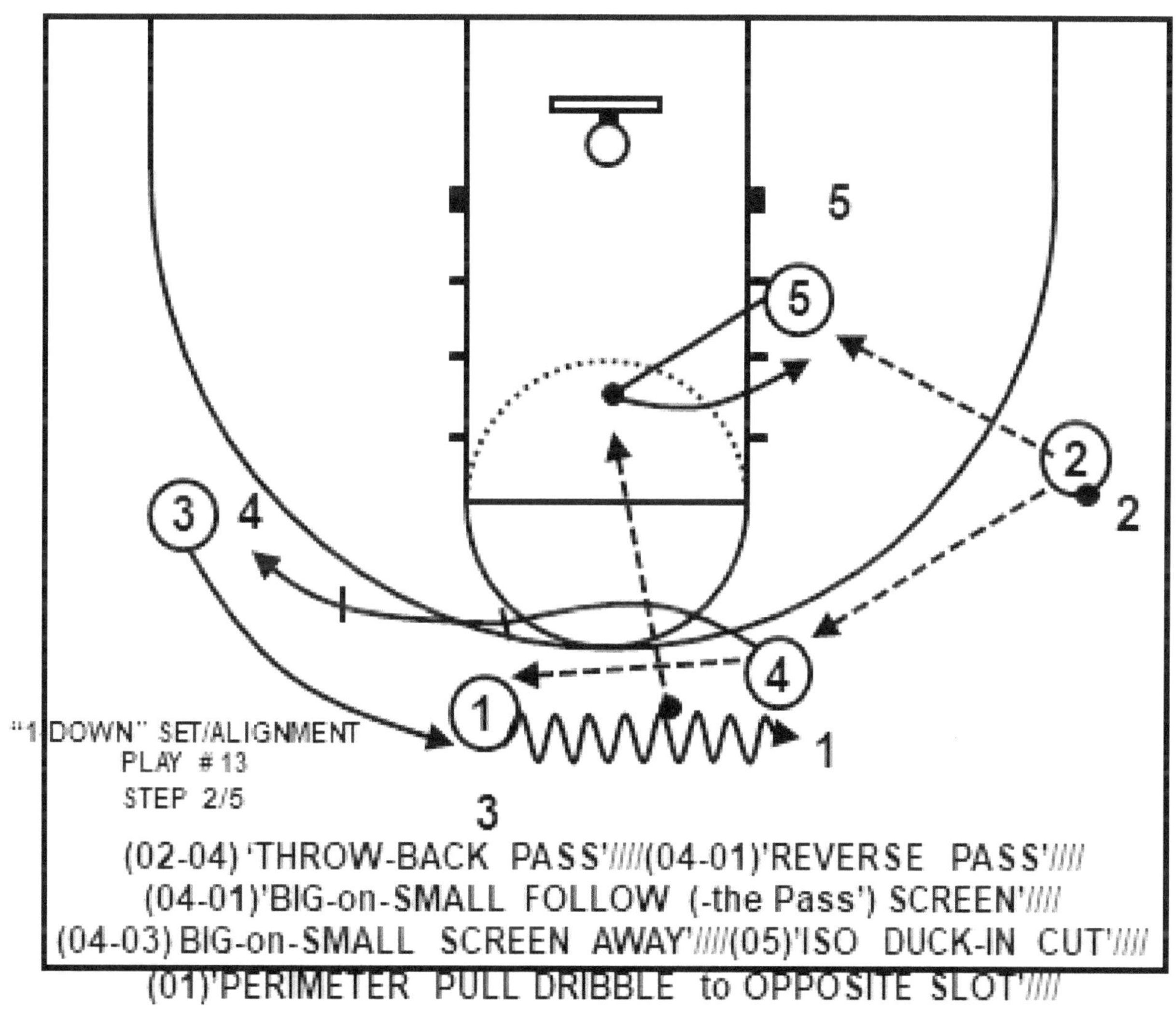

Diagram 10.35

If 01 does not make the pass to 05, 05 empties out to the opposite side of the floor while 01 continues his dribble towards 02. See Diagram 10.36

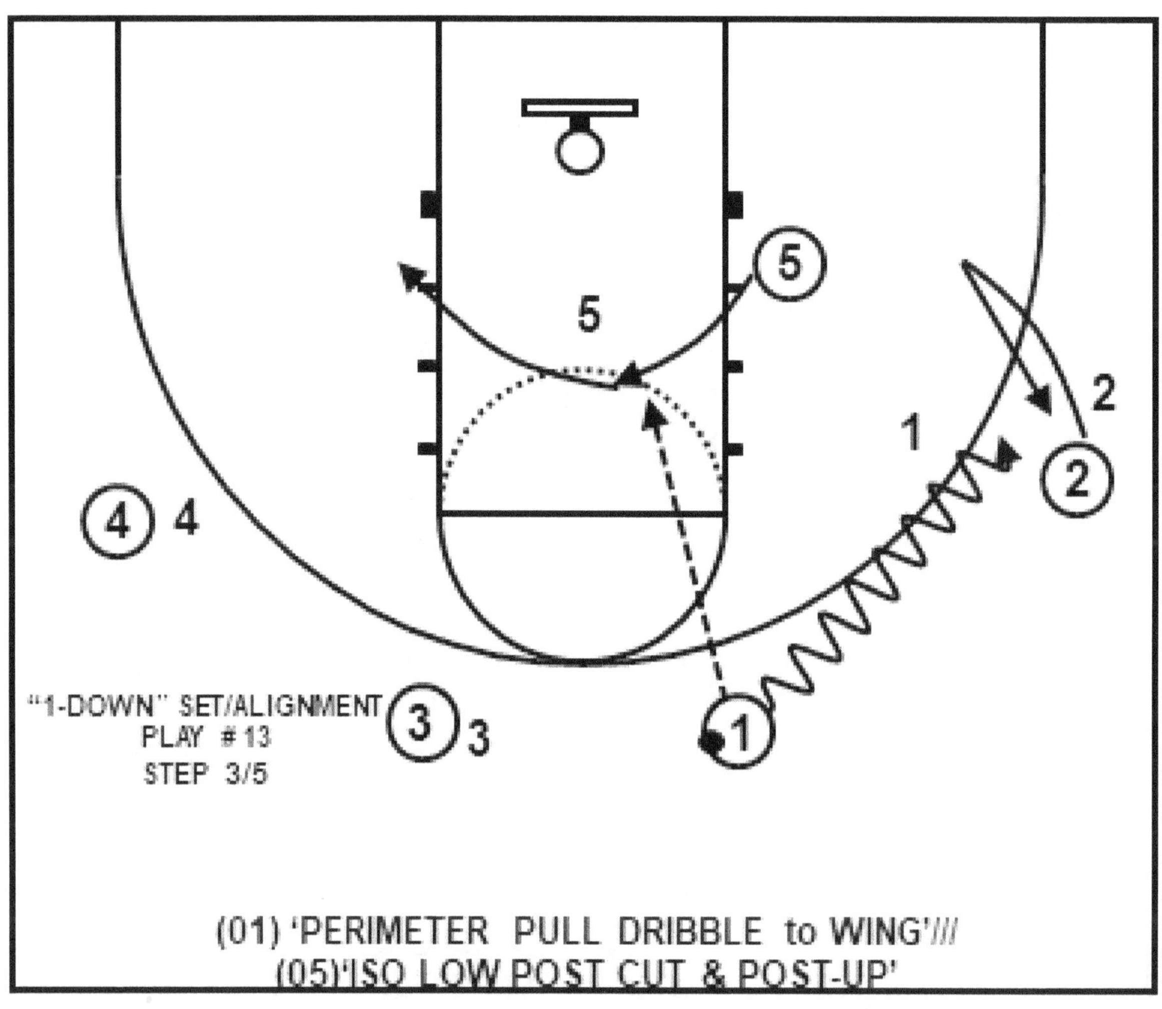

Diagram 10.36

Diagram 10.37 shows 01 making the "Small-on-Big Dribble Hand-Off with 02 and 05 again attacking his isolated defender by another "Duck-In Cut" from the weakside of the lane. If 02 cannot make the pass to 05, he continues towards the top of the key. See Diagram 10.37.

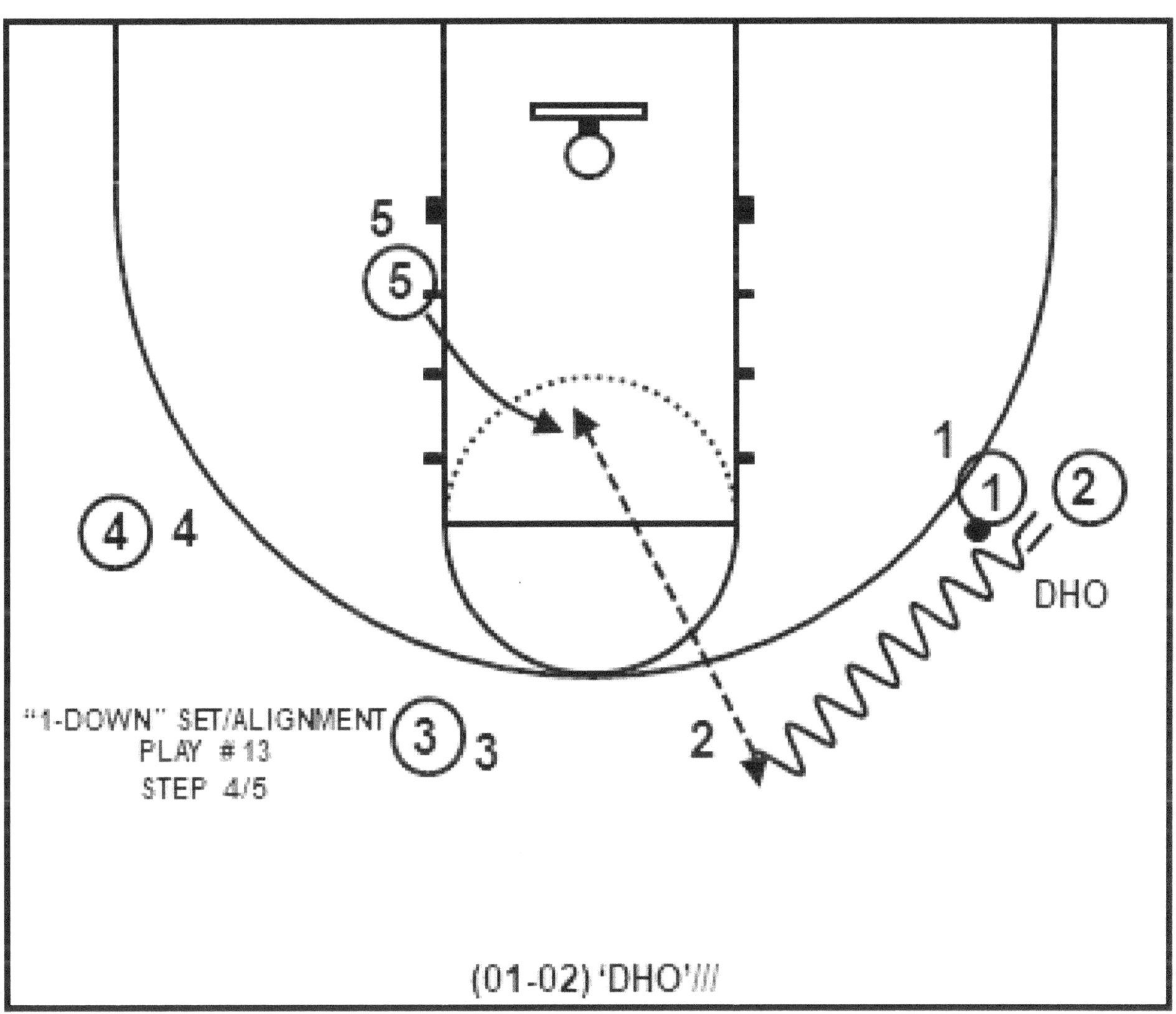

Diagram 10.37

If 05 does not receive the ball from 02, 05 continues his cut towards 02 and the ball to set a "Big-on-Small Long Ball-Screen" at the top of the key. As 02 "dribble-scrapes" off of 05's top right shoulder, 05 then "front pivots" off of his lower left foot and makes his "Rim-Run" to the basket to receive 02's "Lob Pass." 04 diagonally dives to the empty "Block" on his side of the floor and 03 "Flare-Cuts" to the "Deep Corner" while 02 makes his "Perimeter Pull Dribble" towards the opposite side's "Slot." If the wide range of shots from various players from the various locations are not taken, the "4-Out/1-In" Spot-Ups are filled for a smooth and instant transition from this high "Level 3" play into the continuity offense. See Diagram 10.38

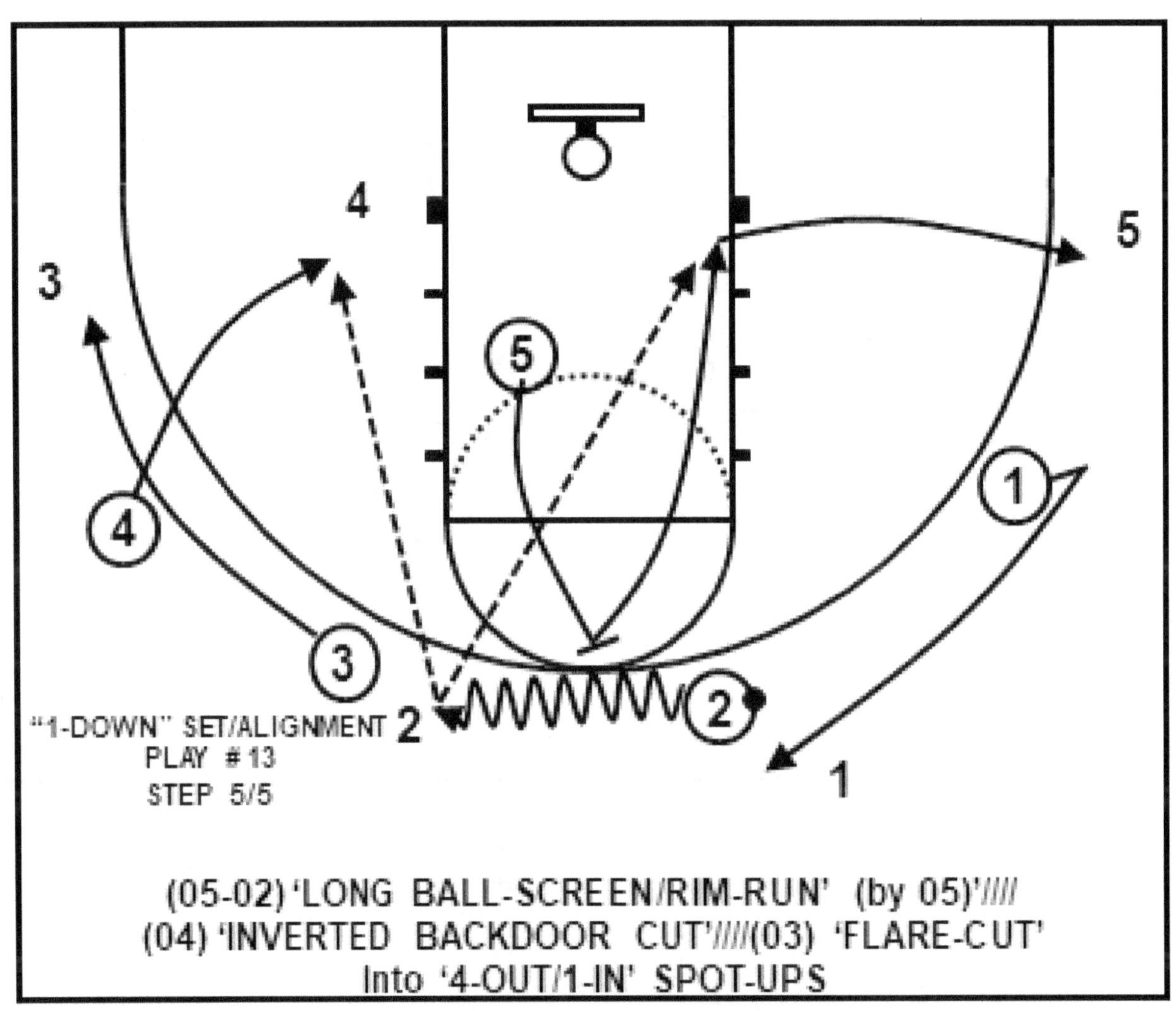

Diagram 10.38

Diagram 10.39 shows the beginning of another sophisticated "Level 3" play with 04 stepping up to set a "Big-on-Small Ball-Screen" near the "Slot." After "dribble-scraping off" of 04's outside left shoulder, 02 looks for 05 to make a slightly different cut—a short "Lob Cut" to the basket. If not open, 05 steps back to the same side to "Iso Post-up his defender. This action not only could give 05 a post-type short "Backdoor Cut" for a quick score, but also then help to set up future "Duck-In Cuts" towards the Dotted Circle area. See Diagram 10.39

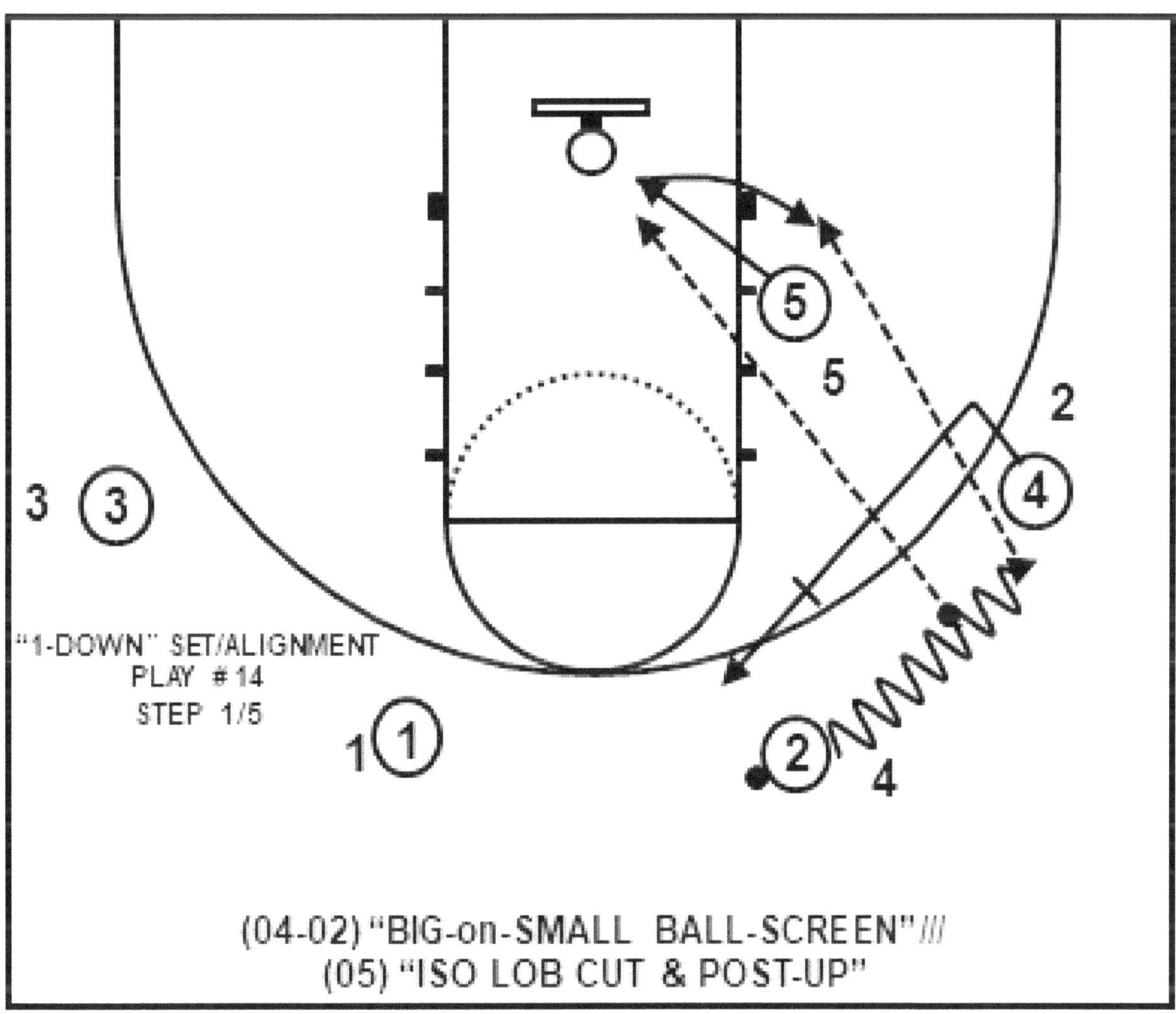

Play # 14   Diagram 10.39

Diagram 10.40 shows 02 turning down the "Inside Pass" to 05 and instead, making a "Throwback Up Pass" out to 04, spotted up at the "Slot." As the ball reaches 04, 05 makes his "Iso Duck-In Cut" into the "Dotted Circle" area. 05 continues across the lane if he does not receive 04's pass. See Diagram 10. 40.

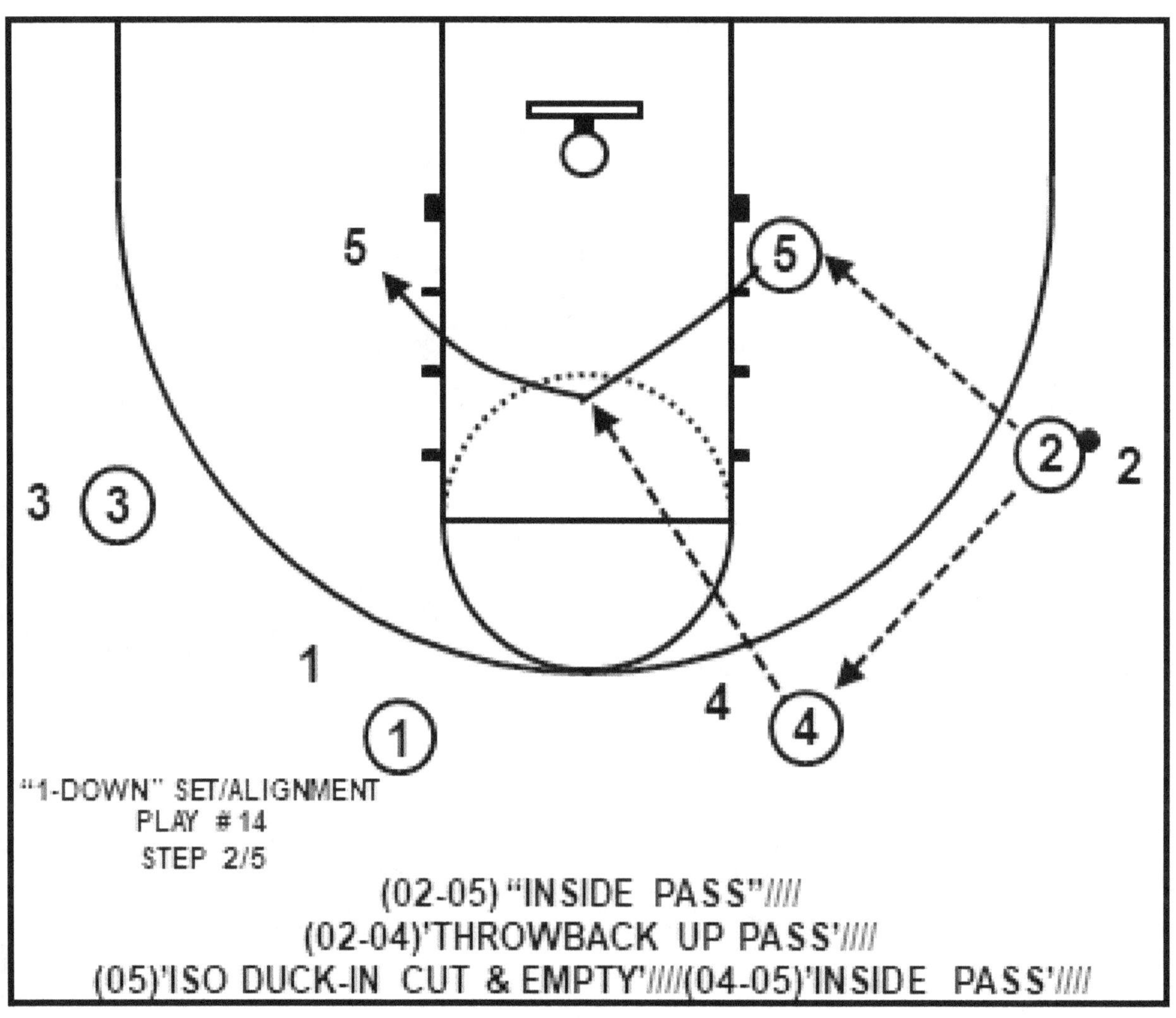

Diagram 10.40

Diagram 10.41 now shows 04 turning down the pass to 05 and instead starting his "Perimeter Pull Dribble" across the top of the key towards 01. 05 makes another "Duck-In Cut" into the middle of the lane, looking for the ball. (He then returns home if he does not receive the ball.)

At the same time, 01 sets his defender up with a "V-Cut" before then changing directions to receive the "Big-on-Small Dribble Hand-Off" from 04 out at the top of the key. After the DHO, 04 continues to set a "Big-on-Small Pin Down-Screen" for 03 to use to break up to the nearest "Slot." 01 now continues across the top of the key towards 02 on the opposite side of the floor. See Diagram 10.41

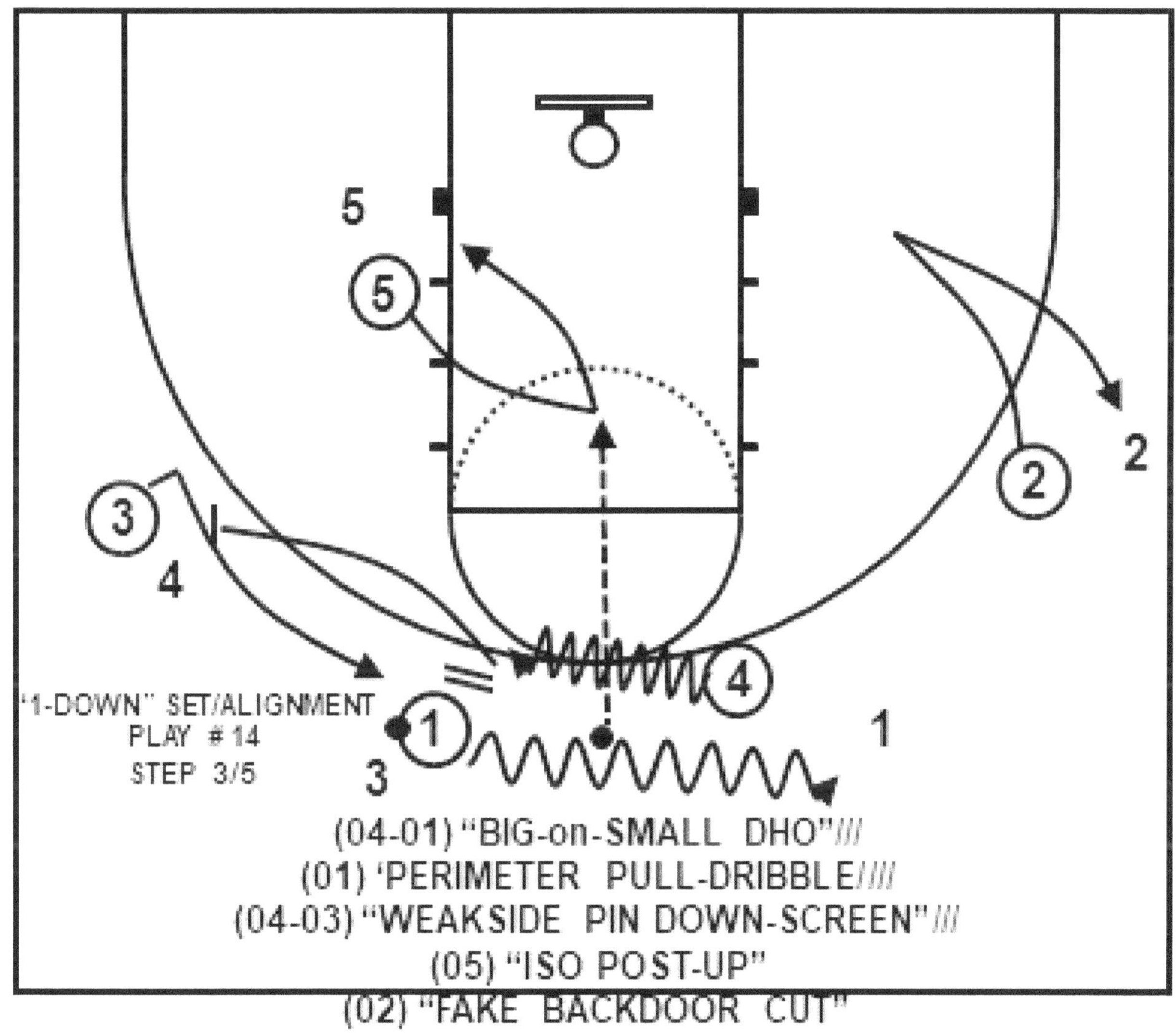

Diagram 10.41

195

Diagram 10.42 illustrates 01 dribbling directly at 02 before then making a short "Pass Hand-Off" to 02. 02 then dribbles up towards the new "Ballside Slot" and 05 continues cutting towards 02. See Diagram 10.42

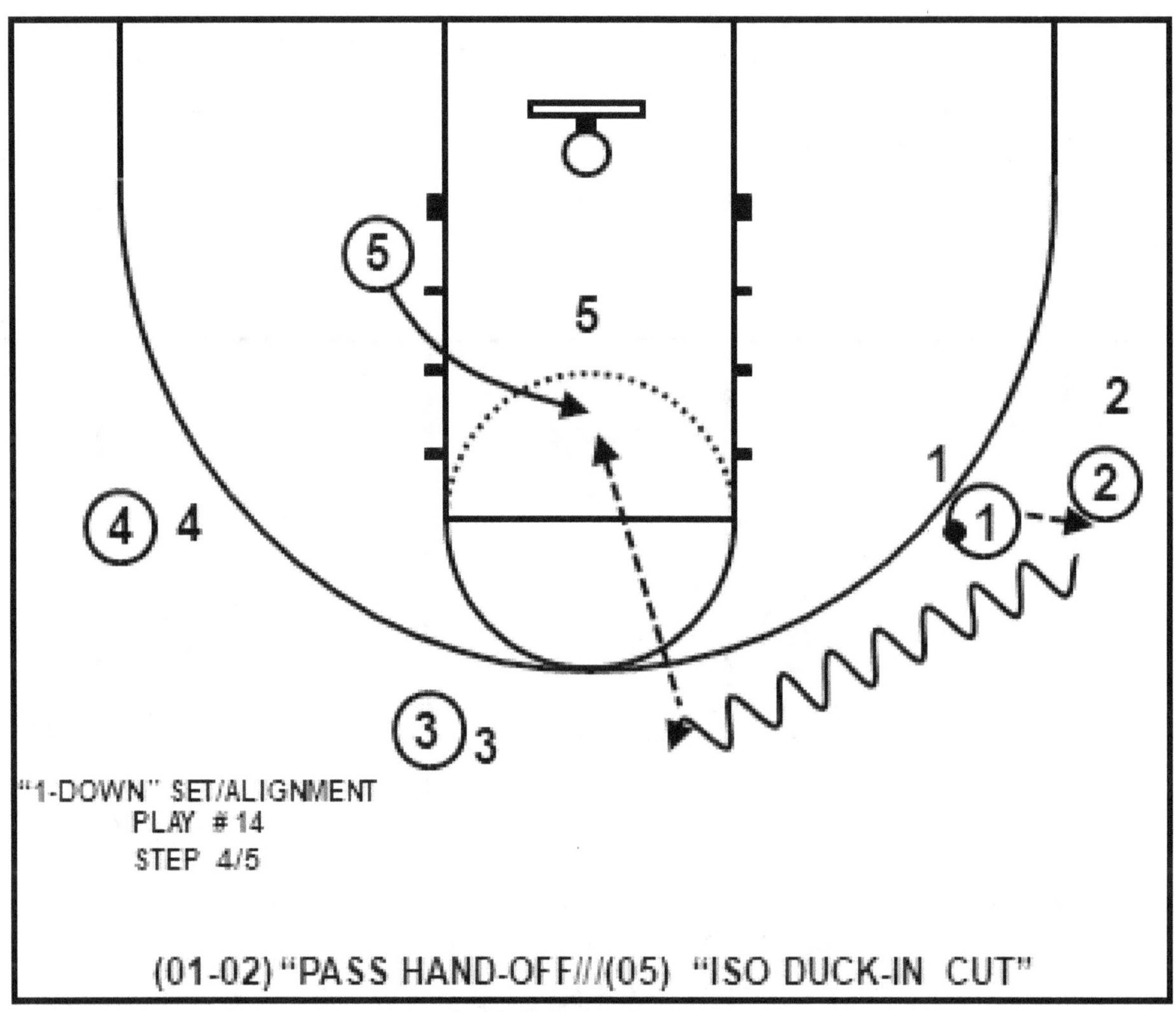

Diagram 10.42

05 steps out of the lane to set a "Big-on-Small Long Pistols Ball-Screen" for 02 to use to dribble towards 03 located at the opposite side's "Slot." This action is similar to Play #17, but in this play the "Long Ball-Screener" (05) does not "Rim-Run," but actually opens up to the dribbler and the ball and "Rolls" through the lane while looking for an "Inside Pass from either 02 or from 04, now in the wide "Deep Corner." 03 circles behind 02 for a "Fake Dribble Hand-Off." Both 01 and 04 have made "Flare-Cuts" to their respective "Deep Corners." This action gives the offense two additional shooting and passing threats as well as stretching the defensive interior by eliminating interior support defense.

The "4-Out/1-In" Spot-Ups are once again filled for another smooth and fluid conversion from this "Level 3" play immediately into the designated continuity offense. See Diagram 10.43

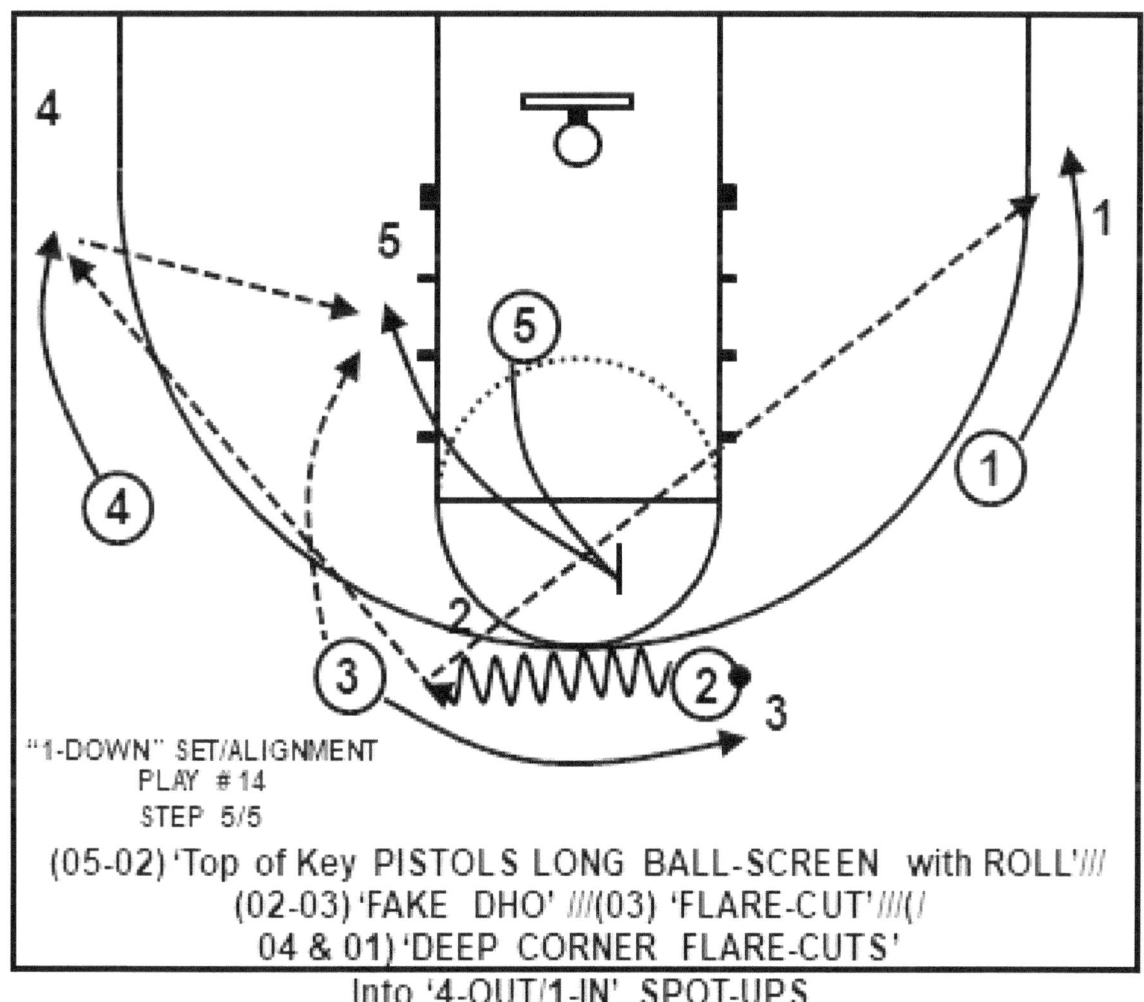

Diagram 10.43

PLAYS/ENTRIES THAT END in

the "HIGH-POST/LOW POST" OFFENSIVE SPOT-UPS

The main difference in this family of plays plays/entries is that all five players will end up in a different group of offensive spot-ups. These "HIGH-POST/LOW-POST" Spot-Ups will have players moved about the court with any of the five ending up in the "Ballside Block," the "Ballside High Post," the "Ballside Wing," the "Weakside Wing," and the "Point" (or top of the key)" These five positions can provide the offense with safe and easy types of ball-reversals, large gaps for dribble penetration, opportunities to deliver the ball inside to whomever (perimeter-type or post-type players) is posting up their defender on the "Ballside Block" or the "Ballside High Post." In addition, the offensive spot-ups can provide a player that can be a perimeter-scoring threat and a legitimate offensive rebounding threat from outside of the arc on his "offensive crashing of the boards" from the Weakside of the floor. The "HIGH-POST/LOW-POST" Spot-Ups also provide ample opportunities for constant and effective defensive transition responsibilities.

Diagram 10.44 begins Play # 15 started out of the "1-DOWN" Set with 01 reversing the ball to 02 and slashing to the new "Ballside High Post" area while 04 steps up to set a "Big-on-Small Ball-Screen" near the "Ballside Slot" area. After screening for 02, 04 then diagonally cuts down to set his second screen-a "Small-on-Big" Diagonal Screen" for 05 to break up to the top of the key. After his second screen, 04 seals his defender and flashes back to the new "Ballside Block."

At the same time, 03 steps up as if to set a "Flare-Screen" possibly for 01 and the "Flare-Cuts" back to his initial "Weakside Wing" area. 03's action helps occupy any support defense that X3 could possibly give. This action therefore places 04 and 01 in isolated post-up locations, 04 on the "Ballside Block" and 01 at the "Ballside High Post." Both 04 and 01 will have advantages with 01 also having a "perimeter-type" opponent trying to defend him a "post-type" location.

If 02 cannot make "Inside Passes" to either 04 or 01 and chooses not to make a "Skip Pass" to 03, this "Level 1" play is quickly over and players are now in their "High-Post/Low-Post" Spot-Ups for a different continuity offense to smoothly begin. See Diagram 10.44

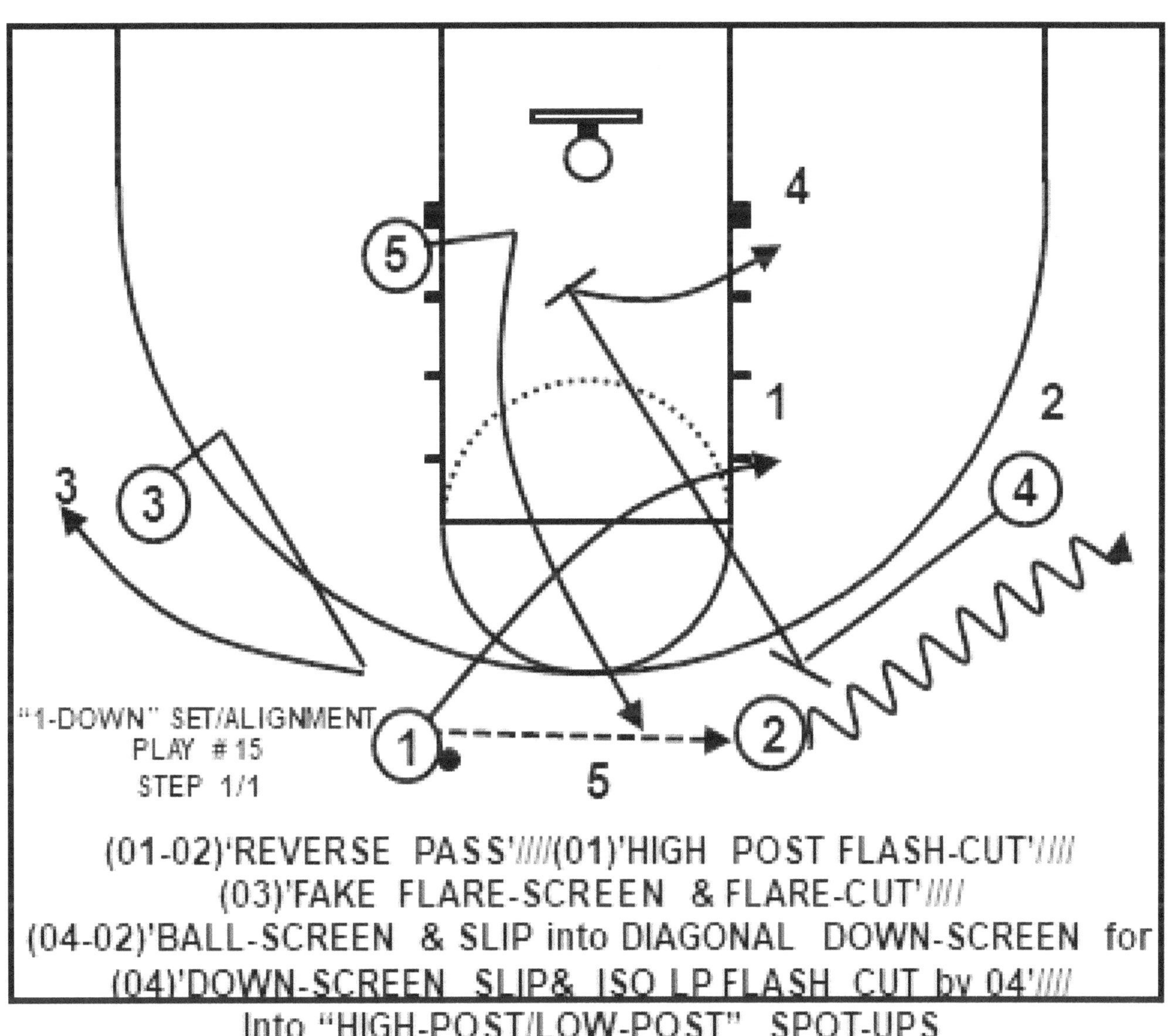

Play # 15   Diagram 10.44

Diagram 10.45 begins Play # 16 with 01 reversing the ball to 02 and 02 then making the quick (02-04) "Wing Pass. 01 makes his "Flare-Cut" to the new "Weakside Wing" that is vacant because 03 is now the player that fakes stepping up to the "Slot" and now becoming the player that flashes to the new "Ballside High Post" area (instead of 01 as in Play # 19). After making the (02-04) "Wing Pass," 02 is the players that breaks down to set the "Small-on-Big" Diagonal Down-Screen for 05 to use to break to the top of the key. After screening X5, 02 seals off his defender and flashes back to the new "Ballside Block," becoming an "inverted and isolated post-up player (as a perimeter-type player against a perimeter-type defender, X2.)

This movement therefore places 02 and 03 in isolated post-up locations, 02 on the "Ballside Block" and 03 at the "Ballside Elbow." Both players will have advantages with each having "perimeter-type" opponents trying to defend them in "post-type" locations.

If 04 cannot make "Inside Passes" to either 02 or 03 and also chooses not to make a "Skip Pass" to 01, the "High-Post/Low-Post" Spot-Ups are filled for the designated continuity offense to immediately start with the next pass that is made. See Diagram 10.45

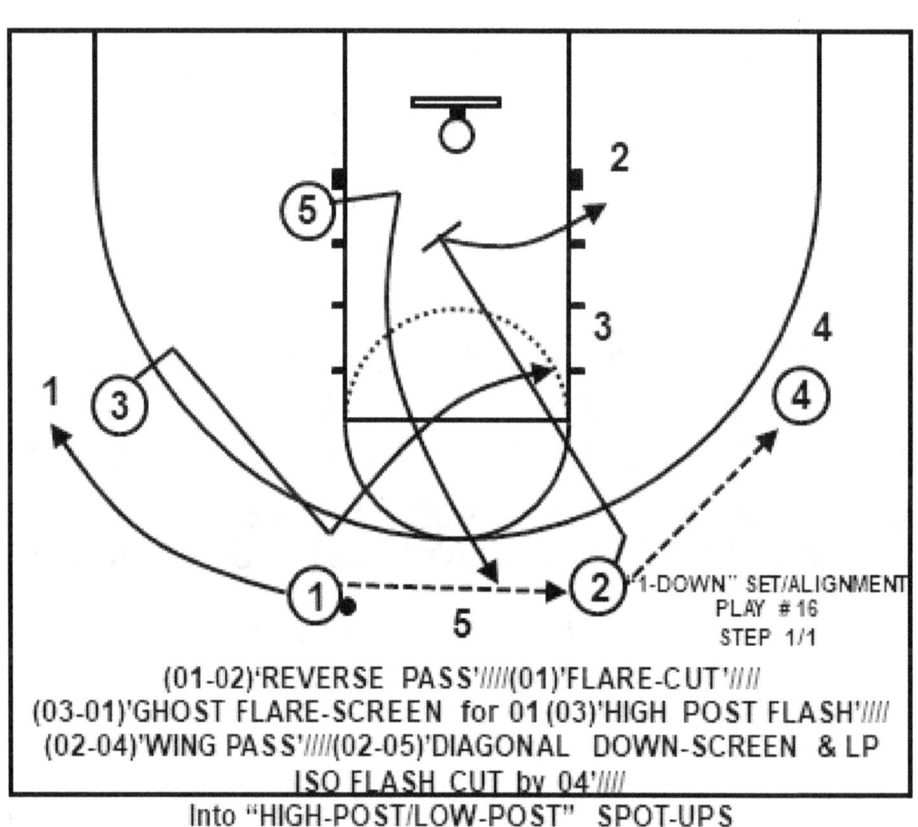

Play # 16   Diagram 10.45

Diagram 10.46 illustrates another quick-hitter (Play # 17(where 05 first begins the play with an "Iso Lob-Cut" directly to the basket. If not open, 05 turns back to break through the lane towards the ball. 02 then makes the "Reverse Pass" to 01, with 05 cutting towards and near the "Nail."

After passing the ball to 03, 01 cuts towards the opposite side of the floor to set a "Brush Screen" for 02 to make a "Brush Cut" off of 01 and continue on to scrape off of 05's outside right shoulder. 02 continues his "Shuffle-Cut" to post his perimeter-type defender in the "Inverted Post-Up" situation on the new "Ballside Block." 02 tries to rub his defender off by also "scraping off of 05's right shoulder" and then looks for the "Inside Pass" from 03. 02 continues his "Shuffle Cut" all the way to the new "Ballside Block" and posts up his perimeter-type defender.

After screening for 02 and receiving the screen from 05, 01 also continues in the same direction with his own inverted "Lob Cut" to the basket, looking for a possible (03-01) "Lob Pass" near the rim.

After setting the "Big-on-Small Scissors Shuffle Back-Screens" for both 02 and 01, respectively, 05 flashes to the new "Ballside High Post." For spacing purposes and for "ball-reversal possibilities, 04 inverts his post-type defender, X4, and breaks to the top of the key. More importantly, this action aligns all five players into the proper "High-Post/Low Post" Spot-Ups for the correct continuity offense to smoothly continue attacking the opposition. See Diagram 10.46

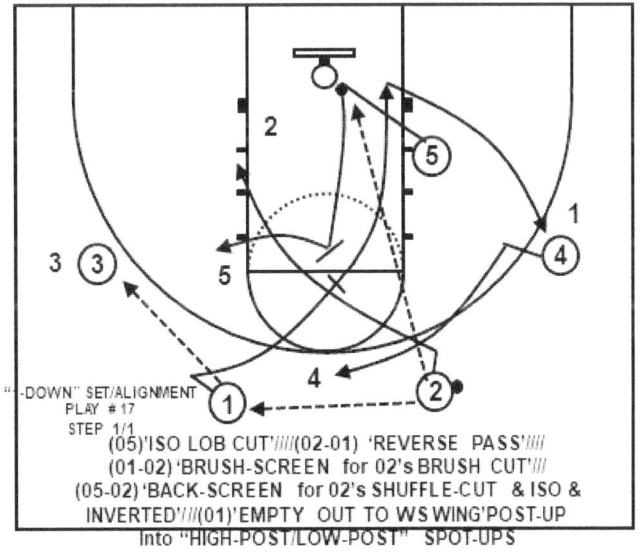

Play # 17   Diagram 10.46

Diagram 10.47 illustrates Play #18 with 05 starting on the offense's left side of the lane and 01 with the responsibilities of crossing the timeline with the dribble. As 01 approaches the "Slot," 05 first makes a "Lob Cut" to the basket and looks for a "Lob Pass" from 01. If not open, 05 then reverses direction to make a strong "Duck-In Cut" into the middle of the lane. If still not open, 01 veers off and dribbles towards 03. 03 fakes the "Small-on-Big DHO and continues to the "Slot" while 01 continues his dribble to the "Wing." 01 looks to make the "Inside Pass" to 05 on his return to the "Ballside Block." If not open, 01 makes the quick "Throwback Up-Pass" to 03. At the same time, 04 steps up and over to set a "Big-on-Small Flare-Screen" for 02 to use to make his "Flare-Cut" to the "Weakside Wing." 04 then slips his screen and steps to the "Slot." This diagram then shows 03 making the "Reverse Pass" to 04 at the new "Weakside Slot." See Diagram 10.47

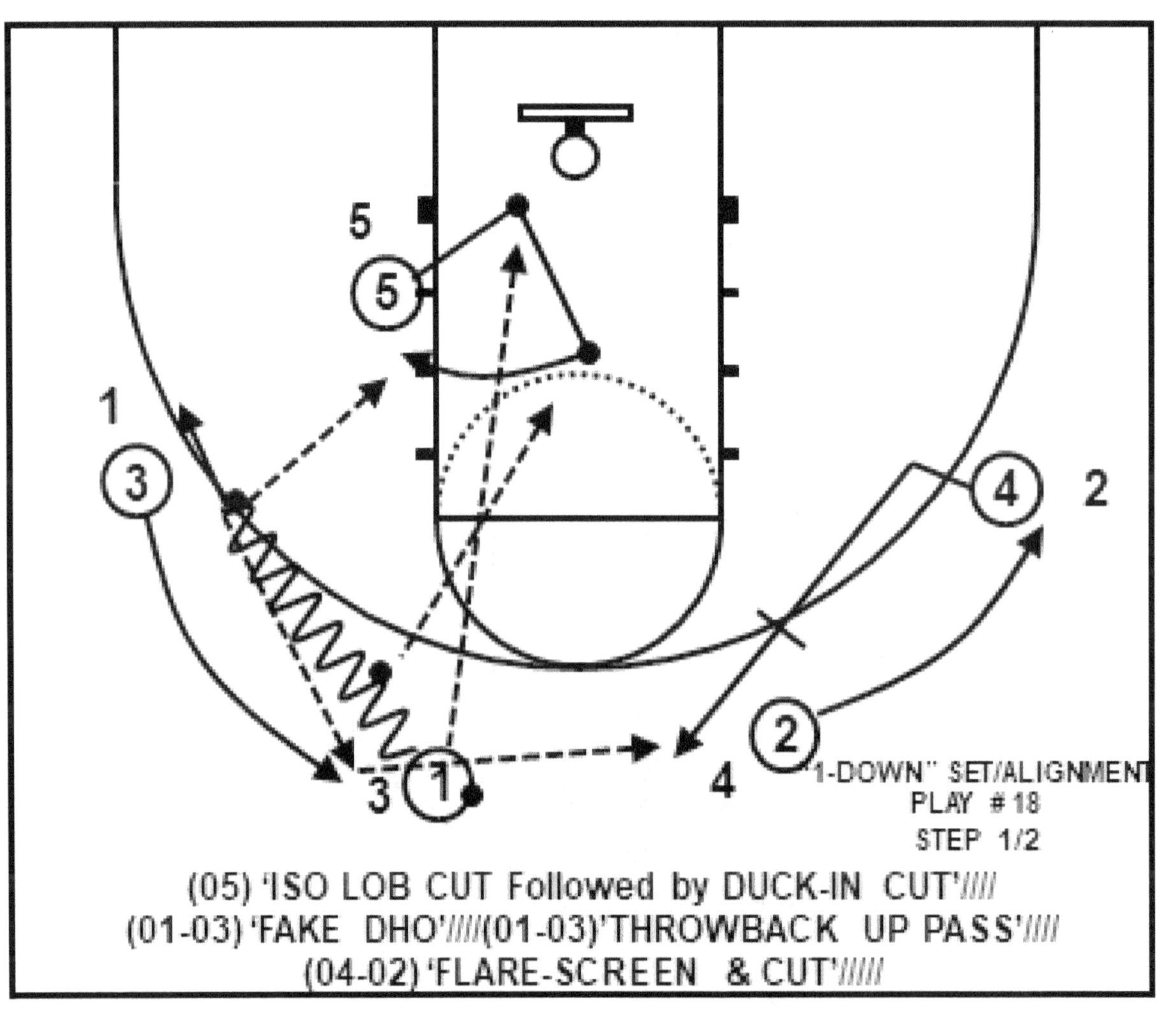

Play # 18   Diagram 10.47

Diagram 10.48 After 04 makes his pass, 03 immediately sets a "Big-on-Small Pin Down-Screen" for 01 to get open at the top of the key. At the same time, 04 diagonally cuts down to set a "Small-on-Big Diagonal Down-Screen" for 05 to use to flash to the new "Ballside High Post" area, while 04 then (swims with a front pivot or gets into X5 and reverse pivots) seals off an opponent and flashes to the new Ballside Mid-Post. If 02 cannot deliver "Inside Passes" to either 04 or 05, a "Skip Pass" to 03 or a "Reverse Pass to 01 should be available. The "High-Post/Low-Post" Spot-ups are filled for that specific continuity offense to immediately begin. See Diagram 10.48

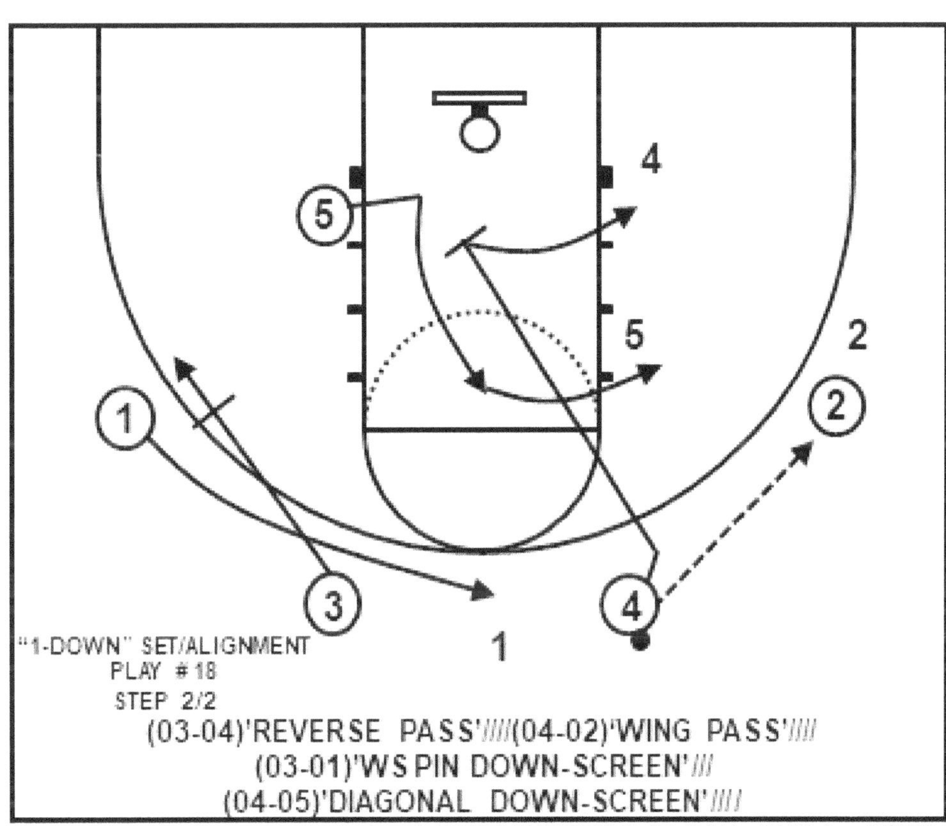

Diagram 10.48

CLOSING

These entries/plays are a group of entries all executed out of the "1-DOWN" set and they include all three levels of skills. Therefore, any coach of any level of completion and age would have the opportunity to take "as is" plays from this chapter or to modify any play to fit his/her needs.

There are many different philosophies on how to attack opposing defenses. This multiple-phase offensive system uses more than one phase/layer/wave of attack, with each phase/wave having a seamless and immediate conversion into the next phase/wave. While this system can be confusing to defenses and difficult to defend, this system can be properly taught and coached so that it can be easily understood and ultimately executed by players of many different levels of (physical talent, mental understand and playing experience.)

In addition, there are several types of offensive schemes and different ways within this system that offenses can attack their defensive counter-parts. Many of these can be integrated within the same offensive system that can attack defenses in various ways. The larger the number of schemes that can be successfully utilized and integrated within the same system, the greater the opportunity an offensive team can find the most efficient and productive schemes that can place both individual and the overall team in the best and most frequent "positions to succeed."

The plays/entries carefully diagrammed down to the small and seemingly unimportant 'V-Cuts' made by countless players before making their more important following cut are also described in detail.

Each play has been carefully studied and evaluated to determine which level of talent and experience must be possessed for that specific team to be able to successfully execute the play. This includes all players' physical skills as well as their mental understanding of the game. Coaches must also have the experience and the associated level of understanding of the game as well as their coaching/teaching of the nuances of each play.

PLAYS/ENTRIES THAT END in the "4-OUT/1-IN" OFFENSIVE SPOT-UPS

The difference in the following plays/entries in this chapter are that all five players will end up in a different group of offensive spot-ups. These "4-Out/1-In Spot-Ups" will have players moved about the court with any of the five ending up in the "Ballside Deep Corner," the "Ballside Slot," the "Weakside Slot," the "Ballside Post," and the "Weakside Deep Corner." These five positions can provide the offense with safe and easy types of ball-reversals, large gaps for dribble penetration, opportunities to deliver the ball inside to whomever (perimeter-type or post-type players) is posting up their defender on the "Ballside Block," and a player that can be a perimeter-scoring threat and a legitimate offensive rebounding threat from outside of the arc on his "offensive crashing of the boards." The "4-Out/1-In Spot-Ups also provide ample opportunities for constant and effective defensive transition responsibilities.

Play # 1, has 01 make the dribble to the FT Line extended, 02 makes the "Pipe Cut" up and out to the "Slot" and 03 rejects the 05-03 Pin Down-Screen and 05 ends up at the same "Weakside Slot." See Diagram 11.1

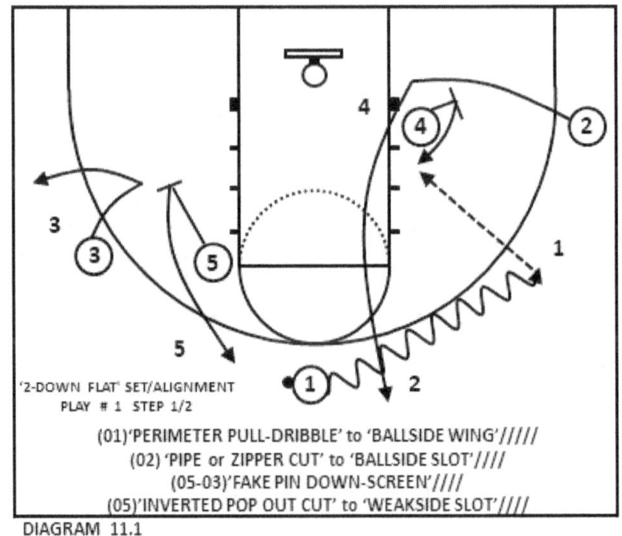

Diagram 11.2 shows 01 turning down the "Inside Pass" to 04 and making the pass out to 02. 05 breaks across the top of the key in the same manner to set the same "Big-on-Small Ball-Screen" for 02 to move the ball to the opposite side of the floor. During the dribble, both 03 and 01 make the same "Drift Cuts" to their respective "Deep Corners." As 02 crosses the imaginary center line and "dribble-scrapes" off of 05's top right shoulder, 04 again flashes across the lane. All the action from every player makes it appear to be the same as other plays that can be executed.

02 breaks contact with 05 and 05 makes a "front pivot" off of his lower left foot to make a "Rim-Run" to the basket. With 04 flashing across the lane and 01 staying wide behind the arc, 05 has plenty of space to make his "Lob Cut" to the rim. This action by 05 is extremely successful when X5 "hard hedges" or "switches" the screen. 02 completes his dribble at the opposite "Slot" and then looks for the same pass receivers in the previous plays. The primary difference in the plays is now 05 is a second interior pass receiver that can be open when and if the defense breaks down or when the defense tries to defend the ball-screen with defensive switches or hard-hedges.

The same "4-Out/1-In Spot-Ups" are filled so that the designated continuity offense can once again smoothly begin on the next pass made by 02. See Diagram 11.2

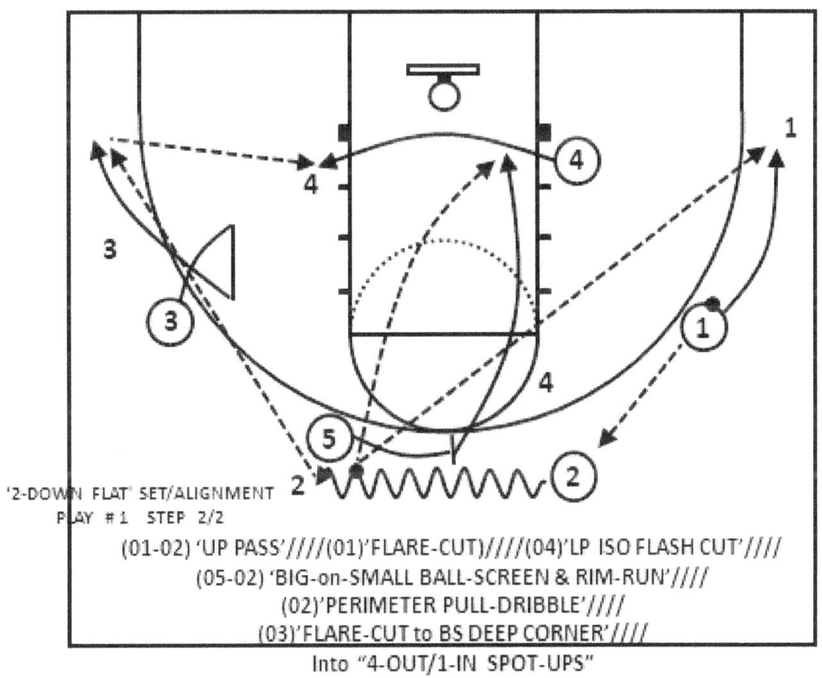

DIAGRAM 11.2

Diagrams 11.3 through 11.5 illustrate Play # 2 with almost identical action of the previous play discussed. Again, 02 runs the baseline until reaching the lane before then making the same "Pipe Cut" vertically up the lane to the new "Ballside Slot." During 02's cut and 01's dribble, 04 again looks to 'shape up' and isolate his defender, X4, down on the newly declared "Ballside Block." 04 should be completely isolated because 05 again sets his "Pin-Screen" for 03, who this time, rejects the screen and returns to the new "Weakside Wing" area and becomes an immediate '3 Pt.' threat off of a likely (01-03) "Skip Pass." After his screen is rejected by 03, 05 pops out to the new "Weakside Slot" and further pulls out the presumed biggest opposing defender further from the basket and 04. See Diagram 11.3

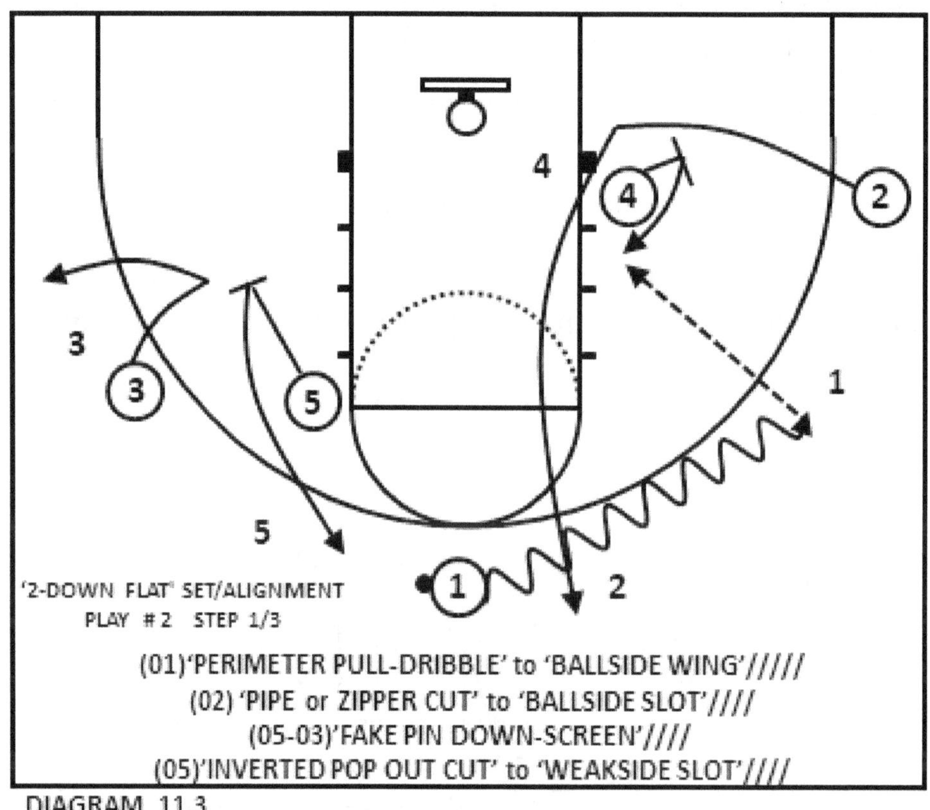

DIAGRAM 11.3

Diagram 11.4 shows the next phase of Play # 2 both 01 and 02 turning down the "Inside Pass" to 04 and the "Skip Pass" to 03 on the weakside. Instead, 01 makes the "Up Pass" to 02 at the "Slot" and 04 again making a hard "Duck-In Cut" into the "Dotted Circle" area.

05 does not come over to screen the ball, but instead breaks away from the ball to go set a "Big-on-Small Pin Down-Screen" for 03 to use to break open at the "Weakside Slot." 05 slips his screen and spots up on the "Weakside Wing" location. See Diagram 11.4

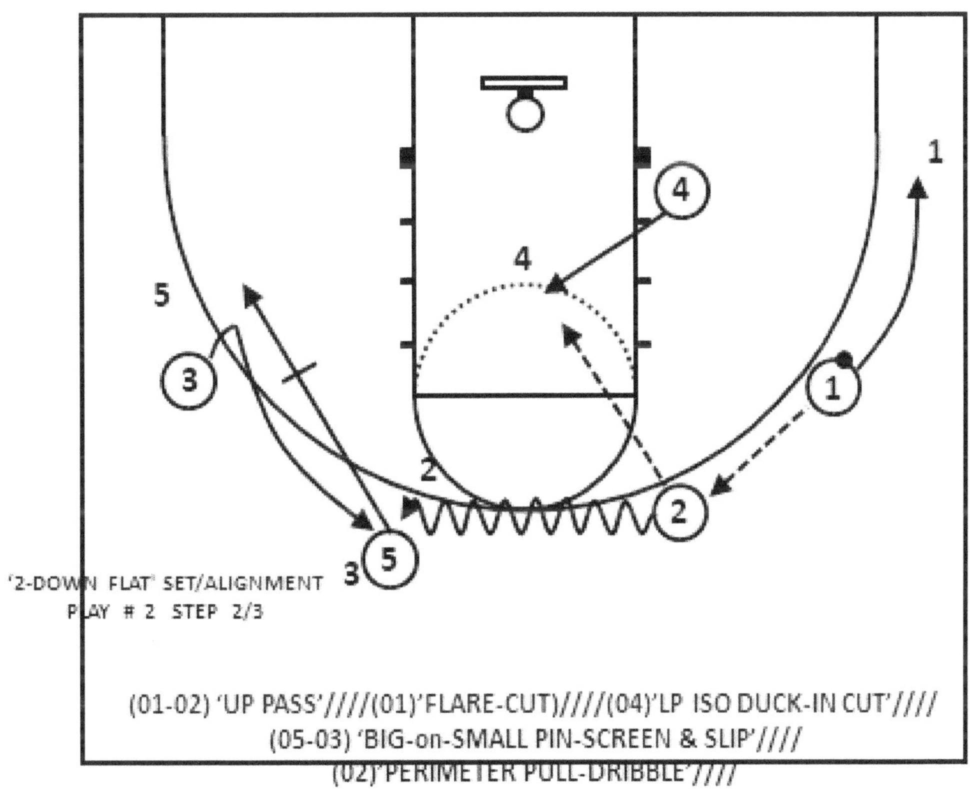

DIAGRAM 11.4

Diagram 11.5 illustrates 03 cutting towards the dribbling 02 to receive a DHO. After handing the ball off to 03, 02 makes a "Flare-Cut" off of 05's "Big-on-Small Flare-Screen." 02 continues his cut towards that side of the floor's "Deep Corner" area. Meanwhile 03 starts his "perimeter pull (drag) dribble" across the top of the key and looks for 04 gaining "position advantage" on his isolated and lone post defender. 01 stays wide and deep on his own side of the floor to further isolate X4 in the paint.

With all four of 04's teammates on the move, all spread out behind various points on the floor behind the arc; each player should have creditable opportunities for "catch and shoot" passes from 02 or "Inside Pass" opportunities for themselves to deliver the ball to 04.

If no shots are taken, the "4-Out/1-In Spot-Ups are filled for a quick transition into the next phase of the offense. See Diagram 11.5

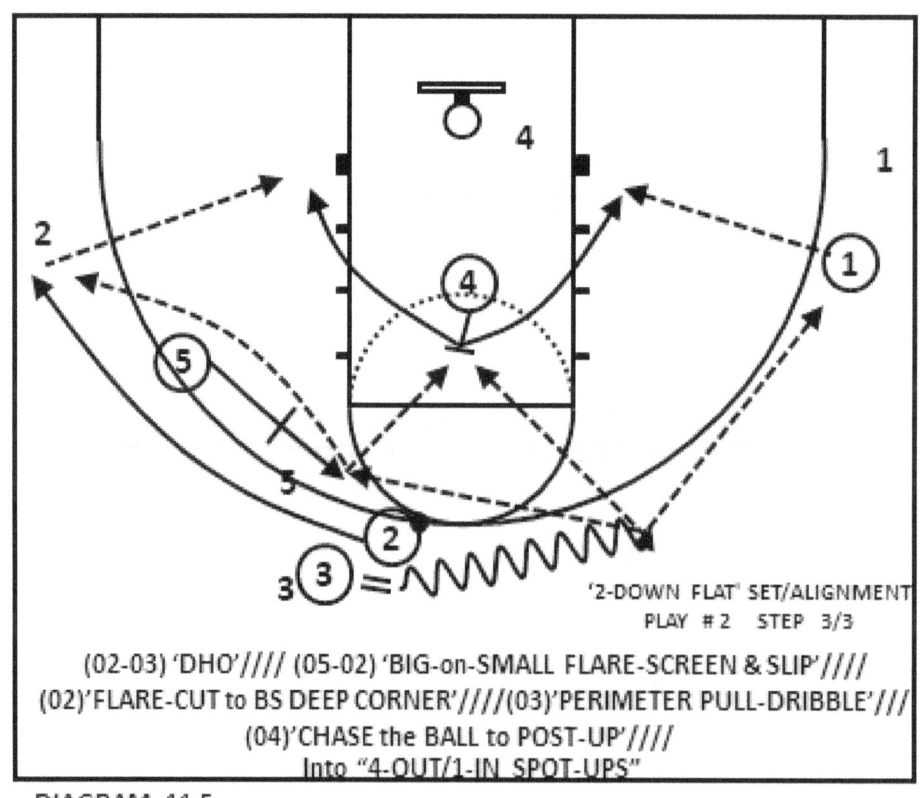

DIAGRAM 11.5

Diagram 11.6 once again repeats the first step of all of the other plays in the "Rejection Screen" family (02's "Pipe Cut," 04's Iso Post-Up, the 05-03 Pin-Screen Rejection and Slip). This fundamentally sound action has legitimate offensive scoring threats that the defense must honor. See Diagram 11.6

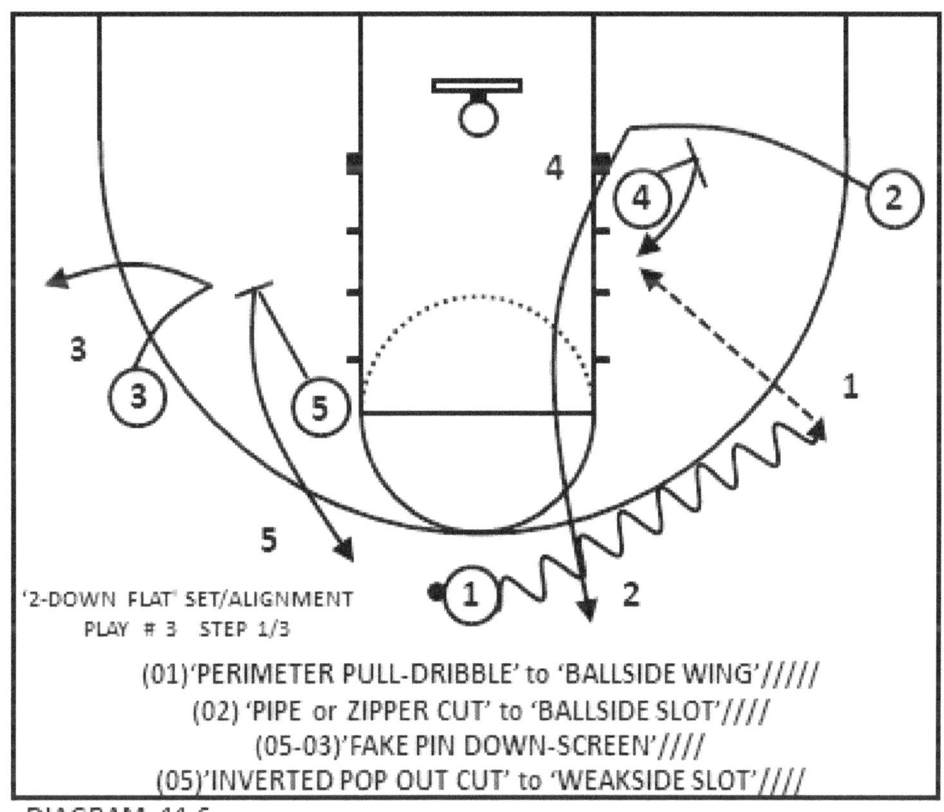

DIAGRAM 11.6

In the next step of Play # 3, 05 makes it appear as if he were executing the second step of Play # 2 with a "Pin Down-Screen" for 03. Instead, the action on the weakside changes with 05 breaking off of his screening route and instead making a hard cut directly to the basket. This "Ghost Pin Down-Screen" that is to be delivered to 03 still has 03 break up to the vacant "Slot," but with no help from the screen. On the initial ballside of the floor, when 02 starts his dribble, 04 steps out as if there were to be a 04-01 "Flex Back-Screen." Instead, 01 breaks in towards 04 before then stepping back out into the "Deep Corner," behind the arc. 04 then attacks his defender by faking the "Flex Screen" and then making a shallow "Duck-In Cut" for 02 (or 01) to give it a look inside. If 05 does not receive the "Inside Pass" from 02 on his cut to the basket, he then empties out and flares out to that new side's "Deep Corner." Diagram 11.7

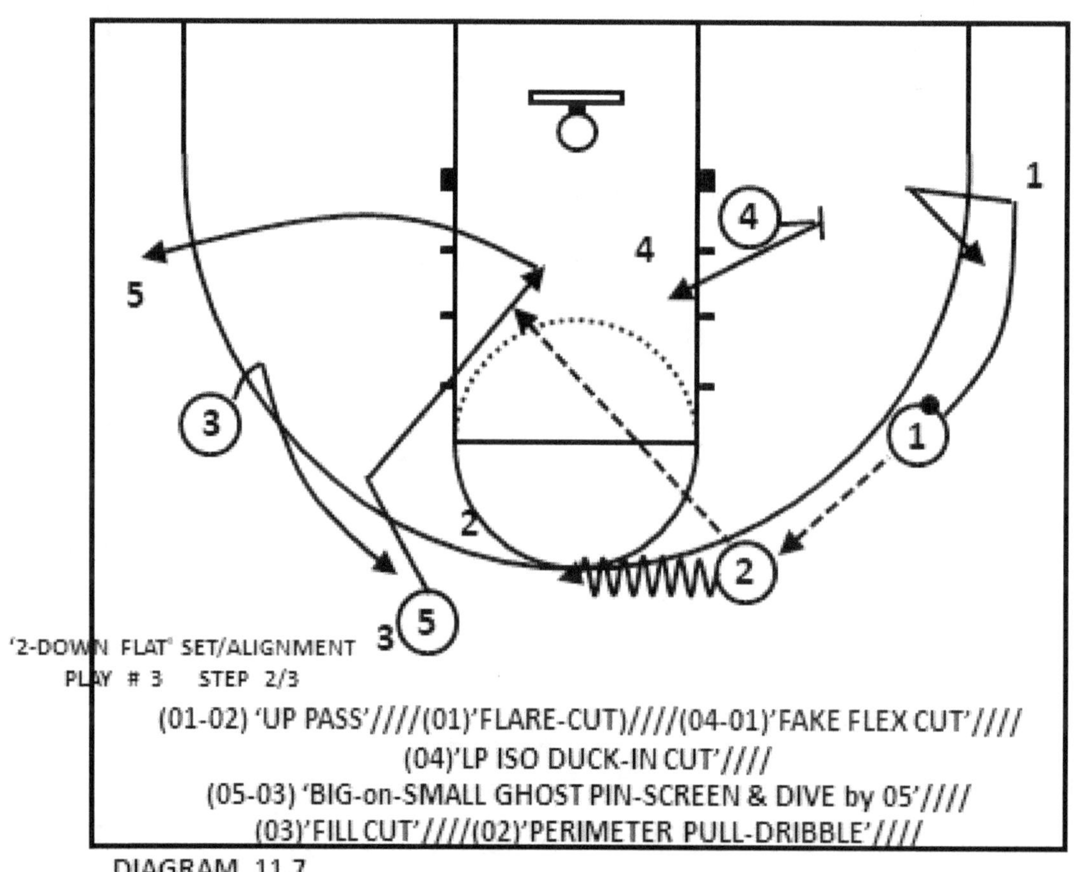

DIAGRAM 11.7

02 continues his "perimeter pull dribble" across the top of the key for 03 to break further up to receive the ball on the 02-03 Reverse Pass and Ball-Screen. After giving up the ball to 03, 02 will scrape off of 05's outside right shoulder for his "Flare Cut" off of 05's "Big-on-Small Flare-Screen" immediately after the 02-03 exchange.

This action is difficult to defend as it is almost identical to screen the screener action, while it is actually "(Flare-)screen the "Follow-the-Pass Ball-Screen.""

04 again attacks his defender with an "Iso Duck-In Cut." Again, with all four of his teammates spread out around the perimeter and all behind the arc, 04 has completely isolated his defender again.

If no shots are taken, the Spot-Ups are again filled for a quick transition into the designated continuity offense. Diagram 11.8

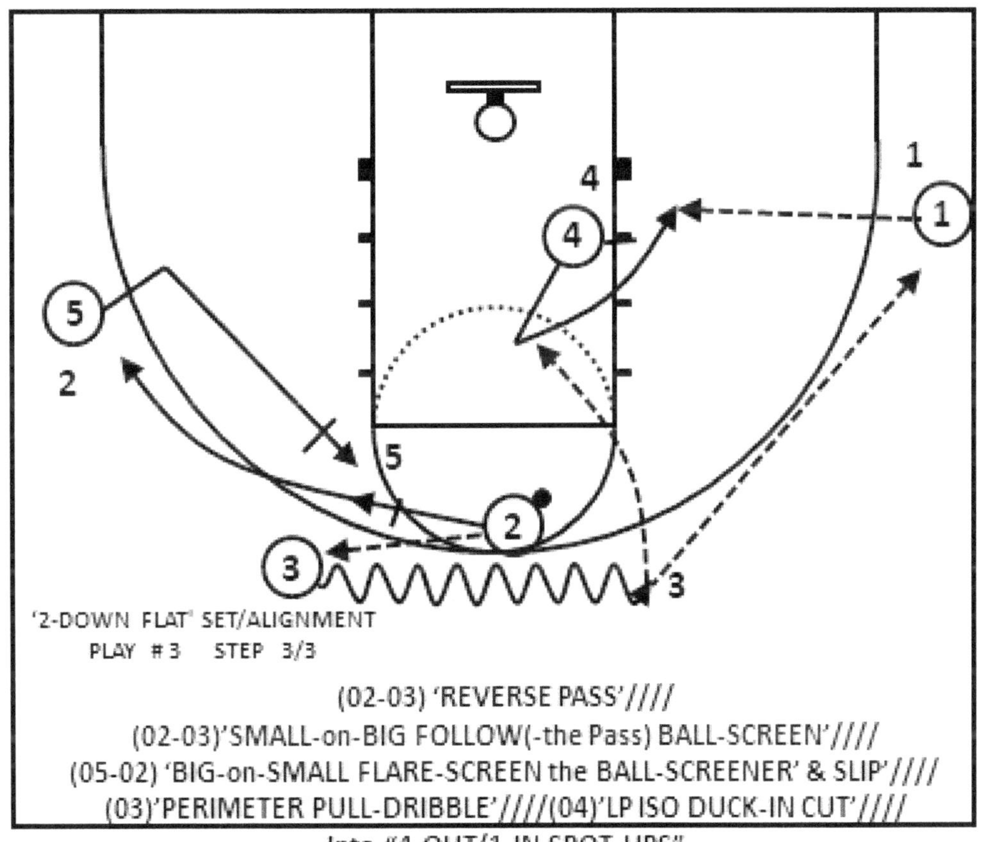

DIAGRAM 11.8

Diagrams 11.9 through 11.12 can be described as Play # 4 being a counter to Play # 3 It all starts again with 01 dribbling to same "Wing" area at the FT Line extended, 02 running towards 04 before making the same "Pipe Cut" up to the same "Ballside Slot."

Diagram 11.9 illustrates another play of the "Rejection Package" of plays between 05 and 03. As usual 01 dribbles to the FT Line extended and 02 makes the same cut towards the basket and towards 04 before then making the same "Zipper Cut" up the FT Lane Line to the newly declared "Ballside Slot." 04 isolates his defender with both 05 and 03 outside of the arc and occupying their individual defenders with their two-man game action. Diagram 11.9

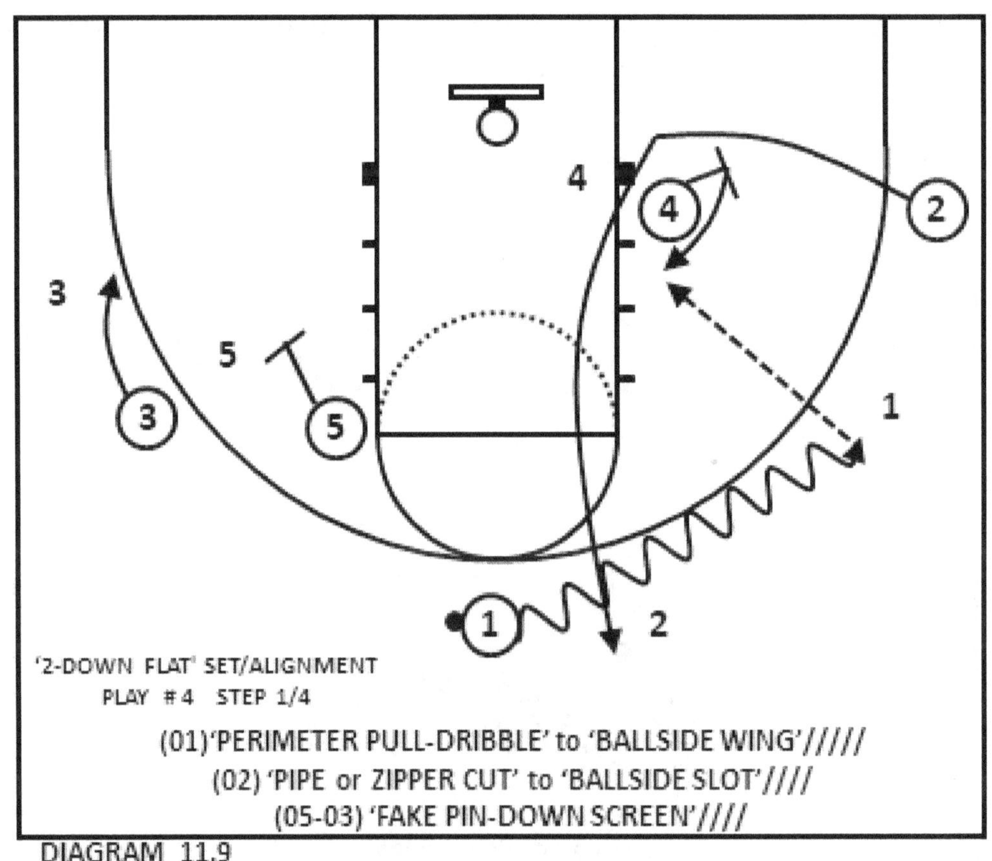

DIAGRAM 11.9

Diagram 11.10 As in the previous plays in the package, 03 again rejects 05's Pin Down-Screen with 05 again popping out to fill the new "Weakside Slot" location. At the same time, 04 makes his strong "Isolated Duck-In Cut" into the "Dotted Circle" area and looks to receive the ball from either 01 or from 02. Diagram 11.10

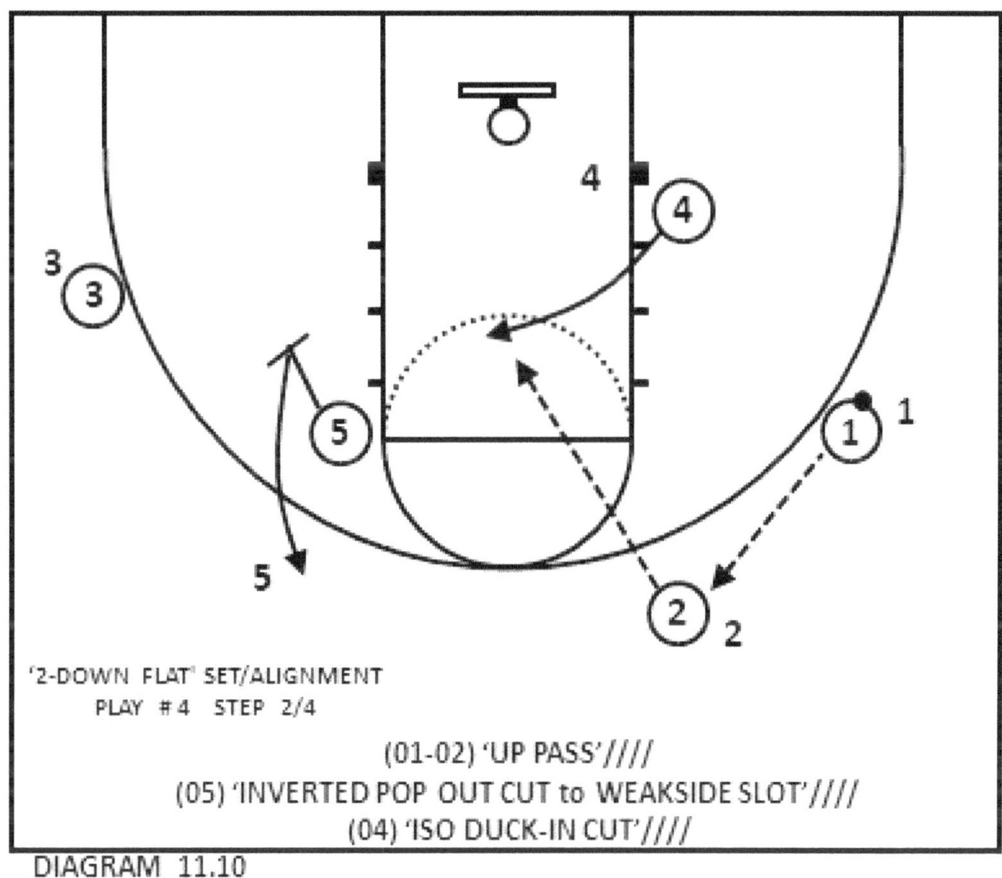

DIAGRAM 11.10

Diagram 11.11 illustrates 02 turning down the "Inside Pass" and making the "Reverse Pass" to 05 with 04 continuing his "chase of the ball around and through the lane, looking for a pass from either 02, 05 or from 03.

After the 02-05 "Reverse Pass," 01 steps up to set a "Small-on-Big Flare-Screen" for 02 to use to make his "Flare-Cut" to the new "Weakside Wing" area. 05 looks for "Inside Pass" to 04 or to passes to 03 or a "Skip Pass" to 02 back on the new "Weakside." Diagram 11.11

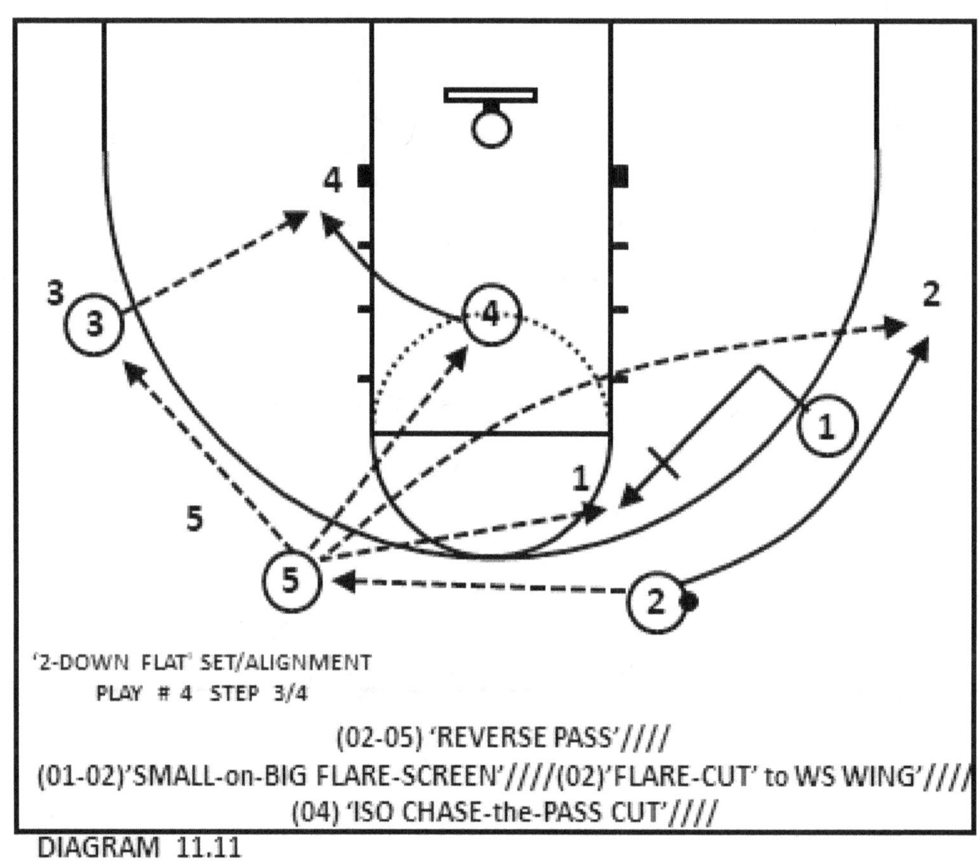

DIAGRAM 11.11

If 05 does not make the "Inside Pass," 05 could make a "Down Pass" to 03, who may have an improved passing angle to make the pass to 04 (now posted up in an isolated "position advantage." If 05 actually makes the "Down Pass" to 03, 05 makes a "Diagonal Rotational Cut' through the lane and eventually out to the new "Weakside Deep Corner." During 05's cut, both 01 and 02 make "Replacement Fill Cuts" from the initial weakside perimeter over towards the new "Ballside." This action helps eliminate any possible helpside defense that helps 04 isolate his defender even more so. In addition, these three perimeter cuts by 05, 01, and 02 reposition players into the "4-Out/1-In" Spot-Ups so that there can be a fluid transition from this set play into the designated continuity offense. Diagram 11.12

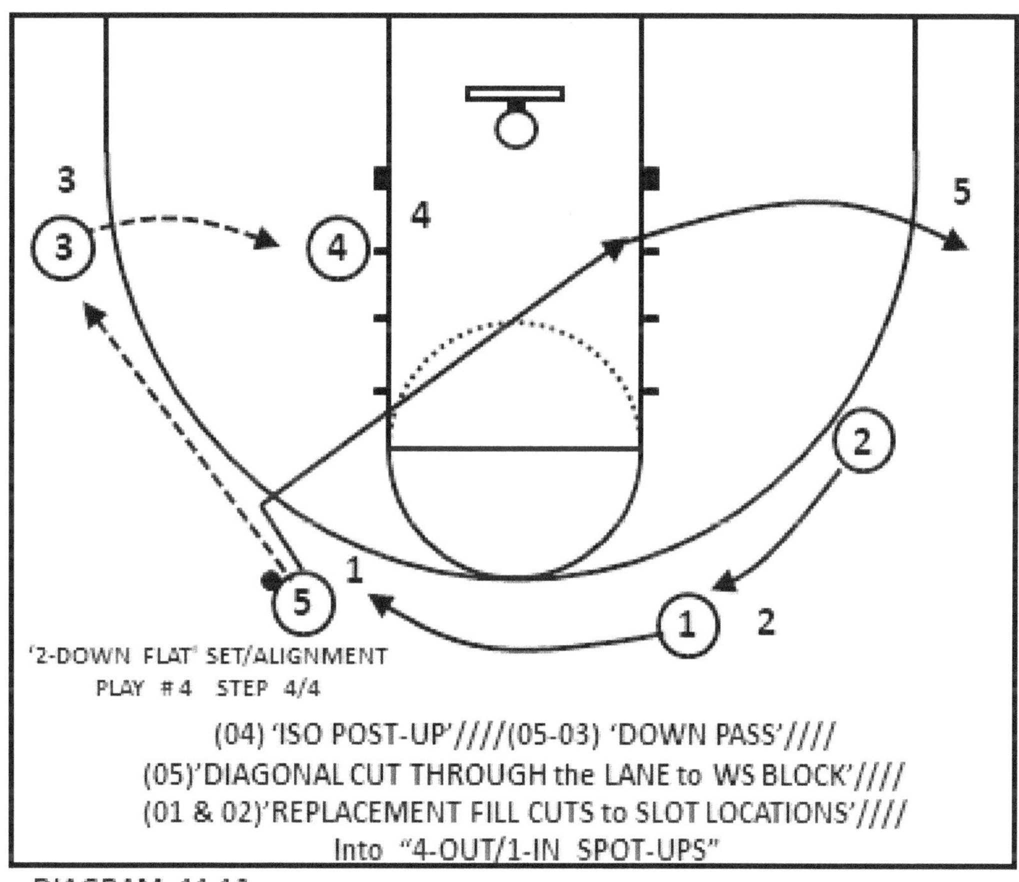

DIAGRAM 11.12

Diagrams 11.13 and 11.14 illustrate a (05-03) "Pin-Down" play that could be used as a counter to any of the four" Rejection" plays (Plays 1 – 4.) 01 makes the same "Perimeter Pull Dribble" towards the FT Line extended on the same right side of the floor. 02 makes the same "Pipe Cut" up the FT Lane Line and 04 executes the identical "Iso Post-Up." The primary difference is that in this Play # 13, 03 sets his defender up to actually utilize 05's "Big-on-Small Pin Down-Screen" for 03 to be the player that pops out to end up in the new "Weakside Slot." 05 then slips to the new "Weakside Wing." Diagram 11.13

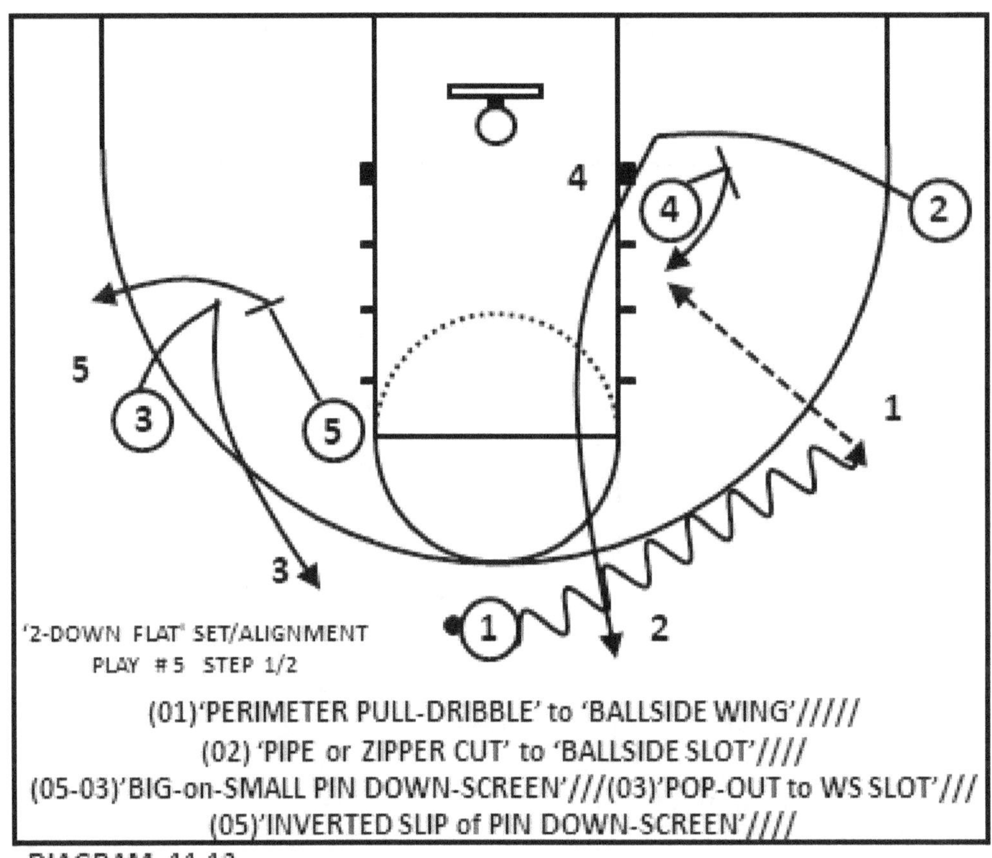

DIAGRAM 11.13

Diagram 11.14 shows 01 making the "Up Pass" to 02 and 02 looking to make the "Inside Pass" to 04 on his "Iso Duck-In Cut." Since 03 is the player that is now located in the "Slot," 03 is the player that sets the "Big-on-Small Ball-Screen" for 02 to "dribble-scrape" off of to the opposite "Slot" location. Since 03 is more of a perimeter scoring threat than 05, 01 steps up to set a "Small-on-Big Flare-Screen" for 03 to use and he then scrapes off of 01's left shoulder to make a "Flare-Cut" to the new "Weakside Wing" area outside of the arc. After screening for 03, 01 slips his screen and steps up to the new "Weakside Wing." As 02 dribbles towards the new "Ballside Slot," 05 makes a "Drift Cut" towards the sideline and the baseline. This action by 05 and 03 helps opens up the area for 04 to fully isolate his defender in the middle of the lane and then a moment later on the new "Ballside Mid-Post."

If no interior shots (by 04) or perimeter shots (by 02, 03 or 01) are taken, the "4-Out/1-In" Spot-Ups are filled for a smooth continuation of a fundamentally sound offensive attack. The switching of personnel (from 05 to 03) to actually make the screen for 02 gives the offense so many other offensive options that also place different offensive personnel with different offensive strengths into those same locations. This makes it more difficult for opposing defenses to predict and prepare to defend the many various offensive actions. Diagram 11.14

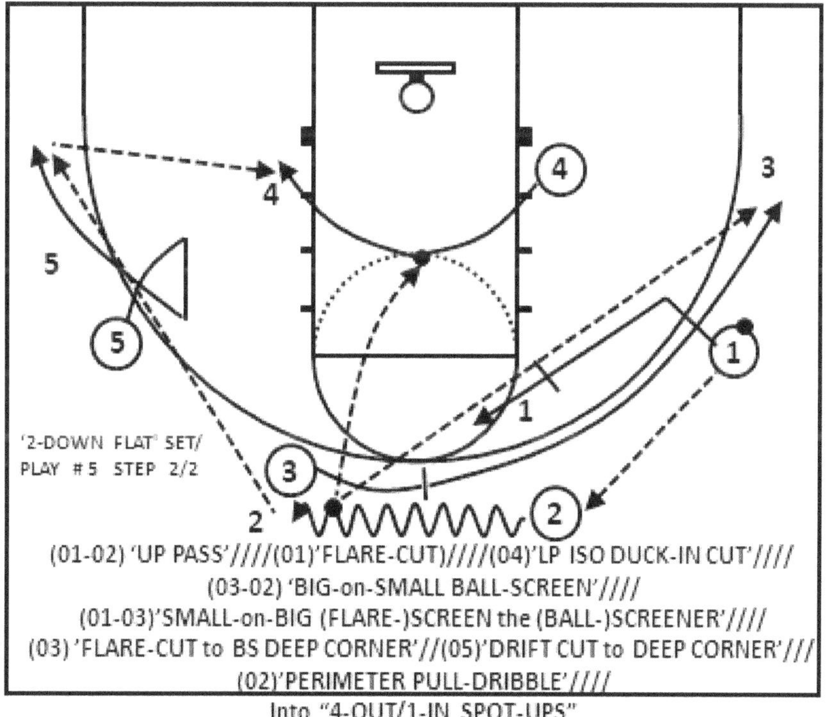

DIAGRAM 11.14

Diagram 11.15 shows once again shows the initial stage of another play that is very similar to the package of players described—Play # 6. Once again, 01 makes the same safe and controlled "Perimeter Pull Dribble" towards the FT Line extended on the same right side of the floor. 02starts to make the same "Pipe Cut" up the FT Lane Line until he slightly modifies the cut to then make it on the outside of the lane and in the form of a "Zipper Cut." 02 ends up at the same "Ballside Slot" while 04 executes the identical "Iso Post-Up" on the same "Ballside Block." The only other difference is that in this Play # 13, 03 sets his defender up to actually utilize 05's "Big-on-Small Pin Down-Screen" for 03 to be the player that pops out to end up in the new "Weakside Slot." 05 then slips to the new "Weakside Wing." Diagram 11.15

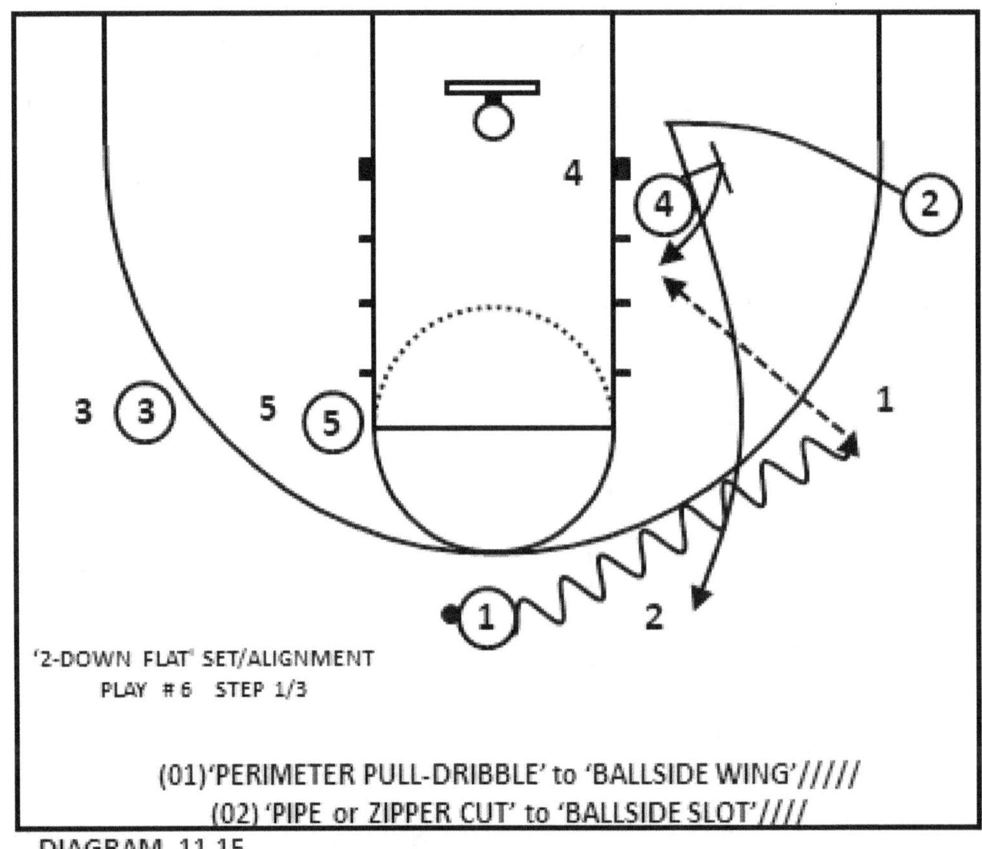

DIAGRAM 11.15

When 01 turns down the "Inside Pass" to 04, he again makes the pass out to 02. 04 makes the same "Iso Duck-In Cut" but breaks even further into the lane. A different form of action is that 01 makes a hard "Give-n-Go Cut" to the basket on the heels of 04's cut towards the ball. 05 then breaks down to set the same "Pin Down-Screen" for 03 use. The diagram then shows 03 scraping off of 05's outside left shoulder to break open to the "Weakside Slot." If 02 does not make the "Lob Pass" to 01, he looks to reverse the ball to 03, now open at the opposite side's "Slot." 01 ends up on the opposite side of the floor on the "Block," while 05 settles outside of the arc at the FT Line extended, further isolating the inverted and perimeter defender X1. 02 then "Flare-Cuts" to the new "Weakside Wing" to also stretch the defense horizontally from 05's sideline to 02's sideline. Diagram 11.16

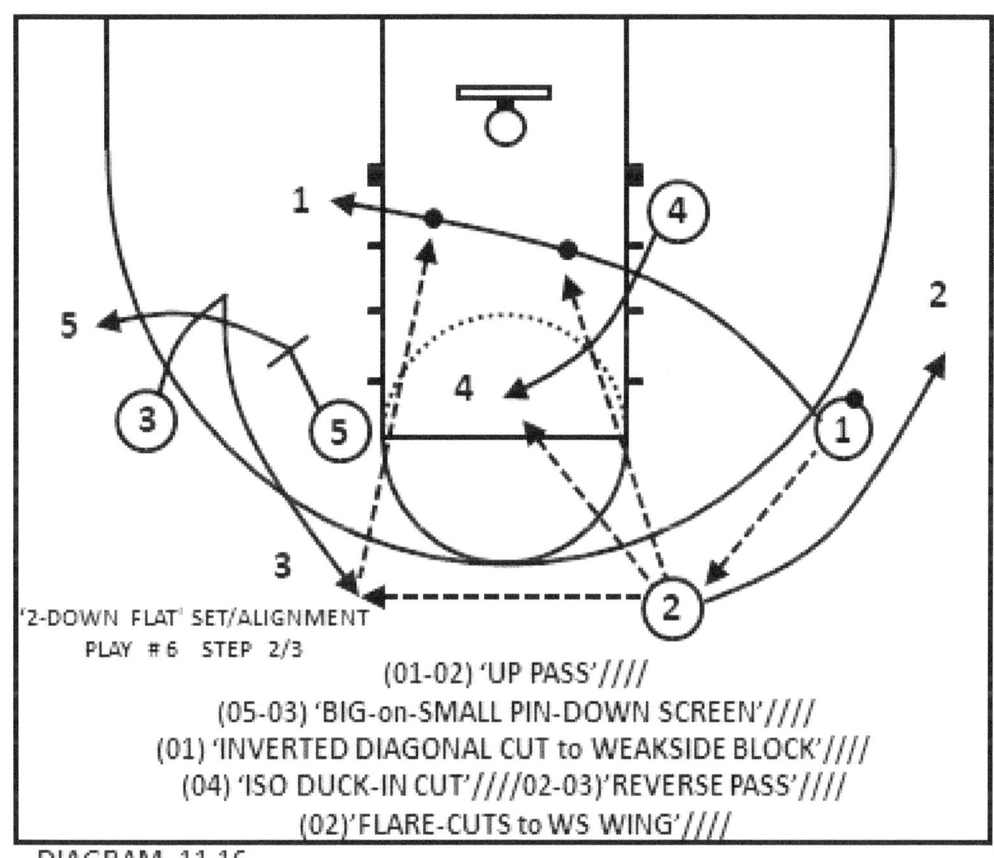

DIAGRAM 11.16

Diagram 11.17 shows the conclusion of the play with 03 having possession of the ball and receiving 04's "Big-on-Small Long Ball-Screen. 03 then "dribble-scrapes" off of 04's top left shoulder and "perimeter pull-dribbles" towards the opposite slot while 02 "Drift Cuts" to the nearest "Deep Corner." At the same time, 05 makes a "Replacement Fill Cut" to step into the newly declared "Weakside Slot" and 01 steps out to the near "Deep Corner" to further horizontally stretch the defense. With either a "Reverse Pivot" or a "Front Pivot' off of the lower right foot, 04 can either "Roll" or "Rim-Run" into the wide open empty lane area.

If 02 or 01 do not have open perimeter shots, if 03 does not have a pull-up jump shot or a penetrating inside shot and if 04 does not receive an "Inside Pass" from a teammate; the "4-Out/1-In" Spot-Ups are filled for the designated continuity offense to fluidly and instantly begin. ." Diagram 11. 17

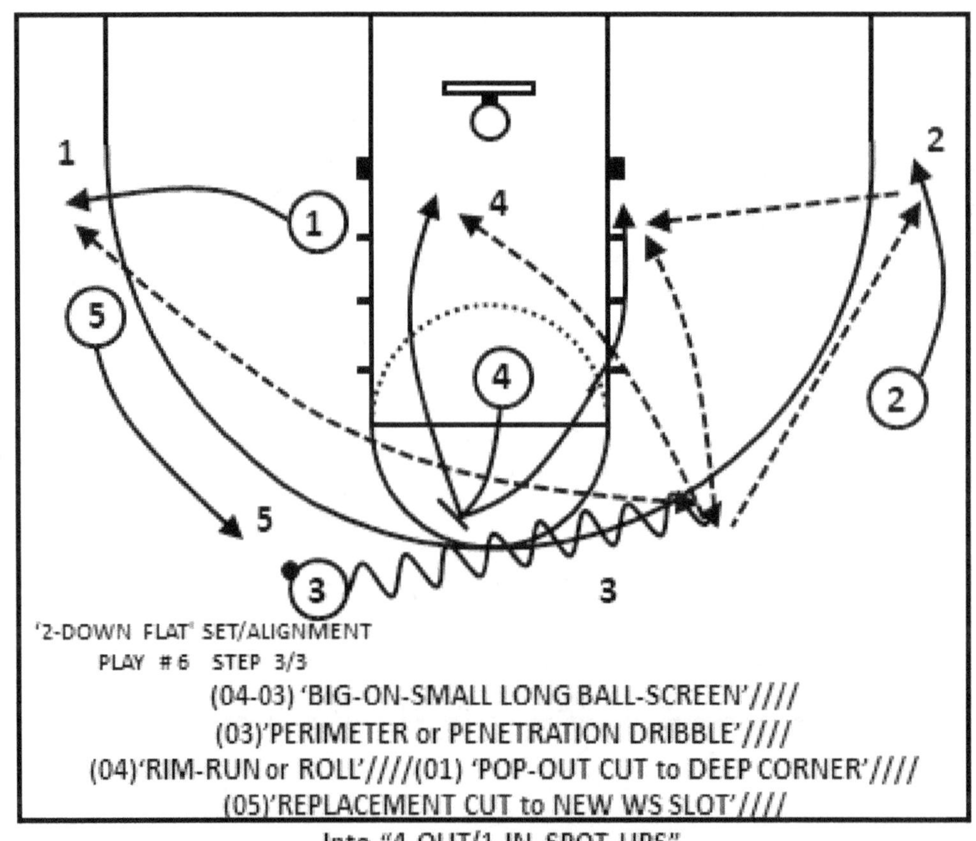

DIAGRAM 11.17

Diagrams 11.18 through 11.20 show the very beginning to the very end of a '3-level' play that somewhat appears to be the same as the previous six plays. 01 "perimeter pull dribbles" towards the same FT Line extended. 02 breaks in towards 04 as if he were going to make the same "Pipe Cut," before stopping short and then breaking out to the FT Line extended on the same side of the floor. It appears that 04 starts to make his same "Duck-In Cut" before then extending it diagonally up across the lane to set a "Back-Screen" for 05 to use to scrape off of either shoulder of 04 before then posting up on the new "Ballside Block." 03 moves about on the perimeter to occupy his defender and to keep him away from being a helpside defender for X5. 01 prepares to make the DHO with 02 near the "Wing" area. ." Diagram 11.18

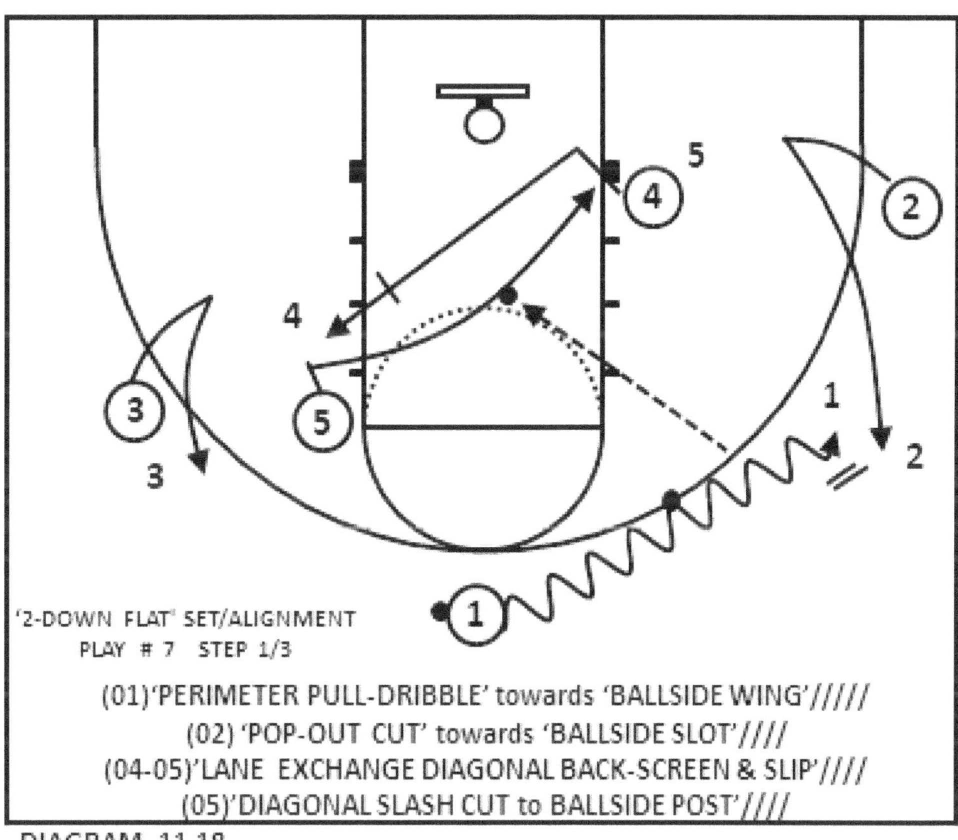

DIAGRAM 11.18

Diagram 11.19 shows 01 looking to hit 04 on his "Duck-In Cut" or to hit 05 on his diagonal cut before then giving up possession of the ball to 02. 02 then dribbles out to the top of the key, with 05 being the player to make his "Iso Post-Up" while 04 steps up closer to 02 and the ball while 01 makes a "Flare-Cut" to the same side's "Deep Corner." Diagram 11.19

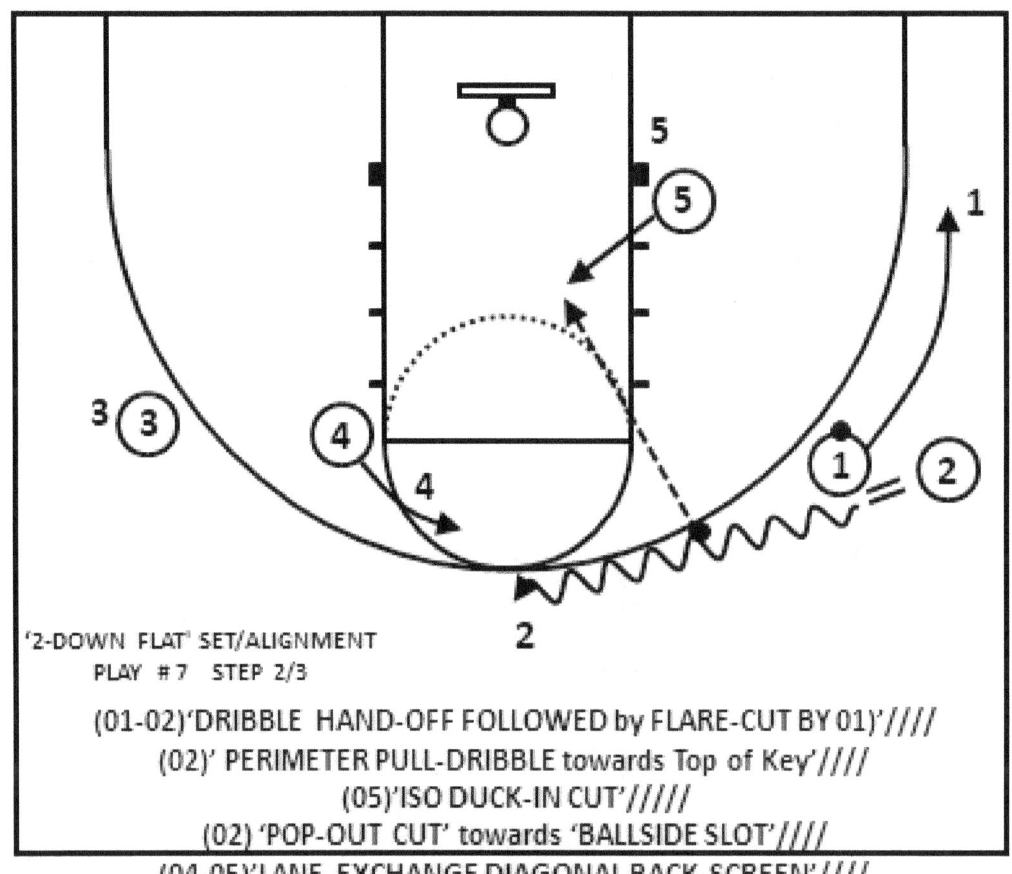

Diagram 11.20 shows the conclusion of Play # 7 with 04 stepping closer to set a "Big-on-Small Ball-Screen" for 02 to use to continue his "perimeter pull dribble" (to the opposite side's "Slot" area.) 03 makes a "Drift Cut" towards his "Deep Corner," preparing for a "catch and shoot" pass from 02, while 04 continues in the same direction to then set a "Big-on-Small" Pin Down-Screen" for 01 to use as he breaks back up as a perimeter scoring threat at the new "Weakside Slot." After ducking in, 05 continues "chasing the path of the ball" and looking for an "inside pass" from either 02 or from 01 on the new "Ballside."

If 02 were to make a "Dribbling Reverse Throwback Pass" to 01 and 01 does not take the shot, 05 would reverse directions and then turn back to follow the path of the ball and to receive possible "Inside Passes" from either 01 or from 04, now spotted up in the opposite "Deep Corner." No shots produced will still reposition all players into the proper "4-Out/1-In" Spot-Ups," allowing for a seamless conversion from this Level 3 play into the designated continuity offense. ." Diagram 11.20

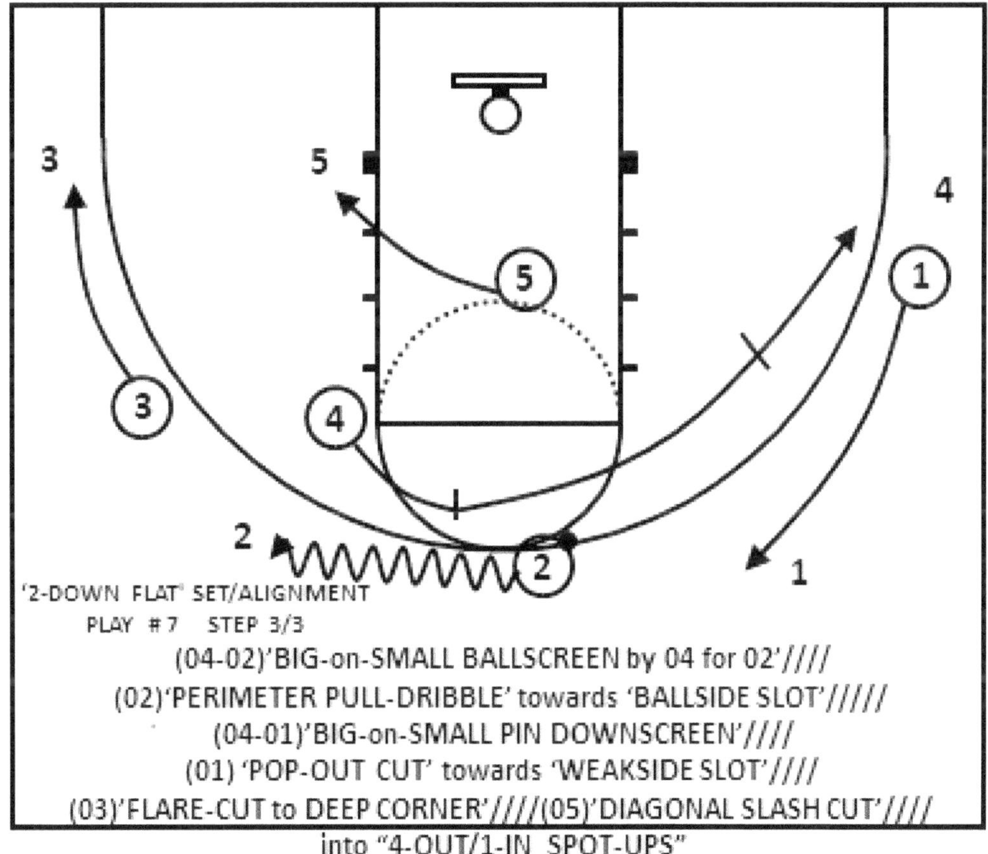

DIAGRAM 11.20

Diagrams 11.21 through 11.23 illustrate Play # 8 from beginning to end. As 01 approaches the top of the key with his dribble and 03 makes his "Iverson Cut" over the top of both 05 and 04 to the opposite "Wing" area. ." Diagram 11.21

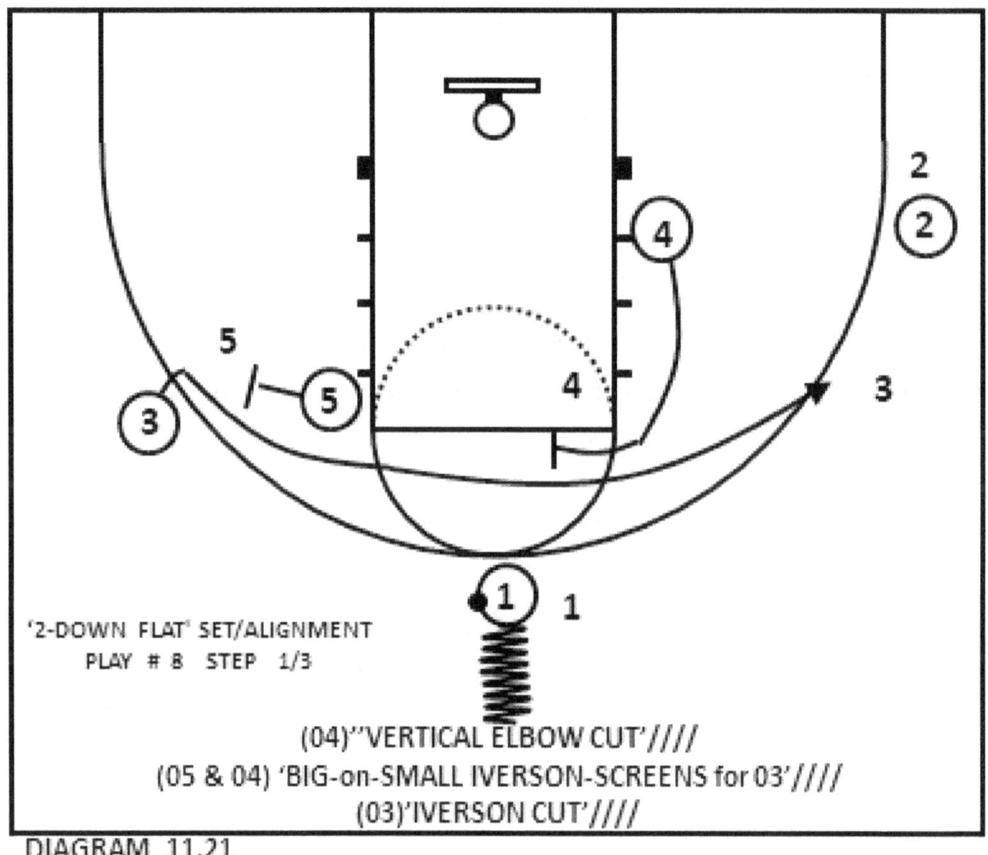

DIAGRAM 11.21

Diagram 11.22 shows 01 making the "Wing Pass" to 03 with 04 setting his "Barkley Screen" to then flash to the new "Ballside High Post." After screening for 05, 04 then slips his screen and makes a "Lob Cut" to the basket and looks for a "Lob Pass" from 03.

At the same time, 02 walks his man up towards 03 before then making a hard "Backdoor Cut." If 03 does not make the pass to 02, 03 then looks to make the pass to 04 and then to 02 who has now posted up his inverted and (now) isolated his perimeter-type defender, X2. ." Diagram 11.22

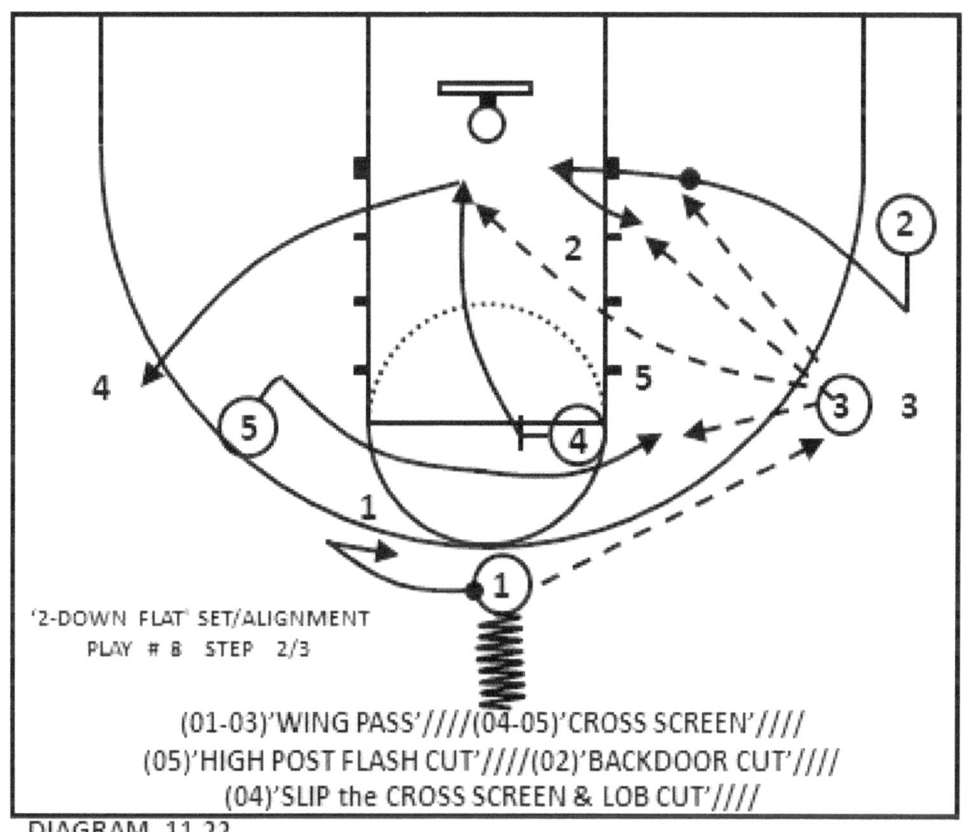

DIAGRAM 11.22

Diagram 11.23 illustrates 03 turning down "Inside Passes" to 04 and 02 and then waiting for 05 to then step out to set a "Big-on-Small" Inside Ball-Screen for 03. 03 should then "dribble-scrape" off of 05's outside right shoulder. As 03 makes either a "penetrating dribble" if the gap is open or a "perimeter pull dribble," 05 should make a "front pivot" off of his inside left foot while 02 steps out towards the "Deep Corner" (to horizontally stretch the interior defense).

At the same time on the weakside of the floor, 04 steps up to set a "Big-on-Small Flare-Screen" for 01 to use to make his "Flare-Cut" to the new "Weakside Wing." This two-man action occupies the helpside defense.

If 03 does not make the "Inside Lob Pass" to 05, a "Skip Pass" to 01 or a "Throwback Reverse Pass" to 02 or any type of shot taken by 03 off of his dribble; the "4-Out/1-In" Spot-Ups are filled for a smooth conversion into the last phase of the offensive attack. ."

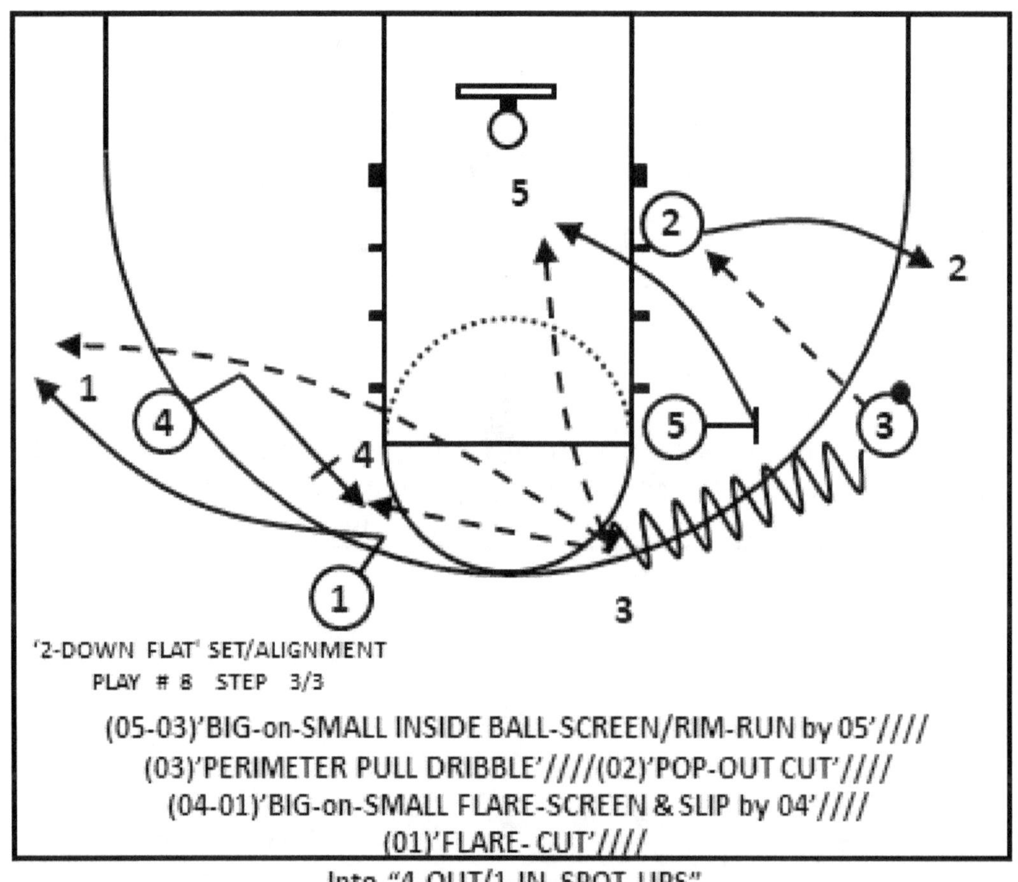

Into "4-OUT/1-IN SPOT-UPS"

DIAGRAM 11.23

Diagram 11.24 illustrates a somewhat different form of action where both 03 and 02 make their respective "Iverson Cuts" off of their "Big-on-Small Iverson Screens." As 01 approaches the top of the key, 03 makes a low "Iverson Cut" underneath 04's "Iverson Screen" and 02 cuts up and over the top off 05's "Iverson Screen." ." Play # 9. Diagram 11.24

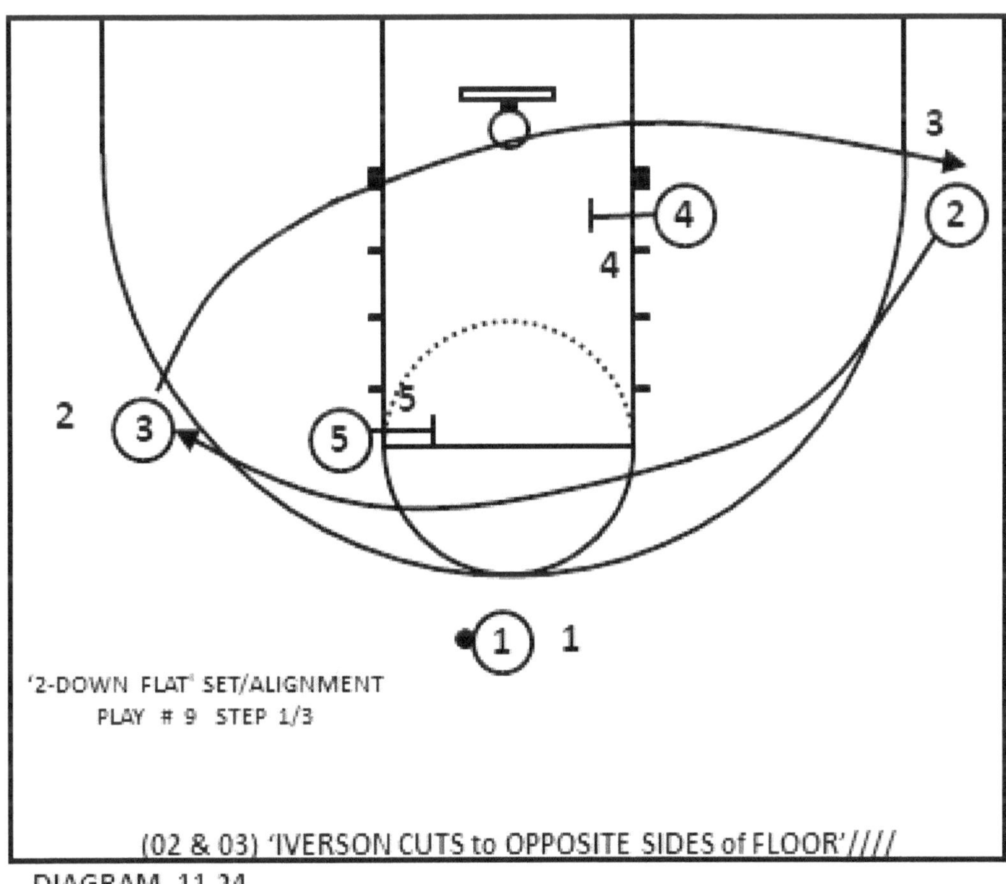

DIAGRAM 11.24

Diagram 11.25 shows 01 make the "Wing Pass" to 02 on the left "Wing" area and 05 immediately making a "front pivot and swim move" off of his lower left foot or a "reverse pivot and seal move" off of the same lower left foot. After gaining a "position advantage" over his post defender, X5, 05 then slides down the lane to post up on the new "Ballside Block." After the pass is made, 01 follows the pass to cut behind 02 while 03 rotates out to the new "Weakside Slot." Diagram 11.25

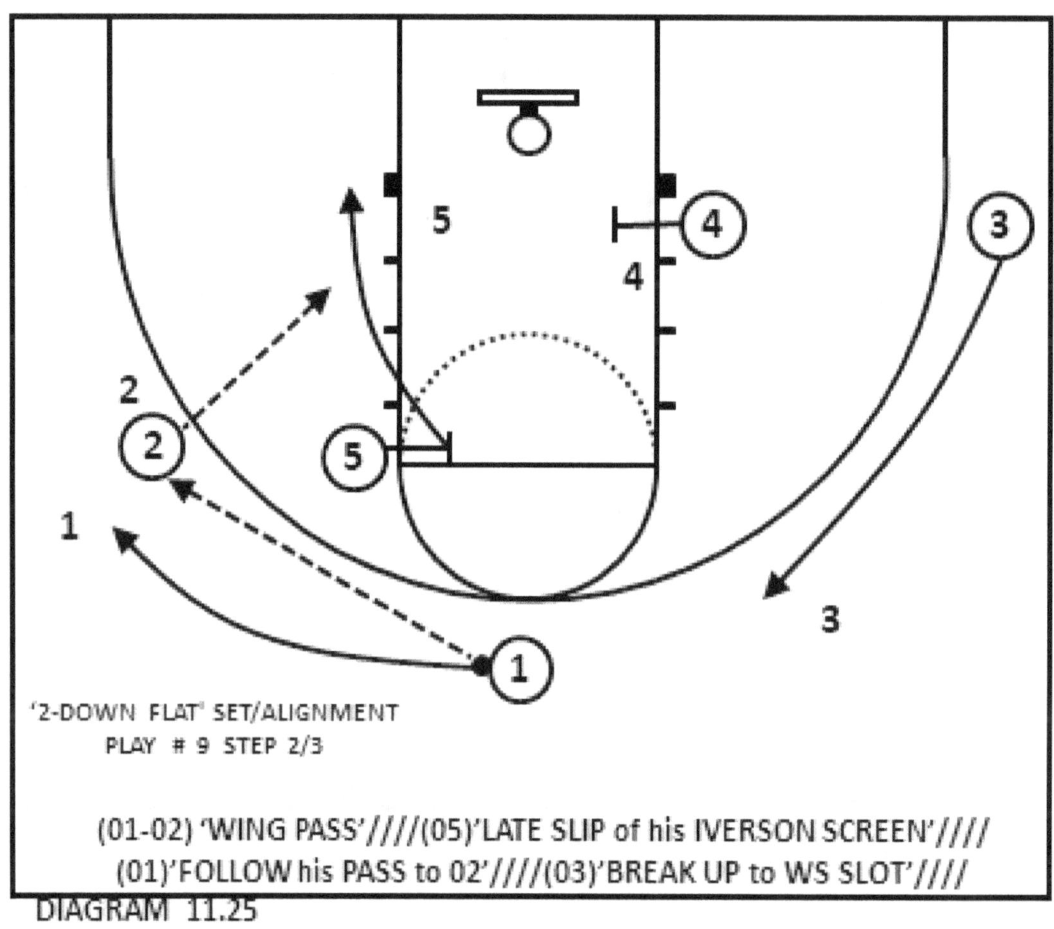

Diagram 11.26 shows the final phase of Play # 9 with 02 flipping the pass back to 01. As the pass is made, 04 breaks diagonally up and across the lane to set a "Big-on-Small Diagonal Back-Screen" for 02 to us (after he has given up possession of the ball to 01.) 02 then runs a "Lob Cut" after scraping off of 04's top left shoulder to shed his defender trying to follow him to the basket. If 01 does not make the "Lob Pass" to 02, 02 then empties out of the lane to stay wide and deep in the "Weakside Deep Corner with 01 making a "perimeter pull down dribble" towards the "Deep Corner" to gain a passing angle for 05 to receive the "Inside Pass" on the "Ballside Block." 04 then slips his "Back-Screen" and slips out to the new "Ballside Slot." This move by 04 fills the final spot of the "4-Out/1-In" Spot-Ups so that the designated continuity offense can immediately begin. ." Diagram 11.26

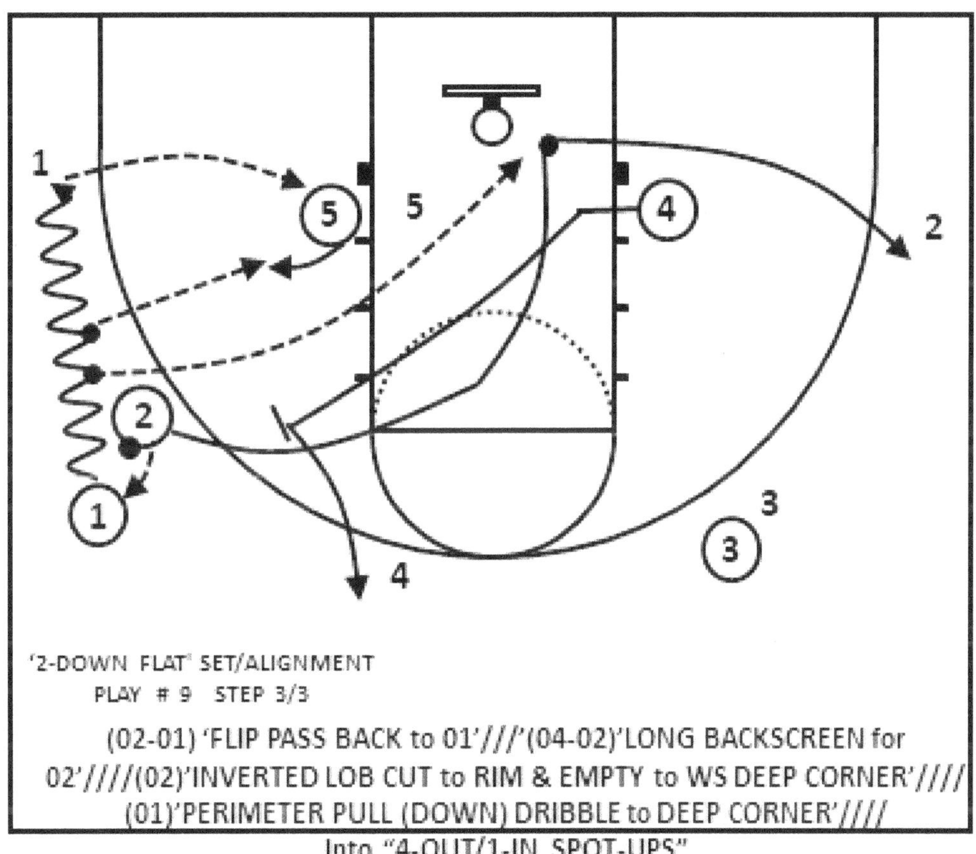

DIAGRAM 11.26

Diagram 11.27 illustrates Play # 10 whose initial actions results in all five players ending up in the same locations they did in the previous Play # 9. The difference is that 02 makes his cut to the opposite "Wing" area by cutting off of 04, through the lane, up and out to the now vacant "Wing" area at the FT Line extended. 03 makes his "Iverson Cut" over the top of 05 to the opposite "Wing" area at the FT Line extended on the opposite side of the floor. ." Diagram 11.27

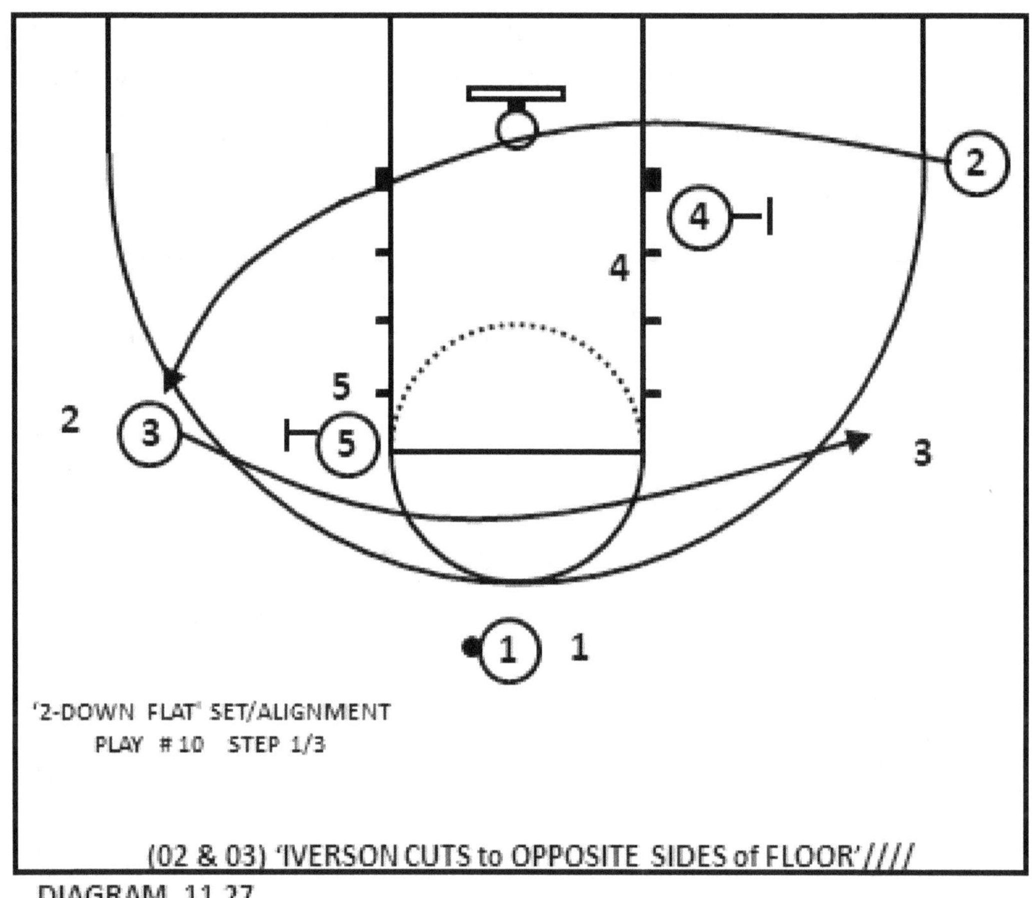

DIAGRAM 11.27

Diagram 11.28 shows the second phase of this play with 01 again making the pass to 02 on the left side of the floor and again following his pass. At the same time, 04 flashes across the lane to the new "Ballside Block" while 05 remains at the new "Ballside High Post" location. 03 again rolls up to the new "Weakside Slot" location. ." Diagram 11.28

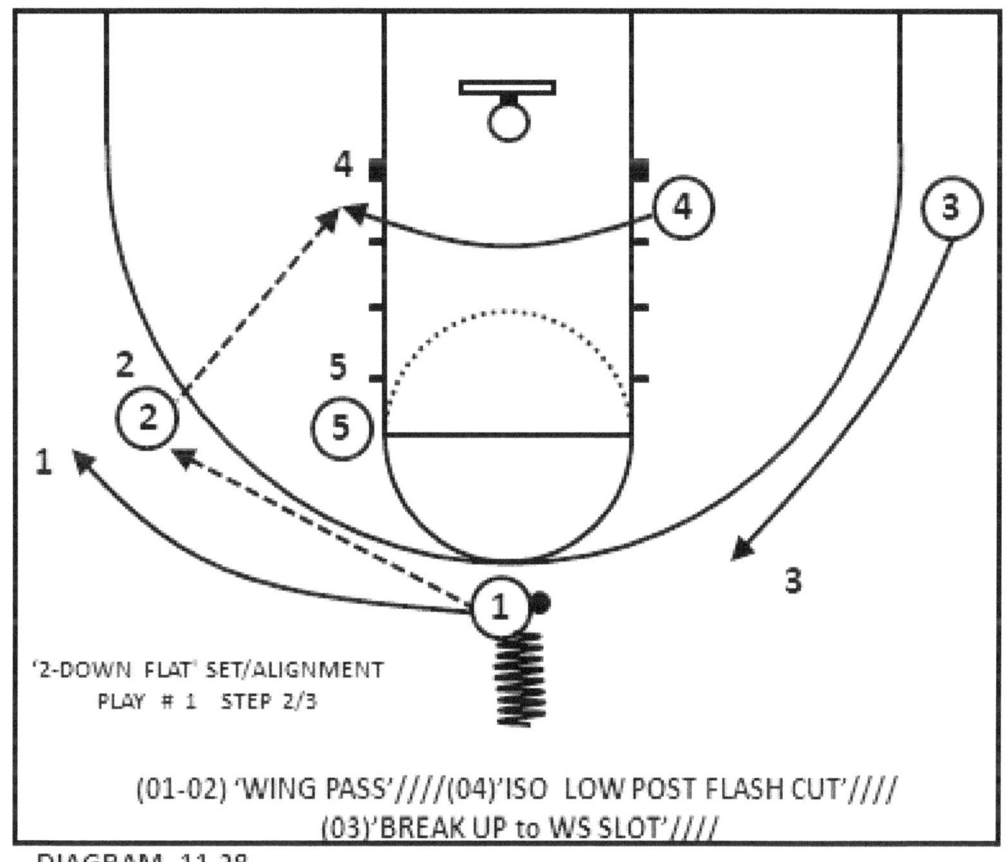

DIAGRAM 11.28

Diagram 11.29 shows the same action as in Play #9's third phase. 02 makes the same "Flip Pass" to 01 and makes the same "Lob Cut" by scraping his defender off of 05's top left shoulder and cutting hard to the rim (before emptying out to the new "Weakside Wing" again.)

If 01 does not make the "Lob Pass" to 02 or the "Inside Pass" to 04 (not 05 in Play # 8 in Diagram 11.22) on his isolated post-up, 01 then looks to make his "perimeter pull down dribble" down to the "Deep Corner," looking to create an improved passing angle to deliver the ball to 04. During the dribble, it is 05's responsibility in this play to step out and invert his defensive "big" to the "Ballside Slot." 02 empties out and moves out to the new "Weakside Deep Corner," and 03 again rotates out to the new "Weakside Slot" creating an even more isolated situation for 04 in this play.

If no shots are taken, the "4-Out/1-In" Spot-Ups are filled for the designated continuity offense to fluidly begin. With no time to reorganize, the opposition must first defend the half-court play with its many options and then immediately stop the continuity offense. ."
Diagram 11.29

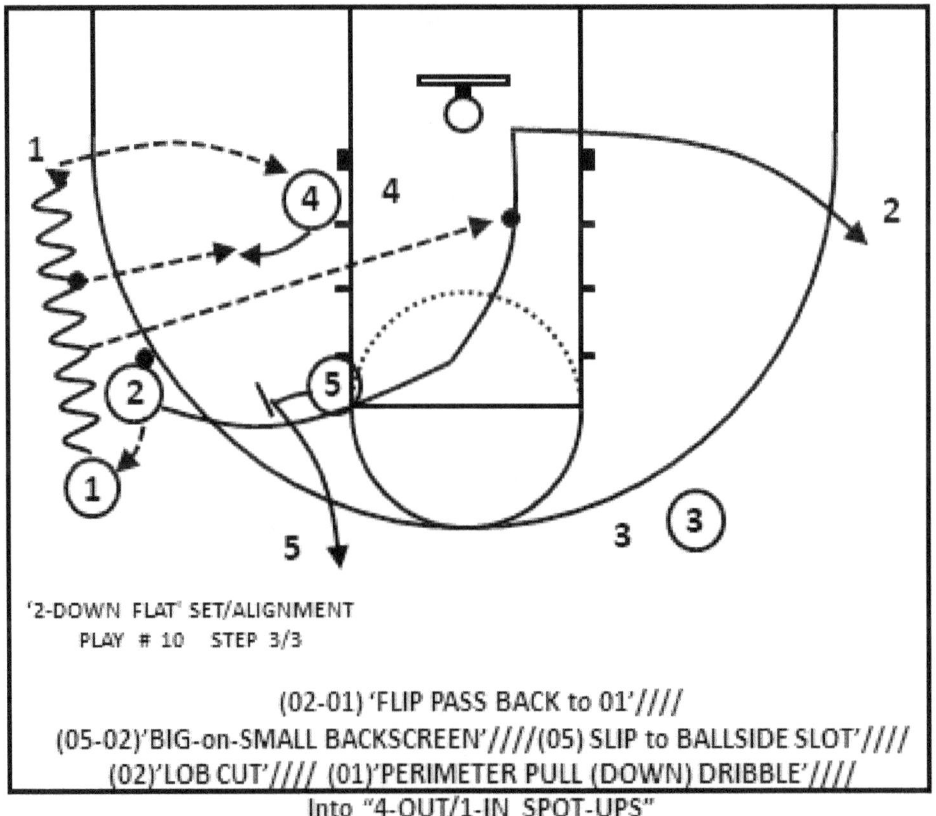

DIAGRAM 11.29

PLAYS/ENTRIES THAT END in
the "HIGH-POST/LOW POST" OFFENSIVE SPOT-UPS

The primary change in this group of plays plays/entries are that all five players will end up in a different group of offensive spot-ups. These "HIGH-POST/LOW-POST" Spot-Ups will have players moved about the court with any of the five ending up in the "Ballside Block," the "Ballside High Post," the "Ballside Wing," the "Weakside Wing," and the "Point." These five positions can provide the offense with safe and easy types of ball-reversals, large gaps for dribble penetration, opportunities to deliver the ball inside to whomever (perimeter-type or post-type players) is posting up their defender on the "Ballside Block," and a player that can be a perimeter-scoring threat and a legitimate offensive rebounding threat from outside of the arc on his "offensive crashing of the boards." The "HIGH-POST/LOW-POST" Spot-Ups also provide ample opportunities for constant and effective defensive transition responsibilities.

Diagram 11.30 illustrates the beginning of Play # 11 where 01 dribbles towards 03. At the same time, 04 flashes straight across the lane to the newly declared "Ballside Mid-Post." Simultaneously, 03 makes a "Lob Cut" by cutting off of 05's top left shoulder and curling towards the basket. In unison with this action, 02 cuts from his "Deep Corner" diagonally towards the top of the key, allowing for 04 to further isolate his defender.

After 03 does not receive the "Lob Pass" from 01, he then empties out of the lane and swings out to the "Weakside Wing" area on the opposite side of the floor.

If no shots are taken, all players are in a new set of continuity offense spot-ups, so that a new continuity offense could smoothly and easily begin. Those spot-ups are the "High-Post/Low-Post" Spot-Ups and a group of continuity offenses could be chosen to execute." Diagram 11.30

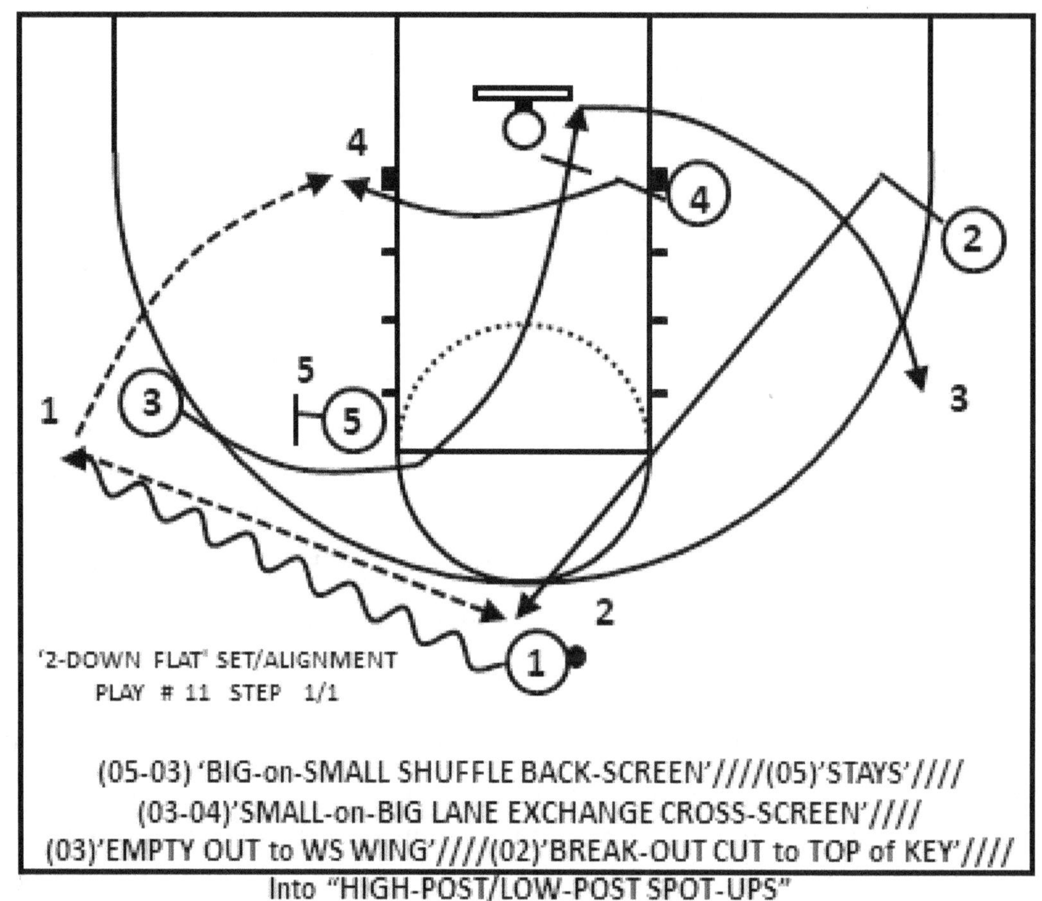

(05-03) 'BIG-on-SMALL SHUFFLE BACK-SCREEN'/////(05)'STAYS'/////
(03-04)'SMALL-on-BIG LANE EXCHANGE CROSS-SCREEN'/////
(03)'EMPTY OUT to WS WING'/////(02)'BREAK-OUT CUT to TOP of KEY'/////
Into "HIGH-POST/LOW-POST SPOT-UPS"

DIAGRAM 11.30

Diagram 11.31 illustrates Play # 12 with 01 bringing the ball to the top of the key and 03 making an "Iverson Cut" over the top of 05 and then over the top of 04 before reaching the opposite side of the floor's "Wing" area. Simultaneously, 02 breaks horizontally along the baseline to the isolated (and inverted) "Mid-Post Block" on the opposite side of the lane.

This action gives 02 a position advantage with the two presumed biggest defenders pulled and stretched out away from the basket. If 02 has average to above-average post-up skills and/or if X2 has average or below-average defensive post-up skills, 02 has an outstanding scoring advantage. ." Diagram 11.31

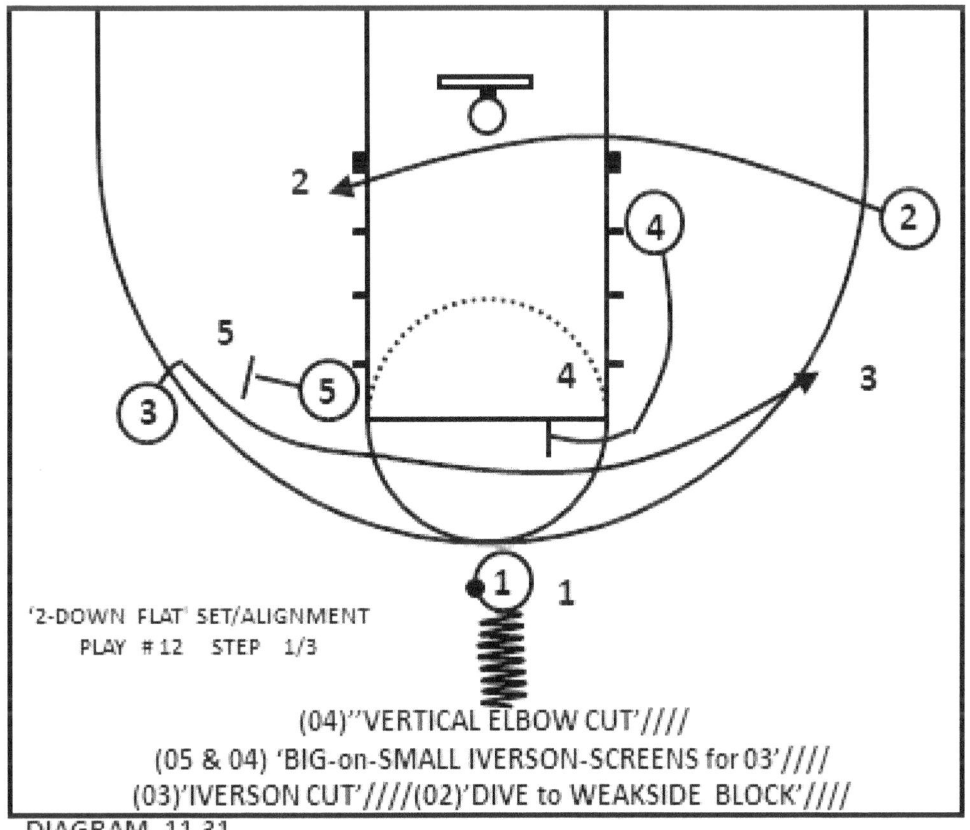

DIAGRAM 11.31

Diagram 11.32 shows 01 not making the "Wing Pass" to 05, but to 03. 01 then makes a "UCLA Cut" off of 04 at the new "Ballside Elbow" area. After the pass is made from 01 to 03, with 05 stretched out horizontally on the new "Weakside Wing" outside on the perimeter, 02 flashes to the top of the key to eliminate any other possible helpside defender. 01 should read his defender and scrape off of either shoulder of 04 before then posting up his inverted (and now isolated) defender on the new "Ballside Block."

If X1 "jumps to the ball," 01 should rub off of 04's inside right shoulder and look for a "Lob Pass" from 03. If the next time Play # 21 is executed and X1 does not "jump to the ball" on the 01-03 "Wing Pass," 01 should scrape off of 04's outside left shoulder and look for a quicker pass from 03. If 01 does not receive the quick pass from 03, 01 then should "Iso Post-Up" his defender down on the "Block." ." Diagram 11.32

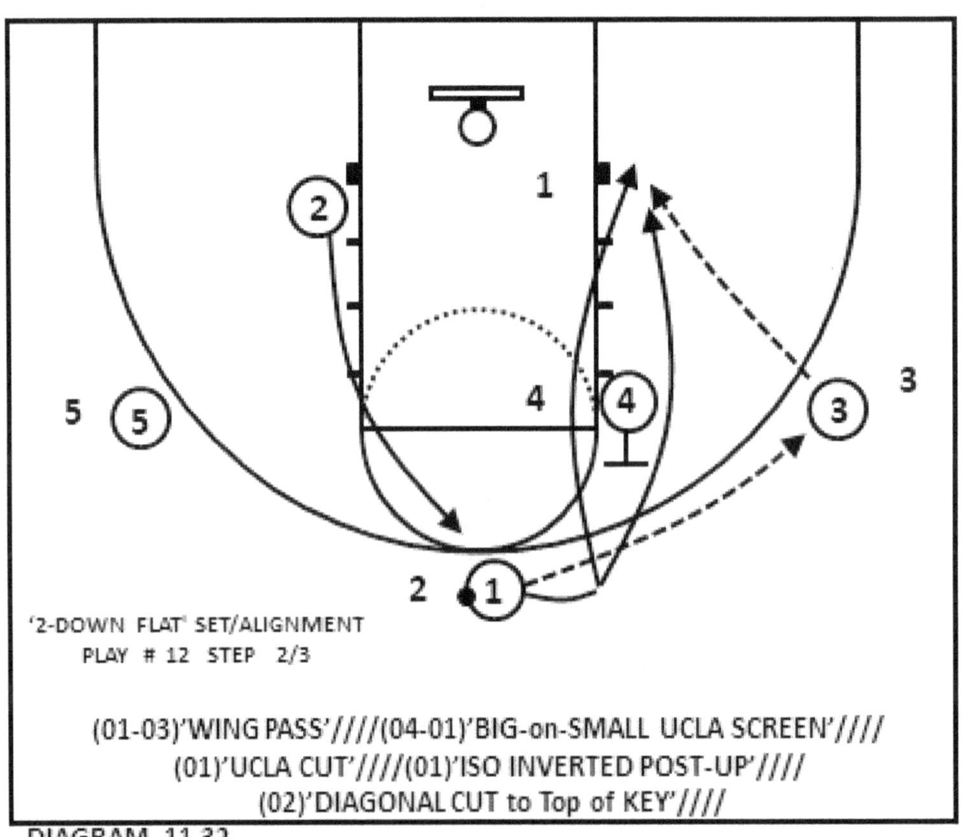

DIAGRAM 11.32

Diagram 11.33 illustrates the end of this play (Play # 12) with 03 not making the pass to 01 at any point in time and instead, making the (03-02) "Reverse Pass."

02 dribble pushes 05 into the "Backdoor Cut" and ultimate "Iso Post-Up" while 04 steps diagonally into the middle of the "Dotted Circle" from the "Ballside High Post" before then diagonally breaking back to the new "Ballside High Post" on the opposite side of the ball. 01 then breaks diagonally up to the top of the key.

This action allows 02 to make possible "Inside Passes to 04, a quick pass to 05 on his cut to the basket, or a "Iso Post-Up" to 05. 02 could have "Skip Pass" opportunities to 03 or a "Reverse Pass" to 01 out on top. Regardless, the "High-Post/Low-Post" Spot-Ups are filled for that specific continuity offense to be able to smoothly begin. ." Diagram 11.33

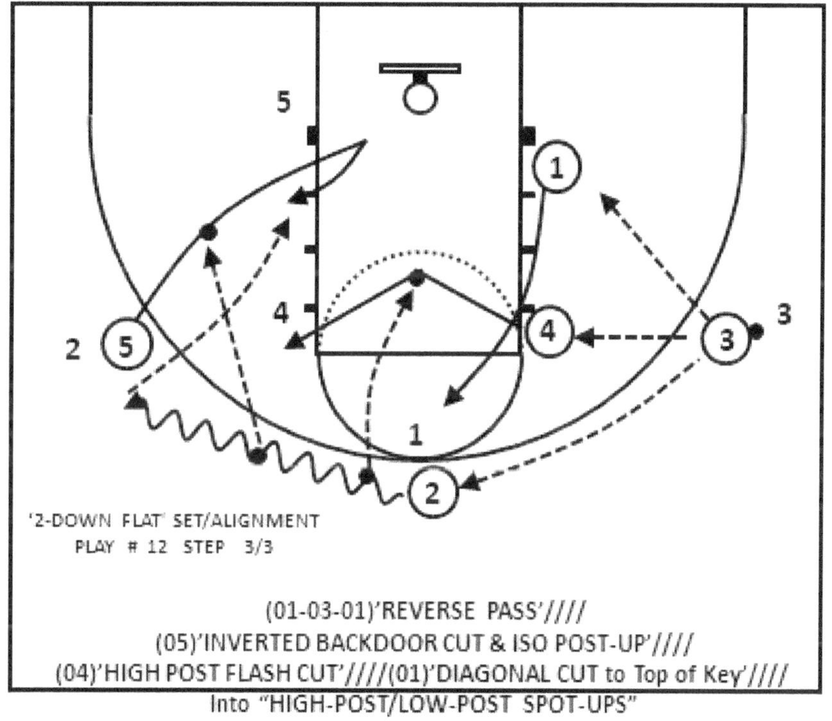

DIAGRAM 11.33

This "2-DOWN " Set alignment is very similar to the "HI-LO STAX" Set and with minor adjustments, most offensive plays/entries from one offensive set can be utilized into the other offensive set. This gives either offensive package numerous more offensive actions that can attack the opposition's defense. Extra plays plus Counter Plays can confuse opposing defenses and give the offense extra advantages to attack the opposition.

CHAPTER 12

PLAYS/ENTRIES EXECUTED FROM THE "2-SQUEEZE SET/ALIGNMENT"

The "2-SQUEEZE" Set

PLAYS/ENTRIES THAT END in the "3-OUT/2-IN" OFFENSIVE SPOT-UPS

After the entry/play/quick-hitter has been executed but no shots have been taken, all five players will end up in a different group of offensive spot-ups. These "3-Out/2-In Spot-Ups" will have players moved about the court with any of the five ending up in the "Ballside Block," the "Ballside Wing," the "Weakside Block," the "Weakside Wing," and the "Point" (at the top of the key). These five positions can provide the offense with safe and easy types of ball-reversals, large gaps for dribble penetration, opportunities to deliver the ball inside to whomever (perimeter-type or post-type players) is posting up their defender on the "Ballside Block," and a player that can be a perimeter-scoring threat and a legitimate offensive rebounding threat from outside of the arc on his "offensive crashing of the boards." The "3-Out/2-In Spot-Ups also provide ample opportunities for constant and effective defensive transition responsibilities.

Diagram 12.1 illustrates the "2-SQUEEZE SET." As the name implies, 02 is the designated player that has the ability to post up on the 'Mid-Post' on either side of the lane. 01 is always the only guard that brings the ball down the floor to initiate the offense and the designated play/entry. The three remaining three players (04, 05 and 03) are "horizontally squeezed" together on the Free Throw Line. With their backs toward their offensive basket, 05 always aligns at the "Nail" position with 04 on the outside of 05's right shoulder and 03 on the outside of 05's left shoulder. With 02 being able to post up on either side of the lane and therefore start on either side of the lane, the offense will have two diverse cosmetic looks and therefore gives the offense a higher level of unpredictability. In this diagram, 02 posts up on the offense's right side of the lane, below 03's initial left 'elbow' location.

There is a significant number of philosophies on how to attack the various types of opposing defenses. This multiple-phase offensive system uses more than one phase/layer/wave of attack, with each phase/wave having a seamless and immediate conversion into the next phase/wave. While this system can be confusing to defenses and difficult to defend, this system can be properly taught and coached so that it can be easily understood and ultimately executed by players of many diverse levels of (physical talent, mental understand, and playing experience.)

In addition, there are several types of offensive schemes and different ways within this system that offenses can successfully attack their defensive counter-parts. Many of these can be integrated within the same offensive system that can attack defenses in various ways. The larger the number of schemes that can be successfully integrated within the same system, the greater the opportunity an offensive team can find the most efficient and productive schemes that can place both individual and the overall team in the best and most frequent "positions to succeed."

The plays/entries carefully diagrammed down to the small and seemingly unimportant 'V-Cuts' made by countless players before making those same player then make their more important cuts are also described in detail.

Each play has been carefully studied and evaluated to determine which level of talent and experience must be possessed for that specific team to be able to successfully execute the play. The most sophisticated plays/entries would fall into the latter of the three levels all based on the team's physical talents and skills, the mental capacities, and the overall team's game experience. In addition, the coaching staff must have a high degree of basketball knowledge as well as very high teaching and coaching skills to educate his/her entire basketball team. The proper breakdown drills must be thoroughly utilized to hone the fundamental skills and techniques needed for individual players and the overall team to execute plays that can be efficient, productive and successful. In addition to the sophistication of the plays as far as the various offensive techniques used, it is almost certain there is a larger number of the various offensive techniques that are weaved into the offensive entry or play. Therefore, there will be additional steps of parts of the higher sophisticated "Level #3" plays.

We define this family of plays as the "Level 3 category" of plays. As just stated, this "Level 3" family of plays will have a much more complex offensive scheme that would require high amounts of physical talent as well as requiring a greater amount of the players (to execute) and the coaches (to teach and coach) mental capacities and experience needed for the offense to be efficient, productive and successful. We feel plays in our defined "Level 3" category could possibly be successful for NBA teams, definitely for college teams and also for many high schools and more experienced AAU teams.

The next lower classification or level of plays would be somewhat lower as far as sophistication, complexity and the actual 'length' of the play (including the number of passes, cuts, screens and other techniques used) in the one particular play's overall series of actions. While all "Level 2" plays in each of the chapters in this book remain to be fundamentally sound, these plays may lack the actual number of techniques/methods that are implemented within that play in comparison to the "Level 3" plays/entries. Therefore, any team that successfully executes the highest "Level 3" plays/entries should easily be able to execute any of these so-called lower "Level 1 and 2" plays/entries, if so desired. It appears most high school teams should be able to execute successfully all aspects of all of the "Level 1 and 2" plays.

The final grouping of plays would be called "Level 1" plays and are not as difficult for offensive players to master their execution of the plays, both physically as well as mentally. Even though the techniques are still fundamentally sound, they may not be as complex to learn and understand in addition to being easier to physically execute. These plays will not take as long of a time to execute the full play because of the lesser number of actual offensive actions implemented within the play.

"Level 1" plays would be lower in the scheme's complexities and the number of techniques used in the execution of this category of plays. This means that these plays will be executed in shorter periods of time before the end of the play and therefore the beginning of the designated continuity offense. More than likely, the fewer number of diagrams will relate to the number of offensive techniques and actions; therefore the lower level of complexity in that particular play/entry.

Obviously, since these "Level 1" plays are still sound, but lack some of the methods used in the two previous more sophisticated and complex levels; these more elementary plays should be able to be utilized by any teams that use either of the two higher level plays. We feel that Middle School/Junior High teams as well as younger AAU teams or organizations should be able to utilize any of the "Level 1" plays successfully, with a possibility that some of those teams that are slightly more advanced (than other teams) could possibly use some plays located in the immediate next immediate level.

Ideas, concepts, and techniques from actual plays from teams of all three levels have been used to modify or to create different combinations of the various techniques and schemes used that will help prove these entries can be successfully used. This allows the author to create numerous plays that use the various schemes to build a library of fundamentally sound plays that will be unique and will be appropriate for a wide range of teams with the various ages and skill levels.

Any team that has the capabilities of executing "Level 3" plays (sometimes called quick-hitters or entries) would then be able to execute the somewhat less complicated and complex plays categorized in both the "Level 2 and Level 1" groups.

Also, any offensive team that can execute "Level 2" plays should then be able to incorporate and implement (the somewhat lower) "Level 1" plays/entries.

The "Level 3" plays that are discussed in this chapter should most likely be slightly too complex for teams that use the Level 1 and 2 plays. Some teams may be able to handle some particular plays that are just a step up from their normal family of plays, such as a team that predominately implements "Level 1" plays may have the capabilities of adding a very small number of "Level 2" plays. Or a team that has a majority of "Level 2" plays may only on rarely have instances to successfully incorporate a "Level 3" play.

With this book having plays in these three presumed categories or levels, the book will reach out and benefit a much larger group of serious basketball coaches from elementary school age to the highest skilled levels that exists.

In addition, an experienced and resourceful coach may be able to mold some plays that include all of the offensive techniques that he/she desires could reshape a specific play that begins in one specific offensive set/alignment and reshape it so that it could begin in a different offensive/set that is more favorable to that coach and his/her coaching staff's liking.

Conversely, that innovative and creative coach may completely like the specific offensive set/alignment and favor the very same offensive actions included in a certain play, but can modify that play so that the ending spot-ups of all five players are conducive to being able to begin the final phase of the offensive attack by using a more favorable offensive continuity offense.

Play # 1 begins with 02 on the left side of the lane and 04 making a "Barkley Cut" and 03 making an "Iverson Cut" to the two "Wing" areas on both sides of the lane and 05 remaining in the center of the FT Line. A slight cosmetic modification in this play could be that 04 and 03 could change which player is the cutter that goes underneath 05 at the "Nail" and which player goes over the top. Diagram 12.13 has 04 make his "Barkley Cut" over 05 and 03 make his "Iverson Cut" under the top of 05. See Diagram 12.1

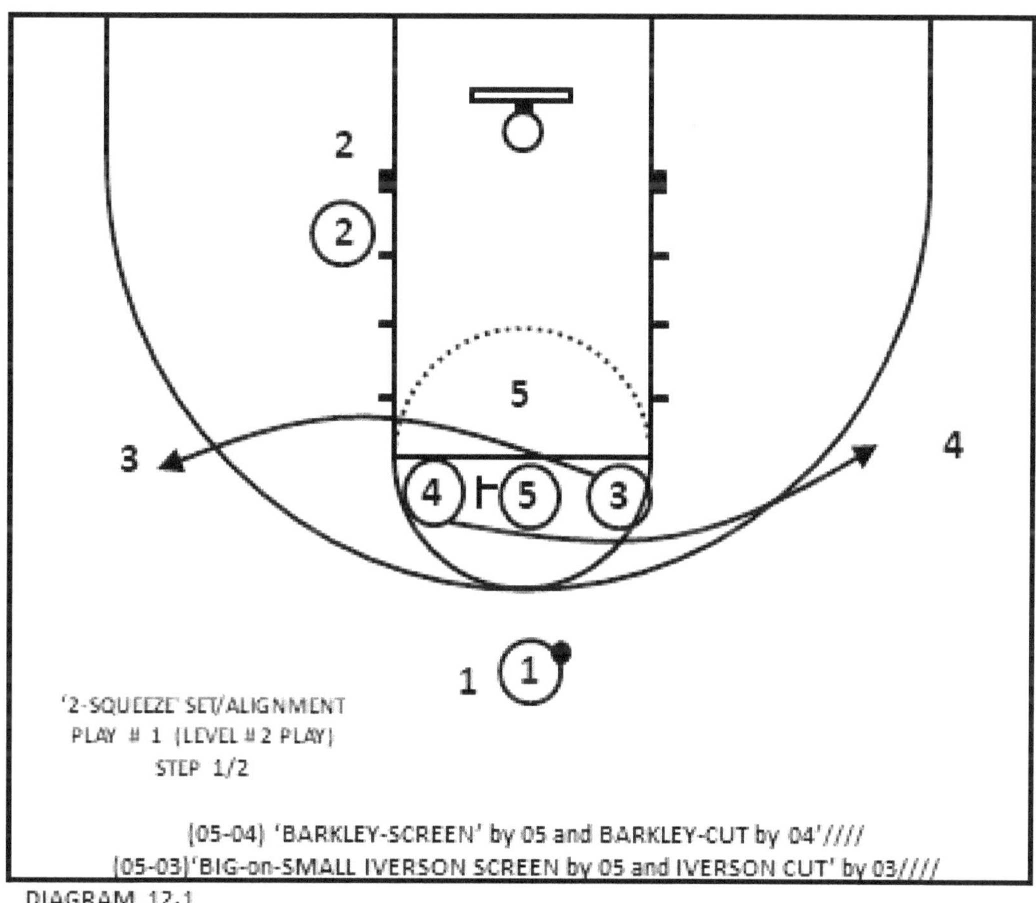

DIAGRAM 12.1

In this instance, 01 must always pass the ball away from 02's initial side of the floor and therefore to the inverted post player, 04, at the FT Line extended on the right side of the offense. Diagram 12.14 shows the continuation of the entry after the 01-04 "Wing Pass." After making the "Wing Pass" to 04, both 01 and 05 diagonally break down to set a "Stagger-Screen" for 02 to use to break up to the top of the key for a possible open '3.' After screening for 02, 05 then makes a "Brush Cut" off of 01 to then flash to the empty new "Ballside Block." With 05 scraping off of 01, a defensive switch would still place X1 on 05 for a distinct 'personnel mismatch advantage' for the offense. 04 would have opportunities for an "Inside Pass" to 05, a pass to 02 for an open '3 Pt.' shot or a "Skip Pass" to 03 on the opposite wing. If 02 does not have an open '3,' the 04-02 "Reverse Pass" ends the actual entry without a shot taken, but has attacked various defenders, moved offensive players and their defenders around the floor and repositioned the offensive players into the proper "3-Out/2-In Spot-Ups" for a smooth and fluid beginning of the next wave of attack. This play also falls into the Level 2 Group, again meaning that any team that has the so-called "Level 1 and Level 2 capabilities" should be able to incorporate this entry into its offensive attack. See Diagram 12.2

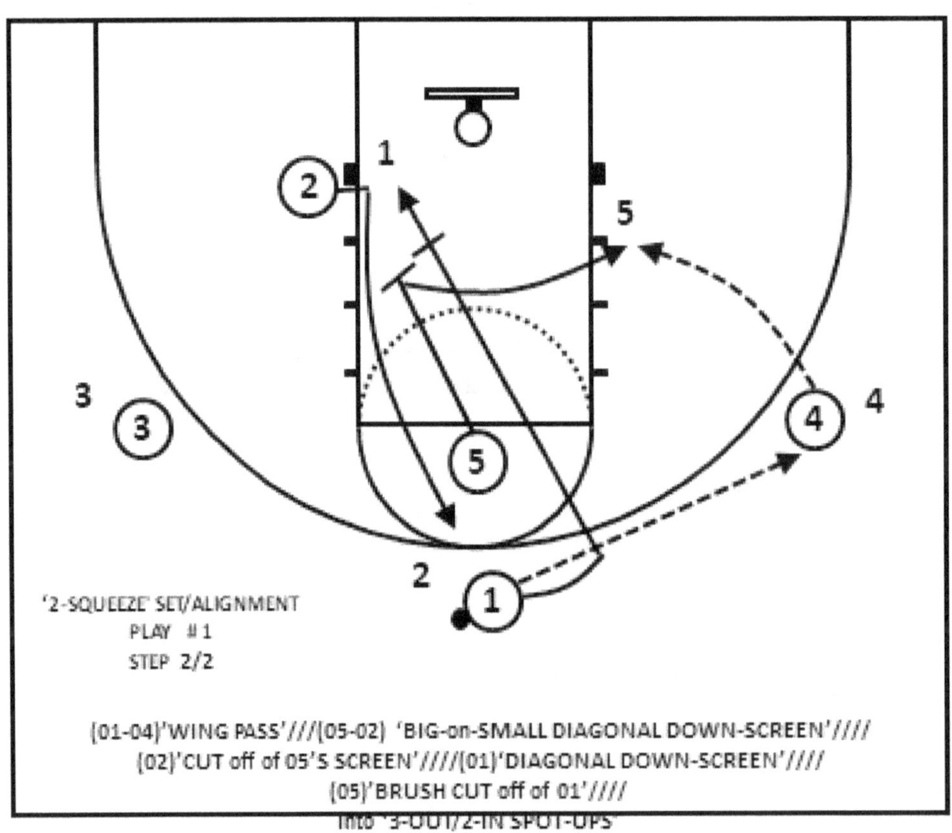

DIAGRAM 12.2

Diagram 12.3 illustrates the beginning of Play # 2, with 02 starting on the left side of the floor. As 01 makes his dribble towards the left "Slot," 02 "L-Cuts" up and out to the FT Line extended on that same left side of the offense. 04 makes his "Barkley Cut" over the top of 05 and 03 to the opposite "Wing" area and 03 makes a short vertical "Pop-Out" to fill the opposite "Slot" position. After 05 "Barkley Screens" for 04 and 04 makes his "Barkley Cut," to the opposite "Wing" area, 05 then remains at the "Nail" location. Keep in mind that with both "2-Guard Slot" locations now filled, both "Wing" locations also filled and 05 at the center of the FT Line; all defenders are stretched out vertically and horizontally away from the basket. See Diagram 12.3

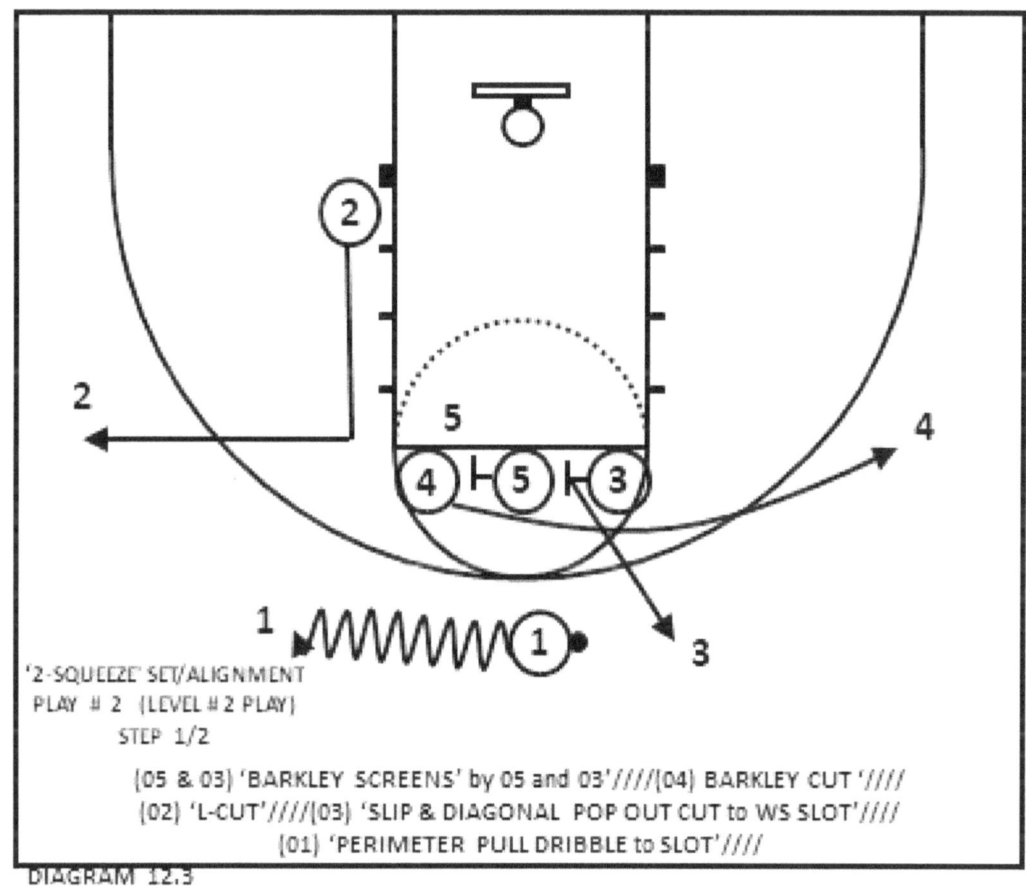

Diagram 12.4 illustrates 01 electing to make the short and safe "Reverse Pass" to 03. 01 then uses 05's "Big-on-Small Back-Screen" and "scrapes off of" 05 on his Shuffle-Cut" to the new "Ballside Block." This cut can be very effective so that this specific entry could use 01's exceptionally good offensive post-up skills and/or to attack X1 (and his presumed defensive weaknesses). 03 immediately looks to make the pass to 01 on his cut as 01 has fully isolated and inverted his own perimeter-type defender. 01 continues to post up on the new "Ballside Block."

03 could then make the "Wing Pass" to 04 (inverted out on the perimeter). 03 immediately then scrapes off of 05's left shoulder and makes a "Lob Cut" towards the basket. 04 can make passes to either 01 or 03 on the interior. After screening for both 01 and 03, 05 steps out to invert his post-type defender, X5, at the top of the key.

If no shots are taken, all players are in the proper "3-Out/2-In Spot-Ups" for the designated continuity offense to immediately and fluidly begin. Diagram 12.16. Play # 9 falls into a Level 2 type of play. So, once again any team that has the so-called "Level 1 and Level 2 skill sets" (physically and mentally) should be able to incorporate this play into its offensive scoring package. The "Level 3" plays that are discussed in this chapter should most likely be slightly too complex for teams using the majority of Level 1 and 2 plays and should be restricted to those types of higher skilled teams. See Diagram 12.4

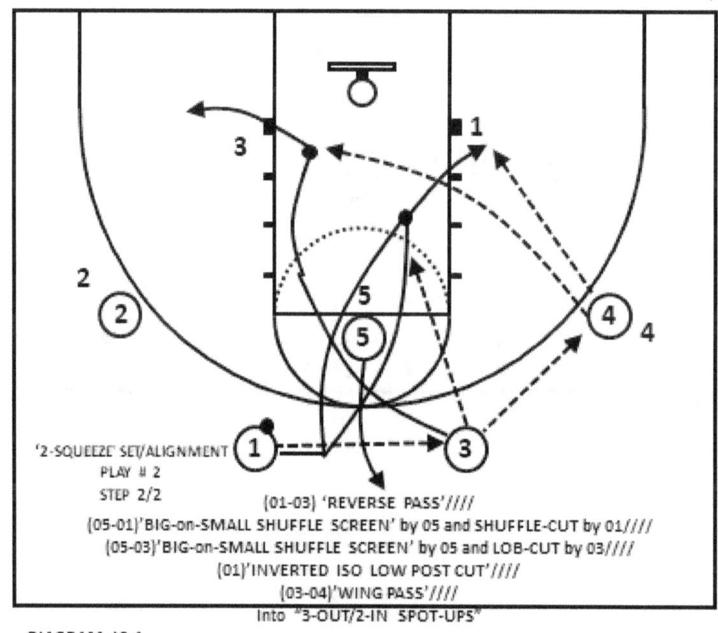

DIAGRAM 12.4

At the very beginning of the action, Play # 3, 02 starts on the left side of the lane with the "Iverson" and the "Barkley Cuts." Play # 3 is shown in Diagram 12.5 with 02 starting on the left side of the lane below 04 with 04 making a "Barkley Cut" off of 05 and 03 making an "Iverson Cut" off of 05. 04 and 03 can make a last second decision on which player cuts over the top of 05 and which one cuts below 05. In this diagram, 03 cuts low under 05 on his "Iverson Cut" and 04 cuts over the top of 05 on his "Barkley Cut." This could be changed up every time this play is executed to increase the deception and disguise of this quick-hitter. See Diagram 12.5

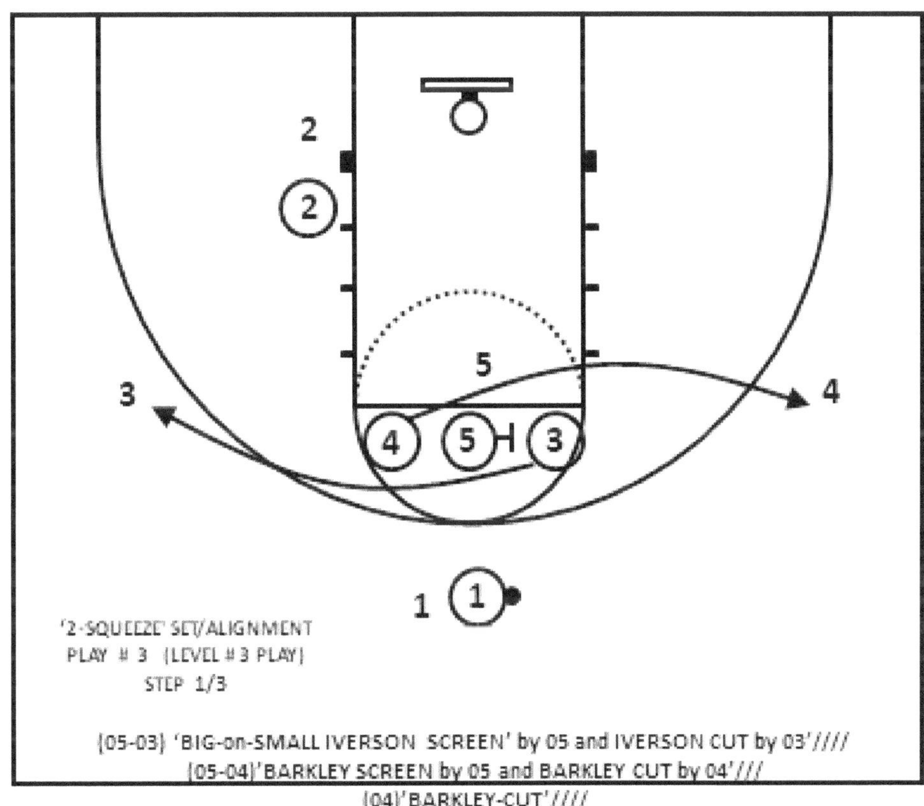

DIAGRAM 12.5

With 03 and 04 now at both wings, Diagram 12.5 shows that 01 could make the initial "Wing Pass" to either player, located on either side of the floor. If 01 elects to make the pass to 04, 02 would immediately be in position for an "inverted and isolated" post-up on his perimeter-type defender. If the ball is passed to 04, away from 02, 02 could simply and quickly flash across the lane to again become an "inverted and isolated post-up player. With 05 at the "Nail" spot and 04 at the FT Line extended, X2 would not have any helpside defensive support. This action could take advantage of 02's offensive interior scoring skills, to attack X2's defensive skills and to take away from X2's own offensive game by fatiguing him or getting him in foul trouble or a combination of all those valid reasons.

After making the 01-03 "Wing Pass," 01 starts to cut away from his pass before reversing directions and then scraping off of 05's left shoulder to make a "Lob Cut" to the basket while attacking a second perimeter-type defender in the lane, X1. See Diagram 12.6

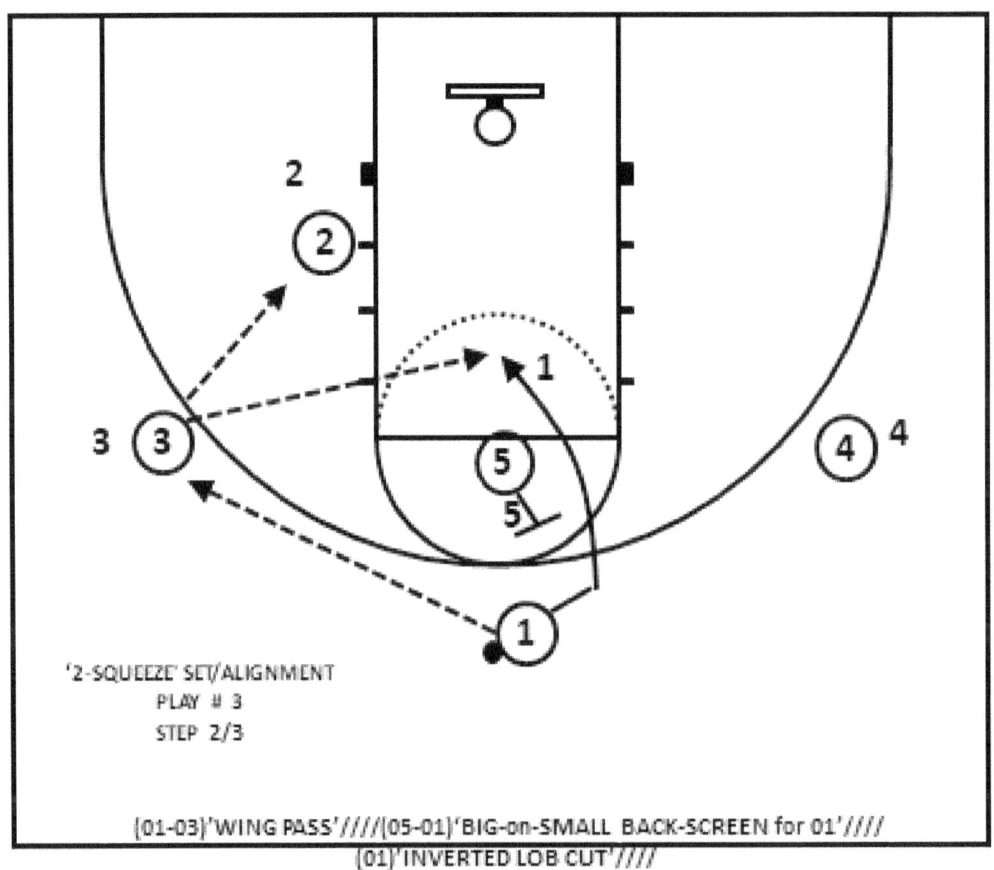

DIAGRAM 12.6

If 01 is not immediately open because his defender is playing him tight and "tagging" him, 01 should stop and reverse his cut to then cut back off of the second screen set by 05—this time, a 05-01 "Big-on-Small Pin-Down Screen" for 01. With X1 taking away 03's Lob Pass by playing 01 tightly, 01 cuts tightly off of 05's 'new ballside shoulder' (the left shoulder). This allows 01 to break free for a probable '3 Pt.' shot at the top of the key, while 05 then slips his screen and diagonally slides down to the vacant "Mid-Post" area on the new weakside.

If this action does not create a shot for 01, it at least occupies and moves off-the-ball defenders to give 02 more possibilities to attack his defender on the 'Ballside Block' as well as to give 01 an opportunity for an open "3 Pt. shot." From there, 01 could turn down his shot and then swing the ball to 04 or 're-reverse' the ball back to 03. Either 02 or 05 would have more opportunities to receive the ball from the two "Wing" areas and attack their defender 'down on the block.' If shots are still not created, opponents have been attacked and forced to move around to defend their men in various situations. Minimally, the offense has placed all five players into the correct "3-Out/2-In Spot-Ups" for the next wave of the attack to fluidly begin. Diagram 12.19. Play # 10 falls into the Level 3 category. This means that only certain types of teams should be able to execute plays at this level of play, but this type of team should be able to execute any and all plays of its choosing from any of the other two levels of the mental and physical heights of play. See Diagram 12.7

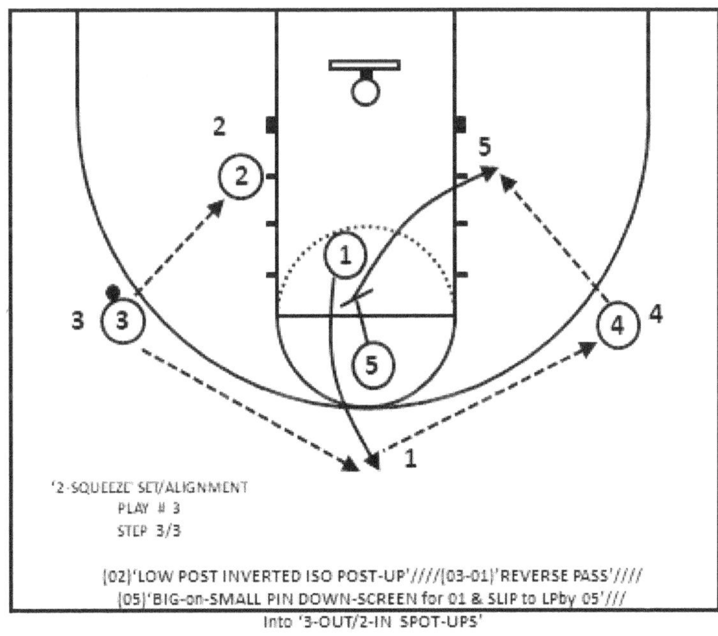

DIAGRAM 12.7

Diagram 12.8 illustrates the beginning of Play # 4, with 02 starting on the left side of the floor. As 01 makes his dribble towards the left "Slot," 02 "L-Cuts" up and out to the FT Line extended on that same left side of the offense. 05 makes his "Barkley Cut" over the top of 03 to the opposite "Wing" area and 03 makes a short vertical "Pop-Out" to fill the opposite "Slot" position. 04 diagonally dives to the basket and looks for an "Inside Pass" from 01. If he is not open, 04 breaks back towards the "Nail" location. If 01 reads that 04 has a different type of "position advantage" on the perimeter better than either 01 or 03's advantages, 01 could look to make a "Lob Pass" to 04 cutting towards the rim. Keep in mind that with both "2-Guard Slot" locations filled (by 01 and 03), both "Wing" locations filled (by 02 and 05) and 04 now at the center of the FT Line, which forces all five opposing defenders to be stretched out vertically and horizontally away from the basket. See Diagram 12.8

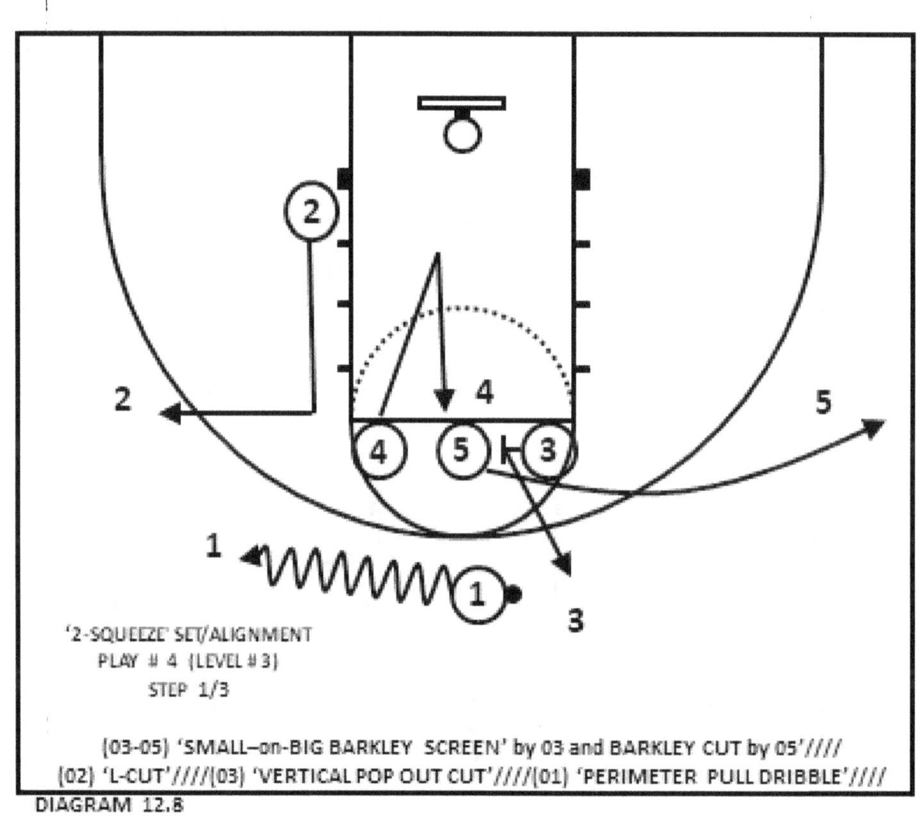

DIAGRAM 12.8

Diagram 12.9 illustrates 01 electing to make the short and safe "Reverse Pass" to 03. 01 then uses 04's "Big-on-Small Back-Screen" and "scrapes off of "05's outside (right) shoulder on his Shuffle-Cut" to the new "Ballside Block." This cut can be very effective to exploit 01's above average post-up skills and/or to attack X1 and his inexperience of playing post-up defense. 03 immediately looks to make the pass to 01 as 01 has fully isolated and inverted his own perimeter-type defender. With 02 at the FT Line extended on the weakside and 04 at the 'nail,' there are no remaining defenders on the weakside of the floor, 01 continues to post up on the new "Ballside Block" and to look for an "Inside Pass" from 05. 05 is at the FT Line extended and has pulled presumably the opponent's biggest defender away from the basket. See Diagram 12.9

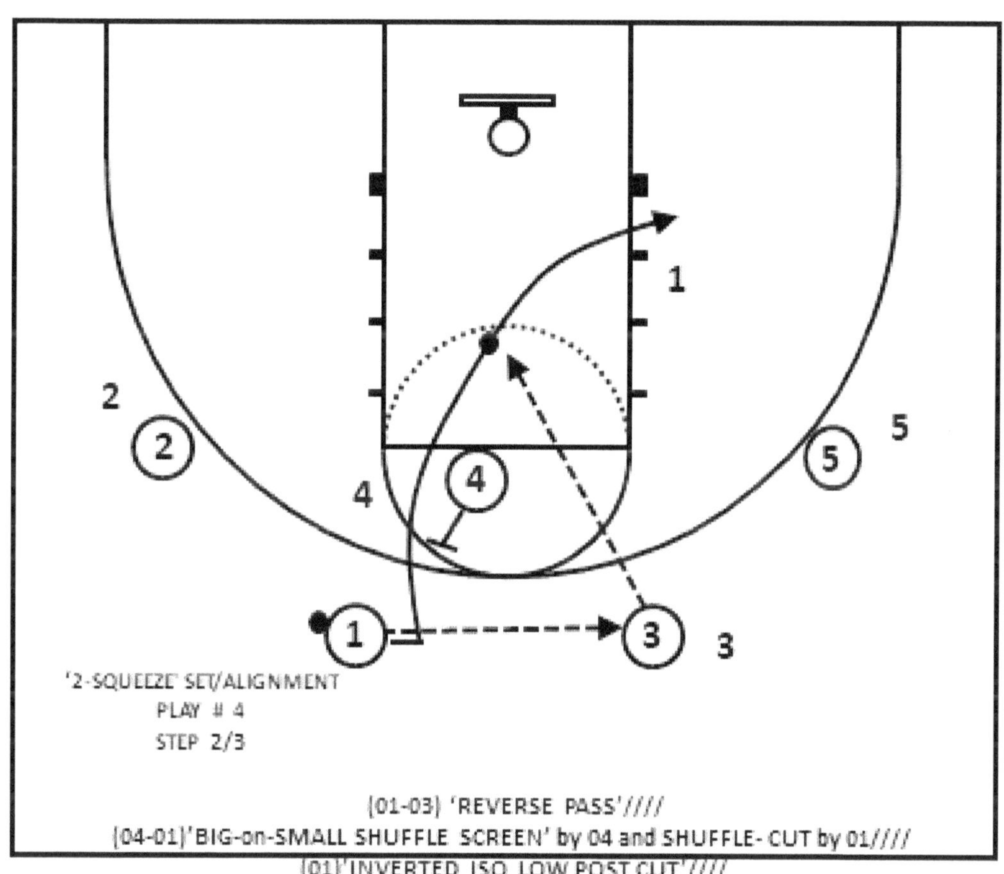

DIAGRAM 12.9

Diagram 12.10 shows 03 turning down passes to 01 on 01's "Shuffle-Cut," then to 05 on the "Ballside Wing" or to 02 on the weakside of the floor. 04 then steps up after setting his 04-01 "Big-on-Small Back-Screen" to then set his second screen-- a "Big-on-Small Ball-Screen" for 03. This screen will help 03 shed his defender so he can make his perimeter pull dribble over to the opposite side of the floor towards the vacant "Slot" location. As 03 breaks contact with 04's top (right) shoulder and continues his dribble towards the "Slot," 04 immediately makes a front pivot off of his left foot to "Rim-Run" to the basket, looking for a "Lob Pass" from 03. At the same time, 01 flashes back across the lane to the opposite side of the floor and looks for "Inside Passes" from either 03 or from 02. With 01 having vacated the area and becoming a new inside scoring threat on the offense's new "Ballside" of the floor and 05 having inverted his own post-type defender out at the FT Line extended on the new weakside; 04 should have all the space needed to attack his defender on his "Lob Cut" to the basket.

03 has primary passing targets to 01 and 04 on the interior, a "Wing Pass" target to 02 or a "Skip Pass" to 05 on the new 'Weakside.' 02 may have a better passing angle to deliver the ball to 01 and 05 could have a better passing to make the "Inside Pass" to 04 after his "Lob Cut." If no shots are produced as a result of the fundamentally sound and fluid movement of all five offensive players, the "3-Out/2-In Spot-Ups" are once again filled for another smooth transition immediately into the designated continuity offense. Play # 11 falls into the highest and most sophisticated Level 3. It must be repeated that this type of team should be able to then also pick and choose any plays/entries that fall into the other two (slightly) lower categories of offensive forms of attack. See Diagram 12.10.

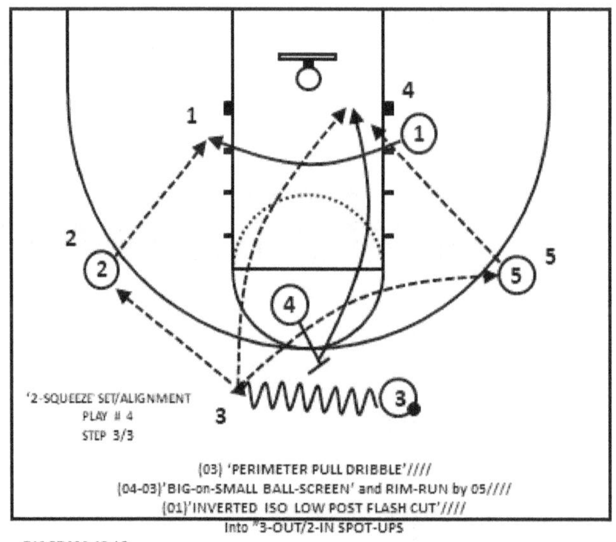

DIAGRAM 12.10

PLAYS THAT END in the "4-OUT/1-IN" OFFENSIVE SPOT-UPS

The difference in the following five plays/entries are that 02 will start on the left side of the lane and in addition, all five players will end up in a different group of offensive spot-ups. These "4-Out/1-In Spot-Ups" will have players moved about the court with any of the five ending up in the "Ballside Deep Corner," the "Ballside Slot," the "Weakside Slot," the "Ballside Post," and the "Weakside Deep Corner." These five positions can provide the offense with safe and easy types of ball-reversals, large gaps for dribble penetration, opportunities to deliver the ball inside to whomever (perimeter-type or post-type players) is posting up their defender on the "Ballside Block," and a player that can be a perimeter-scoring threat and a legitimate offensive rebounding threat from outside of the arc on his "offensive crashing of the boards." The "4-Out/1-In Spot-Ups also provide ample opportunities for constant and effective defensive transition responsibilities.

Diagram 12.11 illustrates the beginning of Play # 5, with 02 starting on the offense's right side of the floor and again 04, 05 and 03 aligned from left to right respectively on the FT Line. 03 steps up to set a "Big-on-Small Ball-Screen" for 01 to use to dribble towards 02, who has broken up to the new "Ballside Wing" area. After 'dribble-scraping off of 03's top left shoulder, 03 then slips his screen and curls to the new "Weakside Slot," opposite of 01 and the ball.

As 01 starts his dribble towards 03 on the right side of the floor, 05 makes a "Barkley Cut" over the top of 04's "Barkley Screen" towards the "Wing" area on the left side of the floor. After setting the "Barkley Screen" for 05, 04 slips the screen and dives to the basket to isolate his lone defender. With 05 and 02 at the two "Wing" areas at the FT Line extended just outside of the arc and with 03 and 01 at the two "Slot" locations; X4 is completely isolated in his attempt to deny 04 the ball in a very high percentage scoring area.

There are countless options and opportunities for all four players outside of the arc to make the "Inside Pass" to 04, or to shoot from their respective perimeter spot-up areas, or to drive and create. If none of the options produce a shot and possession is maintained, the "4-Out/1-In Spot-Ups" are filled for the designated continuity offense to immediately begin. See Diagram 12.11

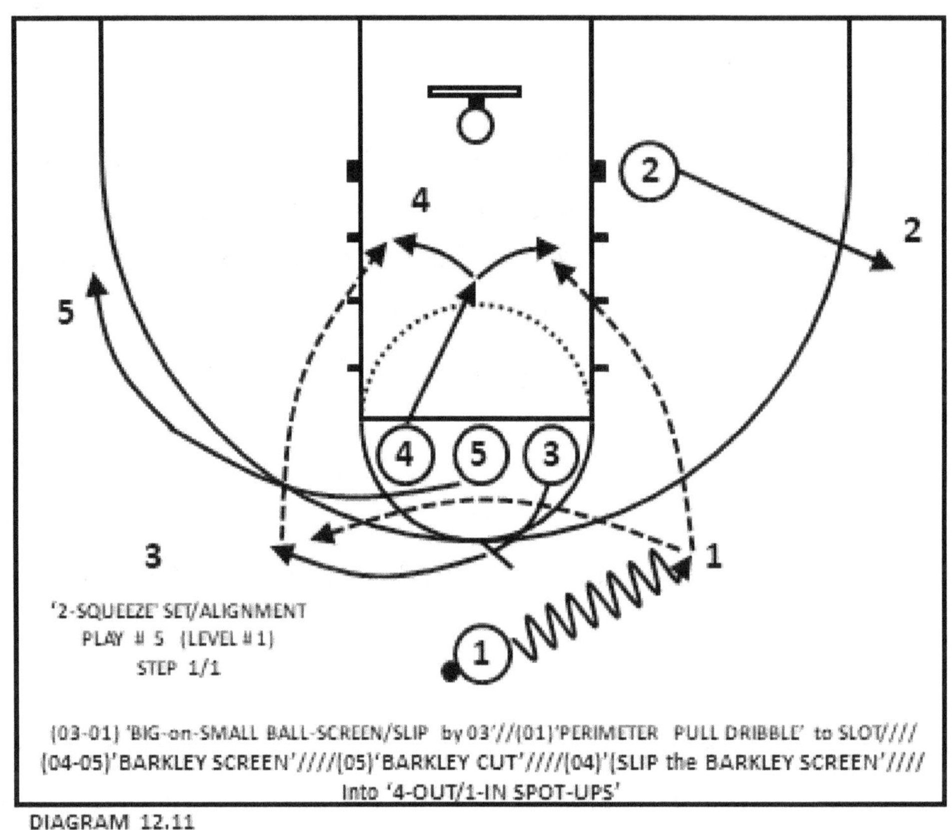

DIAGRAM 12.11

Play # 5 falls into the Level 1 Category, primarily meaning that a team of this level of talent, mental skills and experience should stay within its framework of skills and only utilize plays that are defined as "Level 1" plays.

The beginning of Play # 6 is shown in Diagram 12.12 with 02 making an "L-Cut" up and out to the FT Line extended on his side of the floor while 04 makes his "Barkley Cut" over the top of both 05 and 03. 01 begins his perimeter pull dribble to the "Slot" location on the left side of the floor. After 04 breaks contact with 03 on his cut, 03 then steps out to the new "Weakside Slot" with 05 remaining at the "Nail." See Diagram 12.12

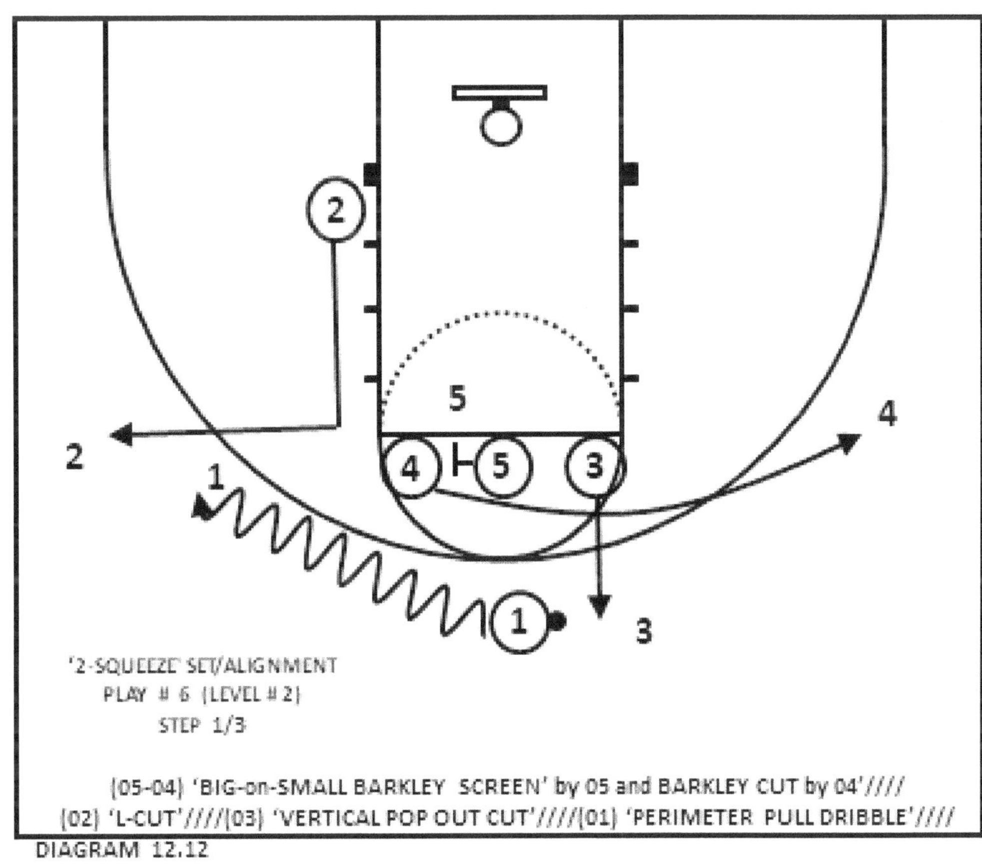

Diagram 12.13 shows the smooth continuation and movement of the play with 01 continuing his dribble towards 02 for the likely (01-02) "Small-on-Big Dribble Hand-Off." Keep in mind, that 05 could read his defender and if he has a direct and clear path to the basket, either 01 or 02 could make the "Lob Pass" to 05. See Diagram 12.13

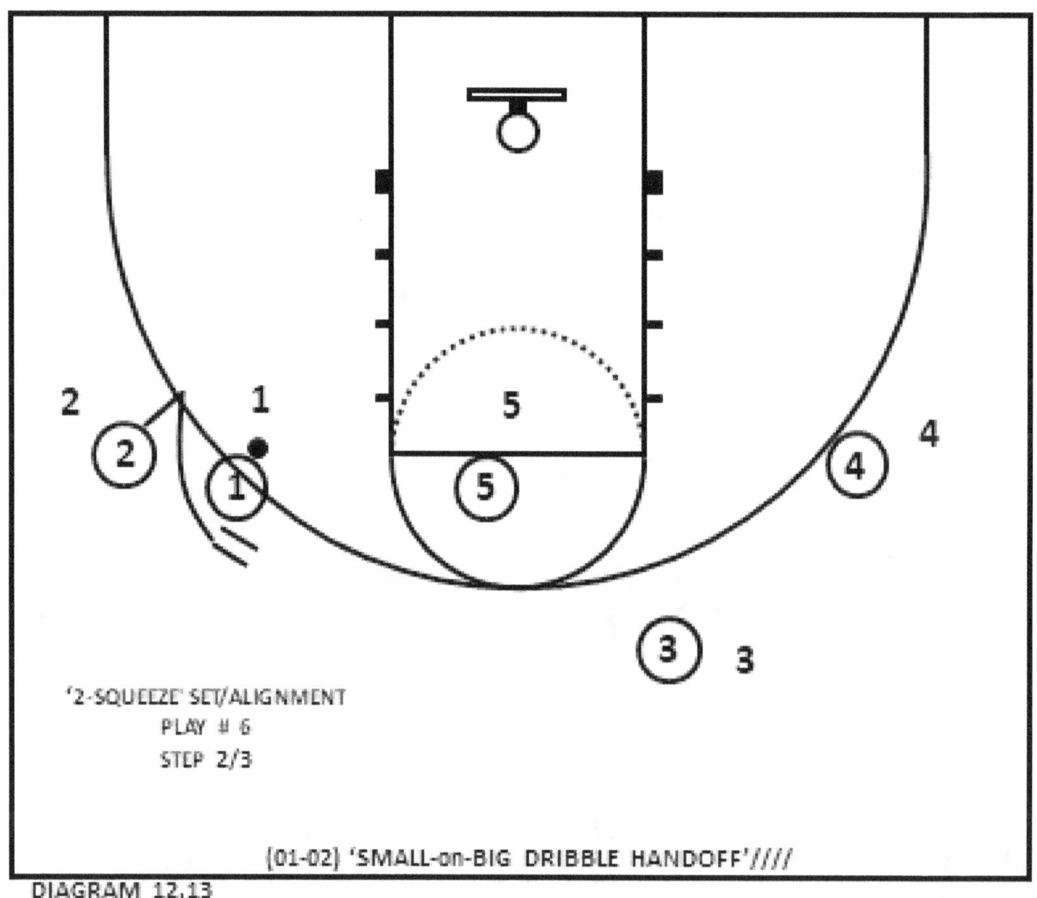

DIAGRAM 12.13

Diagram 12.14 shows the 01-02 DHO with the "Pistols" Action immediately beginning. 05 steps up to set a "Big-on-Small (Pistols) Ball-Screen" for 02 to use. After the hand-off, 01 "Flare-Cuts" to that side of the floor's "Deep Corner" to become 02's potential "Throwback Pass" receiver as well as eliminating a defender in the middle of the action.

As 02 'dribble-scrapes' off of 05's top left shoulder, 05 could either 'Roll' down the lane or 'Rim-Run' to the basket. As 02 approaches 03, to eliminate any support defense that X5 would need to defend either one of 05's cuts to the basket, 04 steps up to "Flare-Screen" for 03 to then "Flare-Cut" to the new "Ballside Deep Corner." This gives 02, one of the better ball-handlers and drivers, opportunities for his own dribble penetration drives and opportunities for passes to either 01 or 03 (both presumed perimeter scoring threats) or a safe pass receiver in 04 at the opposite "Slot."

If no shots are created, the "4-Out/1-In Spot-Ups" are filled so that there can be an immediate and fluid transition from this high-scoring play into the designated continuity offense. Play # 13 falls into Level 2 and possibly the Level 3 categories. That means that this team that has the capabilities of being able to successfully and productively execute this play should easily be able to implement any entries that fits its philosophies and players of the many "Level 1" plays discussed in this book. See Diagram 12.14

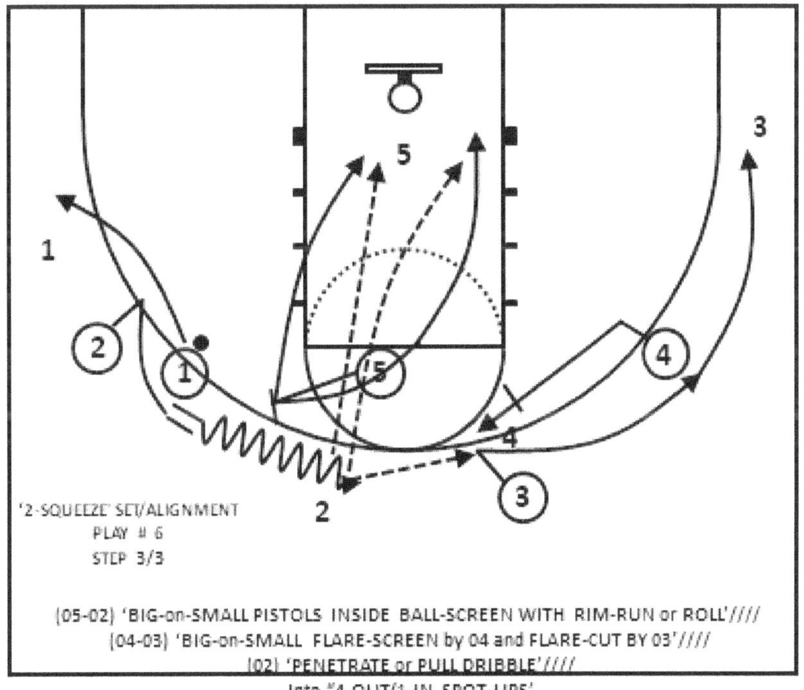

Diagram 12.15 illustrates Play # 7 with 02 on the left side of the lane. 05 breaks over the top of 04's "Barkley Screen" but shortens his "Barkley Cut," by stopping at the "High Post Elbow" area. 03 breaks out to the "Wing" area on his initial side of the floor while 02 remains on the same side of the lane to post up. 04 ends up at the 'Nail' with 01 having approached the top of the key on his dribble. See Diagram 12.15

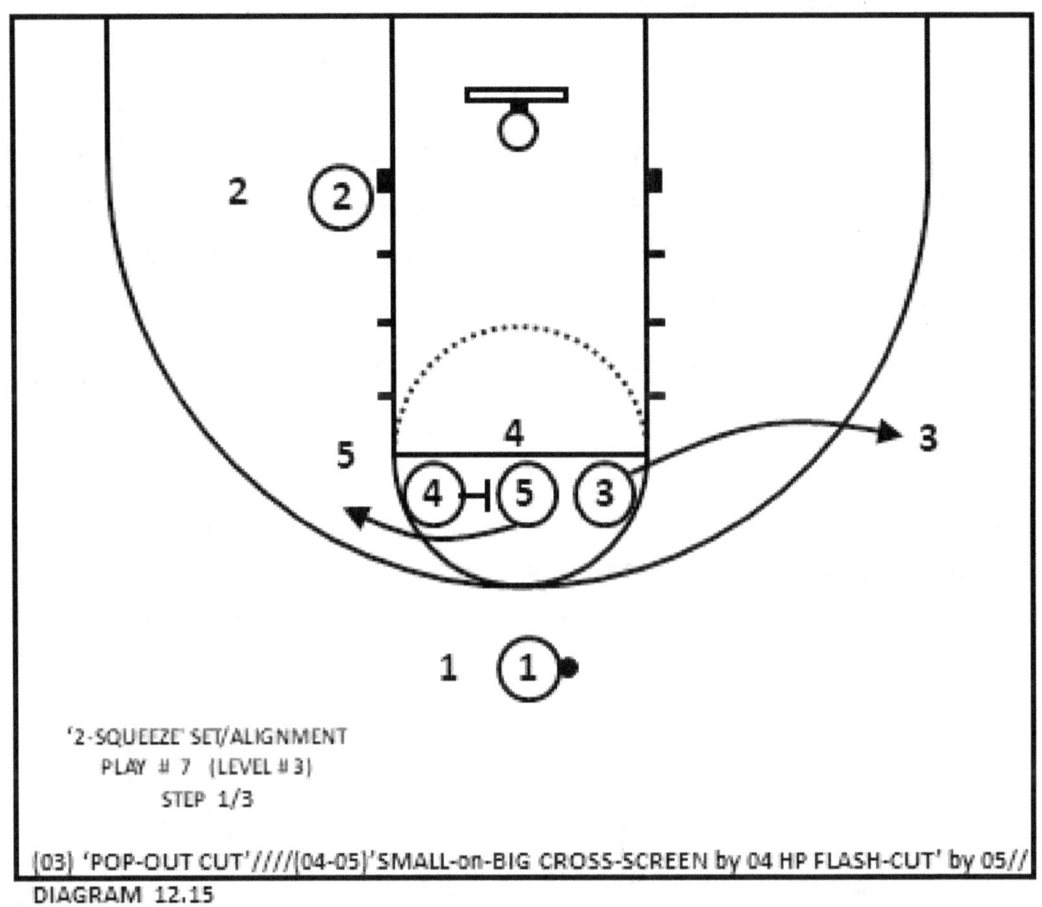

Diagram 12.16 shows 01 making the "Wing Pass" to 03 and 04 crossing over to set a "Cross-Screen" for 05 to flash to the new "Ballside High Post." At the same time, 02 flashes to the new "Ballside Low Post," giving both 05 and 02 inside scoring opportunities with minimal interior helpside defense. After screening for 05, 04 slips his screen and "Flare-Cuts" to the new completely vacant weakside of the floor. This pulls the supposed second biggest interior defender (X4) further from the basket, giving the inverted 02 and 05 more advantageous situations to score in the post. After 01 makes the pass to 03, 01 starts to make a "Flare-Cut" before then breaking back to the top of the key. If shots are not produced or created by the action, all players are now in the correct "High-(Post)/Low-(Post) Spot-Ups for that particular type of continuity offense to be able to immediately begin. See Diagram 12.16

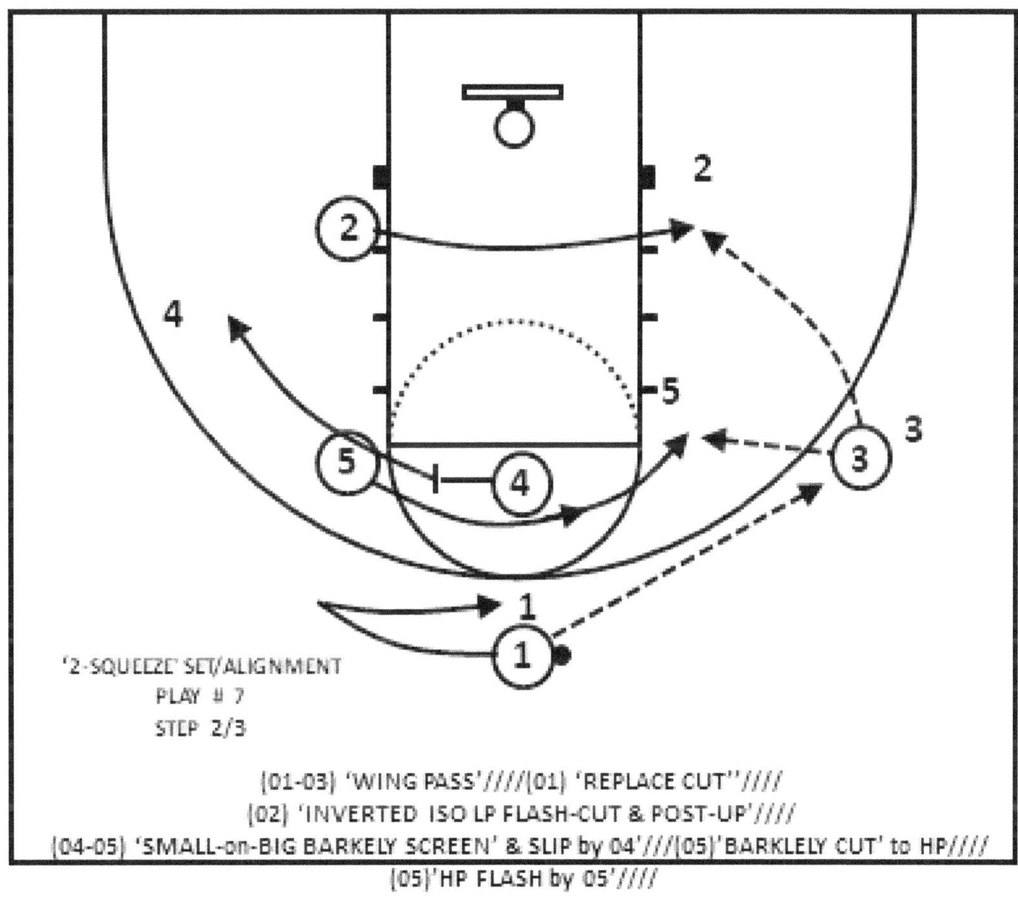

DIAGRAM 12.16

If the coaching staff wants to flow into "4-Out/1-In Spot-Ups" for a different type of continuity offense, when shots are not created; 05 could step out to set a "Big-on-Small Inside Ball-Screen" for 03 to 'dribble-scrape' off of 05's top right shoulder. As contact is broken between 05 and 03, 05 then inverts his defensive 'big' and "Flare-Cuts" to the "Deep Corner." At the same time, 02 can make an "inverted and isolated Duck-In Cut" to attack his perimeter-type defender in the 'paint.' As 03 makes his 'perimeter pull-dribble,' the closest offensive perimeter player to 03 is 01. It is very possible that X1 will want to deny the pass to 01 to prevent the offense from reversing the ball. Therefore, 01 should make a hard "Backdoor Cut" to the basket and look for 03's "Inside Pass." 04 will still prevent his 'big defender' from being involved in support defense for breaking up to fill the "Weakside Slot" location. The actions of 05 and 04 have pulled and stretched both 'defensive bigs' (X4 and X5) further from the basket, allowing all three presumed perimeter-type players, (03, 02 and 01) better opportunities to attack their defenders in areas that the offensive players may have superior offensive skills to those three opponents' inferior defensive skills. Still if no shots are created, players have repositioned themselves into the correct "4-Out/1-In Spot-Ups" for the wanted continuity offense to smoothly begin. Diagram 12.29 Play # 14 falls into both the Level 2 and the Level 3 categories of plays' skill requirements, meaning this team that has the capabilities of being able to execute any "Level 1" plays with success. See Diagram 12.17. # Play 7.

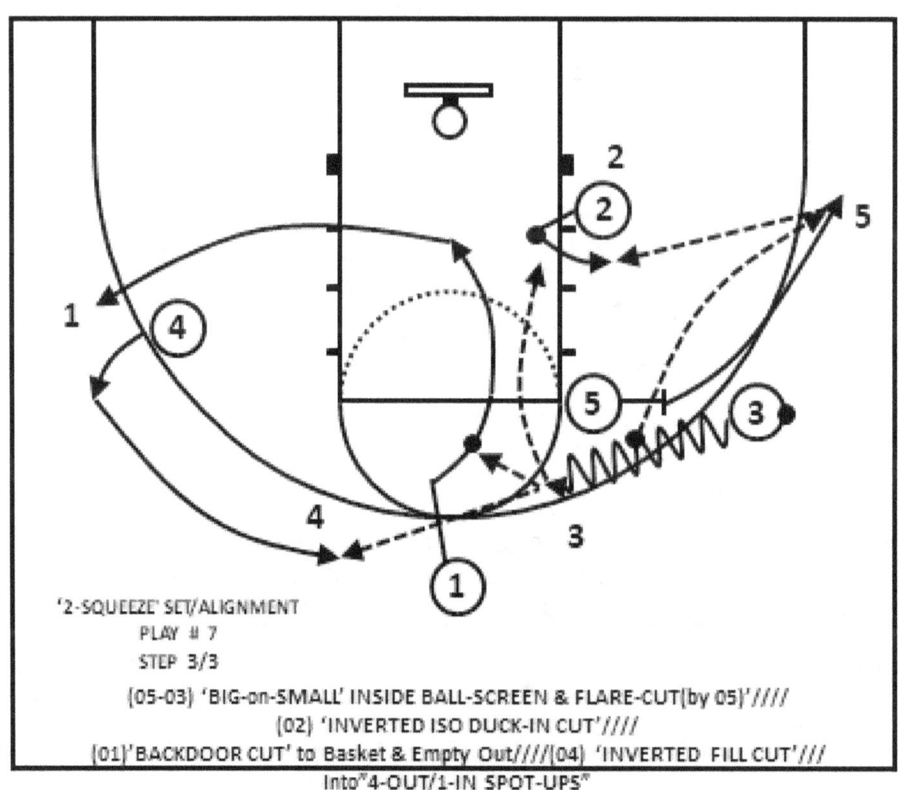

DIAGRAM 12.17

Diagram 12.18 illustrates the beginning of Play #8, another play out of the "2-SQUEEZE" Set. In this quick-hitter play, 02 could start on the offensive right side's "Mid-Post" area. As 01 approaches the top of the key, 04 should make a "Barkley Cut" over the top of 05 to the FT Line extended on the opposite side of the floor. At the same time, 03 makes his "Iverson Cut" underneath 05 to the opposite "Wing" area, while 05 remains at the "Nail" and 02 stays in the "Mid-Post" area on the same side of the lane. See Diagram 12.18

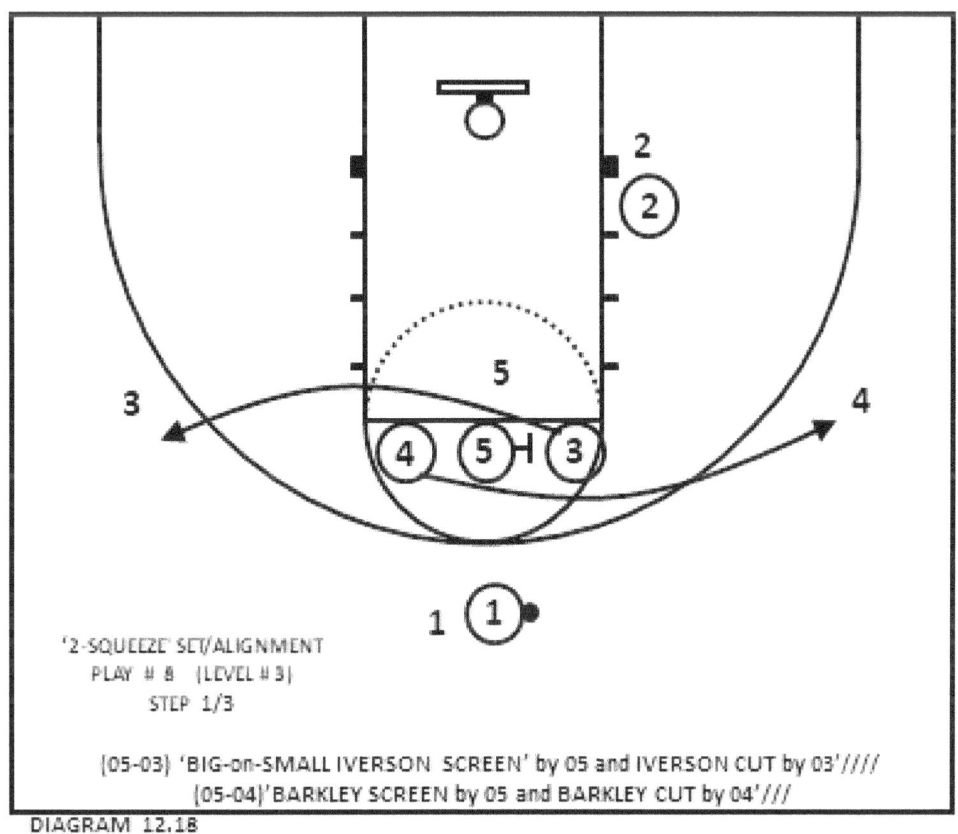

Diagram 12.19 shows 01 making the "Wing Pass" to 03 on the left side of the floor with 02 immediately flashing across the lane to the new "Ballside Block." At the same time, 04 steps up to set a "Big-on-Small Flare-Screen" for 01 to use to "Flare-Cut" to the new "Weakside Wing" area. Also at the same time, 05 drifts away from the ball towards the basket as if on a "Weakside Lob Cut" to the basket. If the cut is not defended tightly by X5, 05 continues to the empty "Weakside Block" area and looks for 03's "Lob Pass."

But this diagram illustrates 05 being defended tightly by X5 on his "Lob Cut," dictating that 05 reverses direction and flashes back towards the new "Ballside High Post Elbow" area and 03 with the ball. With the "Flare-Screen" and "Flare-Cut" action by 04 and 01, with 05 attacking his defender on either cut he makes; there is no one to help the inverted perimeter-type defender, X2, on the new "Ballside Block." While having an obvious "position advantage" over X2, there is a good chance that 02 may also have a "personnel advantage" over X2 in regards to interior post defensive skills and experience. Those possibilities should be taken advantage of with 03 looking to make the "Inside Pass" to the isolated and inverted 02. See Diagram 12.19

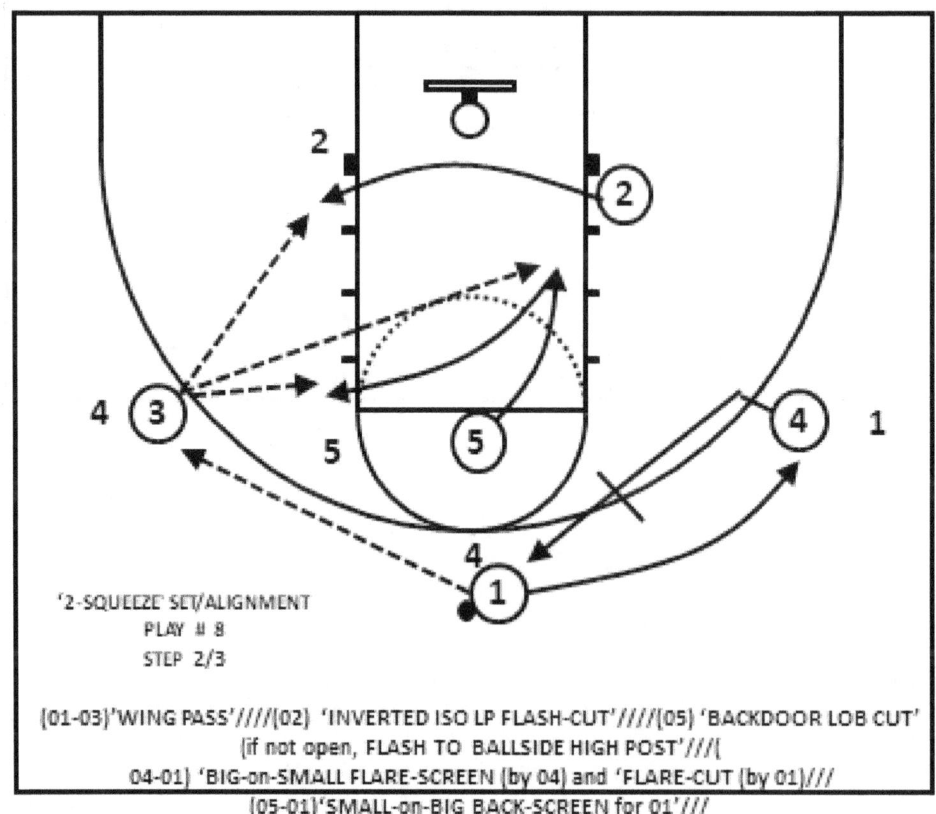

If 03 does not make the pass to 02 or to 05, 03 waits for 05 to step up and out of the 'Elbow' area to set a "Big-on-Small Inside Ball-Screen." 03 should then "dribble-scrape" off of 05's top (left) shoulder to deflect his defender off on his drive towards the middle of the floor. 03 could then make an aggressive hard "dribble penetration" into the lane or a more passive "perimeter pull-dribble" out towards the "Ballside Slot." After 03 breaks contact with 05, 05 could attack his post-type defender by slipping the ball-screen and "Flare-Cutting" towards the "Deep Corner." This action will not only prevent X5 from being able to help out X3 in the lane, but could allow 05 to either utilize his perimeter-type offensive skills or attack X5's lack of perimeter-type defensive talents. At the same time, 02 can attack his perimeter-type defender with an "Iso Duck-In Cut." In addition, as 03 approaches 04 out on top, 04 could attack his post-type defender, X4, by executing more of a perimeter-type offensive cut by "back-dooring his defender" into the 'Dotted Circle' area. If 03 does not make the pass to 04 on his cut to the basket, 04 then empties out to the "Weakside Wing." At the same time 01 steps up to replace 04 at the "Weakside Slot" area, giving 04 space to fill the now-empty "Weakside Wing." If no shots are created from any of these fundamentally sound actions, all players have been moved to be in the new "4-Out/1-In Spot-Ups" for a different continuity offense to immediately begin the final phase/wave of the continuous and never interrupted offensive attack. Play # 15 falls into the more complex and sophisticated Level 3 category. As previously stated, this means that there are only select teams that should have this play/cntry in its arsenal. But it also has been stated that any team that possesses the physical and mental skills to execute this particular play also has the capabilities to execute any of "Level 1 or Level 2" plays that exist in this chapter. See Diagram 12.20

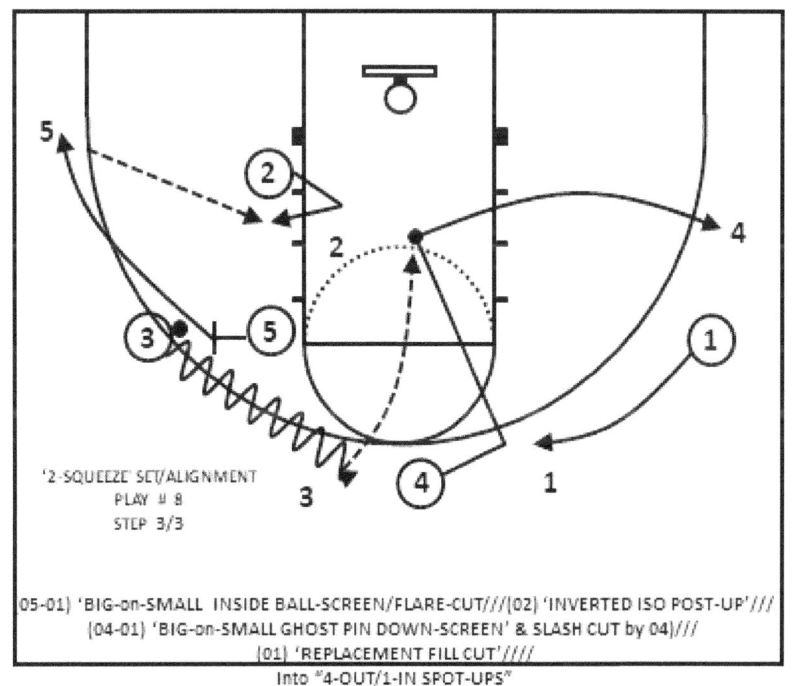

DIAGRAM 12.20

Diagram 12.21 shows the beginning of Play # 9 with the same possible and probable cosmetic appearance and the identical beginning action as the start of Play # 8. 02 could start again on either side of the lane, but will always end up on the new "Ballside Block" area on the same side of the floor that 01 makes his initial "Wing Pass." This can make both plays confusing as well as even more unpredictable to the defense, while still providing different offensive players with different types of scoring opportunities. This diagram shows the (only slight change towards the offense, but a probable bigger difference to the opposing defense) with 03 and 04 slightly changing their respective cuts with 03 making his "Iverson Cut" over the top of 05 and 04 being the cutter that makes his particular cut underneath 05. Communication between 03 and 04 could allow these two players to switch their cuts.

As 01 approaches the top of the circle with the ball, 03 makes his "Iverson Cut" over the top of 05 and 04, but 03 then stops near the "High Post" elbow area on the left side of the floor. At the same time, 04 makes his "Barkley Cut" underneath 05 and extends his cut out to the FT Line extended on the right side of the floor (to invert his 'post-type defender' further from the basket on the perimeter. See Diagram 12.21

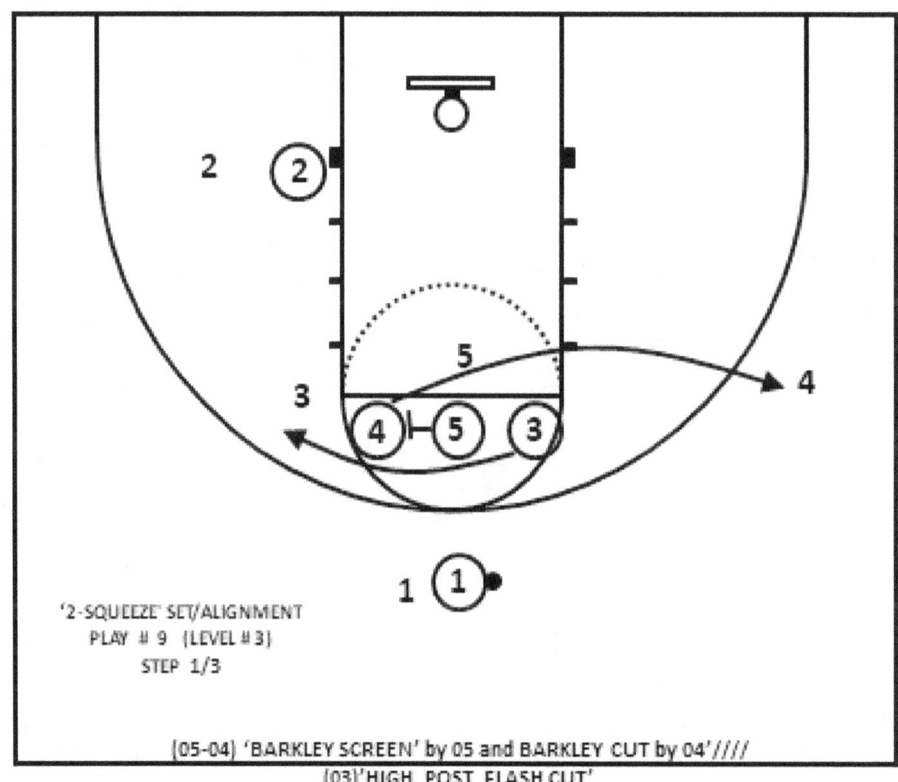

DIAGRAM 12.21

Diagram 12.22 shows 01 making the pass to the inverted 04 out at the FT Line extended, keying 02 to immediately flash to the new "Ballside Block." At the same time, 05 steps over as if to "Cross-Screen" for 03, but instead reverses direction and becomes the player himself that flashes to the new "Ballside High Post." 03 then changes his cut and pops out to the "Top of the Key," while 01 "Flare-Cuts" to the new "Weakside Wing." This action has moved defenders and inverted two position-type players (X2 and X4) into supposedly uncomfortable locations as well as stretching the defense both vertically as well as horizontally. This also isolates 02 and his defender down on the new "Ballside Block" for 04 to look to deliver the ball to him, as well as 05 at the 'Ballside High Post.' See Diagram 12.22

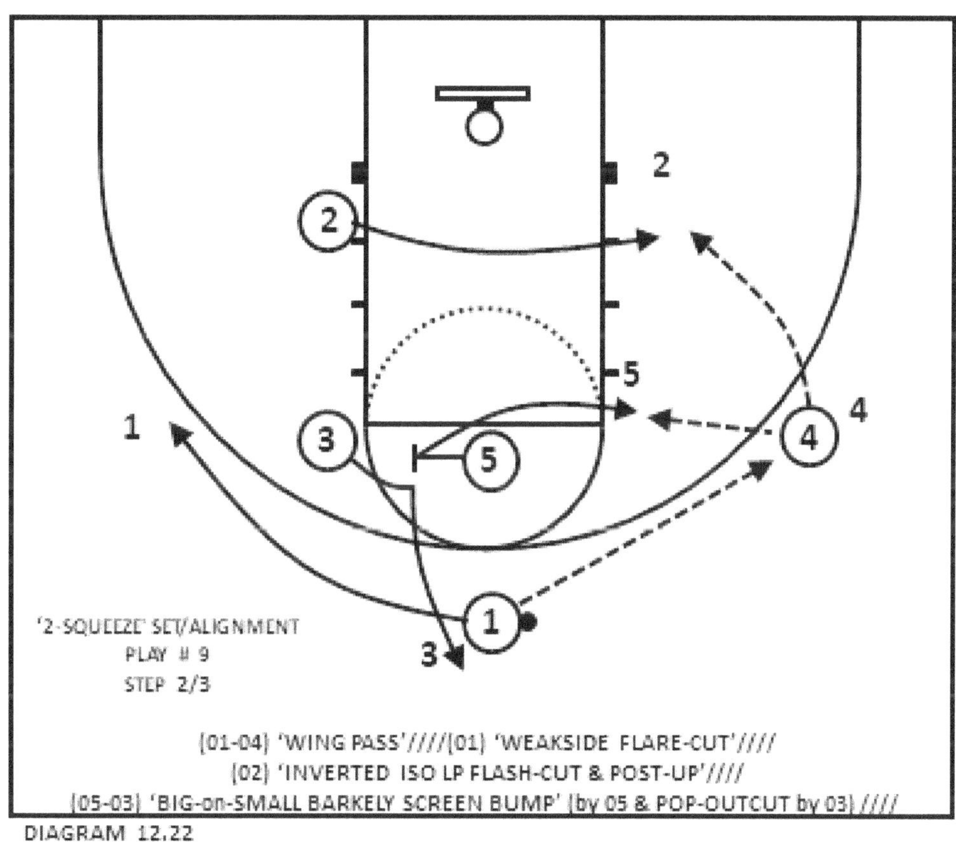

DIAGRAM 12.22

Diagram 12.23 illustrates 04 turning down possible "Inside Passes" to 02 and 05 as well as "Perimeter Passes" to 01 and 03. The new perimeter locations of both 01 and 03 have vertically and horizontally stretched their defenders and pulled them away from the basket, preventing those defenders from being able to help out the interior defenders of 02 and 05, in addition to most likely providing good open '3 Pt.' shot opportunities.

With 04 turning down the possible "Skip Pass" to 01 at the "Weakside Wing" and to 03, now at the top of the key, "Inside Passes" to either 02 on the "Ballside Block" and to 05 on the new "Ballside High Post," 04 could elect to then attack his 'post-type' defender (stretched out on the perimeter) by using 05's "Big-on-Small Inside Ball-Screen." 04 'dribble-scrapes' off of 05's top right shoulder before 05 then slips his screen and "Flare-Cuts" to the "Deep Corner." At the same time, 02 can make another "Inverted and Iso Duck-In Cut" and look for 04's "Inside Pass" from the same side of the lane. Both 04 and 02 have again inverted their specific defenders and look to take advantage of those potential and probable defensive weaknesses, eventual defensive breakdowns, and offensive advantages. See Diagram 12.23

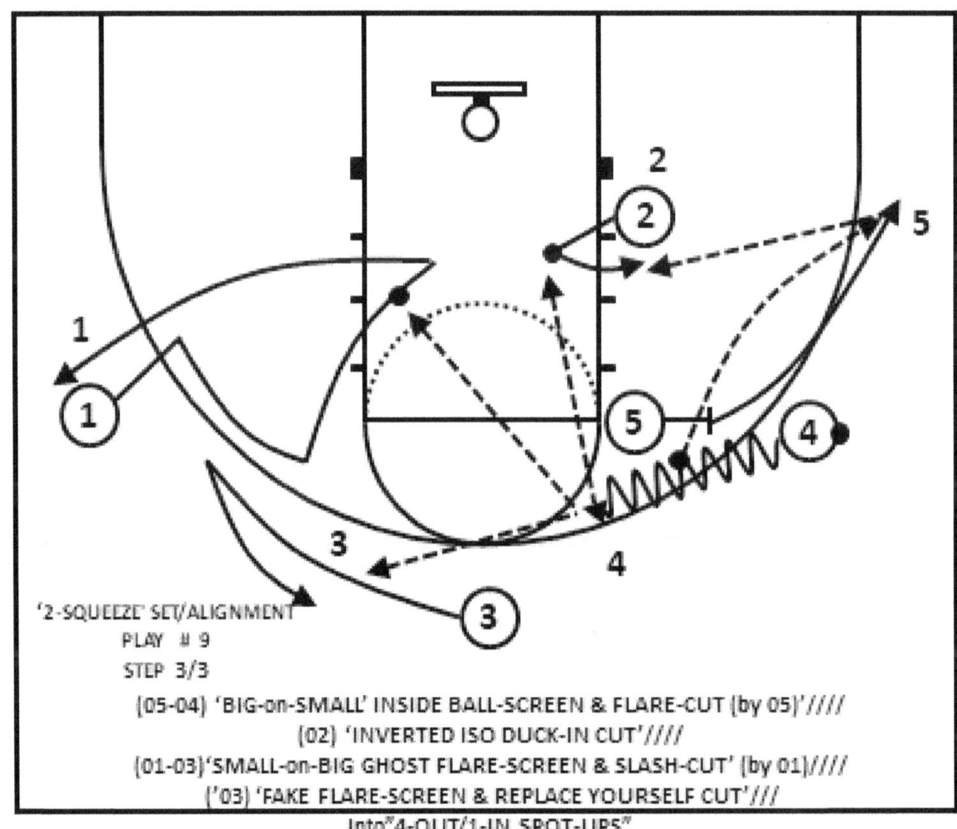

DIAGRAM 12.23

As in other entries/plays where the ball is being dribbled across the floor from one side to the other, the "Weakside Wing" (01 in this instance) can step up as if to set a "Flare-Screen" for 03 to use to take his open '3' after "Flare-Cutting" away from the dribbler towards the "Weakside Wing." In this play, 01 can also cross up the defense with a "Ghost Flare-Screen" and immediate cut to the basket for a potential "Inside Pass" from 04 and score. As if he were going to receive the 01-03 "Flare-Screen," 03 starts his "Flare-Cut" before breaking it off and returning to his initial "Weakside Slot" location. At the same time, if 01 does not receive 04's pass of his surprise 'Basket Cut," 01 then empties out of the lane and circles back out to settle in his initial "Weakside" area," If shots are not created with these different forms of screening and cutting, all players are now in the "4-Out/1-In Spot-Ups" so that the designated continuity offense can fluidly begin.

It should be remembered though that any team that possesses the physical and mental skills to execute this particular play also has the capabilities to execute any of "Level 1 or Level 2" plays that exist in this chapter. Therefore, there would never be a shortage of plays/entries/quick-hitters for a team of his caliber.

PLAYS THAT END in the "HIGH POST/LOW POST" OFFENSIVE SPOT-UPS

The primary difference in this package of the four plays/entries is when any of the plays/entries end with no shot taken but possession of the ball is retained, all five offensive players will end up in a different group of offensive spot-ups on the floor (different than the "3-Out/2-In" spot-ups and different than the "4-Out/1-In" spot-ups. These new spot-up locations/positons will have players moved about the court during the execution of the play with any one of the five ending up in the "Ballside Low Post," one in the "Ballside High Post," one in the "Weakside Wing," one in the "Ballside Wing," and the remaining player at the "Point." As the play concludes without the desired shot taken, these five positions can provide the offense with safe and easy types of ball-reversals, large gaps for dribble penetration, opportunities to deliver the ball inside to whomever (perimeter-type or post-type players) is currently posting up their defender on the "Ballside Block," and the "Ballside High Post," with three perimeter-scoring threats and legitimate offensive rebounding threats.

Diagram 12.24 shows the entire Play # 10 that appears to be similar to other entries/plays previously described. 02 has the freedom to start on either side of the floor. Again, 04 makes his "Barkley Cut" over the top 05 while 03 makes his "Iverson Cut" under

05. Again, the action of 04 and 03 could be easily switched with the proper communication, making the cosmetic look of the play to appear to be different to the opposition's defense.

Regardless of which side of the lane 02 starts on, 01 has the option and the freedom to make a "Wing Pass" to either side of the floor. 05 always then flashes to the new "Ballside High Post" area. The player on the immediate new "Weakside Wing" would then step up to screen for 01 to make his "Flare-Cut" to that now vacant weakside of the floor. 02 would also end up on the new "Ballside Block" to isolate his perimeter-type defender in a high percentage scoring location. See Diagram 12.24

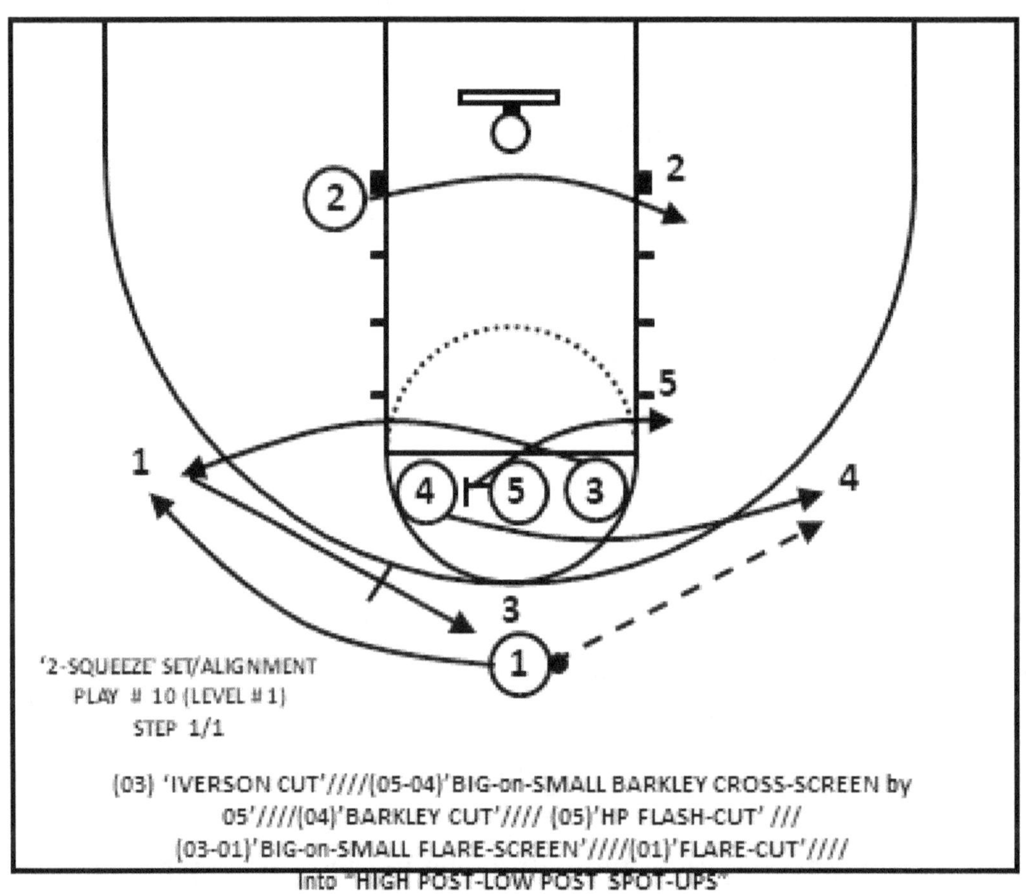

Diagram 12.25 shows the beginning of Play # 11. On this play, 04 makes his "Barkley Cut" over the top of both 05 and 03 while 01 dribbles to the FT Line extended away from 04 and his cut. At the same time 01 that dribbles to the "Wing" area, 02 makes a cut through the "Big-on-Small Elevator Screen" (set by 05 and 03, to the top of the key and looks for 01's "Reverse Pass" for an open '3.'

After screening for 02, 05 slips his screen and dives diagonally across the lane to iso his defender on the new "Ballside Block" while 03 then steps towards 01 and the new "Ballside High Post."

This action in this play also has moved every offensive player and therefore, forced every defender to move into the various locations on the floor. This allows all five offensive players to search for their own particular offensive advantages while constantly looking for their individual opponent's defensive weaknesses. With the desired shot not taken, this action has also repositioned offensive players into the new "High-Post & Low-Post Spot-Ups." These spot-ups will allow for another quick and smooth conversion into the new designated continuity offense. This entry also falls into the Level 1 Group, again dictating that teams of all of the various amounts of physical and mental skills, experience, and knowledge will be able to effectively perform this play. See Diagram 12.25

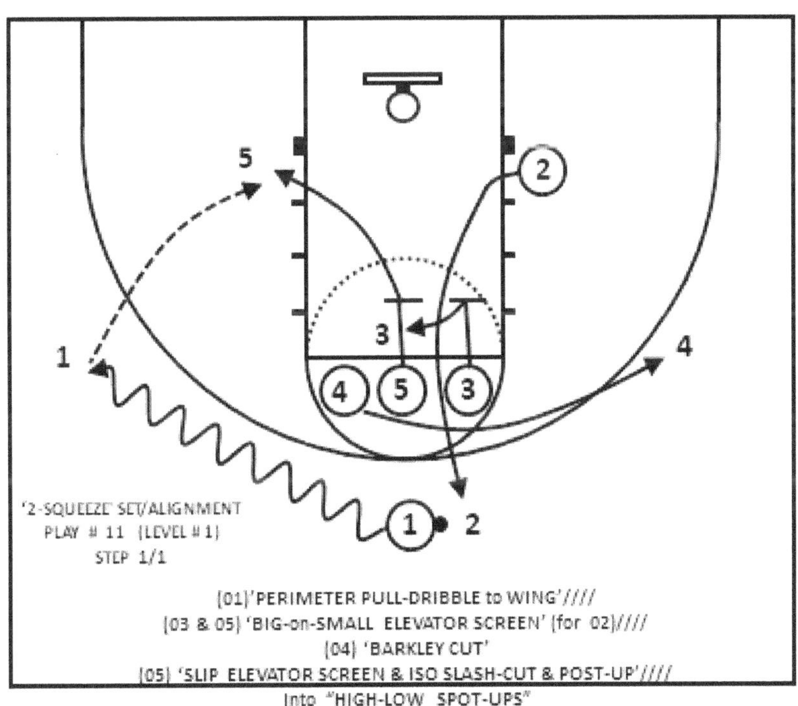

DIAGRAM 12.25

Diagram 12.26 illustrates the beginning of Play # 12. In this play, 02 must start on the left side of the lane and 03 makes an "Iverson Cut" over the top of both 05 and 04 to end up at the "Wing" area outside of the arc at the FT Line extended on the opposite side of the floor from where he started.

Immediately after making the "01-03 Wing Pass," 01 makes a "Flare-Cut" to the "Weakside Wing." At the same time, 02 isolates his defender for an "inverted Post-Up" and then quickly 02 breaks vertically up the Free Throw Lane by using 04 and 05's "Big-on-Small Elevator Screen." 02 cuts between 04 and 05 and breaks up and out to the top of the key behind the '3 Pt. line, preparing his feet and hands for an open shot. 03 could first make the "Inside Pass to 02, before 02 makes his "Pipe Cut" to the top of the key. See Diagram 12.26

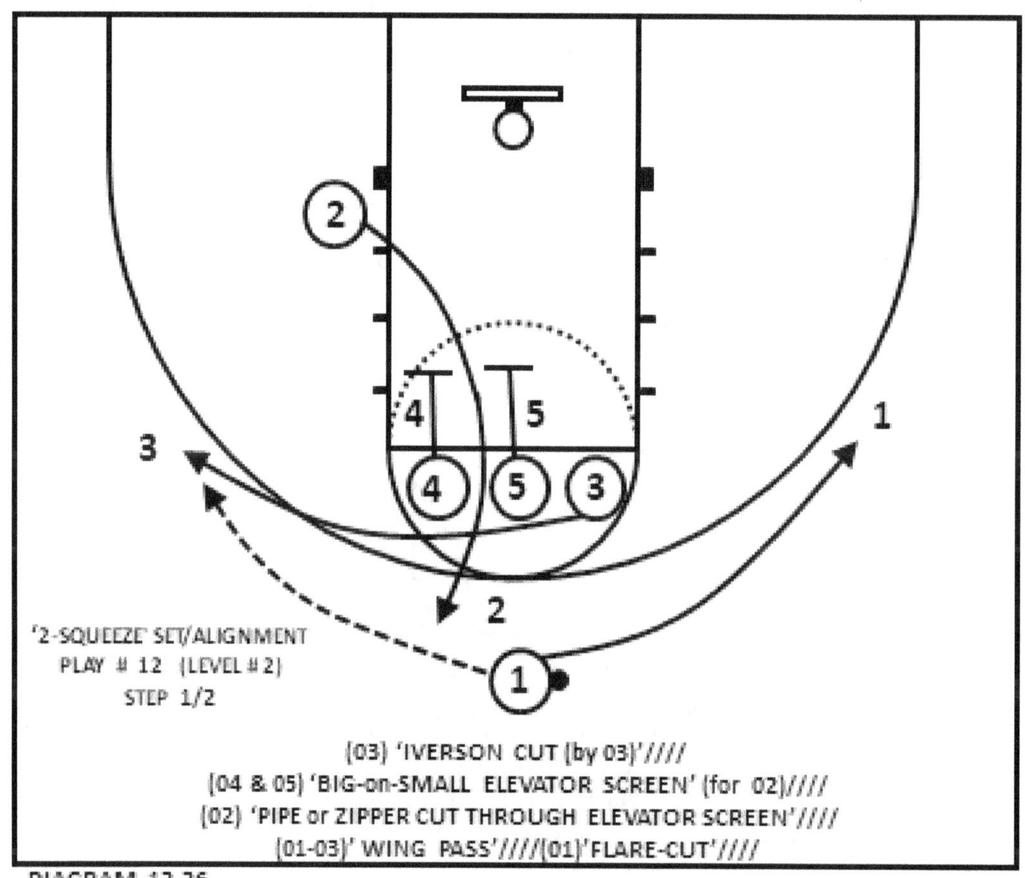

DIAGRAM 12.26

03 should look for a possible 03-01 "Skip Pass" on the "Weakside Wing" or to make the "Reverse Pass" to 02 for a likely open '3' at the top of the key. If 02 is not open for his shot, he should quickly swing the ball on over to 01 on the opposite side of the floor.

After the ball is swung to the opposite side of the floor to 01, 05 should then step over to set a quick "Cross Screen" for 04 to use. From there, 04 and 05 have two possible options. Diagram 12.27 shows 04 and 05 execute their second option. That is that 04 cuts high off of 05's top (left) shoulder and is the post player that flashes to the "Ballside High Post." If 04 cuts high, 05 slips his 05-04 screen and is the designated post player that slashes to the new "Ballside Low Post."

The second option has 04 cut off of 05's top left shoulder and flash to the new "Ballside High Post." If 04 cuts high, 05 reverse pivots after 04 breaks contact and 05 flashes back to the new "Ballside Block." This action is not shown in the diagram.

Regardless of which option 04 and 05 select, all five players end up in the proper "High-Post & Low-Post Spot-Ups. From there, the designated continuity offense can immediately and fluidly begin with the next pass made by 01. Diagram 12.39. With the increased number of offensive techniques and action by more offensive players, we consider Play # 12 to become a more sophisticated play and is placed into a Level 2 play. This means that only the teams considered to be lesser physically and mentally strong and experienced would most likely be wise to avoid this specific play. See Diagram 12.27

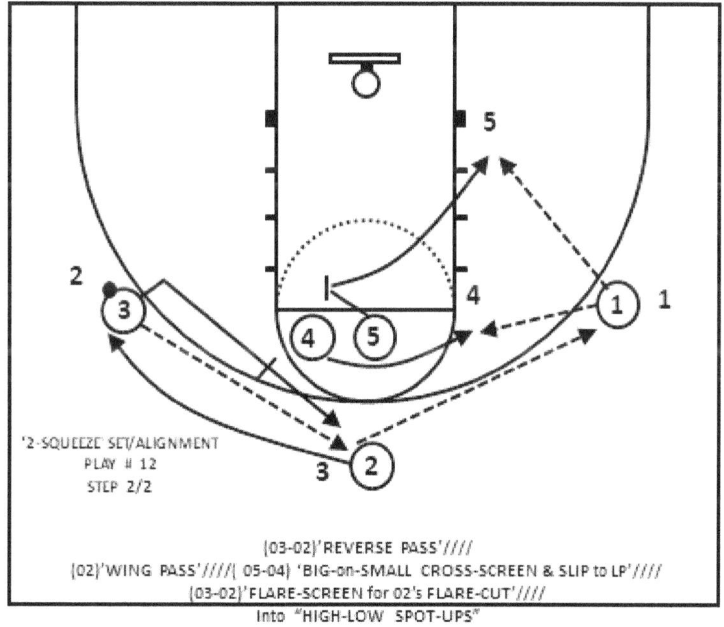

DIAGRAM 12.27

Diagram 12.28 illustrates the beginning action of Play # 13. With 02 starting on the right side of the lane on the "Block" breaking out to the "Wing" position on the same side of the floor, 01 dribbles the ball towards the top of the key. At the same time, 03 makes his "Iverson Cut" over the top of both 05 and then 04 to the opposite side of the floor on the left side of the floor. See Diagram 12.28.

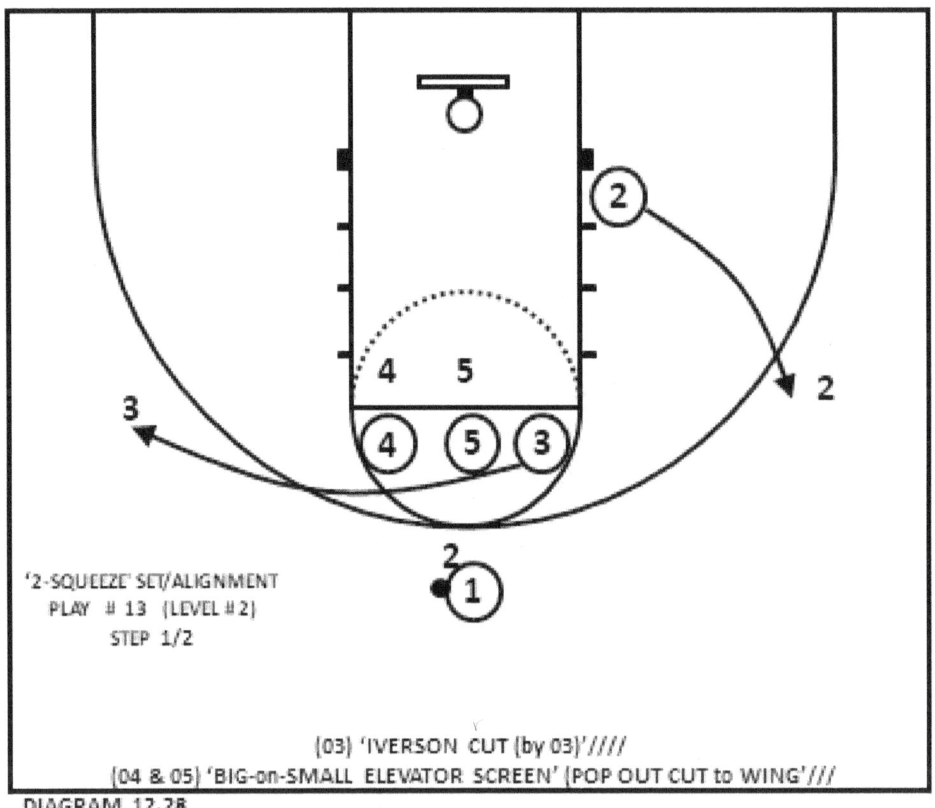

DIAGRAM 12.28

Diagram 12.29 shows 01 making the 01-02 "Wing Pass." At the same time that 02 receives the "Wing Pass" from 01, 05 steps over to screen 04's defender with 04 then scraping and curling tightly off of 05's top left shoulder. As 04 curls to the new "Ballside Block," 05 slips his screen and flashes back towards the ball and 02 towards the new "Ballside High Post." This action completely isolates both 04 and 05 on the interior and gives 02 two outstanding interior passing targets (with high upside scoring opportunities.)

The same diagram shows 01 immediately receiving the 03's "Flare-Screen" to "Flare-Cut" the very wide open weakside of the floor and become an instant perimeter scoring threat within the structure of the play. If 01 were to receive 02's "Skip Pass," 01 would have a wide area to completely isolate his defender on the perimeter and attack him with various types of 'catch and shoot,' 'catch and create' or 'catch and pass' offensive action options.

The "Big-on-Small Flare-Screen" for 01, set by 03 is immediately followed by 03's slip to the top of the key to become the immediate second '3 Pt. Shot" threat at the very vulnerable scoring area—the top of the key. This action has vertically and horizontally stretched the defense and caused the opponent to concentrate on defending their perimeter defense. This action will also weaken its interior, giving 04 and 05 offensive scoring opportunities from the high percentage scoring areas closer to the basket.

To balance out the attack both with interior and exterior scoring threats, 01 is also a very creditable scoring threat behind the arc at the "Weakside Wing" and 03 could easily capitalize on any mistakes made by his own defender at the top of the key (for an open '3.') See Diagram 12.29.

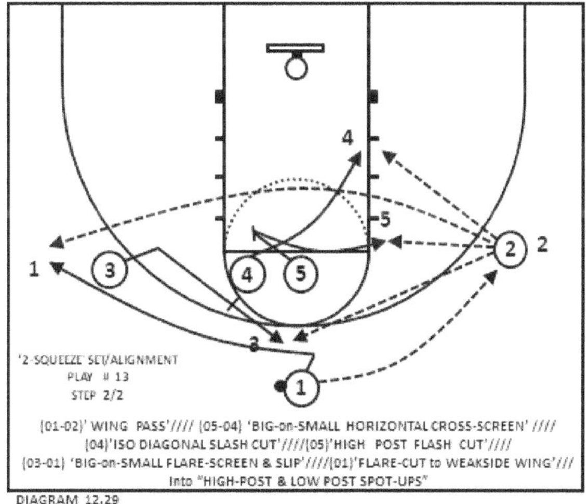

DIAGRAM 12.29

If no shots are taken, a different set of spot-ups are filled with 02 at the "Ballside Wing," 03 at the top of the key, 03 now at the "Weakside Wing," 05 at the new "Ballside High Post" and 04 isolating his defender down on the "Ballside Mid-Post." When 02 turns down his many (interior and perimeter passing) options and reverses the ball to 03 out on top, the actual entry is over and the designated continuity offense that must begin out of the "High-(Post)/Low-(Post) Spot-Ups can fluidly begin. This particular plays also falls into Level 2 Category of the offensive team's sophistication level and degree of difficulty (to execution.) This means that teams that possess "Level 2 or Level 3" skill levels and utilize any continuity offense that operates out of the specific "High Post/Low Post Spot-Up locations could and should incorporate both Play # 19 and Play #20 in their offensive repertoire.

CLOSING

These twenty plays all from the same "2-SQUEEZE" Set can all be very effective forms of action that will use every form of fundamental offensive techniques to gain offensive position and personnel advantages. The practices of inverting and/or isolating post-players out on the perimeter or inverting and/or isolating perimeter players on the interior are used frequently. Different types of ball screens with numerous kinds of actions after the actual screen as well as the many various types of off-ball screens and the countless methods of the action of finishing those screens, are designed within the framework and structure of these plays.

With the different types of fluid movement that each play possesses and the different players that are the primary pass-receivers/potential scorers; there is one constant similarity in each of these plays. And that is the ability of each play that does not produce the desired shot will always reposition all five players into the required and necessary offensive spot-ups that allows the offensive attack to have an immediate and fluid conversion from the actual entry/play into the continuity offense that is to become the last wave of attack. Within the package of plays out of this set/alignment are counters and counter-options to base plays that can cross up and attack defenses that expect certain actions from plays that have been executed. In addition, within the rules and the framework of the continuity offense, it can also possess options to modify specific movements of the continuity. Each continuity offense will have Secondary Break Options, entries/plays from more than one offensive set as well as BLOB and SLOB plays that can immediately flow into those continuity offenses. Additionally, each designated continuity offense will have specific offensive rebounding and defensive transition schemes that assign particular players to execute the required tasks for excellent offensive and defensive results.

CHAPTER 13
PLAYS/ENTRIES EXECUTED FROM THE "2-UP SET/ALIGNMENT"

There are many different philosophies on how offenses can successfully go about attacking (delete to attack opposing) opponent's man-to-man defenses. This multiple-phase offensive system uses more than one phase/layer/wave of attack, with each phase/wave having a seamless and immediate conversion into the next phase/wave. While this system can be confusing to defenses and difficult to defend, this system can be properly taught and coached so that it can be easily understood and ultimately executed by players of many different levels of (physical talent, mental understand, and playing experience.)

In addition, there are several types of offensive schemes and different ways within this system that offenses can attack their defensive counter-parts. Many of these can be integrated within the same offensive system that can attack defenses in various ways. The larger the number of schemes that can be successfully utilized and integrated within the same system, the greater the opportunity an offensive team can find the most efficient and productive schemes that can place both individual and the overall team in the best and most frequent "positions to succeed."

The plays/entries carefully diagrammed down to the small and seemingly unimportant 'V-Cuts' made by countless players before making their more important following cut are also described in detail.

Each play has been carefully studied and evaluated to determine which level of talent and experience must be possessed for that specific team to be able to successfully execute the play. This includes all players' physical skills as well as their mental understanding of the game. Coaches must also have the experience and the associated level of understanding of the game as well as their coaching/teaching of the nuances of each play.

The most sophisticated plays/entries would fall into the first of the three levels all based on the team's physical talents and skills, the mental capacities and the overall team's game experience. In addition, the coaching staff must have a high degree of basketball knowledge as well as very high teaching and coaching skills to educate his/her entire basketball team. The proper breakdown drills must be thoroughly utilized to hone the fundamental skills and techniques needed for individual players and the overall team to execute plays that can be efficient, productive and successful. We define this family of plays as the "Level 3 category" of plays. This "Level 3" family of plays will have a much more complex offensive scheme that would require a very high amount of physical talent as well as requiring a greater amount of the players (to execute) and the coaches (to teach and coach) mental capacities and experience needed for the offense to be efficient, productive and successful. We feel plays in our defined "Level 3" category could possibly be successful for NBA teams, definitely for college teams and also for many high schools and older AAU teams.

The next classification or level of plays would be possibly slightly lower as far as sophistication, complexity and the actual 'length' of the play (and the number of passes, cuts, and screens used) in the play's overall scheme. While all "Level 2" plays in each of the chapters in this book remain to be fundamentally sound, these plays may lack the actual number of techniques/methods that are implemented within that play in comparison to the "Level 1" plays/entries. Therefore any team that successfully executes the highest "Level 1" plays/entries could/should easily be able to execute any of these so-called lower "Level

2" plays/entries, if so desired. Almost all high school teams should be able to execute successfully all aspects of the "Level 2" plays.

The final grouping of plays would be called "Level 1" plays and are not as difficult for offensive players to master the execution of them, both physically as well as mentally. Even though the techniques are still fundamentally, they may not be as complex to learn and understand in addition to being easier to physically execute.

"Level 1" plays would be lower in the scheme's complexities and the number of techniques used in the execution of this category of plays. Obviously, since these "Level 1" plays are still sound, but lack some of the methods used in the two previous more sophisticated and complex levels; these more elementary plays should be able to be utilized by any teams that use either of the two higher level plays. We feel that Middle School/Junior High teams as well as younger AAU teams or organizations should be able to utilize any of the "Level 1" plays successfully, with a possibility that some of those teams that are slightly more advanced (than other teams) could possibly use some plays located in the immediate next immediate level.

Ideas, concepts and techniques from actual plays from teams of all three levels have been used to modify or to create different combinations of the various techniques and schemes used that will help prove these entries can be successfully used. This allows the author to create numerous plays that use the various schemes to build a library of fundamentally sound plays that will be unique and will be appropriate for the wide range of teams with the various ages and skill levels.

With this book having plays in these three presumed categories or levels, the book will reach out and benefit a much larger group of serious basketball coaches from elementary school age to the highest skilled levels that exists.

In addition, an experienced and resourceful coach may be able to mold some plays that include all of the offensive techniques that he/she desires could reshape a specific play that begins in one specific offensive set/alignment and reshape it so that it could begin in a different offensive/set that is more favorable to that coach and his/her coaching staff's liking.

Conversely, that innovative and creative coach may completely like the specific offensive set/alignment and favor the very same offensive actions included in a certain play, but can modify that play so that the ending spot-ups of all five players are conducive to being able to begin the final phase of the offensive attack by using a more favorable offensive continuity offense.

The most sophisticated plays/entries would fall into the first of the three levels all based on the team's physical talents and skills, the mental capacities and the overall team's game experience. In addition, the coaching staff must have a high degree of basketball knowledge as well as very high teaching and coaching skills to educate his/her entire basketball team. The proper breakdown drills must be thoroughly utilized to hone the fundamental skills and techniques needed for individual players and the overall team to execute plays that can be efficient, productive and successful. We define this family of plays as the "Level 3 category" of plays. This "Level 3" family of plays will have a much more complex offensive scheme that would require a very high amount of physical talent as well as requiring a greater amount of the players (to execute) and the coaches (to teach and coach) mental capacities and experience needed for the offense to be efficient, productive and successful. We feel plays in our defined "Level 3" category could possibly be successful for NBA teams, definitely for college teams and also for many high schools and older AAU teams.

The next classification or level of plays would be possibly slightly lower as far as sophistication, complexity and the actual 'length' of the play (and the number of passes, cuts and screens used) in the play's overall scheme. While all "Level 2" plays in each of the chapters in this book remain to be fundamentally sound, these plays may lack the actual number of techniques/methods that are implemented within that play in comparison to the "Level 1" plays/entries. Therefore any team that successfully executes the highest "Level 1" plays/entries could/should easily be able execute any of these so-called lower "Level 2" plays/entries, if so desired. Almost all high school teams should be able to execute successfully all aspects of the "Level 2" plays.

The final grouping of plays would be called "Level 1" plays and are not as difficult for offensive players to master the execution of them, both physically as well as mentally. Even though the techniques are still fundamentally, they may not be as complex to learn and understand in addition to being easier to physically execute.

"Level 1" plays would be lower in the scheme's complexities and the number of techniques used in the execution of this category of plays. Obviously, since these "Level 1" plays are still sound, but lack some of the methods used in the two previous more sophisticated and complex levels; these more elementary plays should be able to be utilized by any teams that use either of the two higher level plays. We feel that Middle School/Junior High teams as well as younger AAU teams or organizations should be able to utilize any of the "Level 1" plays successfully, with a possibility that some of those teams that are slightly more advanced (than other teams) could possibly use some plays located in the immediate next immediate level.

Ideas, concepts and techniques from actual plays from teams of all three levels have been used to modify or to create different combinations of the various techniques and schemes used that will help prove these entries can be successfully used. This allows the author to create numerous plays that use the various schemes to build a library of fundamentally sound plays that will be unique and will be appropriate for the wide range of teams with the various ages and skill levels.

With this book having plays in these three presumed categories or levels, the book will reach out and benefit a much larger group of serious basketball coaches from elementary school age to the highest skilled levels that exists.

In addition, an experienced and resourceful coach may be able to mold some plays that include all of the offensive techniques that he/she desires could reshape a specific play that begins in one specific offensive set/alignment and reshape it so that it could begin in a different offensive/set that is more favorable to that coach and his/her coaching staff's liking.

Conversely, that innovative and creative coach may completely like the specific offensive set/alignment and favor the very same offensive actions included in a certain play, but can modify that play so that the ending spot-ups of all five players are conducive to being able to begin the final phase of the offensive attack by using a more favorable offensive continuity offense.

The "2-UP SET"

PLAYS/ENTRIES THAT END in the "3-OUT/2-IN" OFFENSIVE SPOT-UPS

After the entry/play/quick-hitter has been executed but no shots have been taken, all five players will end up in a different group of offensive spot-ups. These "3-Out/2-In Spot-Ups" will have players moved about the court with any of the five ending up in the "Ballside Block," the "Ballside Wing," the "Weakside Block," the "Weakside Wing," and the "Point" (at the top of the key). These five positions can provide the offense with safe and easy types of ball-reversals, large gaps for dribble penetration, opportunities to deliver the ball inside to whomever (perimeter-type or post-type players) is posting up their defender on the "Ballside Block," and a player that can be a perimeter-scoring threat and a legitimate offensive rebounding threat from outside of the arc on his "offensive crashing of the boards." The "3-Out/2-In Spot-Ups also provide ample opportunities for constant and effective defensive transition responsibilities.

Diagram 13.1 illustrates the "2-UP SET." As the name implies, 01 and 02 are the players located in the two "Slot" locations with 03 and 04 on the two "Wing" positions located at the FT Line extended on both sides of the floor. 05 is the player that that begins at the "nail" location and should possess the abilities to post up on the 'Mid-Post' on either side of the lane.

There are many different philosophies on how to attack opposing defenses. This multiple-phase offensive system uses more than one phase/layer/wave of attack, with each phase/wave having a seamless and immediate conversion into the next phase/wave. While this system can be confusing to defenses and difficult to defend, this system can be properly taught and coached so that it can be easily understood and ultimately executed by players of many different levels of (physical talent, mental understand and playing experience.)

In addition, there are several types of offensive schemes and different ways within this system that offenses can attack their defensive counter-parts. Many of these can be integrated within the same offensive system that can attack defenses in various ways. The larger the number of schemes that can be successfully utilized and integrated within the same system, the greater the opportunity an offensive team can find the most efficient and productive schemes that can place both individual and the overall team in the best and most frequent "positions to succeed."

The plays/entries carefully diagrammed down to the small and seemingly unimportant 'V-Cuts' made by countless players before making their more important following cut are also described in detail.

Each play has been carefully studied and evaluated to determine which level of talent and experience must be possessed for that specific team to be able to successfully execute the play. This includes all players' physical skills as well as their mental understanding of the game. Coaches must also have the experience and the associated level of understanding of the game as well as their coaching/teaching of the nuances of each play.

The most sophisticated plays/entries would fall into the first of the three levels all based on the team's physical talents and skills, the mental capacities and the overall team's game experience. In addition, the coaching staff must have a high degree of basketball knowledge as well as very high teaching and coaching skills to educate his/her entire basketball team. The proper breakdown drills must be thoroughly utilized to hone the fundamental skills and techniques needed for individual players and the overall team to execute plays that can be efficient, productive and successful. We define this family of plays as the "Level 3 category" of plays. This "Level 3" family of plays will have a much more complex offensive scheme that would require a very high amount of physical talent as well as requiring a greater amount of the players (to execute) and the coaches (to teach and coach) mental capacities and experience needed for the offense to be efficient, productive and successful. We feel plays in our defined "Level 3" category could possibly be successful for NBA teams, definitely for college teams and also for many high schools and older AAU teams.

The next classification or level of plays would be possibly slightly lower as far as sophistication, complexity and the actual 'length' of the play (and the number of passes, cuts, and screens used) in the play's overall scheme. While all "Level 2" plays in each of the chapters in this book remain to be fundamentally sound, these plays may lack the actual number of techniques/methods that are implemented within that play in comparison to the "Level 1" plays/entries. Therefore, any team that successfully executes the highest "Level 1" plays/entries could/should easily be able execute any of these so-called lower "Level 2" plays/entries, if so desired. Almost all high school teams should be able to execute successfully all aspects of the "Level 2" plays.

The final grouping of plays would be called "Level 1" plays and are not as difficult for offensive players to master the execution of them, both physically as well as mentally. Even though the techniques are still fundamentally, they may not be as complex to learn and understand in addition to being easier to physically execute.

"Level 1" plays would be lower in the scheme's complexities and the number of techniques used in the execution of this category of plays. Obviously, since these "Level 1" plays are still sound, but lack some of the methods used in the two previous more sophisticated and complex levels; these more elementary plays should be able to be utilized by any teams that use either of the two higher level plays. We feel that Middle School/Junior High teams as well as younger AAU teams or organizations should be able to utilize any of the "Level 1" plays successfully, with a possibility that some of those teams that are slightly more advanced (than other teams) could possibly use some plays located in the immediate next immediate level.

Ideas, concepts and techniques from actual plays from teams of all three levels have been used to modify or to create different combinations of the various techniques and schemes used that will help prove these entries can be successfully used. This allows the author to create numerous plays that use the various schemes to build a library of fundamentally sound plays that will be unique and will be appropriate for the wide range of teams with various ages and skill levels.

With this book having plays in these three presumed categories or levels, the book will reach out and benefit a much larger group of serious basketball coaches from elementary school age to the highest skilled levels that exists.

In addition, an experienced and resourceful coach may be able to mold some plays that include all of the offensive techniques that he/she desires could reshape a specific play that begins in one specific offensive set/alignment and reshape it so that it could begin in a different offensive/set that is more favorable to that coach and his/her coaching staff's liking.

Conversely, that innovative and creative coach may completely like the specific offensive set/alignment and favor the very same offensive actions included in a certain play, but can modify that play so that the ending spot-ups of all five players are conducive to being able to begin the final phase of the offensive attack by using a more favorable offensive continuity offense.

Diagram 13.1 (Play # 1) shows 01 stepping across to set a "Ball-Screen" for 02 to use to exchange the two "Slot" locations. At the same time, 03 "Iverson Cuts" across the underside of 05 while 05 slips the "Iverson Screen" and replaces 03 at the FT Line extended. 04 then makes a "Nail Cut" to replace 05 in the center of the lane. This action simply moves 03, 05 and 04 from their initial locations to each other's locations. See Diagram 13.1

5
3
4
5
4
3
2
1
1
2
"2-UP" SET/ALIGNMENT
PLAY #1
STEP 1/2
(03)'IVERSON CUT'/////(05)'SLIP the IVERSON SCREEN'/////
(01-02)'SMALL-on-BIG BALL-SCREEN & SLIP'/////

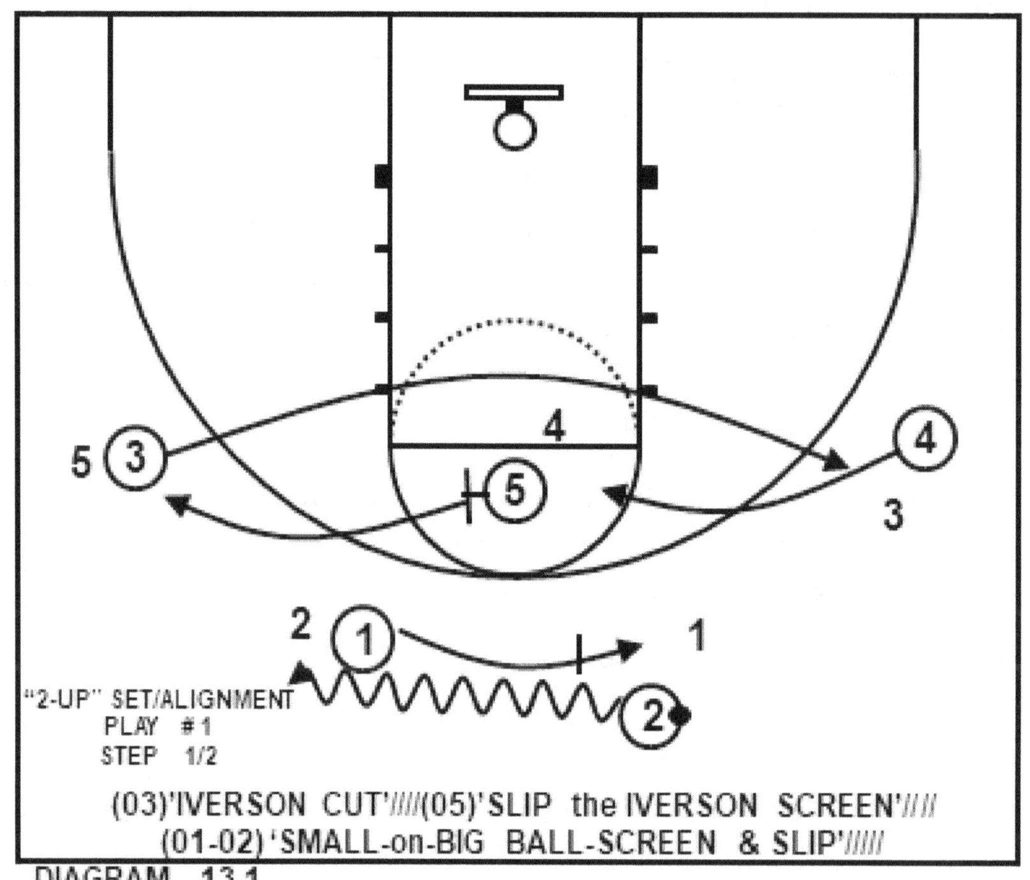

DIAGRAM 13.1

Diagram 13.2 shows 02 then making the "Wing Pass" to 05 at the FT Line extended. From his new location, 01 looks to make a Shuffle-Cut off of 04's "Big-on-Small Shuffle Back-Screen" to the new "Ballside Block." This action inverts perimeter-type player, 01, and further action by 04 and 02 also allows 01 to isolate his perimeter-type defender, X1.

When both 02 and 04 cut over to set a "Stagger-Screen" for 03 to use to break open at the top of the key for an open "3 Pt. Shot," the action also isolates 01 and his (out-of-position) perimeter defender, X1. After stagger-screening for 03, 04 then moves down to the new "Weakside Block" while 02 moves out to the new Weakside Wing" at the FT Line extended. This action gives 01 a great chance to attack X1's defensive weaknesses as well as to provide 03 with an open "3" at the top of the key. Offensive players have moved their defenders as well as repositioned offensive personnel into the "3-Out/2-In" Spot-Ups are filled. See Diagram 13.2

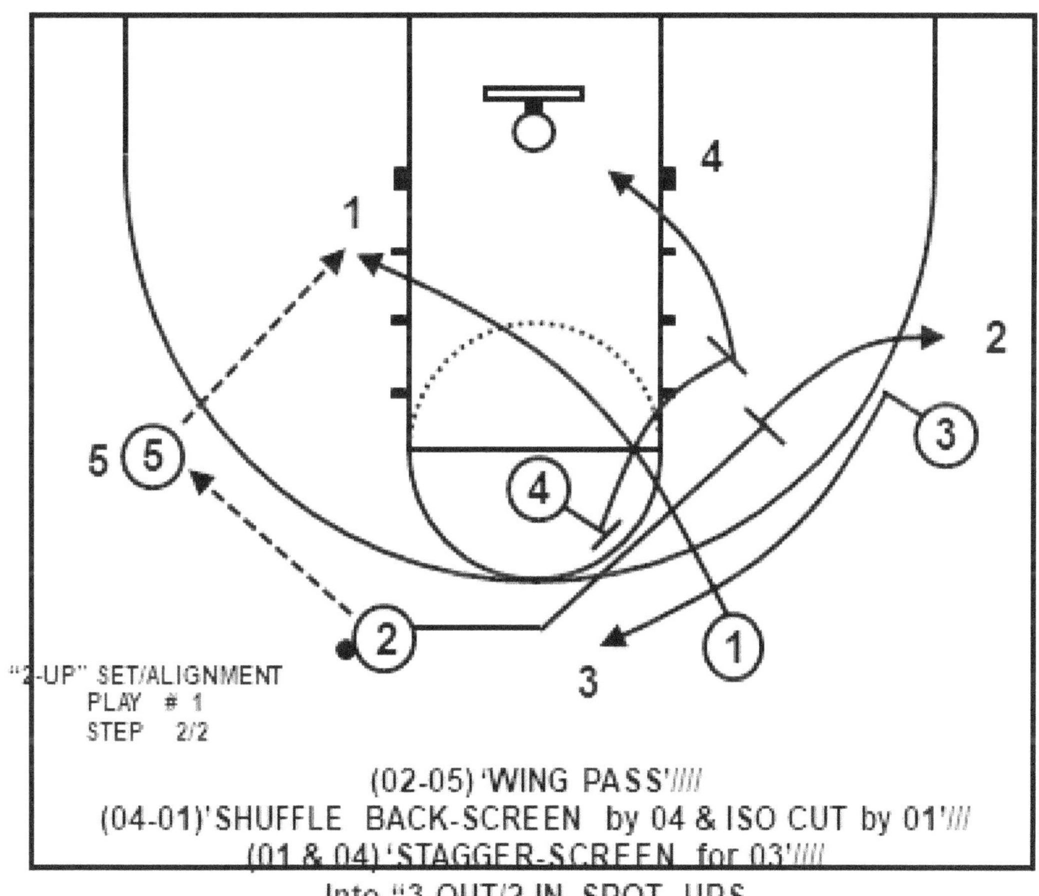

DIAGRAM 13.2

Diagram 13.3 shows the exact beginning action of Play # 2 as in Play # 1 (Diagram 13.1). Again, 02 "dribble-scrapes" off of 01's top right shoulder to the opposite "Slot" location while 01 then slips his screen to fill the new "Weakside Slot." 03 makes the same "Iverson Cut" underneath 05 and 04, while 05 slips his "Iverson Screen" to fill the vacated "Wing" spot on the left side of the floor. 04 steps in to fill the now empty "Nail" location. See Diagram 13.3

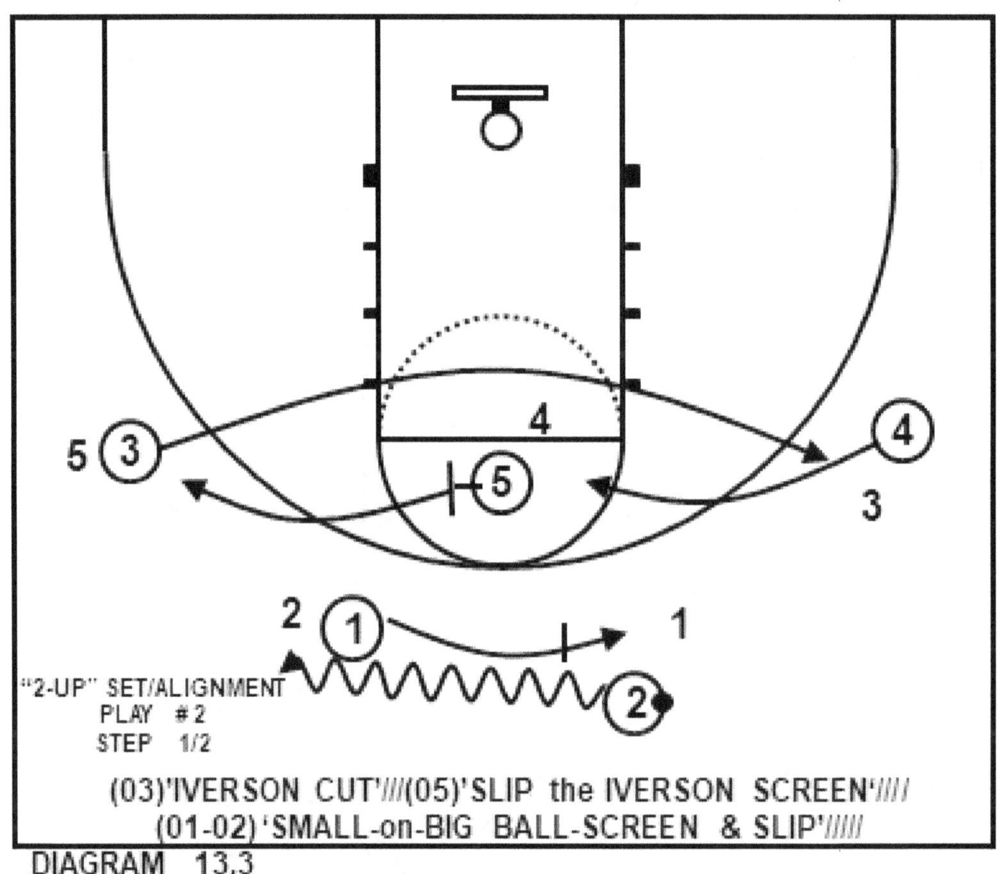

Diagram 13.4 shows 02 then making the same "Wing Pass" to 05 at the FT Line extended. From the same location, 01 looks to make a Shuffle-Cut off of 04, (identical to Play 1) now at the "Nail," before then "bumping" 04 to become the actual "Shuffle-Cutter." This allows 04 to diagonally "Slash Cut" to the new "Ballside Block," (instead of 01) looking for the same "Inside Pass" from 05. To eliminate helpside defense that X4 needs to keep the ball out of 04's hands, both 02 and 01 cut over to set a "Stagger-Screen" for 03 to use to break open at the top of the key for an open "3 Pt. Shot." 01 then slips his screen and moves down to the new "Weakside Block" while 02 slips his screen and slides out to the FT Line extended. This action gives 04 a great "Inside Shot" opportunity as well as 03 an open perimeter shot out on top behind the arc. In addition, the "3-Out/2-In" Spot-Ups are filled for the next and final phase of the offense to develop. See Diagram 13.4

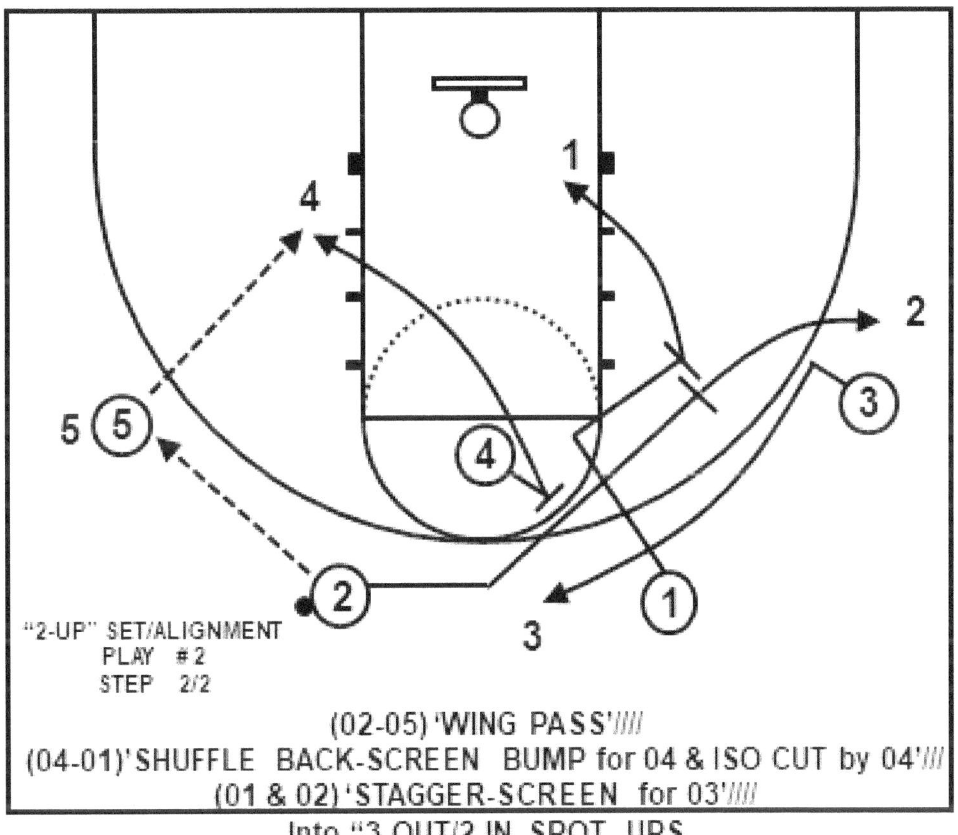

DIAGRAM 13.4

Diagram 13.5 shows Play # 3 that is another play within this 3-play package (Plays 8, 9 and 10) that very similar actions throughout the entire play. Play # 3 has 03 still be the "Iverson Cutter" but he cuts over the top of both 05 and 04's "Iverson Screens." With 03 ending up at the same "Wing" area on the same right side of the floor, both 05 and 04 again slip their screens as they move over on position to the left. Instead of 02 having possession of the ball and receiving 01's "Ball-Screen & Slip" (also often known as "Pick-n-Pop"), 01 starts with the ball and makes a "Small-on-Big" DHO with 02 taking the ball to the "Slot" on the opposite side of the floor. See Diagram 13.5

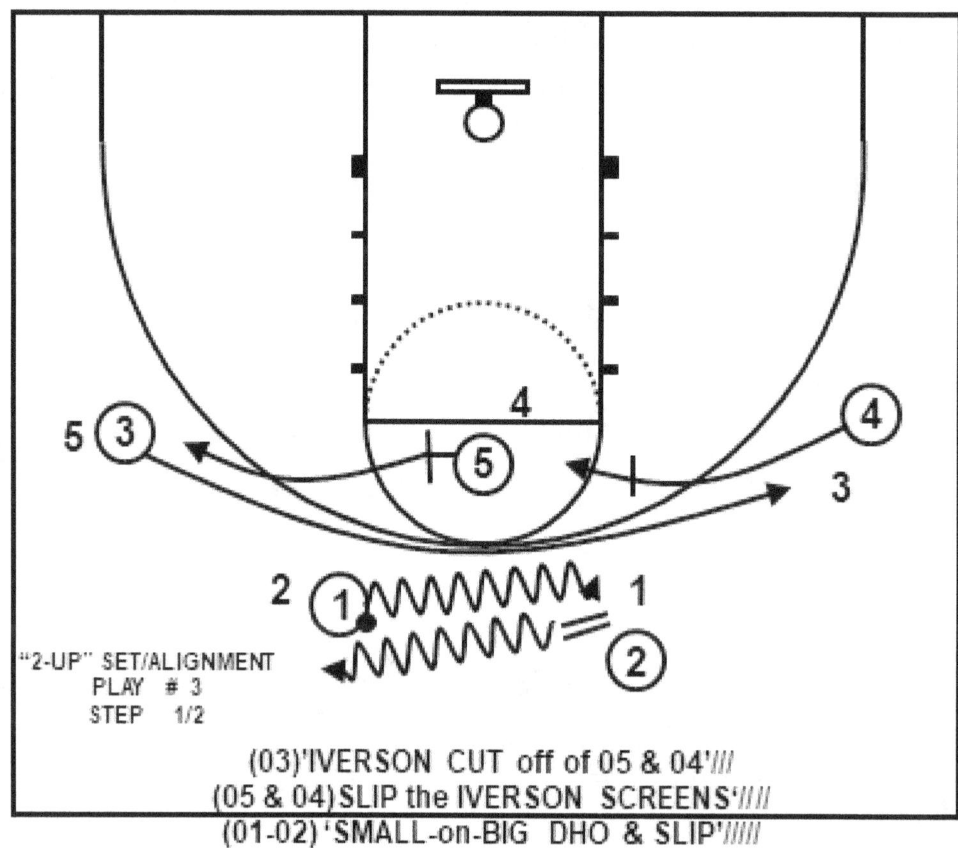

DIAGRAM 13.5

Diagram 13.6 illustrates 02 maintaining possession of the ball until he makes the "Wing Pass" to the inverted "Wing," 05 at the FT Line extended. To change up this play, with designated players at the new "Nail" and the new "Weakside Wing" (04 and 01) normally being the two players designed to cut to the new "Ballside Block," it is changed up in this third play. The passer, (02) starts to go over to screen after making the (02-05) "Wing Pass," and now cuts back to make a hard "Give-n-Go Cut" towards the basket and the new "Ballside Block." At the same time, both 01 and 04 fake the "Back-Screen Shuffle-Cut" Action and both head over to set another "Stagger-Screen" for 03 to use to get open for a '3

Pt. Shot' at the same top of the key area. After their screens, both 04 and 01 move into the same locations so that the "3-Out/2-In" Spot-Ups are once again filled. See Diagram 13.6

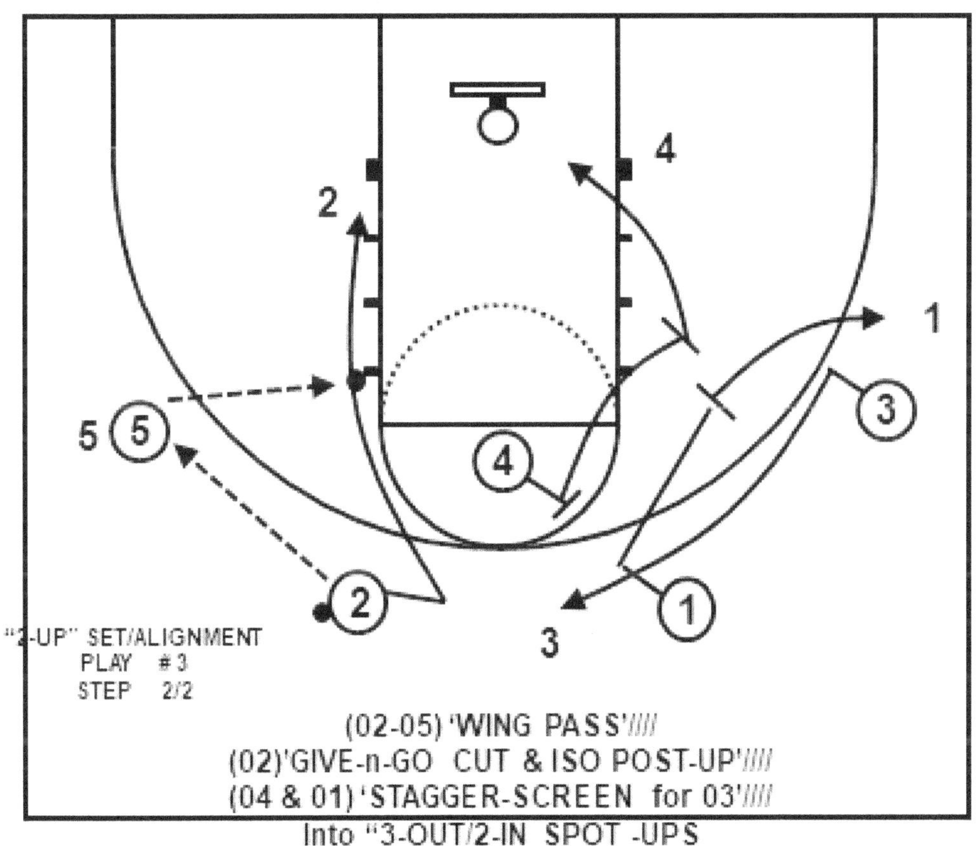

DIAGRAM 13.6

Play # 4 begins in Diagram 13.7 with a quick ball-reversal from 02 to 01. As soon as the ball is out of 02's hands towards 01, 04 steps up to set a "Big-on-Small Flare-Screen" for 02 to scrape off of 04's outside left shoulder and "Flare-Cut" to the new "Weakside Wing." At the same time, 05 starts to cut away from the ball as if to screen (away from the ball) for 04. After a step, he reverses direction and diagonally "slash cuts" across the lane to the new "Ballside Mid-Post." With 01 and 03 being on the ballside and outside of the arc and with 04 and 02 being the only offensive players on the weakside as well as executing a two-man game on the weakside, there can be no opponent's interior help that X5 would need to be a successful interior defender on 05. If 01 does not make the pass to 05, a (01-03) "Wing Pass" may allow 03 to have a better passing angle to deliver the ball to 05. In addition, 01 could make a "Skip Pass" to 02 on the opposite side of the floor for an open '3.' See Diagram 13.7

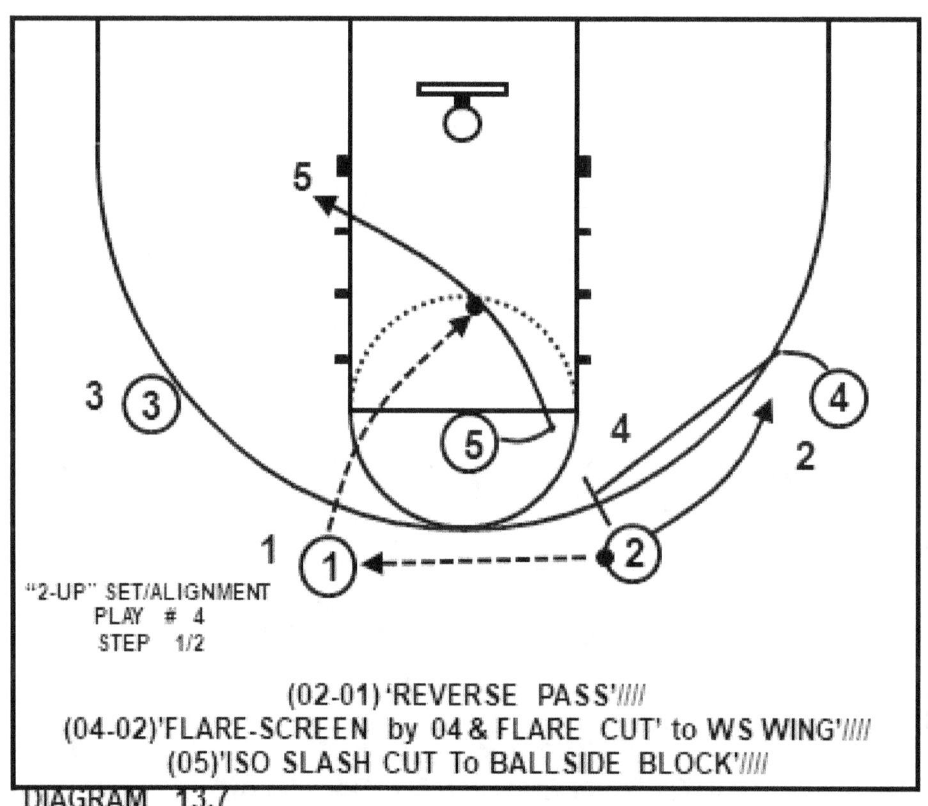

Diagram 13.8 demonstrates the next action of this play with 01 electing to dribble towards the opposite side of the floor. 02 can step up a short distance while 04 makes a longer cut for the player to set a double "Big-on-Small Double Ball-Screen" for 01 to use.

As 01 "dribble-scrapes" off of 02's top left shoulder towards the FT Line extended, the action of all four off-the-ball players begins. 05 flashes across the lane to the new "Ballside Block," while 03 steps up to set a "(Big-on-Small Flare-)Screen the (Ball-)Screener action for 02 to then "Flare-Cut" to the new "Weakside Wing." After screening for 02, 03 slips his screen and steps to the top of the key. When 01 breaks contact with 02, 04 should make a "front pivot" off of his lower right foot" and make a "Lob Cut" to the basket.

While 01 has four genuine pass receivers with all being legitimate scoring threats, the "3-Out/2-In" Spot-Ups are properly filled for the offensive attack to smoothly flow into the last phase of the attack. See Diagram 13.8

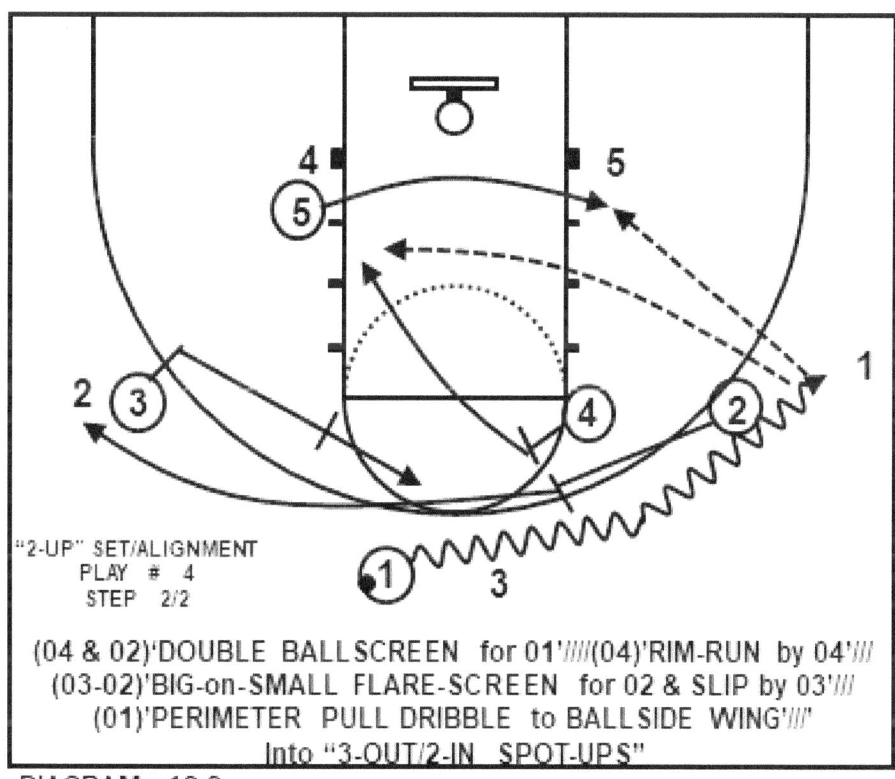

DIAGRAM 13.8

Play # 5, executed out of the same "2-UP Set" is a counter play to Play # 4. After 02 again reverses the ball to 01, 05 and 04 again both make the same initial cuts towards each other. In this play, 05 steps back towards 01 and the ball while 04 "Ghost Flare-Screens" 02's defender and becomes the player that slashes across the lane to the new "Ballside Mid-Post." 02 again makes the "Flare-Cut" to the new "Weakside Wing." See Diagram 13.9

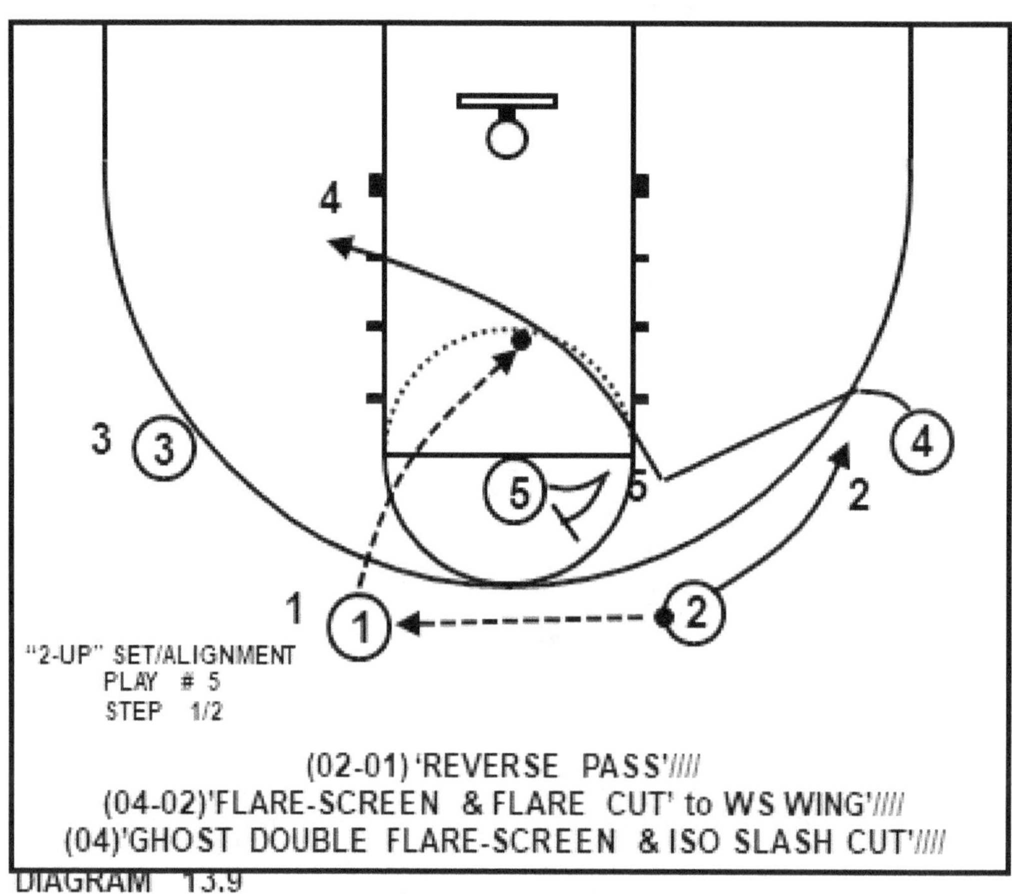

Diagram 13.10 shows the completion of Play # 5 with 02 breaking back up but this time with 05 near the "Weakside Slot" (just inside the arc) to set the same type of "Big-on-Small Ball-Screen" for 01 to use to free himself "with the ball up at the FT Line extended. 01 again "dribble-scrapes" off of 02's outside left shoulder. This time, when 01 breaks contact with 02, 05 makes a "Reverse Pivot" off of his lower right foot and rolls down the lane to post up on the new "Ballside Mid-Post." In this play, 02 "front pivots" off of his lower right foot and cuts diagonally down to set a "Small-on-Big Diagonal Pin Down-Screen" for 04 to use to break to the top of the key. In this play, 03 remains on the new "Weakside Wing," spotted up, stretching the defense and looking for a 01-03 'Skip Pass." 01 has three major passing targets: 05 posting up, reversing the ball to 04 at the top of the key and a possible "Skip Pass" to 03 on the "Weakside Wing."

Even if shots are not created by entry, this play repositions all five players into the correct "3-Out/2-In" Spot-Ups for the continuity offense to fluidly begin. See Diagram 13.10

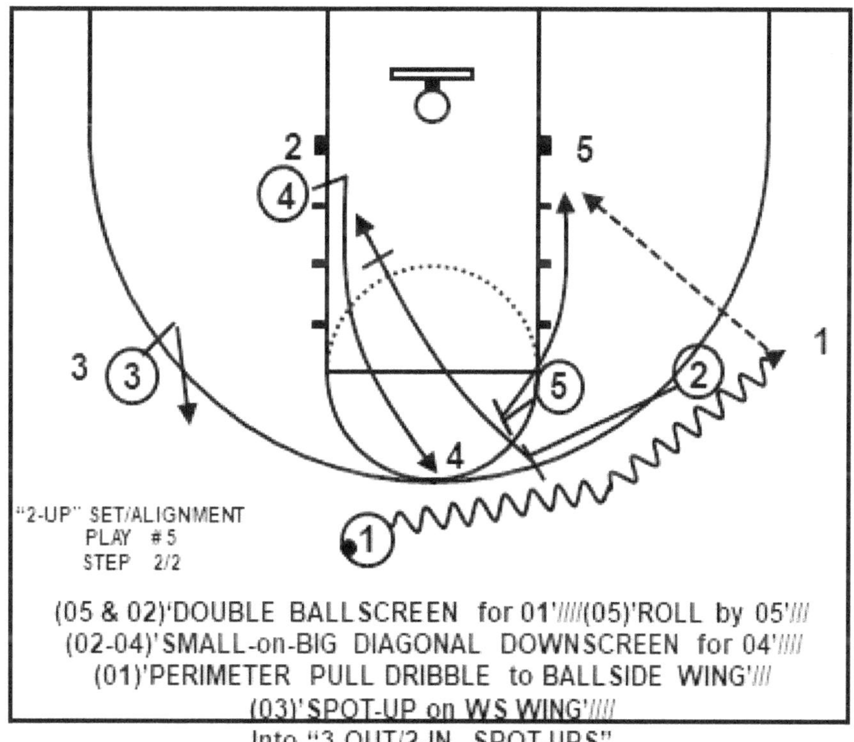

DIAGRAM 13.10

Play # 6 is shown in Diagrams 13.11 and 13.12. Even though the play could be executed on either side, this diagram has 02 be the player that does not start the play on his side of the floor with his dribble. Instead, 02 reverses the ball to 01 with 03 immediately stepping up to set a "Big-on-Small Ball-Screen" for 01 to use. As 01 "dribble-scrapes" off of 03's outside right shoulder, 03 makes a "Reverse Pivot" off of his inside left foot to roll to the basket. 03's other option, dependent upon how X3 defends the ball-screen, could be to make a "Front Pivot" off of the same inside left foot and make a "Rim-Run" to the basket.

As the two-man game between 01 and 03 is being executed, 02 makes a "Replacement Fill Cut" towards the new "Ballside Slot." On the weakside of the floor, 05 breaks across to set a high "Cross Screen" for 04 to break to the now empty "Nail" spot. This action helps eliminate interior support defense that the perimeter-type defender, X3, will need to stop 03 on the "Ballside Block." See Diagram 13.11

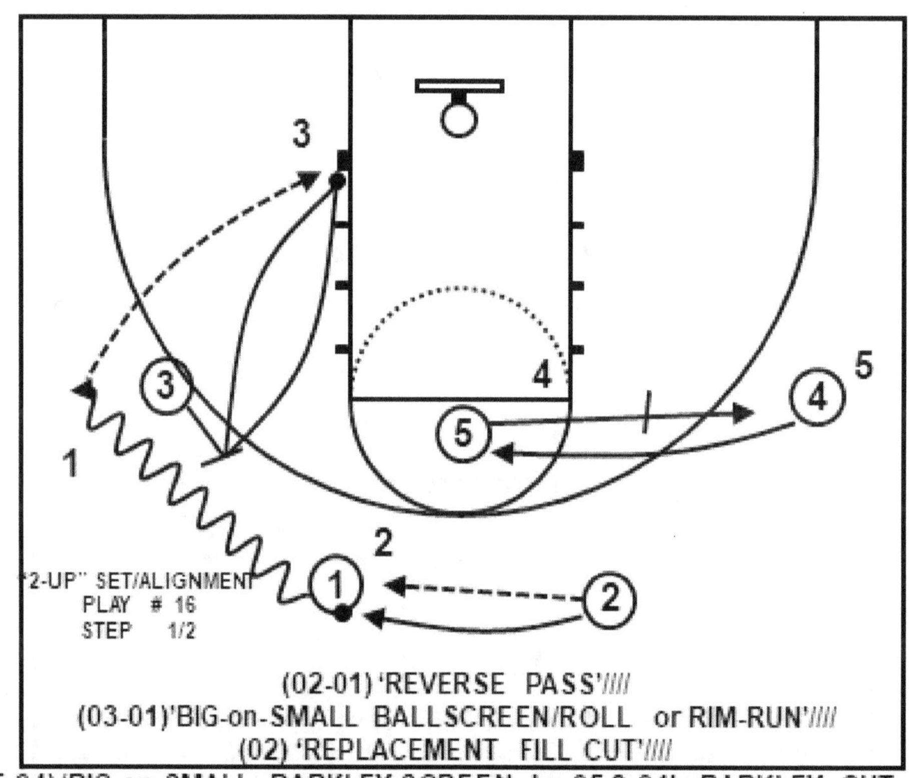

(05-04) 'BIG-on-SMALL BARKLEY-SCREEN by 05 & 04's BARKLEY CUT   2
DIAGRAM   13.11

Diagram 13.12 illustrates the conclusion of Play # 13 with 01 killing his dribble and turning down any type of pass that could possibly be made to 03.

01 then makes the (01-02) "Up Pass" to 02. As 02 starts his perimeter pull dribble towards the top of the key, 04 steps up to the top of the key to set a "Big-on-Small Ball-Screen" for 02 to use to dribble to the opposite "Slot." As 02 "dribble-scrapes" off of 04's top left shoulder, 04 front pivots off of his lower right foot so that 04 can "Rim-Run" to the basket on the new weakside half of the lane. That side of the lane is open because 03 has emptied out of the initial "Ballside Block" area to cut across the lane.

As 02 approaches 05, 05 cuts to set a "Big-on-Small Pin Down-Screen" for 03 to cross the lane and to then scrape off of 05's outside right shoulder and continue to the new "Ballside Wing." After screening for 03, 05 seals off his defender and posts him up on the newly declared "Ballside Block."

All five offensive players have repositioned themselves into the proper "3-Out/2-In" Spot-Ups. See Diagram 13.12

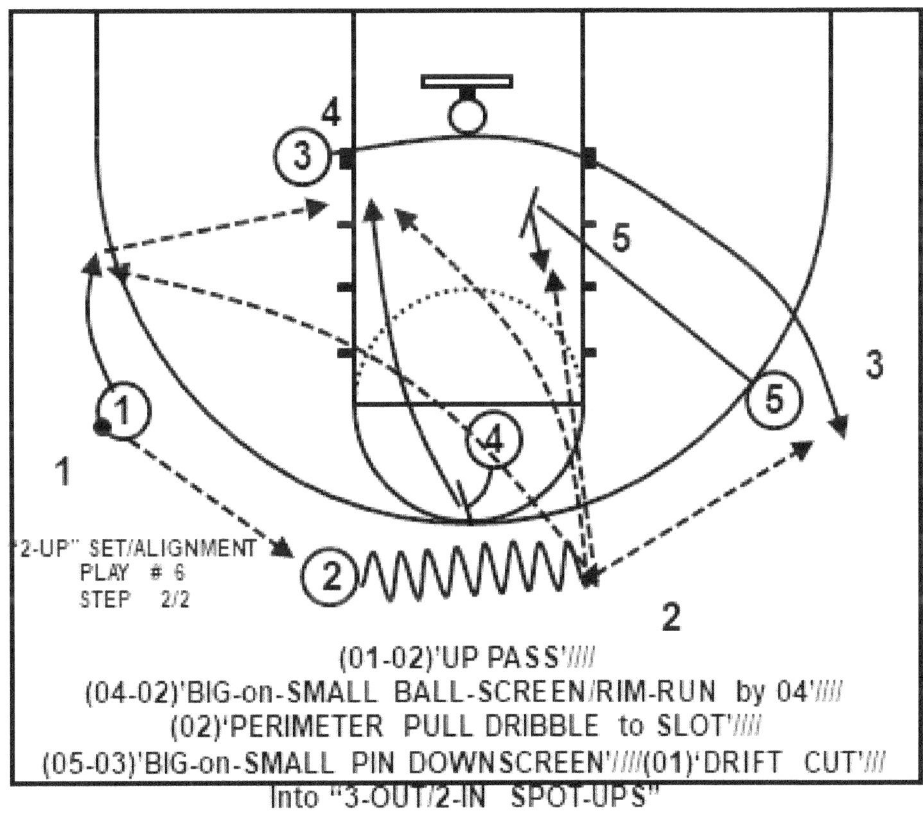

DIAGRAM 13.12

Diagram 13.13 illustrates the beginning of still another Level 2 play that is # Play 14. After 02 swings the ball to the other side of the floor to 01, 02 diagonally cuts towards 05 to set a "Small-on-Big Pin Down-Screen" for 05 to invert his (post-type) defender, X5, out on the new "Weakside Slot." After screening for 05, 02 slips his screen and steps out to the new "Ballside Slot."

At the same time 01 receives the ball, 03 starts his route as if to set another "Ball-Screen" for 01 (as he did in Play # 13.) After one or two steps, 03 breaks off of his screening route towards 01 and makes a direct "Slash Cut" towards the basket; executing a "Ghost Ball-Screen" with 02. With the interaction between 02 and 05 and with 04 staying spread out high and wide, 03's action becomes a perimeter invert and isolation post-up for himself against a perimeter-type defender, X3. See Diagram 13.13

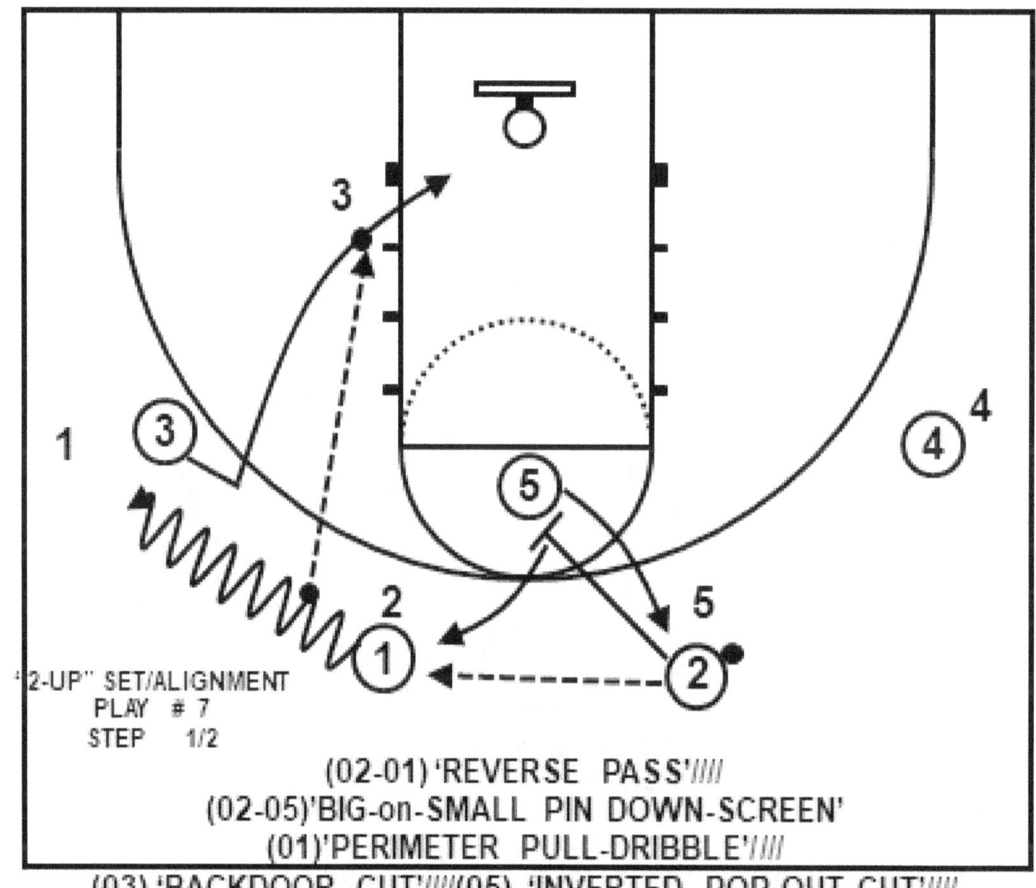

DIAGRAM   13.13

Diagram 13.14 shows 01 turning down the "Inside Pass" to 03 and instead, making an "Up Pass" to 02 at the "Slot." When the (01-02) pass is made, 03 makes an inverted and isolated "Duck-In Cut" and looks for the ball from 02. At the same time, 05 steps over to set a "Big-on-Small Ball-Screen" and 02 "dribble-scrapes" off of 05's top left shoulder for 05 to then make a "reverse pivot" off of his lower right foot. As 02 makes a "perimeter pull dribble" towards the opposite "Slot," 04 "spots-up" near the sideline and slightly lower than the FT Line extended. This stretches the opposition's defense both vertically as well as horizontally. As the play ends with various teammates having different types of possible open shots, the "3-Out/2-In" Spot-Ups are filled. See Diagram 13.14

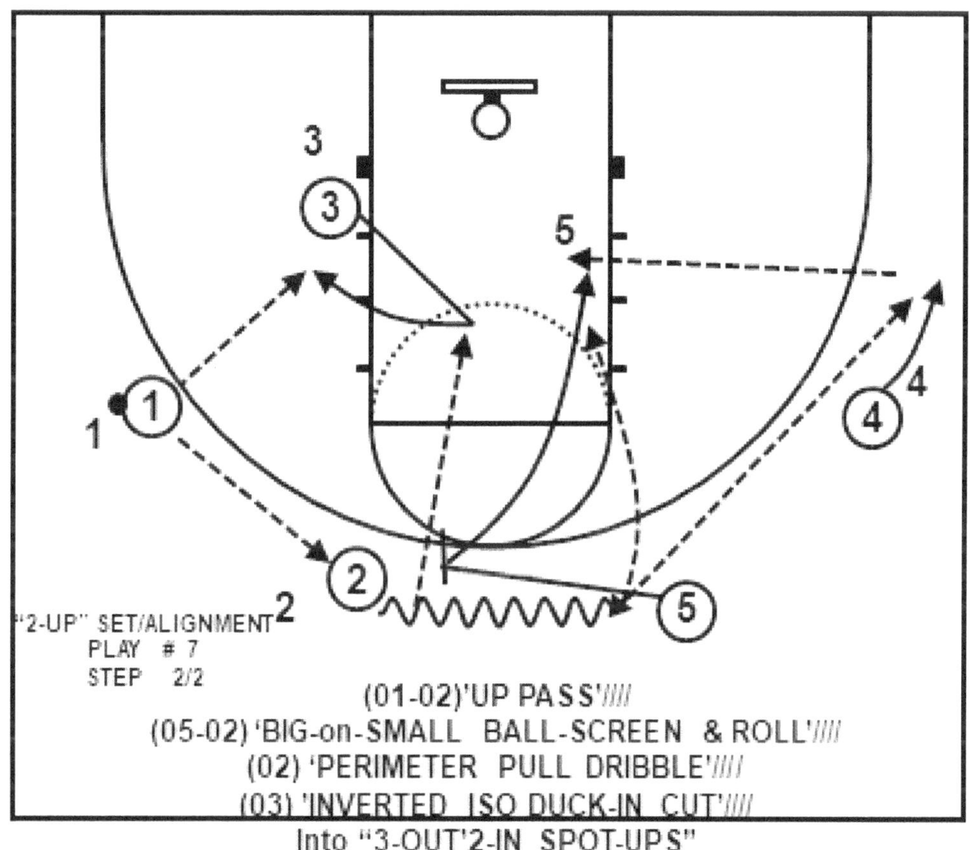

DIAGRAM 13.14

Diagram 13.15 begins the illustration of Play # 8, the first Level 3 play described. This entry starts with the basic (05-01) "Big-on-Small Shuffle Back-Screen after 01 has reversed the ball to 02. 05 then slips his screen and fills the newly vacated "Slot." 01 should read his defender and choose the appropriate shoulder of 05 he should make contact with on his direct cut to the basket. See Diagram 13.15

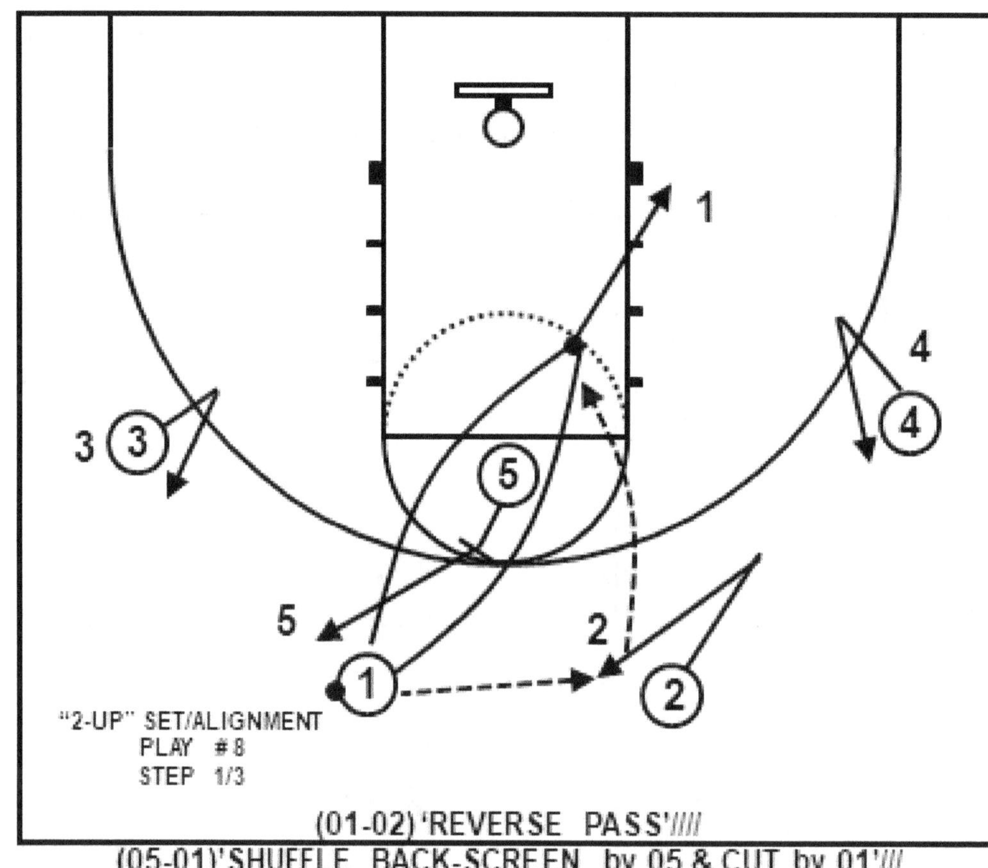

Diagram 13.16 illustrates 02 turning down the pass to 01 and waiting for the presumed (04-02) "Ball-Screen." After one to two steps by 04 towards 02 and the ball, 04 immediately reverses the direction of his cut to finish the execution of the (04-02) "Big-on-Small Ghost Ball-Screen" and "Diagonal Slash Cut" across the lane to the opposite "Block." This action should catch the defense, particularly X4 off-guard and make the opposition defense-less.

02 then reverses the ball to 05 since 05 and 03 both will have very good passing angles and opportunities to deliver the ball to 04 on his initial cut or later post-up. After making the pass to 05, 02 "Flare-Cuts" to the new "Weakside Wing." See Diagram 13.16

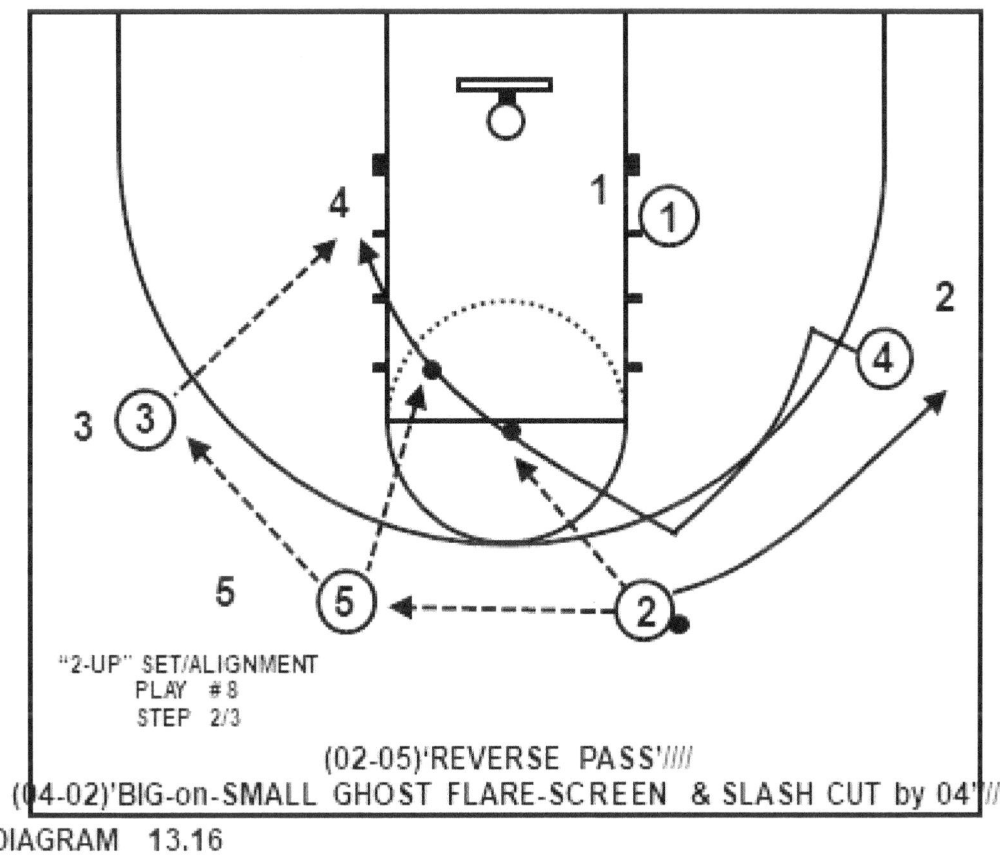

DIAGRAM 13.16

If 03 receives the ball from 05, 05 immediately cuts diagonally down to set a "Big-on-Small Down Pin-Screen" for 01 to use to break up to the top of the key. This two-man game allows to 04 further isolate his defender down on the new "Ballside Block." In addition, with 02 spread out near the sideline outside of the arc, 02's location helps spread the defense even thinner. All five players are spotted up in the proper "3-Out/2-In" Spot-Ups. See Diagram 13.17

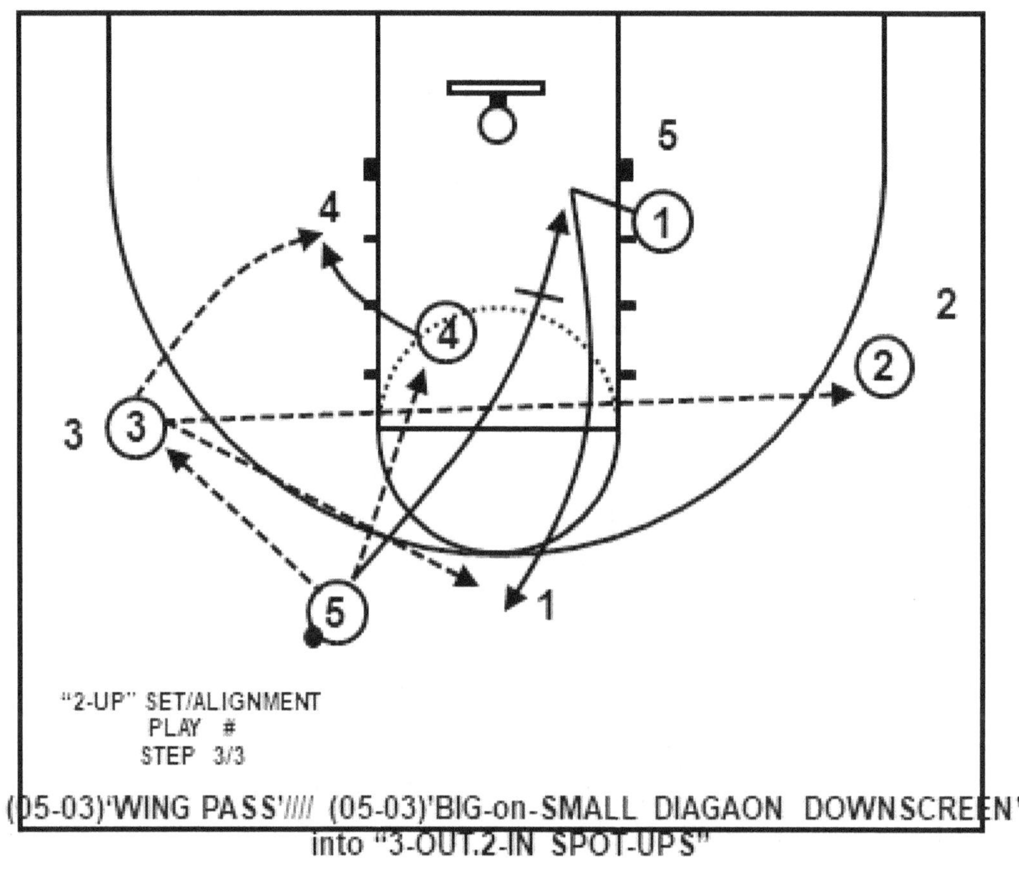

DIAGRAM 13.17

Diagram 13.18 illustrates the beginning of the second Level 3 play (Play # 9) out of the "2-UP" Set. 02 brings the ball down the floor and makes the quick "Reverse Pass" to 01. Immediately 04 then steps up to set a "Big-on-Small Flare-Screen" for 02 to use to then "Flare-Screen" to the new "Weakside Wing" area. See Diagram 13.18

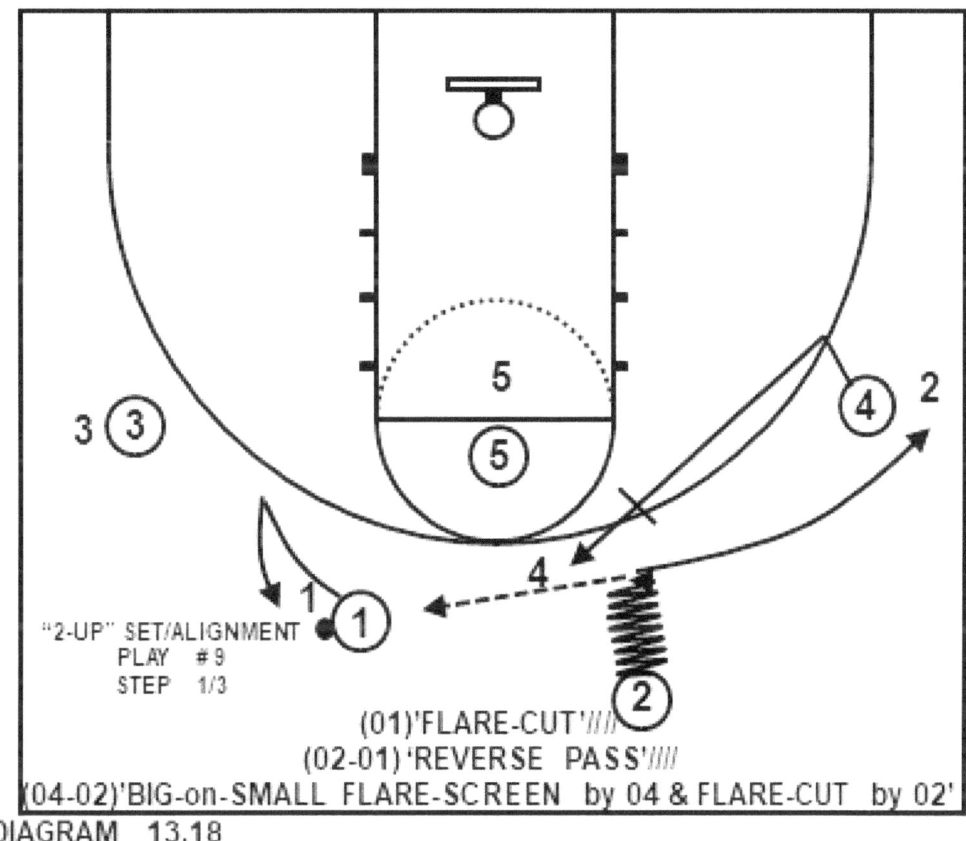

Diagram 13.19 shows 01 then "re-reversing" the ball to 04, now spotted up on the "Slot" vacated by 02. After making the pass to 04, 01 makes the standard "Shuffle Back-Screen Cut" off of 05 and 05 quickly steps out to again fill the "Slot," just like in Play # 15 (in Diagram 13.27) If 04 cannot hit 01 after 01 makes a short cut to the basket, 01 stops and returns to align at the "Nail" (where 05 originated.) See Diagram 13.19

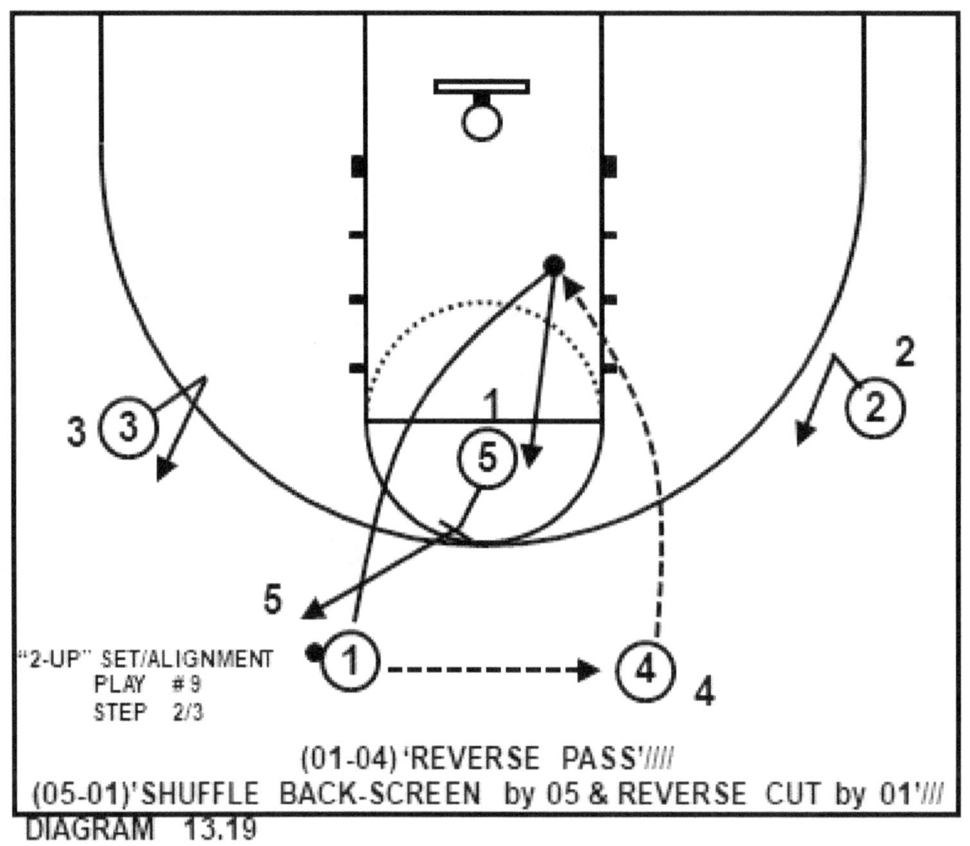

Diagram 13.20 illustrates the ending of the Level 3 play/entry with 04 making the pass back to 05, after 05 has inverted his position and his post-type defender, X5. 05 then makes a "Wing Pass" to 03, leading to both 04 and 05 making "Scissors Cuts" off of 01 (at the "Nail.")

This "Small-on-Big Back-Screen" for both 05 and 04 attack the two inverted post-type defenders, X5 and X4. The fact the actual screener is presumed to be the opposition's smallest defender, X1 will discourage defensive switches by X1 on either 05 or 04.

03 looks to hit 04 on his "Slash Cut" or to make a "Lob Pass" to 05 on his "Scissors Shuffle-Cut Back-Screen." His other pass receivers are to 01 popping out to the top of the key after setting the screen or to 02 spotted up on the new "Weakside Wing." This action gives the offense four legitimate pass receivers as well as placing all five offensive players into the proper "3-Out/2-In" Spot-Ups. This gives the opposition's defense no time to recover or reorganize at the conclusion of this play. See Diagram 13.20

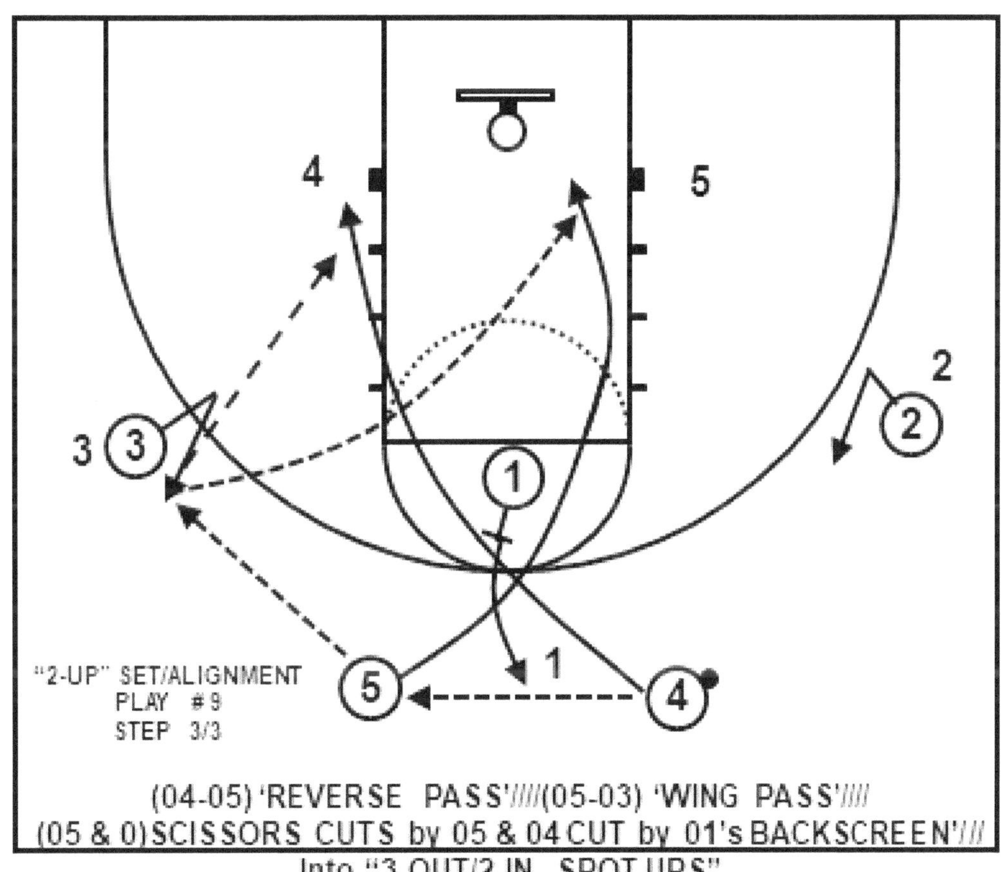

DIAGRAM 13.20

PLAYS/ENTRIES THAT END in the "4-OUT/1-IN" OFFENSIVE SPOT-UPS

The difference in the following plays/entries to be discussed is that all five players will end up in a different group of offensive spot-ups. These "4-Out/1-In Spot-Ups" will have players moving about the court with any of the five ending up in the "Ballside Deep Corner," the "Ballside Slot," the "Weakside Slot," the "Ballside Post," and the "Weakside Deep Corner." These five positions can provide the offense with safe and easy types of ball-reversals, large gaps for dribble penetration, opportunities to deliver the ball inside to whomever (perimeter-type or post-type players) is posting up their defender on the "Ballside Block," and a player that can be a perimeter-scoring threat and a legitimate offensive rebounding threat from outside of the arc on his "offensive crashing of the boards." The "4-Out/1-In Spot-Ups also provide ample opportunities for constant and effective defensive transition responsibilities.

Diagram 13.21 illustrates a Level 1 play (Play # 10) out of the "2-UP Set" that will flow into the "4-Out/1-In" Spot-Ups at its conclusion with no shots being taken.

While the action could start on either side of the offensive set/alignment, 02 is the player in this diagram that dribbles directly at 04, causing 04 to make a hard aggressive "Backdoor Cut" to the basket. 02 kills his dribble possibly slightly deeper than the nearest "Slot" position. If 02 does not make the quick pass to 04, 04 stops his cut and then breaks back out to the open "Deep Corner" position. As 04 vacates the "Ballside Block" area and breaks out behind the arc, 01 then scrapes off of 05 and attacks his defender by cutting through the lane to again fill the "Ballside Block." 01 looks to make the pass to 01 or possibly a "Down Pass" to 04, who may have a better passing angle (to deliver the ball to 01.)

After setting the screen for 01, 05 makes a "Reverse Pivot" off of his right foot to make a "Rim Run" Cut to the basket. If 02 does not make the "Lob Pass" to 05, 05 rotates out to the wide and vacant "Weakside Deep Corner." At the same time, 03 rotates up to fill the newly declared "Weakside Slot." The conclusion of this action repositions all players into the "4-Out/1-In" Spot-Ups. See Diagram 13.21

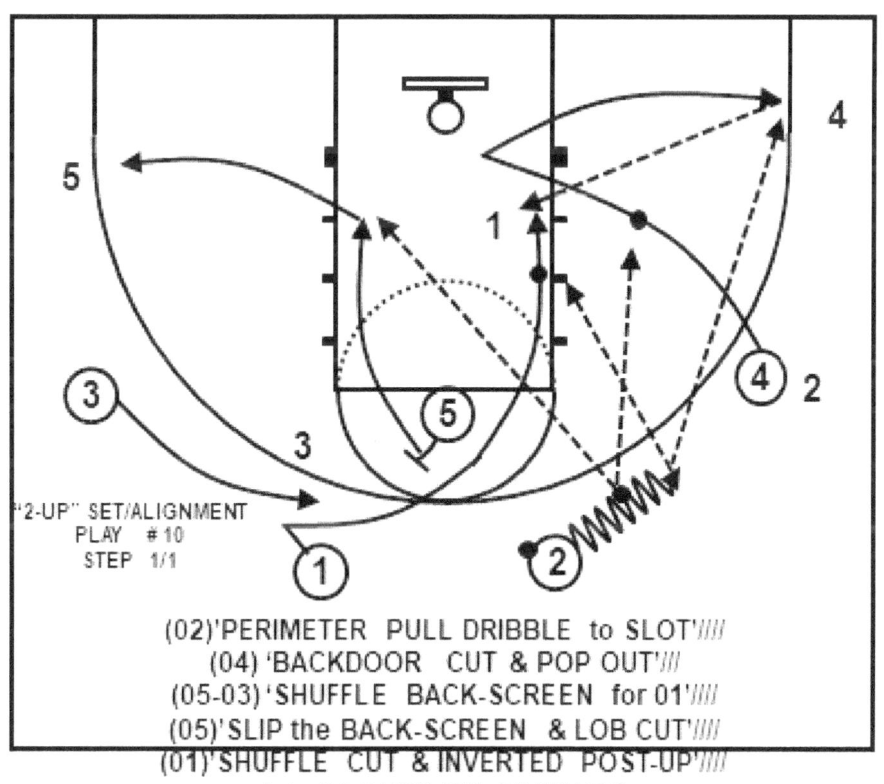

Play # 11 is a Level 2 play that is shown in Diagrams 13.22 and 13.23. 02 makes the "Reverse Pass" to 01 and immediately sets a "Pin Down-Screen" for 05 to pop out to the now empty "Weakside Slot." 02 slips his screen and fills the now empty "Ballside Slot."

01 then makes a "Wing Pass" to 03 and then follows his pass to receive a "Flip Pass" back from 03. After returning the ball to 01, 03 makes his "Lob Cut" to the basket. If 03 does not receive 01's "Lob Pass," 03 remains at the new "Ballside Block" to invert and isolate his individual defender, X3. With 05 and 04 the presumed two biggest defenders and are stretched horizontally and vertically, this action fully isolates X3. See Diagram 13.22

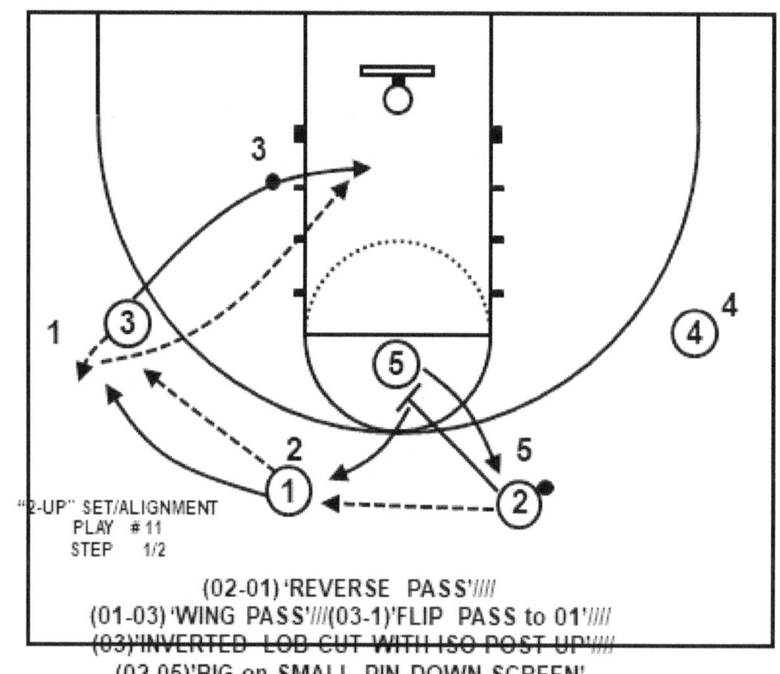

Diagram 13.23 shows 01 turning down the pass to 03 and making the "Up Pass" to 02 at the "Slot." 05 then breaks across the top of the key to set a "Big-on-Small Ball-Screen" for 02 to use as 02 "dribble-scrapes" off of 05's top left shoulder. When 02 breaks contact with 05, 05 makes a "Reverse Pivot" off of his lower right foot and "rolls" down the lane to post up his defender down on the new "Ballside Block." To eliminate helpside defense, 03 makes a vertical "Up Cut" to the new "Weakside Slot." At the same time, 04 and 01 both make "Flare-Cuts" towards their respective Deep Corners. This repositions players into the "4-Out/1-In" Spot-Ups for the next wave of attack to continue. See Diagram 13.23

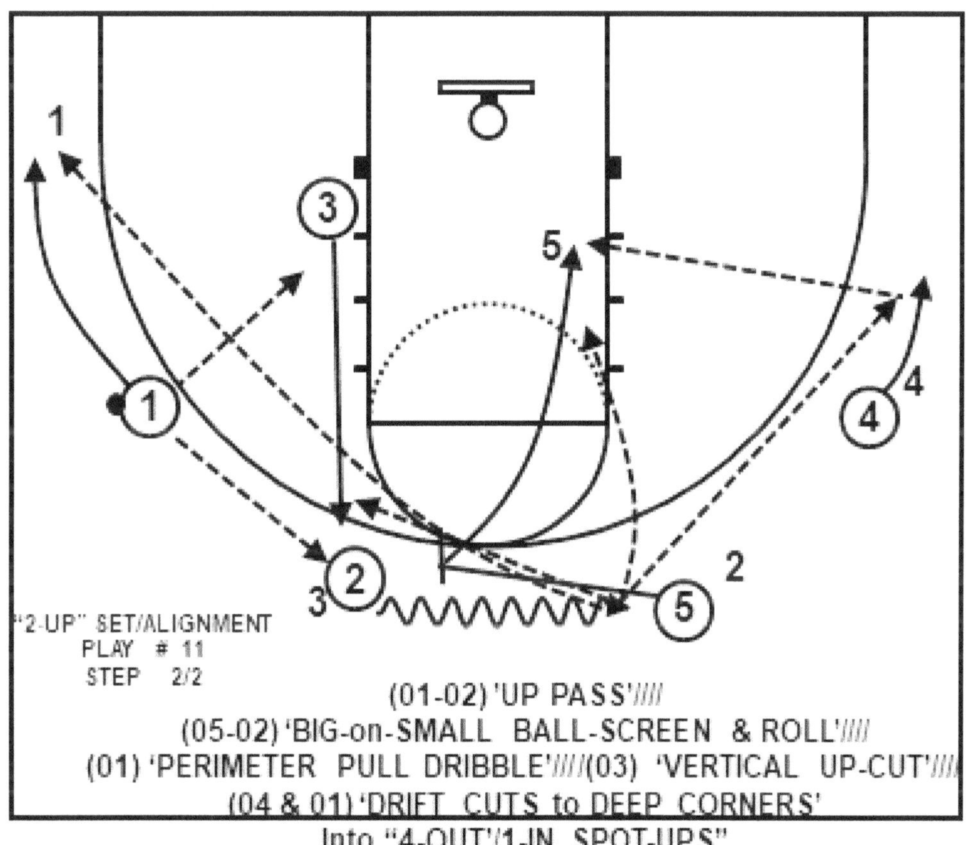

Diagram 13.24 shows another Level 2 play (Play # 12) that is a Counter Play to Play # 11 with 02 again reversing the ball to 01 and immediately setting the same screen for 05. 05 uses the screen in the same manner and fills the same "Weakside Slot." 02 pops out to again fill the opposite "Slot."

Instead of making the same (01-03) "Wing Pass," 03 makes a hard "Backdoor Cut" to the basket. If 01 cannot make the pass to the cutting 03, 01 continues his dribble and fills 03's "Wing" Spot-up area at the FT Line extended. 03 remains posted up on the new "Ballside Block, with 02 and 05 now at the two "Slot" locations and 04 spotted up at the "Weakside Wing" area on the opposite side of the floor. See Diagram 13.24

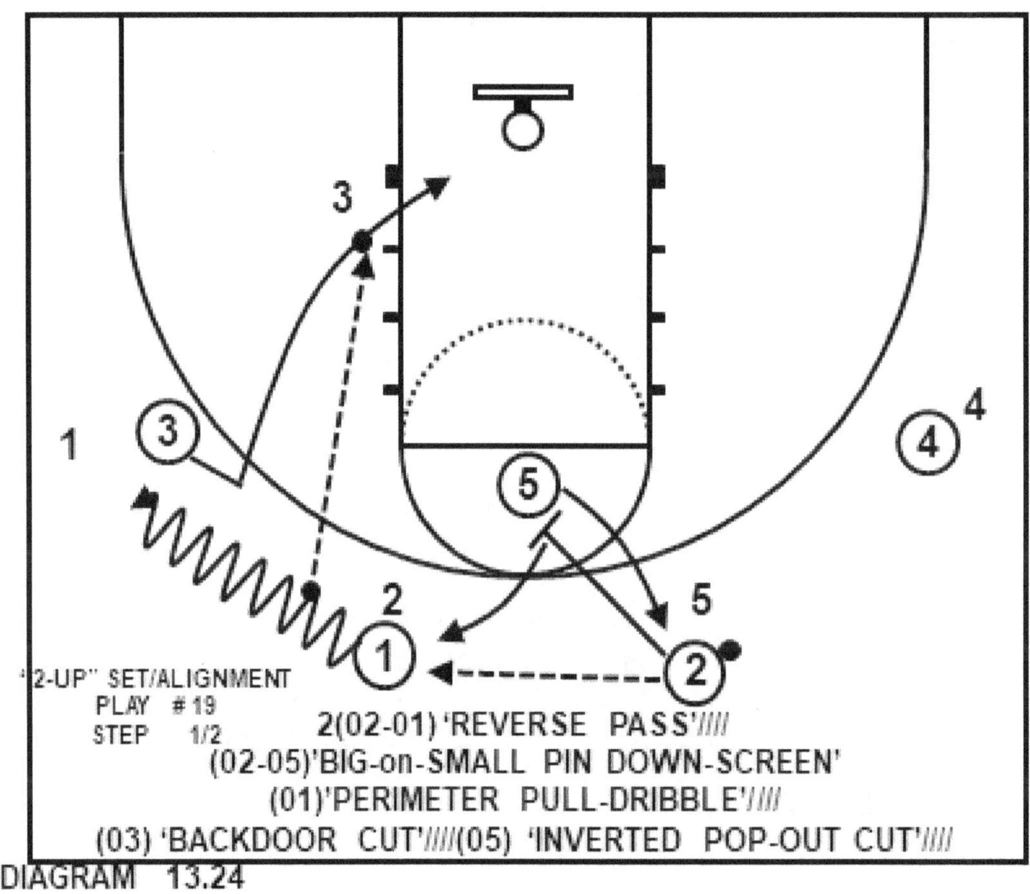

Diagram 13.25 illustrates 01 not being able to make the pass to 03 on his "Backdoor Cut" and instead (again) passing the ball out to 02. As in Play # 18, 05 steps across to set the same type of "Big-on-Small Ball-Screen" for 02 to use to perimeter pull dribble across the floor to the opposite "Slot" position. Where Play # 13 differentiates from Play # 18 is that in this play, 03 flashes across the lane to post up on the new "Ballside Block" (versus making an "Up-Cut") and 01 steps up to execute a (01-05) "(Small-on-Big Back-)Screen (the Ball-)Screener" action with 05. 05 uses the screen to scrape off of 01's outside right shoulder and then curl to make a "Lob Cut" to the rim, looking for 02's "Lob Pass." 01 then slips that screen to step into the vacant "Weakside Slot." If 02 does not connect with 05 on the pass, 05 empties out to the new "Weakside Deep Corner." These actions by all of the offensive players again repositions each player into one of the proper "4-Out/1-In" Spot-Ups for the designated continuity offense to once again have a smooth conversion into the designated continuity offense. See Diagram 13.25

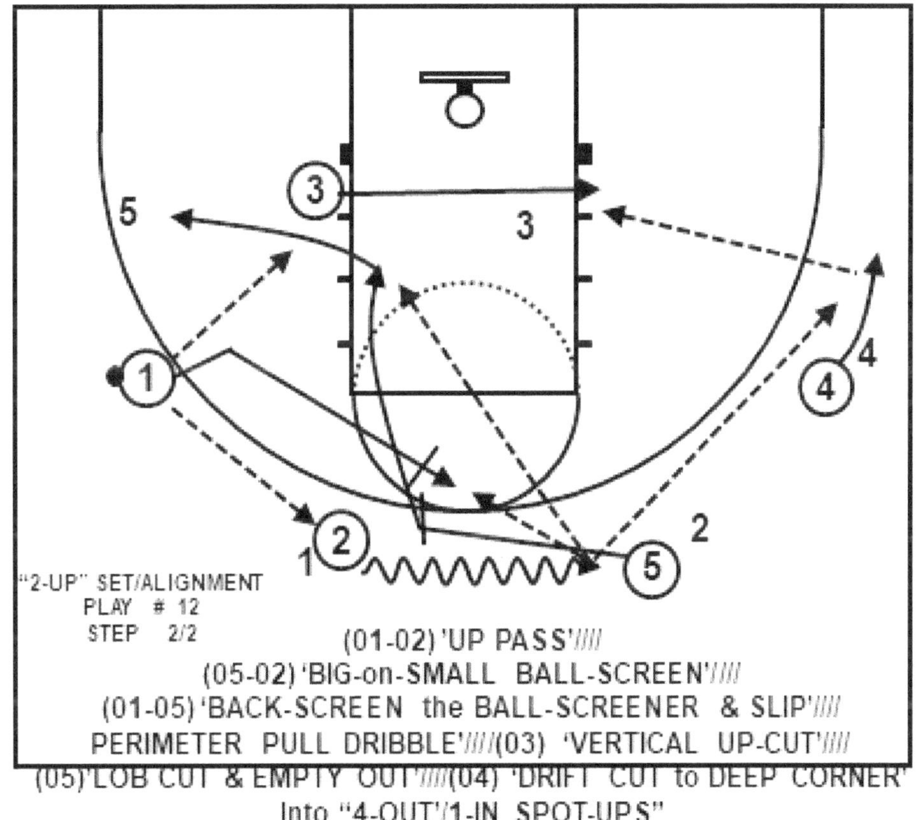

Diagram 13.25

Diagram 13.26 shows the beginning Play # 13, another Level 2 play, with 02 reversing the ball to 01. At that point, 03 steps up to set a "Big-on-Small Ball-Screen" for 01 to use. 01 "dribble-scrapes" off of 03's outside right shoulder and 03 "reverse pivots" off of his inside left foot, opens up to the ball and rolls to the basket. 01 kills his dribble at the FT Line extended. 02 makes a "Replacement Fill Cut" to the "Slot" where 01 started. 05 pops out to make an "Inverted Replacement Fill Cut" to the "Slot" position where 02 began. See Diagram 13.26

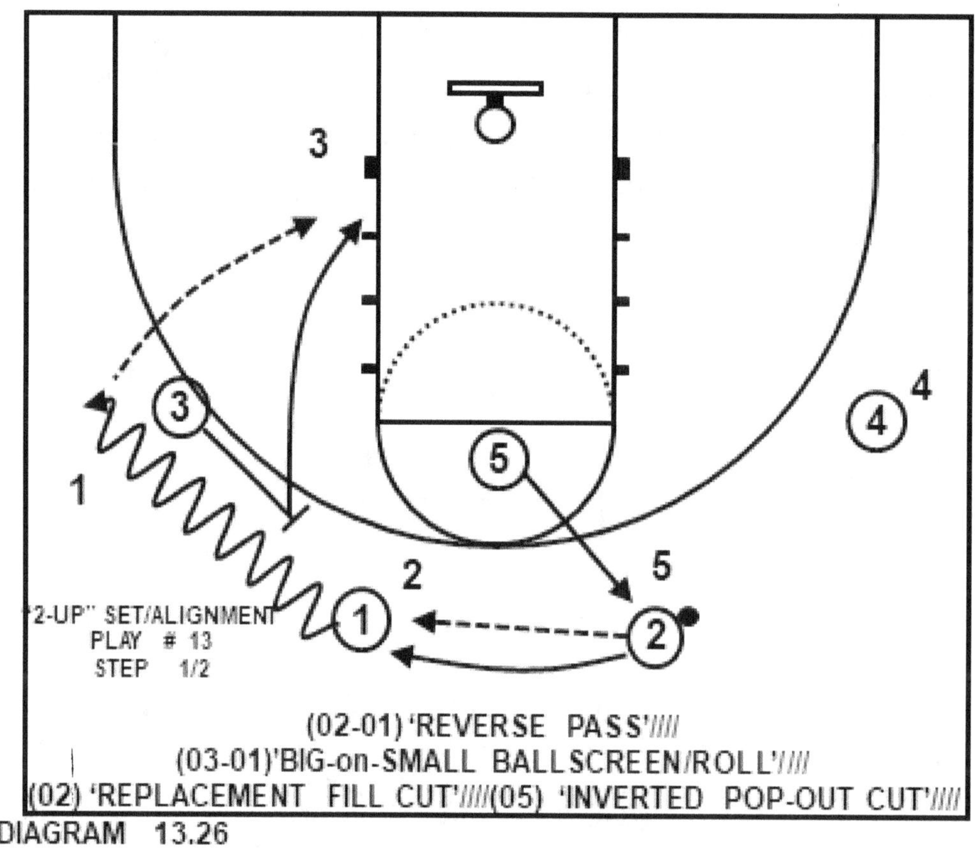

Diagram 13.27 shows the conclusion of Play # 13 with 01 passing the ball back to 02. As 02 starts to reverse the ball via dribble, 05 cuts towards 04 to set a "Big-on-Small Ram Screen" and then makes his "Flare-Cut" to the new "Ballside Deep Corner." After using 05's screen, 04 continues to break up towards the ball and 02 to set a "Big-on-Small Ball-Screen" for 02 to continue across the imaginary center line.

As 02 "dribble-scrapes" off of 05's top left shoulder, 03 makes a strong "Iso Duck-In Cut" into the "Dotted Circle." If 02 does not make the pass to 03, 03 cuts across the lane to post up on the new "Ballside Block." 05 should then make a "front pivot" off of his lower right foot and then "Rim-Run" towards the basket, while looking for 02's "Lob Pass." If 04 does not receive 02's pass, 05 then curls out towards the new "Weakside Deep Corner. 01 slips up to the "Weakside Slot" and 02 kills his dribble at the "Ballside Slot." If this action does not produce a shot, the "4-Out/1-In" Spot-Ups are properly filled for the final phase of the offense to fluidly begin. See Diagram 13.27

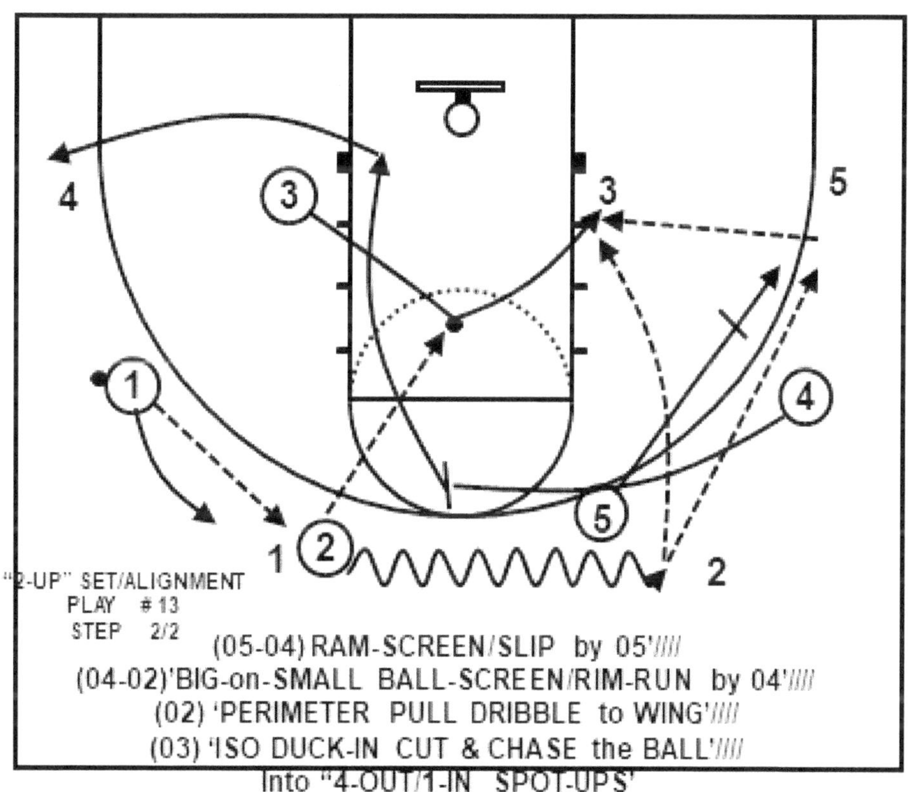

DIAGRAM 13.27

PLAYS THAT END in the "HIGH POST/LOW POST" OFFENSIVE SPOT-UPS

The major change in this group of the four plays/entries (one Level 1 play, one Level 2 play and two Level 3 plays) is when either play ends with no shot taken, all five offensive players will reposition themselves in a different group of offensive spot-ups on the floor called the "High Post/Low Post" Spot-Ups. (These new spot-up locations/positons will have players moved about the court during the execution of the play with any one of the five ending up in the "Ballside Low Post," one in the "Ballside High Post," one in the "Weakside Wing," one in the "Ballside Wing," and the remaining player at the "Point." If any plays end without the desired shot taken, these five positions will give the offense the important advantages such as the abilities to have safe and easy types of ball-reversals, spreading defenders for more frequent dribble penetrations, more "Inside Pass" opportunities for whomever (perimeter-type or post-type players) is currently posting up their defender on the "Ballside Block," and the "Ballside High Post." The actions still provide with three perimeter-scoring threats and with a fundamentally sound offensive rebounding plan.

Diagram 13.28 shows the beginning of Play # 14 with 02 beginning the play with a (04-02) "Big-on-Small Ball-Screen" with 04 reading the defensive positions of X4 and electing to "roll to the basket" or to "rim-run" to the basket as 02 finishes his dribble at the FT Line extended.

To occupy potential opposing helpside defenders, 05 steps out to "Iverson Screen" for 03 to flash to the new "Ballside High Post," and then 05 steps out to the now vacant "top of the key." This area is open because at the same time of the (04-02) "Ball-Screen," 01 "Flare-Screens" to the new "Weakside Wing" location. This keeps opposing defenders, especially the presumed biggest defender, X5 from trying to help out his post defender, X4. This gives 04 an even greater advantage of receiving the ball from 02 and scoring from a very close range in more of an isolated situation.

Still, if no shots are taken, the new "High Post/Low Post" Spot-Ups are filled to continue the transition from "play to continuity." See Diagram 13.28

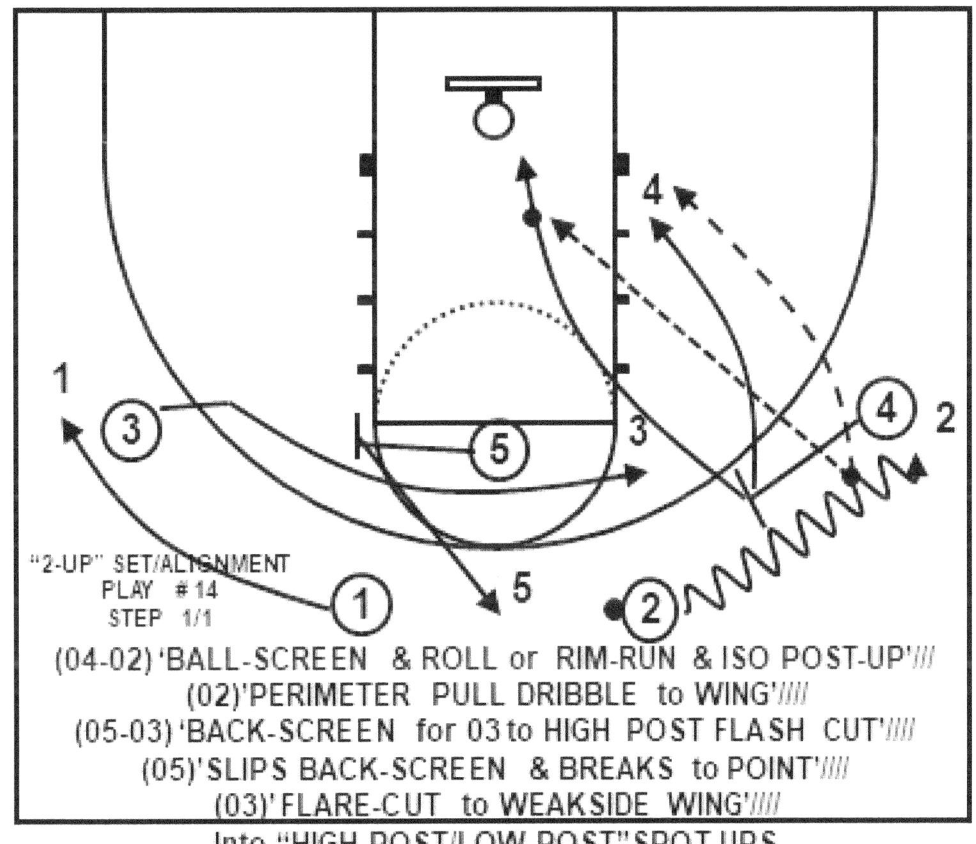

DIAGRAM 13.28

Diagrams 13.29 and 13.30 illustrate the first Level 2 play in this package of plays with 02 cutting across to set a "Ball-Screen/Slip" for 01 to reverse dribble to the now vacant "Slot" on the right side of the floor. As 02 then slips his screen, 04 then steps adjacent to 05 at the "Nail."

From there, 03 makes an "Iverson Cut" off of the "Double Big-on-Small Iverson Screens" set by 05 and 04. At the same time, 05 sets a "Big-on-Small Iverson Screen" with 04 who has stepped adjacent to 05 at the "Nail." See Diagram 13.29

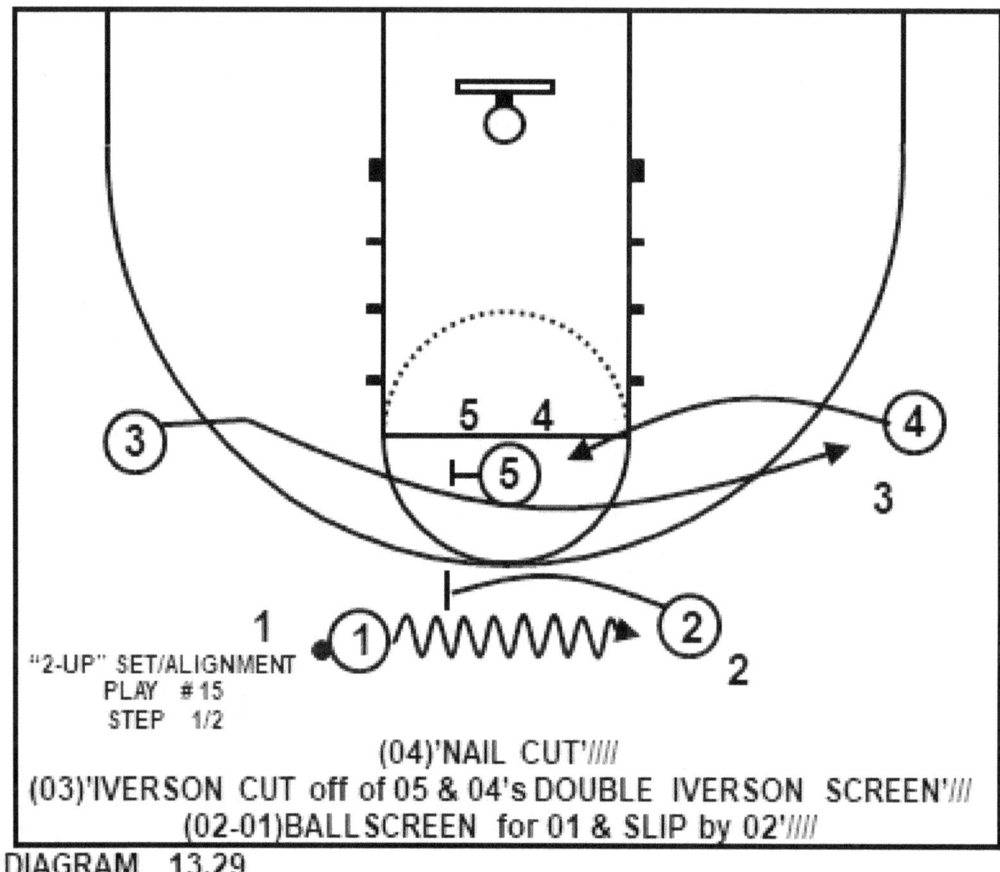

As the ball is "Wing Passed" from 01 to 03, 02 then makes a "Shuffle-Screen Cut" off of 04 as he ends up isolated and inverted down on the newly designated "Ballside Block." After setting the screen for 02, 04 then "Flare-Cuts" to the new "Weakside Wing" while 05 then flashes to the new "Ballside High Post." 01 moves to the top of the key and the "High Post/Low Post" Spot-Ups are now filled to continue the attack. See Diagram 13.30

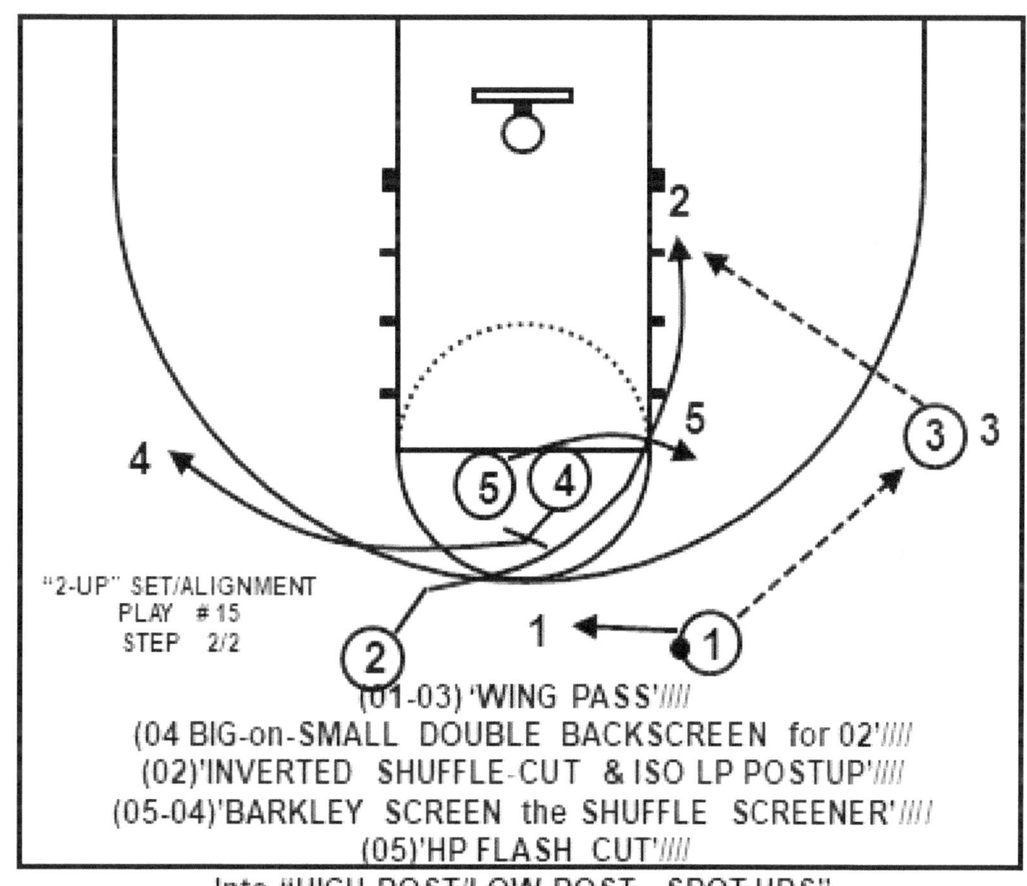

Diagrams 13.31 through 13.33 show Play # 16 as a simple but sophisticated Level 3 play that is somewhat similar to Play # 14. 01 makes the "Reverse Pass" to 02 and 02 immediately flips the ball back to 01, who has followed his pass and has cut towards 02.

After flipping the ball to 01, 02 slides over before then receiving the (03-02) "Flare-Screen." 02 "Flare-Cuts" to the new "Weakside Wing" and prepares his feet, hands and shoulders for a quick "catch and shoot off of 01's "Skip Pass."

With the ball now back in 01's hands, 04 steps up to set the (04-01) "Big-on-Small Ball-Screen" for 01 to use to "dribble-scrape" to the same "Wing" at the FT Line extended. During the screen for 01, 05 immediately "Slash Cuts" to the new "Ballside Block" and after 01 breaks contact with 04's outside left shoulder, 04 slips his screen to make a "Rim-Run" to the basket. See Diagram 13.31

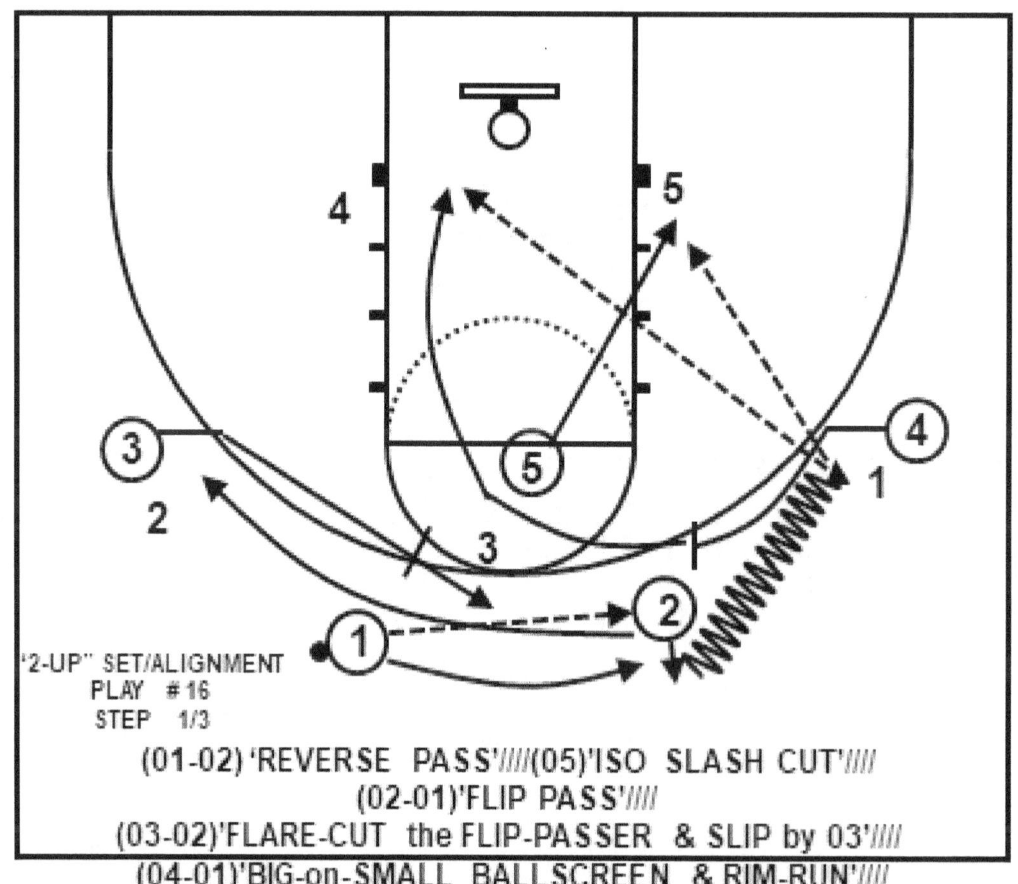

If 01 does not make "Inside Passes" to either 05 or 04 or the "Skip Pass" to 02; 01 should reverse the ball to 03, who has slipped his "Flare-Screen" and stepped over to the "top of the key." When 03 receives the pass, 05 makes a diagonal "Lob Cut" to the basket and 04 makes an aggressive "Duck-In Cut" into the "Dotted Circle" area. See Diagram 13.32.

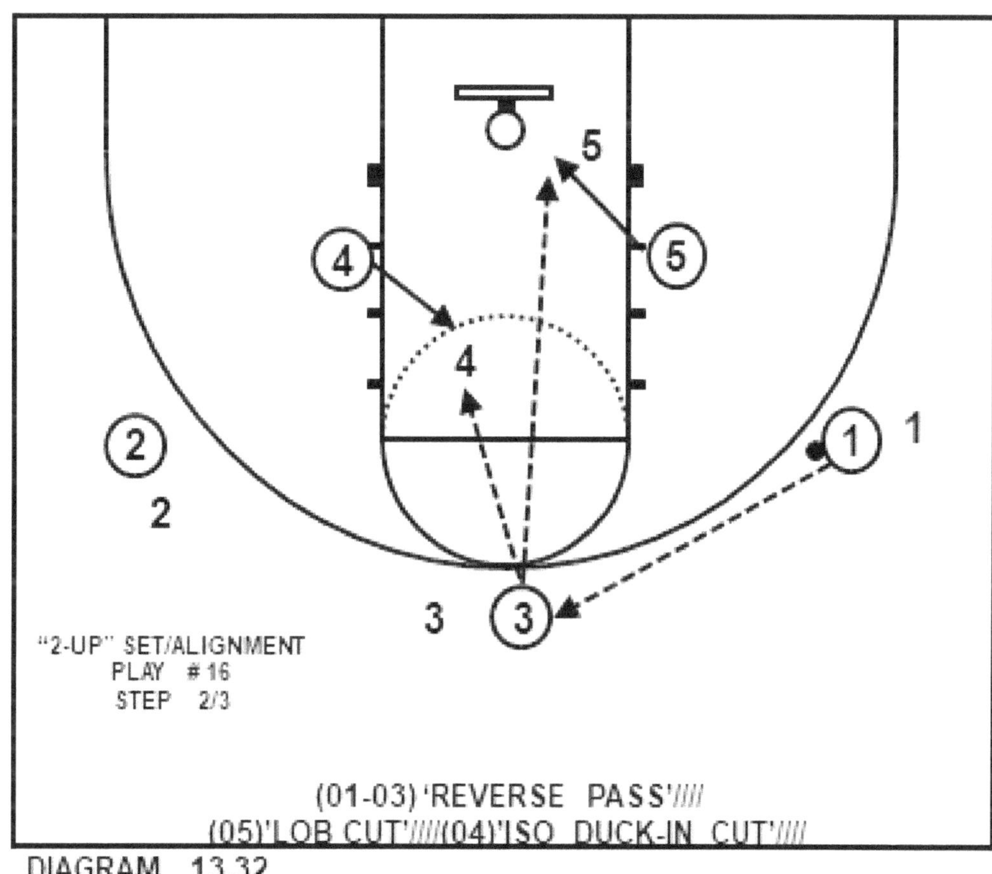

DIAGRAM   13.32

Diagram 13.33 shows the end of the play with 03 not able to make passes to either 04 or to 05. 02 then steps up to set a (02-03) "Small-on-Big Ball-Screen" for 03 to dribble to the FT Line extended on the left side of the floor. After 02 sets the "Ball-Screen" for 03, 01 then steps up execute "(Flare-)Screen the (Ball-)Screener" action for 02 to use on his "Flare-Cut" to the opposite side of the floor. After setting that screen, 01 then fills the "Point" Spot-Up.

During the (02-03) "Ball-Screen," 04 seals off his defender and slides back down to the new "Ballside Block." At the same time, 05 flashes from under the basket to the new "Ballside High Post." This fills all of the "High Post/Low Post" Spot-Ups for the designated continuity offense to fluidly begin. See Diagram 13.33

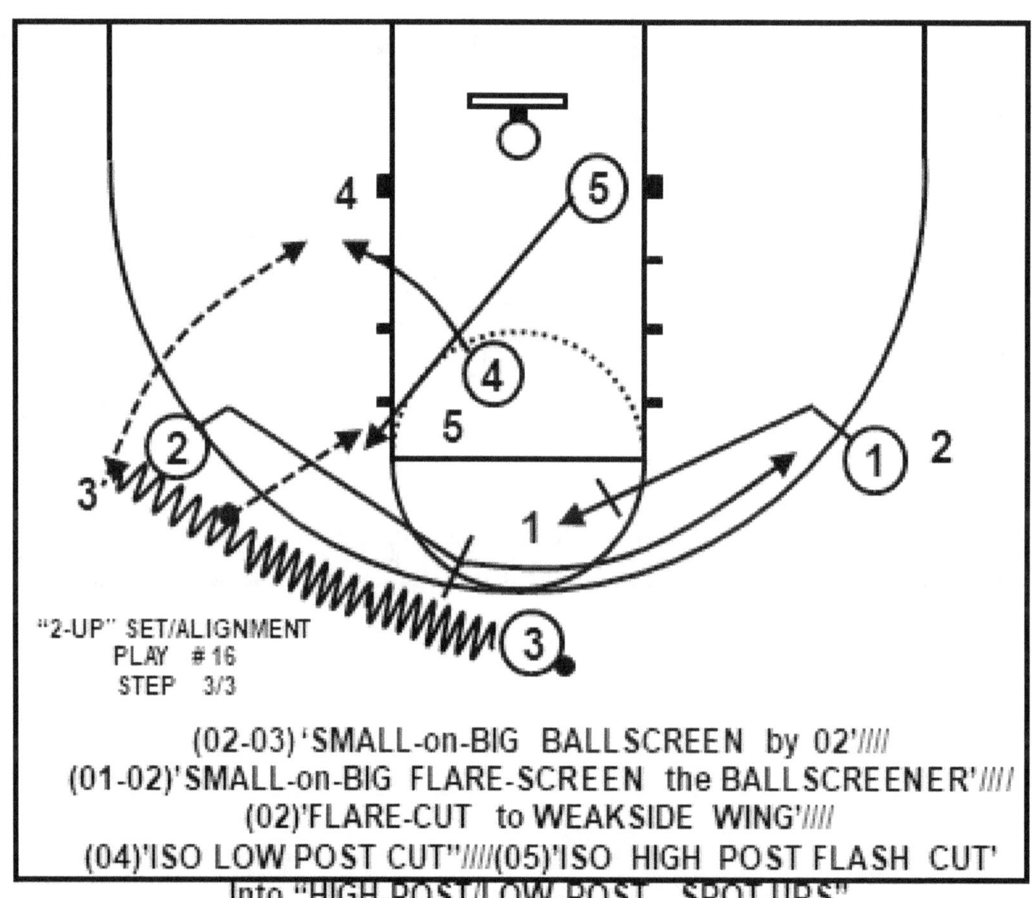

DIAGRAM 13.33

Diagrams 13.34 through 13.37 show a more complicated and sophisticated Level 3 play, called Play # 17. 02 dribbles towards 04 and executes a smooth DHO with 04 for 04 to dribble out to the same side's "Slot." At the same time, 03 steps up to set a "Flare-Screen" for 01 to use to make a "Flare-Cut" to the new "Weakside Wing" area. 05 remains at the "Nail" while the remaining four players all changes locations. See Diagram 13.34

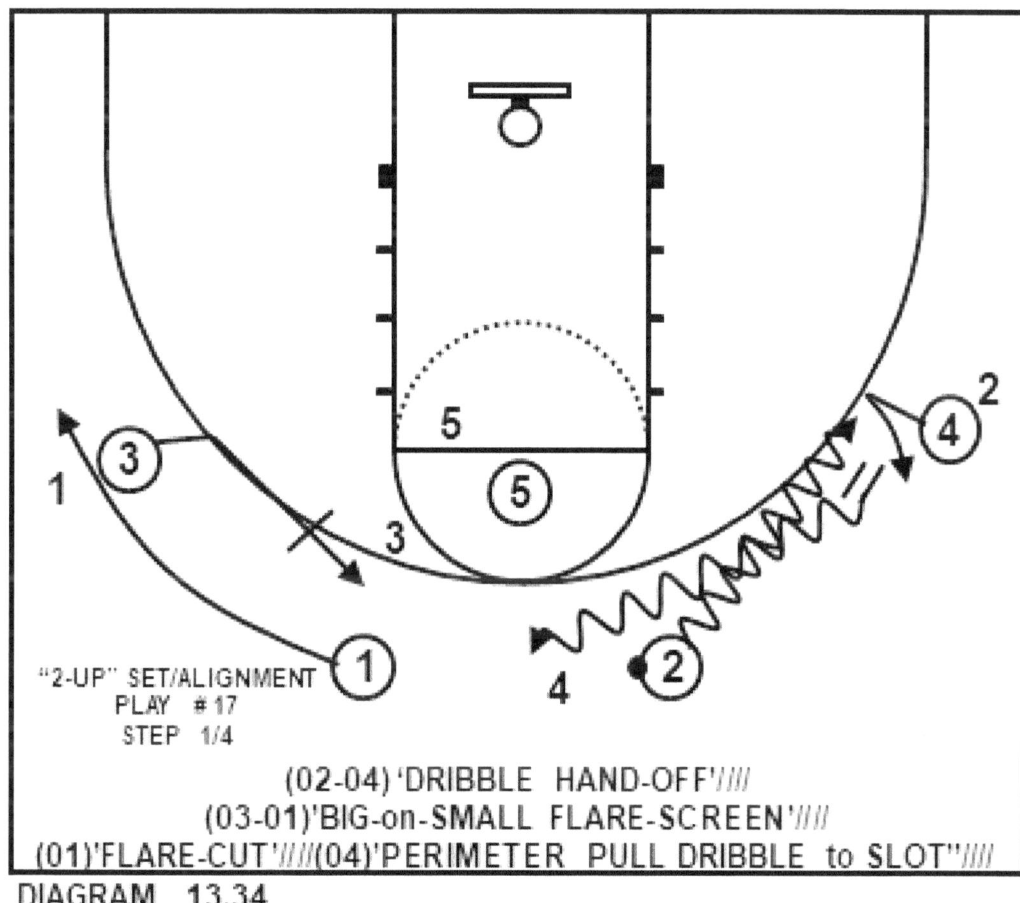

Diagram 13.35 shows 04 dribbling the ball out to the "Slot" before 04 makes a "Reverse Throwback Pass" to 02. After making the pass back to 02, 04 makes a "Shuffle-Cut" off of 05's right shoulder and looks for a "Lob Pass" from 02. While 03 appears to make the same type of "Shuffle-Cut" as 04, 03 "bumps" 05's "Shuffle Back-Screen," causing 05 to be the player that diagonally slashes from the "Nail" to the new "Ballside Block." 03 pops out to the top of the key to become a potential '3 Pt.' shooter or a Passer. See Diagram 13.35

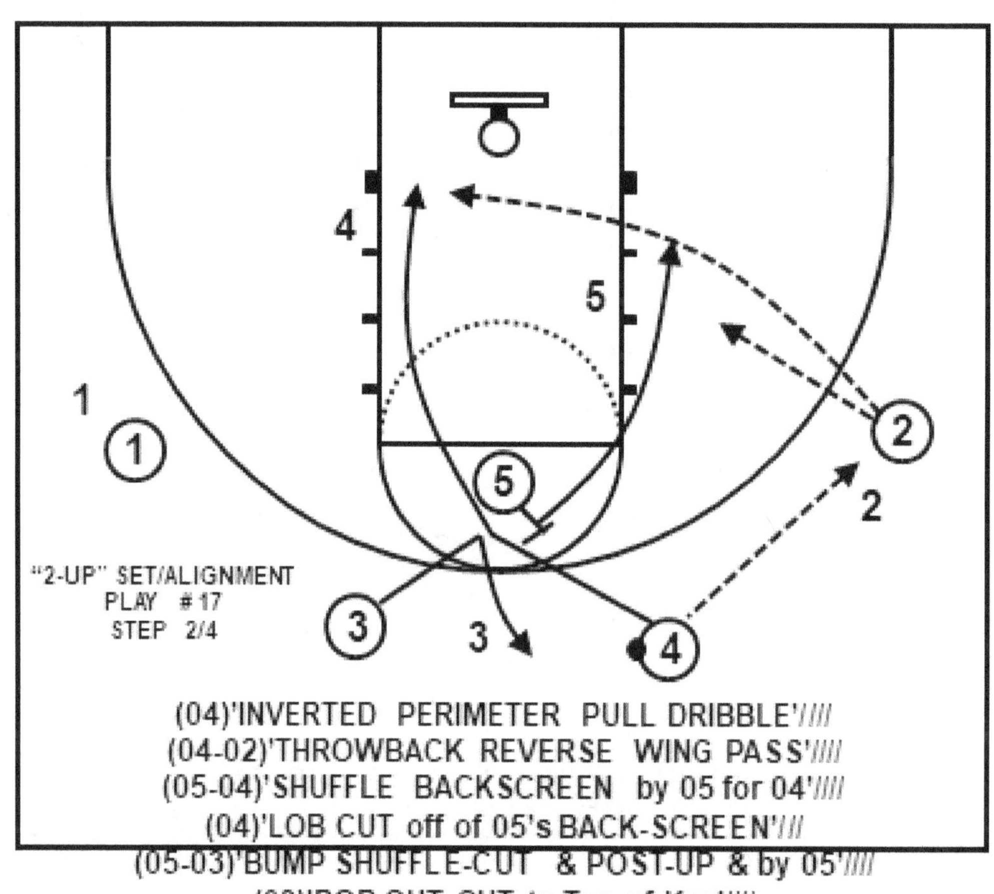

Diagram 13.35

Diagram 13.36 shows 05 making a "Lob Cut" to the basket and 04 making an "Iso Duck-In Cut" into the "Dotted Circle" area, with both looking for the "Inside Pass" from 03 out at the top of the key. With 01 and 02 both spotted up outside of the arc near the "Wings" on both sides of the court, they both become perimeter scoring threats as well as stretch the defense from sideline to sideline. These spot-up locations further isolate both 04 and 05 and make them more successful inside scoring threats.. See Diagram 13.36

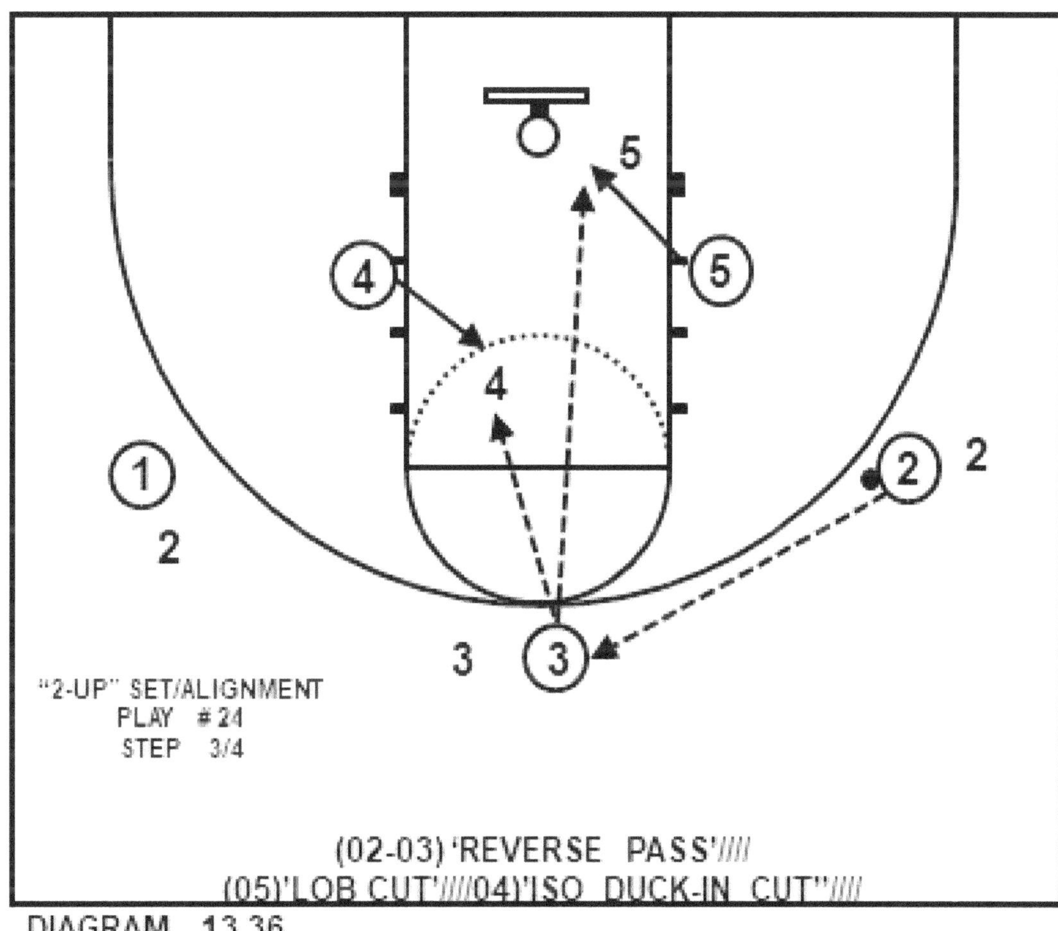

DIAGRAM 13.36

Diagram 13.37 shows the action with 04 sealing off his defender and then flashing to the new "Ballside High Post." From under the basket, 05 simply makes a simple direct "Low Post Flash Cut" across the lane to the new "Ballside Block."

Diagram 13.49 shows the end of the play with 03 not able to make passes to either 04 or to 05. 01 then steps up to set a (01-03) "Small-on-Big Ball-Screen" for 03 to dribble to the FT Line extended on the left side of the floor. After setting the screen for 03, 01 then continues across the top of the key to set a "Small-on-Big" Pin Screen for 01 for 02 to use to break to the "Point" Spot-Up for a possible open '3.' 01 then flows to the now vacant "Weakside Wing." This fills all of the "High Post/Low Post" Spot-Ups for the designated continuity offense to fluidly begin. See Diagram 13.37

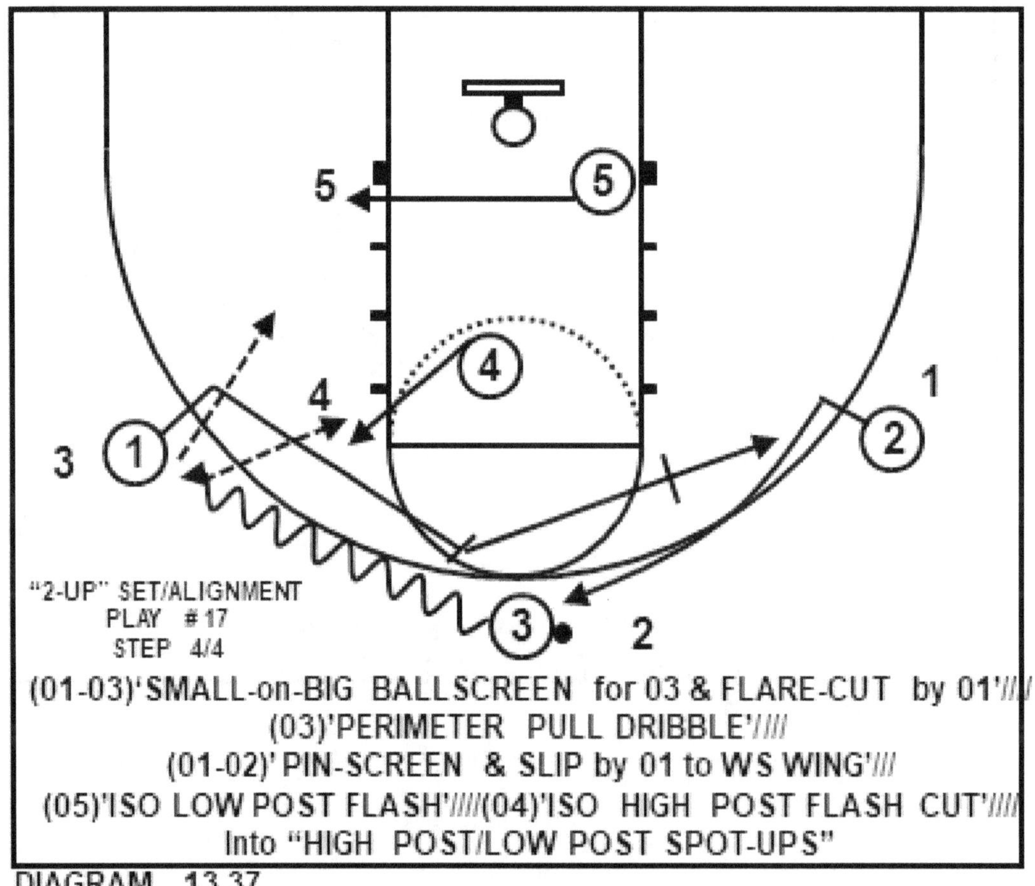

DIAGRAM 13.37

There are many different philosophies on how to attack opposing defenses. This multiple-phase offensive system uses more than one phase/layer/wave of attack, with each phase/wave having a seamless and immediate conversion into the next phase/wave. While this system can be confusing to defenses and difficult to defend, this system can be properly taught and (physical talent, mental understand and playing experience.)

In addition, there are several types of offensive schemes and different ways within this system that offenses can attack their defensive counter-parts. Many of these can be integrated within the same offensive system that can attack defenses in various ways. The larger the number of schemes that can be successfully utilized and integrated within the same system, the greater the opportunity an offensive team can find the most efficient and productive schemes that can place both individual and the overall team in the best and most frequent "positions to succeed."

The plays/entries carefully diagrammed down to the small and seemingly unimportant 'V-Cuts' made by countless players before making their more important following cut are also described in detail.

Each play has been carefully studied and evaluated to determine which level of talent and experience must be possessed for that specific team to be able to successfully execute the play. This includes all players' physical skills as well as their mental understanding of the game. Coaches must also have the experience and the associated level of understanding of the game as well as their coaching/teaching of the nuances of each play.

PLAYS/ENTRIES THAT END in the "4-OUT/1-IN" OFFENSIVE SPOT-UPS

The difference in the following plays/entries are that all five players will end up in a different group of offensive spot-ups. These "4-Out/1-In Spot-Ups" will have players moved about the court with any of the five ending up in the "Ballside Deep Corner," the "Ballside Slot," the "Weakside Slot," the "Ballside Post," and the "Weakside Deep Corner." These five positions can provide the offense with safe and easy types of ball-reversals, large gaps for dribble penetration, opportunities to deliver the ball inside to whomever (perimeter-type or post-type players) is posting up their defender on the "Ballside Block," and a player that can be a perimeter-scoring threat and a legitimate offensive rebounding threat from outside of the arc on his "offensive crashing of the boards." The "4-Out/1-In Spot-Ups also provide ample opportunities for constant and effective defensive transition responsibilities.

Diagram 14.1 illustrates Play # 1-a Level 1 play. As 01 dribbles towards 02, 03 cuts through the lane and off of 05's "Big-on-Small Pin Screen" for 03 to the new "Ballside Deep Corner." At the same time, 02 steps up to set a "Big-on-Small Ball-Screen" for 01 to use to dribble to the "Ballside Slot." After screening for 01, 04 steps up to set a "(Big-on-Small Back-)Screen the (Ball-)Screener" action. 02 curls tightly off of 04's outside right shoulder and makes a "Lob Cut" to the basket. After screening for 02, 04 slips his screen and breaks to the new "Weakside Slot." If 01 does not make the "Lob Pass" to 02 or to make an "Inside Pass" to 05, (who has sealed off his defender after screening for 03), or perimeter passes to either 03 or 04; the players are in the "4-Out/1-In" Spot-Ups for other continuity offenses to begin. See Diagram 14.1

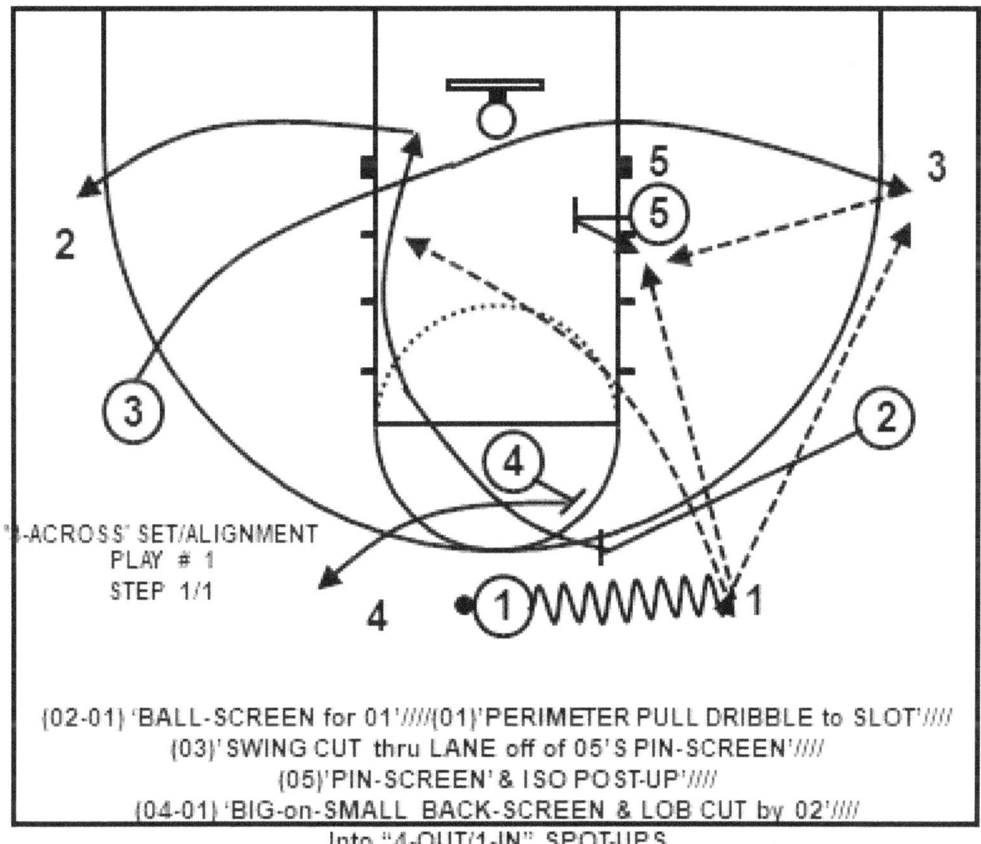

DIAGRAM 14.1

2

Play # 2 illustrates, a Level 2 Play, that flows into the same "4-Out/1-In" Spot-Ups. This play (# 12) has 01 make a "Wing Pass" to the side of the floor that is away from 05. 01 then follows his pass to break towards 02 and the ball. 02 then flips the pass back to 01 near the FT Line extended. From the "Nail" position, 04 steps towards the ball before then diagonally cutting down to set a "Diagonal Down-Screen" for 05 to use to break to the new "Ballside High Post." 03 remains on the new "Weakside Wing" and spots up as a perimeter scoring threat, stretching the defense from sideline to sideline. 05 and 04's actions actually isolate both interior defenders, weakening their effectiveness. See Diagram 14.2

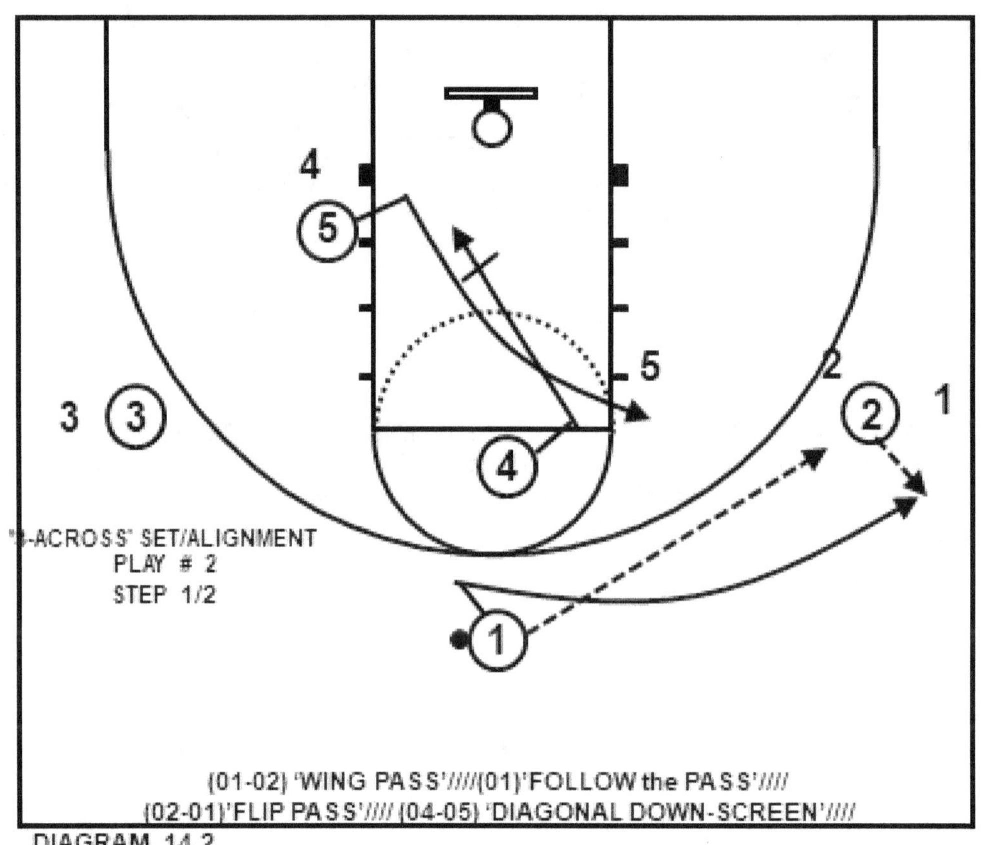

2

Diagram 14.3 shows that after the (02-01) DHO, 01 "Flare-Cuts" to the "Ballside Deep Corner." As 02 regains possession of the ball, 05 steps up to set a "Big-on-Small Inside Ball-Screen. 05 reads the defense to either make a "Rim-Run" or a "Roll" through the lane. At the same time, 04 makes a vertical "Up Cut" to the new "Weakside Slot," while 03 "Flare-Cuts" to his nearest "Deep Corner" on the "Weakside." With 03 and 01 flattening out their respective defender down towards the baseline and stretching the defense, 04 also makes a "Vertical Up Cut" up to the new "Weakside Slot." 02 "dribble-scrapes" off of 05's top right shoulder and looks to attack X5 or his own defender with a penetrating or a perimeter pull dribble. This gives the offense many scoring options both on the interior as well as the perimeter by actually all five players. This action also repositions the same five offensive players into the "4-Out/1-In" Spot-Ups. See Diagram 14.3

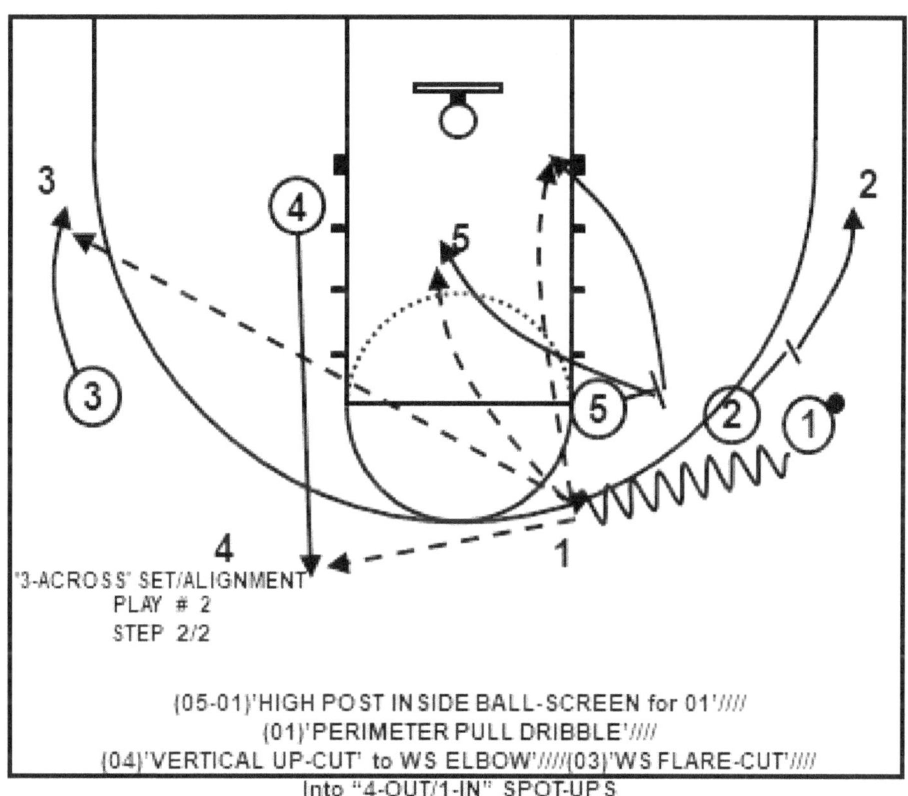

DIAGRAM 14.3

2

Diagram 14.4 illustrates the beginning of a Level 3 play (Play # 3)that is a counter to the previous Play # 2, where 01 makes the first pass to 03 at the "Wing" on the left side of the ball. 01 follows his pass while 04 breaks towards the ball as he does in Play # 12 (to get the proper screening angle) before then starting to set his "Diagonal Down-Screen" (for 05). Instead, 04 then breaks off of his screening route to then quickly slash to the new "Ballside Block" for his "Iso Post-Up against his lone post defender, X4. After so many "Diagonal Down-Screens" have already been used, 04's "Ghost Down-Screen" could and should catch X4 off-guard, giving 04 a potential "position advantage" on the new "Ballside Block." The weakside defenders (X5 and X2) both must react to the cuts their two individual offensive players actually make.

Without 04's screen, 05 still flashes to the new "Ballside High Post," while 02 rotates over to the new "Weakside Slot." See Diagram 14.4

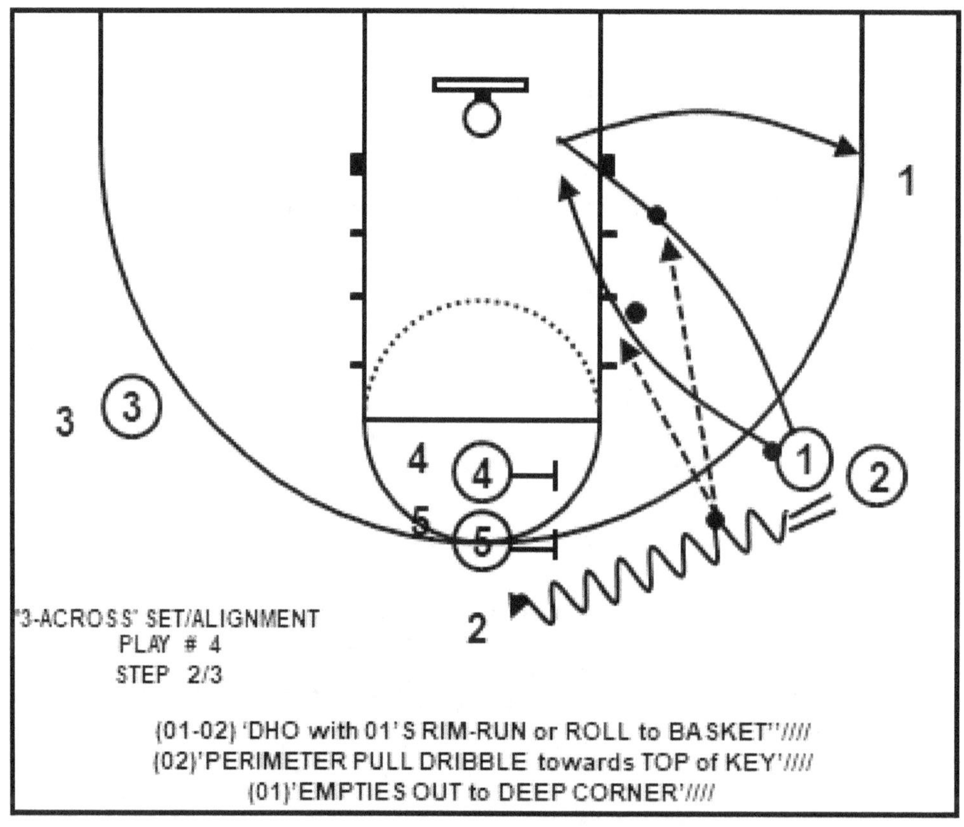

Play # 3   Diagram 14.4

After the (01-03) "Wing Pass" is completed, 03 flips the ball back to 01 while 05 steps up and over to set a "Big-on-Small Inside Back-Screen" for 03 to use, while 04 remains isolated on the new "Ballside Block." 03 then runs off of 05's top left shoulder to make a "Lob Cut" to the basket. 02 remains at the "Weakside Slot" with 01 having the ball at the FT Line extended.

01 looks to make the "Lob Pass" to 03, attacking his perimeter-type defender with his "Lob Cut" or 01 can look to make the "Inside Pass" to his isolated teammate, 04, on the "Ballside Block." 02 could be another potential perimeter pass receiver at the new "Weakside Slot."

After 03 has scraped off of 05's top shoulder, 05 should be another potential pass receiver at the "Ballside High Post." See Diagram 14.5

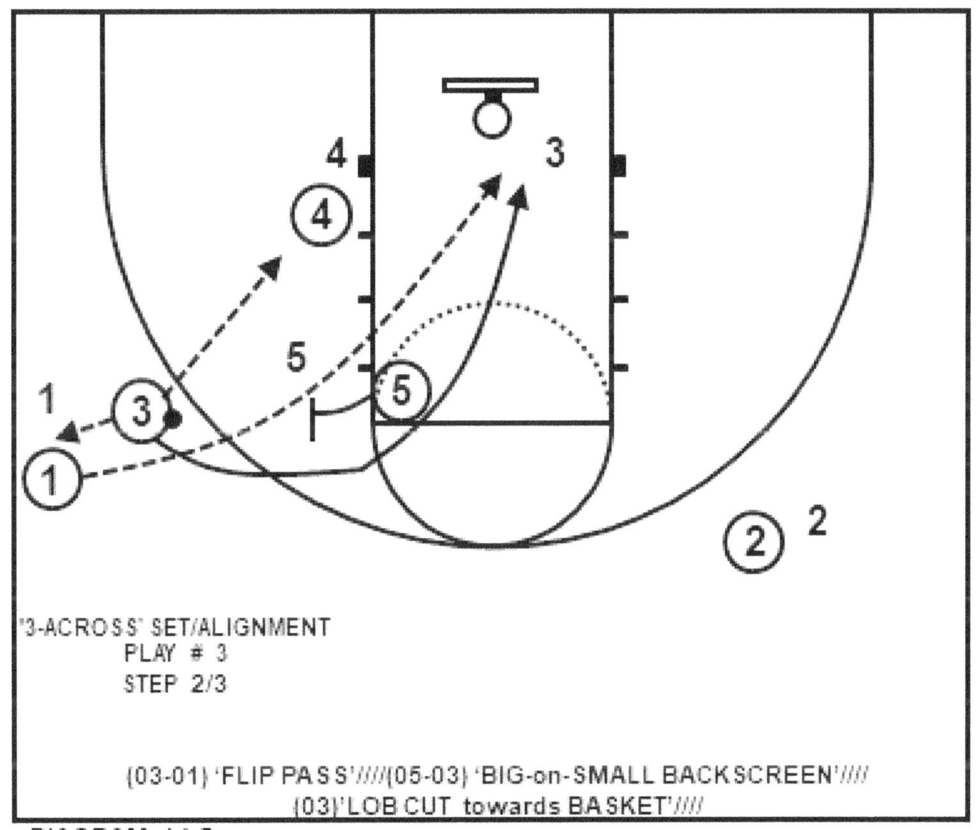

Diagram 14.6 shows 01 not making the passes to either 04 or to 03. 03 then empties out to the new "Weakside Deep Corner." 05 then steps up to set a "Big-on-Small Inside Ball-Screen" for 01 to "dribble-scrape" off of 05's top left shoulder. After 01 breaks contact with 05, 05 makes a "front pivot" off of his lower right foot and continues with a "Lob Cut" to the basket. As 05 starts his "Rim Run" to the basket, 04 makes an inverted "Pop Out Cut" to the initial "Ballside Deep Corner." 04 and 03's actions spread the defense horizontally from sideline to sideline, giving 05 much more room and space to operate within the lane. This weakens the defense and gives the offense still another advantage. 01 and 02 occupy the two "Slots" and become two additional perimeter scoring threats. In addition, 01, with the use of 05's "Inside Ball-Screen" could become an interior scoring threat with a penetrating drive off of 05's screen. With all of the possible scoring threats, if no shots are taken, this action still places e all offensive players in the correct "4-Out/1-In" Spot-Ups, ending the Level 3 play. See Diagram 14.6

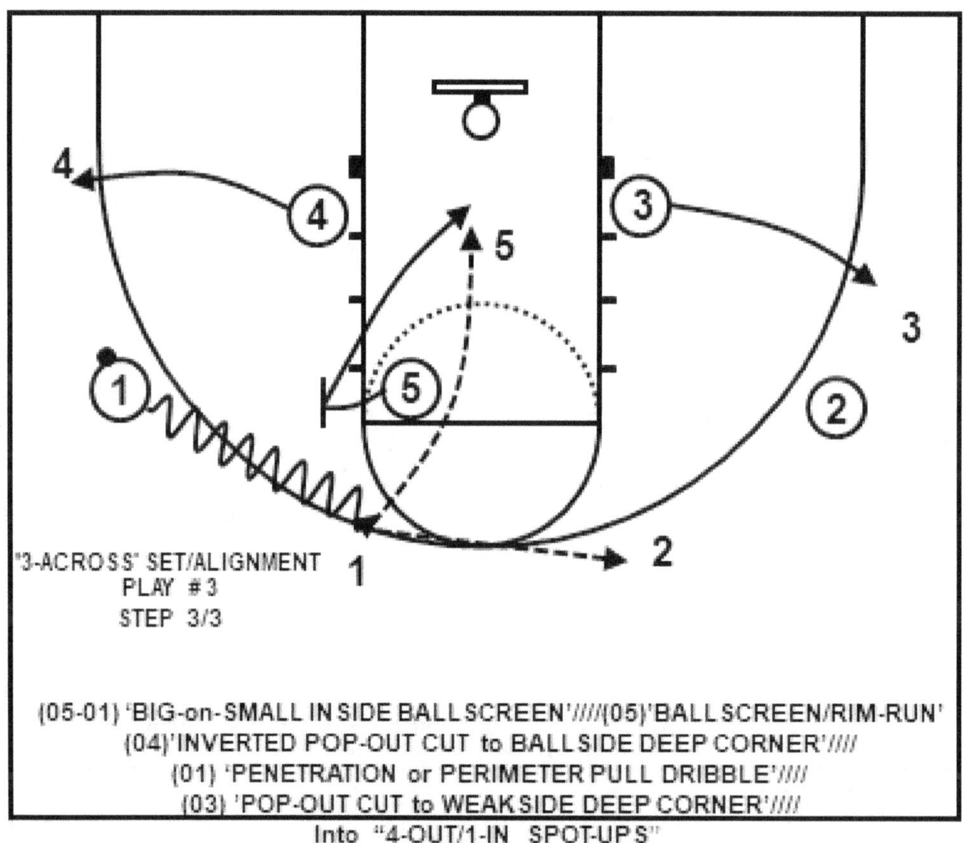

DIAGRAM 14.6

Diagram 14.7 is another more sophisticated Level 3 play (Play # 4) where 01 dribbles towards 02 and away from 03 and 05. In this play, 02 makes the same type of "Backdoor Cut" as he does in Play # 6. If and when 02 does not receive the quick pass, 02 plants his outside right foot and front pivots off of that foot to break back out to the FT Line extended This allows him to continually open up to the passer and keep his eyes on the basketball. 01 continues his dribble to meet 02 at the FT Line extended. At the same time 05 breaks up diagonally to align vertically just above 04 at the "Nail." See Diagram 14.7

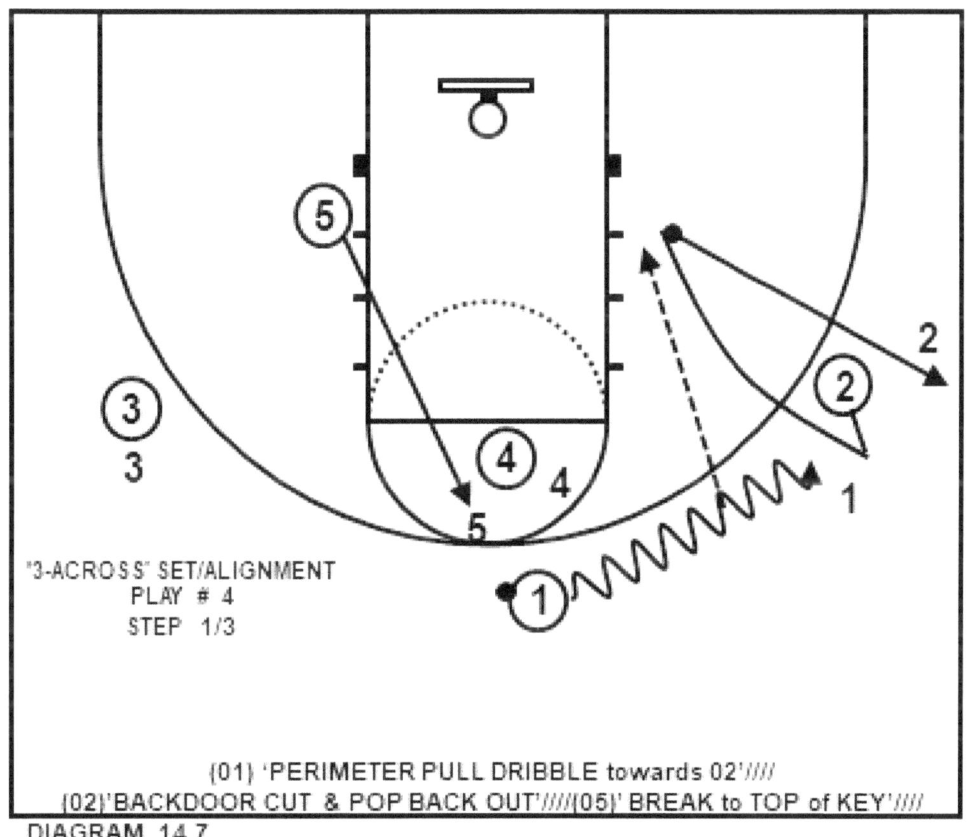

DIAGRAM 14.7

1

Diagram 14.8 shows 01 making the DHO to 02 before 01 then "Rolls" (similar to a "Ball-Screen/Roll") or "Rim-Runs" (similar to a "Ball-Screen/Rim-Run.") If 01 does not receive the quick pass from 02 after either cut to the basket, 01 should immediately break out to that side's "Deep Corner."

02 then makes a "perimeter pull dribble" from the "Wing" area out towards the top of the key, where 04 and 05 are prepared to set a "Big-on-Small Ball-Screen" for 02 to continue his pull dribble (to the opposite "Slot." See Diagram 14.8

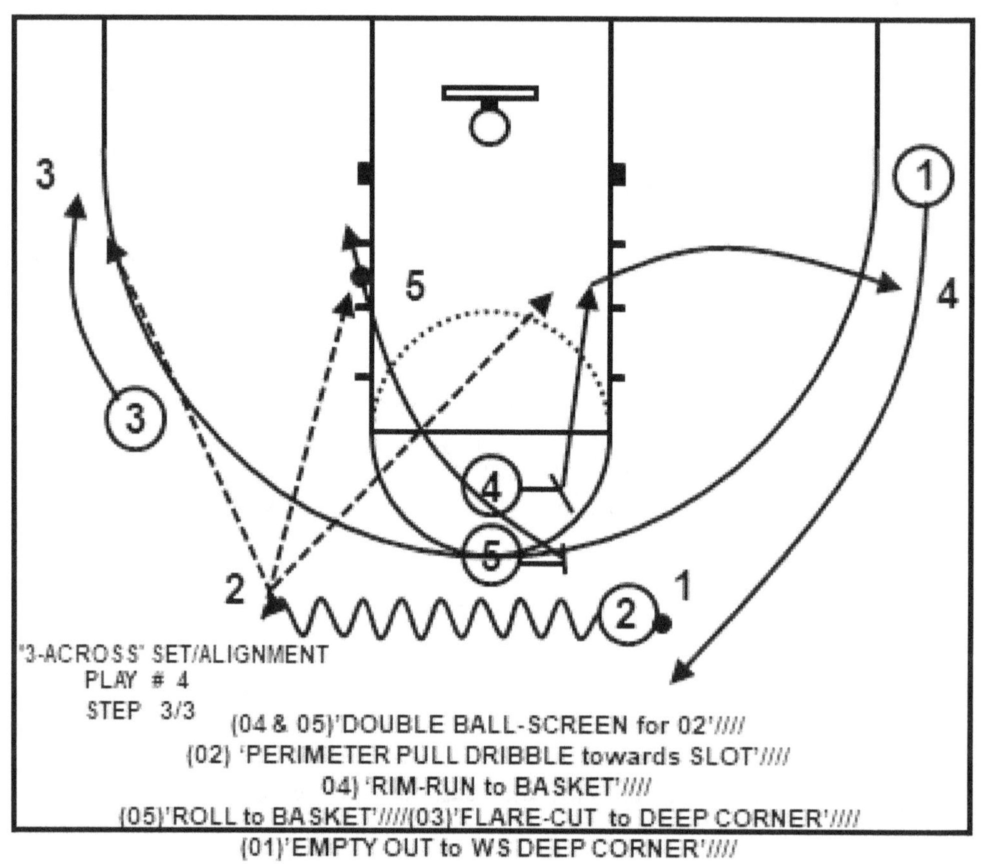

Diagram 14.8

If 02 does not make the interior passes to either 05 or to 04, he looks to make the "Down Pass" to 03 or a "Reverse Pass" to 01, now at the "Weakside Slot." Diagram 14.27 shows the "4-OUT/1-IN Spot-Ups are filled for the next phase of the offense. See Diagram 14.9

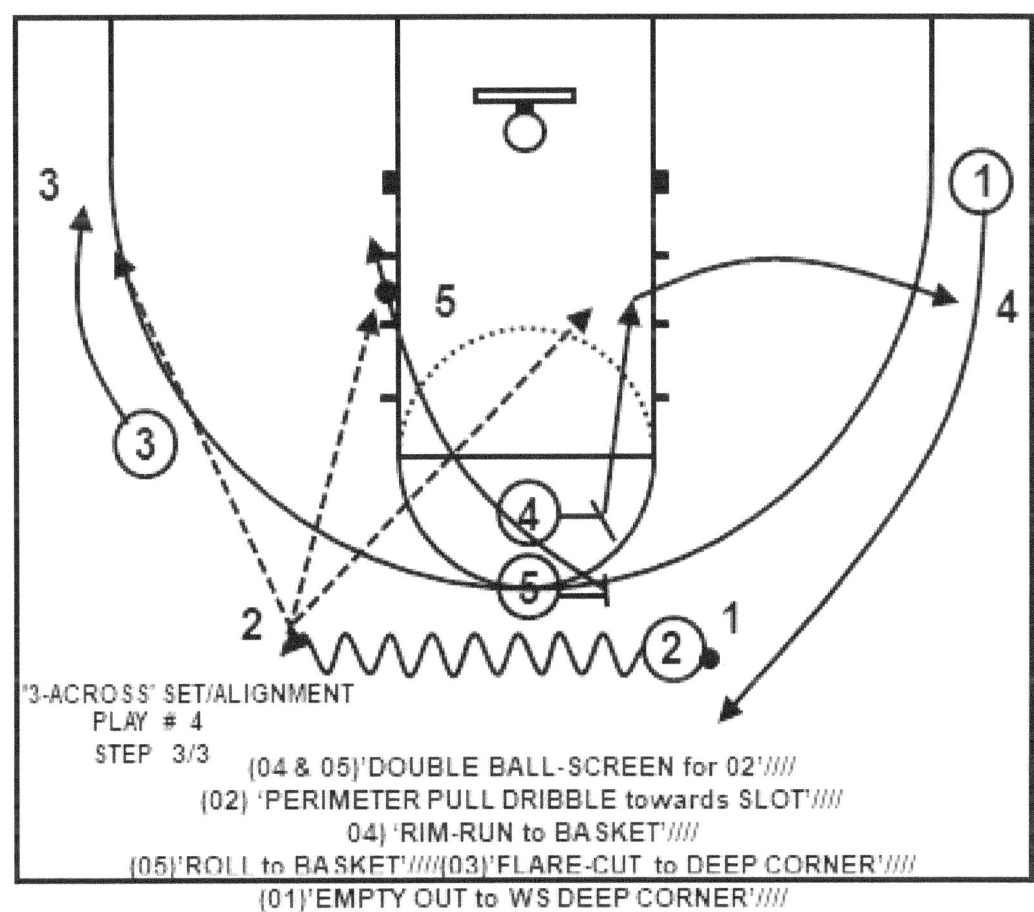

Diagram 14.9

Diagram 14.10 illustrates another top level play (Play # 5) with 01 dribbling a shorter distance to the "Slot" on the right side of the floor. This action then keys 04 to break out to the opposite side's "Slot." When 01 makes a "Throwback Reverse Pass" to 04, 05 steps up to set a (05-02) "Big-on-Small Back-Screen" for 02 to break towards the basket on his "Lob Cut" that will continue through the lane to the opposite side of the floor. 04 looks to make a "Lob Pass" to 02 who has inverted and isolated his perimeter-type defender, X2. See Diagram 14.10

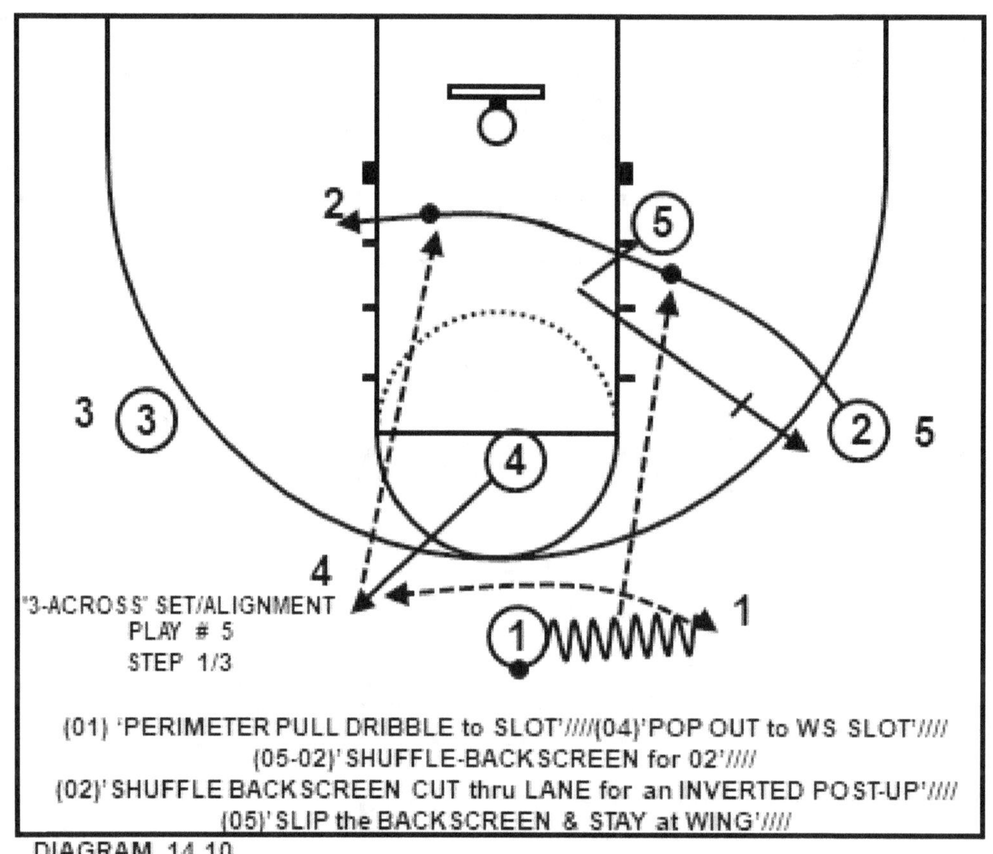

DIAGRAM 14.10

Diagram 14.11 illustrates 04 not able to make a pass to 02 and instead 04 makes a "Wing Pass" to 03. Immediately 02 vertically breaks up the lane line to set a "Small-on-Big UCLA Back-Screen" for 04 to use. Dependent upon X4's defensive reaction to the (04-03) "Wing Pass," 04 should rub off of either shoulder of 02 and end up isolated on the new "Ballside Block."

To occupy the potential helpside defenders, 05 steps up to set a "Big-on-Small Flare-Screen" for 01 to use to "Flare-Cut" on the "Weakside" of the floor. This two-man action pulls the presumed biggest defensive opponent even further from 04 and the basket, giving 04 an even greater offensive advantage over X4 or X2 if X2 has possibly switched the (02-04) "UCLA Screen." This allows 04 and 02 to both be isolated on the "Ballside Block" and the "Ballside High Post" with minimal support defense. See Diagram 14.11

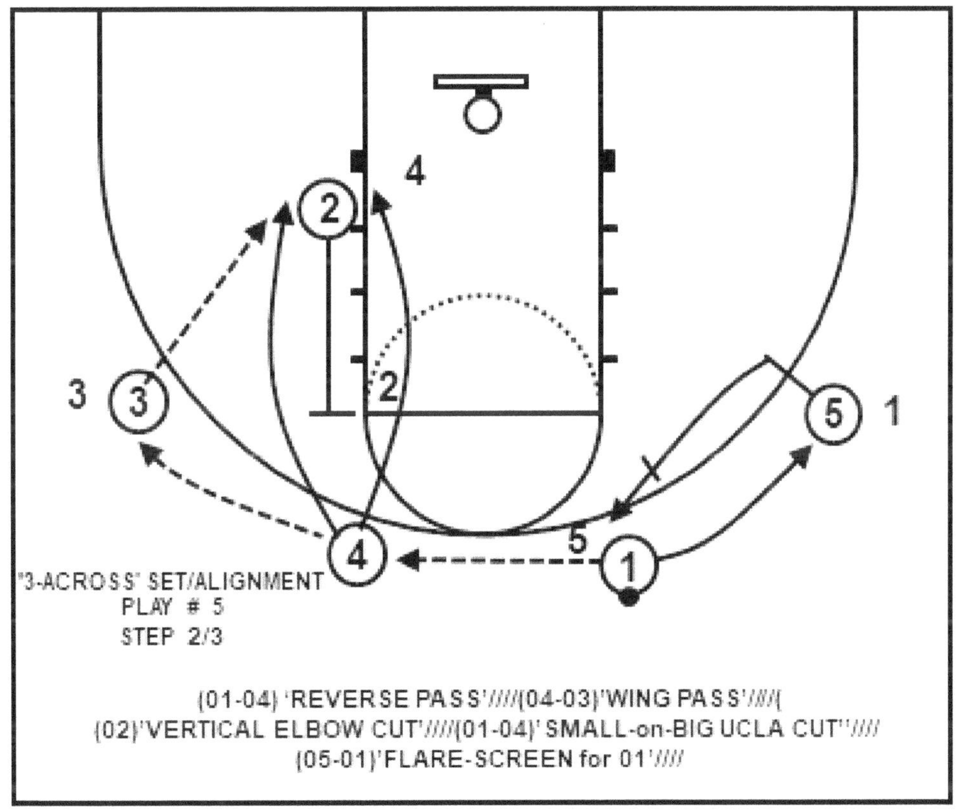

DIAGRAM   14.11

Diagram 14.12 shows the final action of Play # 5, with 02 stepping out towards 03 to set an "Inside Ball-Screen" for 03 to attack the middle of the defense. As 03 "dribble-scrapes" off of 02's top left shoulder, 02 makes a "Front Pivot" off of his lower right foot towards the "Deep Corner" on the same side of the floor. At the same time, 04 makes an "Isolated and Inverted Duck-In Cut" into the "Dotted Circle" area. As 03 dribbles out towards the "Slot," 03 could make a "Throwback Reverse Pass" to 02 in the "Deep Corner." 03's next pass receiver, 04, should be able to isolate his defender, X4, in the middle of the lane.

The next pass receiver could be 05 on the weakside of the floor. As 03 approaches 05 during his perimeter pull dribble, 05 makes a "Backdoor Cut" to the basket, while 01 breaks up to the now empty "Weakside Slot." If 03 cannot make the "Inside Pass" to on his cut to the basket, 05 then empties out to the same side's "Deep Corner." This action attacks several individual defenders and when shots are not taken, the "4-Out/1-In" Spot-Ups are filled. See Diagram 14.12

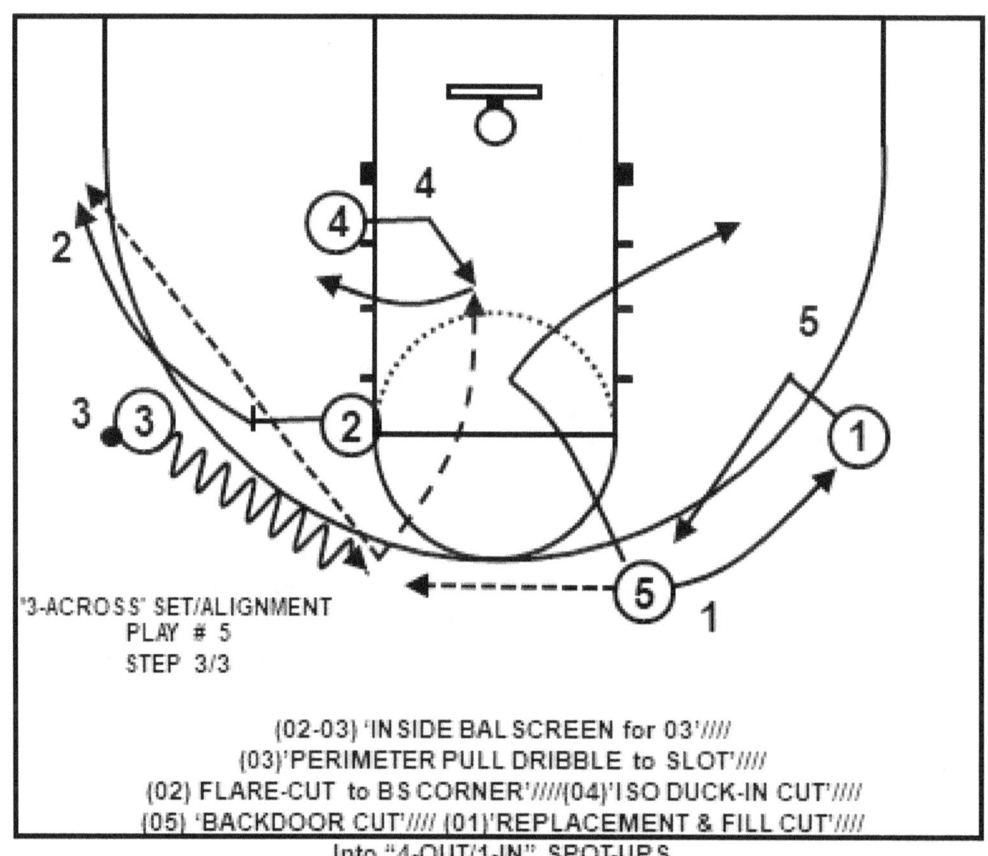

DIAGRAM 14.12

Diagram 14.13 illustrates Play # 6, another Level 3 play with 03 and 02 both making "Iverson Cuts" over and underneath 04, respectively. 03's usual destination is to the "Wing" area on the right side of the floor, but in this play, 05 steps up for 03 to curl tightly off of 04 before then also receiving the (05-03) "Big-on-Small Diagonal Back-Screen." These two screens allow 03 to invert and to isolate his perimeter-type defender and end up on the newly declared "Ballside Block." With 02 making his "Iverson Cut" to the new "Weakside Wing," this gives 01 space to dribble to the FT Line extended to the new "Ballside Wing." Dribbling to that wing will allow 01 an excellent passing angle to deliver the ball to 03 on the "Block." With 05 ending up at the "Nail" and 04 then stepping out at the top of the key, and 02 now at the new "Weakside Wing" area, there can be no helpside support that X3 would need to deny 03 the ball in such a high percentage scoring area. See Diagram 14.13

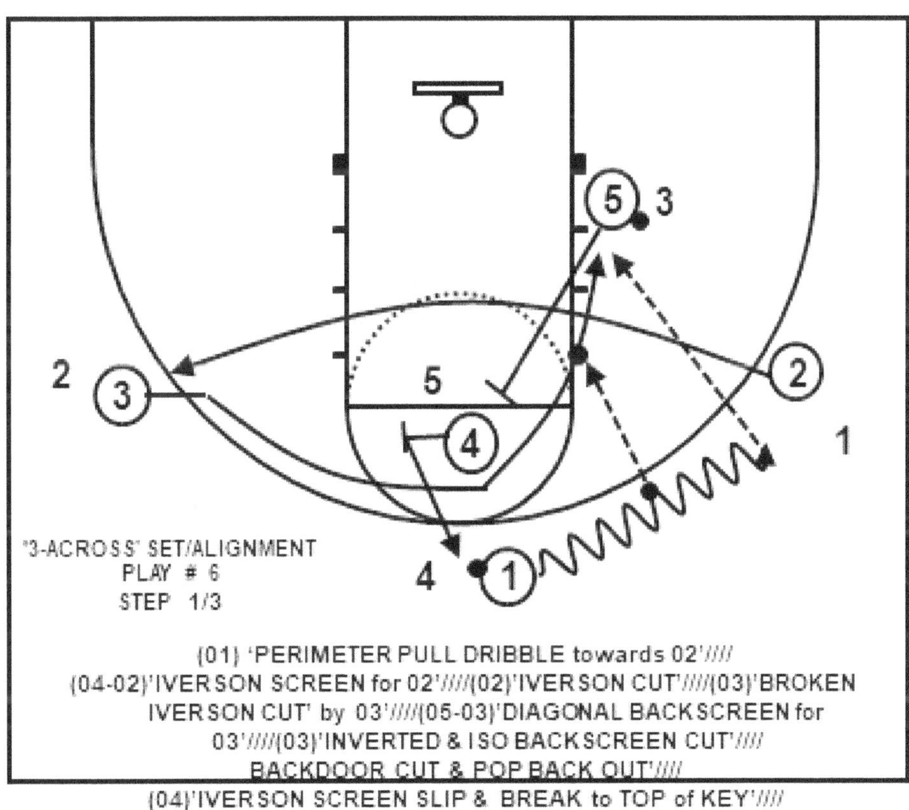

DIAGRAM 14.13

But if somehow 01 does not make the pass to 03, Diagram 14.32 shows 01 reversing the ball to the inverted 04 out on top. The ball should then be quickly swung to 02 on the opposite side of the floor.

When 04 makes that pass to 02, 05 should first jab step towards 02 and the ball before then changing directions to diagonally down-screen for 03 to flash to the new "Ballside High Post." Instead of completing the screen for 03, 05 should quickly break off his screening route. 05 should then actually "Ghost Down-Screen" 03 by slipping to the new "Ballside Block," while 03 continues to flash to the "Ballside High Post" (without the help of 05's screen.) At the same time, to give 01 an open shot as well as to eliminate helpside defense that X5 and X3 would need, 04 diagonally "Pin Screens" for 01 to cut to the top of the key. This gives 02 three potential highly successful scoring threats in 05, 03 and 01. See Diagram 14.14

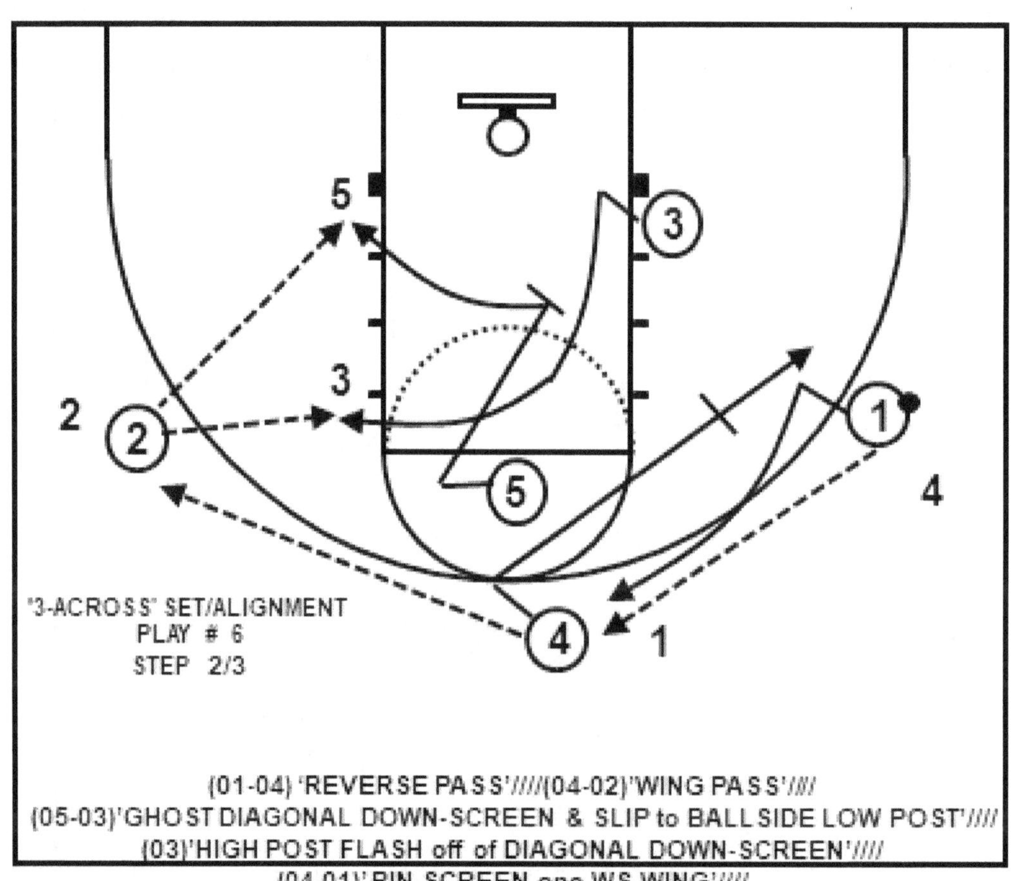

DIAGRAM 14.14

Diagram 14.15 illustrates the end of this play/entry and with 02 turning down all three passing target possibilities. With no passes made by 02, 03 then steps up and out to set an "Inside Ball-Screen" for 02 to use to "perimeter pull dribble" towards the "Ballside Slot." With 05's strengths presumably on the interior and 03's scoring strengths on the perimeter, after 02 "dribble-scrapes" off of 03's outside left shoulder, 05 makes an "Iso Duck-In Cut" into the "Dotted Circle" while 03 makes a "Flare-Cut" towards the "Ballside Deep Corner." This provides two additional scoring threats on the initial Ballside of the floor both on the interior (05) and the perimeter (to 03).

On the weakside of the floor, as 02 approaches 01 on the dribble, 01 makes a hard "Backdoor Cut" while 04 steps up to fill the now vacant "Weakside Slot." This gives the dribbling 02 two more pass receiving threats as well as reposition all players into the proper "4-Out/1-In" Spot-Ups. See Diagram 14.15

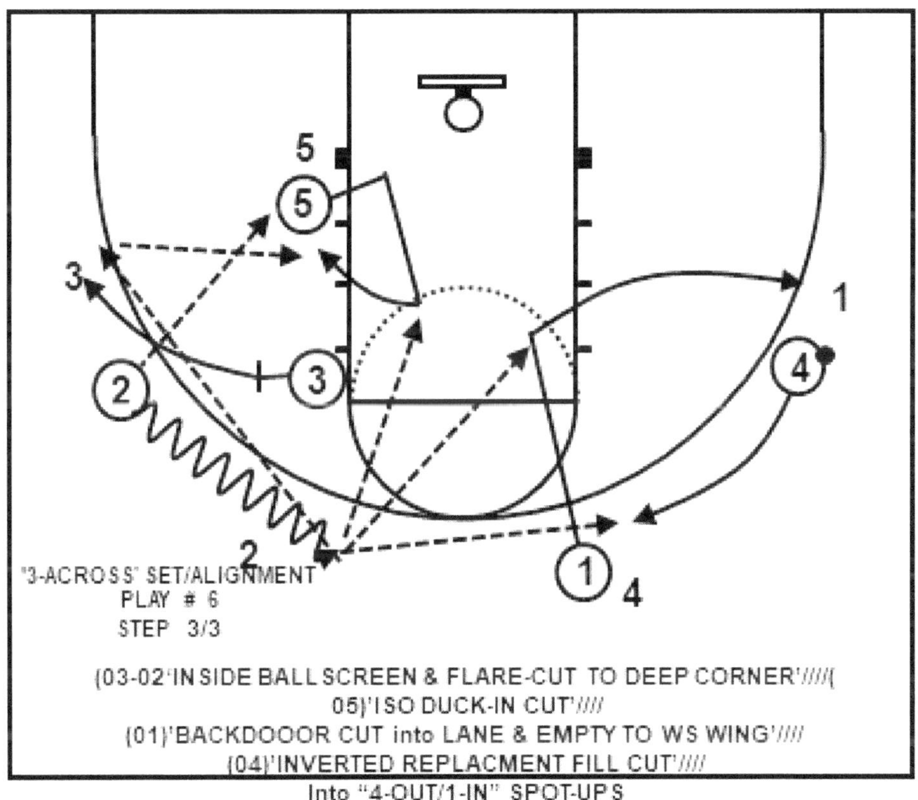

DIAGRAM 14.15

When plays do not create the desired shots, this package of plays/entries will at least reposition players in a group of offensive spot-ups that are different than the other two series of plays. From these different spot-ups, this will give a team the opportunity to flow into different various continuity offenses; These different continuity offenses will have the abilities to attack individual defenders as well as the overall team defense in addition to being able to use different offensive skills of different individual players.

These "HIGH-POST/LOW-POST" Spot-Ups will have players moved about the court with any of the five players ending up in the "Ballside Block," the "Ballside High Post," the "Ballside Wing," the "Weakside Wing," and the "Point" (or top of the guy)" These five positions can provide the offense with safe and easy types of ball-reversals, "skip passes" that could produce highly successful '3 pt. shots,' large gaps for dribble penetrations by any of the players, opportunities to deliver the ball inside to whomever (perimeter-type or post-type players) is posting up their defender on the "Ballside Block," or the "Ballside High Post." The spot-up location on the "Weakside Wing" will also have the capabilities of placing a player that can be a perimeter-scoring threat. This player can become a legitimate offensive rebounding threat from outside of the arc on his "offensive crashing of the boards" opportunities. The ""HIGH-POST/LOW-POST" Spot-Ups also provide ample opportunities for constant and effective defensive transition responsibilities to prevent the opposition's offensive transition opportunities.

Play # 7 is a Level 1 play that is executed out of the same "3-ACROSS" Set. Diagram 14.16 illustrates 03 stepping up and over to set a "Big-on-Small Ball-Screen" for 01 to "dribble-scrape" off of 03's outside right shoulder towards the "Wing" location on the left side of the floor. As that action takes place 04 breaks from the "Nail" towards 01 and the ball before diagonally "Slash Cutting" down to the newly designated "Ballside Block." This becomes an isolated cut because, at the same time, 05 flashes diagonally up and over to the new "Ballside High Post.

To occupy any possible helpside defense that X4 and X5 would need, 02 steps up to set a (02-03) ("Small-on-Big Flare-) Screen the (Ball-)Screener. After screening for 03, 02 slips his screen and steps up to the top of the key behind the arc for a likely open '3 Pt.' Shot. 03 should have an open '3 Pt. Shot off of 01's "Skip Pass."

If no shots are taken, the "High-Post/Low Post" Spot-Ups are filled for the next phase of the offense to smoothly and instantly begin. See Diagram 14.16

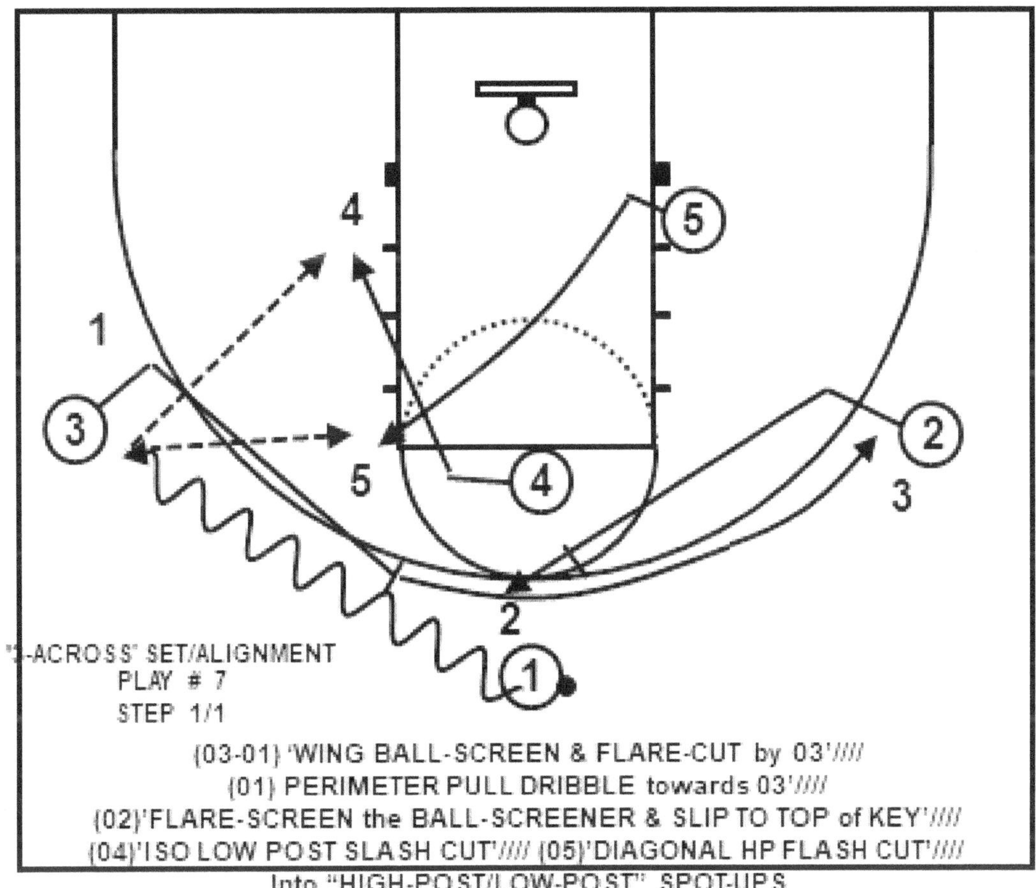

Diagram 14.17 illustrates another simple Level 1 Play (Play # 8) that is a Counter to Play # 7. With 05 aligned on the same right side of the floor and 03 stepping up to set the same "Big-on-Small Ball-Screen" for 01 to again use, 04 steps over towards the Ballside High Post before sliding down to the new "Ballside Block." Where this play changes up from the initial play's action is that 05 breaks up to diagonally set a (05-03) ("Big-on-Small Diagonal Back-)Screen the (Ball-)Screener." After screening for 03, 05 slips his screen to slide out to the top of the key and in this play, 02 is the player that makes a horizontal straight cut from his "Wing" through the "Nail" to the new "Ballside High Post." After making the "Lob Cut" and not receiving 01's "Lob Pass", 03 then curls and lifts out to the new "Weakside Wing."

This action again attacks individual defenders and now places 02 at the "Ballside High Post," (instead of 05), 05 at the top of the key (instead of 02), and 03 ending up at the same "Weakside Wing." Even though players have switched ending spot-up locations, the same "HIGH POST/LOW POST" Spot-Ups are once again filled to continue the offensive attack. See Diagram 14.17

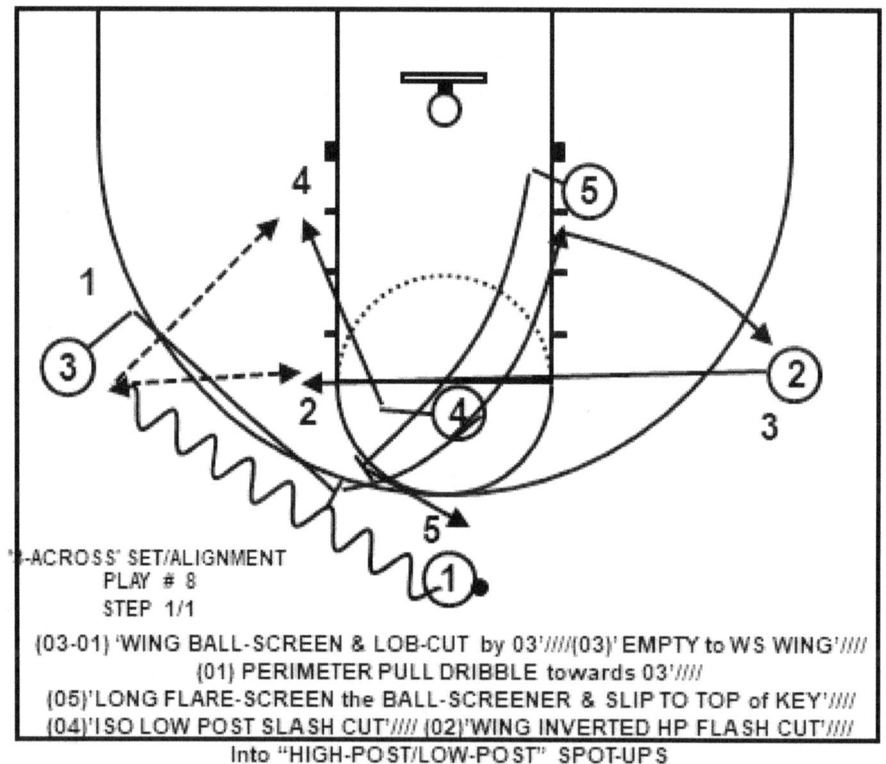

DIAGRAM 14.17

Diagrams 14.18 and 14.19 show the beginning and end of a more complex Level 2 play out of the same offensive alignment/set. In this Play #9, 01 makes the "Wing Pass" to 02, with 05 starting on the "Block" on that same side of the floor.

04 immediately steps up to set a "Big-on-Small Diagonal Back-Screen" for 01. 01 makes a "V-Cut" jab step before then scraping off of 04's right shoulder to use to make a "Lob Cut" to the rim on the weakside half of the FT Lane.

After screening for 01, 04 breaks down to set a "Pin Down-Screen" for 05 to use to break out to the top of the key. As 04 breaks down facing 05, 05 then scrapes off of 04's left shoulder and breaks to the top of the key outside of the arc. This action between 04 and 04 give 01 a moment for isolation on 01's inverted cut to the basket. In addition, it opens up a possibility for 04 on the new "Ballside Block" in an isolation move. 05's cutting action also stretches and weakens the overall interior defense by pulling presumably the biggest defender, X5, further from the basket. 03 spots up on the "Weakside Wing" to stretch and weaken the support defense horizontally. See Diagram 14.18

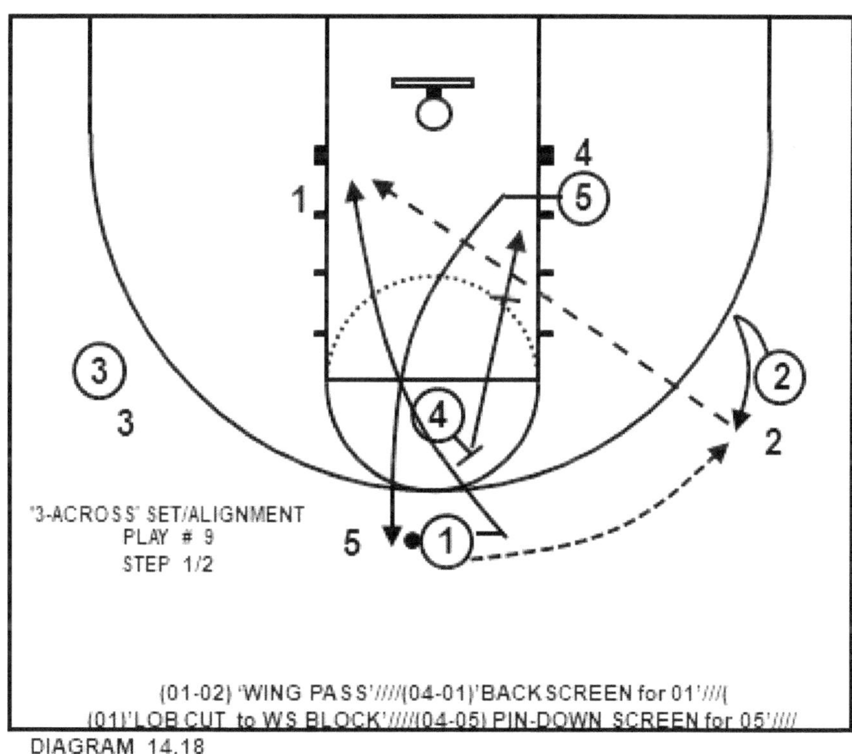

DIAGRAM 14.18

If neither 01 or 04 are open on the interior, 03 makes the somewhat rare horizontal cut across the "Nail" to the new "Ballside High Post." 02 could make the pass to 03 on his "Flash Cut" or to 05 inverted out at the top of the key. At the same time, 01 breaks out diagonally to the now vacant "Weakside Wing" (where 03 just exited) and 04 empties out of the "Ballside Block" to make an "Iso Duck-In Cut."

With 02 receiving the 02-05 "Reverse Pass," 05 could make the pass to (04) on his "Duck-In Cut," to 03 on his "High Post Flash Cut" or to swing the ball over to 01."

If 03 receives the 02-03 Pass, 03 could have a "catch and shoot" shot, a quick pass to 04 on his "Duck-In," a quick "Kick-Out Pass" to 05 or continue the direction of 02's pass and make a quick "Relay Pass" over to 01."

When 01 receives the quick pass from 05 or the even quicker pass from 03, 01 would also have "catch and shoot" shot possibilities, an "Inside Pass" to 04, now posted up in his "Iso Post-Up" or a "Skip Pass" back to 02 on the opposite side of the floor.

Still, if all shots are turned down, the "HIGH-POST/LOW-POST" Spot-Ups are filled for the smooth conversion to take place. See Diagram 14.19

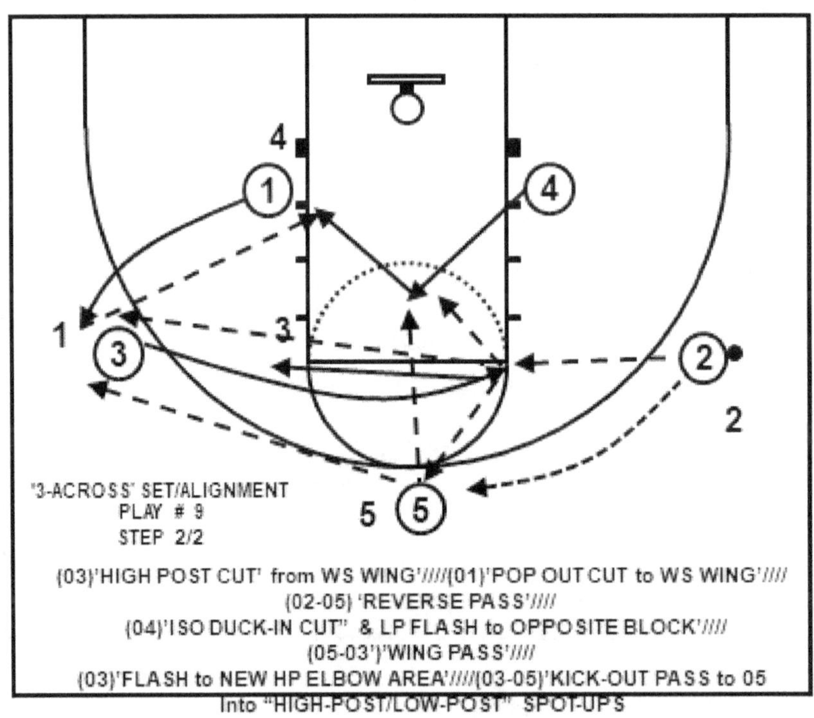

DIAGRAM 14.19

Diagrams 14.20 and 14.21 illustrate the entire Play # 10—another Level 2 Play from this offensive set. 03 and 02 make the usual "Iverson Cuts" over and underneath 04, respectively. See Diagram 14.20

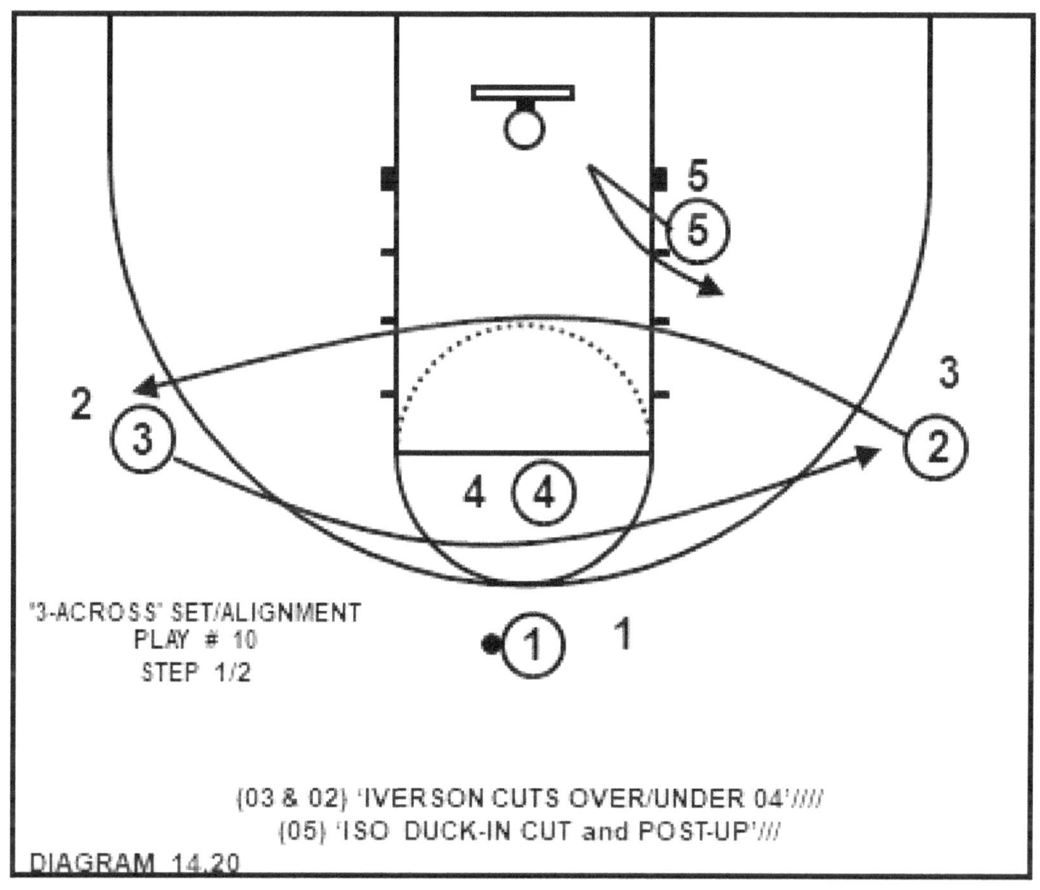

Diagram 14.21 illustrate 01 making the "Wing Pass" to 02 on the right side of the floor. 05 immediately steps up to set a "Diagonal Back-Screen" for 04 to spin off of either one of 05's shoulders to then "Iso Post-Up" on the new "Ballside Block." As 04 breaks contact with 05, 01 steps down to set a (01-05) "(Small-on-Big Pin Down-)Screen the (Back-)Screener." After screening for 05, 01 then slips his screen and steps towards the new "Ballside High Post." This action gives 02 passing opportunities of 04 at the "Ballside Block," 01 at the "Ballside High Post," 05 at the top of the key and 03 at the "Weakside Wing." These are the same "HIGH POST/LOW-POST" Spot-Ups for the continuity offense to immediately begin. See Diagram 14.21

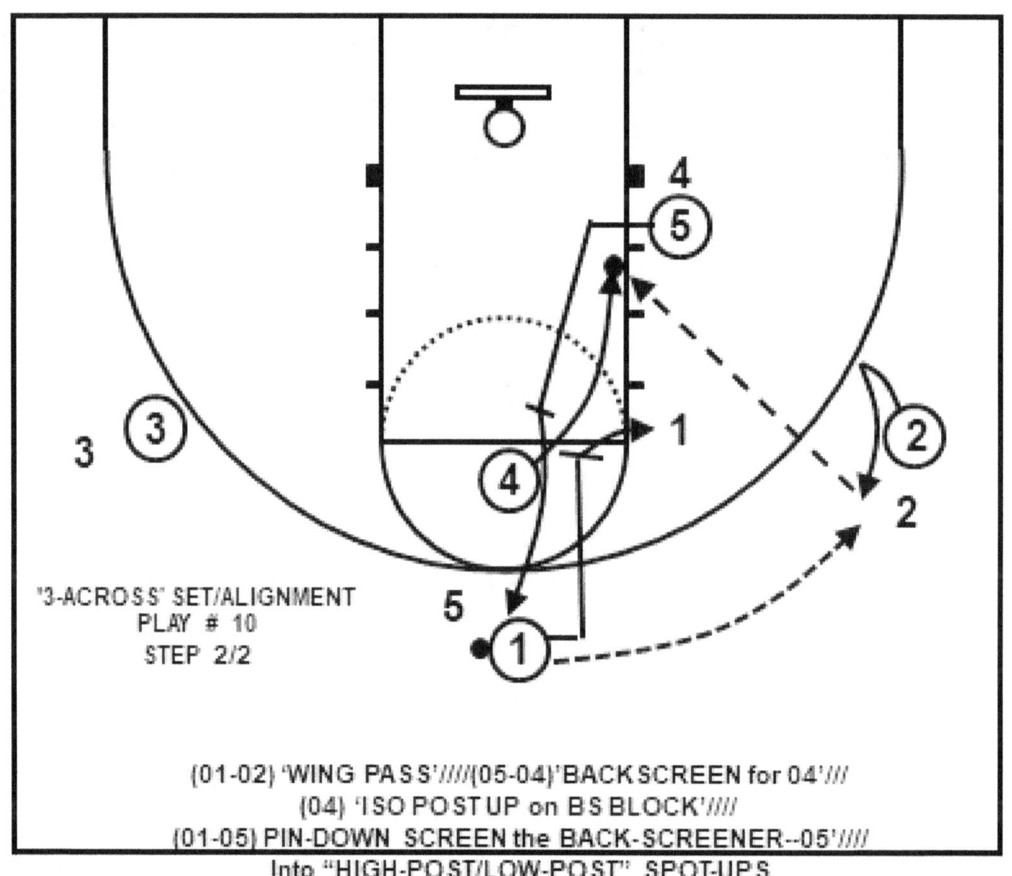

DIAGRAM 14.21

Diagram 14.22 shows the beginning of Play # 11—a more complex Level 3 play that begins with 03 dribbling towards the "Slot" that is away from the side of the floor that 05 begins. 03 and 02 make the "Iverson Cuts" over and underneath 04. After both 02 and 03 make their "Iverson Cuts" off of 04, 04 then steps out on the perimeter to fill the empty "Weakside Slot." 05 breaks from the "Block" to replace 04 at the "Nail." See Diagram 14.22

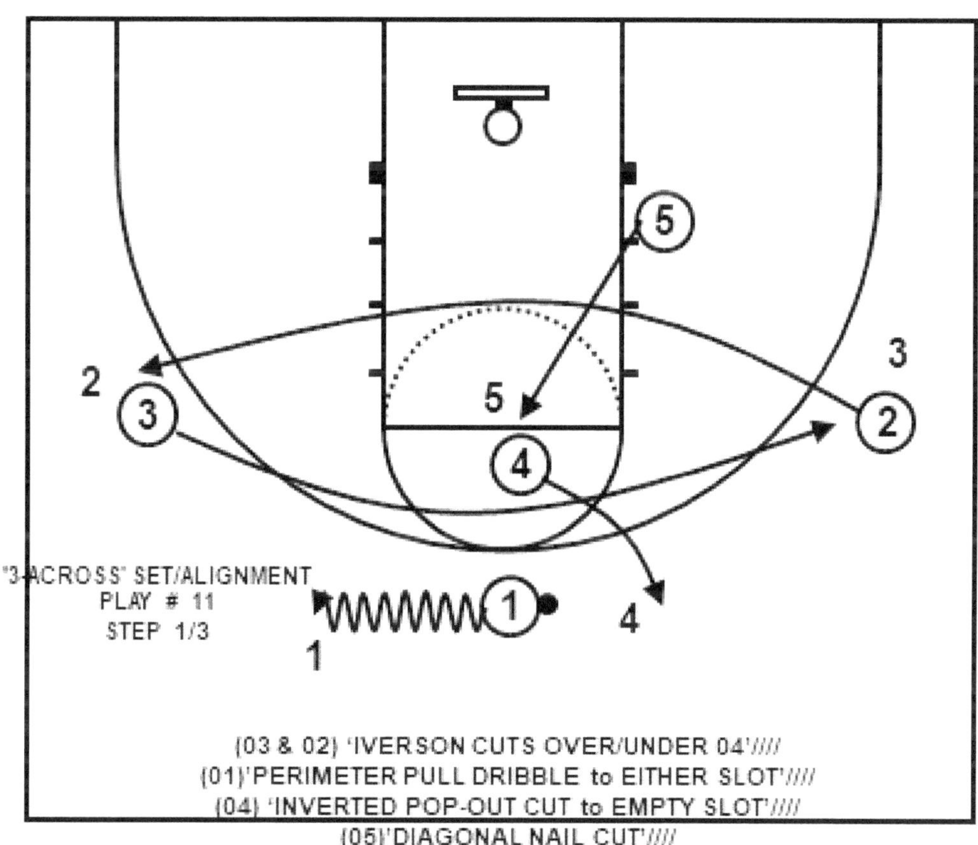

DIAGRAM 14.22

01 kills his dribble at the "Slot" and then makes the immediate "Wing Pass" to 02. Instantly, 04 makes his "Inverted and Isolated Shuffle Cut" off of 05's "Shuffle Back-Screen" located near the "Nail." 04 should read his defender and adjust his cut to either scrape off of the right shoulder or the left side of 05 and to then continue diagonally through the lane to the new "Ballside Block." After 04's cut to the newly declared "Ballside Block," 05 and 01 break over to set a "Stagger-Screen" for 03 to use as he breaks up to the top of the key. This action not only gives 02 an outstanding target for a highly successful '3 pt. shot' opportunity, but will help destroy any possible interior defensive support that X4 would need to successfully defend his man. Again, the presumed biggest defender's offensive man influences that defender out away from the basket. See Diagram 14.23

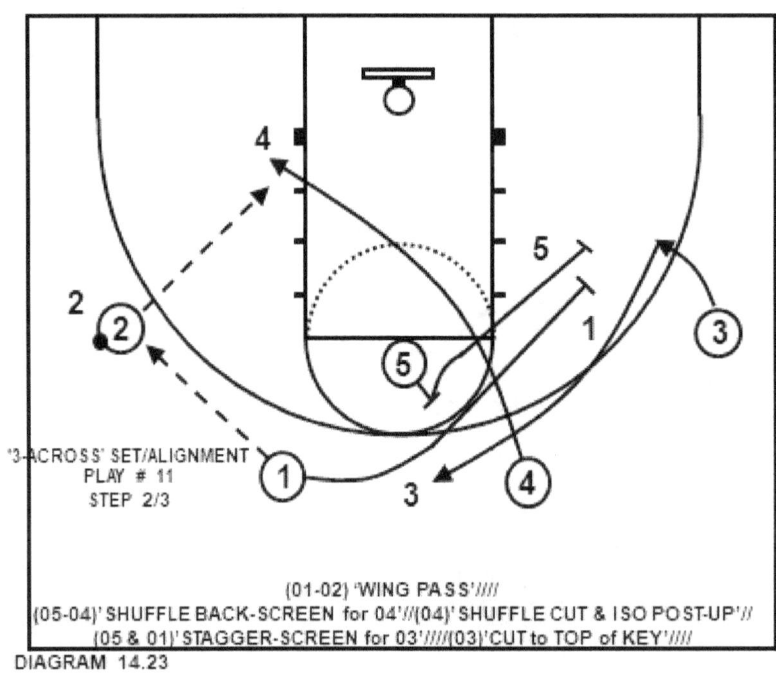

Diagram 14.24 illustrates 02 looking to make the "Inside Pass" to 04, now isolated and posted up on the new "Ballside Block." In addition, the "Stagger-Screens" set by 05 and 01 not only give 03 an open '3 Pt. shot opportunity at the top of the key but also their screens occupy the only existing weakside defenders and allow 04 to be isolated even for a longer period of time. Still, if no shots are taken, the "HIGH-POST/LOW-POST" Spot-Ups ae once again filled.

If 02 cannot deliver the ball to 04, he can look to make a "Skip Pass" to 01 or to make a pass to 03 now at the top of the key for an open '3 Pt' Shot opportunity.

If 02 makes the pass to 03 on top but no shot exists, 03 can swing the ball to 01 on the opposite side of the floor. This "Wing Pass" would dictate that 05 slide down the lane with 04 flashing to the new "Ballside High Post." This gives 01 two different interior pass receiving targets that should have outstanding scoring opportunities.

In addition, after the (03-01) "Wing Pass," 02 would step up to set a "(02-03) "Small-on-Big Flare Screen" for 03 to use to make a "Flare-Cut" to the newly declared "Weakside Wing." This two man action would give 01 two additional passing targets on the perimeter as well as the same action would help eliminate interior support defense that is needed by X4 and X5.

If shots are not taken, the "HIGH-POST/LOW-POST" Spot-Ups ae once again filled. See Diagram 14.24

PLAYS/ENTRIES THAT END in the "4-OUT/1-IN" OFFENSIVE SPOT-UPS

The difference in the following plays/entries are that all five players will end up in one of the different offensive spot-ups. These "4-Out/1-In Spot-Ups" will have players moved about via cuts, screens, dribbles and after every play each player could (and will) result in spotting up in any of the five ending up in the "Ballside Deep Corner" or "Ballside Slot," the Weakside Deep Corner and the Slot," and the "Ballside Mid-Post," and the "Weakside Deep Corner."

These five spot-up positions can also give the offense safe and easy types of ball-reversals, large gaps for dribble penetration, opportunities to deliver the ball inside to whomever (perimeter-type or post-type players) is posting up their defender on the "Ballside Block." The two "Deep Corners" horizontally and vertically spread the opposition's defense to weaken the interior and not allow a complete coverage of both interior and perimeter players. Players that are perimeter-scoring threats and a legitimate offensive rebounding threats from outside of the arc have opportunities for weakside offensive rebounding, defensive transition as well as "skip pass "catch and shoot" possibilities after "skip passes" are made from any of the three locations on the ballside to either "weakside perimeter" location.

Diagram 15.1 (called Play # 1) shows a Level 2 Play. The same action between 02, 03 and 04 take place as in a previous play, making this play a good Counter to that play. The diagram again shows 03 first faking a "Flex-Screen" and then making an "Iverson Cut" over the top of 04 to the opposite "Wing" area. 02 fakes the "Flex-Cut" off of 03 and then makes an "L-Cut" up to the "Wing" area on the same side of the floor. While 03 seems to be the apparent pass receiver, 01 makes the pass to 05 at his initial location. **Diagram 15.1.**

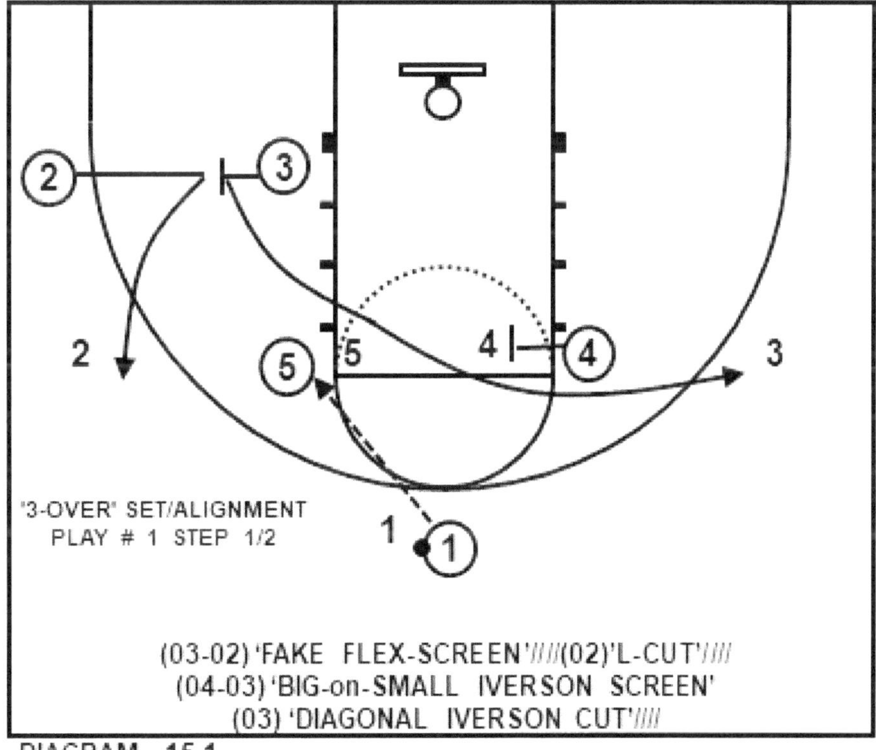

DIAGRAM 15.1

With the ball being initially close to 02 and 03 for somewhat normal and obvious passes, the defense should have a good deal of denial pressure on those two receivers. With 05 being an inverted post-type player situated on the perimeter and 05 receiving the (01-05) Pass, 05 will have a much improved passing angle to make the "Blind Pig Pass" to 02 on his "Backdoor Cut" to the basket. So as soon as the ball is in the air towards 05, the two closest teammates to 05 ae 02 and 04. 02 changes his "L-Cut" breaking out direction to make the cut to the rim. If he does not receive the quick pass, he then spreads out towards the "Deep Corner" on his side of the floor. On the opposite side of the floor, 04 also makes a "Backdoor Cut" when the ball reaches 05's hand and he also curls out to the "Deep Corner" on his side of the floor. Both 01 and 03 rotate out to fill the two "Slot" locations.

05 looks to make interior passes to either 02 or 04 and perimeter passes to either 01 and 03. If no shots are taken and with 05 sliding down a couple of steps in the lane, this action fills the "4-Out/1-In" Spot-Ups for the designated continuity offense to immediately begin. **Diagram 15.2.**

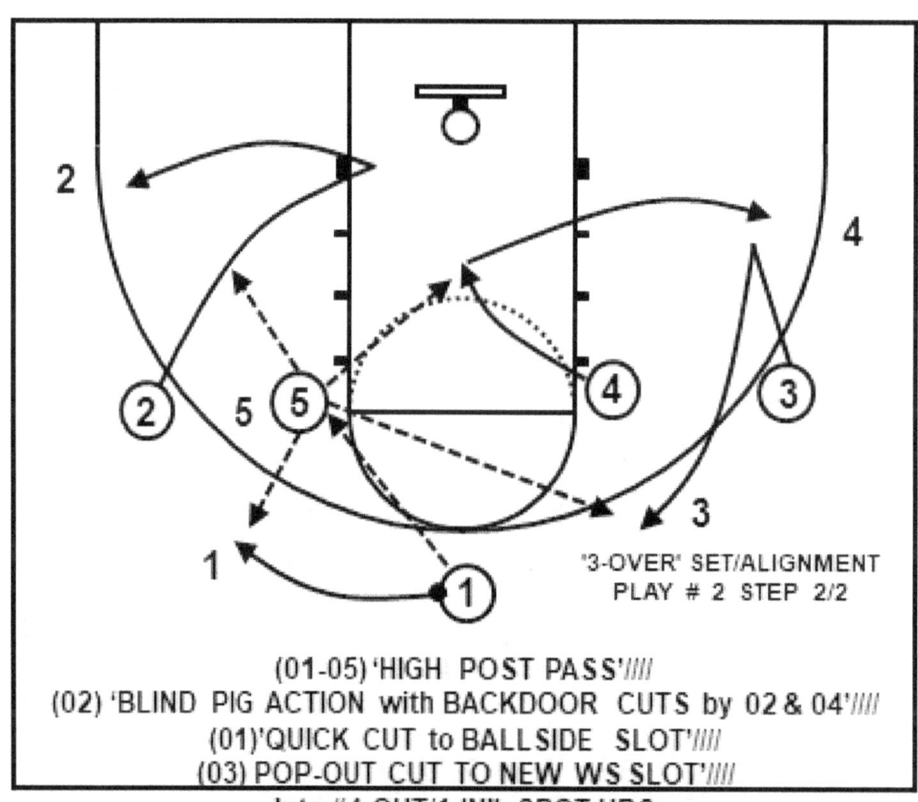

DIAGRAM 15.2

Diagram 15.3 shows another play (Play # 13-a Level 3 Play) where the 03-02 "Flex-Screen" action appears to start to take place, but 02 changes direction and breaks diagonally up to "Iverson Cut" up and over both 05 and 04 to the opposite "Wing" area. After 02 breaks up, 03 then breaks out to the "FT Line" extended on the opposite side of the floor as 02. This transfigures the "3-OVER" Set into the "5-UP" Set—a "1-4 High" Alignment. **Diagram 15.3.**

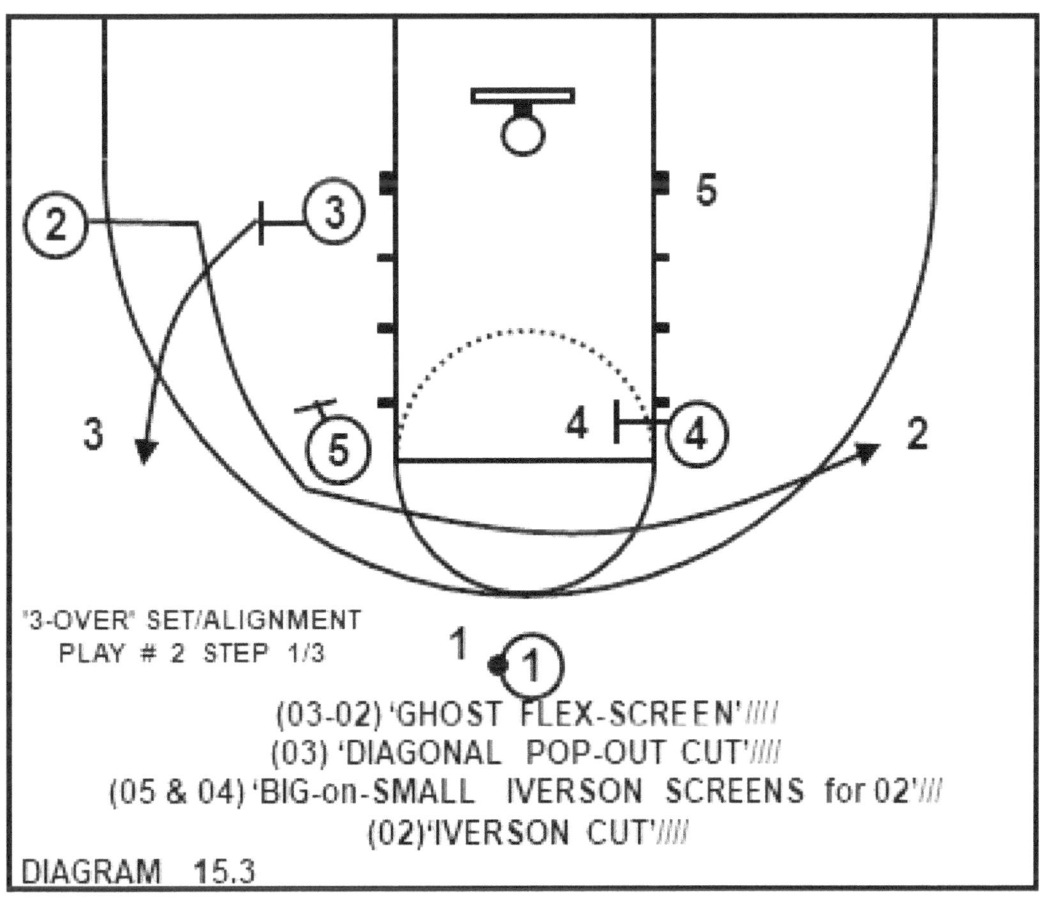

Diagram 15.4 shows 01 making the "01-03 Wing Pass" and immediately making a "Give-n-Go Cut" just before 05 cuts across to set the high "Cross-Screen" for 04 to fill the new "Ballside High Post" area. After screening for 04, 05 slips out to the new "Weakside Slot" (with 02 remaining at the "Weakside Wing." **Diagram 15.4.**

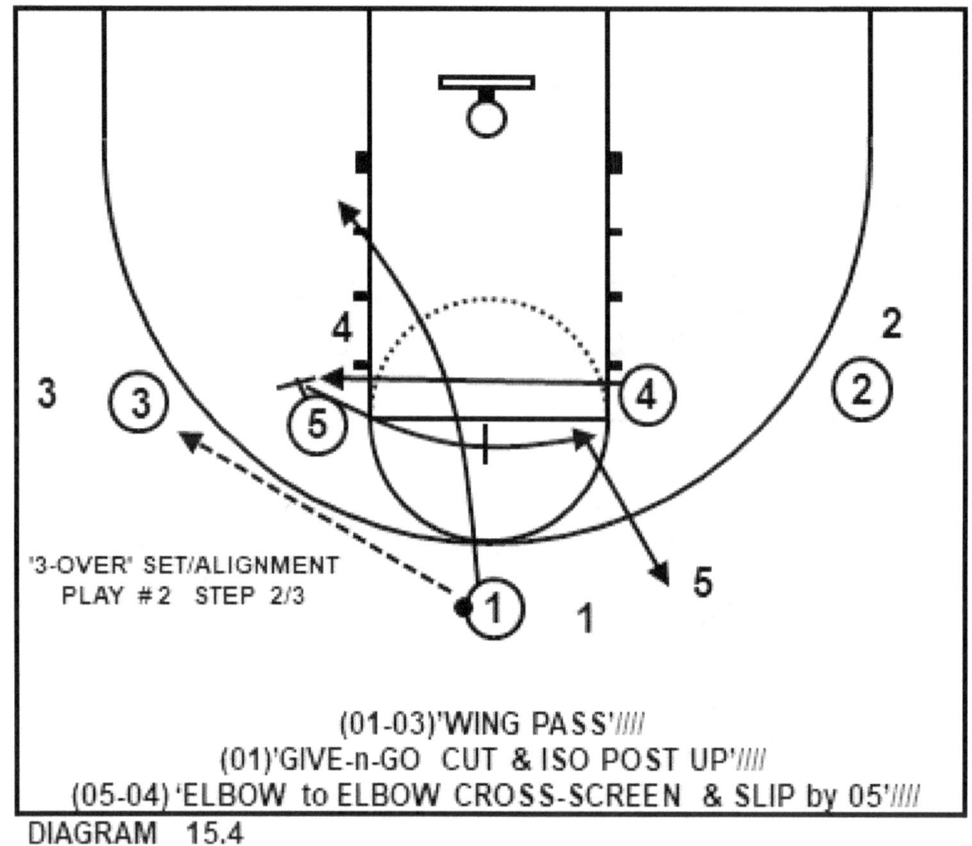

Diagram 15.5 illustrates 03 turning down passes to the inverted and isolated 01 on the new "Ballside Block" and to 04 at the "Ballside High Post." 03 should look heavily for helpside defenders trying to keep X1 from being isolated as well as X4. If an extra defender is sagging, 03 should look to make the "Skip Pass" to 02 across the lane on the "Weakside Wing" area. When those shots are not available or are not taken, 04 steps further out to set a "Big-on-Small Inside Ball-Screen" for 03 to attack the middle defense of the opposition.

When 03 attacks the middle with a "dribble-scrape" off of 04's top left shoulder," 04 should make a "front pivot" off of his lower right foot and step towards the basket with his "Rim-Run." To add a perimeter shot scoring threat and to eliminate help defense on 04, 01 breaks out behind the arc on the sideline near the FT Line extended and also the "Deep Corner."

The weakside action has 05 start to step towards 02 for "(05-02) Big-on-Small Pin Down-Screen" during 03 "perimeter pull dribble." Instead, 05 cuts off the screening route and makes a strong and aggressive "Ghost Pin Down-Screen," cutting hard towards the weakside part of the lane. 02 continues to fill the "Weakside Slot" area. No shots still repositions all five players into the appropriate and proper "4-Out/1-In" Spot-Ups. **Diagram 15.5**.

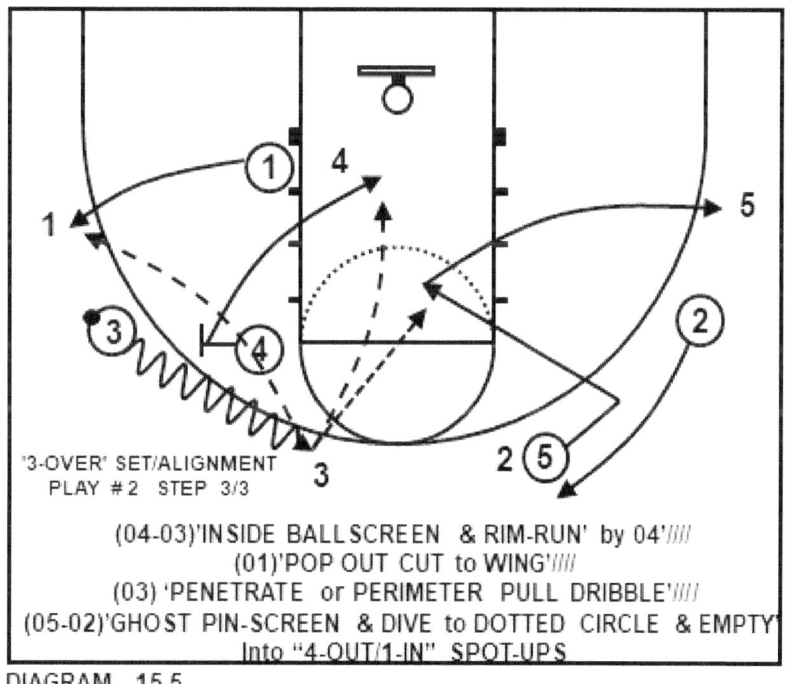

DIAGRAM 15.5

Diagram 15.6 illustrates Play # 3, a Level 2 play with different types of action than previous plays. Both 05 and 04 step just outside of the arc near the "Slot" on their side of the floor and 01 then makes the pass to 05. Upon making the pass to 05, 01 receives a "Flare-Screen" from 04 to use to "Flare-Cut" to the FT Line extended on the new "Weakside Wing."

02 quickly breaks up to the FT Line extended on his own side of the floor. With all four teammates outside of the arc and both big defenders, X5 and X4 far from the basket, 03 makes an inverted "Iso Duck-In Cut" and looks for the ball from 05 for his high percentage shot. **Diagram 15.6**.

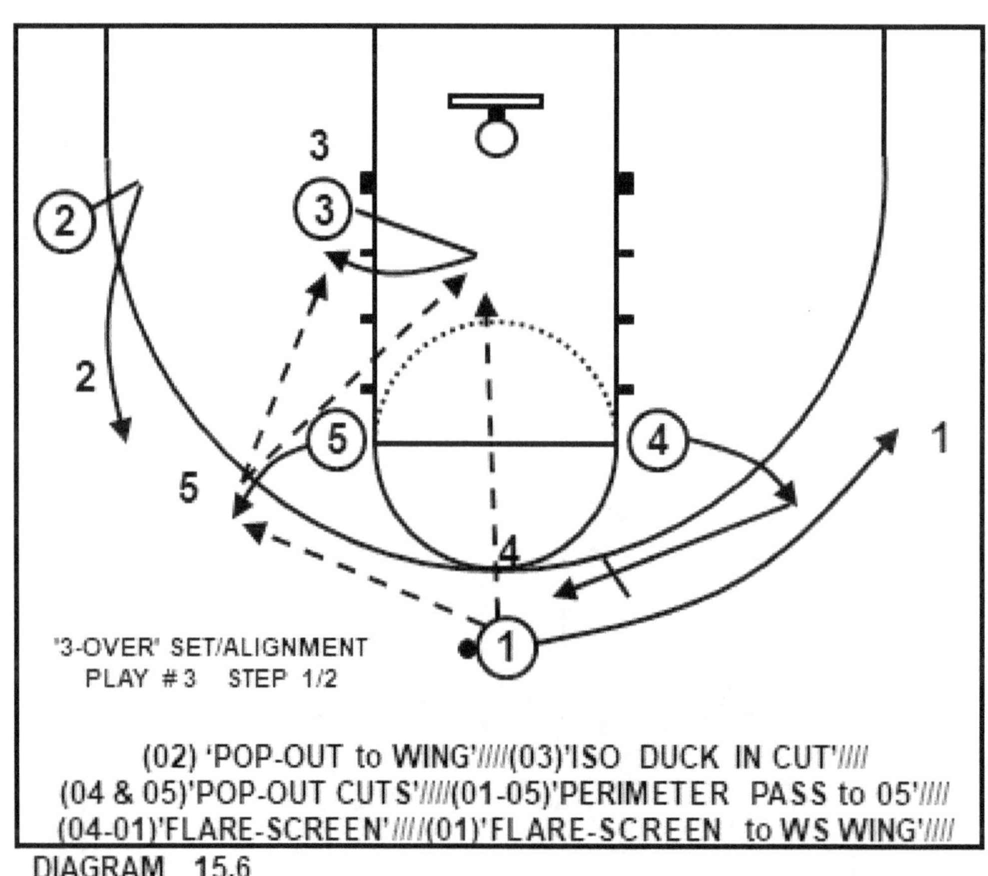

DIAGRAM 15.6

If the pass is not made inside by 05, 02 continues breaking up and over to receive the "Big-on-Small Pass Hand-off. 02 takes the ball and continues across the top of the key with 04 stepping over to set a "Big-on-Small Ball-Screen" and 03 flashes across the lane to make another inverted post-up. After 02 dribbles tightly off of the top left shoulder of 04, 04 then makes a "front pivot" off of his lower right foot to make a "Rim-Run" to the basket. With 02 "drag dribbling across the top of the key off of 04's screen and approaching 01, 01 makes a "Flare-Cut" deeper into the corner. 01 becomes a potential "catch and shoot" scoring threat, an "Inside Passing" threat (to 03) or possibly a "creator" with the ball. After the hand-off with 02, 05 slips back up behind the weakside defenders to the new "Weakside Slot." **Diagram 15.7.**

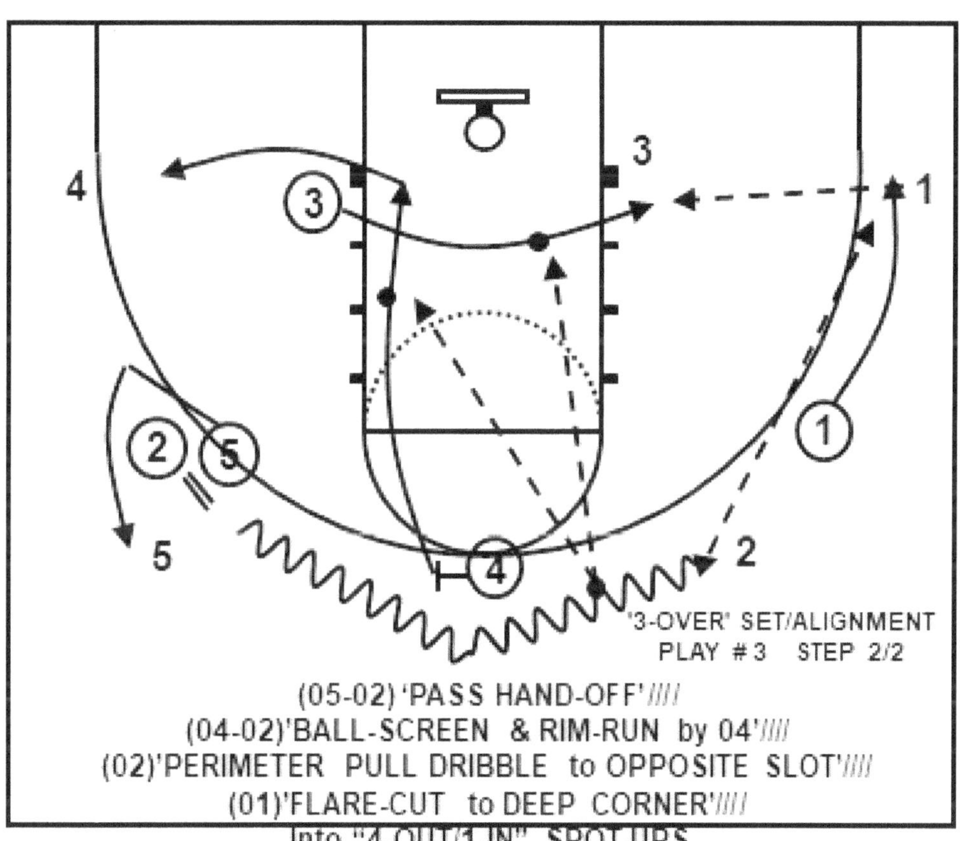

DIAGRAM 15.7

The main difference in this group of "HIGH-POST/LOW-POST" Spot-Ups compared to the other two types of spot-ups is that there is both a "Ballside Block' and a "Ballside High Post." There are "Ballside and Weakside Wings" and a "Point" with no weakside interior position or "Deep Corner" locations. As in the other continuity spot-ups, all players will have been moved about the court after the execution of each play and the appropriate continuity offense will be able to smoothly transition from these "High-Post/Low Post" Spot-Ups. While these five positions are slightly different than the other two groups of spot-ups, this group can also provide the offense with safe and easy types of ball-reversals, dribble penetration, opportunities, ways to deliver the ball inside to whomever (perimeter-type or post-type players) is posting up their defender on both the "Ballside Block," and "Ballside High Post." As in the other groups, but just in different locations on the floor, there are a number of perimeter-scoring threat and interior scoring threat possibilities in addition to offensive rebounding and defensive transitioning methods that can be implemented.

Diagram 15.8 illustrates Play # 4, (a lower Level 1 Play that gives that the opposition a great deal of movement by all five players to attempt to defend. It also could be considered part of the so-called family that includes Plays 10, 11 and 12 (even though those plays end up in a different spot-up family.)

02 is the first player that breaks up first over the top of 05 and then of 04 with his "Iverson Cut." Before the pass to 02 is made, 05 "Ghost Iverson Screens" 02 diagonally slashes across the lane to the empty "Block." After 04 "Iverson Screens" for 02, 04 either "front pivots and swims" or "reverse pivots and swings" around to seal off his own defender near the new "Ballside High Post."

01 makes the "Wing Pass" to 02 and immediately gets into position for the proper screening angle to "Pin Down-Screen" 03's defender for 03 to break to the top of the key. With 02 having the ball, 02 has immediate interior scorers available in 05 and 04, an outside scoring threat in 03 at the top of the key and a "skip pass" receiver in 01 on the "Weakside Wing." Even if shots are turned down, all of the "HIGH/POST/LOW POST" Spot-Ups are filled to continue the offensive attack. **Diagram 15.8.**

'3-OVER' SET/ALIGNMENT
PLAY # 4   STEP 1/1
(05-02)'GHOST IVERSON SCREEN, SLIP & ISO SLASH CUT'/////
(04)'IVERSON SCREEN, SLIP & HP POST SEAL'/////
(02)'IVERSON CUT'/////(01-02)'WING PASS'/////
(01-03)'DIAGONAL DOWN-SCREEN'
Into "HIGH POST/LOW POST SPOT-UPS'

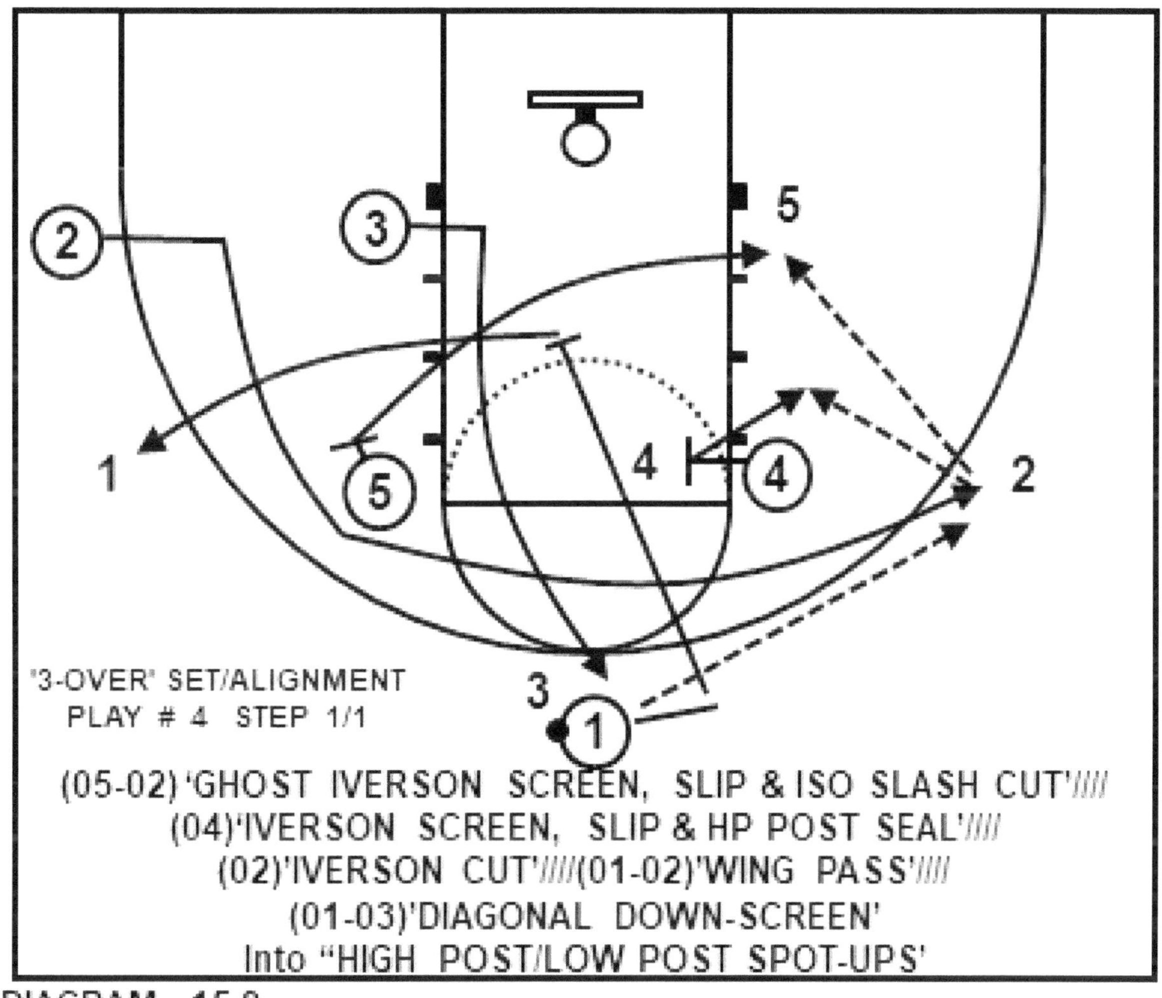

DIAGRAM   15.8

Diagram 15.9 illustrates Play # 5, another Level 1 play that possesses all types of movement for individual opponents to attempt to defend. 03 breaks vertically up towards 05 before then making his horizontal "Iverson Cut" over the top of 05 and 04. 05 then receives 04's "(Barkley-)Screen the (Iverson-)Screener" near the opposite side's "Elbow" area before spotting up at the opposite side's "Wing" area. After 03 breaks contact with 04's top left shoulder, 04 seals his defender off and slashes to the new "Ballside Block." This then places 05 at the new "Ballside High Post" after his "Barkley Cut."

To occupy any possible helpside defenders, 01 screens 02's defender on the "Weakside Wing" to give the play an immediate outside scoring threat in 03 at the top of the key. The same "HIGH-POST/LOW-POST" Spot-Ups are filled for the same continuity offense to begin after the next pass is made. Play # 5 **Diagram 15.9.**

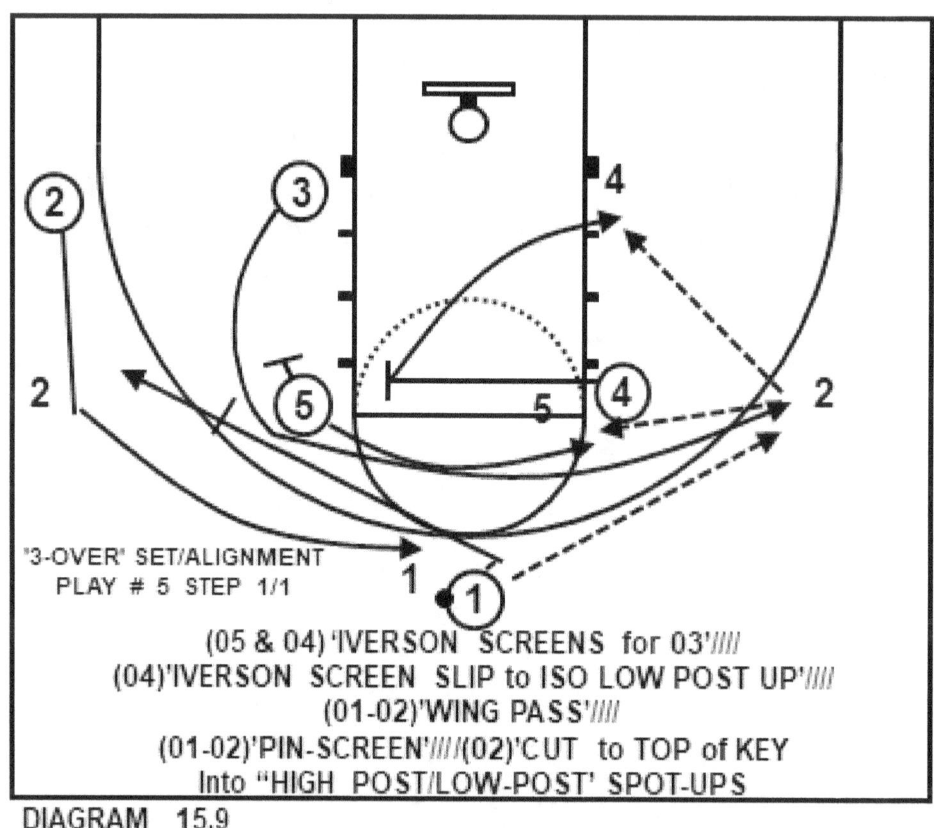

DIAGRAM 15.9

Diagram 15.10 shows the beginning of Play # 6, a Level 2 entry, where this play could also be fitted in a previous group of plays, Plays 1 through 12—various types of "Flex or Fake Flex" action. Again, those previous plays all end up in "3-Out/2-In" Spot-Ups and are located in a different book.

As 01 dribbles towards the top of the key, 02's first steps are towards 03 as if he is to become a "Flex-Cutter" (off of the potential "Flex-Screener," 03.) Instead, 03 "Ghost Flex Screen" 02 and cuts across the lane himself to post up. 02 then changes directions and makes his "Iverson Cut" over the top of both 05 and 04's "Big-on-Small Iverson Screens." **Diagram 15.10.**

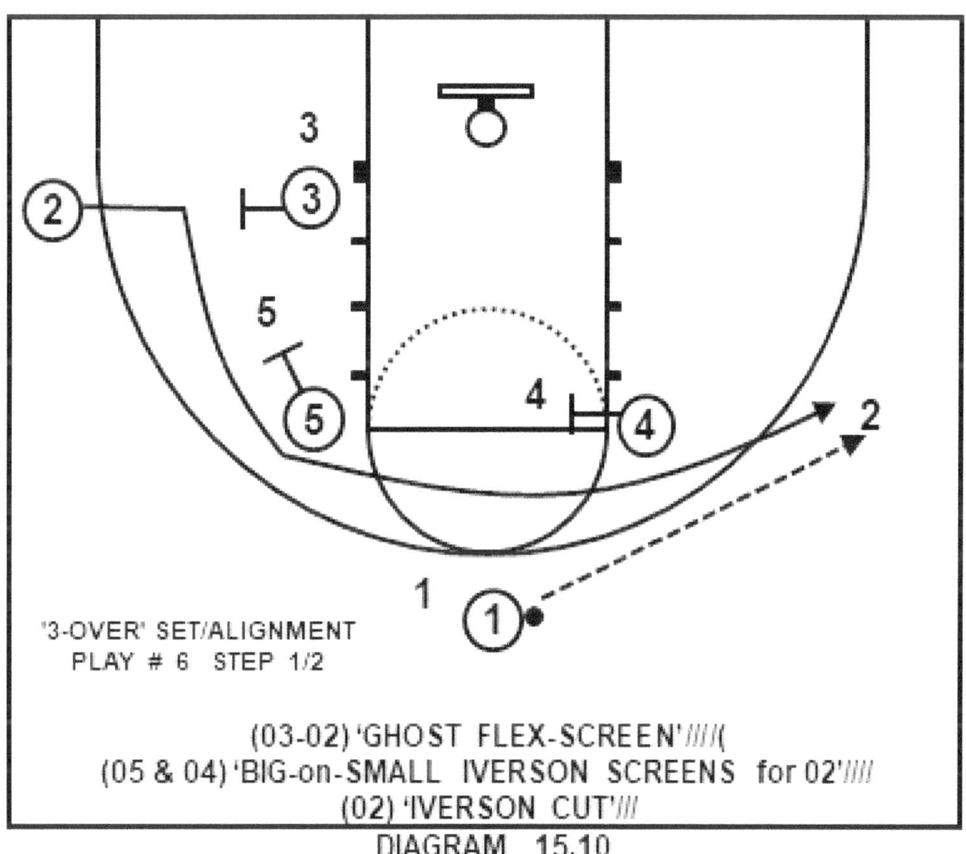

DIAGRAM 15.10

After 01 makes the "Wing Pass" to 02, 01 "Flare-Cuts" to the opposite "Weakside Wing" away from his teammates, but making himself a perimeter scoring threat in the form of a potential "Skip Pass" from 02. As 03 inverts and isolates his perimeter-type defender on the "Ballside Block," 04 occupies off-ball defenders and also creates two new scoring threats—one for 05 at the new "Ballside High Post" and the other at the top of the key for himself. This is done by 04 cutting across the "Nail" to set a high "Cross-Screen" for 05 to flash to the new "Ballside High Post." After screening for 05, 04 slips his screen and steps out to the top of the key, completing the filling of the "HIGH-POST/LOW-POST" Spot-Ups for the final phase of the offense to immediately continue. **Diagram 15.11.**

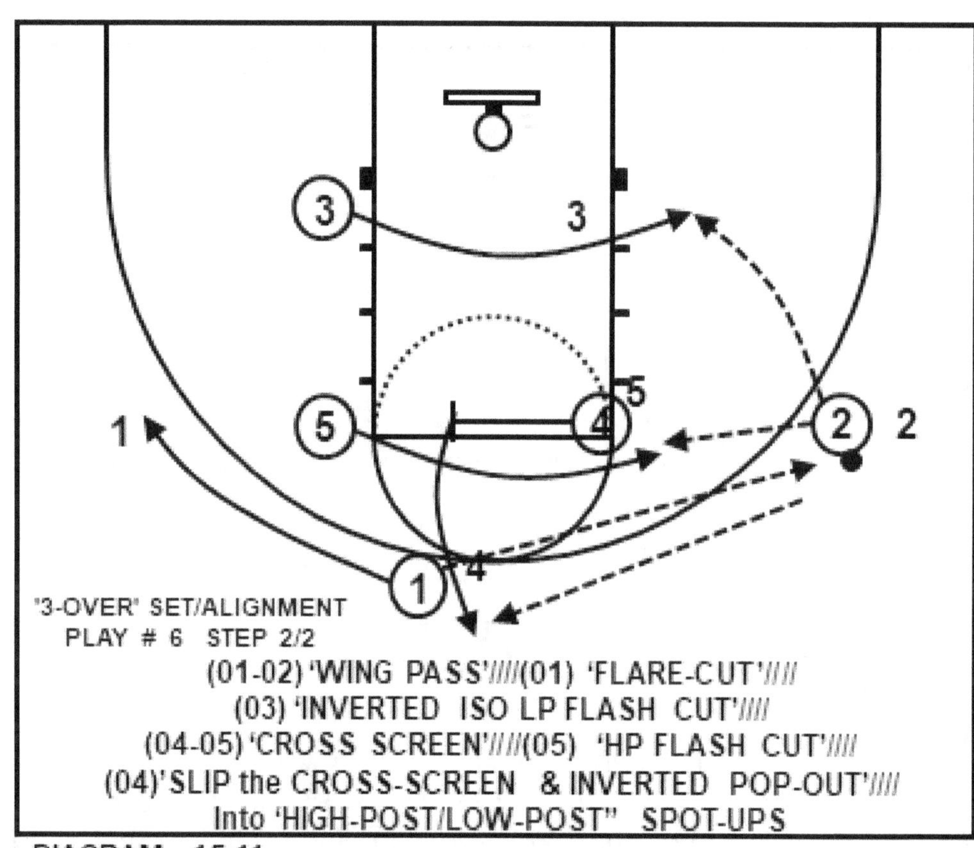

DIAGRAM 15.11

Somewhat similar initial action is shown in Diagram 15.12 in Play # 7. 05 makes a "Barkley Cut" across the "Nail" and over the top of 04 towards the "Wing" area on the opposite side of the floor. As that action starts, 03 makes a direct cut out to the FT Line extended on the opposite side of the floor, while 02 runs horizontally to the empty "Block" and then diagonally up through the lane to set a (02-04) "(Small-on-Big Diagonal Back-)Screen the (Barkley) Screener." **Diagram 15.12**

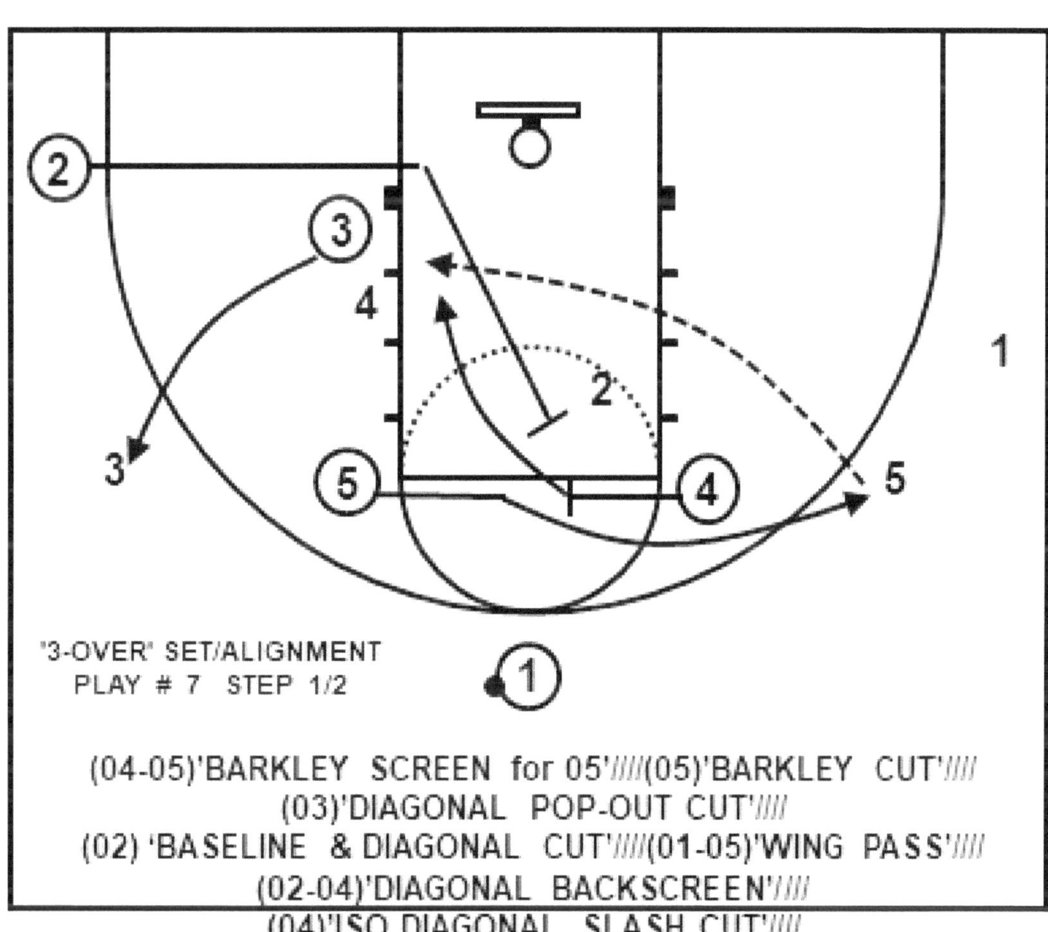

DIAGRAM 15.12

With 05 having the ball outside of the arc (with X5) forced to defend 05 out on the unfamiliar and uncomfortable perimeter area, 04 would have only minimal help (from X2) in the defense trying to stop 05's" Lob Pass" to 04. Still, if no "Lob Pass is made, 05 should reverse the ball to 01 who quickly swings the ball to 03. After making the pass to 03, 01 positions himself for the proper screening angle to then set a (01-02) "(Pin Down-)Screen the (Back-)Screener."

If shots are still not taken, the spot-ups are once again filled for the designated continuity offense to fluidly and immediately begin. **Diagram 15.13**

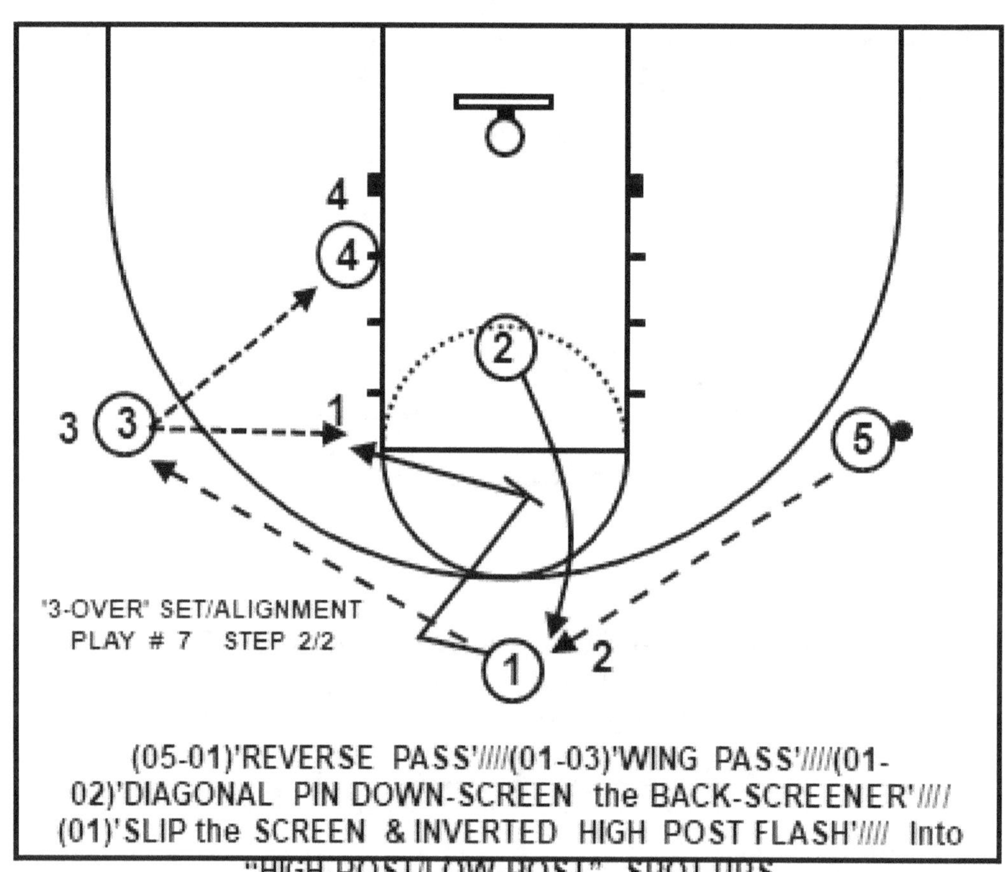

DIAGRAM 15.13

Play # 8 is another Level 2 play that is demonstrated in Diagrams 15.14 and 15.15 As 01 dribbles towards the top of the key, he sees 02 cutting towards 03 and the basket. 01 then immediately dribbles to the FT Line extended on the left side of the floor. 03 screens for 02 before 02 then makes a "Pipe Cut" vertically up the lane and cuts through the "Big-on-Small Twisted Elevator Screen" set by 04 and 05 near the "Nail."

01 looks to hit 03 after 03 has screened for 02 and then sealed his perimeter-type defender (X3) off in the isolated and inverted situation. **Diagram 15.14**.

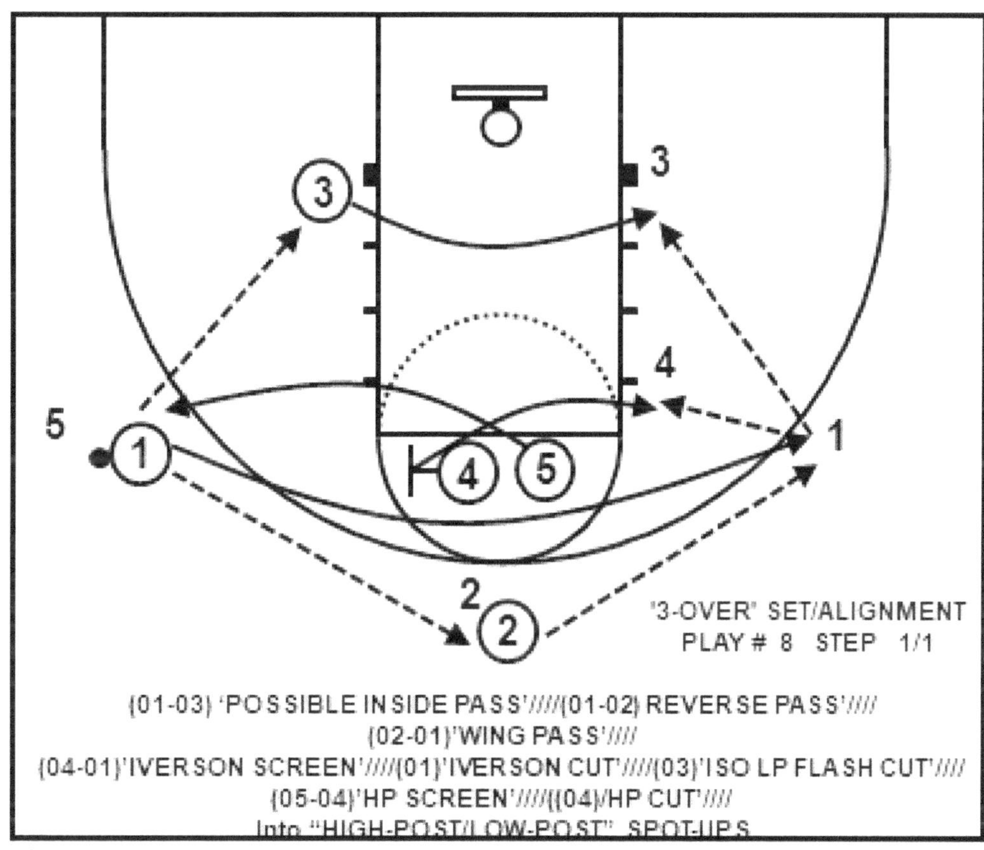

DIAGRAM 15.14

Diagram 15.15 shows the continuation of the entry with 01 turning down the "Inside Pass" to 03 and reversing the ball to 02 out on top. After making the 01-02 "Reverse Pass," 01 makes an "Iverson Cut" over the top of 04 and 05 and cuts to the opposite "Wing" area. 02 then quickly swings the ball over to 01 at the opposite "Wing" area. After screening for 01, 04 then receives a (05-04) "(Barkley-)Screen the (Iverson-)Screener" for 04 to flash to the opposite side's "High Post." At the same time, 03 flashes across the lane to the new "Ballside Mid-Post." The 02-01 "Wing Pass" gives 01 'catch and shoot" possibilities, "creating" opportunities off of the dribble and "Inside Pass" opportunities (to either 03 or to 04.) This pass and the following action repositions all five players into the "HIGH-POST/LOW-POST" Spot-Ups for a smooth continuation into the continuity. **Diagram 15.15.**

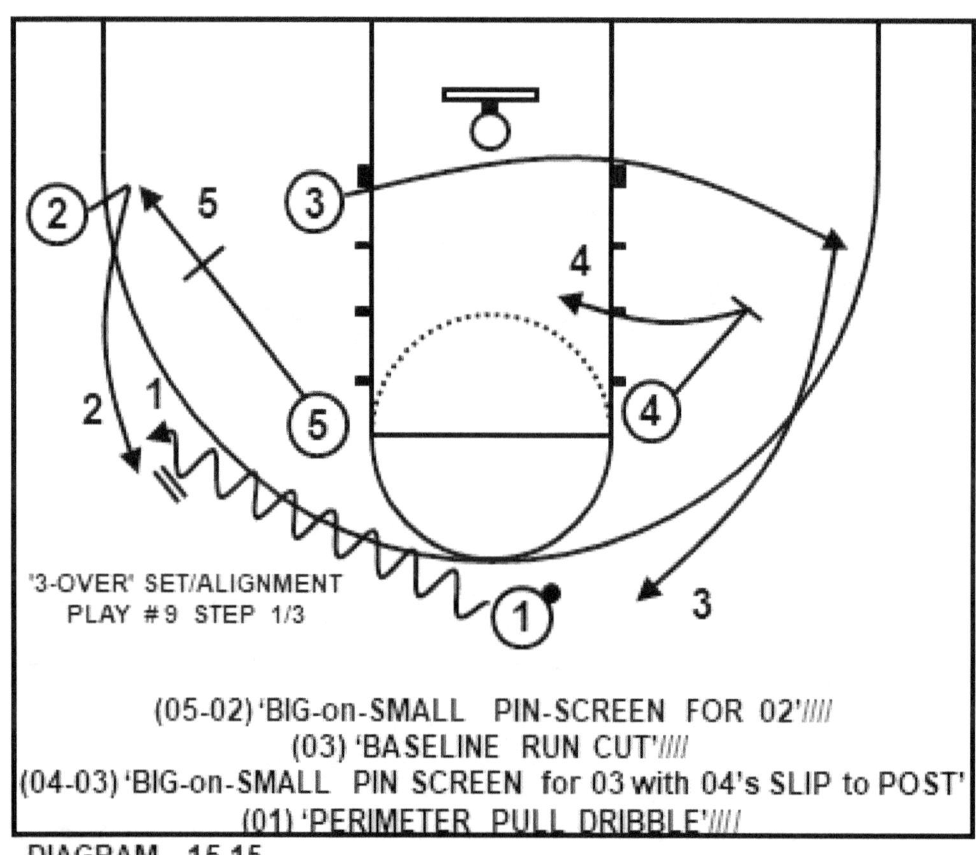

DIAGRAM 15.15

Diagrams 15.16 through 15.18 show the entire Play # 9, a Level 3 play. 03 empties out to the opposite side of the floor almost to the "Deep Corner." This action (or called "False Motion") basically realigns players into the "Horns" Set. From there, 04 sets a "Big-on-Small Ghost Pin Down-Screen" for 03 to use to break up to his new side's "Slot" location. On the other side, with 02 already in his "Deep Corner" position, 05 breaks down to set his own "Big-on-Small Pin Down-Screen" for 02 to break up towards the "Wing" area on his own initial side of the floor.

The difference between 04 and 05's screens is that 04 will then "Ghost" his screen and step back towards the "Mid-Post" area while 05 will continue down towards the "Deep Corner" where 02 began his cut.

As 02 breaks up off of 05's screen, 01 continues his dribble to make a DHO near the FT Line extended. **Diagram 15.16.**

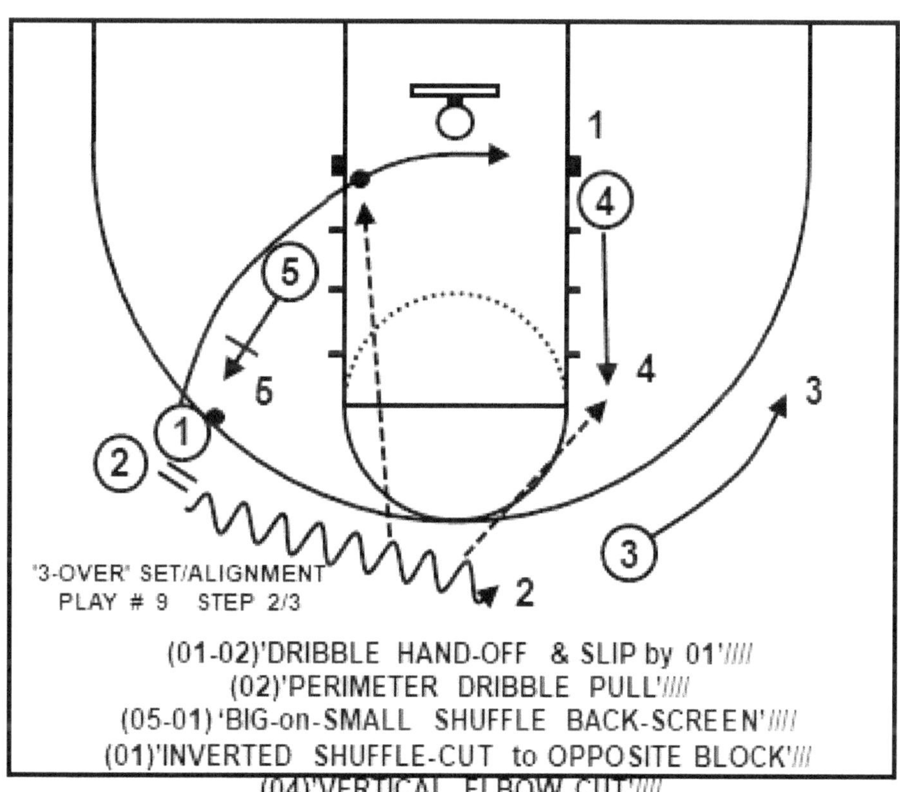

DIAGRAM 15.16

Diagram 15.17 shows 02 receiving the ball on the 01-02 DHO and dribbling towards the top of the key. As the ball is handed off by 01 to 02, 05 steps up to set a "Big-on-Small Shuffle Back-Screen" for 01 to use to cut to the basket and eventually through the lane to invert his perimeter-type defender, X1. During 02's dribble, 02 looks to hit 01 on his cut to the basket and at the same time, 04 makes a vertical "Elbow Up-Cut" to possibly receive the ball from 02 on his continued dribble. Diagram 15.17.

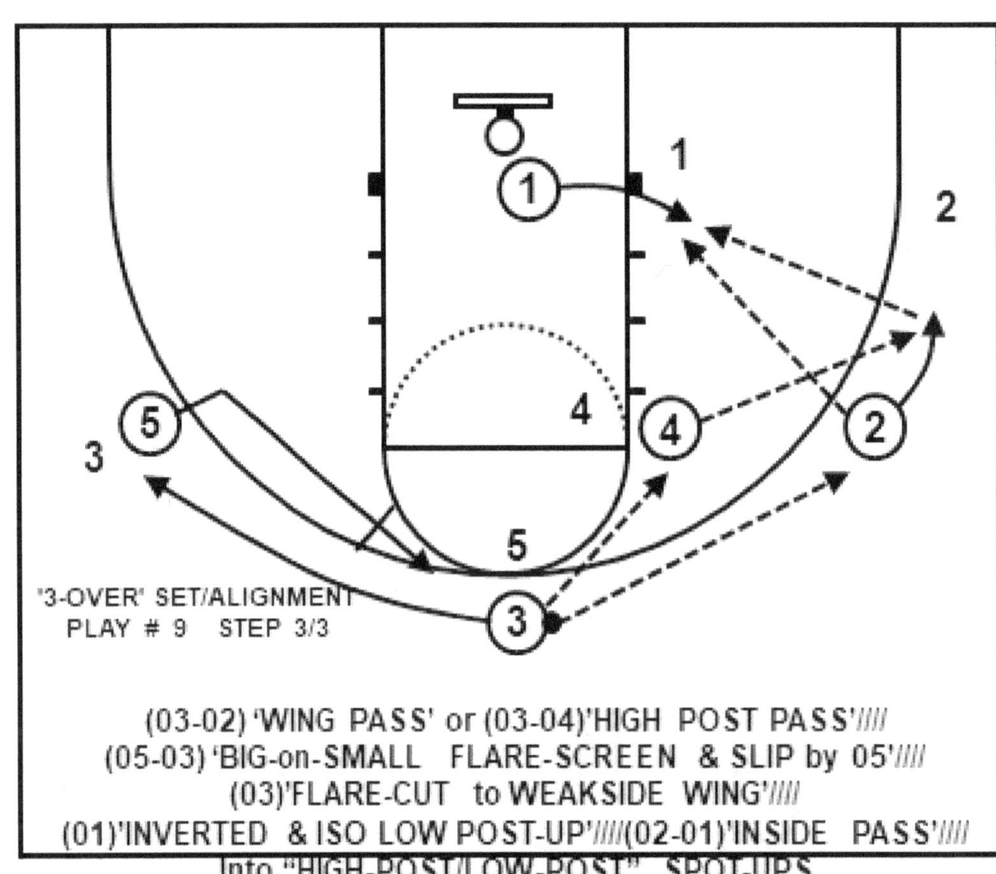

DIAGRAM   15.17

02 could make passes to 04 or to 03 that can then be relayed on to 01 now posting up on the new "Ballside Block." After the pass, 05 should step up to set a "Big-on-Small Flare-Screen" for 02 to use on his "Flare-Cut" to the new "Weakside Wing." This occupies both X2 and X5, and makes it especially important that X5 stays out of the 'defensive picture' in helping X1 and X4 defend their two men posting up on the "Ballside Block" and "Ballside High Post" respectively.

This action also moves and therefore causes their defenders to move that could expose defensive weaknesses or breakdowns, giving the offense advantages and opportunities to utilize. These coordinated and planned movements repositions into the "HIGH-POST/LOW-POST" Spot-Ups.

The "3-OVER" Set is a very good and somewhat unique offensive alignment that can use many of the same actions that a "HORNS" Set can use in addition to being able to execute actions such as high "Ball-Screens" and low "Flex-Screens" besides its own set of more unique and less common forms of offensive attack.

Just like every play that is a part of every offensive alignment, there is free-flowing actions of many kinds that always remains fundamentally sound and structured within the framework of the offense. Each play from this offensive set also provides the easy conversion into the final phase of the overall offensive attack, be it a continuity offense or a motion-type offensive phase.

This multiple-phase offensive system uses more than one phase/layer/wave of attack, with each phase/wave having a seamless and immediate conversion into the next phase/wave. While confusing to defenses and problematic to defend, this system can be properly taught and coached so that offensive players can comprehend and ultimately execute the plays while having many different levels of (physical talent and playing experience.)

Many of these types of offensive schemes can be integrated within the same offensive system that can attack defenses in various ways. The more the schemes the greater the opportunity an offensive team can find the most efficient and productive schemes that can place both individual and the overall team in the best and most frequent "positions to succeed."

The smallest of techniques of all of the plays/entries carefully diagrammed are also described in detail.

Every entry/play has been carefully studied and evaluated to determine which level of talent and experience must be possessed for that specific team to be able to successfully execute the play. This includes all players' physical skills as well as their experience and their mental understanding of the game. This also includes coaches that must teach and coach their players to provide those players with the experience, the knowledge and their new and understanding of the game.

The most sophisticated plays/entries would fall into the final of the three levels all based on the team's physical talents and skills, the mental capacities and the overall team's game experience. In addition, the coaching staff must have a high degree of basketball knowledge as well as very high teaching and coaching skills to educate his/her entire basketball team. The proper breakdown drills must be thoroughly utilized to hone the fundamental skills and techniques needed for individual players and the overall team to execute plays that can be efficient, productive and successful. We define this family of plays as the "Level 3 category" of plays. This "Level 3" family of plays will have a much more complex offensive scheme that would require a very high amount of physical talent as well as requiring a greater amount of the players (to execute) and the coaches (to teach and coach) mental capacities and experience needed for the offense to be efficient, productive and successful. We feel plays in our defined "Level 3" category could possibly be successful for NBA teams, definitely for college teams and also for many high schools and older AAU teams.

The next classification or level of plays would be possibly slightly lower as far as sophistication, complexity and the actual 'length' of the play (and the number of passes, cuts and screens used) in the play's overall scheme. These "Level 2" plays remain to be fundamentally sound, these plays may lack the actual number of techniques/methods that are implemented within that play in comparison to the "Level 3" plays/entries. Therefore any team that successfully executes the highest "Level 3" plays/entries could/should easily be able execute any of these so-called lower "Level 2" plays/entries, if so desired. Almost all high school teams should be able to execute successfully all aspects of the "Level 2" plays.

The final grouping of plays would be called "Level 1" plays and are not as difficult for offensive players to master the execution of them, both physically as well as mentally. Even though the techniques are still fundamentally, they may not be as complex to learn and understand in addition to being easier to physically execute.

"Level 1" plays would be lower in the scheme's complexities and the number of techniques used in the execution of this category of plays. Obviously, since these "Level 1" plays are still sound, but lack some of the methods used in the two previous more sophisticated and complex levels; these more elementary plays should be able to be utilized by any teams that use either of the two higher level plays. We feel that Middle

School/Junior High teams as well as younger AAU teams or organizations should be able to utilize any of the "Level 1" plays successfully, with a possibility that some of those teams that are slightly more advanced (than other teams) could possibly use some plays located in the immediate next immediate level.

Ideas, concepts and techniques from actual plays from teams of all three levels have been used to modify or to create different combinations of the various techniques and schemes used that will help prove these entries can be successfully used. This allows the author to create numerous plays that use the various schemes to build a library of fundamentally sound plays that will be unique and will be appropriate for the wide range of teams with the various ages and skill levels.

With this book having plays in these three presumed categories or levels, the book will reach out and benefit a much larger group of serious basketball coaches from elementary school age to the highest skilled levels that exists.

In addition, an experienced and resourceful coach may be able to mold some plays that include all of the offensive techniques that he/she desires could reshape a specific play that begins in one specific offensive set/alignment and reshape it so that it could begin in a different offensive/set that is more favorable to that coach and his/her coaching staff's liking.

Conversely, that innovative and creative coach may completely like the specific offensive set/alignment and favor the very same offensive actions included in a certain play, but can modify that play so that the ending spot-ups of all five players are conducive to being able to begin the final phase of the offensive attack by using a more favorable offensive continuity offense.

PLAYS/ENTRIES THAT END in the "4-OUT/1-IN" OFFENSIVE SPOT-UPS

The difference in the following family of plays/entries are that all five players will end up in these "4-Out/1-In Spot-Ups" that could individually called the "Ballside Deep Corner," the "Weakside Deep Corner." the "Ballside Slot," the "Weakside Slot," and the "Ballside Post." "These five positions also can provide the offense with successful ball-reversals, more possibilities for dribble penetration, opportunities to attack the defense with interior passing to either perimeter-type or post-type players. These "4-Out/1-In Spot-Ups will also give the offense strong methods of attacking the defense with offensive rebounds, particularly from the weakside as well as a successful defensive transition scheme.

Diagram 16.1 introduces a Level 1 play, numbered Play # 1, where 05 is the elected post player to set the screen. Therefore, 01 "perimeter pull dribbles" to the left "Slot" for

05 to step up to set a "Big-on-Small Long Ball-Screen." At the same time, 02 breaks up as if to set a screen for 01. Instead he "ghosts ball-screens" 01 and then receives a "Big-on-Small Long Flare-Screen 02, now located up near the new "Weakside Slot." 02 then "Flare-Cuts" to the new "Weakside Deep Corner," while 04 remains at the new "Weakside Slot."

After 01 breaks contact with 05's outside right shoulder, 05 reads X5 and how X5 attempts to defend the screen (either by a switch, a trap, a hard-hedge or a 'drop coverage;' 05 attacks with a "Roll" through the lane or a "Rim-Run/Lob Cut" towards the weakside half of the lane. 03 remains "spotted up" in his "Deep Corner" with 02 returning after his action to his side's "Deep Corner." 01 ends up on the "Ballside Slot" and 04 on the "Weakside Slot," while 05 "chases the ball" to post up on the "Ballside Block."

This play gives the offense different methods and locations to attack various defenders and also repositions players into the correct "4-Out/1-In" Spot-Ups. Diagram 16.1.

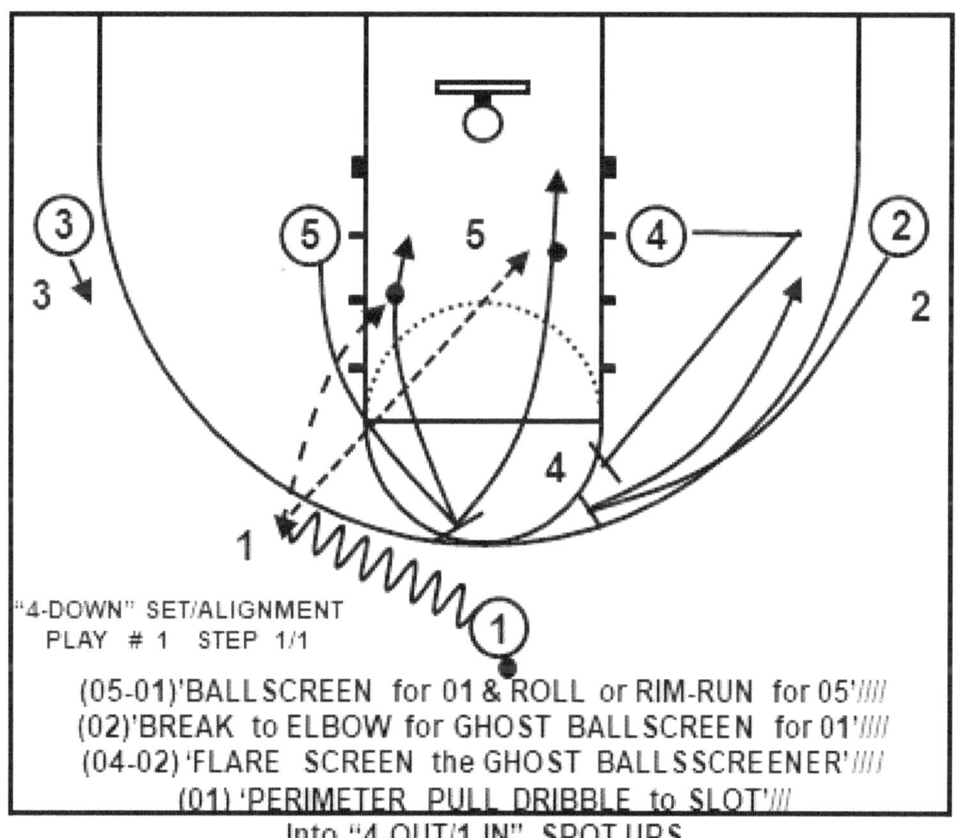

DIAGRAM 16.1

Play # 2 is a Level 2 play that is shown in Diagrams 16.2 and 16.3. While the play could be executed also towards the left side and immediately involve 03, 01 dribbles towards 02 in this action. This forces 02 to execute a "Pipe Cut" in and up the lane to the new "Ballside Slot." 01 can look to immediately make the pass to 04, who could seal off his defender or to reverse the ball to 02 out on top. Diagram 16.2.

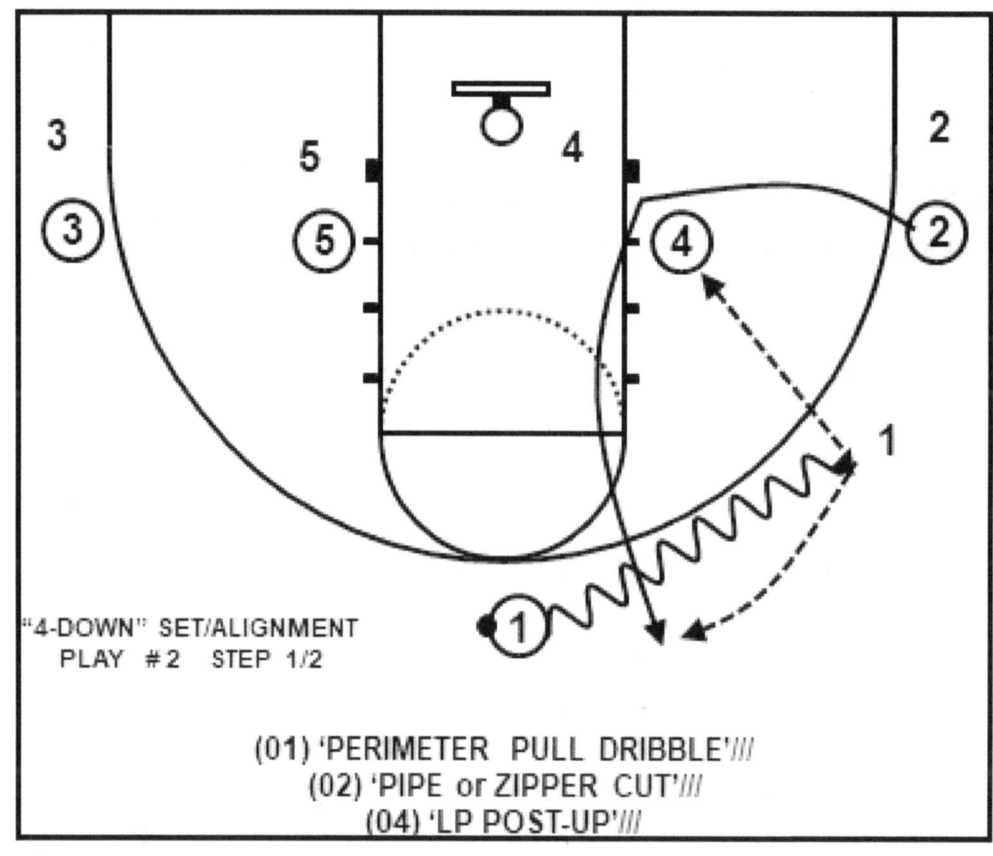

DIAGRAM   16.2

If the ball is reversed to 02, 05 again steps up diagonally to set a "Big-on-Small Long Ball-Screen" for 02 to use to advance the ball to the other side of the floor. As 02 "dribble-scrapes" off of 05's top right shoulder and breaks contact, 04 flashes across the lane to post his defender on the opposite side of the floor. At the same time, 05 makes a "front pivot" off of his lower left foot and makes a "Rim-Run/Lob Cut" to the backside of the lane and looks for 02's "Lob Pass." 03 makes a "Lift Cut" to the FT Line extended to become a potential passer (to either 05 first or primarily to 04 on the new "Ballside Block."

01 rotates to the new "Weakside Slot" to occupy the lone weakside defender. If 05 does not receive the "Lob Pass" from 02 or 03, he empties out to then occupy the "Weakside Deep Corner." If "Inside Shots" are not taken by 04 and 05 while perimeter shots are not taken by 01, 02 or 03; the "4-Out/1-In" Spot-Ups are filled to maintain the offensive attack on a scrambling defense. Diagram 16.3.

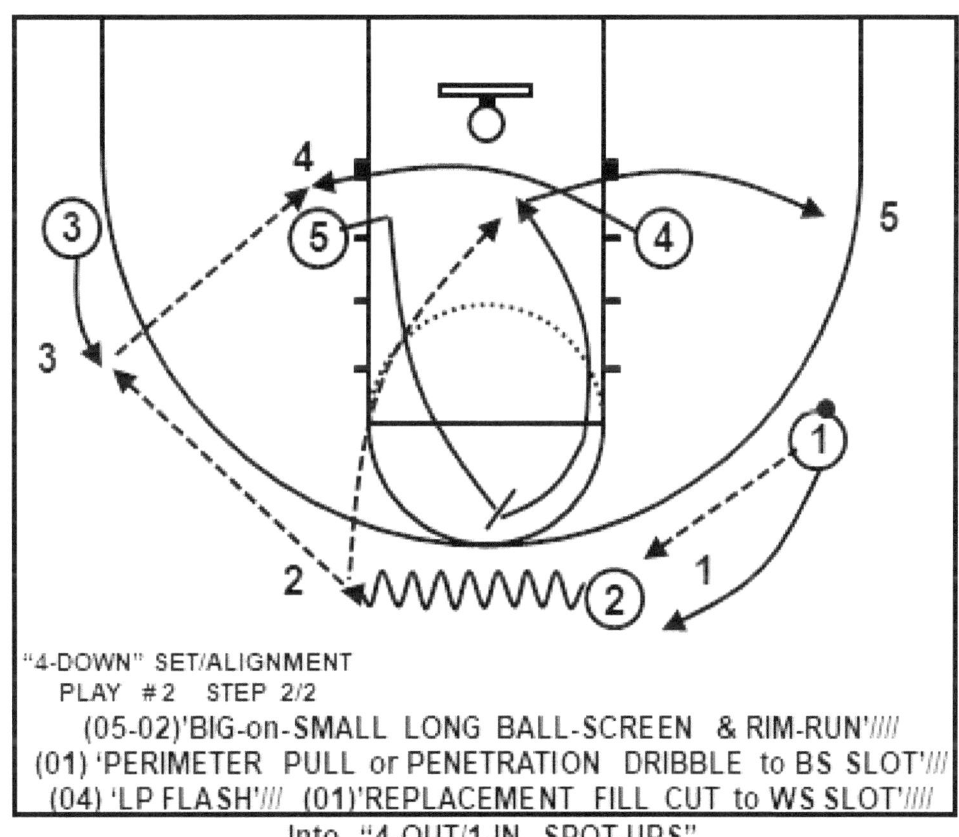

DIAGRAM 16.3

Play # 3 is another Level 2 play that is a Counter to the previous Level # 2 play. Again, this play could be started on either side of the floor, but Diagram 16.4 shows it being run to the right side of the floor again.

Again, 01 "perimeter pull dribbles" to the right "Wing" area with 02 executing the same "Pipe Cut" up and out to the same "Slot" location. Diagram 16.4.

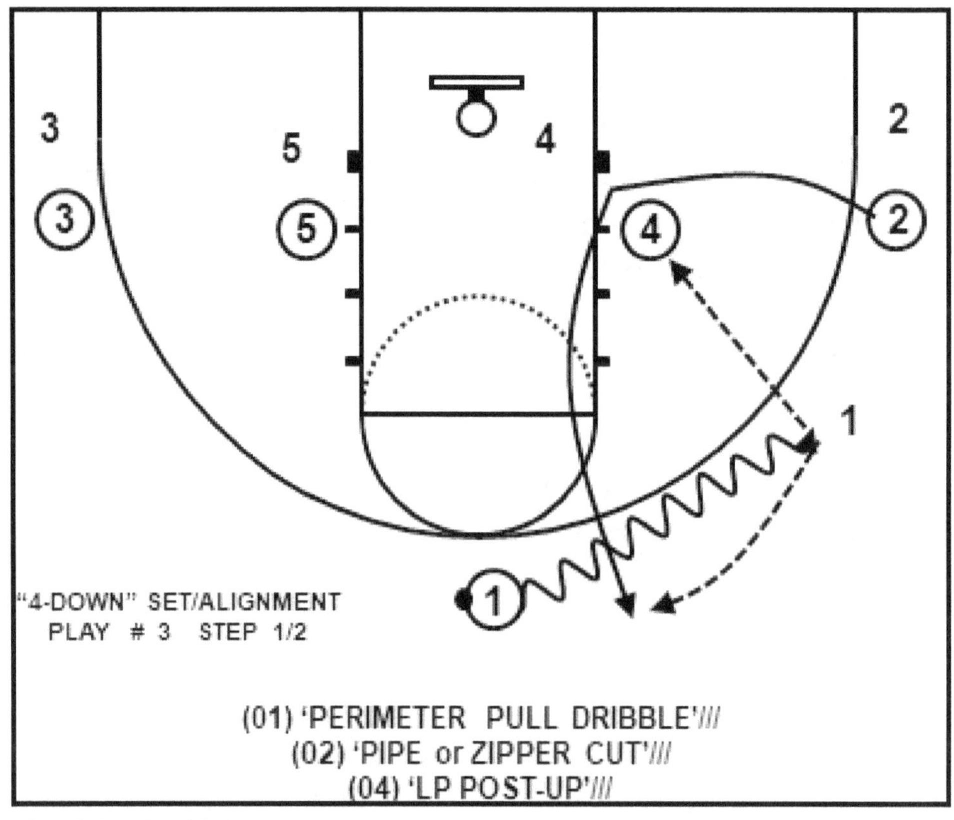

DIAGRAM 16.4

Diagram 16. 5 illustrates the identical action of 05 stepping up to set the same "Big-on-Small Long Ball-Screen" for 02 to use. At the same time 04 can change his action up by making an "Iso Duck-In Cut" into the "Dotted Circle" area. As 02 "dribble-scrapes off of 05's top shoulder again, 04 then steps out to the new Weakside Slot."

In this instance, 05 switches up his route to the basket by making his screen a "Ball-Screen/Roll" down the left side of the lane. 03 again lifts to become an immediate pass receiver for 02 since 03 may have an improved passing angle to deliver the ball to 05. As 02 dribbles towards the "Ballside Slot," 01 makes a "Drift Cut" towards his side's "Deep Corner" and looks for a possible (02-01) "Skip Pass" or a (04-01) "Down Pass" after a (02-04) "Reverse Pass."

Regardless of the passes made, the same "4-Out/1-In" Spot-Ups are filled to continue the attack. Diagram 16.5.

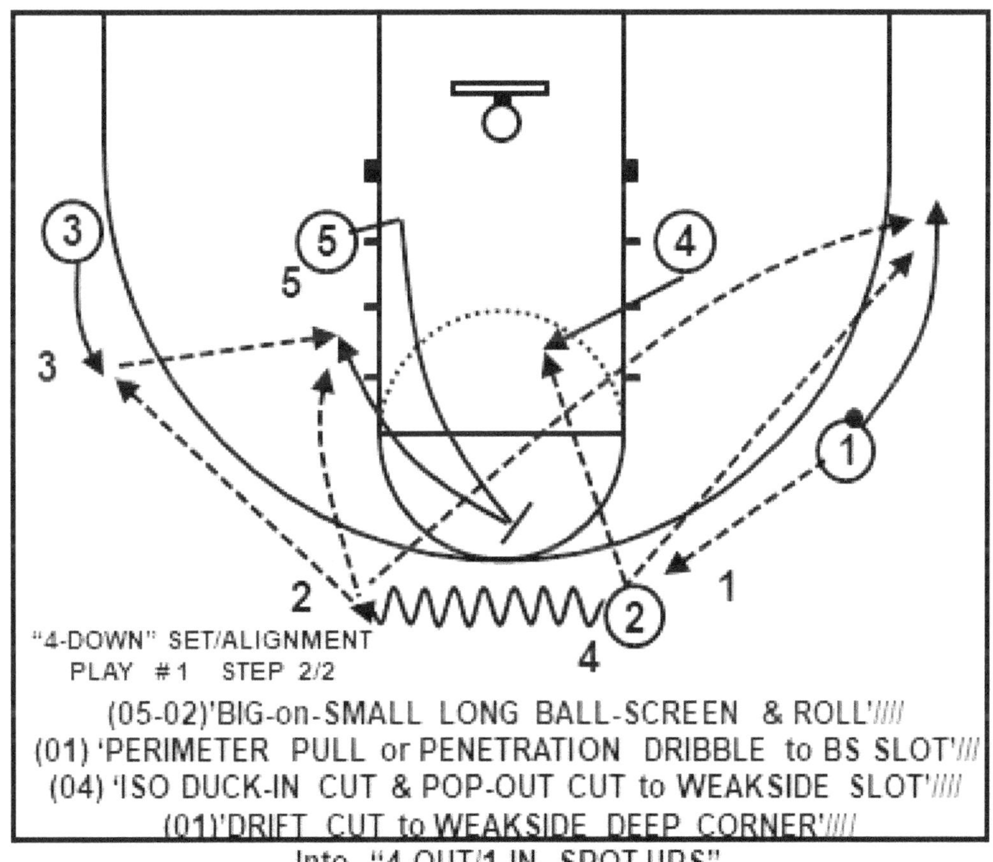

DIAGRAM 16.5

Diagram 16.6 shows the beginning of Play # 4, a Level 2 play where the actual play could start with 01 making a "perimeter pull dribble" towards either "Slot." That beginning dribble keys the movement of each player. When 01 advances the ball towards the right side, 04 times his "Iso Duck-In Cut" into the Dotted Circle when 01 is close enough to the "Slot" that he can easily deliver the ball to 04.

Depending upon how X4 attempts to defend 04, 01 should read the defender and either make a "Lob Pass" towards the basket and away from X4 or a "Bounce Pass" towards 04's free hand but away from the defender.

02 makes a quick dash towards the "Block" and then back out to the "Deep Corner" to both stretch and occupy his defender. 05 and 03 make it initally appear as if they are running some "Weakside Flex Action" before 03 breaks back out vertically towards the vacant new "Weakside Slot" and 05 out towards the new "Weakside Deep Corner." This gives 03 and open perimter shot at the "Slot" and also horizontally pulls the presumed biggest defender away from 04 and the basket. Diagram 16.6.

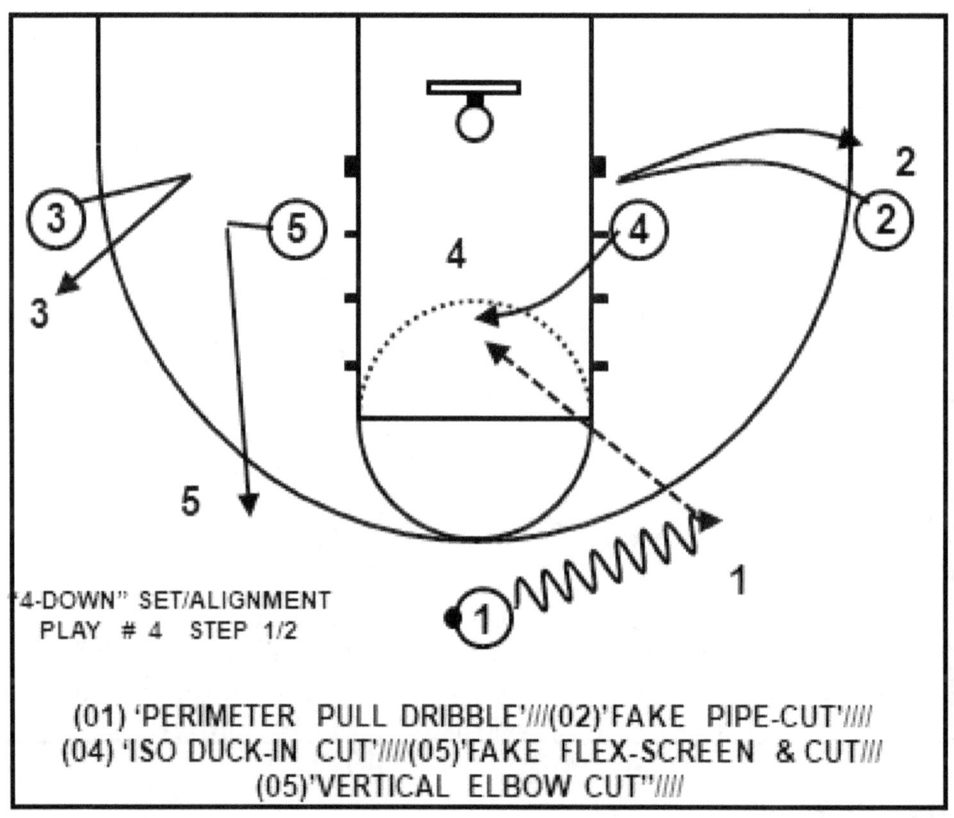

DIAGRAM 16.6

If 01 elects not to make the "Inside Pass" to 04, he has the option to make a "Down Pass" to 02 for scoring and driving options for 02. 02 may have the best "passing angle" to deliver the ball to 04, on his "return cut" to the "Ballside Block."

01 could also reverse the ball to 03 for 03 to attack defender out on the perimeter. After 01 makes the pass to 03, 02 quickly breaks up to set a "Flare Back-Screen" for both 02 and 01 to replace each other in the respective new "Weakside Slot" and new "Weakside Deep Corner" locations. With 03 at the new "Weakside Slot," 03 is prepared for a (01-03) "Reverse Pass" that could quickly lead to quick aggressive actions by 03 off of 01's pass, such as "catch and shoot," "catch and drive" or "catch and "Inside Pass" to 04, who continues to follow the flight of the perimeter pass. 05 remains "spotted up" in his "Deep Corner" for a possible "Down Pass" from 03, leading to shots, drives or passes to either 04 or a "Skip Pass" to 02.

If no shots are taken, the action by all five players has attacked and moved individual defenders as well as placed all five offensive players into the proper "4-Out/1-In" Spot-ups for the last phase of the overall offensive attack. Diagram 16.7

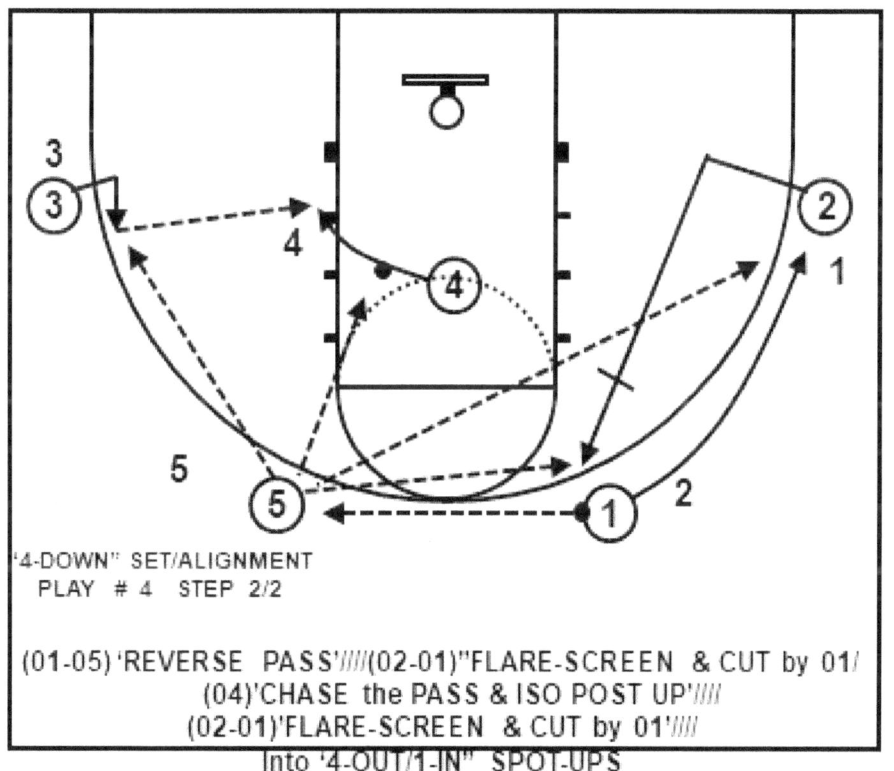

DIAGRAM 16.7

Diagram 16.8 shows the beginning of Play # 5, another Level 2 play where the actual play starts very similar to Play # 14 with 01 making a "perimeter pull dribble" towards either "Slot." Again, this means that either Play # 14 and Play # 15 could be executed toward the left side of the floor. As in Play # 14, 01's dribble to one slot or the other dictates which players become the initial 'Ballside' players (04 and 02 in both plays in these discussions and which become the first 'Weakside' players (05 and 03) in both instances. When 01 goes to the right with his dribble, 04 executes the same "Iso Duck-In Cut" into the Dotted Circle when 01 is available to make the pass to 04.

Again, 01 should read the 04's post defender and either make a "Lob Pass" towards the basket and away from X4 or a "Bounce Pass" towards 04's free hand but away from the defender.

02 again pops in and out back to his "Deep Corner" to again occupy his defender out wide. 03 ends up out horizontally towards the sideline and 05 is now the player that makes the "Vertical Up Cut" straight to the vacant new "Weakside Slot." 05 agains stretches the defense vertically away from the basket and pulls the presumed biggest defender, X5, further out away from 04 and the basket. Diagram 16.8.

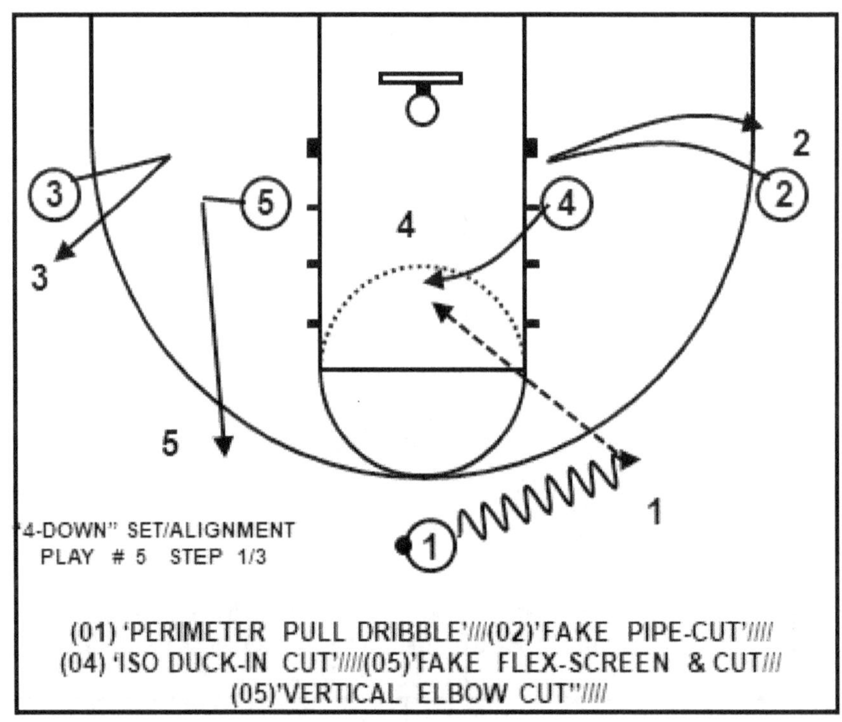

DIAGRAM 16.8

If 01 does not make the "Inside Pass" to 04 or the "Down Pass" to 02, he should make the "Reverse Pass" to the inverted 05 out on the "Weakside Slot." If 05 cannot make the quick pass to 04 in the middle of the lane, 05 should quickly swing the ball over to 03, who has popped out near the sideline at the FT Line extended.

04 continues his cut to reach the 'Nail,' and 05 quickly sprint cuts off of 04's left shoulder to curl around 04 towards the basket, while looking for 03's "Lob Pass."

As 05 continues his cut towards 04, 01 then begins his cut and times his movements as to use 05 as a "Big-on-Small Brush-Screener" before then using 04 as a stationary "Big-on-Small Shuffle Back-Screener." 01 scrapes off of 04's right shoulder and cuts to the new "Ballside Block," constantly looking for 03's "Inside Pass."

To help eliminate interior support, 02 rotates up to the FT Line extended to his new "Weakside Wing" area. After screening first for 05 and then for 01, 04 slips his screens and steps out to the top of the key. Diagram 16.9.

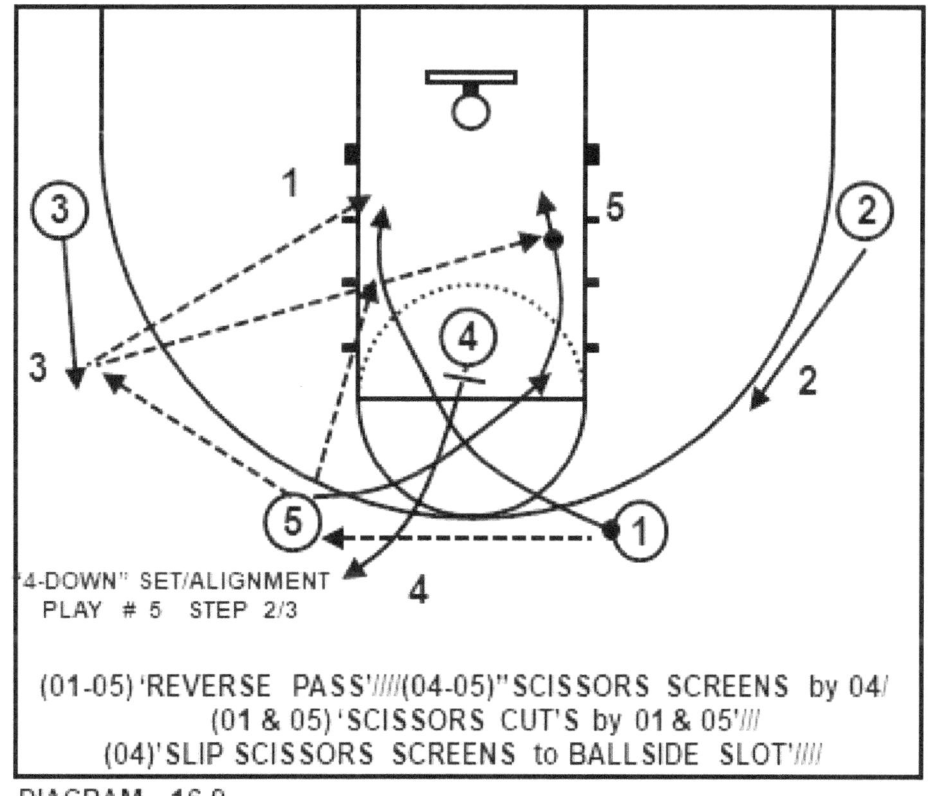

DIAGRAM 16.9

Upon receiving the ball, 03 has countless options: "catch and shoot" off of the pass, "catch and pass ("Lob Pass" to 05, "Inside Pass" to 01, "catch and drive" or "Down Dribble" to the "Deep Corner." This gives the offense other options as well as placing all five offensive players into the proper "4-Out/1-In" Spot-Ups to seamlessly flow into the designated continuity offense—the final attacking phase of the offense. Diagram 16.10.

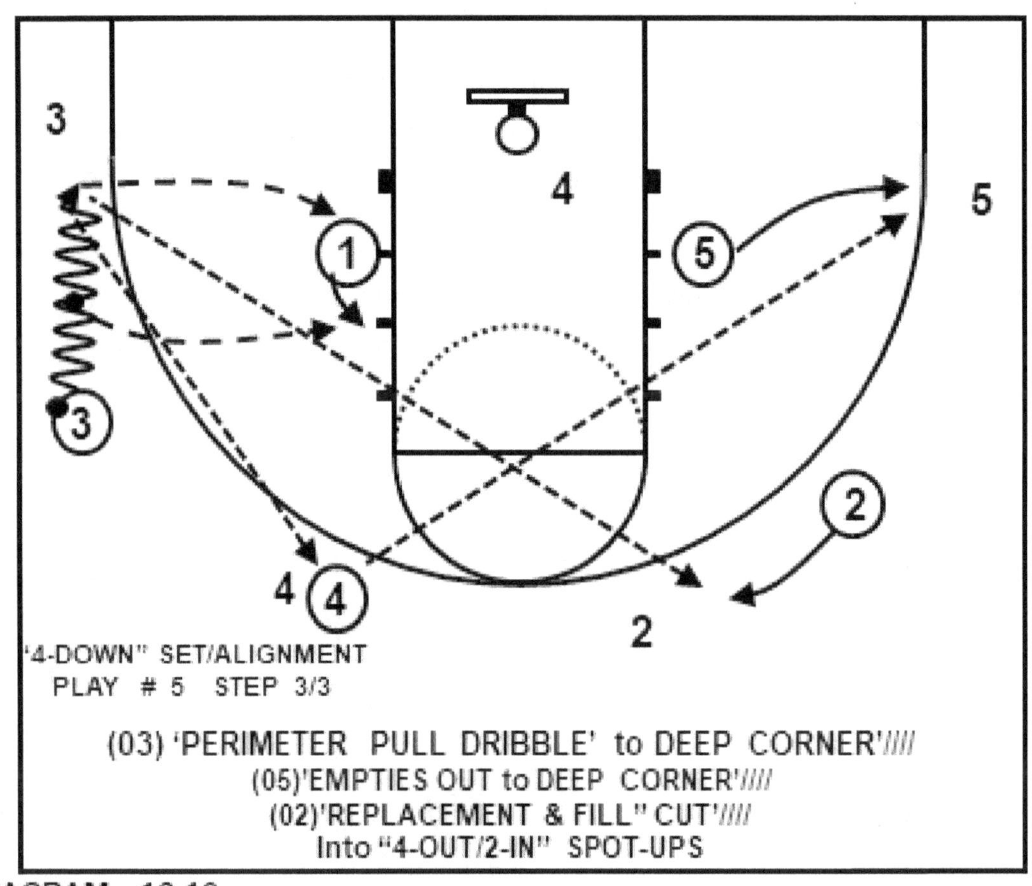

DIAGRAM   16.10

The main difference in this family of plays plays/entries are that all five players will end up in a different group of offensive spot-ups. These "HIGH-POST/LOW-POST" Spot-Ups will have players moved about the court with any of the five ending up in the "Ballside Block," the "Ballside High Post," the "Ballside Wing," the "Weakside Wing," and the "Point" (or top of the guy)" Though different from the other two sets of offensive spot-ups, these spot-ups can also allow continuity offenses that utilize these spot-ups with the same ball-reversals, driving gaps for dribble penetration, opportunities to deliver the ball inside to two different ballside post pass receiving locations as well as an excellent perimeter shooting location on the weakside of the of the offense. The spot-ups again offer some very strong weakside rebounding opportunities from the perimeter.   Defensive conversion should still be good with a fundamentally strong scheme.

Play # 6 is another Level 2 play that is executed out of the "4-DOWN" Set, but if no shots are taken, the five offensive players have repositioned themselves into the correct "HIGH-POST/LOW-POST" Spot-Ups. This allows this specific play and any other plays that end up in these particular positions to immediately and smoothly flow into an entirely different continuity offense.

Diagram 16.11 shows the beginning of Play # 6 that appears to be similar to Plays 4 and 5, even though this particular play is in an entirely different package of plays (all that flow into various continuity offenses that originate from the "HIGH-POST/LOW-POST" Spot-Ups. Again, because of the symmetry of the "4-DOWN" Offensive Set, each play could be executed to either side of the floor.

In this diagram, 01 elects to dribble towards the right side of the floor with 02 rotates up towards 01. At the same time, 04 makes his usual aggressive isolated "Duck-In Cut," into the middle of the lane. If 01 does not make the quick pass to 04, he intersects with 02 to make a DHO with 02. Diagram 16.11.

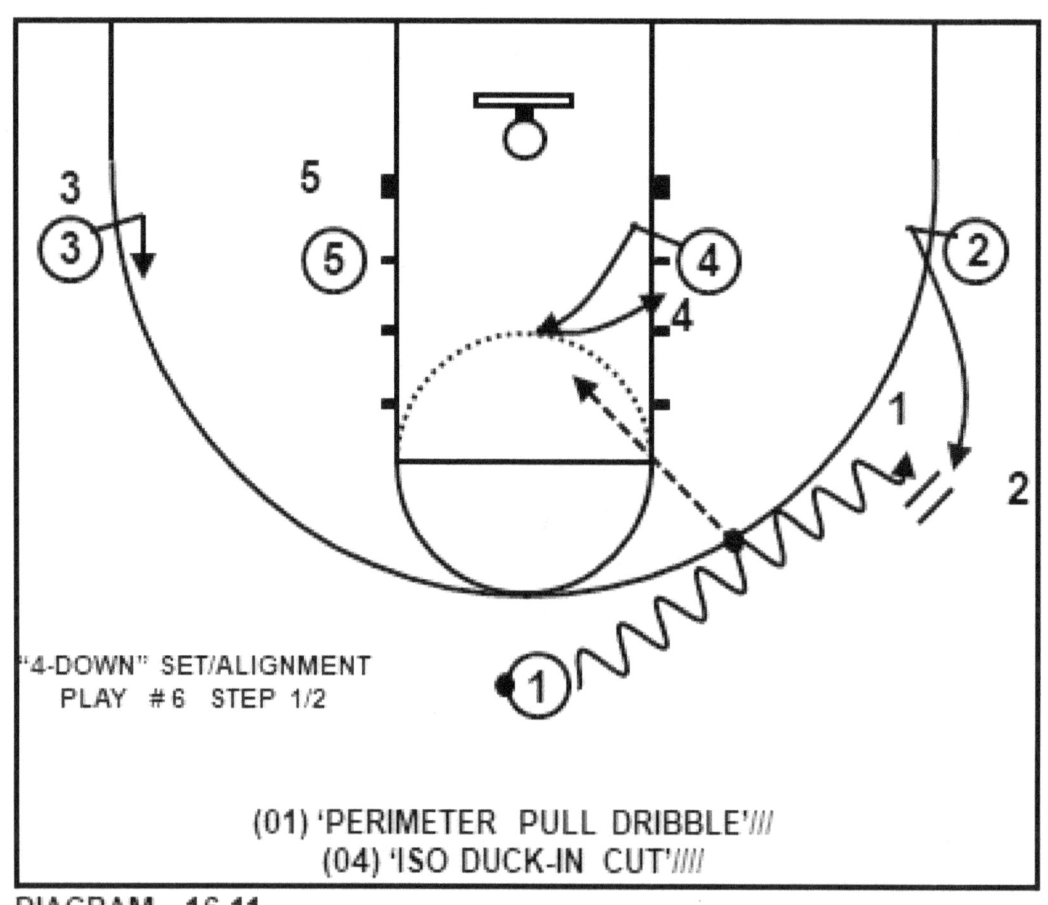

DIAGRAM 16.11

As 02 takes the hand-off and makes a perimeter pull dribble towards the top of the key, 03 breaks directly up to the FT Line extended and looks to receive 02's "Wing Pass." When this pass is denied, 05 makes a "Vertical Up Cut" up to the new "Weakside High Post" area to receive the ball from 02. 03 then makes the "Backdoor Cut" to the basket. The action mainly between 05 and 03 is offensive action called the "Blind Pig" action. To further isolate 03 now down on the "Block," 04 breaks up diagonally towards 02 at the top of the key.

02 makes the pass to either 03 or to 05 and immediately breaks to the empty "Wing" area at the FT Line extended. With 03 inverted and isolated down on the new "Ballside Block," 04 now at the top of the key and 02 now at the "Wing," and 01 remaining at the new "Weakside Wing," the "HIGH-POST/LOW-POST" Spot-Ups are filled for a continuous and fluid transition from this "Blind Pig" play immediately into a designated continuity offense. Diagram 16.12.

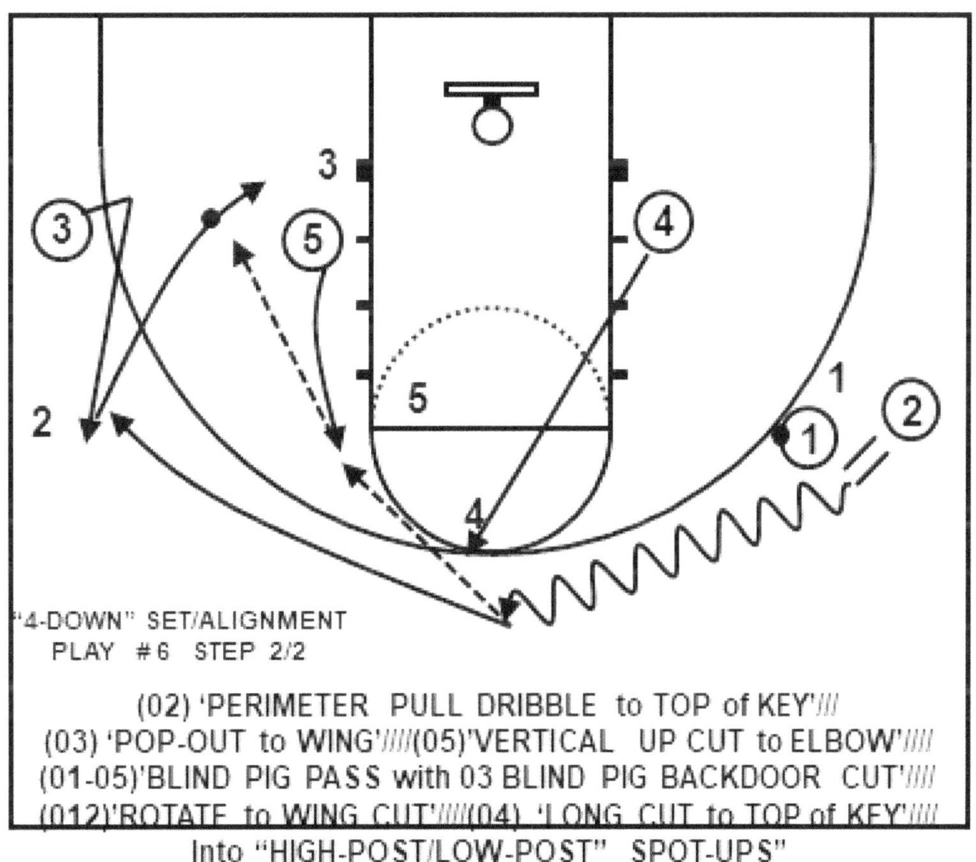

DIAGRAM 16.12

Diagram 16.13 illustrates Play # 7, another Level 2 play, with different action beginning with various types of action compared to previous plays. After 04 diagonally breaks up across the lane to the opposite "High Post, 03 makes an "Iverson Cut" from his left "Deep Corner" position over the top of 04 and on over to the opposite "Wing" location.

At the same time, 02 runs the baseline and makes his "Iverson Cut" from his "Deep Corner under 05 and out to the opposite "Wing." Diagram 16.13

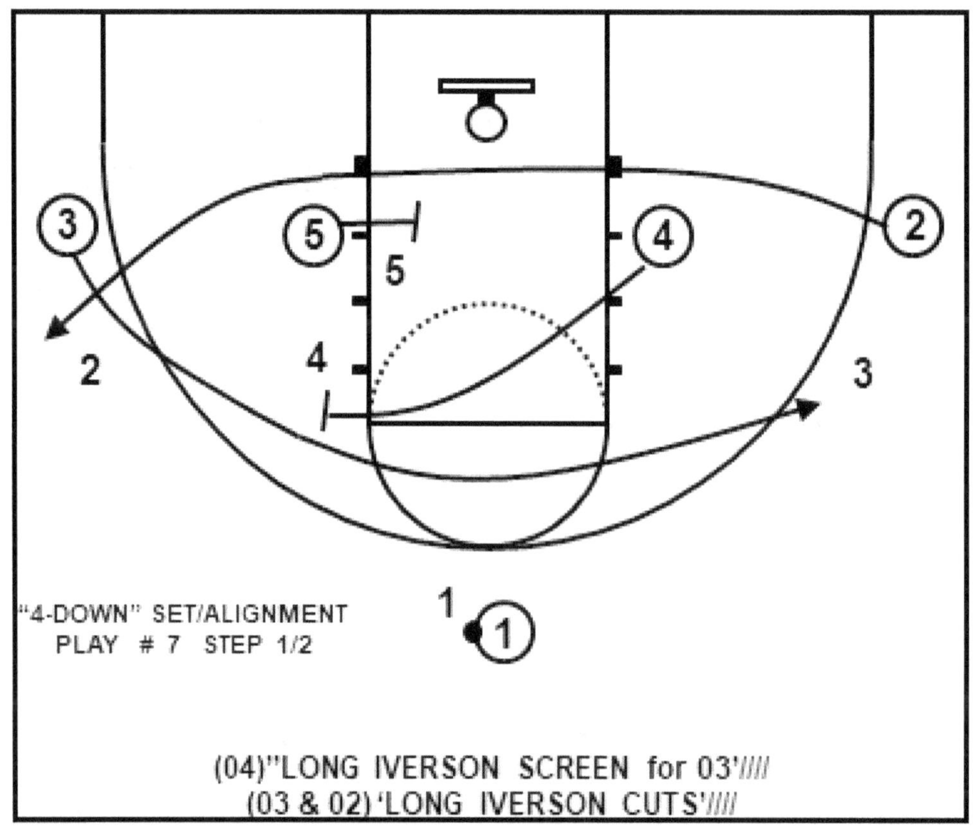

DIAGRAM   16.13

Diagram 16.14 illustrates one of the two options 01 has. While he could immediately make the "Wing Pass" to 02 and place players in the proper "HIGH-POST/LOW-POST" Spot-Ups with 02 looking to make passes primarily to 05 or to 04 on the interior or a "Skip Pass" to 03 on the "Weakside Wing," or a simple "Reverse Pass" immediately back to 01 at the top of the key.

The option shown in the diagram has 01 make the initial "Wing Pass" to 03, possibly because 02 could be denied the (01-02) "Wing Pass" with an aggressive X2. Using that denial pressure on 02 works to the offense's advantage when 01 makes the pass to 03.

There, 02 quickly scrapes off of 04's top left shoulder with 04's "Big-on-Small Shuffle Back-Screen" and diagonally cuts through the lane to the new "Ballside Block." Using the proper timing, 05 then diagonally flashes across the lane from low side to the high side with his "High Post Flash Cut."

After the pass is made by 01, 04 then slips his screen for 02 and steps up to set a "Big-on-Small Flare-Screen" for 01 to then "Flare-Cut" to the newly designated "Weakside Wing," with 04 then slipping the screen to the top of the key. If interior shots (to 02 or 05) or perimeter shots by (03, 01 or 04) are not taken, the "HIGH-POST/LOW-POST" Spot-Ups are filled. If no shots are taken, the designated continuity offense could smoothly and immediately begin.   Diagram 16. 14.

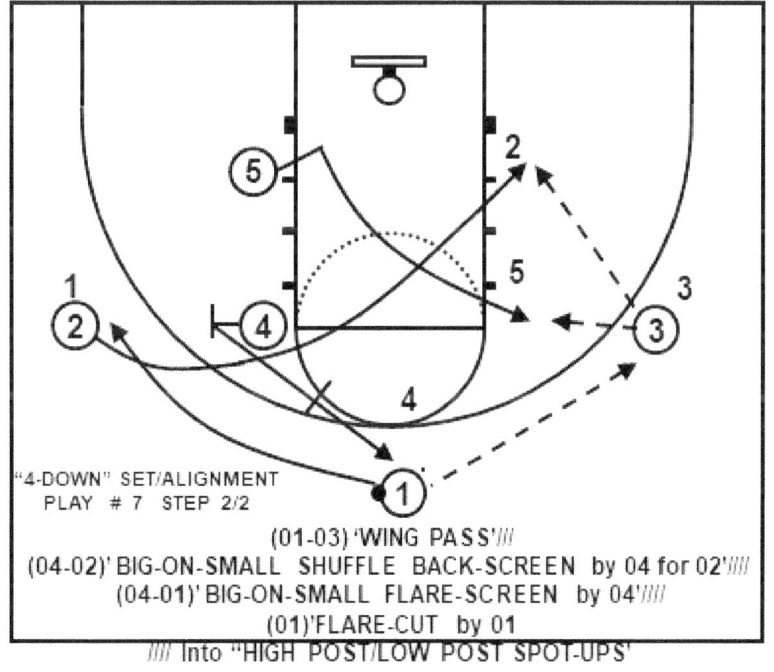

DIAGRAM 16.14

Play # 8 is a Counter to Play # 7 in that the initial action is identical to the beginning movements of Play # 17. Once again, 04 is the post player that seemingly is the non-threatening scoring player that simply flashes to the high post area to become an "Iverson Screener" for 03 to use again. 03 breaks up and around 04 to end up on the same right "Wing" area. 02 runs the baseline and cuts off of 05's lower shoulder as he makes the same "Iverson Cut" as in the previous play. 05 again sets the same "Iverson Screen" for 02 to use to break to the same "Wing" area at the FT Line extended on the opposite side of the floor. Diagram 16.15

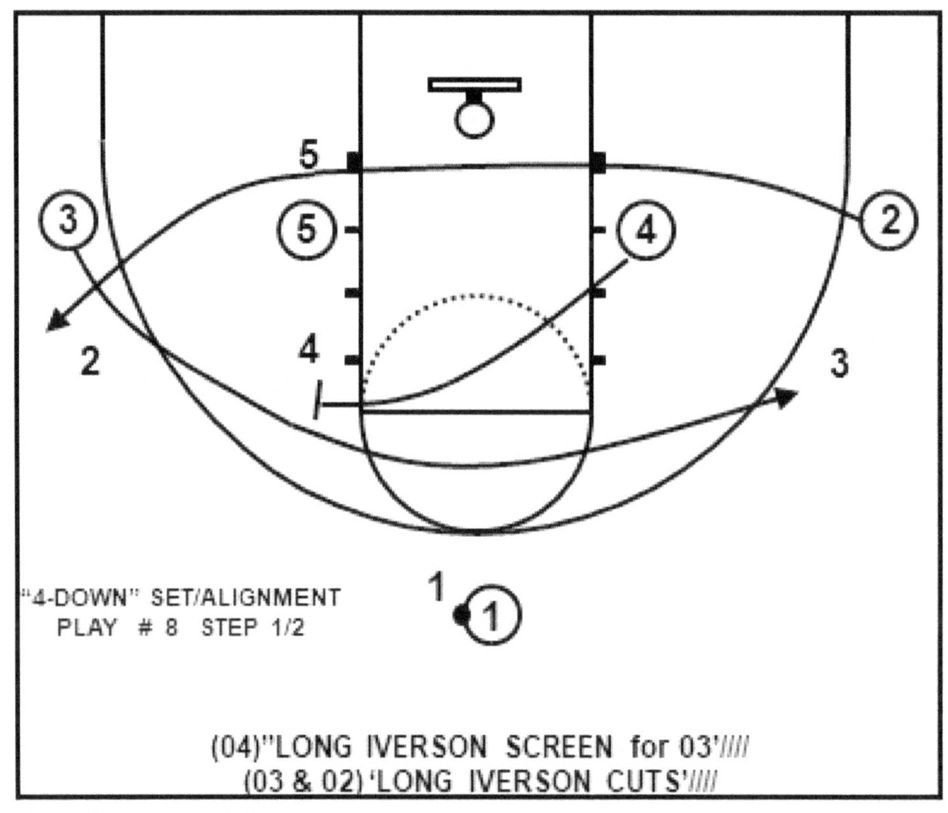

DIAGRAM 16.15

On this play, 01 makes the pass to 02 and immediately 05 steps up to "head-hunt" the unsuspecting X4 for a modified form of a "UCLA Back-Screen," with 04 receiving 05's surprise screen and cutting to the new "Ballside Block." 05 then remains at the new "Ballside High-Post. To occupy any semblance of interior support defense as well as to give 02 two perimeter scoring threat pass receivers, 03 steps up to set a "Flare Back-Screen" for 01 to use after making the (01-02) "Wing Pass." Both players becoming legitimate perimeter scoring threats with 04 becoming the primary interior scoring threat.

If shots are not taken, all five players are already in the proper "HIGH-POST/LOW-POST" Spot-Ups" for the final phase of the offense to fluidly begin. Diagram 16.16

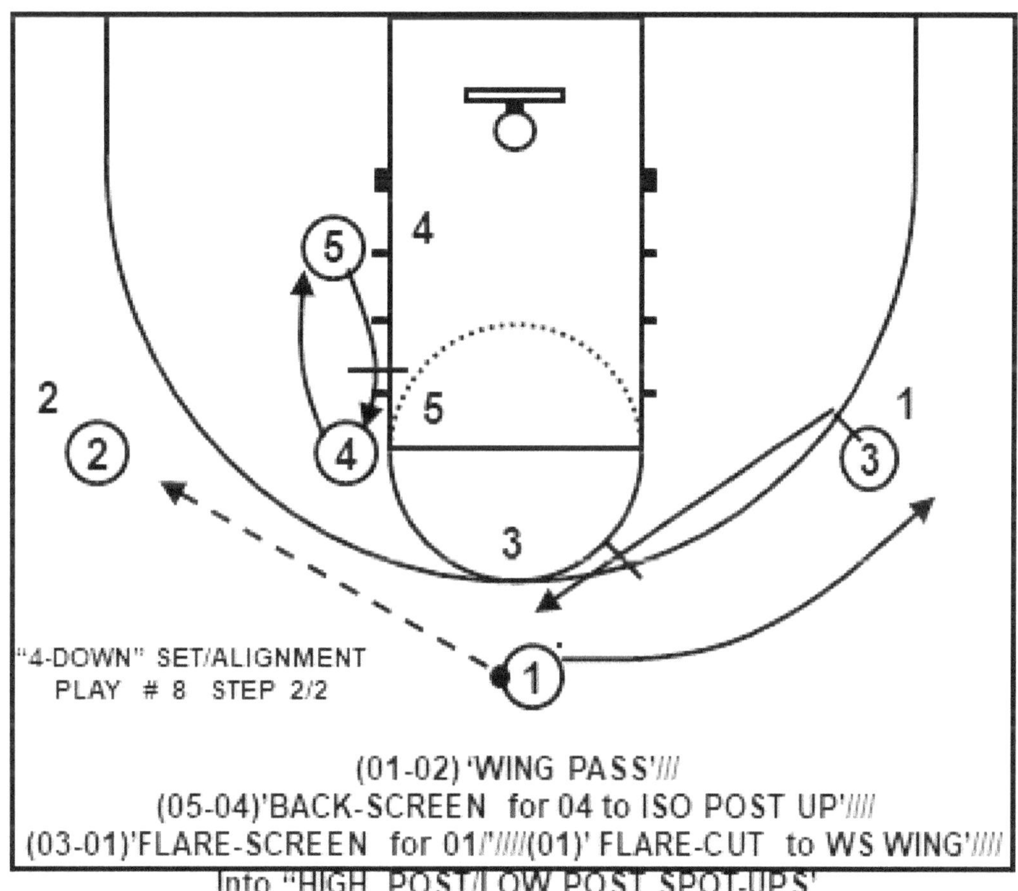

DIAGRAM 16.16

Play # 9 is another Level 2 play that begins in Diagram 16.17. While the play could be executed to either side, this diagram shows the play being started on the left side of the floor with 03 breaking up to set a "Big-on-Small Long Ball-Screen" for 01 to use to "perimeter-pull dribble to the offense's left "Wing" area at the FT Line extended.

At the same time that 01 breaks contact with 03's top right shoulder, 02 has sprinted up to the top of the key to set a "Small-on-Big (Flare-)Screen the (Ball-)Screener for 03 to use to continue to the new "Weakside Wing." 02 then remains at the top of the key after slipping his screen for 03. There, 03 and 02 become credible and realistic '3 Pt.' Scoring threats in their new 'spot-up' locations.

Also, simultaneously, 05 spins out to set a "Big-on-Small Lane Exchange Cross-Screen" for 04 to rub his defender off of 05's screen. Dependent upon how X4 is playing 04, 04 could "fake low and scrape high off of 05's top right shoulder to flash across the lane to the new "Ballside Block," or 04 could "fake high and scrape low off of 05's low left shoulder to reach the same "Block." 01's primary targets are to make the "Inside Pass" to 04 or a "Skip Pass" to 03. Diagram 16.17.

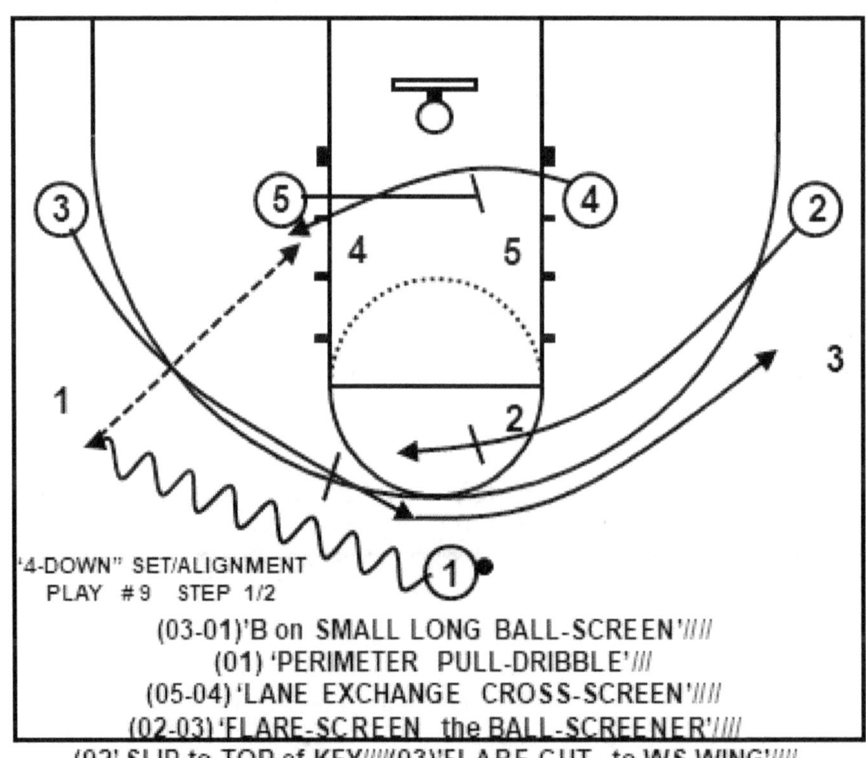

DIAGRAM 16.17

If 01 does not have the shot and elects not to make passes to either 04 or to 03 for quick "catch and scores" action, 01 can reverse the ball to 02 now at the top of the key. If not open for his own '3 Pt.' shot, 02 could swing the ball quickly over to 03 for a possible shot of his own.

If no shots are taken, 05 turns as if to set another "Lane Exchange Cross-Screen." 04 could then scrape off of either shoulder to flash to the new "Ballside" of the lane. He has the option again of cutting off either shoulder. The difference is that 05 will set the screen for 04 and then flash back to either the "Block" or to the "High Post," the opposite spot that 04 has gone. In this case, 04 scrapes off of 05's top left shoulder and flashes to the new "Ballside High Post," with 05 then reversing off of his lower right foot to open up to the ball and then flashing to the new "Ballside Block."

To eliminate any possible helpside defense, 01 again steps up to set a "Small-on-Big Back Flare-Screen" for 02 to use to "Flare-Cut" to the new "Weakside Wing" on the left side of the floor. If no interior shots are open (to 05 and 04) and no perimeter shots (to 02 or to 01) are available, the same "HIGH-POST/LOW-POST" Spot-Ups are again filled for a quick and fluid transition into the final phase of the relentless attack on the defense. Diagram 16.18.

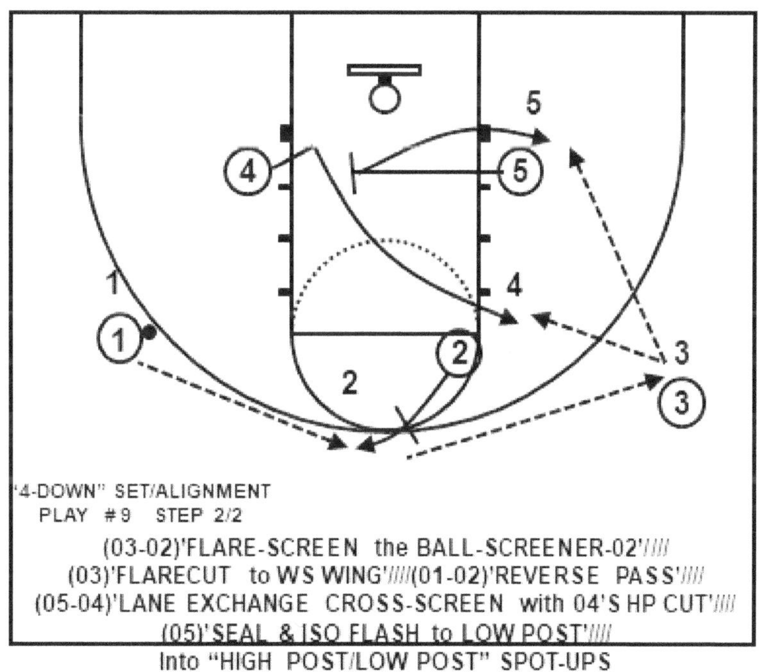

DIAGRAM 16.18

While this play could be executed first with 03 and 01 on the right side, Diagram 16.19 illustrates Play # 10 to the right side. 02 sprints up to set a "Long Ball-Screen" for 01 near the "Slot" area and while 01 "dribble-scrapes" off of 02's top left shoulder, 01 looks to make the "Inside Pass" to 04 on his "Isolated Duck-In Cut" in the middle of the "Dotted Circle" area.

To help isolate X4, 05 makes a "Vertical Up Cut" towards the newly declared "Weakside High Post with 03 also breaking vertically up to the new "Weakside Wing" area. After screening for 01 and 01 dribbling to the new "Ballside Slot," , 02 slips and screen to make a small "Flare-Cut" to the new "Weakside Slot" area. Diagram 16.19

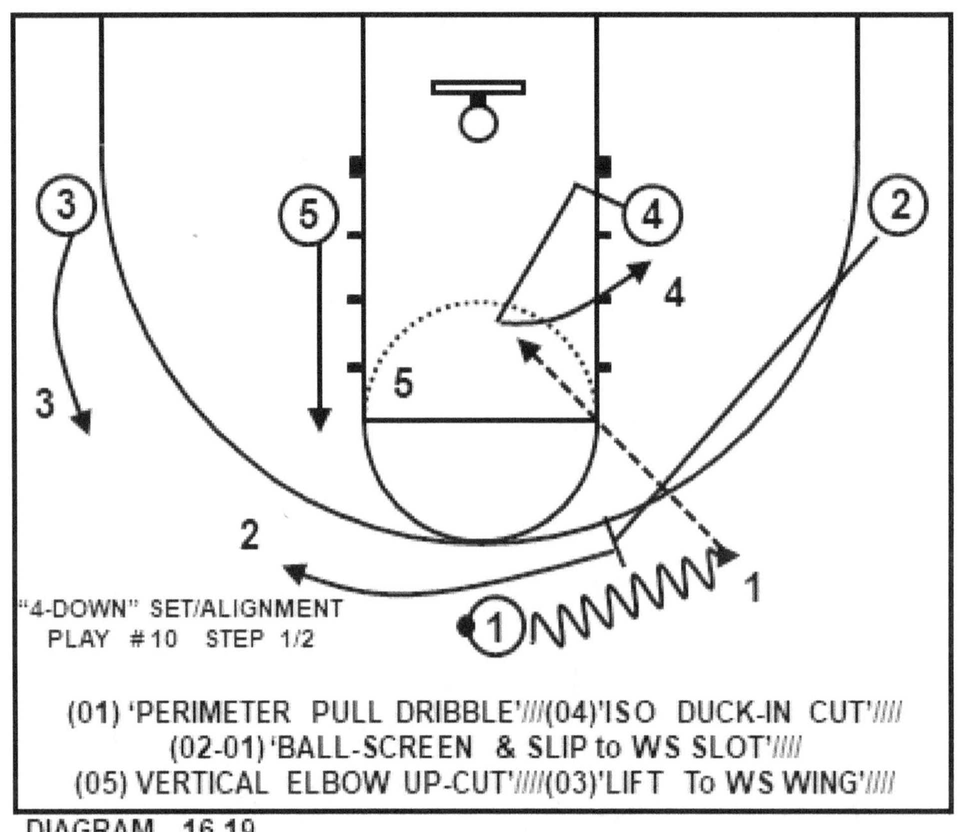

DIAGRAM 16.19

If 01 cannot hit 04 for an isolated score in the middle of the lane and does not have an opportunity to create, he makes the short "Reverse Pass" to 02. 02 immediately swings the ball on over to 03 and with 05 at the "High-Post" on the same side as 03 and 05, 02 uses 05 to rub his defender off and make an inverted "UCLA Cut" to the new "Ballside Mid-Post." This places X2, a perimeter defender, into an unfamiliar and uncomfortable defensive situation.

02 should read his defender and scrape off of either shoulder, dependent upon how X2 and X5 play the action. To then isolate 02's defender even more so, 04 breaks up from his position to the top of the key, stretching the interior defense and allowing 02 to also isolate his defender.

An option or a Counter Play that could easily and quickly be added would be for 02 to make the pass to 03 and then "Bump" 05 so that 05 becomes the new "UCLA Cutter/Iso Post-Up player.

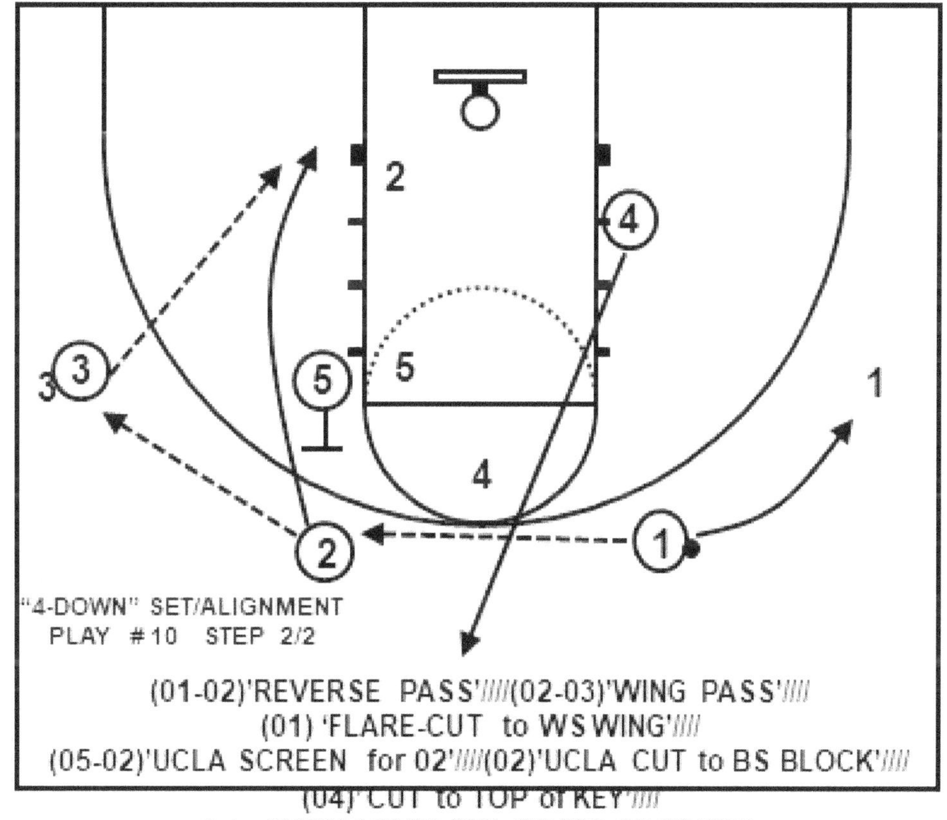

Diagram 16.20

In this Play # 11, either post player is the designated "Long Ball-Screener," dependent upon which side of the floor is the chosen side. Diagram 16.21 shows the play starting to the right side of the floor, therefore having 04 break up from his initial position to set the "Big-on-Small Long Ball-Screen."

01 "dribble-scrapes" off of 04's top left shoulder while 05 makes a custom "Vertical Up Cut" to the opposite "perimeter-like" "Slot" that pulls up his "big" defender away from the basket. With 05 being the logical "Reverse Pass" Recipient, X5 could put some denial pressure on 05 in this somewhat uncomfortable area.

Therefore, when 02 breaks into the lane and diagonally up to set a surprise "Small-on-Big Diagonal Back-Screen for 05 to use, 05 then scrapes off of 02's outside right shoulder and cuts diagonally to the new "Ballside Block" on the right side of the lane.

After screening for 05, 02 has ended up in the middle of the lane, while 03 has lifted his defender up to the new "Weakside Wing" and 04 has slipped his screen for 01 to end up at the top of the key. Diagram 16.21.

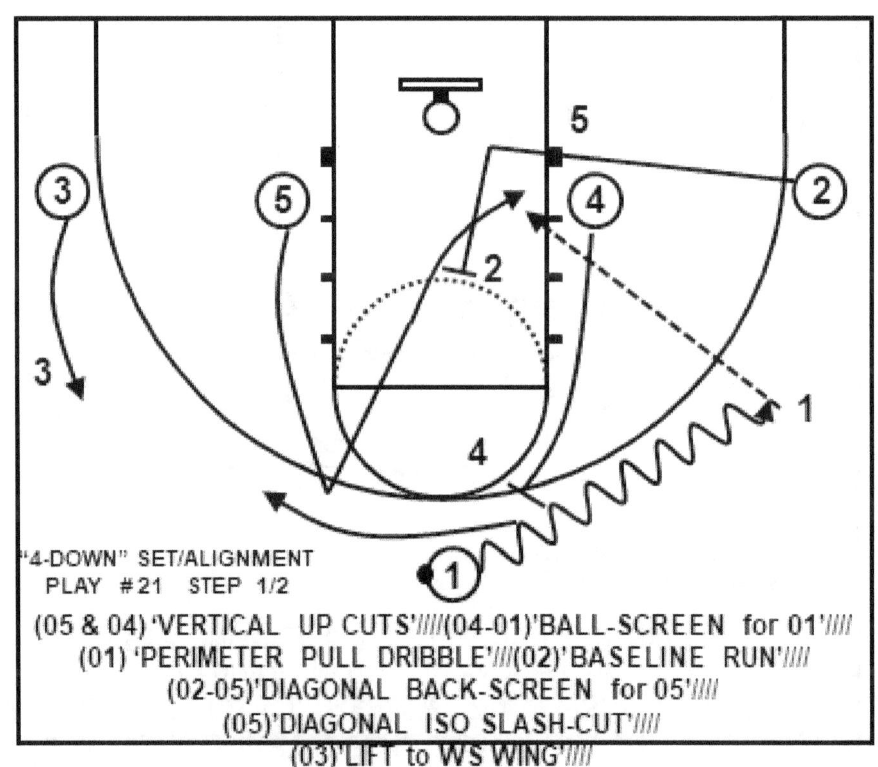

Diagram 16.21

After 01 has looked to make the pass to 05 and turned it down, 04 has quickly stepped into the lane to set a "Big-on-Small (Pin-)Screen the (Back-)Screener for 02 to step out to the top of the key for an open '3 Pt.' After screening for 02, 04 slips his screen and flashes to the "Ballside High Post" as an additional scoring threat. 03 remains spotted up on the "Weakside Wing," continually stretching the opposition and weakening the interior defense.

If shots are not taken, the same "HIGH-POST/LOW-POST" Spot-Ups are filled so that the designated continuity offense can fluidly and seamlessly begin. Diagram 16.22.

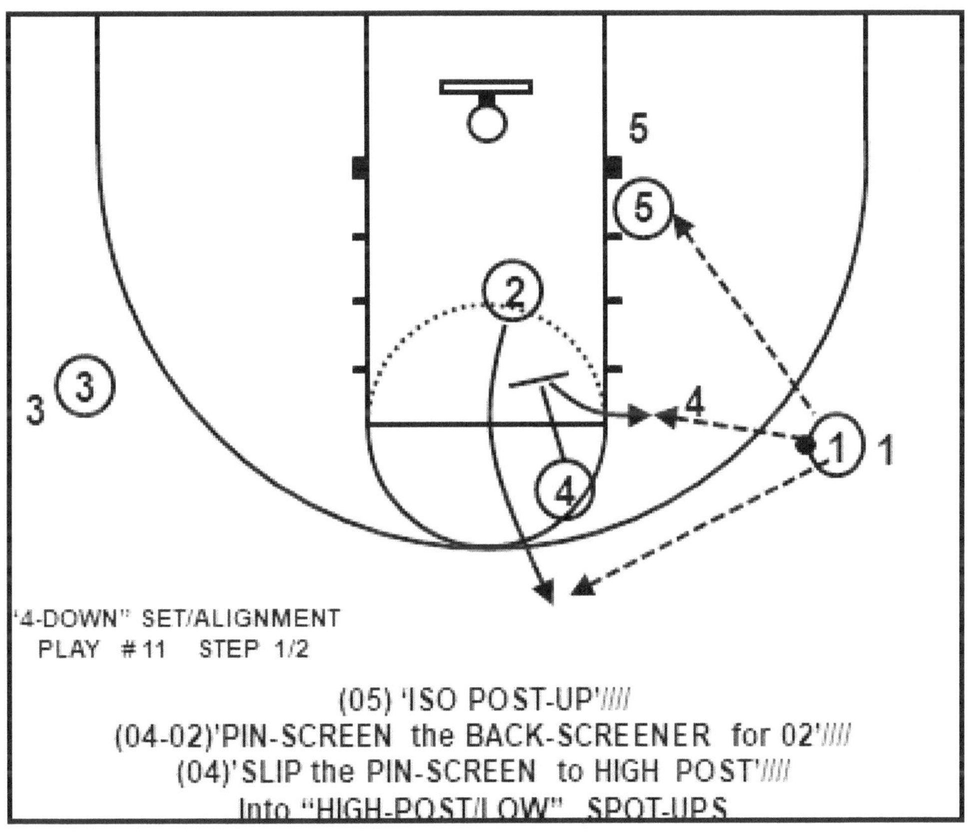

Diagram 16.22

As stated previously, the "4-DOWN" Set is a symmetrically balance d offensive alignment that allows the offense to attack either side of the floor in the very same manner. This gives the offense another advantage of unpredictability. Flattening out the defense with four offensive players along the baseline also gives 01 the freedom and spacing to individually attack his own solo defender, allowing for specific offensive advantages when they present itself. 03 and 02, spotted up in their respective "deep corners" allows the offense to maximize "catch and shoot" players that may not have the offensive skills to create their own shots, particularly off of the dribble. Having two offensive players on the two respective "blocks" allows the offense to have constant interior scoring threats. Creative coaches can use a variety of actions to then use any of the four 'off-the-ball' players to break out towards the FT Lines extended on their own side of the floor as well as to utilize the many different types of "Long Ball-Screens" with the various ending types of actions that can be used after the screen has been set for 01. This makes the "4-DOWN" Set an unpredictable and multiple type of action scoring alignment.

.

There are many different philsophies on how to attack opposing defenses. This multiple-phase offensive system uses more than one phase/layer/wave of attack, with each phase/wave having a seamless and immediate conversion into the next phase/wave. While this system can be confusing to defenses and difficult to defend, this system can be properly taught and coached so that it can be easily understood and ultimately executed by players of many different levels of (physical talent, mental understand and playing experience.)

In addition, there are several types of offensive schemes and different ways within this system that offenses can attack their defensive counter-parts. Many of these can be integrated within the same offensive system that can attack defenses in various ways. The larger the number of schemes that can be successfully utilized and integrated within the same system, the greater the opportunity an offensive team can find the most efficient and productive schemes that can place both individual and the overall team in the best and most frequent "positions to succeed."

The plays/entries carefully diagrammed down to the small and seemingly unimportant 'V-Cuts' made by countless players before making their more important following cut are also described in detail.

Each play has been carefully studied and evaluated to determine which level of talent and experience must be possessed for that specific team to be able to successfully execute the play. This includes all players' physical skills as well as their mental understanding of the game. Coaches must also have the experience and the associated level of understanding of the game as well as their coaching/teaching of the nuances of each play.

The most sophisticated plays/entries would fall into the first of the three levels all based on the team's physical talents and skills, the mental capacities and the overall team's game experience. In addition, the coaching staff must have a high degree of basketball knowledge as well as very high teaching and coaching skills to educate his/her entire basketball team. The proper breakdown drills must be thoroughly utilized to hone the fundamental skills and techniques needed for individual players and the overall team to execute plays that can be efficient, productive and successful. We define this family of plays as the "Level 3 category" of plays. This "Level 3" family of plays will have a much more complex offensive scheme that would require a very high amount of physical talent as well as a greater amount of the players (to execute) and the coaches (to teach and coach) mental capacities and experience needed for the offense to be efficient, productive and successful. We feel plays in our defined "Level 3" category could possibly be successful for NBA teams, definitely for college teams and also for many high schools and older AAU teams.

The next classification or level of plays would possibly be slightly lower as far as sophistication, complexity and the actual 'length' of the play (and the number of passes, cuts and screens used) in the play's overall scheme. While all "Level 2" plays in each of the chapters in this book remain fundamentally sound, these plays may lack the actual number of techniques/methods that are implemented within that play in comparison to the "Level 1" plays/entries. Therefore, any team that successfully executes the highest "Level 1" plays/entries could/should easily be able to execute any of these so-called lower "Level

2" plays/entries, if so desired. Almost all high school teams should be able to execute successfully all aspects of the "Level 2" plays.

The final grouping of plays would be called "Level 1" plays and are not as difficult for offensive players to master the execution of them, both physically as well as mentally. Even though the techniques are still fundamentally, they may not be as complex to learn and understand in addition to being easier to physically execute.

"Level 1" plays would be lower in the scheme's complexities and the number of techniques used in the execution of this category of plays. Obviously, since these "Level 1" plays are still sound, but lack some of the methods used in the two previous more sophisticated and complex levels; these more elementary plays should be able to be utilized by any teams that use either of the two higher level plays. We feel that Middle School/Junior High teams as well as younger AAU teams or organizations, should be able to utilize any of the "Level 1" plays successfully, with a possibility that some of those teams that are slightly more advanced (than other teams) could possibly use some plays located in the immediate next immediate level.

Ideas, concepts and techniques that will help prove these entries can be successfully used. This allows the author to create numerous plays that use the various schemes to build a library of fundamentally sound plays that will be unique and will be appropriate for the wide range of teams with various ages and skill levels.

With this book having plays in these three presumed categories or levels, the book will reach out and benefit a much larger group of serious basketball coaches from elementary school age to the highest skilled levels that exists.

In addition, an experienced and resourceful coach may be able to mold some plays that include all of the offensive techniques that he/she desires could reshape a specific play that begins in one specific offensive set/alignment and reshape it so that it could begin in a different offensive/set that is more favorable to that coach and his/her coaching staff's liking.

Conversely, that innovative and creative coach may completely like the specific offensive set/alignment and favor the very same offensive actions included in a certain play, but can modify that play so that the ending spot-ups of all five players are conducive to being able to begin the final phase of the offensive attack by using a more favorable offensive continuity offense.

PLAYS/ENTRIES THAT END in the "3-OUT/2-IN" OFFENSIVE SPOT-UPS

After the entry/play/quick-hitter has been executed but no shots have been taken, all five players will end up in a different group of offensive spot-ups. These "3-Out/2-In Spot-Ups" will have players moved about the court with any of the five ending up in the "Ballside Block," the "Ballside Wing," the "Weakside Block," the "Weakside Wing," and the "Point" (at the top of the key). These five positions can provide the offense with safe and easy types of ball-reversals, large gaps for dribble penetration, opportunities to deliver the ball inside to whomever (perimeter-type or post-type players) is posting up their defender on the "Ballside Block," and a player that can be a perimeter-scoring threat and a legitimate offensive rebounding threat from outside of the arc on his "offensive crashing of the boards." The "3-Out/2-In Spot-Ups also provide ample opportunities for constant and effective defensive transition responsibilities.

The "HORNS" SET/ALIGNMENT

The "HORNS" Set is another symmetrically balanced offensive set as the offense positions 03 and 02 in the two opposite "Deep Corners" outside of the arc and along the baseline on an imaginary line that would extend from one side and "Block" to the opposite "Block and out to the sideline. This action spreads those defenders from sideline to sideline and also vertically flattens out the defense, but not so deep towards the baseline that there isn't room for 03 and 02 to create and attack towards the baseline.

The two offensive "Bigs," 05 and 04 start at the "Elbow" positions on both sides of the floor. They immediately are high enough to force the two defensive "Big Counterparts," X5 and X4 to be a good distance from the basket, to also be in positions to easily and quickly set ball-screens for 01 to use, to be able to pin down-screens for their respective teammate below them in the "Deep Corner" as well as to be able to flash (and isolate) their defender to the "Block" on the opposite side of the lane. With two players on each side of the lane plus 01 with the ball centered up; there is no designated initial strong and weak side of the offense, meaning that every quick-hitter/play/entry could actually be run towards either side of the floor. With each play being able to be executed towards either side of the floor, the number within the family of plays doubles without the actual complexity level increasing to a high degree.

Play # 1 is Level 3 play that is fully diagrammed in Diagrams 17.1 through 17.4. While the play could be 'mirrored' the opposite direction, this time 03 is the player that makes the "Iverson Cut" over the top of both 05 and 04 to the "Wing" on the right side of the floor, while 02 runs the baseline before curling out to the opposite "Wing" area. Both 05 and 04 remain at the respective "Elbow" positions after their "Iverson Screens" are set for 03. **Diagram 17.1**.

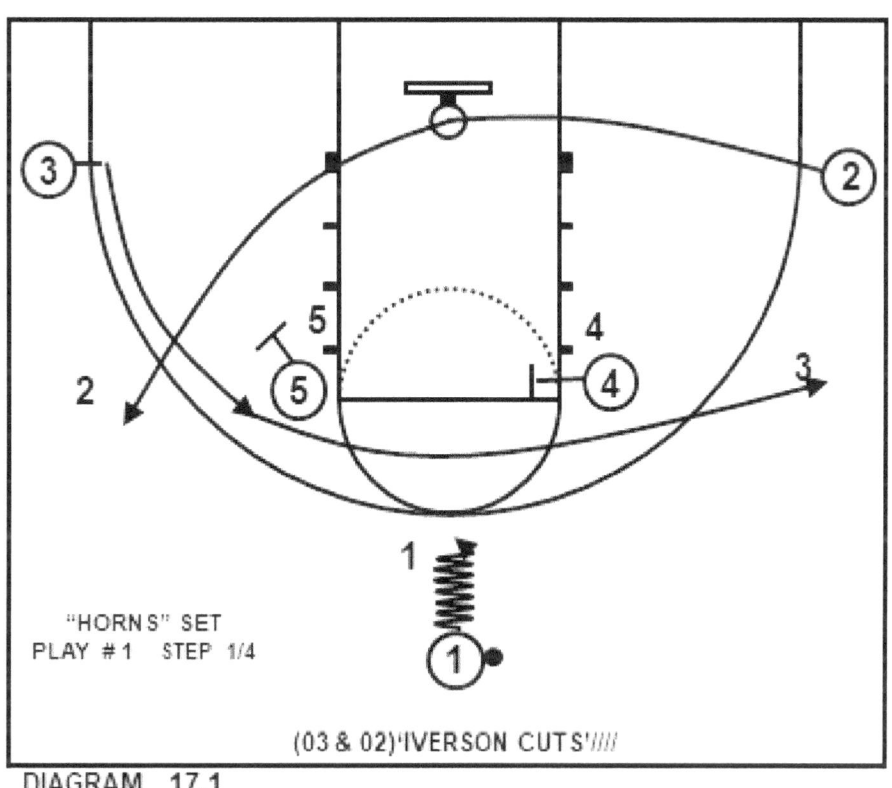

DIAGRAM 17.1

With 03 and 02 making their "Iverson Cuts" to the opposite sides of the floor, the repositioning of these two players still makes the new repositioning a symmetrically balanced alignment. Therefore, with 01 having the ball still centered up; the initial attack could be executed towards either side of the floor.

In this case, 01 makes the pass to 02 on the left side of the floor. 01 immediately makes a "UCLA Cut" off of 05's UCLA Back-Screen at the left "Elbow." 01 should read his defender and then scrape off of either the outside right or the inside left shoulder before cutting towards the "Ballside Block."

At the same time, 04 steps out from his "Elbow" location to the new "Weakside Slot" to pull the presumed second biggest defender, X4, further from the ball and from the basket. **Diagram 17.2**.

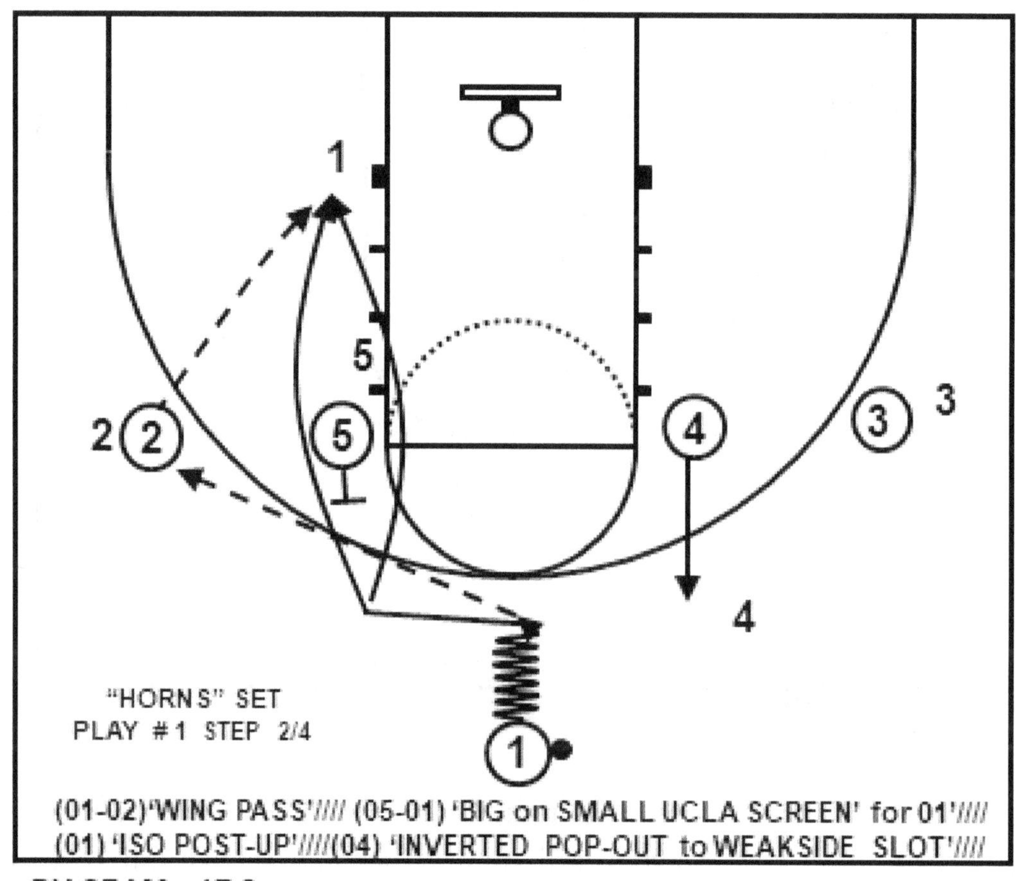

DIAGRAM 17.2

If 02 or 01 do not take the shot, 05 steps out to set a "Big-on-Small Inside Ball-Screen" for 02 to use to "penetrate dribble" or to "perimeter-pull dribble" out towards the top of the key. As 02 breaks contact with 05, 05 "reverse pivots off of his right foot" to "open up to the ball" and rolls diagonally through the lane to post up on the opposite side of the lane. If 02 cannot make the "Inside Pass" off of his dribble, 02 should make the pass to 04 (who may possess the proper angle to provide the ball to 05 on his continued cut across the lane.) **Diagram 17.3**.

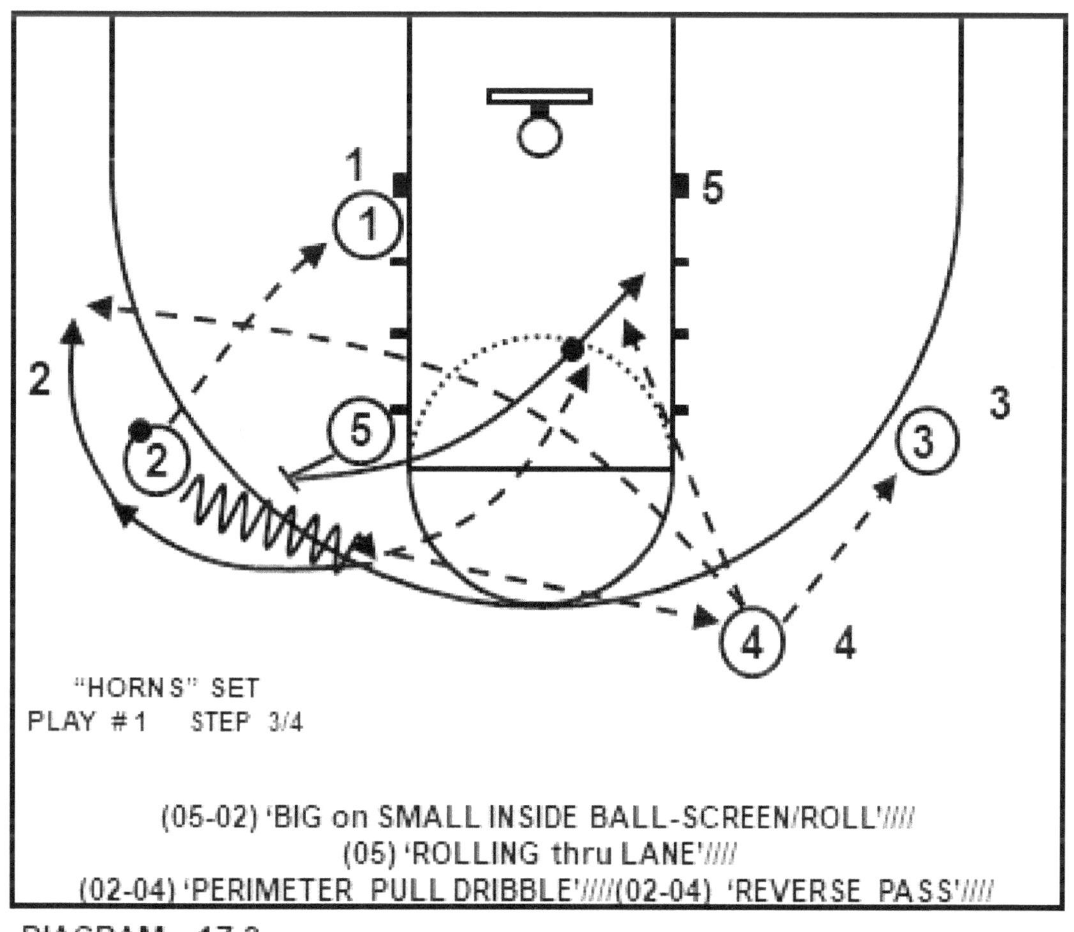

DIAGRAM 17.3

If 04 does not have the angle and opportunity to make the "Inside Pass" to 05, 03 may be the player that can make the pass. After 04 makes the "Wing Pass" to 03, 04 takes one step towards the ball before breaking down diagonally to set a "Big-on-Small Diagonal Pin-Screen" for 01 to use to break up to the top of the key. This (04-01) screen accomplished three objectives: it minimizes weakside defense that 05 can take advantage of, it gives 03 a second perimeter shot passing target (along with 02 on the "Weakside Wing,") and it helps fill all five the "3-Out/2-In" Spot-Ups for a smooth conversion into the last phase of the offense. **Diagram 17.4**.

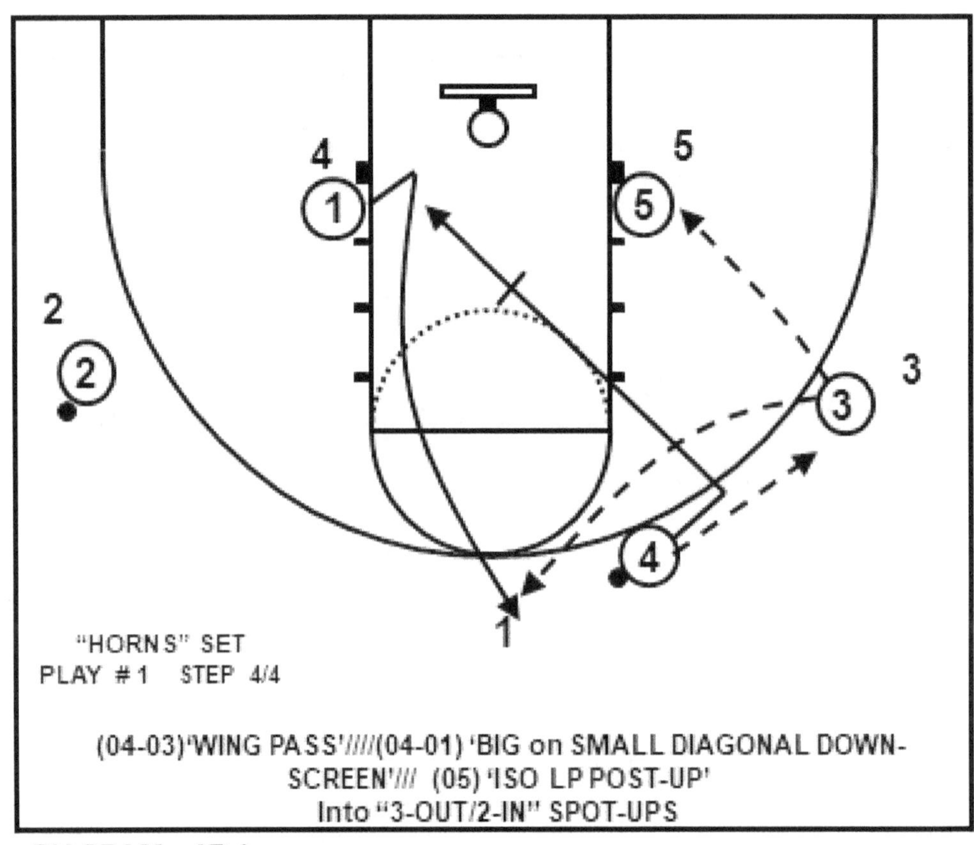

DIAGRAM 17.4

PLAYS/ENTRIES THAT END in the "4-OUT/1-IN" OFFENSIVE SPOT-UPS

The difference in the following plays/entries are that all five players will end up in a different group of offensive spot-ups. These "4-Out/1-In Spot-Ups" will have players moved about the court with any of the five ending up in the "Ballside Deep Corner," the "Ballside Slot," the "Weakside Slot," the "Ballside Post," and the "Weakside Deep Corner." These five positions can provide the offense with safe and easy types of ball-reversals, large gaps for dribble penetration, opportunities to deliver the ball inside to whomever (perimeter-type or post-type players) is posting up their defender on the "Ballside Block," and a player that can be a perimeter-scoring threat and a legitimate offensive rebounding threat from outside of the arc on his "offensive crashing of the boards." The "4-Out/1-In Spot-Ups also provide ample opportunities for constant and effective defensive transition responsibilities.

Diagram 17.5 illustrates Play # 2, a Level 1 play with 04 the designated player (instead of 05) stepping up to set a "Big-on-Small Ball-Screen/Roll" for 01 to use to dribble to the new "Ballside Slot." On the newly designated "Weakside" of the, 05 pops out to the new "Weakside Slot" while 03 starts to break up before then slipping back down to the new "Weakside Deep Corner." 02 remains spotted up in his initial "Deep Corner." This action stretches the opposition's defense both north/south and east/west; therefore isolating 04 even more in the lane. If the "Inside Pass" to 04, if a "Down Pass" to 02, or a "Skip Pass" to 03 are not able to be made; the "3-Out/2-In" Spot-Ups are filled for an instant transition into the designated continuity offense. **Diagram 17.5.**

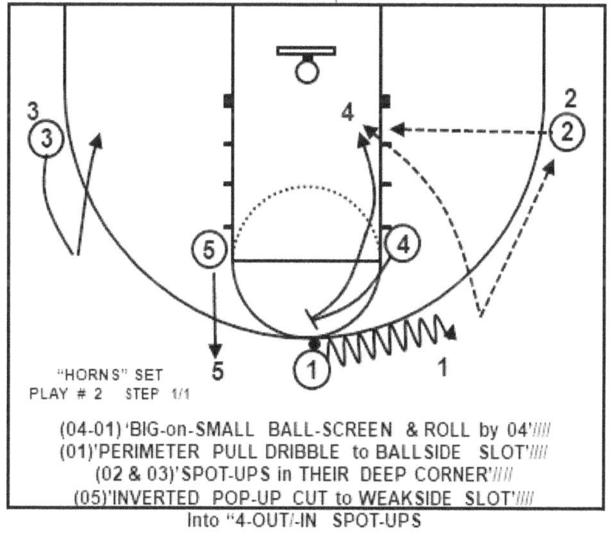

Play # 2   Diagram 17.5

Play # 3 is a Level 2 play that is also run out of the "HORNS" Set, but if shots are not taken will reposition players into the different "4-Out/1-In" Spot-Ups. This will allow various continuity offenses to immediately begin.

It is designated that 05 is the player that steps just outside of the arc on top with 03 breaking up towards the FT Line extended. 01 makes the pass to 05 and starts to break down to set a "Diagonal Stagger-Screen" with 04 for 02 to use to break out towards the "Slot" position on his side of the floor. While reading X1's anticipation of helping X2 or actually switching with X2 onto 02 on his break-out cut, 01 breaks off the screening route to actually set a "Ghost Stagger-Screen" and make a "Diagonally Slash Cut" across the lane to be an isolated "Post-Up Player."

04 continues cutting down to turn the (01 & 04) "Stagger-Screen" for 02 into a "Diagonal Pin-Screen" for 02. This action that turned into a two-man action on the weakside of the play eliminates the interior support that the perimeter-type defender, X1, needs to successfully defend 01. Diagram 17.6.

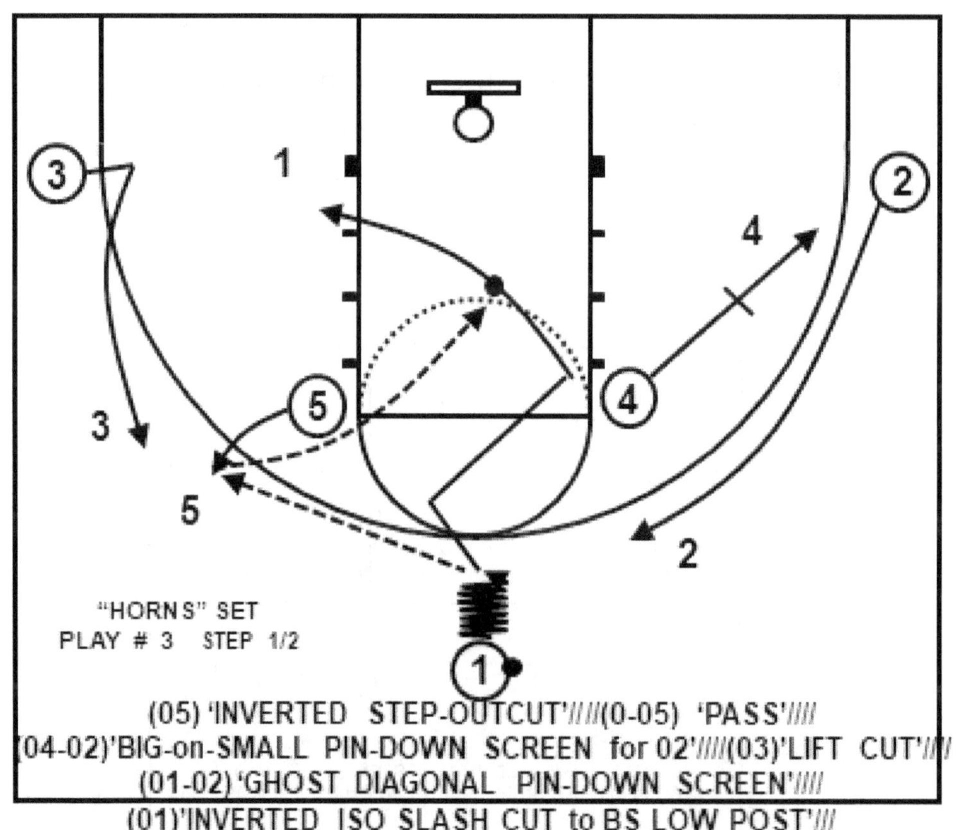

DIAGRAM 17.6

Diagram 17.7 shows the conclusion of Play # 3 with 05 not making the pass to 01. 01 then steps back out on the perimeter to the "Deep Corner" on the same side of the floor. At the same 03 continues his cut up from the FT Line extended to break towards 05 and the ball. 05 makes a quick short "Flip Pass" and immediately makes a "Front Pivot" off of his inside right foot to "Rim-Run" to the basket and the empty interior area.

If 03 turns down the "Inside Pass" to 05, he then "perimeter-pull (drag) dribbles" out towards the top of the key area. As 03 makes his "drag dribble" across the top of the floor, 05 "chases" the ball across the lane to post up his defender. At the same time, 04 steps back up to set a "Big-on-Small Flare-Screen" for 02 to use to "Flare-Cut" towards the wide sideline and the "Deep Corner."

This gives 03 a "dribbling and creating" opportunity, an "Inside Pass" to 05, a "Throwback Reverse Pass" to 01 in the "Deep Corner," or a "Skip Pass" to 02 that could lead "catch/shot/create/pass (inside to 05) opportunities." If shots are not taken, the new "4-Out/1-In" Spot-Ups for the final phase of the offense to instantly and fluidly begin. **Diagram 17.7.**

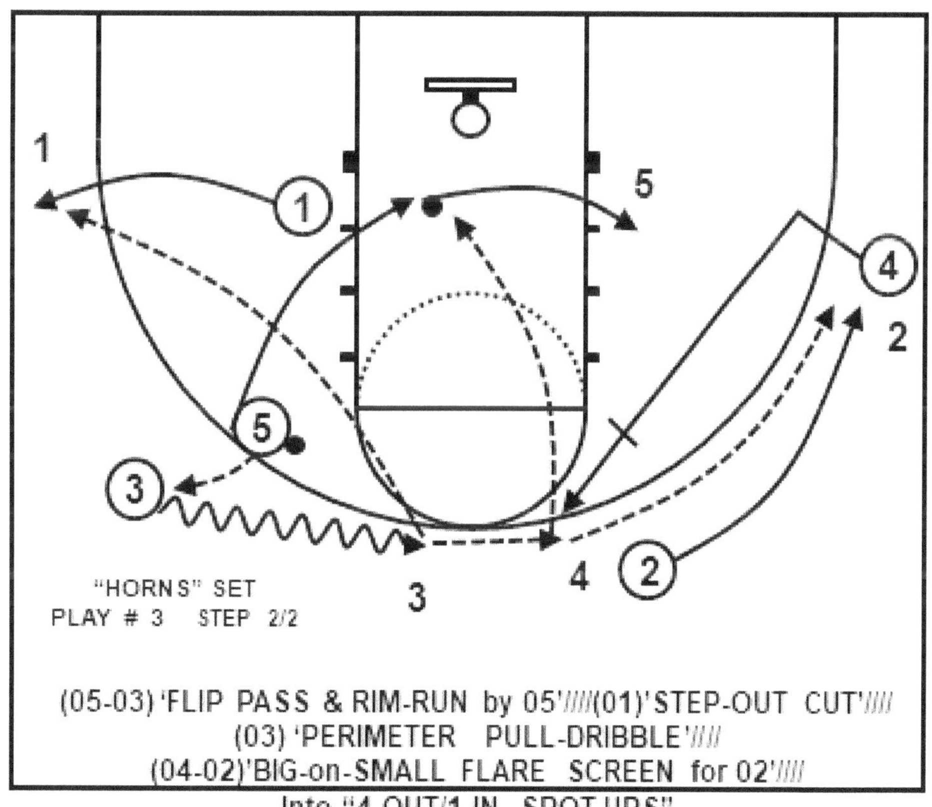

Diagram 17.7

Diagrams 17.8 and 17.9 show Play # 4, a Counter to Play # 3. This Level 2 play is executed towards the left side of the floor with 05 again stepping outside of the arc, with 03 also again breaking up to the "Wing" area on his side of the floor. 01 makes the same pass to 05. Again 01 and 04 both start to set the same "Stagger-Screen" for 02, but 04 is the player that breaks off the screening route and becomes the player that slashes across the lane to the "Ballside Block." 01 switches with 04 and becomes the "Diagonal Pin-Screener" for 02 to break up to the "Weakside Slot." **Diagram 17.8.**

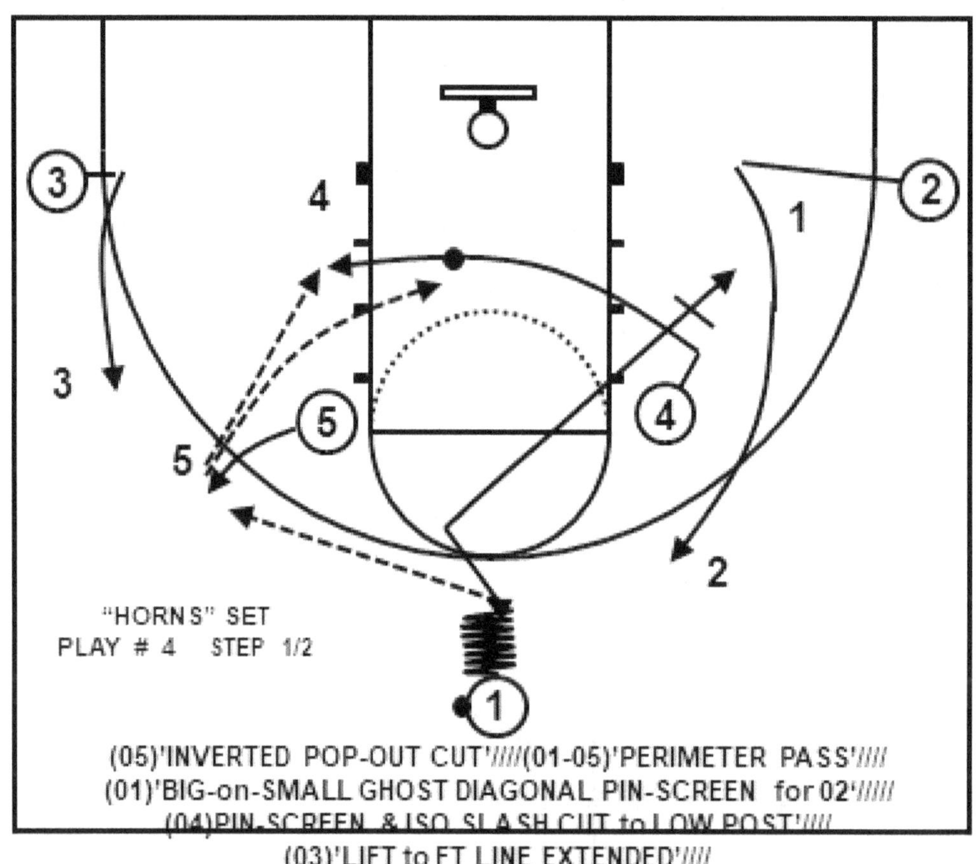

DIAGRAM 17.8

Diagram 17.9 shows 05 making a "Big-on-Small DHO" for 03 to become the same player to dribble out across the top of the key. After the DHO, 05 makes the same pivot and the same "Rim-Run" to the basket, looking for 03 to make the same "Lob Pass." If 04 does not receive the (03-04) "Inside Pass," 04 empties out of the lane to the "Deep Corner." If 03 does not make the penetrating dribble to the middle of the lane, 03 looks to make the same possible "Skip Pass" to 02 (after the same type of "Flare-Cut.")

The end of this Counter play has positioned 01 to be the "Flare-Screener" for 02 to make the same "Flare-Cut" to the "Deep Corner" that he does in Play #10. If no shots are taken, the same "4-Out/1-In" Spot-Ups are filled for the same continuity offense to be able to be started. **Diagram 17.9.**

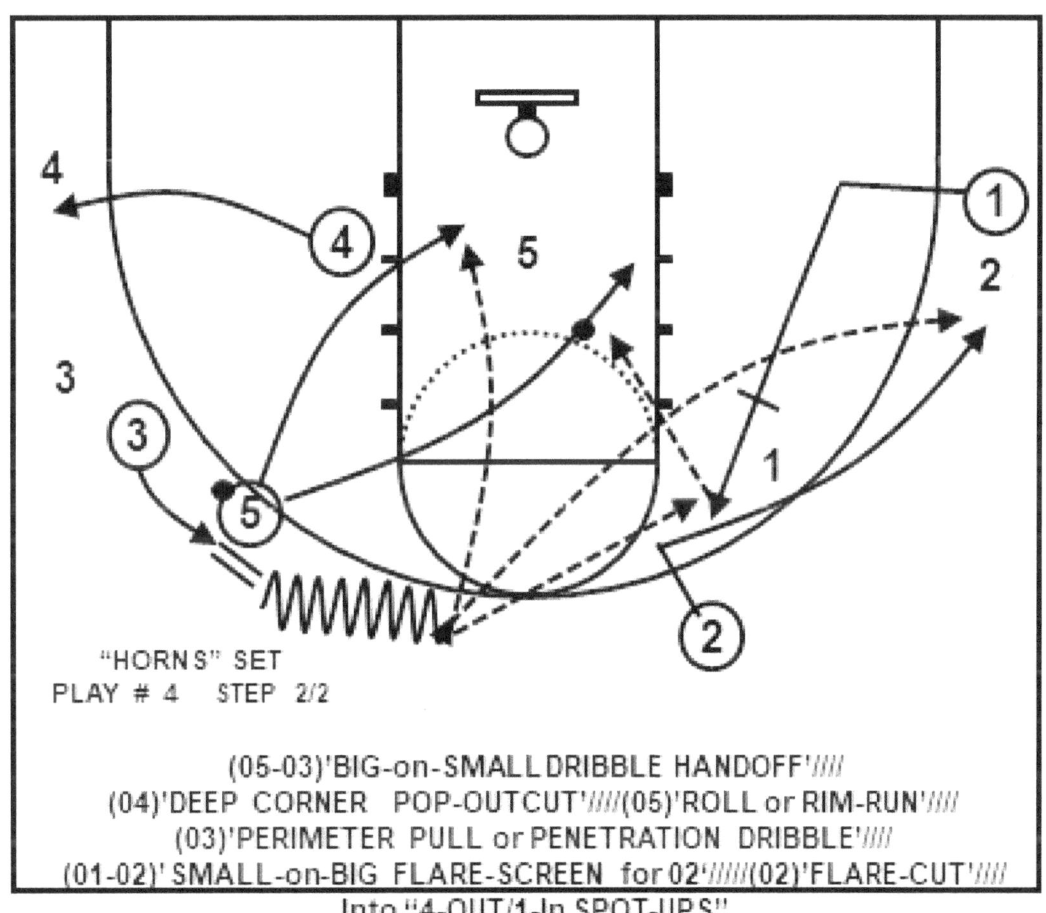

DIAGRAM 17.9

Play # 5 is illustrated in Diagrams 17.10 through 17.12 with 04 being the designated "Post Player" to step out just inside of the arc and to receive the (01-04) Pass. At the same time, 02 makes an "L-Cut" up to the "Wing" area on the same side of the floor. Immediately afterwards, both 01 and 05 angle over to set a "Stagger-Screen" for 03 to break up towards the top of the key.

Instead, 03 rejects the "Stagger Screen" and makes a hard "Backdoor Cut" across the lane to the new "Ballside Block." After the rejection, 01 slips out to the "Wing" area and 05 pops out to the new "Weakside Slot." 04 looks to make the "Inside Pass" to 03 on his cut across the lane or his "inverted and isolated post-up." **Diagram 17.10**.

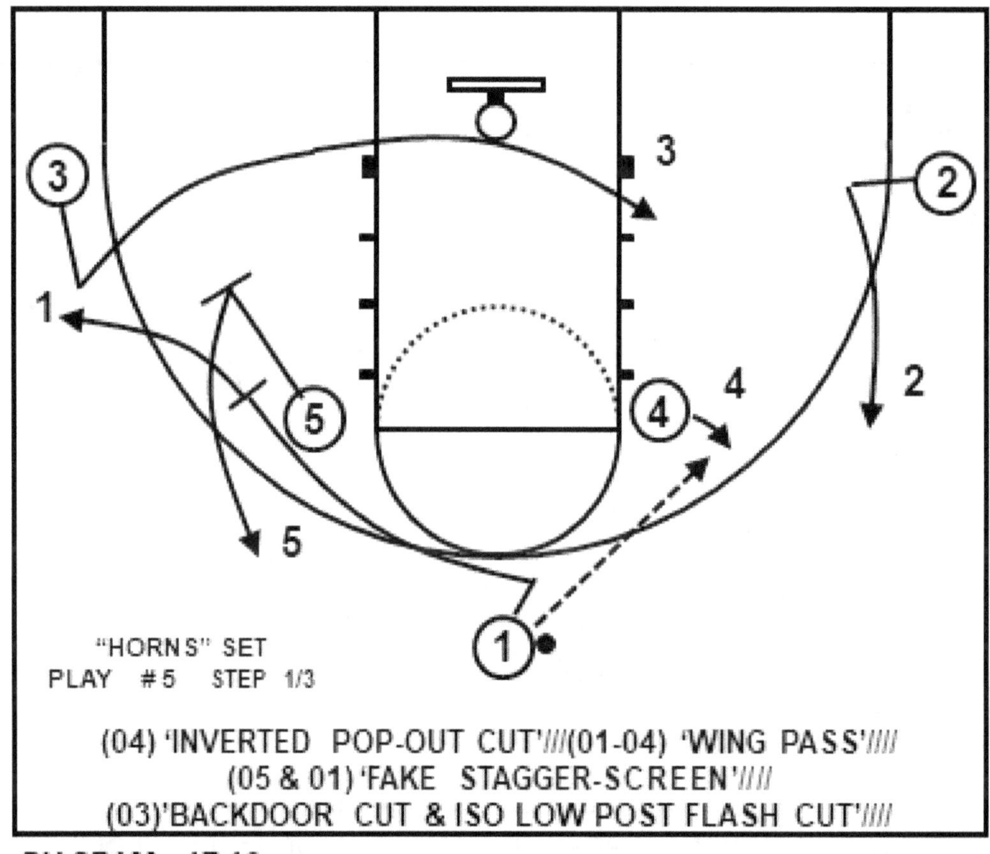

DIAGRAM 17.10

Diagram 17.11 shows 04 not making the pass to 03 and electing to dribble out towards 02 at the FT Line extended. There, there is a "Big-on-Small DHO" with 04 handing the ball off to 02 for his "perimeter-pull dribble" off of 04's top right shoulder. 04 immediately front pivots off of his lower left foot and runs towards the "Ballside Block" where 02 has ended up (after his "Backdoor Cut.")

If 02 does not penetrate towards the middle, he should elect to make a "perimeter pull dribble." When that dribble takes place, 05 breaks across the top of the key to set a "Big-on-Small (Drag) Ball-Screen" for 02 to continue to the opposite side of the floor. As that action out on top takes place, 04 continues the cut off of the "Small-on-Big Lane Exchange Back-Screen" to end up on the opposite side of the lane. **Diagram 17.11**.

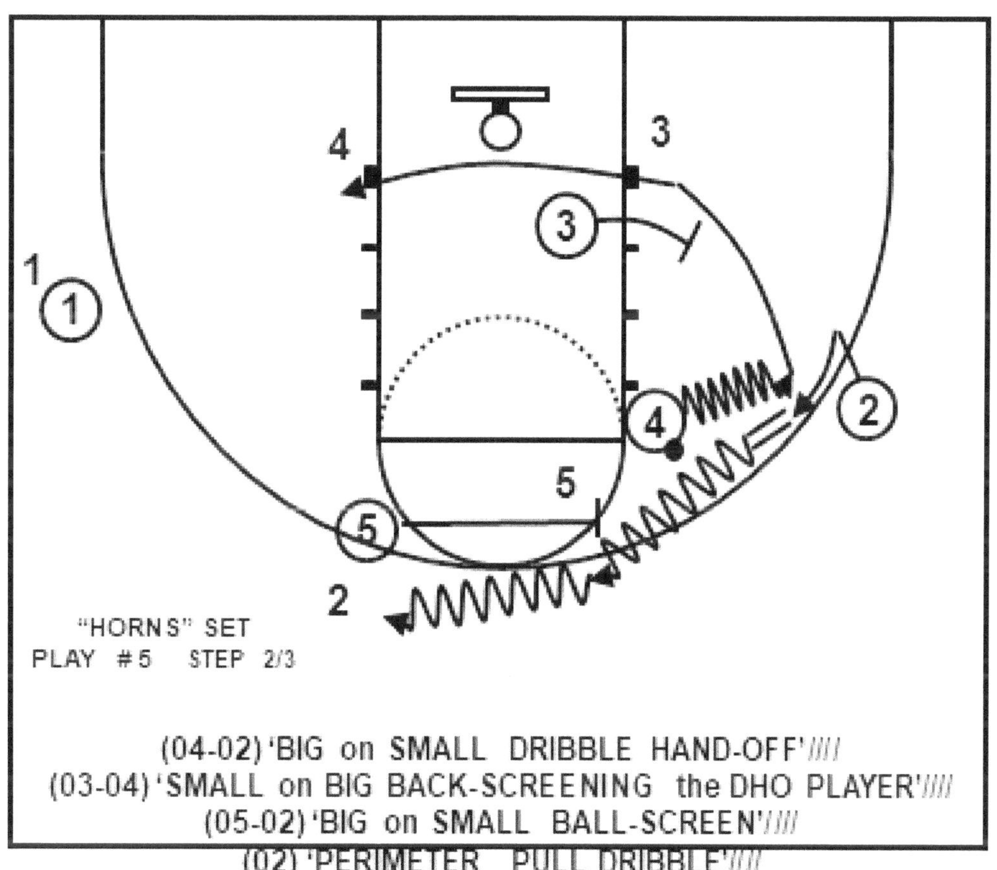

DIAGRAM 17.11

As 02 breaks contact with 05's top right shoulder and continues across the top of the key, 02 looks to make the "Down Pass" to 01 in the "Deep Corner" or the "Inside Pass" to 04. To isolate 04 down on the new "Ballside Block," the two man weakside action consists of 05 cutting down to set a (05-03) ("Big-on-Small Vertical Pin Down-)Screen the (Back-)Screener with 03 then breaking up to the new "Weakside Slot." After his second screen, 05 slips out to the new "Weakside Deep Corner."

If shots are not taken by the primary receivers/scorers (04, 02 or 01) this fundamentally sound action that takes place on both sides of the floor have attacked each individual defender as well as repositioned the five offensive players into the proper "4-Out/1-In" Spot-Ups. This leads to a smooth transition or conversion into the final phase of the offensive attack. **Diagram 17.12.**

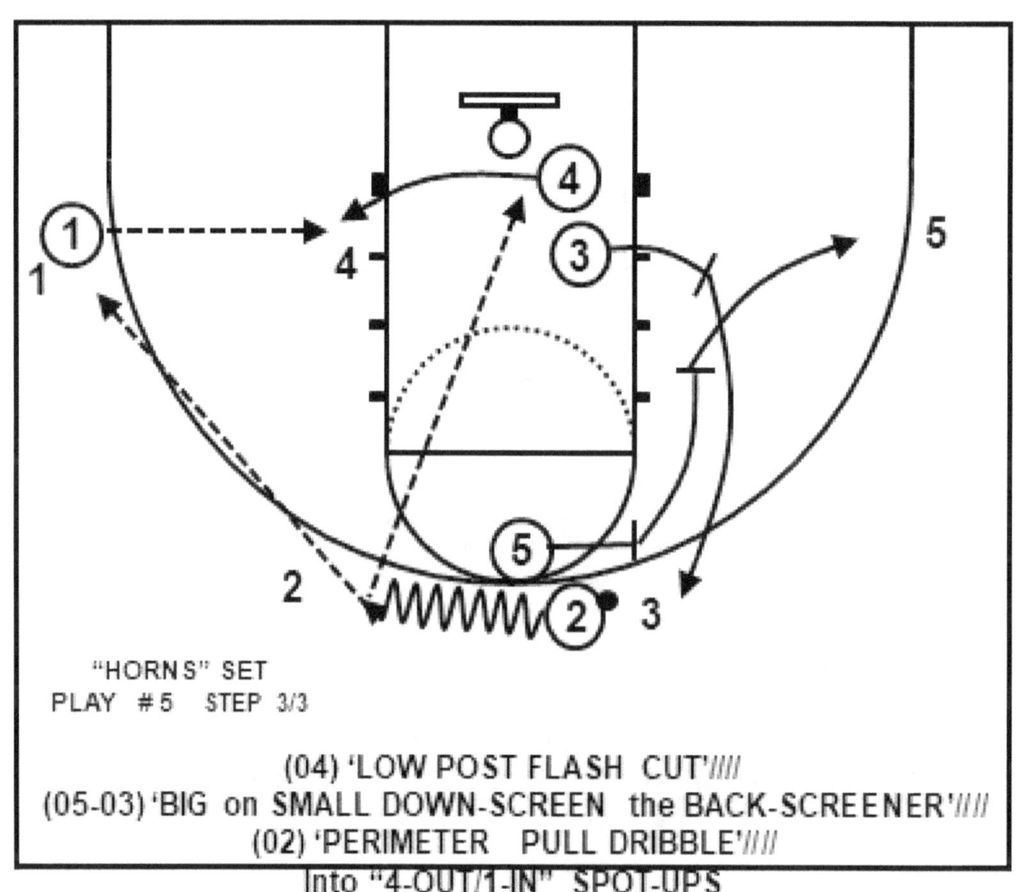

DIAGRAM 17.12

Play # 6, a Level 3 play, is shown in its entirety in Diagrams 17.13 through 17.15. As 01 elects to dribble towards the "Slot" on the right side, while 03 and 02 make their respective "Iverson Cuts" and end up at the FT Line extended on the opposite sides of the floor. After 03 scrapes off of 05's top left shoulder, 05 pops out to the "Slot" position. When 03 breaks contact with 04's top left shoulder, 04 turns back to flash to the new "Ballside High Post." **Diagram 17.13**.

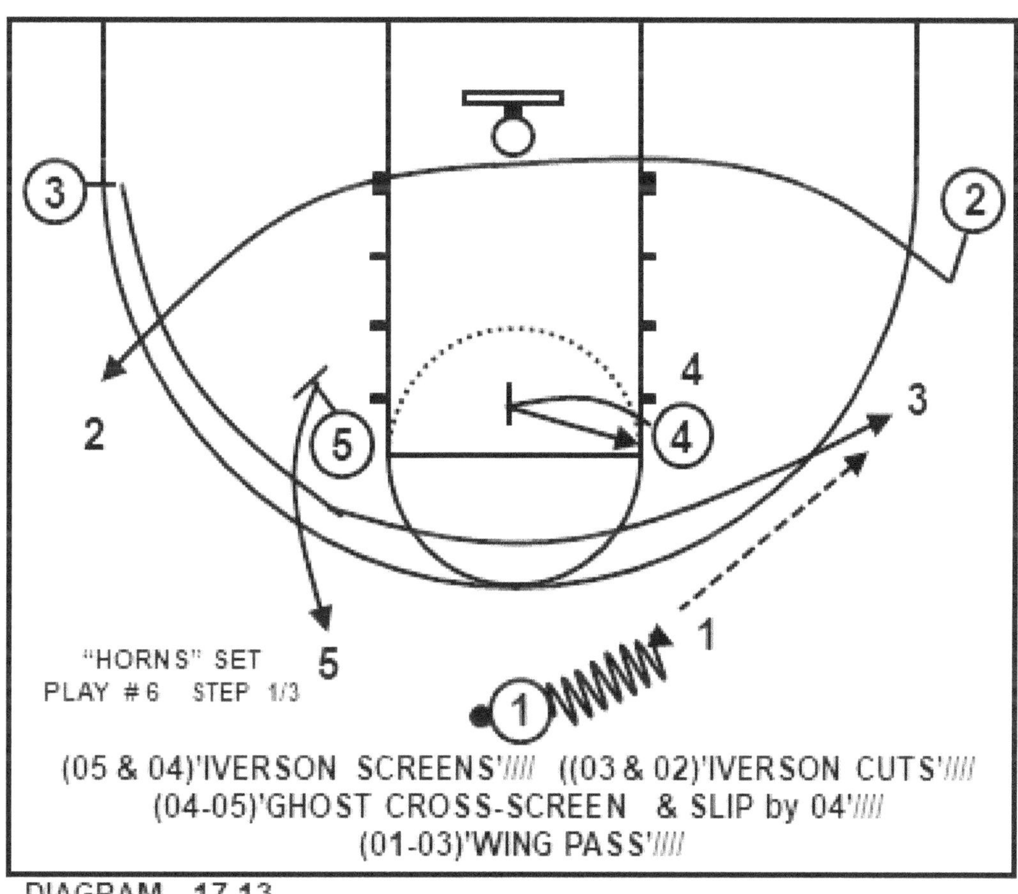

DIAGRAM   17.13

With every player outside of the arc and above the FT Line extended except for 04, 01 looks to make the pass to 03 so 03 can quickly hit 04 on his dive from the new "Ballside High Post" to the "Ballside Block." Not only has 04 isolated his defender, but the actual biggest defender, X5, is as far as possible from 04.

If 03 does not make the pass to 04, he would pass the ball back to 01 and immediately make a "Give-n-Go Cut" through the vacated "High Post" and diagonally through the lane to the opposite side's "Block." **Diagram 17.14.**

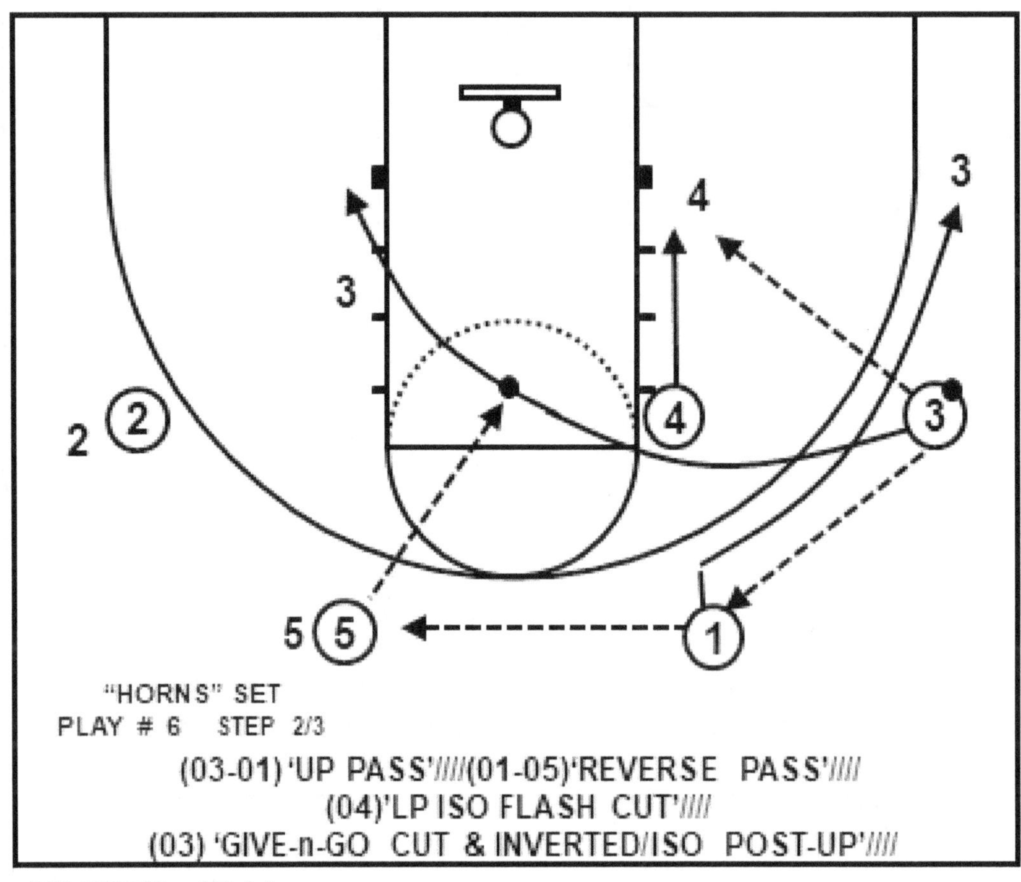

DIAGRAM 17.14

Diagram 17.15 shows 05 inverting his post-type defender and receiving a "Long Ball-Screen" from 04. 05 attacks his defensive 'big' with a "perimeter-pull (drag) dribble" across the top of the key off of 04's top left shoulder. As 05 breaks contact with 04, 04 should "reverse pivot" off of his lower right foot, open up to the ball and 05 so he can roll down the lane to post up on the "Block." 03 would make a "Vertical Up-Cut" to fill 05's now empty "Slot." At the same time, 02 makes a "Drift Cut" into the new "Weakside Deep Corner." This makes 03 and 02 viable shooting threats with a possible "Reverse Throwback Pass" to 03 or a "Skip Pass" to 02. The cuts made by 03 and 02 will also fully isolate 05 on his "Screen/Roll" by eliminating any possible weakside defensive help that X4 would need. 05 would also have a third perimeter scoring threat with 01 staying wide and deep to spot-up in the new "Ballside Deep Corner."

This action attacks X4 from different locations on the floor off of 05's pass possibilities. In addition, the action repositions all five players into the fundamentally sound all-important "4-Out/1-In" Spot-Ups for the final phase of the offensive attack to smoothly begin. **Diagram 17.15.**

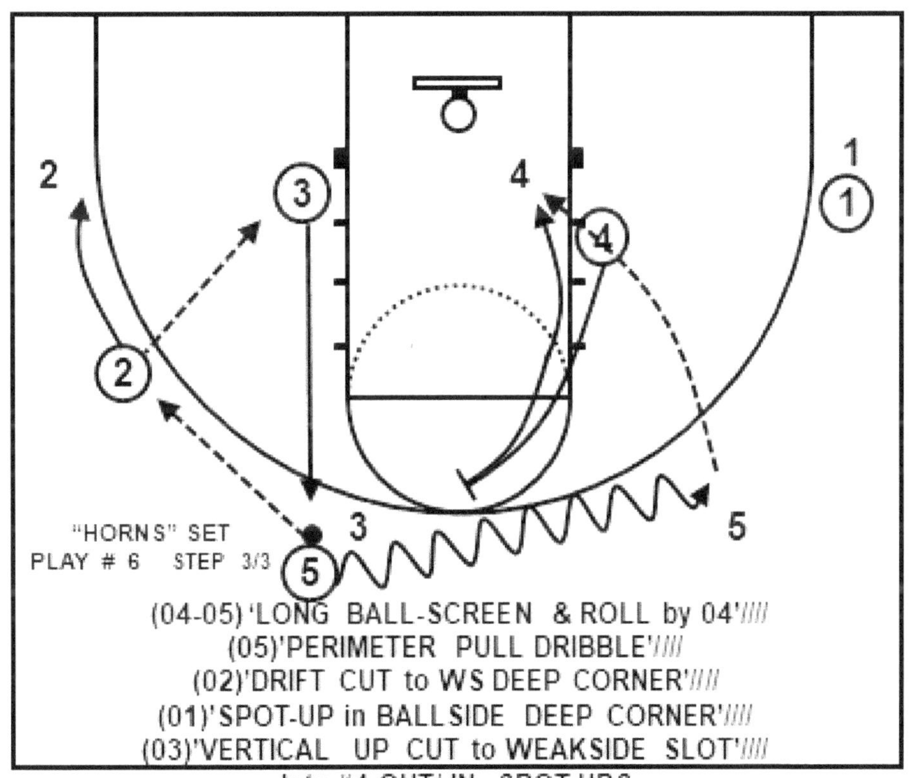

DIAGRAM 17.15

Diagrams 17.16 through 17.18 show the full Play # 7, a Counter Play to Play # 5. This play could also be run towards either side of the floor, but to show the similarities as well as the differences in the two plays; this play will also be started with 01's pass to the same play on the same side of the floor.

The diagram shows 01 making the pass to 04 and immediately cutting again away from the ball to set the presumed same "Stagger-Screen" for 03. As 03 breaks up towards the screen and the "Slot," 01 breaks off of his screening route to "diagonally slash across the lane" to post up on the opposite side of the lane. 05 continues cutting towards 03 to actually make the two-man action as a (05-03) "Pin-Screen" with 01 (instead of a "Stagger-Screen"). At the same time, 02 breaks up and out to the "Wing" area on his side of the floor at the FT Line extended. **Diagram 17.16.**

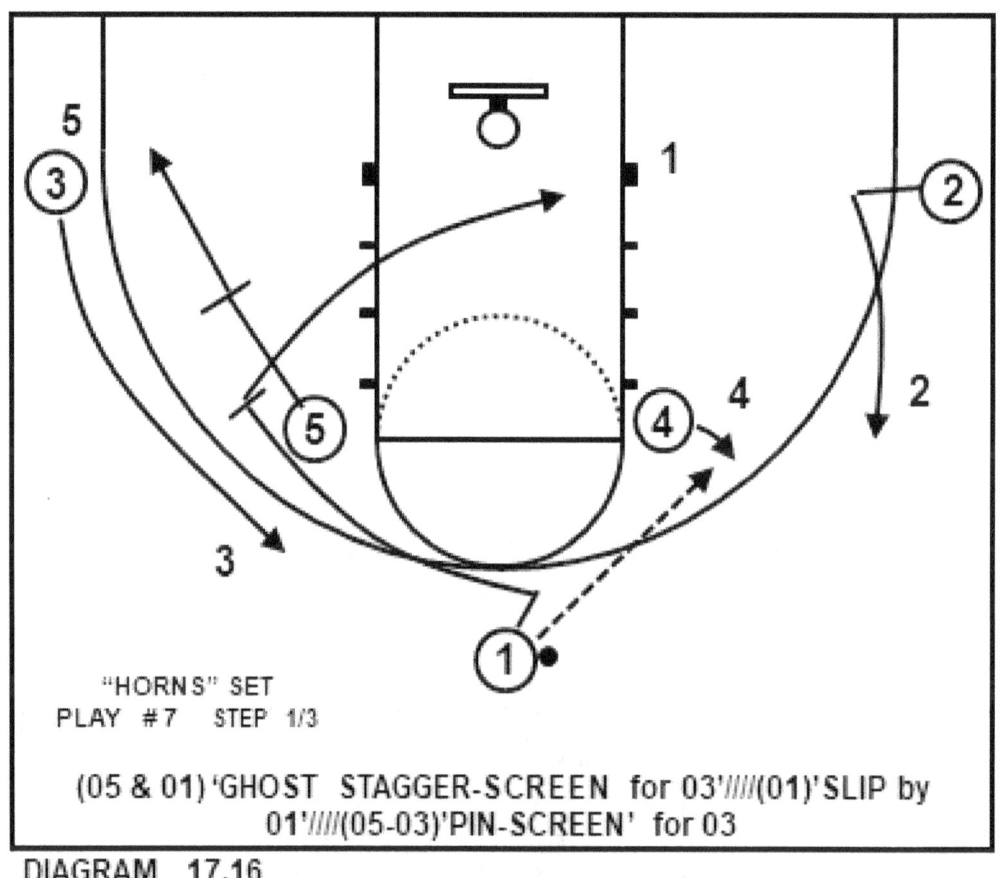

DIAGRAM 17.16

Diagram 17.17 shows 04 making a quick "Flip Pass" to 02, who should first look to make a quick "Inside Pass" to 01, now inverted as well as isolated on the new "Ballside Block." After making the pass to 02, 04 steps out to set a "Big-on-Small Inside Ball-Screen" for 02 to use for either a "penetration dribble" into the lane or a "perimeter pull (drag) dribble" out across the top of the key. As 02 "dribble-scrapes" off of 04's top right shoulder, 04 then front pivots off of his lower left foot to then "Flare-Cut" to the "Deep Corner" on the same side of the floor. At the same time, 01 attacks his perimeter-type defender with an "Iso Duck-In Cut" into the "Dotted Circle" area. Regardless of how X1 attempts to defend 01 in the middle of the lane, 02 and 01 should be able to successfully attack his perimeter-type defender.

As 02 continues dribbling the ball out on top, 03 steps over to set a "Ball-Screen" for 02 to use to continue advancing the ball across the top of the key. To move the ball to the opposite "Slot," 02 should "dribble-scrape" over the top of 03's top right shoulder with 03 slipping his screen and then "spotting up" at the near "Slot." This action is commonly called "Pick and Pop." **Diagram 17.17.**

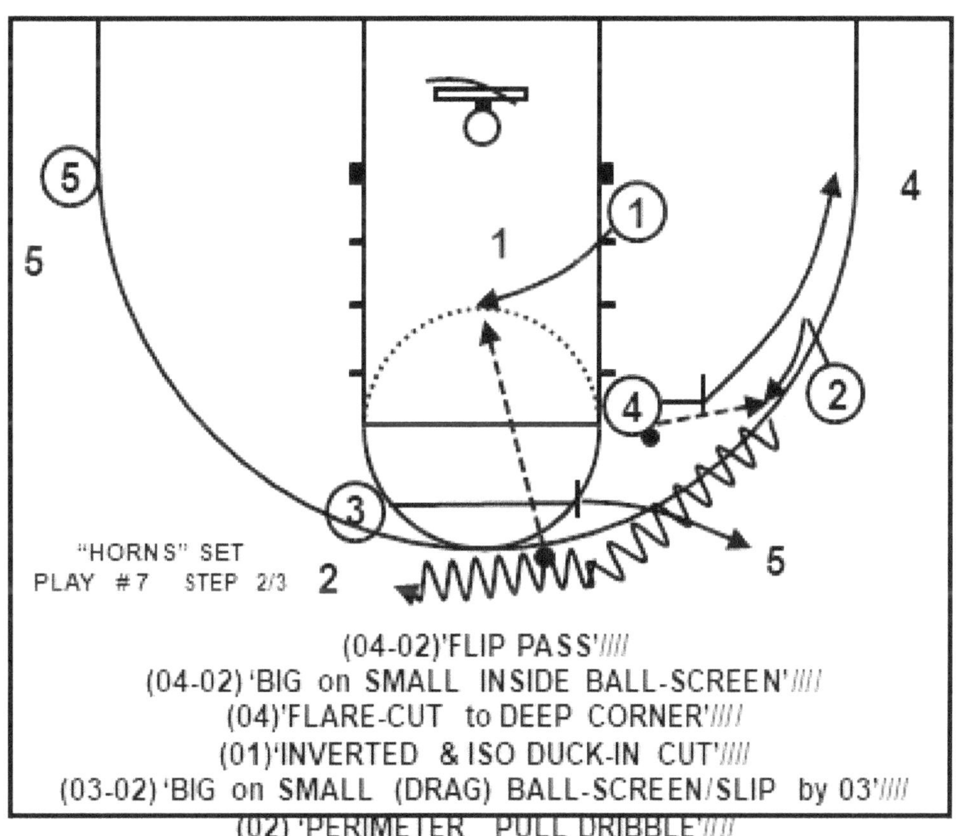

DIAGRAM 17.17

From the new "Ballside Slot," 02 has three perimeter pass opportunities (a "Down Pass" to 05, a "Reverse Throwback Pass" to 03 and a possible "Skip Pass" to 04 in the "Deep Corner" and one "inside pass" possibility to 01 in the 'paint'.

The ball could easily be moved from one side of the floor to the other with 01 following the perimeter flight of the ball. When the next pass is made, with the "4-Out/1-In" Spot-Ups already being filled, the designated continuity offense can seamlessly begin.

Using both Play # 5 interspersed with Play # 7 will keep opposing defenses constantly off-balance. 03 is the lone player that will be used to "iso post up" his perimeter-type defender, X3, in Play # 5. If Play # 5 was executed on the opposite side of the floor, 02 would be the player that would be the designated "Iso Post-Up player." While Play # 7 has 01 become the player to individually attack his defender in the 'paint," he would also be the player regardless of which side the ball is entered. These two plays could provide success for each other by the deception that is implemented in each. **Diagram 17.18.**

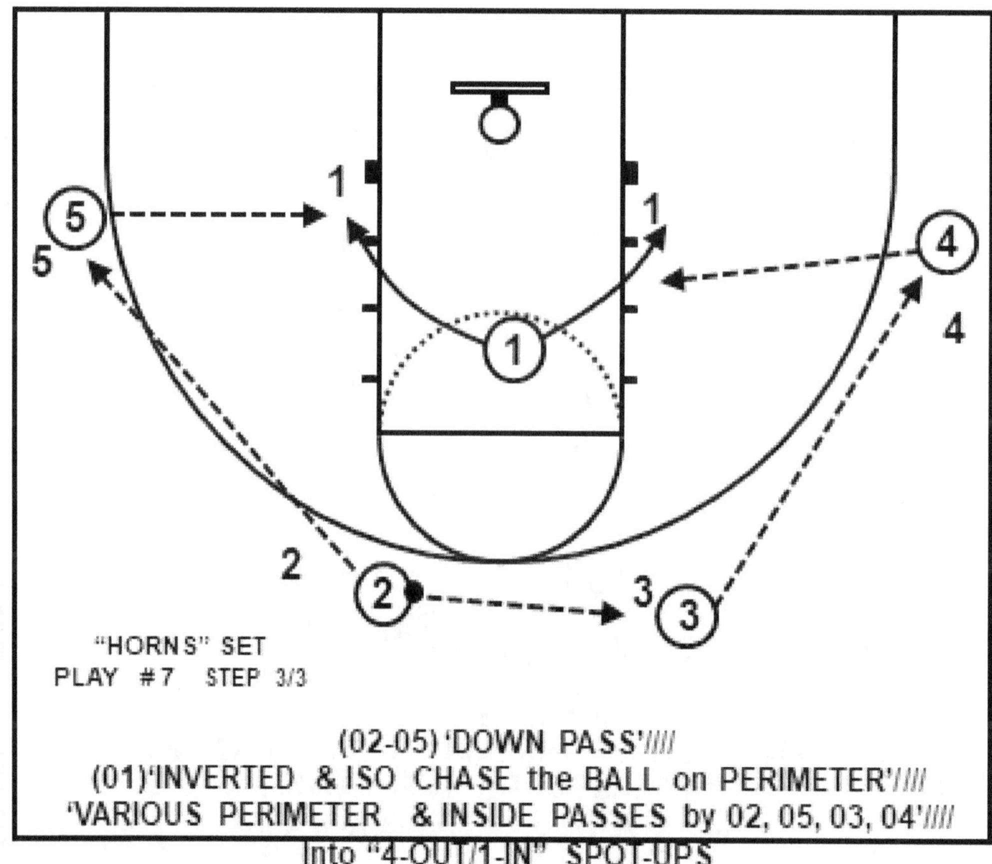

DIAGRAM 17.18

Play # 8, another Level 3 play is shown in Diagrams 17.19 through 17.21. While having the freedom to attack either side of the floor, 04 has been designated to be the player (instead of 05) to step up to set a "Big-on-Small Ball-Screen" for 01 to dribble slightly deeper than the FT Line extended on the right side of the floor. As 01 "dribble-scrapes" off of 04's top left shoulder and approaches 02, 02 then makes a hard "Backdoor Cut" to the basket. If he does not receive the pass on his cut, 02 will then "button-hook" his defender to become an inverted and isolated post-up player on the "Ballside Block." **Diagram 17.19**

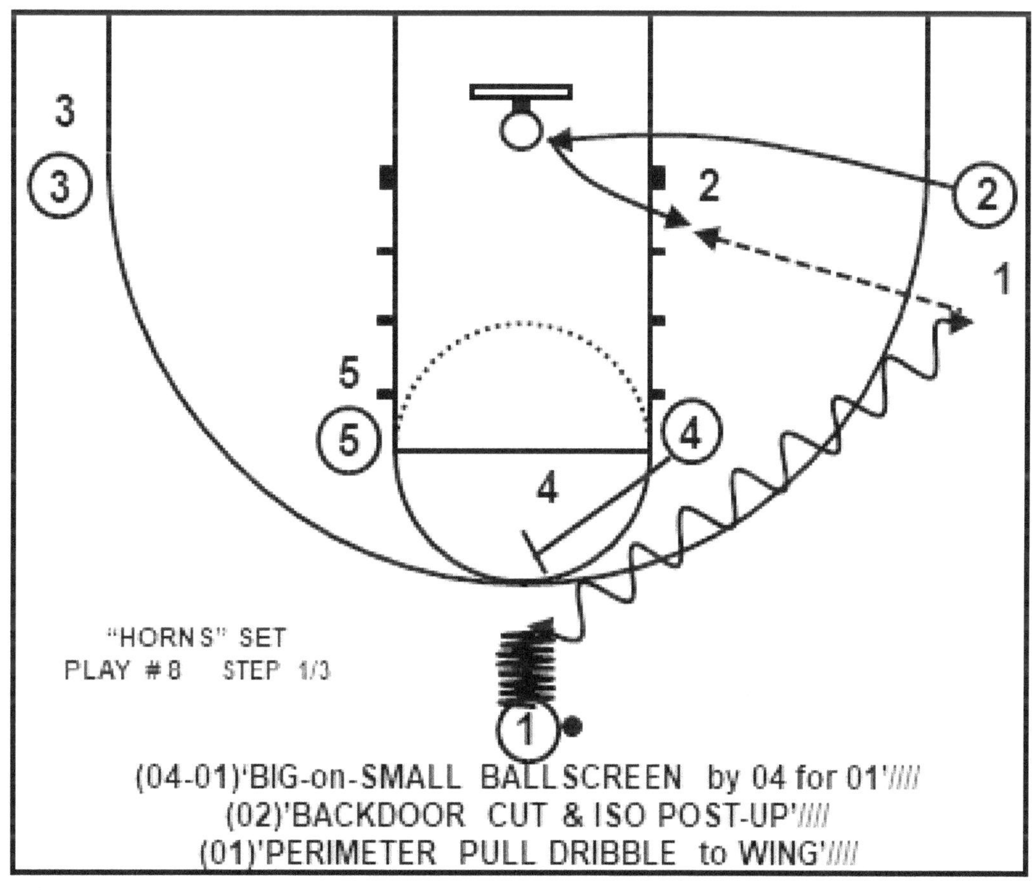

DIAGRAM 17.19

As 01 dribbles to his spot which will be very conducive for 01 to make the "Inside Pass" to 02, 04 cuts over to set a "Pin-Screen" for 05 to use to break to the new "Ballside Slot." After screening for 05, 04 continues cutting diagonally down to set his second "Pin-Screen" for 03 to use to break up to the newly designated "Weakside Slot." 04 then remains in the "Weakside Deep Corner." This action not only gives 01 two very legitimate perimeter scoring opportunities but also to the fully isolated and inverted 02, against a perimeter-type defender, X2. **Diagram 17.20.**

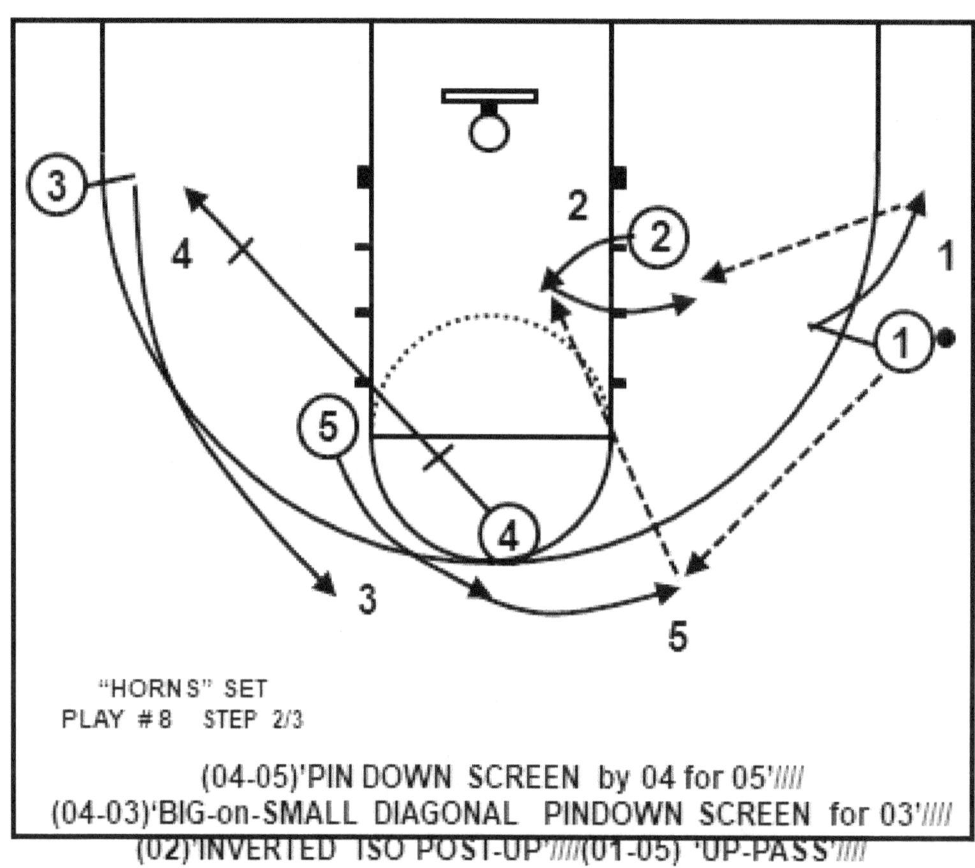

DIAGRAM   17.20

If no shots are taken, 05 could reverse the ball to 03 and follow the pass with a "Big-on-Small Ball-Screen" at the far sided "Elbow" area. This screen would allow for a quick and instant re-reversal with 03 then making a "perimeter-pull (drag) dribble" back towards the initial right side of the floor. After receiving the (initial) "Reverse Pass" from 05, 03 "dribble-scrapes" off of 05's top left shoulder" and continues to the "Slot" back on the right side.

When 03 dribbles to the imaginary center line, 02 makes another "Isolated and Inverted Duck-In Cut;" but returns to the same "Block" if 03 cannot make the pass to 02. At the same time, after screening for 03, 05 then makes a "front pivot" off of his lower right foot to "Rim-Run" to the basket. If 03 does not make the "Lob Pass" to 05 on his "Lob Cut," 05 should then roll out of the lane and spot-up in the new "Weakside Deep Corner." Simultaneously, 04 rotates up to fill the vacant "Slot" where 03 begins his dribble. This action helps eliminate weakside support defense that the perimeter-defender, X2, would need to defend 02 on the "Block." This play has attacked various defenders in different locations during the three phases of the play. It has also moved offensive players as well as their individual defenders and repositioned them into the proper "4-Out/1-In" Spot-Ups so that the designated continuity offense can seamlessly begin. **Diagram 17.21**.

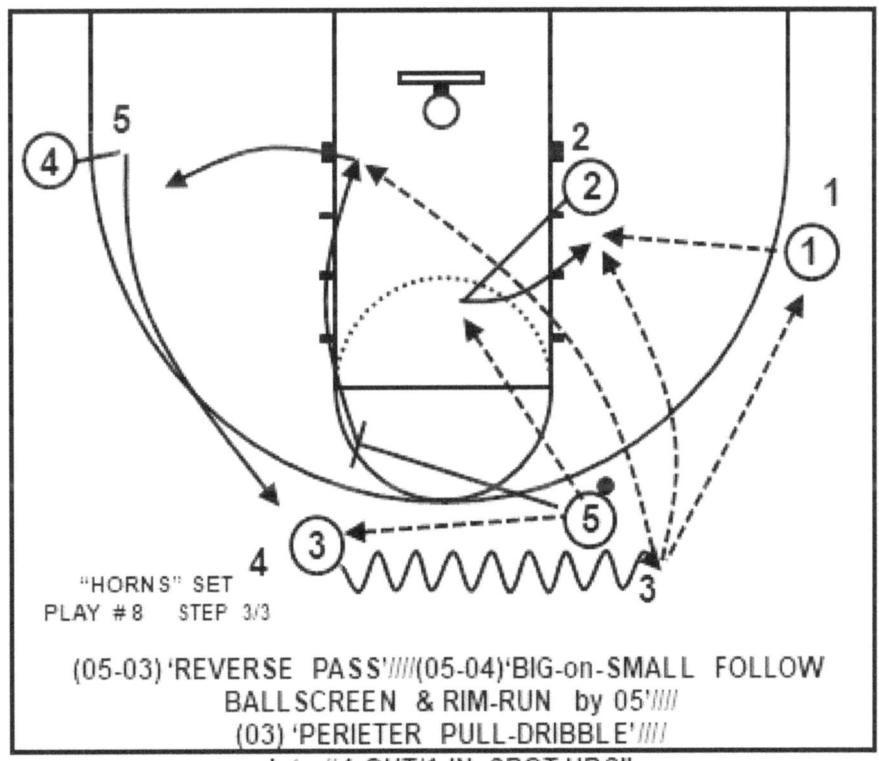

DIAGRAM 17.21

Play # 9 is a Level 3 play that begins with Diagram 17.22 and ends with Diagram 17.24. It has been designated that 05 break across towards the "Nail" for 04 to make his "Barkley Cut" off of either shoulder of 05 with 04 ending up at the "Wing" area on the opposite side of the floor. After "Barkley Screening" 04's defender, 05 then slips just inside of the arc near the "Slot" location on the right side of the floor. **Diagram 17.22**.

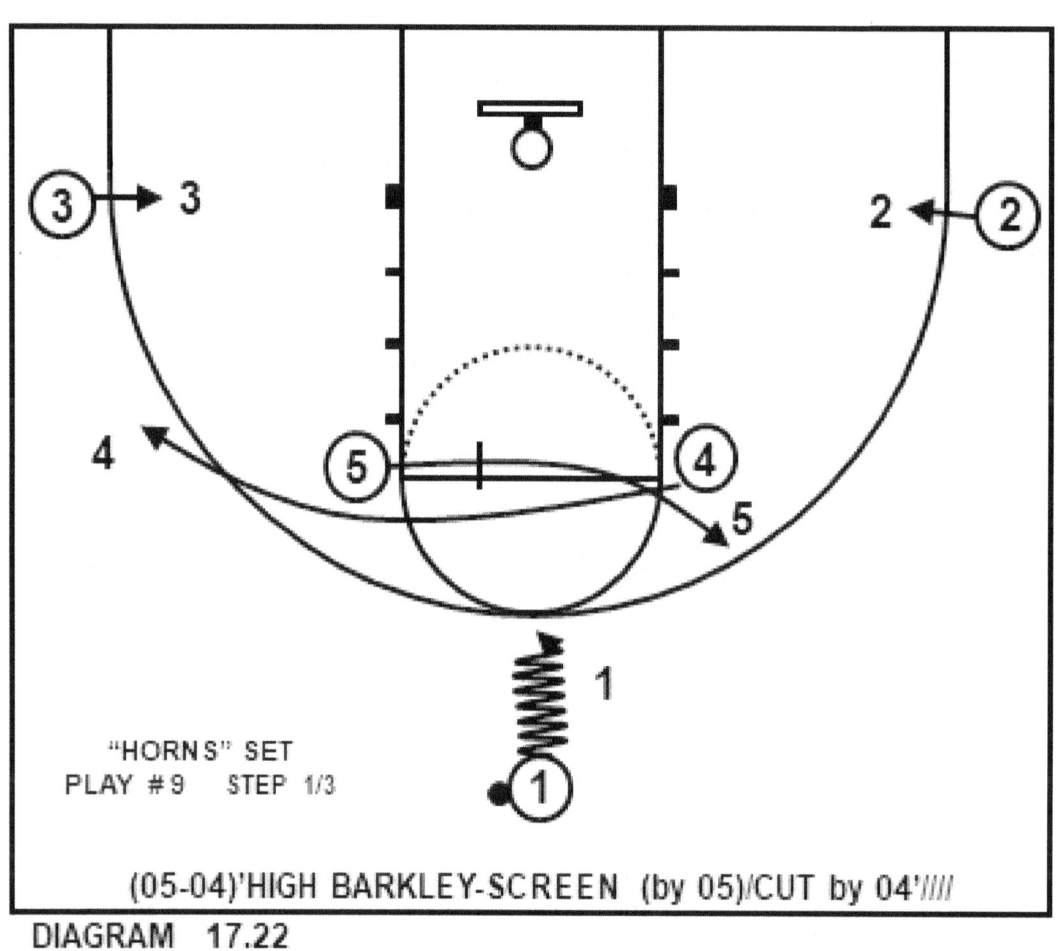

DIAGRAM 17.22

Diagram 17.23 shows 01 making the pass to 04 and immediately stepping towards the ball for two steps before then slashing across the "Nail" to set a "Small-on-Big Brush Screen" 05 05 to use to break to the newly declared "Ballside Block." Using this perimeter-type "Brush Screen" set by a perimeter-type player, 01, should give X5 defensive problems in keeping up with 05's "Brush Cut" off of 01. After screening first for 05, 01 continues diagonally down to set a "Small-on-Big Diagonal Pin Down-Screen" for 02 to break up to the new "Weakside Slot." **Diagram 17.23**

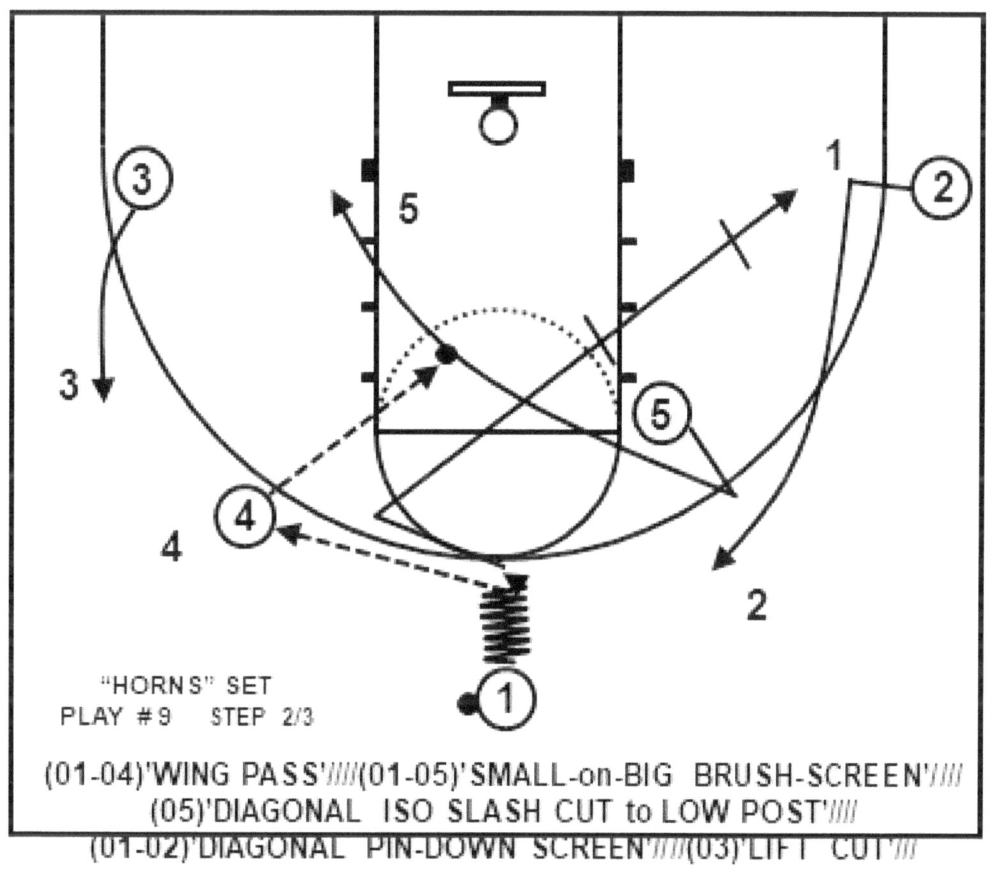

04 looks first to hit 05 on his cut to the "Block," then to 03 at the FT Line extended and also to reverse the ball to 02 on the opposite "Slot." If nothing develops, 03 continues to cut towards 04 to receive the (04-03) DHO. After the hand-off, 04 "Flare-Cuts" to the "Deep Corner" while 05 posts his defender up in an isolated situation. In addition to 04's cut, 03 looks to "penetrate-dribble" or to "perimeter-pull dribble" out towards the empty "Ballside Slot."

As 03 dribbles out towards 02, 02 is the expected pass receiver and most likely is somewhat denied the ball with X2 overplaying 02. That is when 02 makes a hard "Backdoor Cut" all the way into the "Dotted Circle" area. If 03 does not make the quick pass to 02, 02 then empties out to the near "Deep Corner" while 04 breaks up to fill the "Weakside Slot" position. 03's top targets should be 05 posting up, 02 on his cut to the basket, to 03 on the "Reverse Throwback Pass" and to 01 cutting up towards the "Slot." If none of these passes help create a shot, the action has at least moved every offensive player as well as each defender and has repositioned offensive players into the proper "4-Out/1-In" Spot-Ups. From there, the next phase of the offense can fluidly and immediately begin. **Diagram 17.24.**

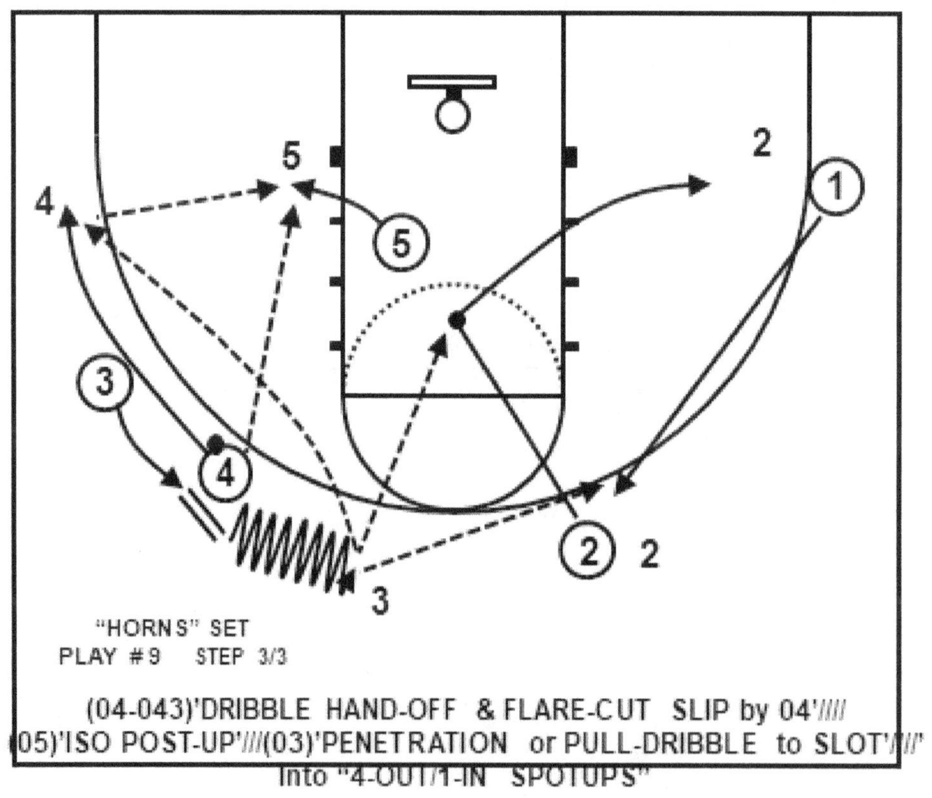

DIAGRAM 17.24

the "HIGH-POST/LOW POST" OFFENSIVE SPOT-UPS

The main difference in this family of plays/entries are that all five players will end up in a different group of offensive spot-ups. These "HIGH-POST/LOW-POST" Spot-Ups will have players moved about the court with any of the five ending up in the "Ballside Block," the "Ballside High Post," the "Ballside Wing," the "Weakside Wing," and the "Point" (or top of the guy)" These five positions can provide the offense with safe and easy types of ball-reversals, large gaps for dribble penetration, opportunities to deliver the ball inside to whomever (perimeter-type or post-type players) is posting up their defender on the "Ballside Block," and a player that can be a perimeter-scoring threat and a legitimate offensive rebounding threat from outside of the arc on his "offensive crashing of the boards." The ""HIGH-POST/LOW-POST" Spot-Ups also provide ample opportunities for constant and effective defensive transition responsibilities.

Play # 10 a Level 2 Play, is a play that begins out of the very same offensive set/alignment as the previous plays described, the "HORNS" Set. But this family of plays has a different set of offensive "spot-ups" that each play that does not take a shot results in a repositioning of players. These different locations are called the "HIGH-POST/LOW-POST" Spot-Ups. This particular package of spot-ups allows an offensive team to immediately flow into another group of continuity offenses with no interruptions or delays.

Again, each play could have the freedom and capability to be started towards either side of the floor. Diagram 17.25 shows Play # 10 to be executed towards the right side of the floor with 01 dribbling directly to the "Wing" area on the right side of the floor. This then dictates that 04 break down to the "Block" and 02 to dive to the same "Block" for 02 to then make a "Pipe Cut" up the Lane Line to the top of the key. 04 then tries to seal his defender off for an "Isolated Post-Up" in the new overload (with no weakside interior support). At the same time as 02's "Pipe Cut," 05 should cross over to the newly designated "Ballside High Post" trying to use 02 as a "Brush-Screener" approximately at the "Nail." To eliminate even the very last of weakside defensive support, 03 breaks up to the FT Line extended, stretching the defense both "east and west." **Diagram 17.25.**

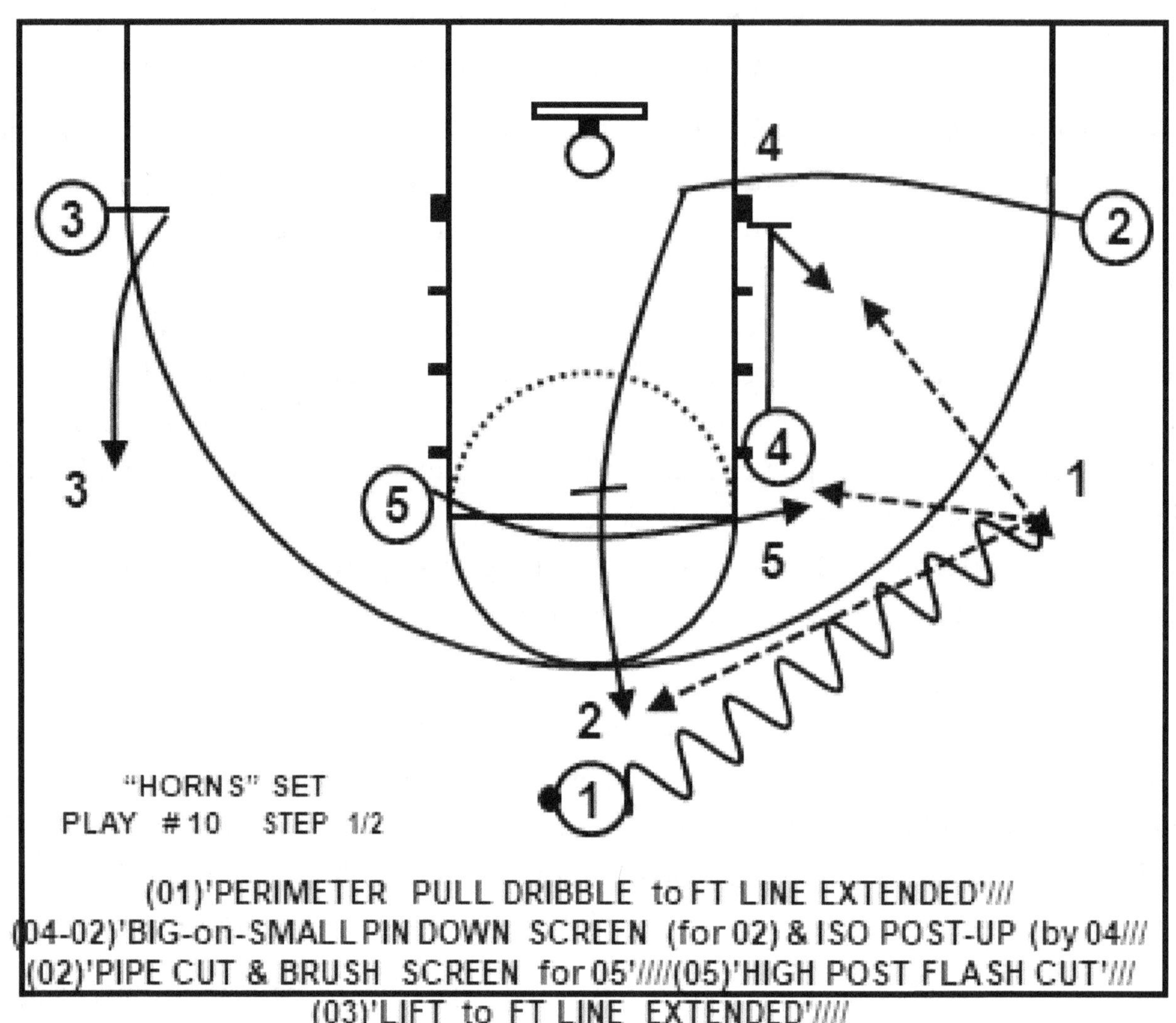

DIAGRAM 17.25

Diagram 17.26 illustrates 01 not making the possible three primary scoring threats, 04 on the "Block," 05 at the "Ballside High Post," and 03 at the "Weakside Wing" (for a possible '3' off of a "Skip Pass.") If those passes are not made, 01 could reverse the ball to 02 out on top of the key. He also could have a possible '3' available, but if not 03 should step up and over to set a "Big-on-Small Ball-Screen" for 02 to then advance the ball to the opposite wing area. After 03 screens for 02, 01 should step up to set a "Small-on-Big (Flare-)Screen the (Ball-)Screener" so that 03 then can "Flare-Cut" to the newly designated "Weakside Wing" area.

During 02's "perimeter-pull dribble," both 05 and 04 step horizontally into the lane before diagonally flashing to the opposite side of the lane. Their "(Post) X-Cuts" switches 04 from the initial "Ballside Block" into the new "Ballside High Post" and 05 from the original "Ballside High Post" into the new "Ballside Block" on the opposite side of the lane. This action attacks and moves every one of the five defenders but still places offensive players into the correct spot-ups for the newly desired continuity offense to begin with no pause or delay. **Diagram 17.26.**

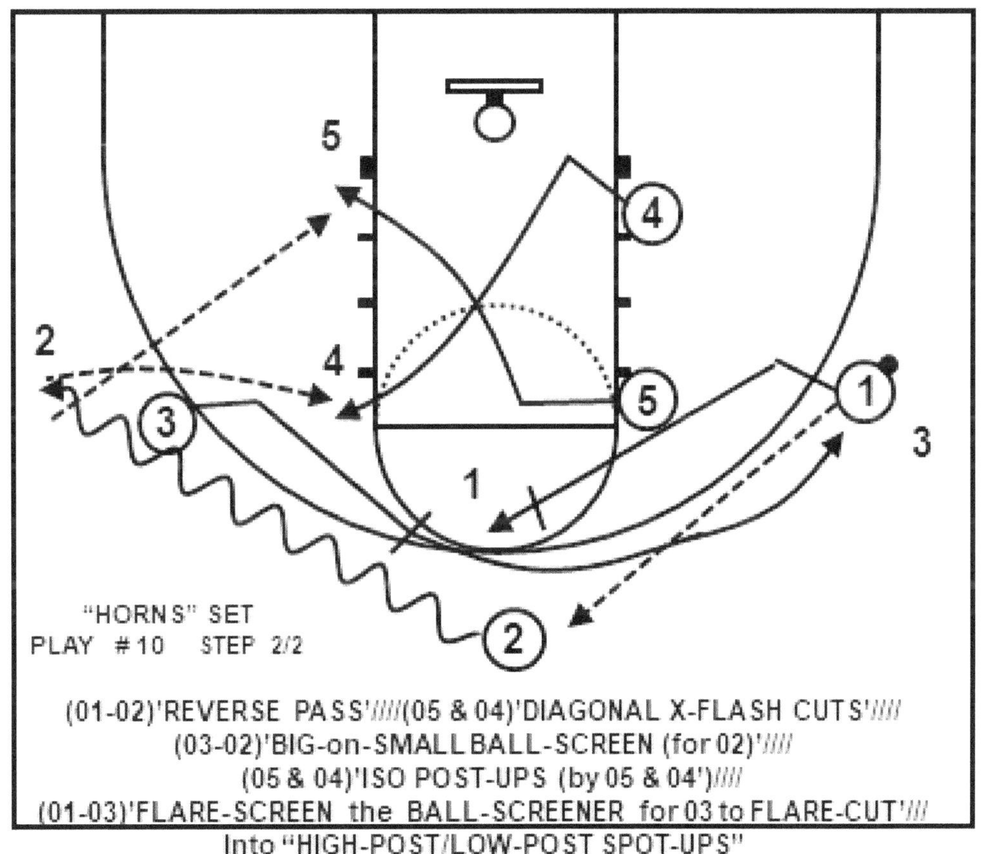

DIAGRAM 17.26

Diagrams 17.27 and 17.28 show the complete Play # 11, another Level 2 play that starts in the "HORNS" Set and ends in the "High-Post/Low-Post" Spot-Up locations. This play actually appears or slightly appears to be any of the following plays that can be executed out of the "Horns" Set:" Plays 1, 6, 13 and 14.

In addition the sole designated "Iverson Cutter" (03) could be switched to the opposite perimeter player (02) making it even less predictable for the defense to know what is to come. In this action, 03 makes his "Iverson Cut" over the top of 05 and 04's "Iverson Screens" and ends up on the "Wing" area on the opposite side of the floor. **Diagram 17.27.**

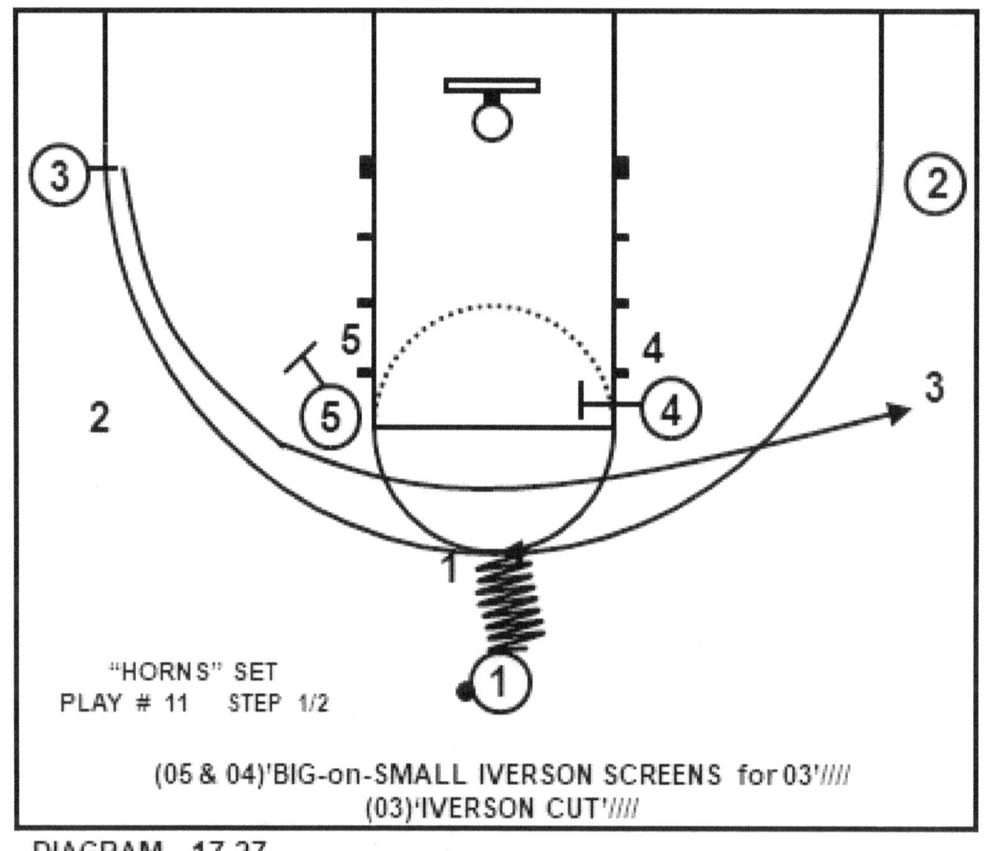

DIAGRAM 17.27

01 makes the "Wing Pass" to 03 which dictates that 04 cuts across to set a high "Cross-Screen" for 05 to flash across to the new "Ballside High Post." After making the pass to 03, 01 "Flare-Cuts" to the new "Weakside Wing." After screening for 05, 04 slips his screen and pops out to the top of the key. At the same time, 02 makes a "Backdoor Cut" to the basket and if he does not receive 03's quick pass, he stops to turn to make an "Inverted Iso Post-Up on the new "Ballside Block." The action by all four of his teammates will leave

02 completely isolated and make his perimeter-type defender very vulnerable in an area where he most likely has little defensive experience and skills.

03's primary receiver should be 02, with 05 also being an outstanding scoring threat. If there is weakside defensive support, it most likely will come from X1. That is why 01 has repositioned himself to be the top perimeter scoring threat on the "Weakside Wing" and could quickly receive the ball from 03's "Skip Pass" or a quick "Reverse Pass" from 04.

If shots are not taken, the new "High-Post/Low-Post" Spot-Ups are accurately filled with the final phase of the offense immediately ready to begin. **Diagram 17.28.**

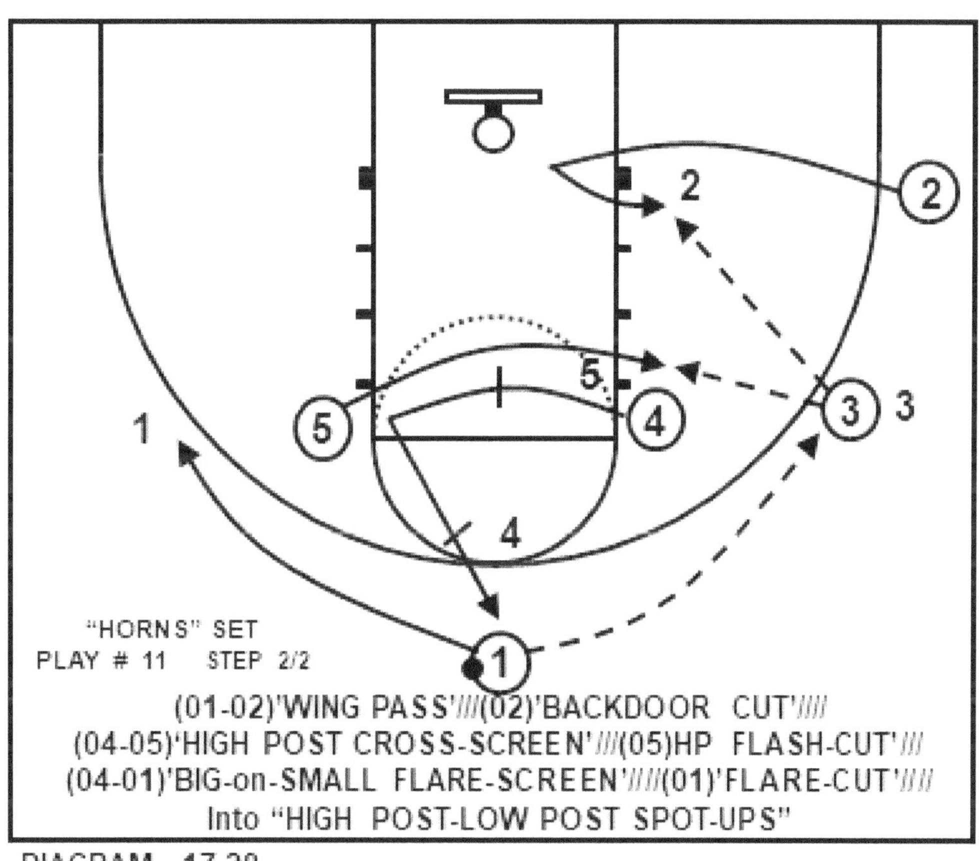

DIAGRAM   17.28

Diagrams 17.29 and 17.30 show the complete Play # 12, another Level 2 play. This shows the initial action side to be the right side of the floor, even though the play could be 'mirrored' to the left side. Both 05 and 04 start to break down to their teammates in their respective "Deep Corners." With it being determined that 01 is heading towards the right side of the floor, 04 breaks down to set a "Ram-Screen" for 02 to continue up to then set a "Ball-Screen" for 01 to continue to the "Slot" on the right side of the floor. 04 then slips his screen and pops out to the "Wing" area. After screening for 01, 02 slips his screen and "Flare-Cuts to the opposite "Wing" area.

On the opposite side, 05's "Pin-Screen" is rejected by 03 so that 03 can make a "Backdoor Cut" to the basket and on through the lane to the opposite side of the floor to invert his perimeter-type defender and "Iso post him up" on the new "Ballside Block." 05 then slips his screen and steps towards the basket on the weakside of the floor. **Diagram 17.29.**

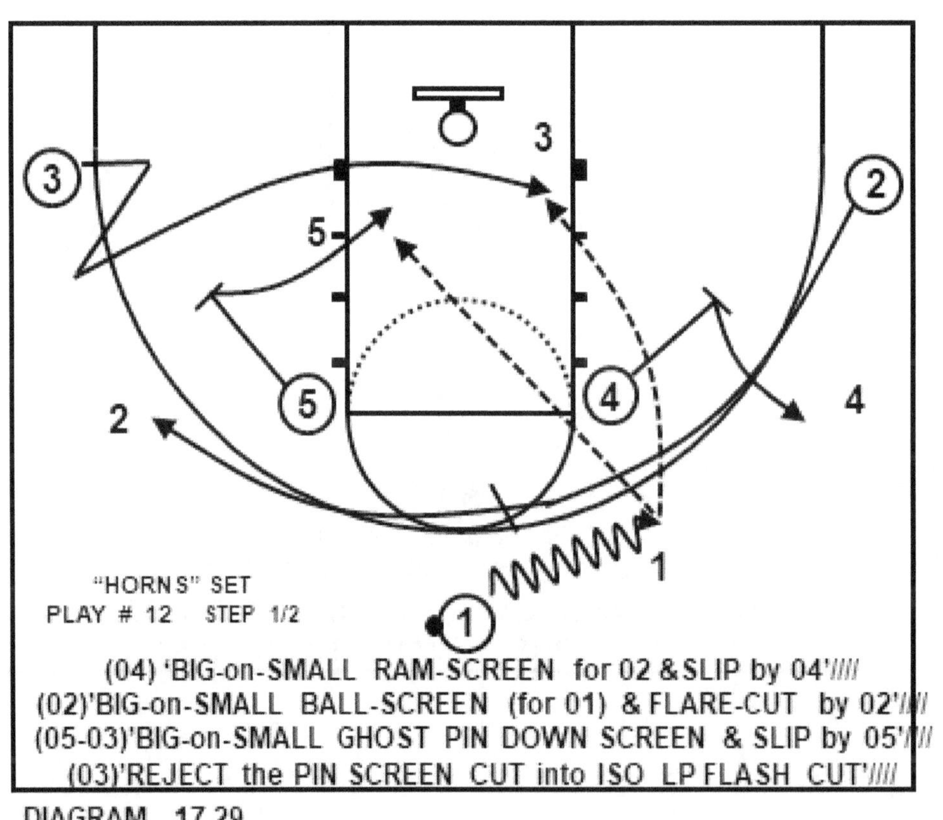

DIAGRAM 17.29

If 01 cannot make "Inside Passes" to either 03 or to 05, he should make the "Wing Pass" to 04, who may have an improved passing angle to deliver the ball to 03 on the "Ballside Block." With 04 now having possession of the ball and to become more of a scoring threat, 05 flashes across the lane to the new "Ballside High Post." This isolates both 03 and 05 even more so for 04 to be able to make various types of passes to either player in addition to the two perimeter scoring threats that 04 has (with 02 floating on the "Weakside Wing" or to 01 at the top of the key.)

If shots are not produced, all five players have repositioned themselves into the correct and fundamentally sound "High-Post/Low-Post" Spot-Ups for the last phase of the offense to instantly begin. **Diagram 17.30.**

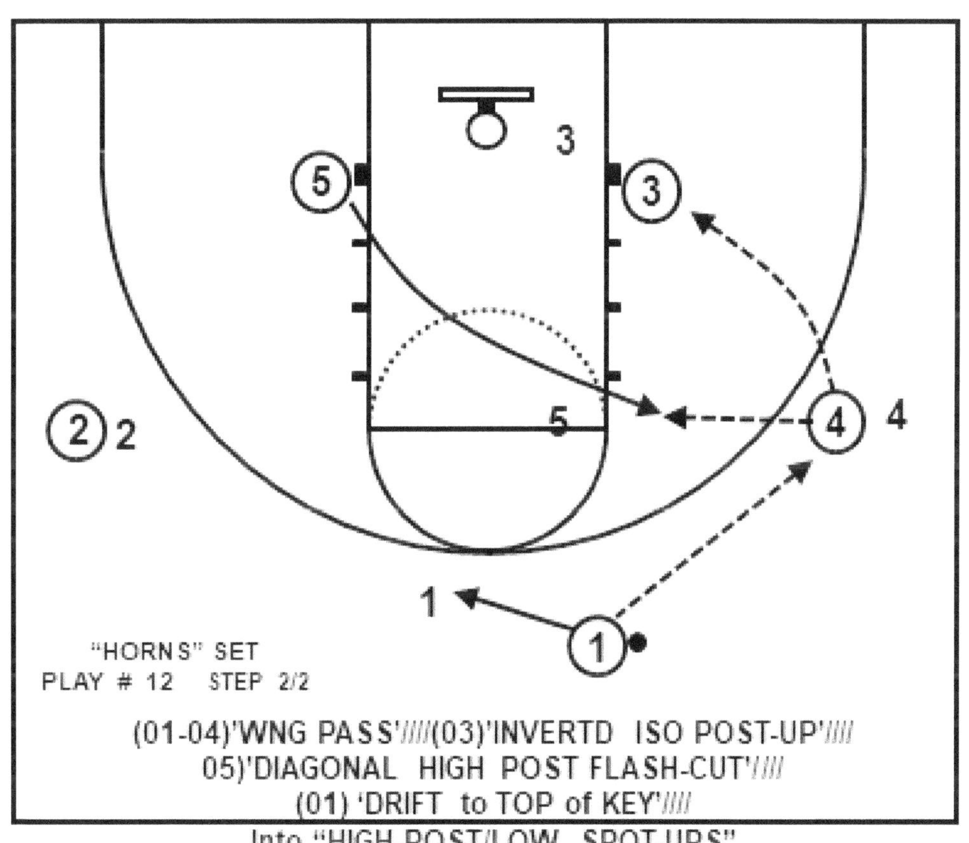

DIAGRAM 17.30

Play # 20 is a Level 3 play that begins almost identical to Plays , 1, 6 and 14 with the two perimeter players that start in their respective "Deep Corners" before ending up on the "Wing" areas on their opposite sides of the floor from where they began. In addition, Play 11 hs actions that are very similar to these nine different entries. This again makes it confusing for opposing defenses to anticipate which play is actually going to be executed.

Diagram 17.31 shows 03 making his "Iverson Cut" over the top of both 05 and 04 and their "Big-on-Small Iverson Screens" while 02 runs the baseline through the lane to the opposite side of the floor. Both players end up at the opposite "Wing" areas while 01 dribbles towards the "Slot" position nearest 03. **Diagram 17.31.**

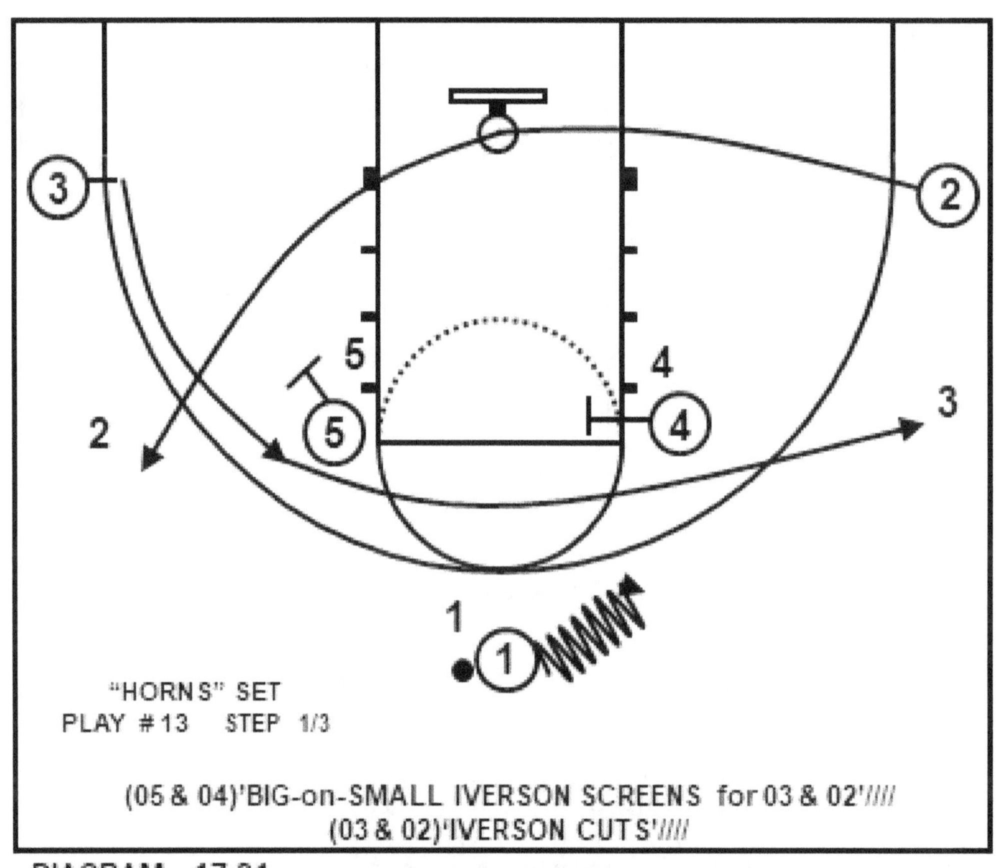

DIAGRAM   17.31

After 03 breaks contact with 05 and 04, 04 cuts across the top of the FT Line to set and past the "Nail" to set a "Cross-Screen" for the post-type offensive player, 05, to make more of a perimeter-type "Shuffle-Cut" off of 04's top left shoulder as he cuts to the new "Ballside Block." After screening for 05, 04 slips his screen to invert his post-type defender out on the new "Weakside Slot." **Diagram 17.32**.

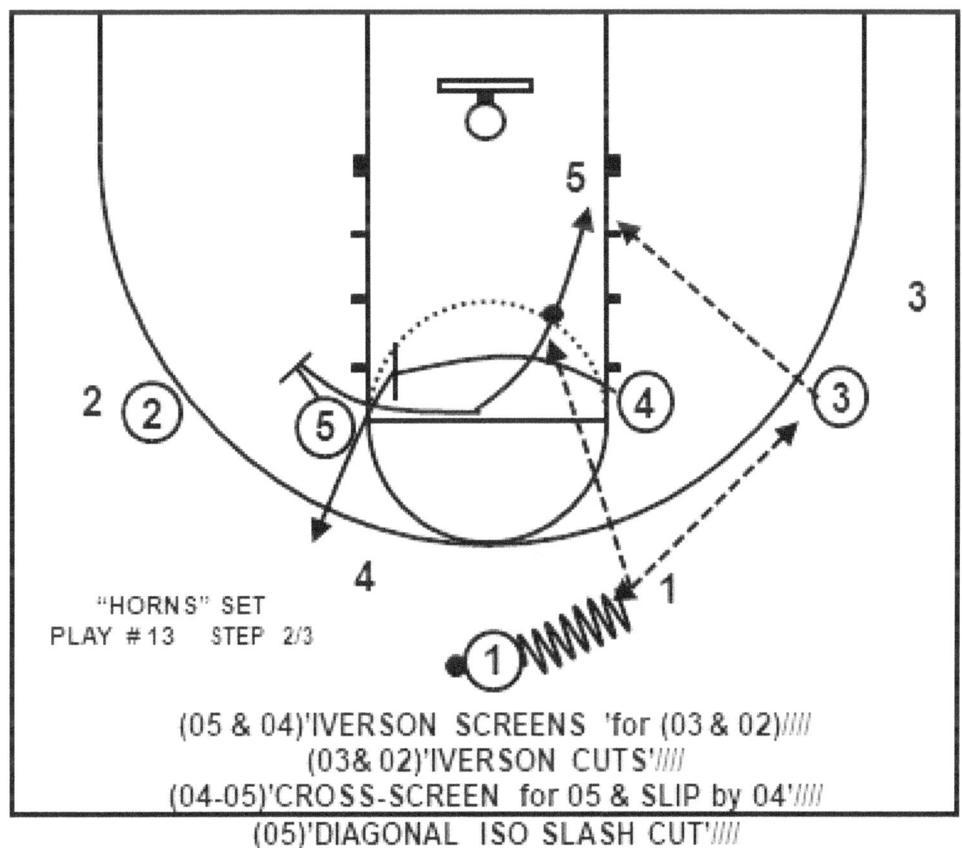

DIAGRAM 17.32

If 01 or 03 cannot hit 05 on his cut to the "Block," the ball is reversed to 04 and quickly swung on over to 02. After 01 makes his "Reverse Pass," 01 breaks over to set a "Small-on-Big" Pin Screen" for 03 to break to the top of the key and for 01 to spot-up to the new "Weakside Wing."

04 breaks towards 02 as if to set a "Big-on-Small Follow(-the-Pass) Screen" for 02. Instead, 04 "Ghosts" this screen and immediately cuts hard to the basket and the new "Ballside Block." At the same time, 05 flashes diagonally up across the lane to the new "Ballside High Post." These cutting actions by 04 and 05 give them opportunities for either to receive the pass from 02 and place them in high percentage scoring probabilities. In addition to the actions by 01 and 03, both 04 and 05 isolate their individual defenders to a great extent and give them opportunities to score close to the basket.

In addition, if shots are not taken; the "High-Post/Low-Post" Spot-Ups are filled for a smooth conversion into the final phase of the offensive attack. **Diagram 17.33**.

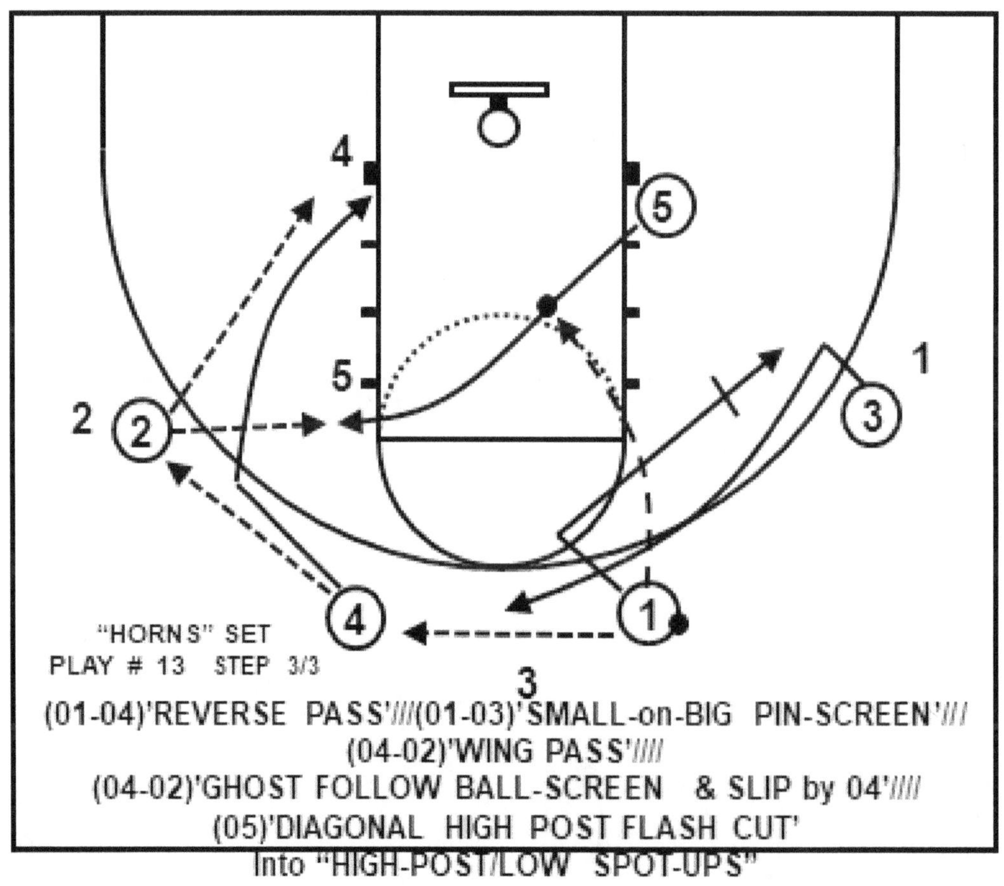

DIAGRAM 17.33

Play # 14 is another Level 3 play where both 03 and 02 make their "Iverson Cuts" to the opposite sides of the floor. To demonstrate that plays/entries such as 1, 6 and 14 could change up which player is the player that cuts over the top of 05 and 04; 02 becomes the player that cuts over the top of 04 and 05 while 03 is the baseline runner that cuts through the lane underneath 05 and 04 to end up on the "Wing" area on the opposite side of the floor. **Diagram 17.34.**

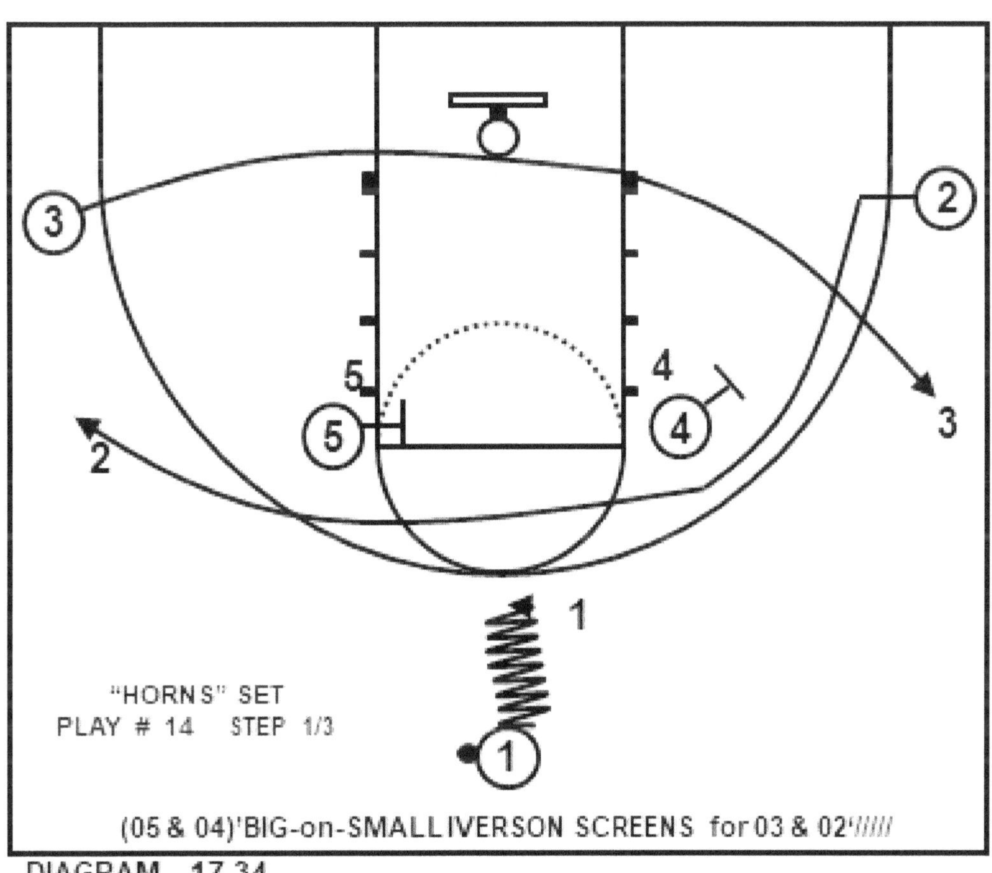

DIAGRAM 17.34

Diagram 17.35 shows 01 electing to make the "Wing Pass" to 02 on the left side (while the play could actually have started with a (01-03) "Wing Pass" to the opposite side of the floor. After making the pass to 02 on the left side of the floor, 04 is the player who steps up to set a "Big-on-Small Back-Screen" at the top of the key. 01 scrapes off of 04's outside left shoulder and curls through the lane to the new "Ballside Block" while 04 remains at the top of the key. This action not only inverts 01's defender, a perimeter-type defender but with 04 and 03 both outside of the arc; fully isolate X1 down on the "Ballside Block." 02 looks to make the quick "Inside Pass" first to 01 and then also to 05 at the new "Ballside High Post." **Diagram 17.35**.

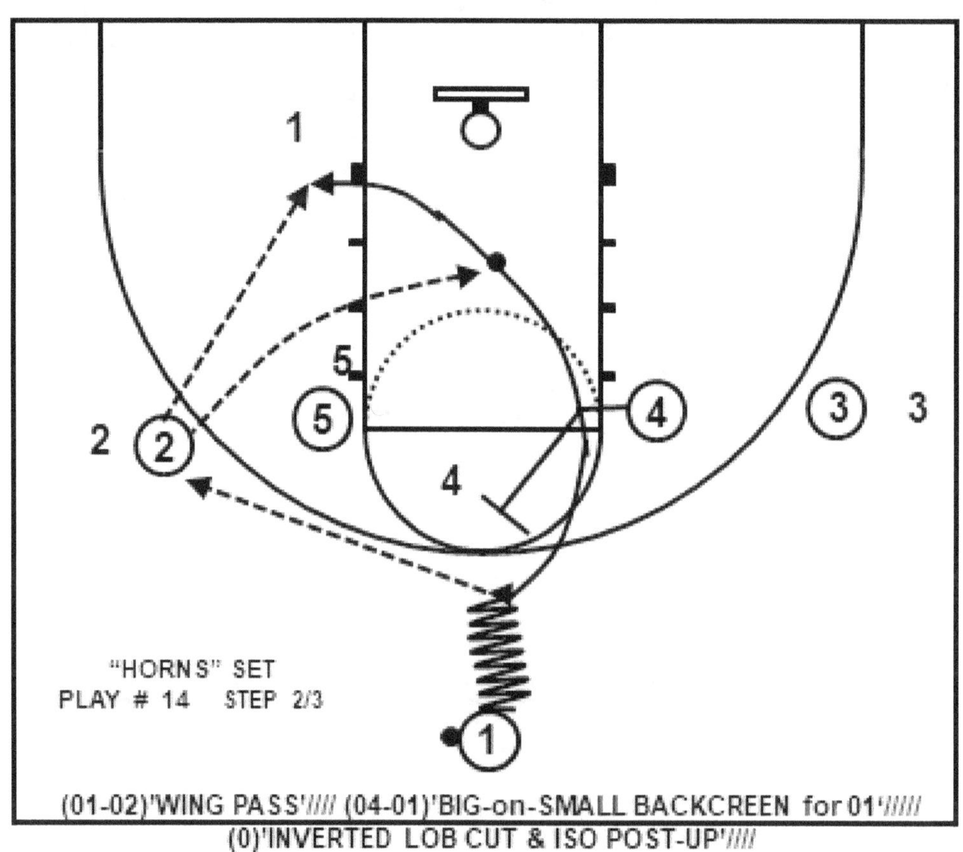

DIAGRAM   17.35

02's passing targets should first be to 01 or 05 in the 'paint' areas but also for a possible "Skip Pass" to 03 on the "Weakside Wing." If 02 turns those three passes down, he can simply make the "Reverse Pass" to 04 who has inverted his post-type defender out on top of the key behind the arc.

04 should quickly swing the ball over to 03 with 05 and 04 both looking to start together a "Stagger-Screen" for 02 to use to break out to the top of the key for a likely '3.' After starting in that direction, 04 breaks off that route and slashes across the lane to post up on the new "Ballside Block." At the same time, 05 continues towards 02 to not "Stagger Screen" (with 04) but to set a "Big-on-Small Pin-Screen" for 02 to still become the primary perimeter scoring threat in this play/entry. As 04 cuts through the lane, 01 sets his defender up to then diagonally break from underneath the basket up to the new "Ballside High-Post."

The synchronized actions by 01, 02, 04 and 05 all have helped not only isolate 04 on the new "Ballside Block," but also for 01 on the new "Ballside High-Post." 03's top inside passing threats are 04 first and then 01. His top perimeter scoring threat in this movement (when the play is executed towards this side of the floor) is 02 at the top of the key.

If all three primary scoring threats are not utilized for taking the shot, the movement of the players has repositioned each player into the proper spot-ups for the designated continuity offense to immediately and seamlessly begin. **Diagram 17.36.**

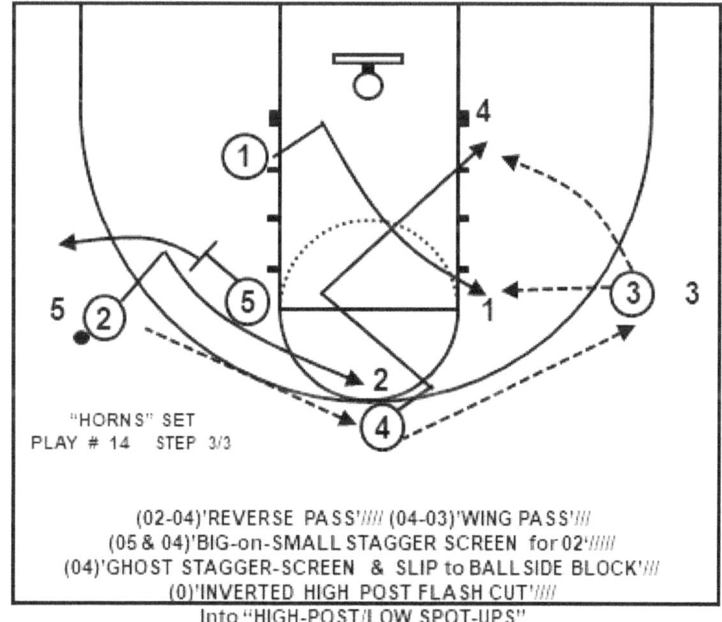

DIAGRAM 17.36

CLOSING

While it has been discussed often, the coaching staff has many decisions to make. They must decide on the most advantageous continuity offense that will meet the skill set of their present players, the coaching staff's offensive philosophies, the type of Primary and Secondary Fastbreaks (Odd-Front or Even-Front Breaks Options, depending on the continuity offense(s) chosen), the best one or two offensive alignments/sets that will be the most efficient and productive for individual and overall team performance, the specific plays and the actual number of plays that should be implemented within the half-court package of plays. In addition, the Baseline and Sideline Plays along with the number of plays chosen must be determined.

It must be emphasized that "Quality trumps Quantity" in the decision in selecting the number of continuity offenses, the number of sets/alignments and the number of plays (from each alignments) that are to be implemented. Don't allow too many plays or alignments to mentally bog down the offensive team.

Again, it must be brought to the coaching staff's attention that the continuity offense(s) chosen will be the main determination of which Secondary Break Options, offensive alignments and plays/entries are incorporated within the current season's offensive arsenal.

The plays/entries carefully diagrammed down to the small and seemingly unimportant 'V-Cuts' made by countless players before making their more important following cut are also described in detail.

Each play has been carefully studied and evaluated to determine which level of talent and experience must be possessed for that specific team to be able to successfully execute the play. This includes all players' physical skills as well as their mental understanding of the game. Coaches must also have the experience and the associated level of understanding of the game as well as their coaching/teaching of the nuances of each play.

The most sophisticated plays/entries would fall into the last of the three levels all based on the team's physical talents and skills, the mental capacities and the overall team's game experience. In addition, the coaching staff must have a high degree of basketball knowledge as well as very high teaching and coaching skills to educate his/her entire basketball team. The proper breakdown drills must be thoroughly utilized to hone the fundamental skills and techniques needed for individual players and the overall team to execute plays that can be efficient, productive and successful. We define this family of plays as the "Level 3 category" of plays. This "Level 3" family of plays will have a much more complex offensive scheme that would require a very high amount of physical talent as well as requiring a greater amount of the players (to execute) and the coaches (to teach and coach) mental capacities and experience needed for the offense to be efficient, productive and successful. We feel plays in our defined "Level 3" category could possibly be successful for NBA teams, definitely for college teams and also for many high schools and older AAU teams.

The next classification or level of plays would be possibly slightly lower as far as sophistication, complexity and the actual 'length' of the play (and the number of passes, cuts and screens used) in the play's overall scheme. While all "Level 2" plays in each of the chapters in this book remain to be fundamentally sound, these plays may lack the actual number of techniques/methods that are implemented within that play in comparison to the "Level 1" plays/entries. Therefore any team that successfully executes the highest "Level 1" plays/entries could/should easily be able execute any of these so-called lower "Level 2" plays/entries, if so desired. Almost all high school teams should be able to execute successfully all aspects of the "Level 2" plays.

The final grouping of plays would be called "Level 1" plays and are not as difficult for offensive players to master the execution of them, both physically as well as mentally. Even though the techniques are still fundamentally sound, they may not be as complex to learn and understand in addition to being easier to physically execute.

"Level 1" plays would be lower in the scheme's complexities and the number of techniques used in the execution of this category of plays. Obviously, since these "Level 1" plays are still sound, but lack some of the methods used in the two previous more sophisticated and complex levels; these more elementary plays should be able to be utilized by any teams that use either of the two higher level plays. We feel that Middle School/Junior High teams as well as younger AAU teams or organizations should be able to utilize any of the "Level 1" plays successfully, with a possibility that some of those teams that are slightly more advanced (than other teams) could possibly use some plays located in the immediate next immediate level.

Ideas, concepts and techniques from actual plays from teams of all three levels have been used to modify or to create different combinations of the various techniques and schemes used that will help prove these entries can be successfully used. This allows the author to create numerous plays that use the various schemes to build a library of fundamentally sound plays that will be unique and will be appropriate for a wide range of teams with various ages and skill levels.

With this book having plays/entries in these three presumed categories or levels, the book will reach out and benefit a much larger group of serious basketball coaches from elementary school age to the highest skilled levels that exists.

In addition, an experienced and resourceful coach may be able to mold some plays that include all of the offensive techniques that he/she desires could reshape a specific play that begins in one specific offensive set/alignment and reshape it so that it could begin in a different offensive/set that is more favorable to that coach and his/her coaching staff's liking.

Conversely, that innovative and creative coach may completely like the specific offensive set/alignment and favor the very same offensive actions included in a certain play, but can modify that play so that the ending spot-ups of all five players are conducive to being able to begin the final phase of the offensive attack by using a more favorable offensive continuity offense.

The "HI-LO STAX SET"

PLAYS/ENTRIES THAT END in the "3-OUT/2-IN" OFFENSIVE SPOT-UPS

At the conclusion of every entry/play/quick-hitter where no shots have been taken, all five players will always be repositioned into a different family of offensive spot-ups. One of these groups of spot-ups is called the "3-Out/2-In Spot-Ups." After each play every player will have been repositioned around the court with any one of the five players ending up in the "Ballside Block," the "Ballside Wing," the "Weakside Block," the "Weakside Wing," and the "Point" (at the top of the key). These five positions can provide the offense with safe and easy types of ball-reversals, large gaps for dribble penetration, opportunities to deliver the ball inside to whomever (perimeter-type or post-type players) is posting up their defender on the "Ballside Block," and a player that can be a perimeter-scoring threat and a legitimate offensive rebounding threat from outside of the arc on his "offensive crashing of the boards." The "3-Out/2-In Spot-Ups also provide ample opportunities for constant and effective defensive transition responsibilities and well as maximum offensive rebounding.

Diagram 18.1 illustrates the "HI-LO STAX" Set with 01 always being the lone primary ball-handler bringing the ball to the top of the key. 03 always starts at the "Elbow" area on the left side of the floor stacked just below 05 who is also aligned at the left "Elbow."

On the opposite side of the floor, 04 starts on the "Ballside Notch" above the Block, while 02 stacks just below 04.

Play # 1 illustrates a Level # 3 play with 04 "Pin-Screening" for 02 to pop out to the "Deep Corner" on his side of the floor. After screening for 02, 04 then breaks out to the "Wing" area on his side of the floor.

On the left side of the floor, 03 slips up to set a quick "Small-on-Big Back-Screen" for 05 to spin off of and slide down the "Block" on his side of the floor. After screening for 05, 03 steps up to set a second screen—a "Big-on-Small Ball-Screen" for 01 to use to reach the "Wing" area on the left side of the floor. 03 then slips his second screen and pops out to the "Top of the Key." This last screen by 03 can also be called "Pick and Pop."

01's primary target is to make the "Inside Pass" to 05 posted up on the new "Ballside Block." With 02 and 04 having weakened the defensive weakside by stretching the defense both horizontally and vertically, 05 should be basically able to isolate his defender on the "Ballside Block." **Diagram 18.1.**

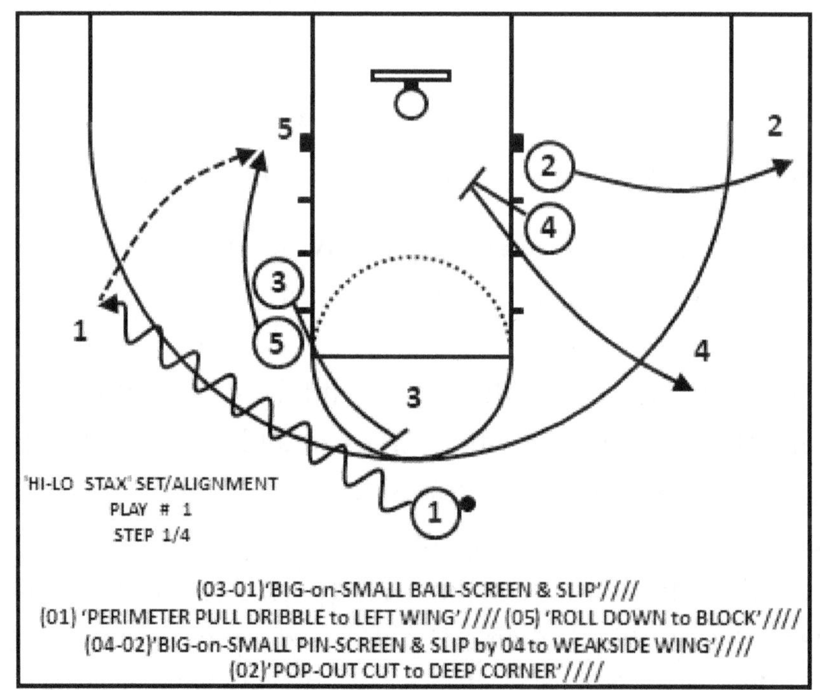

DIAGRAM 18.1

Diagram 18.2 shows that 01 has the ball and looks initially to make the "Inside Pass" to 05. With 02, a perimeter player extended out to the "Weakside Deep Corner," 04, a post-type player stretched out at the "Weakside Wing" area and 03, another perimeter-type player out at the "Top of the Key;" 01 could make "Skip Passes" particularly to 02 or 03 or to 04. **Diagram 18.2.**

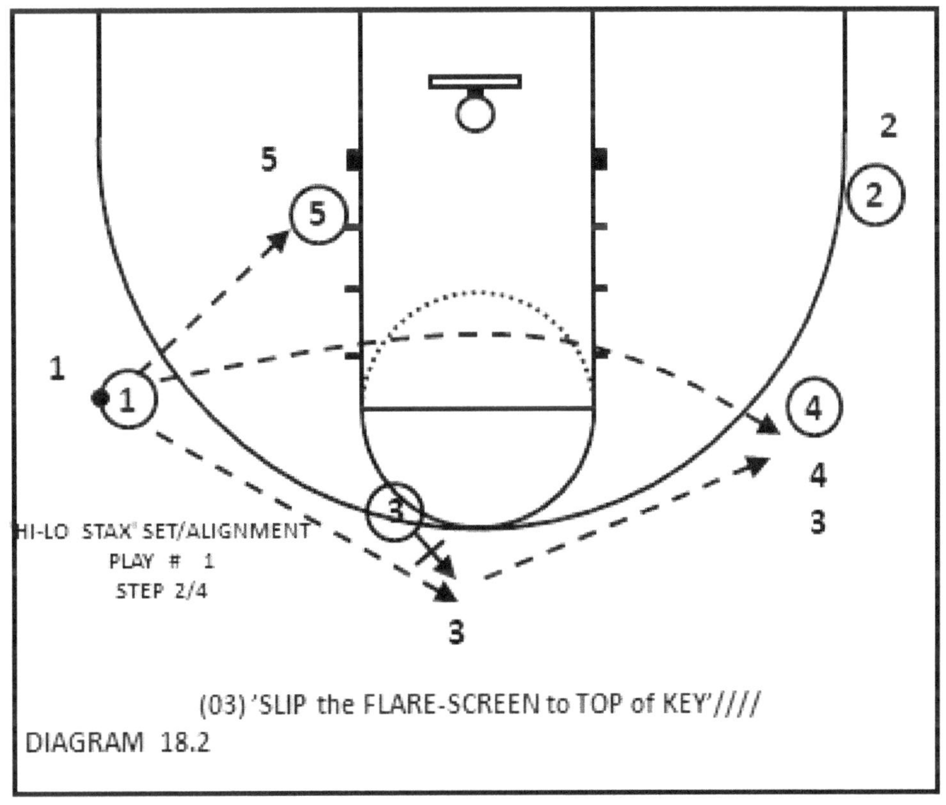

Diagram 18.3 shows the fourth and final step of Play # 1 with 01 making the (01-03) 'Up Pass" to 03 out on top. 05 starts to steps out as if to set a "Shuffle Back-Screen for 01" before he "Ghosts" the screen and he then flashes towards the "Nail." 01 starts to make the normal "Shuffle Back-Screen Cut" that he would have used if 05 had completed the screen. He then breaks back out to the "Wing" area he started from.

With 04 and 02 spread out behind the arc along with 03 (on "Top) and 01 (at the "Wing,") 05 should have the luxury of receiving the ball from 03 and attacking X5 in a complete isolation scenario or to make quick "Kick-Out Passes" to any of his four teammates. When 05 makes the "Kick-Out Pass" to 02, 04 dives to the "Ballside Block and then empties out to the opposite side. If 04 receives 05's pass, 02 is the teammate that dives to the basket and if he does not receive the quick touch pass from 04, he continues through the lane to the opposite side of the lane. After 05 makes the pass to either 04 or 02, 05 continues cutting to the new "Ballside Block." **Diagram 18.3**

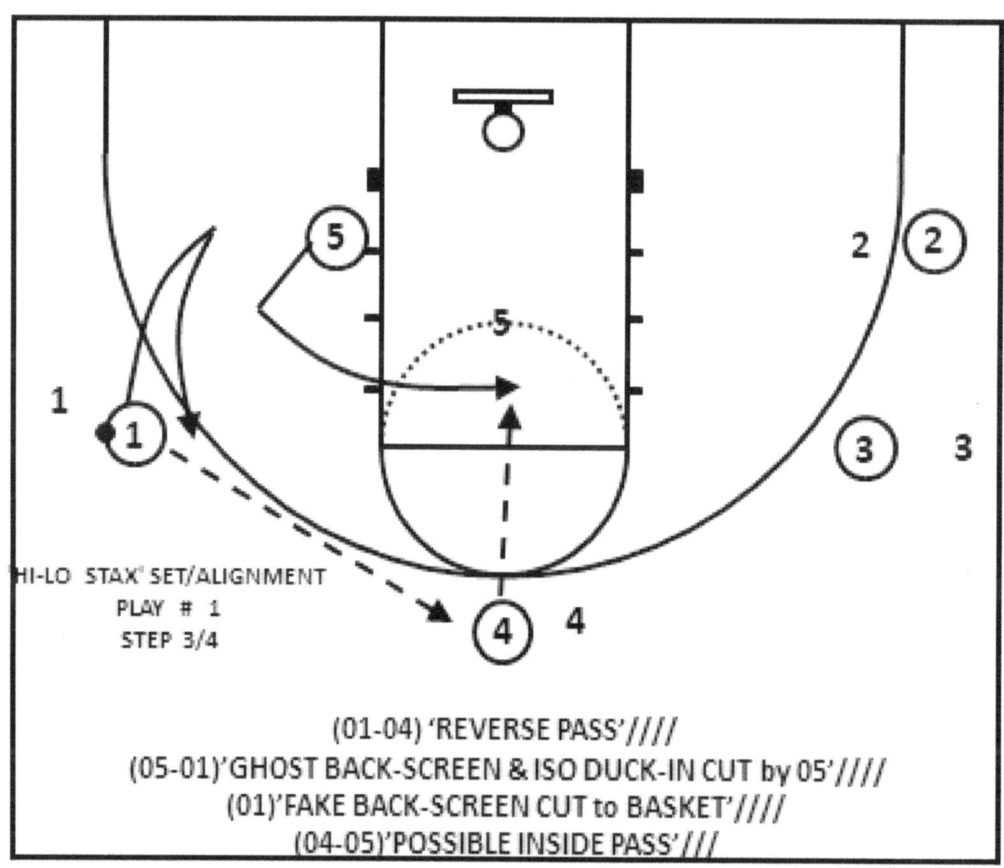

DIAGRAM 18.3

Diagram 18.4 shows making that quick pass to 04 with 02 being the (first) cutter looking for 04's pass. 05 immediately follows 02's "basket cut." If no shots are created, the "3-Out/2-In" Spot-Ups are then filled for the final phase of the attack immediately ready to begin. **Diagram 18.4**.

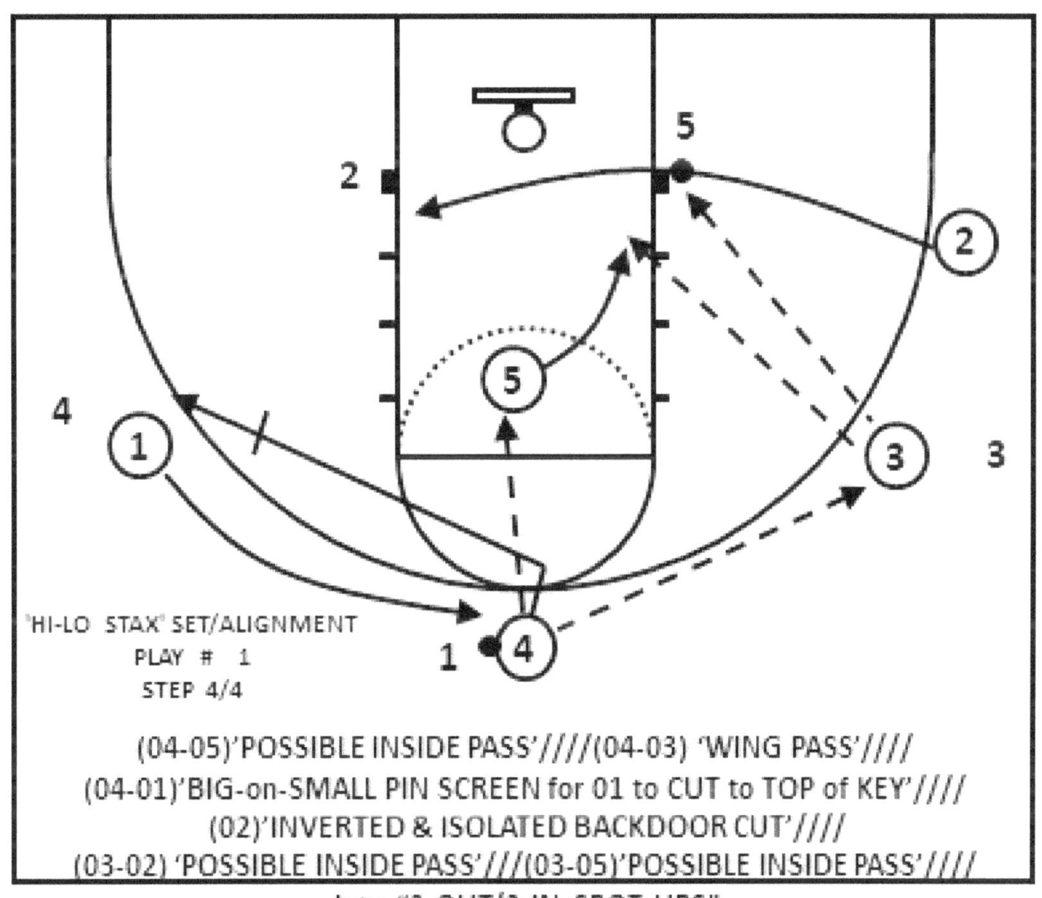

DIAGRAM 18.4

The primary difference in the following plays/entries are that all five players will end up in a different group of offensive spot-ups. These "4-Out/1-In Spot-Ups" will have players moved about the court with any of the five ending up in the "Ballside Deep Corner," the "Ballside Slot," the "Weakside Slot," the "Ballside Post," and the "Weakside Deep Corner." These five positions can provide the offense with safe and easy types of ball-reversals, large gaps for dribble penetration, opportunities to deliver the ball inside to whomever (perimeter-type or post-type players) is posting up their defender on the "Ballside Block," and a player that can be a perimeter-scoring threat and a legitimate offensive rebounding threat from outside of the arc on his "offensive crashing of the boards." The "4-Out/1-In Spot-Ups also provide ample opportunities for constant and effective defensive transition responsibilities.

Diagram 18.5 illustrates the complete Play # 2, a Level 1 play/entry. This play begins with very similar action as several previous plays—05 "Pin-Screening" for 03, (who in this instance, breaks out to the "Slot" position on their side of the floor. 05 then becomes the player that breaks out to the FT Line extended. On the "lower stack" side of the floor, 04 sets his usual "Pin-Screen," and stays on his "Block" and waits for 03. 02 uses the screen to break out to the wide and "Deep Corner" on his side of the floor.

01 dribbles over towards 03 at the "Slot" for a (01-03) DHO. 03 then "perimeter-pull (drag) dribbles" over the top of the key to the opposite "Slot." During 03's " drag dribble," 04 then seals his defender off before making his frequent (but delayed in this case) "Iso Duck-In Cut." Either 03 or 02 should have the proper locations to be able to make the "Inside Pass" to 04 on his return from the middle of the lane to the new "Ballside Block."

This action is a very short play that immediately after the (01-03) DHO, repositions all players into the new "4-Out/1-In" Spot-Ups for a different continuity offense that can be instantly executed. **Diagram 18.5.**

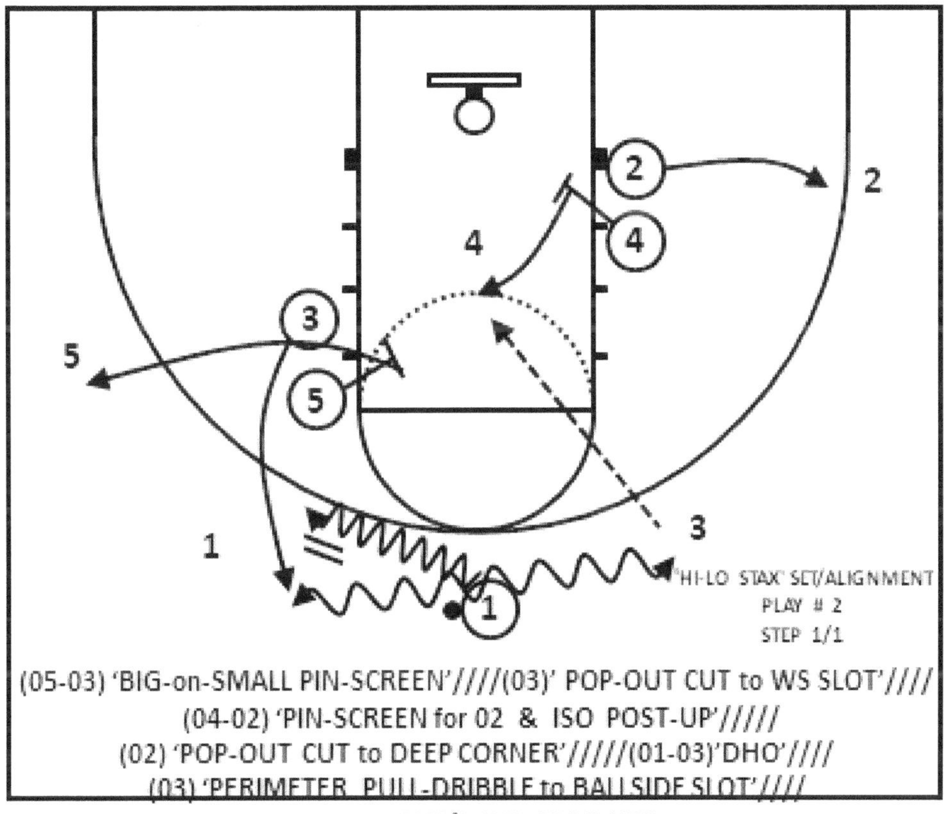

DIAGRAM 18.5

Play # 3 another Level 2 play starts with a 04-02. "Pin-Screen" for 02 and then slipping across the lane to the opposite "Block." 03 pops out to his "Wing" position off of 05's "Pin-Screen" before then making an "Iverson Cut" off of 05's "Iverson Screen." 03 then cuts through the "Nail" location over to the opposite "Wing" area.

After "Iverson-Screening" for 03, 05 slips out just outside of the arc to receive the initial pass from 01. 01 then follows his pass by cutting towards 05. **Diagram 18.6.**

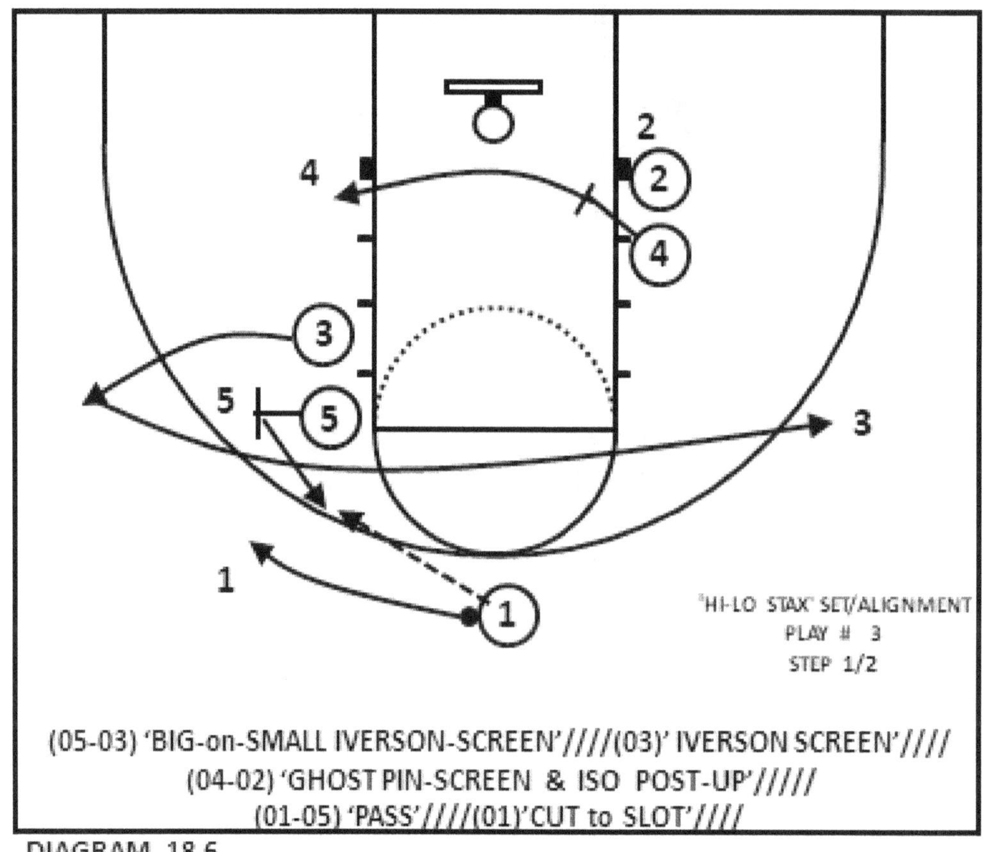

DIAGRAM 18.6

Diagram 18.7 shows 05 making a "Flip Pass" to 01 and 02 immediately breaking up diagonally through the lane to set a (02-05) "Small-on-Big Back-Screen." After making the "Flip Pass" to 02, 05 spins off of 02's screen and runs a "Lob Cut" to the basket, waiting for 01's "Lob Pass." With 04 posting up on the new "Ballside Block" and 05 running towards the rim, 02 steps up to the "Ballside Slot" and 03 filling the new "Weakside Slot." 01 has the opportunity to also make a "perimeter-pull (down) dribble" towards the "Deep Corner" (while looking for an "Inside Pass" to 04 or a possible "Skip Pass" to 03. If no shots are taken, the "4-Out/1-In" Spot-Ups are filled for a fluid continuation of the overall offensive attack. **Diagram 18.7**.

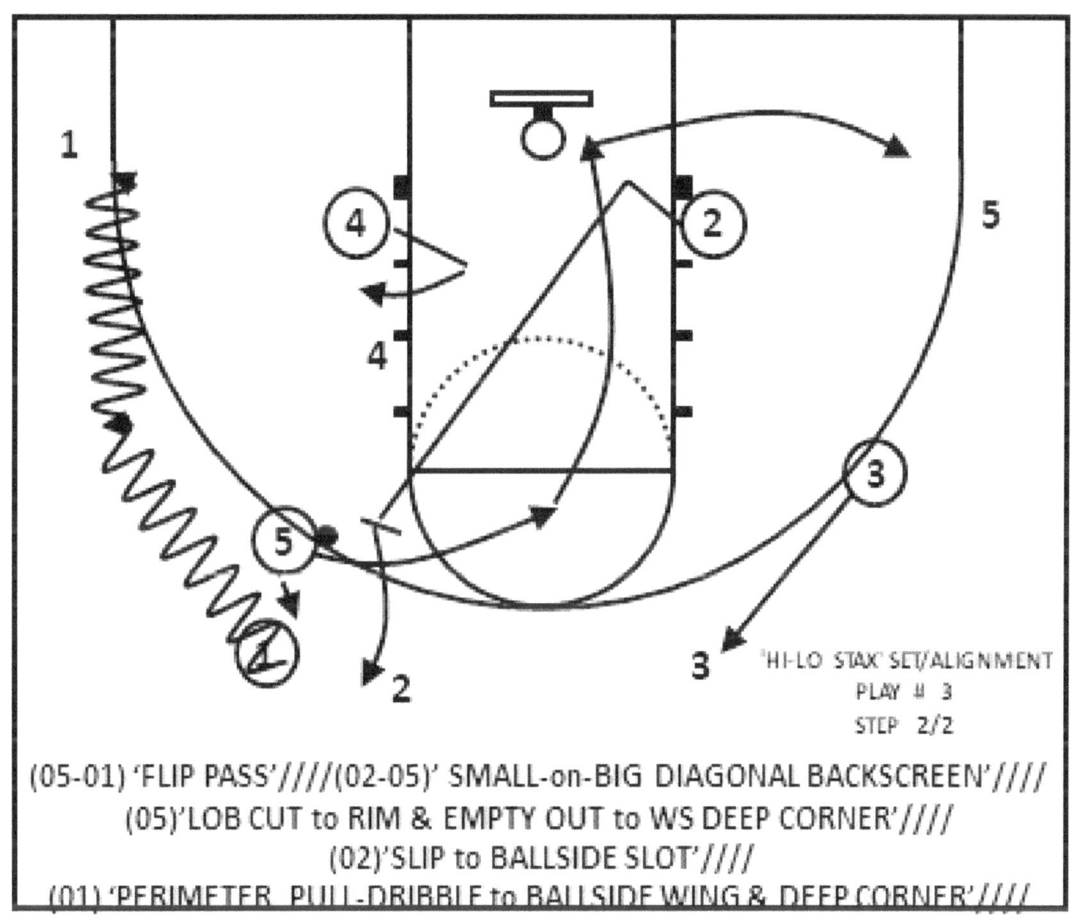

DIAGRAM 18.7

Play # 4 is a Level 2 Play that is fully shown in Diagrams 18.35 and 18.36. Again, this play has a "Counter" partner with the previous play in that the beginning action very much resembles Play # 13 as well as other play beginnings (such as Plays 5, 6, and 7.) This means that 04 sets the same "Pin-Screen" for 02 to break out to the perimeter—this time the "Deep Corner." On the "high stack" side, 05 sets the same "Pin-Screen" for 03 to break out to his same "Wing" area at the FT Line extended. After screening for 03, 05 slips the screens and makes an inverted cut out to the perimeter "Slot" position.

As 04 and 05 set their screens, 01 again perimeter-pull dribbles towards the "low stack" side and reaches the opposite "Slot" location. During his dribble, he primarily looks to how X4 is attempting to defend 04 on his (more than isolated) "Duck-In Cut." **Diagram 18.8.**

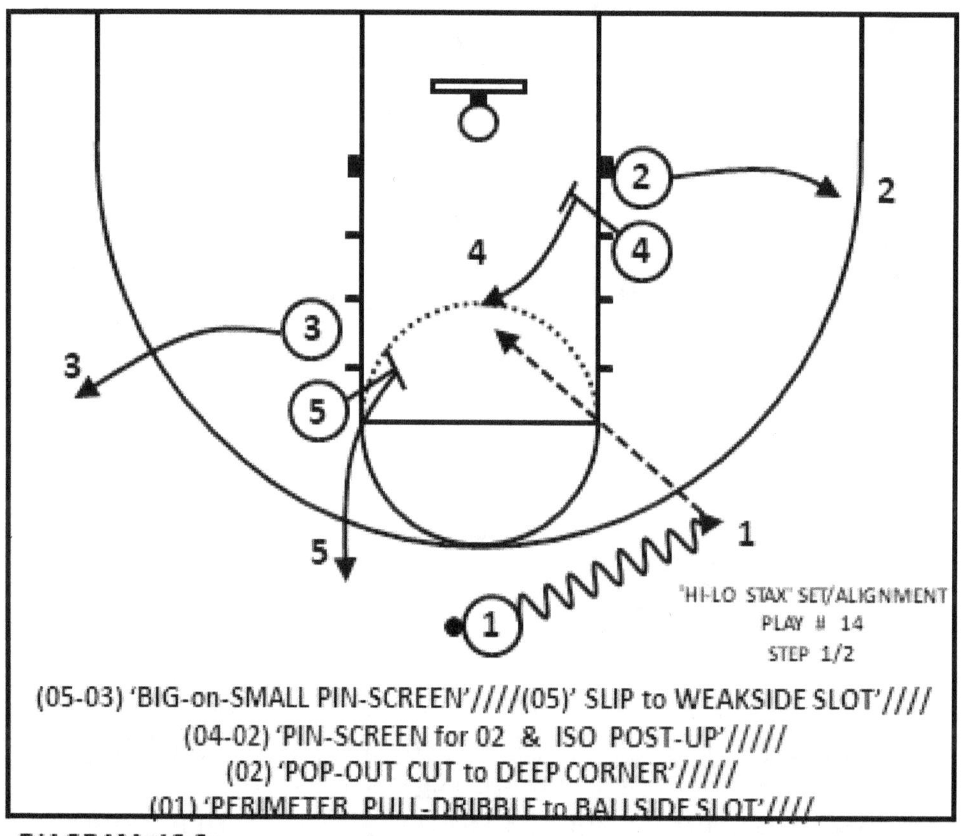

DIAGRAM 18.8

Once again, this play temporarily repositions players in the same "Odd Front Secondary Break" Spot-Ups before the play is concluded. Various half-court options could then be executed or any of the actual "Secondary Break" Options could continue the play before any (and all) options flow into the ending "4-Out/1-In" Spot-ups.

In this play, 01 has decided to reverse the ball to 05, who has pulled presumably the biggest opponent on the floor out away from the basket and behind the arc. While common action could be a "(04-01) Chin-Screen" followed by other various actions. In this play, the offense is attempting to "counter" the more common and frequently used "Chin" action with the following movement. As 01 releases the ball to 05, he starts to set his defender up before cutting off of 04's outside left shoulder. Many defenders will have been taught to "jump to the ball" when the pass is made and to go "ballside" (the right side of 04 on the "Chin" screen.)

To take advantage of that fundamentally sound defensive technique, 02 slips in from his "Wing" position to (horizontally) "pin" in X1 with 01 "bumping the Chin-Screener (04) and flare-cutting off of 02's top left shoulder to the now vacant "Weakside Wing." There still exists an interior cutter in that 04 is still the "Chin Screener" and then actually switches to become the "Chin-Cutter." 04 then diagonally slashes across the lane to become the "Iso Cutter and Post-Up player on the new "Ballside Block."

With the "Weakside" being occupied by the (02-01) "Flare-Screen" (after the (04-01) "Bump Chin-Screen," X4 should have absolutely no help in defending his post-type defender on the new "Ballside Block." In addition, a simple (05-01) "Skip Pass" should provide the offense with an open '3' on the weakside. It should not be forgotten that 02 will be a formidable perimeter threat at the "Slot" after slipping his (02-01) Flare-Screen."

If all of this action does not create the desired shot, the "4-Out/1-In" Spot-Ups are filled for the continuation of the overall offensive attack. Diagram 18.9.

4
3
1
2
3
4
5
1
5
'HI-LO STAX' SET/ALIGNMENT
PLAY #4
STEP 2/2
(01-05) 'REVERSE PASS'////(04-01)' BUMP CHIN BACK-SCREEN'///
(04) 'BUMPED CHIN-CUT thru LANE to OPPOSITE BLOCK'////
(02-01)'FLARE-SCREEN for 01////(01) 'FLARE-CUT'////
(02) 'SLIP the FLARE-SCREEN to WEAKSIDE SLOT'////
Into "4-OUT/1-IN" SPOT-UPS

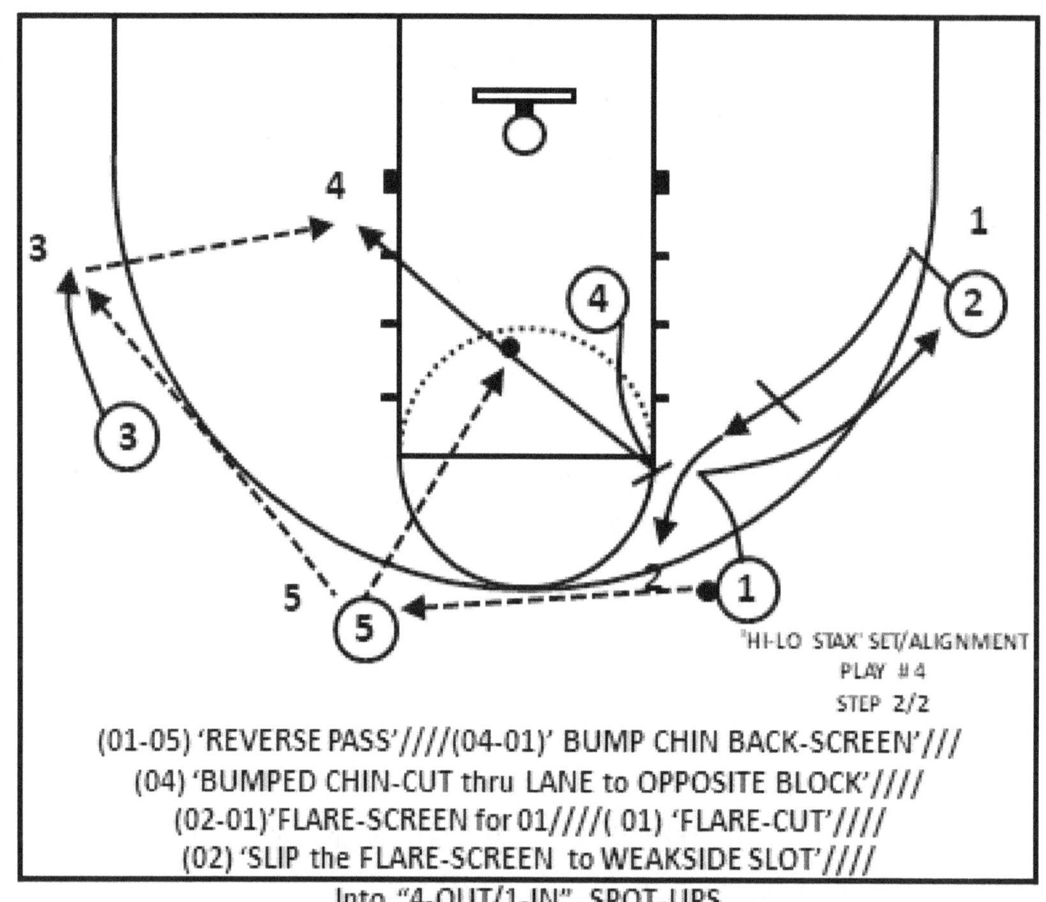

DIAGRAM 18.9

Play # 5 is a Level 3 play that is a Counter to Play # 4 in that Play # 5 actually executes the "(04-01) "Chin Screen" action (while the previous play executes the "Bump Chin Screen" action.) The double "Pin-Downs" by both 05 and 04 that are followed by 04's "post seals and post-ups" look very similar to Plays 5, 6, 7 10, and 14. As 01 "perimeter dribble-pulls" to the "Slot" on the right side of the floor, 05 pops out to the "Slot" on the left side as 04 makes the identical "Duck-In Cut" he does in Play # 15. **Diagram 18.10.**

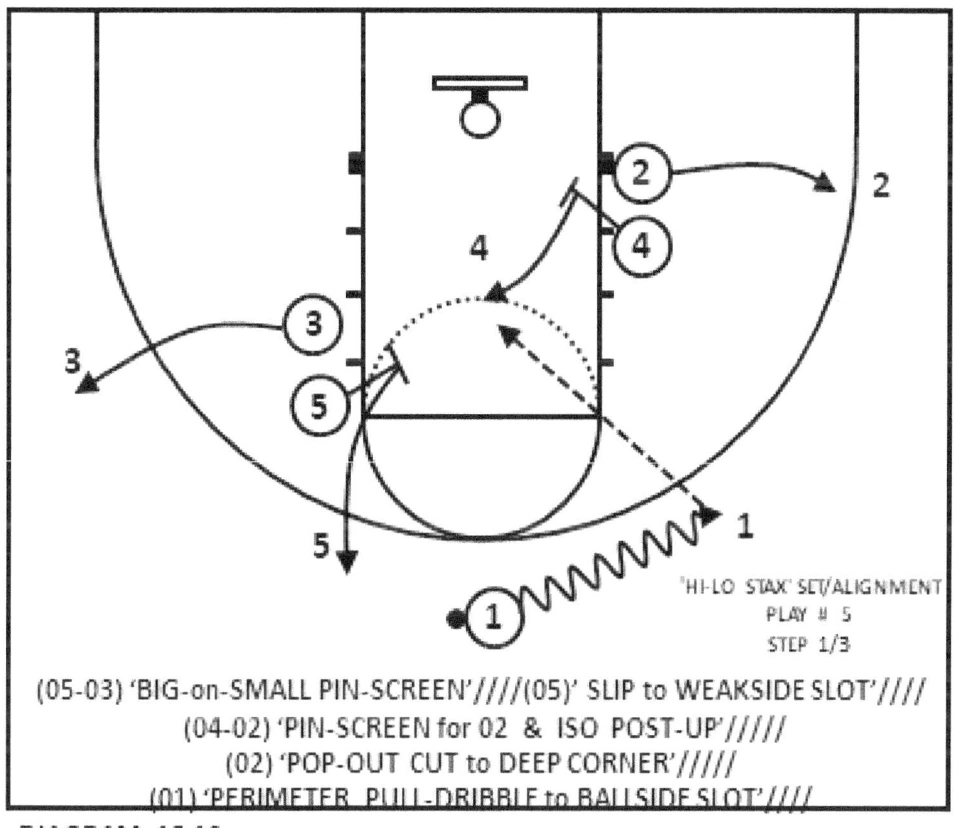

DIAGRAM 18.10

Diagram 18.11 shows 01 electing to not make the "Inside Pass" to 04 and instead (again) reversing the ball to the inverted post-type player, 05, out on the "Slot." 01 executes his "Chin-Screen (Shuffle) Cut through and across the lane to the new "Ballside Block." As the cut is made and 05 looks to make the "Inside Pass" to 01, 03 makes a "Drift Cut" towards the "Deep Corner." If 05 cannot make the pass to 01, a "Down Pass" to 03 may allow 03 to deliver the ball to 01. After "Chin-Screening" for 01, 04 slips his screen and steps out to the new "Weakside Slot." With 02 now on the weakside of the floor, 02 has the space and the freedom to drift and float behind helpside defenders and be prepared for possible "Skip Passes" from either 03 or from 05. With 01 being a perimeter-type player that is now inverted and somewhat isolated, 05 and 03's primary receiver should be 01. Their next receiver could be 02 on the opposite side of the floor. **Diagram 18.11.**

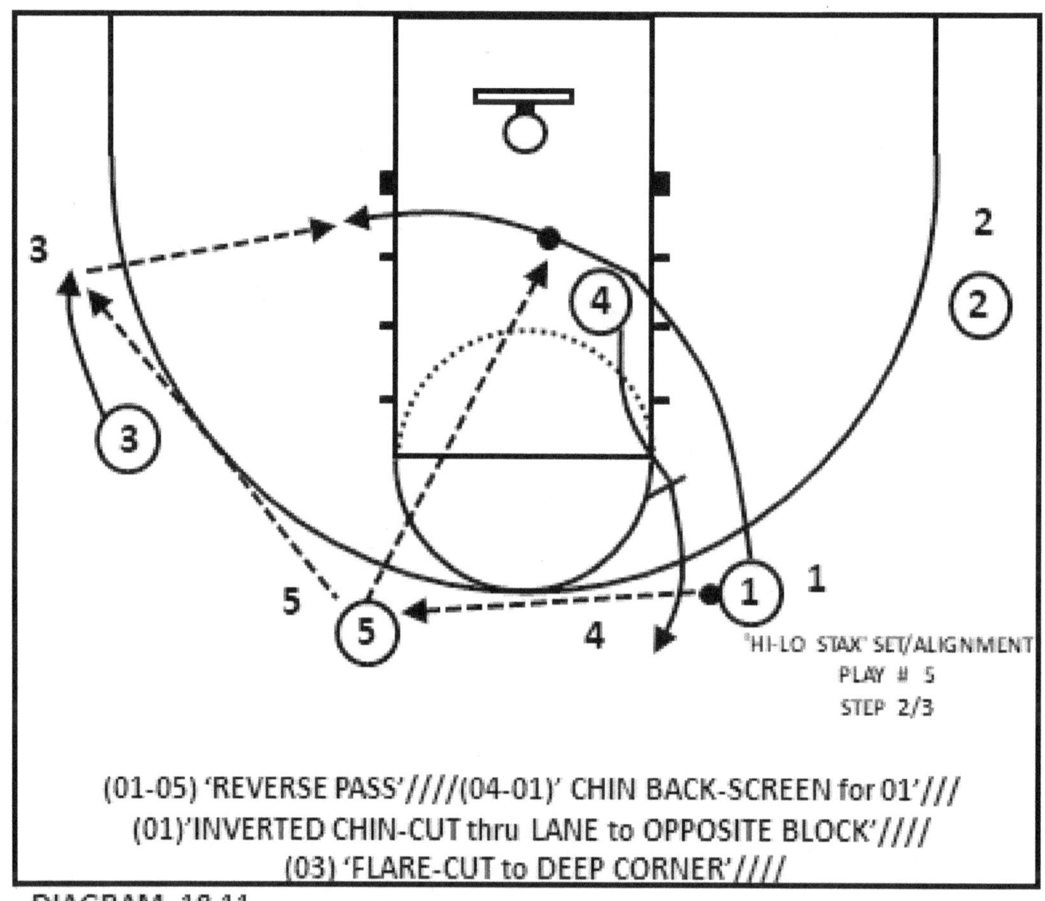

DIAGRAM 18.11

If those two receivers are not able to get their designed shots, 05 could simply reverse the ball out on top to 04. 03 would immediately execute his "Flex Cut" off of 01's "Small-on-Big Flex Back-Screen." If 04 cannot hit 03 cutting through the lane, he looks to hit 05 off of his "Flare-Cut" or to 01 on his Vertical Elbow Cut." If neither are open, 02 breaks up to receive the (04-02) DHO while 04 continues drifting down to the "Deep Corner."

The "4-Out/1-In" Spot-Ups are again filled so that the designated continuity offense can fluidly and instantly begin the final phase of the attack. Diagram 18.12.

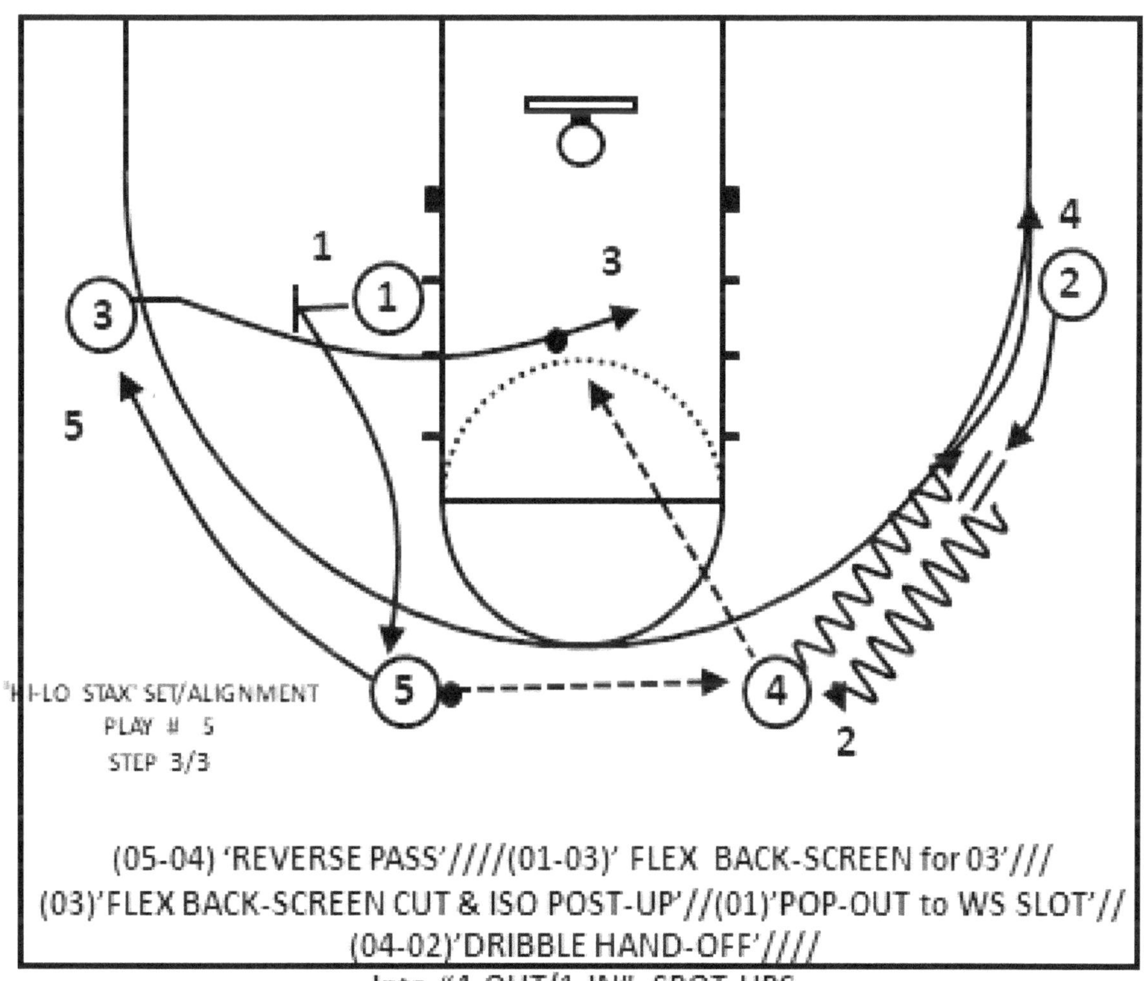

DIAGRAM 18.12

Play # 6 is a Level 3 play that appears in many ways to be the same plays/entries as other plays. Again, as 01 dribbles towards the "Wing" area on the right side of the floor, 02 executes the same "Zipper" Cut while 04 attempts to post up his isolated defender. The weakside defenders are occupied with 05 "Pin-Screening" for 03 to break out to the new "Weakside Slot," followed by 05 slipping the initial screen and then stepping out to the "Wing" area. **Diagram 18.13**

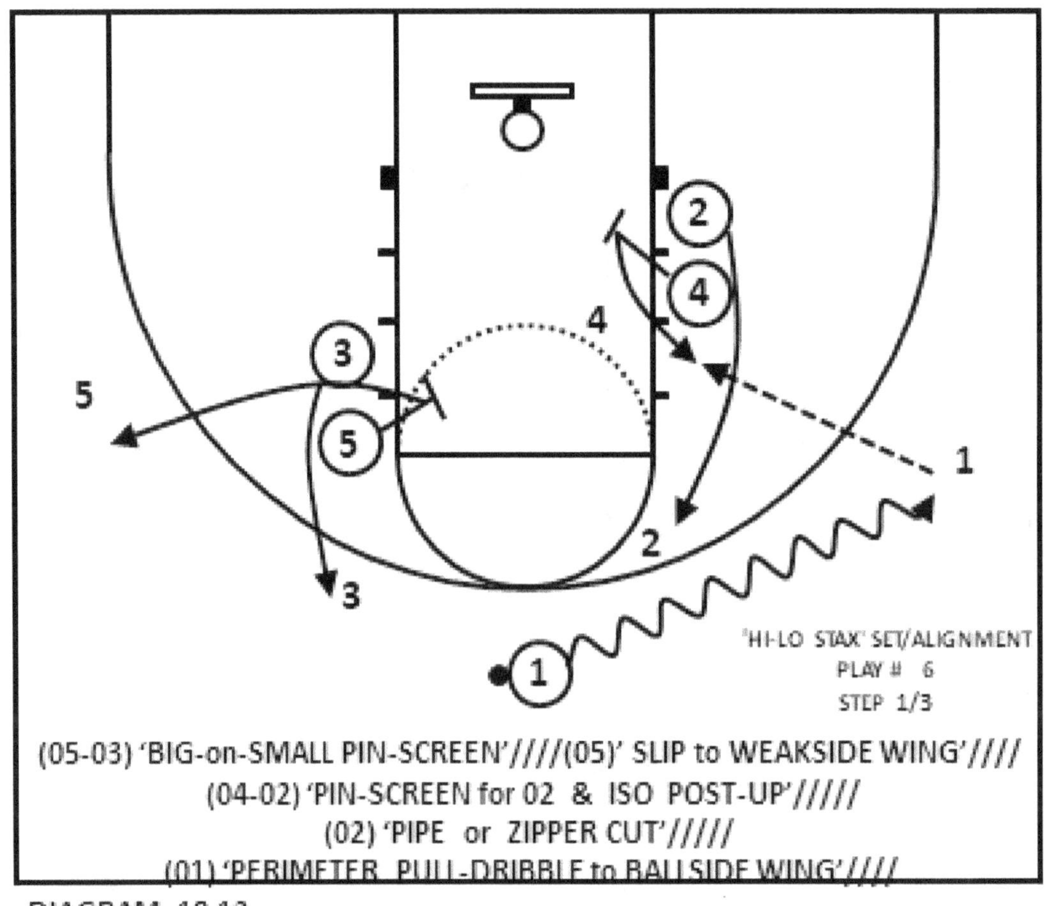

DIAGRAM 18.13

01 looks to make the "Inside Pass" to 04 or the "Up Pass" to 02 at the "Slot." As the ball is in the air, 03 breaks over to set a "Small-on-Big Ram-Screen" that 05 will use to break towards the "Top of the Key" location. Diagram 18.14.

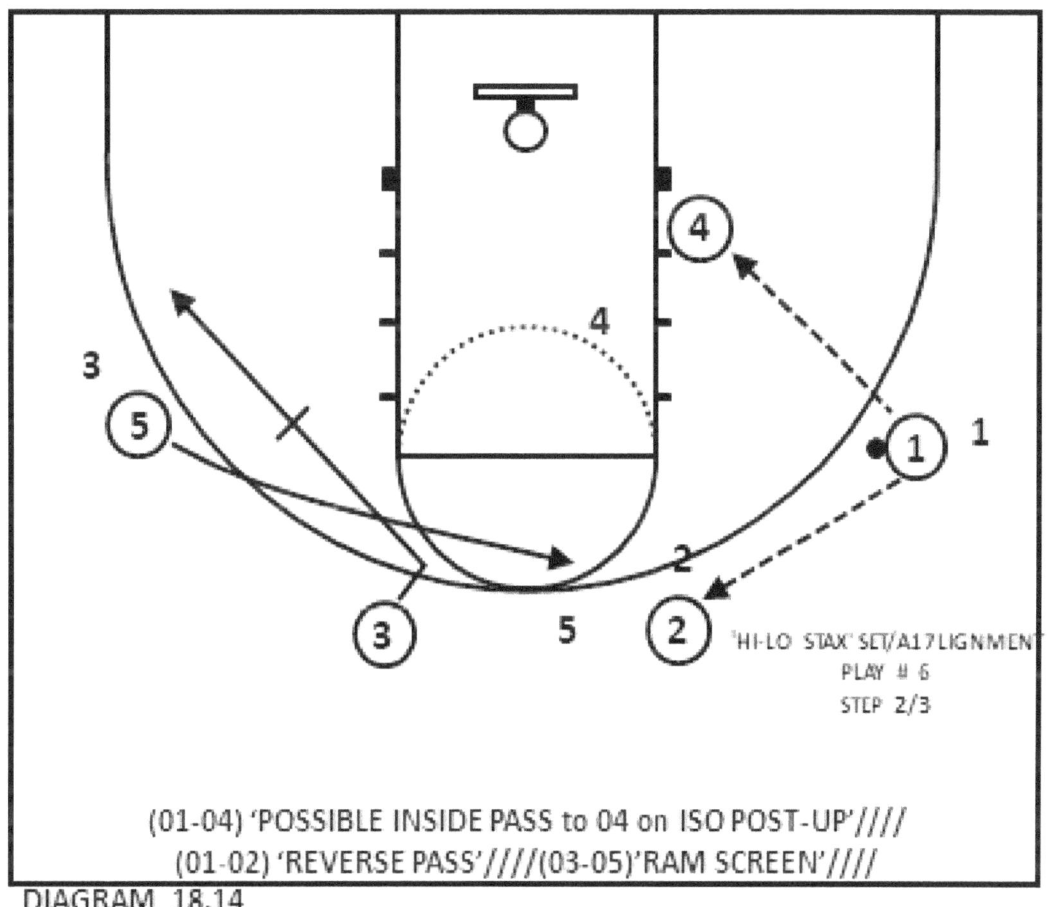

DIAGRAM 18.14

Diagram 18.15. illustrates the final part of Play # 6 with 05 continuing his cut over to then set a "Big-on-Small Ball-Screen" for 02 to use to "perimeter (drag) dribble-pull" across the top of the key to the opposite "Slot" location. In a continual motion, 05 then continues in the same direction to set a ""Big-on-Small Brush-Screen" for 01 to use as he scrapes off of 05's top right shoulder. 01 continues cutting diagonally across and through the lane to post his defender up on the new "Ballside Block." 04 leaves his "Ballside Block" location and steps out further into his new "Weakside Deep Corner." At the same time, 03 flares out towards the "Ballside Deep Corner," looking for 02's "Down Pass." With that pass, 03 could look for "catch/shoot or catch/create or catch/pass (to 01.) This action has repositioned all players into the "4-Out/1-In" Spot-Ups so there can be an immediate transition from the actual play into the designated continuity offense.

Regardless, the "4-Out/1-In" Spot-Ups are filled for the designated continuity offense that is tied in with these specific spot-ups is ready to continue the attack. **Diagram 18.15.**

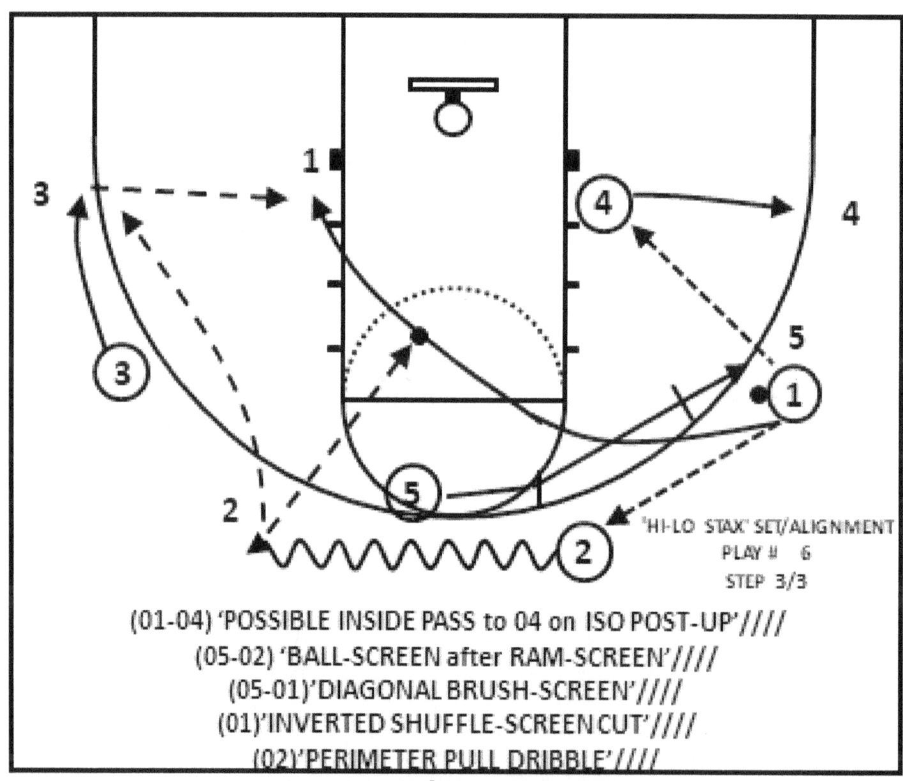

DIAGRAM 18.15

PLAYS/ENTRIES THAT END in

the "HIGH-POST/LOW POST" OFFENSIVE SPOT-UPS

The main difference in this family of plays plays/entries is that all five players will end up in a different group of offensive spot-ups. These "HIGH-POST/LOW-POST" Spot-Ups will have players moved about the court with any one of the five players ending up in the "Ballside Block," the "Ballside High Post," the "Ballside Wing," the "Weakside Wing," and the "Point" (or top of the guy)" These five positions can provide the offense with safe and easy types of ball-reversals, large gaps for dribble penetration, opportunities to deliver the ball inside to whomever (perimeter-type or post-type players) is posting up their defender on the "Ballside Block," and a player that can be a perimeter-scoring threat and a legitimate offensive rebounding threat from outside of the arc on his "offensive crashing of the boards." The ""HIGH-POST/LOW-POST" Spot-Ups also provide ample opportunities for constant and effective defensive transition responsibilities.

Diagram 18.16 illustrates a Level 1 play that initially resembles several other plays (that actually flow into other offensive spot-ups, rather than the "HIGH-POST/LOW-POST" Spot-ups that will be discussed now.

Play # 7 starts with 05 and 04 again "Pin-Screening" their teammate on the same side of their own stack. 04 sets his (04-02) "Pin-Screen" for 02 to break out to the "Wing" area on his side of the floor and then turns to face 01 dribbling to the "Wing" where 03 has also relocated. After 05 has set his customary screen for 03 to use to break out to the "Wing" area, 05 continues across the lane to then set a (05-04) "(Diagonal Down-)Screen the (Pin-)Screener" for 04 to use to then flash to the new "Ballside High Post."

After setting the screen, 05 reverses directions to turn back and flash to the new "Ballside Block." At the same time, 03 loops around 01 and the ball and then receives 02's "Flare-Screen" for 03 to end up "Flare-Cutting" to the new "Weakside Wing."

This action places 05 on the new "Ballside Block," 04 on the "Ballside High Post", 01 on the "Ballside Wing" with the ball, 03 at the new "Weakside Wing" and 02 now settled in at the "Top of the Key." With each player repositioned at these new "HIGH-POST/LOW-POST" Spot-Ups for the new appropriate continuity offense to fluidly and smoothly begin. **Play # 7 Diagram 18.16**.

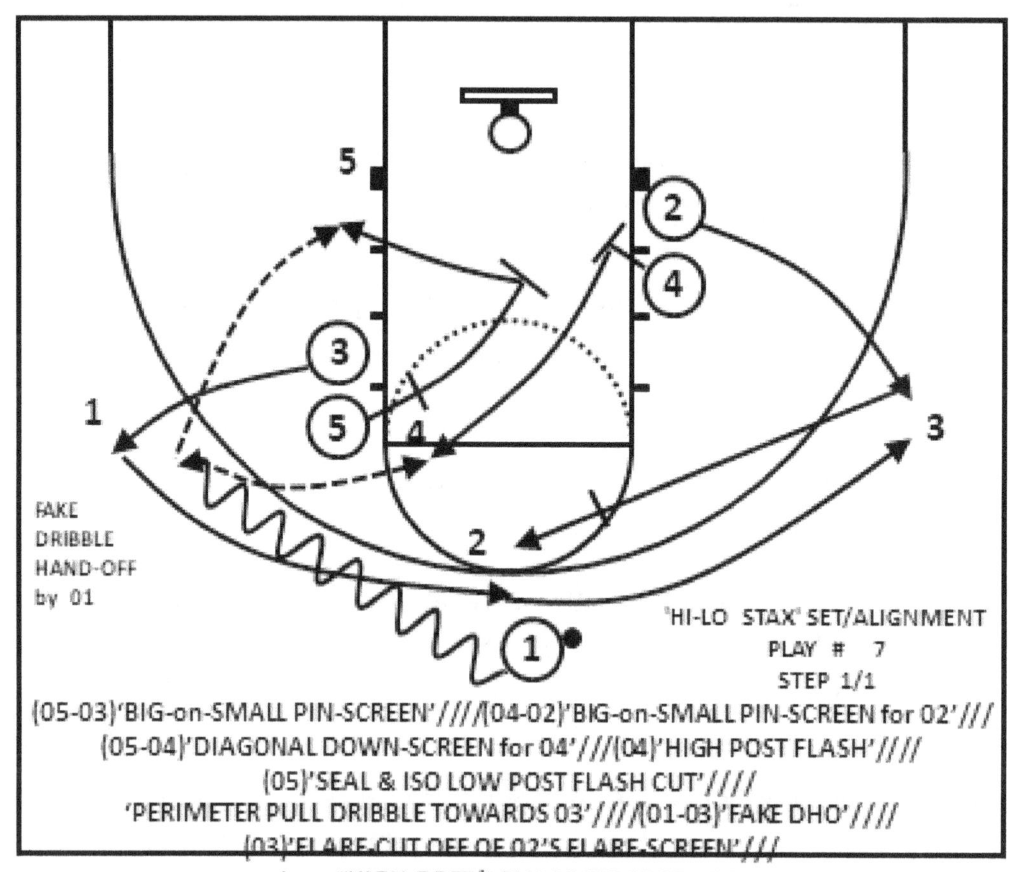

DIAGRAM 18.16

Play # 8, a Level 2 Play, is shown in Diagrams 18.17 and 18.18. It starts with the standard "Big-on-Small Pin-Screens" by 05 and 04 for 03 and 02 respectively. 01 dribbles towards 03 in the "Wing" area while 02 has popped out to his "Wing" area.

After 05 has screened for 03, 05 continues diagonally across the lane to execute a "(Lane Exchange Cross-)Screen the (Pin-)Screener" action with 04. 04 ends up on the new "Ballside Block" with 05 settling in on the "Block" across the lane.

At the same time of the interior screen, 01 makes a DHO with 03 for 03 to either make a "Penetration Dribble" to attack his defender in the lane or a "Perimeter Pull Dribble" out towards the top of the key. **Diagram 18.17.**

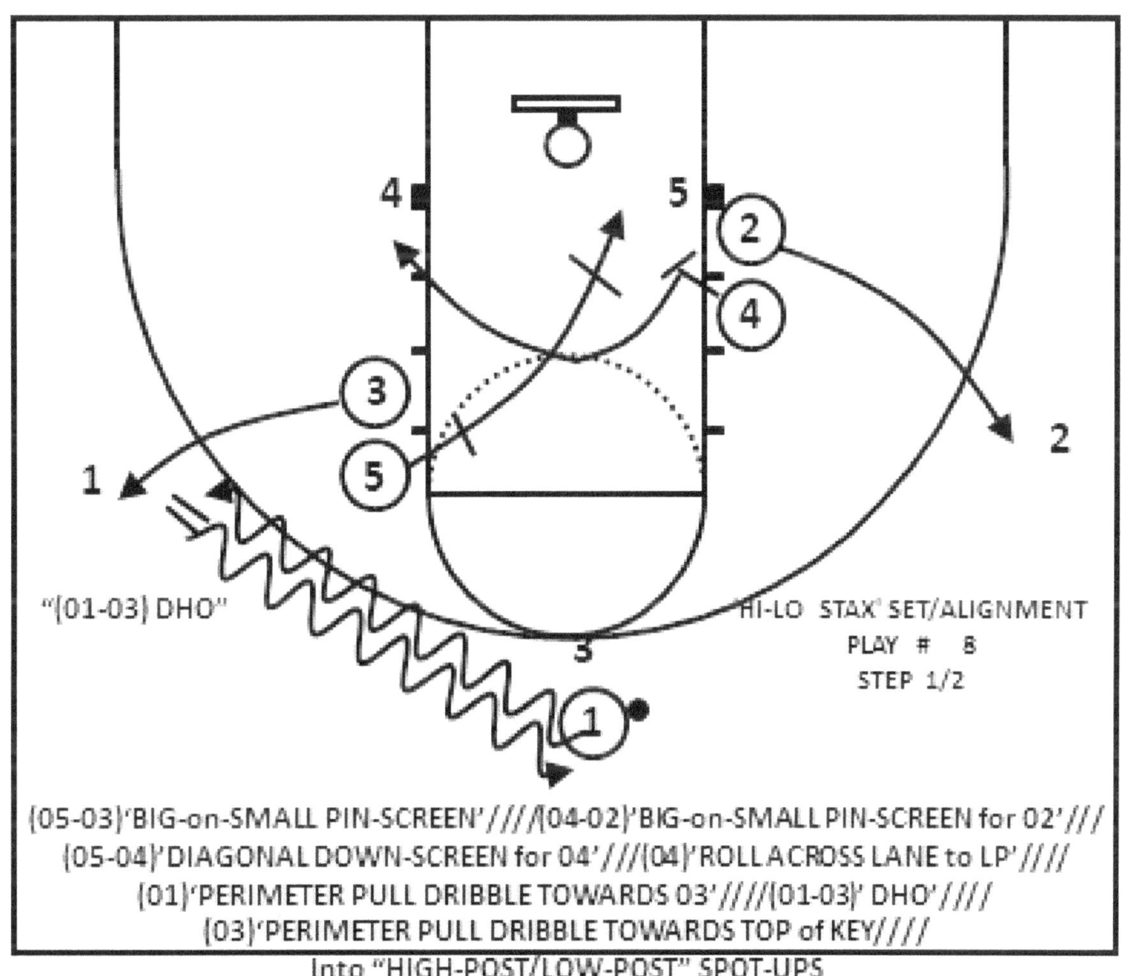

DIAGRAM 18.17

As 01 "Perimeter Pull Dribbles" to the top of the key, 05 makes a "Duck-In Cut" into the "Dotted Circle" area and looks for 03's "Bounce Pass" into the lane. At the same time, 04 turns towards the basket and looks for 03's "Lob Pass." With 04 underneath the basket and 05 in the "Dotted Circle" area, both players follow the direction of 03's next "Wing Pass."

This diagram shows 03 continuing the swing of the ball with a (03-02) "Wing Pass" to 02, causing 05 to flash to the new "Ballside High Post" and 04 cutting across the lane to the new "Ballside Block."

The Wing that does not receive 03's "Wing Pass" (01 in this diagram) should step up and over to set a "Flare-Screen" for 03 to use on his "Flare-Cut" away from the ball. 01 then slips his "Flare-Screen (for 03) and steps to the top of the key to fill one of the five "HIGH-POST/LOW-POST" Spot-Ups for the specific continuity offense to be able to smoothly begin. **Diagram 18.18.**

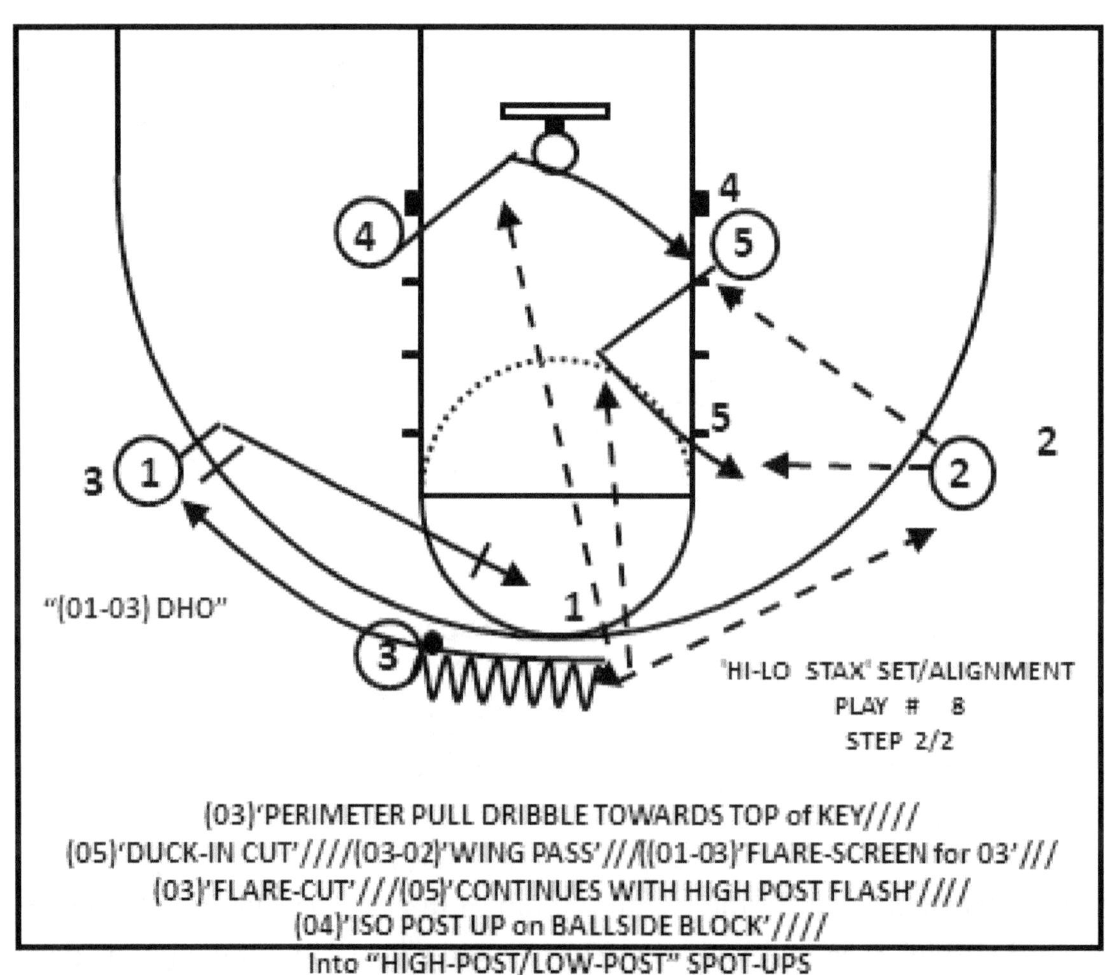

DIAGRAM 18.18

Play # 9, another Level 2 Play, is a Counter to Play # 7 and is shown in Diagrams 18.17 and 18.18. It starts with the standard (05-03) and (04-02) "Big-on-Small Pin-Screens." In this play 01 again dribbles towards the "high stack" side where 03 has broken out to the same "Wing" area and with 02 has breaking out to his "Wing" area on the opposite side of the floor.

After the (05-03) Screen, again 05 breaks towards 04 to diagonally cross the lane to set the same "(Lane Exchange Cross-)Screen the (Pin-)Screener" action for 04 to use to flash to "Block" across the lane. After screening for 04, 05 empties out to the opposite side of the lane.

As the interior screening action takes place, 03 gains possession of the ball with the (01-03) DHO. Once again, reading the defense, 03 can elect to make a "Penetration Dribble" into the lane or a "Perimeter Pull Dribble" to pull defenders out away from the lane. **Diagram 18.19.**

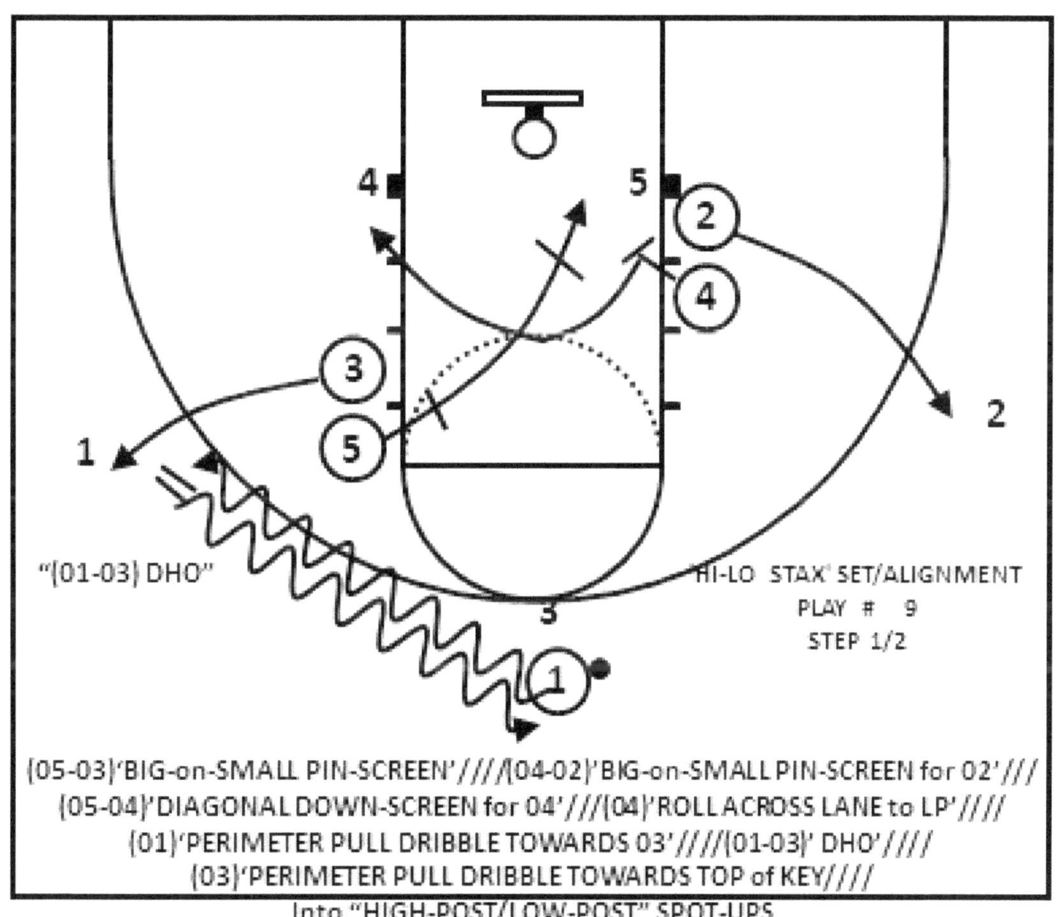

DIAGRAM 18.19

When and if 03 makes a "Perimeter Pull Dribble" and reaches the imaginary center line, 04 changes his route and becomes the player that makes the "Duck-In Cut" into the "Dotted Circle" area while 05 changes his cut also and steps towards the basket. 05 is the player looking for the "Lob Pass" while 04 becomes the player waiting for the "Bounce Pass" on his "Duck-In Cut."

If neither are open, 03 can make a "Wing Pass" to either side of the floor. In this diagram, 03 makes the (03-012) "Throwback Reverse Pass." Once the new "Ballside" is declared, 04 (the new "Duck-In Cutter) now becomes the player that flashes to the new "Ballside High Post" while 05 (the new "Lob Cutter") now becomes the player that flashes and posts up on the new "Ballside Block."

When 03 changes up and makes a "Throwback Reverse Pass" back to where the action started (to 01,) 02 is the player that steps up and over to set a (02-03) "Flare-Screen" for 03 to "Flare-Cut" to the newly designated "Weakside Wing."

With the ball in 01's hands on the left side of the floor, 05 on the new "Ballside Block," and 04 now at the new "Ballside High Post;" the HIGH-POST/LOW-POST" Spot-Ups are filled on the left side of the floor and the designated continuity offense can immediately begin. **Diagram 18.20.**

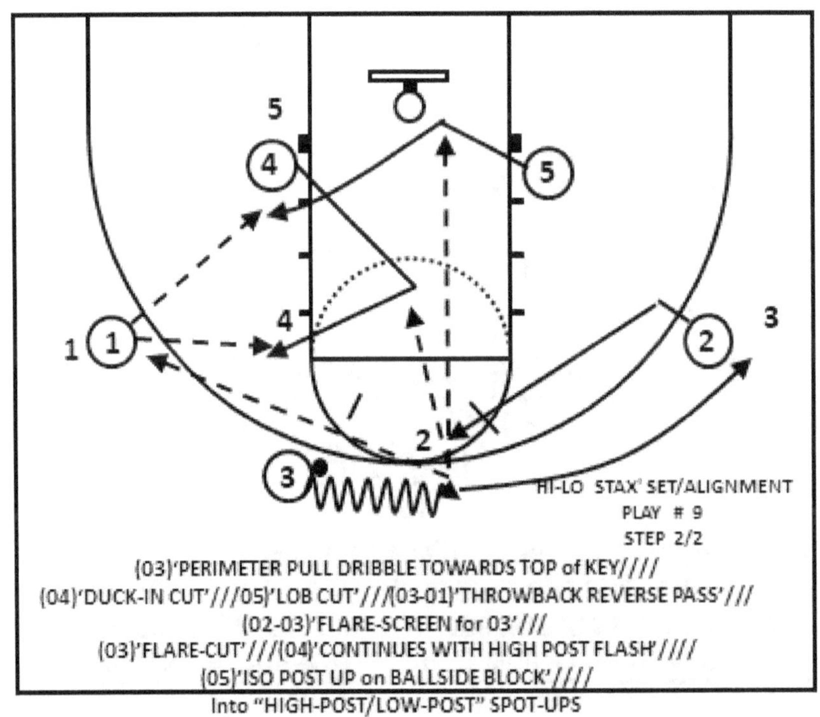

DIAGRAM 18.20

This offensive set is more of an unusual set in today's offense since there is a minimal amount of two-man offensive stacks being used. Even more unique is the fact that there are two offensive stacks and that they both are located at different heights on the court. This can cause the first set of problems in that it is harder to prepare.

There will obviously be different forms of "Pin Down-Screens" that can be used a few times or at a majority of the time. Inside action as long as perimeter attacks are available in the twenty plays. Different types of screens, both on-the-ball and off-the-ball screens can and should be utilized at various locations on the floor. Almost every type of offensive cut is available during at least a couple of the plays demonstrated. Both sides of the floor also can and will be used to attack opposing defenses. Along with many other positive attributes comes the fact that there can be numerous types of continuity offense that can seamlessly flow from any of the three sets of offensive spot-ups. This makes this alignment a key and productive offensive set/alignment that should be part of the overall offensive system.

It has often been discussed that the coaching staff has many decisions to make regarding the offensive system it is constructing. While half-court plays/entries, out-of-bounds plays and Secondary Fastbreaks are tremendous sources of scoring points and are extremely important, when those initial phases of offense do not produce the shots, the only method remaining is the final phase of the offense to be productive. And that final phase will always be the continuity offense or the motion-type offense that the previous phase(s) place them.

It is important that the Secondary Break, the actual half-court plays and the out-of-bounds plays all score points and are effective during their execution, the continuity offense will very likely be the largest point-producing phase of the overall system. Therefore, it is likely the most important decision that must be made is what is the most productive and efficient continuity or motion-type offense that will meet the skill set of their present players and the coaching staff's overall offensive (and even defensive) philosophies. The proper continuity offense should give the offensive team the proper amount of structure as well (with counter options within the continuity) the freedom, the fluid movement and high levels of unpredictability for opposing defenses to contend with, using many fundamentally sound types of action (including various on-ball screens, off-ball screens, cuts and various forms of dribbling and passing opportunities.)

The desired continuity offense will help determine the type of Primary and Secondary Fastbreaks (Odd-Front or Even-Front Breaks Options) the system needs to utilize, solely based on the required ending spot-up locations. Every Secondary Break Option that is used that does not produce a shot reposition players in the identical spot-ups of the continuity offense for an immediate and seamless transition into that continuity offense.

The ending spot-ups of the designated continuity offense will be a large factor and determine the most productive plays that result in the very same spot-ups every Secondary Break Option ends up in their player movements.

After selecting the half-court plays that are fundamentally sound, fluid and high-scoring, it must be determined that those plays must have the very same spot-ups that are required for the smooth and immediate execution of the continuity offense.

Those half-court quick-hitters/plays/entries that are chosen (directly from the selected continuity offense) would then factor into the best one or two offensive alignments/sets that will allow those plays to be successfully executed.

In addition, the Baseline and Sideline Out-of-Bounds Plays also will be chosen by each play having the play-ending spot-ups locations required by the chosen continuity offense.

It should also be realized that the quicker and more fluid the transitions are between the initial phase (be it the Secondary Break Options phase, the Half-Court Plays/Entries phase or the Out-of-Bounds Plays phase) into the final phase (the designated Continuity Offense or the Motion-type Offense); the productivity and success the final phase will be.

It must be emphasized again that "Quality trumps Quantity" in the decision to select the number of continuity offenses to be executed, the number of sets/alignments and the number of plays (from each of the alignments) that are to be employed. It is very important that coaches don't allow too many plays or alignments to mentally bog down their offensive team.

It must be remembered that the Level order of plays begins with Level 1 plays being the most basic and the actual shorter in length and lesser amount of fundamentally sound types of action. Level 2 plays step in with a greater number of different types of actions that will take longer to execute before spotting up in the proper locations for the same quick transition into the designated Continuity Offense. Level 3 plays reach the maximum in length, sophistication, degrees of difficulty and numbers of the various offensive attacking techniques and methods.

With every play discussed as labeled as a specific Level of play, it must be remembered that older, more skilled and more experienced teams should/could have a variety of different levels of plays; such as Level 1, 2 and 3 plays. Somewhat younger teams and less experienced teams could have only Level 2 and 1 plays; where the very youngest of teams could have only Level 1 plays and a minimal number of those to be successful offensively.

This book will help every coach at every level, regardless of the experience of the coaching staff and/or the players' skill levels and experience. Young, less experienced and less talented players should be coached the Level 1 plays and a variable but minimal number of the many types of offensive cuts, on and off-ball screens that could be utilized in their plays used.

Older, better skilled, and more experienced players can maintain some Level 1 plays while advancing to higher Level 2 plays/entries along with an increased number of cuts and screens that could be added to their offensive attacks.

Older and far better talented and more experienced players have all of the Level 3 plays in addition to retaining some Level 2 plays to keep in their offensive schemes. These players should maximize on the wide number of offensive cuts that could be used on the perimeter as well as the interior. In addition, the number of off-ball screens as well as the number of on-ball screens could be increased dramatically as well as the many actions that can follow both types of screens.

This book also can be the foundation for the younger coaches but also the more veteran coaches to keep adding to their Level 2 and 3 plays. New techniques, different cuts and ways to utilize those cuts can be improvised. Creative coaches can simply use the various cuts, the various screens to create their own Level 1, Level 2 or Level 3 plays as they expand their knowledge and change their philosophies on offense.

This book could be a "starter" and a "progression ladder" book for young coaches that becomes a valuable book as that coach progresses along with the level of his/her teams. As the coach progresses in experience and knowledge, as his/her teams progress in skills and competition levels, so can the offensive schemes, techniques, concepts and plays/entries used in the ever-changing offensive system. The progressions of all of these important components of an offensive system are all included in this detailed and wide range of ideas within this single book.

There is so much information that is to be dispersed that the initial book is split into two different books.

In "Book 1 of 2 Books, "there are almost 180 plays/entries/actions that are executed out of nine different offensive alignments described. Book 1 of 2 Books thoroughly discusses in detail three different offensive continuities that begin from three different groups of offensive spot-ups that each play will end up in. Each offensive entry/play that is shown in this book will have the ability to then smoothly transition into one of the offensive continuities described. This initial book will include over 350 diagrams clearly discussing each play/entry where each play will flow into one of the three continuity offenses.

Book 1 includes chapters that contain specific actions that cover the various offensive actions such as a specific chapter on "On-Ball Screens," another chapter covering the various types of " Off-Ball Screens and the various actions that could follow. There is also a chapter that describes the various types of offensive cuts with examples of each in specific forms of action. Another chapter covers the different kinds of dribbles that can be executed while another chapter explains the various types of dribbles that can be utilized while executing the actions. Each type is explained and then illustrated in additional offensive plays.

In "Book 2 of 2 Books," there are a total of over 110 additional plays with over 265 diagrams that clearly describe and demonstrate those plays. Each of these plays also can be executed from one of the nine different offensive alignments/sets that are illustrated, giving an even greater volume of plays a coaching staff can choose from.

To expand the knowledge, both books go together hand in hand and are necessary for the over all building and construction of a coach's own Offensive System.

Coach Kimble took the Head Basketball Coaching position at Deland-Weldon (IL) High School where the varsity accumulated a five year record of 91-43 that included 2 Regional Championships, 2 Regional Runner-Ups and 1 Sectional Tournament Runner-up.

From there, he moved to Dunlap (IL) High School. His five year record at Dunlap amounted to an overall 90-45 record that included two Regional Runners-up, one Regional Championship, one Sectional and one Super-Sectional Championship and a final 2nd Place Finish in the Illinois Class A State Tournament.

Coach Kimble then moved to Florida where he became an Assistant Basketball Coach at Central Florida Community College in Ocala, FL. The next year, he became the Offensive Coordinator in charge of the team's overall offense. For the next two years, he retained that Offensive Coordinator responsibility while also becoming the Associate Head Basketball Coach, with a 2 year record of 44-22. The four year overall record while at CFCC was "73 -58".

Coach Kimble then became the Head Basketball Coach at Crestview (FL) High School for the following 10 years. Excluding the initial year, the overall record averaged almost 18 wins each year for the next 9 years.

Coach Kimble has worked over 100 weeks of basketball camps and has spoken at several coaching clinics and camps. He also has had over 100 articles published in the following publications such as: *The Basketball Bulletin of the National Association of Basketball Coaches, The Scholastic Coach and Athletic Journal, Coach and AD, Winning Hoops, and Basketball Sense,* as well as contributing articles submitted and all diagrams drawn for the following books: the *NABC's Coaching Basketball* in two separate editions.

He has authored six other books through Coaches Choice titled, *The Basketball Coaches Complete Guide to the Multiple Match-up Zone Defense," "The Basketball Coaches' Complete Guide to Zone Offenses," "Coaching Basketball's Speed Game, "Coaching Basketball's Multiple 2-1-2 Full-Court Zone Press," The Basketball Coaches' Complete Guide to Footwork, Balance and Pivoting" and "Implementing the SPEED GAME."*